Hispanic First Names

HISPANIC FIRST NAMES

*A Comprehensive Dictionary
of 250 Years of
Mexican-American Usage*

Compiled by

Richard D. Woods

Bibliographies and Indexes in Anthropology, Number 1

Greenwood Press
Westport, Connecticut • London, England

Library of Congress Cataloging in Publication Data

Woods, Richard Donovon.
    Hispanic first names.

    (Bibliographies and indexes in anthropology,
ISSN 0742-6844   ; no. 1)
    English and Spanish.
    Bibliography: p.
    1. Names, Mexican American. 2. Names, Personal—
Spanish. 3. Names, Personal—United States. I. Title.
II. Series.
CS2375.U6W66   1984   929.4'4'08968073   84-6633
ISBN 0-313-24193-7 (lib. bdg.)

Library of Congress Catalog Card number: 84-6633
ISBN: 0-313-24193-7
ISSN: 0742-6844

First published in 1984

Greenwood Press
An imprint of Greenwood Publishing Group, Inc.
88 Post Road West, Westport, Connecticut 06881

Printed in the United States of America

10 9 8 7 6 5 4 3

Contents

Acknowledgments

No reference book is ever the result of an isolated effort. The present book, being no exception, owes something to many individuals during its various stages of development.

Archbishop Francis J. Furey had the foresight to consolidate all of the Catholic birth records from thirty south Texas counties. This archive must be one of the greatest sources of Hispanic name lore in the United States. Sister Magdalan Connolly, responsible for keeping these records current, filed the names of recent births and extended the archives to the 1980s.

Another source for names, the informal ones, was Dr. Peter Boyd-Bowman of SUNY at Buffalo. He appears to be one of the first scholars in the United States to collect examples of Spanish diminutives and to attempt to determine the rules governing their formation. Thanks go to him for generously allowing me to incorporate his findings into my book.

Funding and research time, two indispensable elements to any project, came through the efforts of Dr. Jean S. Chittenden and Dr. George N. Boyd, chair of the Department of Foreign Languages and Dean of Humanities and Arts, respectively, at Trinity University.

Twentieth-century technology allowed for the organization and retrieval of the data. Dr. Aaron H. Konstam gave his valuable time writing a computer program for first names and finding student assistants capable of carrying out the project. Such were the roles of Sharon and Don Gardner, whose interest extended beyond that of manuscript editing. Kate Ruckman, veteran of a previous reference book of mine, designed the first program to put names into machine-readable form. José Gracia-Medrano entered all computer data while miraculously deciphering my handwriting. Richard Silva also helped in the early stages of computerizing archival data.

My work-study student, Claudia Gláfira Vizcarra, assisted in the multiple tasks involved in manuscript preparation. More importantly, her willingness to be called "Gláfira," meaning "polished, fine, elegant" in Greek, inspired anyone interested in the revival of classical names. Josie Cruz graciously assisted in proofing the manuscript. Danny Rodríguez and Patsy Padilla Cárdenas served as informal consultants on name usage. Finally, my wife Mary for several years tolerated the presence of boxes of 3 x 5 cards in our home. Her reward goes beyond mention here, for the data within prove that her name, at least in its Spanish form "María," is the most popular in the Mexican-American community.

Abbreviations

Full Word	Abbreviation
and	&
Arab	Ar.
century	cen.
combination	comb.
Dictionary of Saints	DS.
diminutives	**Dim:**
Egyptian	Egyp.
English Equivalent	**EE:**
Feast	F.
feminine	f.
figuratively	fig.
French	Fr.
German	Ger.
Greek	Gk.
Hebrew	Heb.
Italian	Ital.
Latin	Lat.
martyr	M.
martyred	mart.
martyrs	Mm.
masculine	m.
mythology	myth.
New Testament	NT
numbers	1, 2, etc.
Old Testament	OT
Persian	Pers.
Phoenician	Phoen.
saint	S.
saints	Ss.
Scandinavian	Scan.
Semitic	Sem.
Spanish	Sp.
Teutonic	Teut.
times	x
variants	**Var:**
virgin	V.
virgins	Vv.

Sample Entry

The following entry, typical for this dictionary, is duplicated
here to alert the user to both format and abbreviations.

Casiano[1] (Cah see ah' noe)[2] m.[3] **EE:** Cassianus.[4] Lat. "Helmet
of steel." 21 x in DS. 4th cen. teacher tormented to death
by pagan pupils. F. 8/13.[5] **Dim:** Chano.[6] **Var:** Assiano,
Caciana, Cacianna, Casanio, Cascina, Casin, Casinero,
Casiono, Cassiana, Cassinta, Gasino, Quesino.[7]

1. Main entry
2. Transliteration. Apostrophe indicates that the accent falls on
   the preceding syllable.
3. Gender
4. English Equivalent
5. Description. In this case it has the Latin origin, frequency of
   occurrence in Dictionary of Saints and saint's day, August 13.
6. Diminutive(s)
7. Variant(s)

Introduction

The given name in any culture is a unique possession often connoting ethnicity, religious tradition, age, and a degree of adherence to a dominant culture. Differing from the surname, the first name has its own peculiarities. Historically, it is the older form of identification and needed the aid of a surname only when the proliferation of "Juan" and other popular forms mandated more refinement in recognition. Indeed, the ancestors of the Mexican Americans had established the first permanent surnames in the Iberian Peninsula by the fifteenth century.

A name given at birth is not only the older of the two labels that one carries through life, it is selected from a repository of names accumulated since Adam. The Roman Martyrology has almost 5,000 brief biographies of the beatified and canonized. Unsatisfied with this selection, imaginative parents wishing to distinguish their offspring may coin their own name, for example, "Celésforo" (see) comes from elements of "Celestino" and "Telésforo"; the same is true of the more readily recognizable "Anaberto" (see).

In this same vein, a first name is indicative of parental or familial interest in the destiny of the bearer. To be christened "Pelayo" (Pelagio) relates the individual to the caudillo of the Reconquest of eighth-century Spain. "Eulalia," with more cultural resonance, unites the child to an even earlier peninsula and to popular Catholicism. This Christian maiden, put to death during the persecution of Diocletian in the fourth century, enjoys a legend of two miracles: in the moment of death a white dove issued from her mouth; heaven sent a snowfall over her dispersed ashes.

Be it "Pelayo" or "Eulalia," a given name is subject to mutations and whimsicality as evidenced by the numerous variants and diminutives. Perhaps three examples best illustrate this. "Francisco" (see) has 76 forms; "Hermenegildo" (see) has 118; and "Genoveva" (see) 116. Yet the less formal "Pancho," "Merejo," and "Vevo" derive respectively from these traditional forms. By contrast the surname, whether patronymic, personal, or toponymic, has suffered relatively few changes, and "Calvo," "Gutiérrez," and "Huerta" remain basically intact since their medieval origins.

At baptism the infant or convert is brought into the Christian community through a name linking him to the saints: apostles, martyrs, and virgins found in the aforementioned Roman Martyrology or the better known Catholic Calendar. Perhaps forgotten today for their miracles, devotion, and sufferings, "Viridiana," "Eudoxia," and "Mechilda" persist through their names in the Spanish-speaking world.

Certain characteristics profile this world. Although interpreters of culture note individualism, personalism, the supremacy of the family, and a distinct perception of time, more tangible facets lend themselves to measurement: Catholicism, comprehension of the Spanish language, and the system of naming. Because of the distinctiveness of Spanish surnames, they are recognizable in any Anglo context. Likewise, the baptismal name accompanying them may be just as identifiable by its vowel ending or frequent termination in "n," "s," or "l" and its stress on the penultimate syllable. Almost invariably, the first name in this culture has either two or three syllables. Ethnicity is implied in both family and baptismal names.

The latter, especially in the United States and in a southwestern context, suggests an adherence to Spanish values as opposed to an Anglo name that may mean attraction to the dominant culture and even assimilation. The Gómez parents christening their son "John" in preference to "Juan" do more than select one form over another. Their choice is symptomatic of accommodation to Anglo standards and heralds perhaps even more acculturation.

Regardless of their choice, be it Anglo or Spanish, the parents may inadvertently identify their son as belonging to a certain generation or age group. If the name is not standard, meaning timeless and always in vogue, it may mature and decline simultaneously with its owner. Classical baptismal choices such as "Juan," "Carlos," and "Francisco" endure betraying no age group. Contrariwise, "Eustorgio," "Eufemio," "Ildefonso," and "Sacramento" label the bearer as elderly and dating back to the nineteenth century. To illustrate further, women's names are subject to the same rules. Whereas "María," "Carmen," and "Ana" adorn every generation, "Clementina," "Graciela," and "Ponciana" rarely are in the name pool for female infants.

To summarize, the first name is almost a code word that communicates nationality, religion, age and even degree of Americanization of its bearer. As a cultural label highly connotative, this form merits a more profound study.

The arrangement and analysis of first names in a dictionary format is a desirable reference tool. Several works of this nature, extant in the Spanish language but generally unavailable in the United States, communicate only with the users who have a reading knowledge of Castilian. These reference books fail to register with any ease of accessibility the variants and diminutives of Spanish names. In collections of American names, Spanish names are neglected. Only the most popular ones or those operative in both cultures, "Irma," "Daniel," and "Amanda," appear in standard name dictionaries.

The present dictionary facilitates the retrieval of names selected from the Mexican-American culture but meaningful to the Spanish-speaking area of this hemisphere. Within the United States, the dictionary has wide applicability, for in a survey of Hispanic names of this country (Cuban, Puerto Rican, etc.) 92 percent of the male names and 88 percent of the female names appear in the present work. In other words, the dictionary achieves approximately 90 percent coverage within this country.[1] On a broader basis, that is, comparing this dictionary with names in use in Spanish America, the results are not quite as satisfying: 80 percent of the female names and 94 percent of the male names from Spanish America may be found here.[2] Yet these figures based on both internal and external comparisons, suggest the universality of naming patterns.

Furthermore, it might be of interest to speculate on the lower correspondences of female names both between Mexican Americans and other U.S. Hispanics and Spanish Americans. One possiblity is the male bias of the data. Phone directories, still listing males as heads of house-

---

1. The survey was based upon a comparison between the names I gathered from Mexican-American sources and those in a book entitled, Spanish Surnamed American College Graduates, 1971-72. (Washington, D.C.: Cabinet Committee on Opportunity for the Spanish Speaking). Eight hundred colleges and universities were contacted and the names of their graduates were placed in this book according to state. Thus any identifiably Spanish name was included regardless of national origins. Since one of the criteria for the First Name Dictionary was names recognizable as Spanish, the same rule applied to Spanish Surnamed American College Graduates.
2. One of the few name frequencies extant on Spanish America is Raymond L. Gorden's Spanish Personal Names (Yellowsprings, Ohio: Antioch College, 1968). The frequency lists provided in the appendixes made a comparison with my list relatively easy.

holds, would give preference to masculine names, thus giving them a
greater potential for correspondences in both the United States and
Spanish America. The Spanish Surnamed American College Graduates
probably reflects the tradition of a greater number of males attending
colleges than females.[3] Hence more male names are available for
comparison. Finally, the supposed inferior status of the female in
Hispanic cultures perhaps allows for a greater liberality in christening
forms. Whereas the male, or breadwinner, needs a solid name, the female
in her secondary role can be the bearer of a "cute" name. The resultant
inventiveness would tend to give a lower frequency of name correspondences for females.

Regardless of its sex bias, as seems evident from the above data,
the dictionary will also be useful for the parent wishing to bestow a
Spanish name, to the bearer who is curious about appropriate variants
and diminutives of his own name, and to anyone desiring to know the
pronunciation and history of a Spanish name. Yet of more significance,
this compilation lists names once popular but now forgotten except in a
nineteenth century census or an obscure birth record. The "Anselinos,"
"Moraimas," "Profetos," and "Zósimos," rescued from anonymity due to the
injustice of a name system, may hope for revival because of the present
work.

To accomplish the above, attention has been paid to finding and
identifying Spanish first names. The Spanish form because of its vowel
ending is often readily identifiable and makes selection easy, for
example, "Evangelina," "Famoso," "Gumersindo," and so forth. Certain
names, functioning in both cultures, also merit inclusion, for example,
"Carolina," "Christina," "Gabriel," and "Leonor." Contrariwise, other
names, blatantly Anglo such as "Jack," "Bill," and "Dick," were rejected. Admittedly at times the decision is more judgmental. Probably
the best guide for omission is the consistent occurrence of a name in
Anglo dictionaries. Here the Anglo culture with its preferences,
spellings, pronunciations, and peculiarities will be emphasized over the
Hispanic.

The broad criteria in collecting were regional, temporal, and
inner-ethnic. In order to insure that Mexican-American names predomi-
nated, sources from the Southwest, especially in its cities and in its
historical documents from the eighteenth, nineteenth, and twentieth
centuries, monopolized concentration. In addition, all economic, social
and religious backgrounds within the ethnic communities were
represented.

The diversity of Spanish names was possible through four sources:
(1) phone directories (listed in a special section of the bibliography)
from 757 locations were perused to find surnames and simultaneously
first names. (2) The San Antonio Catholic Chancery, the administrative
head for thirty south Texas counties, archives all baptismal records for
this large area. (3) The New Mexico Genealogical Society published the
1850 census in three volumes. Search in these commemorative editions,
and archival work in Santa Fe actualized retrieval of names for
nineteenth-century New Mexico. Finally, miscellaneous secondary sources
such as Frederick C. Chabot's With the Makers of San Antonio (San
Antonio, Tx: Artes Graficas, 1937), Fray Angelico Chavez'
Origins of New Mexico Families (Santa Fe: Historical Society of New
Mexico, 1954), and Leon Rowland's Los Fundadores (Fresno: Academy of
California Church History, 1951) provided additional data. These and
supplemental works appear in the bibliography.

Frequency of occurrence played no part in the selection. To illustrate, "María" and "José," the most common names, appear only once, the
same as names of less popularity. However, in the Catholic Chancery of
San Antonio, the "Martínez" name was found to be the largest. Using
this family as a sample, that is, suggesting that its christening
patterns are indicative of the entire Mexican-American community, the
following names were abstracted and ranked as to popularity:

Males	Females
José	María

3. op. cit. Cabinet Committee on Opportunity for Spanish Speaking.

Juan	Guadalupe
Manuel	Mary
Jesús	Margarita
Guadalupe	Glorita
Luis	Juanita
Pedro	Rosa
Francisco	Juana
David	Linda
Miguel	Francisca

(For a more detailed idea of the incidence of certain forms, the reader is advised to turn to page 195, which has a tabular count of baptismal names.)

Once located the names were then alphabetized and arranged into families. For example, all of the variants of "Beatriz" (see) and "Francisco" (see) were entered under the appropriate parent form, for example, "Cisco" under "Francisco"; "Tiche" under "Beatriz." Although both are diminutives and derivatives, they appear in appropriate alphabetical order but only with a cross-reference to the root name. Beyond these are gradations of information depending upon the existence and availability of sources and fecundity of the name in generating equivalents in English as well as variants and diminutives in Spanish.

Each entry has one or more of the following components:

1. Main entry: The name is written in its Spanish form and with the accentuation in this language. The Spanish speaker will determine the correct pronunciation from the main entry. Although an effort was made to follow the general rules of Spanish pronunciation, there are some names about which native speakers could not agree upon accentuation, for example, "Lisias," "Emanuelem," "Martia," "Odom," "Petram," "Rosaelia." Consequently, these forms carry no written accentuation, as it would only mislead the user to a pronunciation arbitrarily chosen.

2. Transliteration: The name is divided to approximate the sounds of American Spanish, and consequently, the English user will arrive at a near rendering of this through syllables transliterated into English. The international phonetic alphabet was not used, as its complexity would inhibit the nonexpert.

3. Gender: Spanish first names enjoy the flexibility of being masculine or feminine depending upon the final vowel. Thus "Pedro," ending in "o," indicates that the bearer is male; whereas "Pedra," ending in "a," denotes female. Yet most names have been standardized to the masculine form. Therefore, the user is cautioned that entries such as "Pedro m." should not be interpreted to mean that the name is limited only to males. A simple vowel change incorporates the female. However, more care must be exercised with nontraditional endings:

Mercedes	f.
Penelope	f.
Raul	m.

It appears that names relating to the Holy Family, the various denominations of the Virgin, or significant events in the Christian calendar, in their unchanged form, can be given to either sex. Examples of such versatile religious names are:

Anunciación mf.	Encarnación mf.	Presentación mf.
Asunción mf.	Natividad mf.	Redención mf.
Concepción mf.	Pasión mf.	Refugio mf.
Consuelo mf.	Paz mf.	Rosario mf.

Probably other Catholic names that denote an abstract concept in the life of Christ or Mary, although generally feminine, also can be masculine. Thus "Consejo," "Dolores," "Luz," "Piedad," and "Visitación," labelled only as feminine (f.) in the present work, also may enhance a male name. As christening forms for boys, these become part of a compound name, for example, "José de la Luz," "José de la Paz," "Juan Encarnación," "Juan Concepción," and so forth. In a society where sex roles are important, the bearer probably would prefer the masculine component of his name.

In extreme cases, if a name is relatively obscure, no gender is

noted. Trying to determine this suggests the anarchy of first names.
Tradition and custom may regularize the "a" and "o" endings. However,
often the giver of the name makes up his own rules and erodes efforts at
systematization. "Raquel," normally female, may also be rendered
"Raquela" or "Raquelo" by hypercorrective parents. Likewise, "Asunción"
and "Concepción" may be safely feminine in "Asunciona" and
"Concepciona."

4. English Equivalent: Whenever possible an equivalent in English
is given. This can be identical, such as "Daniel," "Mercedes," and
"Carmen," christening forms equal in both languages; it may be a translation of the less recognizable "Carlos-Charles" or "Juana-Jane, Jean,
or Joan." Still others, apparently unique to Spanish, have neither an
equivalent nor a likeness in English. Consequently, the absence of this
component cautions that no translation was located. Useful for English
equivalents are the U.S. Department of Justice's Foreign Versions
(Washington, D.C.: GPO, 1969) and Evelyn Wells' What to Name the Baby
(Garden City, N.Y.: Doubleday and Co., Inc., 1946). Those curious
about Spanish names into English might well consult the glossary on page
199.

Of related interest is a phenomenon peculiar to Spanish Catholic
culture but absent in the Anglo-Saxon. Certain Roman Catholic concepts
are universal and articulable in both languages. However, though the
Spanish devotional forms such as "Sacramento," "Concepción," "Custodio,"
"Presentación," and "Pasión" may be safely rendered "Sacrament,"
"Conception," "Custodia," "Presentation," and "Passion" in English, they
are never used as names in the Anglo world. To have listed them as such
would have misguided the user.

5. Description: This is the key component for each entry and information legitimizing the inclusion of the name is broadly interpreted.
The data here can be a definition, that is, "Pedro" is from the Greek
meaning "rock"; "Viridiana" is the name of a twelfth-century saint;
"Macedonia" is a biblical placename. To clarify further, this component
for the entry means verifying data suggesting a root word or previous
use of the name under consideration.

When possible the saint's day is indicated by the abbreviation "F"
(feast) and the date, and the initials "DS" mean Dictionary of Saints.
Often the popularity of a saint is indicated by the number of times he
appears in this basic reference. When only one saint could be selected
among several possible candidates, two criteria were invoked: the saint
enjoying the most fame was chosen for inclusion; in default of the latter, that is, no one of significance, the most interesting life and
martyrdom were incorporated to adorn the annotation of a Mexican-
American first name.

All possible resources were perused for definitions and other data.
These works, among others, include:

(a) Drake. Saints and Their Emblems.
(b) Enciclopedia universal europeo americano.
(c) Holweck. A Biographical Dictionary of the Saints.
(d) Kolatch. The Name Dictionary: Modern English and Hebrew Names.
(e) Sainz de Robles. Ensayo de un diccionario universal.
(f) Serdoch. Diccionario onomatológico.
(g) Smith. Baptismal and Confirmation Names.
(h) Stewart. American Given Names.
(i) Tibon. Diccionario etimológico comparado.
(j) Wells. What to Name the Baby.
(k) Withycombe. The Oxford Dictionary of English Christian Names.

Unfortunately, many of the names collected from the Catholic Chancery seem to be orphaned forms in regard to information as to origin,
saint lore, or compatibility with other name families. Nothing can be
found on them in the standard reference sources listed above. Therefore, in accordance with the criteria for inclusion, these 2,543 names
had to be excluded. This negative result can be attributed to several
causes: the names are misspelled and too distorted to be rescued; they
are coined and therefore do not appear in any standard reference; they
are a combination of more familiar names or their diminutives but their
union precludes recognition by the usual means. These names remain
outside the dictionary not only for the absence of supporting data but
their inclusion would have teased the etymologist and frustrated the lay

user.

6. Diminutives: This part consists of the abbreviated and often
affectionate forms that act as a substitute for baptismal names, for
example, "Jando," "Jano," and "Xandro" for "Alejandro"; and "Nico,"
"Tonio," and "Tuco" for "Antonio." Since almost every name in Spanish
becomes diminutive by the suffixing "ito" and "ita," this form is generally omitted. Consequently, the readily identifiable "Alejandrito" and
"Antonito" do not appear.

Peter Boyd-Bowman is especially noteworthy for his research of
diminutives or the hypocoristic forms of standard names. He did field
studies in Mexico and in his article (see below) he comments on the lack
of attention to this form of popular culture. Boyd-Bowman not only
collected diminutives, many of which appear in the present work, but
more importantly he determined the phonetic rules for their formation.
Although his "Cómo obra la fonética infantil en la formación de los
hipocorísticos" is seminal, sources from other authors also provided
information: Saul Pollock's Spanish and Mexican Given Names (Los
Angeles: Committee for Social Research, 1940); U.S. Department of
Justice's Foreign Versions (Washington, D.C.: GPO, 1969); and H.L.A.
Van Wijk's "Los hipocorísticos hondureños" (Romantische Jahrbuch Vol.
XV, 1964).

7. Variants: Orthographic and phonetic differences comprise the
final data of the name families. "Inocencio" may also be rendered
"Innocencio," "Ynosencio," and "Inocercio," three examples of the
eighty-seven variants. Likewise "Beatriz" may be changed orthographi-
cally to "Viatrix" or phonetically to "Beztrix." These listings are
mainly the result of careful plodding through the baptismal archives of
the Catholic Chancery of San Antonio, Texas.

8. Finally, several of the entries have "see also" references.
These alert the user to names that are cognates rather than equivalents.
Or occasionally two names that are from the same sources have a separate
independence. And although they could be subsumed under a single group-
ing, custom dictates their autonomy.

Adela, see also Adelaida
Alicia, see also Elizabeth
Elena, see also Eleanor
Eloisa, see also Luis
Fernando, see also Hernando
Jacobo, see also Santiago

The present work's originality is based on two contributions: (1)
its accumulation of core names, their diminutives, and their variants;
(2) its organization of these proliferating names, through the use of
the computer, into a format that indicates their interrelationship and
allows for easy retrieval of information, for example, "Genovevo" may be
found under the parent name or any of its eleven diminutives or 105
variants. The user's awareness of this and of the dictionary's four
component parts will maximize retrieval of information.

(1) the name entries with their pronunciation, definition, saint
lore, diminutives, and variants.

(2) an appendix with tables of the most frequently occurring
names. Because frequency is not a concern of the dictionary proper,
these materials are isolated and analyzed in a separate section. An
explanation of methodology precedes the lists of popular names.

(3) an English-Spanish glossary that enables access through an
English baptismal name. For example, the name "Henry" (Henry, see
Enrique) directs the user to all of the data under the entry "Enrique."
Here, "Henry" will be listed along with other information, as one of the
English equivalents.

(4) an extensive bibliography on both sources for finding first
names and also information on these names.

Hispanic First Names

Name Entries

A

Aarón (Ah roan') m. **EE:** Aaron, Aron. Of Egyp. origin but meaning unknown. Brother of Moses; 3 Ss. **Var:** Aarona, Arón, Arona, Aronida, Arrón, Erón,

Aarona   see **Aarón.**

Abacum (Ah bah coom') m. **EE:** Abachum. 3rd cen. S. mart. for ministering to Christians. F. 1/19.

Abalardo   see **Abelardo.**

Abán (Ah bahn') m? **EE:** Aban. In Pers. myth., Muse of liberal arts & mechanics.

Abangelina   see **Evangelina.**

Abaristo (Ah bah rees' toe) m. **EE:** Evaristus. Gk. "To be agreeable." 3 Ss. **Var:** Avaristo, Ayarsito,

Abdénago (Ahb day' nah go) m. **EE:** Abdenago. 1 of 3 companions of Daniel cast into furnace. **Var:** Abdeniago, Abedmago, Adbonego, Avendio.

Abdeniago   see **Abdenago.**

Abdías (Ahb dee' ahs) m. **EE:** Abdias. Heb. "Slave of God." 3 Ss. 1 in 900 B.C. foretold destruction of Edom.

Abdiel (Ahb deal') m. **EE:** Abdiel. Heb. "Servant of God." Prophet who withstood Satan.

Abdón (Ahb doan') m. **EE:** Abdon. Sem. "Servant of God." 3rd cen. S. mart. in Rome. **Dim:** Nona. **Var:** Abedón.

Abdulia (Ahb doo' lee ah) m. **EE:** Abdul. Ar. "Servant of Allah."

Abedardo   see **Abelardo.**

Abedmago   see **Abdenago.**

Abedón   see **Abdón.**

Abegail (Ah' bay guile) f. **EE:** Abby, Abigail, Gail. Heb. "My father is joy." Wise, beautiful wife of David. **Var:** Abgel, Abigael, Abigil, Abrigail, Avigail.

Abejundio (Ah bay hoon' dee oh) m. **EE:** Bee. Sp. "Abejuno" means "relating to the abeja (bee)."

Abel (Ah bell') m. **EE:** Abel, Abell, Able. Heb. "Breath of vanity." 2nd son of Adam & Eve. Slain by Cain. 5 x in DS. **Var:** Abelón, Abiel, Avel.

Abelado   see **Abelardo.**

Abeladro   see **Abelardo.**

Abelandio   see **Abelardo.**

Abelando   see **Abelardo.**

Abelardo (Ah bay lahr' doe) m. **EE:** Abelard. Teut. "Nobly resolute." Peter Abelard's love for Heloise, great romance of medieval France. **Dim:** Beluch, Lalo. **Var:** Abalardo, Abedardo, Abelado, Abeladro, Abelandio, Abelando, Abelcardo, Abeloido, Ablardo, Afelardo, Alelarda, Alvelardo, Arelardo, Avelarde, Avelardo, Ebelardo, Evalardo, Evilardo.

Abelcardo   see **Abelardo.**

Abelena   see **Abelino.**

Abelia   see **Abelino.**

Abeliano   see **Aurelio.**

Abelibaldo (Ah bay lee ball' doe) m. **EE:** Abelbald. Comb. of Abel (see) & Ger. "baldo," "audacious."

Abelicio (Ah bay lee' see oh) m. **EE:** Abelicio. Abelicea, elm-like tree.

Abelinda   see **Abelino.**

Abelino (Ah bay lee' no) mf. **EE:** Avelin, Hazel. From city Avellino, place of "avellanos" (hazelnut trees). **Dim:** Lina, Minina. **Var:** Abelena, Abelia, Abelinda, Aberlina, Avalino, Aveleno, Avelia, Avelimo, Avelín, Avelinda, Avelino, Avellino, Averlino, Obelino.

Abeloido   see **Abelardo.**

Abelón   see **Abel.**

Abenamar (Ah bay nah' mar) m. **EE:** Abenamar. 1 of classics of Sp. literature. Minister of 10th cen. Moorish king.

Abenicio (Ah bay nee' see oh) m. **EE:** Aventinius. 4 x in DS. **Var:** Abenincio, Avenicio.

Abenincio   see **Abenicio.**

Aber   see **Alberto.**

Aberardo (Ah bay rar' doe) m. **EE:** Aberardo. Scottish S. of 8th cen. F. 2/9.

Aberhán   see **Abraham.**
Aberlina   see **Abelino.**
Abertano (Ah bear' tah no) m. **EE:**
Avertanus. Confessor & S. F.
2/25. **Var:** Avertano.
Abeto   see **Alberto.**
Abgel   see **Abegail.**
Abiel   see **Abel.**
Abigael   see **Abegail.**
Abigil   see **Abegail.**
Abil (Ah beel') m. **EE:** Abella.
Form of Lat. "asella," "the
beautiful." **Var:** Abila, Abilano,
Abiliano, Abilica, Abilio,
Aviel, Avilio.
Abila   see **Abil.**
Abilano   see **Abil.**
Abiliano   see **Abil.**
Abilica   see **Abil.**
Abilio   see **Abil.**
Abimelech (Ah bee may' leck) m.
EE: Abimelech. Heb. "Father is
king." Canaanite king who took
Sarah into harem.
Abinadi (Ah bee nah' dee) m? Heb.
"Father of liberality." 4 x in
Bible.
Abirio (Ah bee' ree oh) m. **EE:**
Abiram, Abiron. Heb. "Father is
exalted." Heb. rebel against
Moses & Aaron; swallowed by
earth.
Ablardo   see **Abelardo.**
Abondio   see **Abundio.**
Aboundio   see **Abundio.**
Abraam   see **Abraham.**
Abraán   see **Abraham.**
Abrahá   see **Abraham.**
Abraham (Ah bra ahm') m. **EE:** Abe,
Abraham, Abram. Heb. "Exalted
father." Father of Jews who
accepted 1 true God; founder of
Jewish & Arab tribes. 5 x in DS.
Dim: Brancho. **Var:** Aberhán,
Abraam, Abraán, Abrahá, Abrahán,
Abram, Abrama, Abrán, Abrana,
Abrom, Ahbrán, Arvrana, Avrán,
Habrán, Ibrahim, Ibrain.
Abrahán   see **Abraham.**
Abram   see **Abraham.**
Abrama   see **Abraham.**
Abrán   see **Abraham.**
Abrana   see **Abraham.**
Abrasia (Ah bra' see ah) f? **EE:**
Abrasia. Sp. "Abrasar," "filled
with violent passion"?
Abrielo   see **Gabriel.**
Abrigail   see **Abegail.**
Abrisio   see **Abursia.**
Abrom   see **Abraham.**
Absalón (Ahb sah lone') m. **EE:**
Abishalom, Absalom, etc. Heb.
"Father of peace." Rebellious
3rd son of David; noted for long
hair.
Abulina   see **Apolonio.**
Abundencio   see **Abundio.**
Abundio (Ah boon' dee oh) m. **EE:**
Abundius. Lat. "Abundius," "full
of good works." 8 x in DS. **Dim:**
Abunito. **Var:** Abondio, Aboundio,
Abundencio, Abundo, Abunelia,
Agundio, Agundo, Albundio,
Apundia, Augundio, Aundio,

Avundio.
Abundo   see **Abundio.**
Abunelia   see **Abundio.**
Abunito   see **Abundio.**
Abursia (Ah boor' see ah) m. **EE:**
Abercius. Abercius, 4 Ss., 3 Mm.
Main, 2nd cen. bishop in Persia.
F. 10/22. **Var:** Abrisio.
Acacio (Ah cah' see oh) m. **EE:**
Acacius, Acathius. Gk. "Honor-
able." 5 Ss. **Var:** Acarcius,
Accasius, Alcasio, Anicacio,
Anicasio, Arcarcio, Arcario,
Arcasio, Ecasio, Enacasio.
Acadro   see **Arcadio.**
Acansión   see **Asunción.**
Acapito   see **Agapito.**
Acarcius   see **Acacio.**
Acario (Ah cah' ree oh) m. **EE:**
Acario. 1 of 1st bishops of
Noyon, France in 7th cen. In-
voked against evil disposi-
tions. F. 11/27. **Var:** Alacrio,
Alcairo, Alcariae, Alcario,
Alcarius.
Accasius   see **Acacio.**
Acedonio   see **Macedonio.**
Acela (Ah say' la) f. **EE:** Asella.
Lat. "Asinus," "little burro."
5th cen. S. mentioned in St.
Jerome for virtue & austerity.
Dim: Acelino. **Var:** Acelie,
Asael, Asalia.
Acelie   see **Acela.**
Acelino   see **Acela.**
Acencención   see **Asunción.**
Acencio   see **Asunción.**
Acención   see **Asunción.**
Acenete   see **Asenet.**
Acenseón   see **Asunción.**
Aches   see **Mercedes.**
Achimedes   see **Arquímedis.**
Aciano (Ah see ah' no) m. **EE:**
Aciano. Blue bottle flower.
Acilino (Ah see lee' no) m. **EE:**
Aquila. Lat. "Aquilinus," "like
an eagle." 13 Ss. **Var:** Acilnio,
Ancilino, Aquilina.
Acilnio   see **Acilino.**
Acineción   see **Asunción.**
Acinta (Ah seen' tah) f. **EE:**
Acindynus. Form of Acindynus? 3
Mm.
Aciono (Ah see oh' no) m. **EE:**
Aciono. One who makes stirrups?
Also form of Asunción (see).
Acionsión   see **Asunción.**
Acisclo (Ah sees' cloe) m. **EE:**
Acisclus, Ascylus. Lat.
"Acisculus," "instrument for
shaping stones." Name of 4th
cen. M. put to death at Cordova.
F. 11/1. **Var:** Acisius, Acisla,
Asislo.
Acisius   see **Acisclo.**
Acisla   see **Acisclo.**
Acorinio (Ah co ree' nee oh) m.
EE: Acorinio. Acorina, chemical
used in making perfume.
Actaniano   see **Octavio.**
Actaviano   see **Octavio.**
Actavio   see **Octavio.**
Adabelia (Ah dah bay' lee ah) f.
EE: Adabelia. Comb. of Adela &
Abelino (see both).

Adaberta   see **Adalberto.**
Adadea (Ah dah day' ah) f? **EE:**
    Adadea. In myth., Adad is god of
    thunder.
Adaelaida   see **Adelaido.**
Adaido   see **Adelaido.**
Adal   see **Adalberto.**
Adalaida   see **Adelaido.**
Adalberto (Ah dahl bare' toe) m.
    EE: Adalbert. Ger. "Of noble
    lineage." 10th cen. patron S. of
    Poland & Bohemia. F. 4/23. **Dim:**
    Adal, Beto. **Var:** Adaberta,
    Adalverto, Addiberto, Adelberto,
    Adialberto, Edilberto.
Adalena   see **Adela.**
Adalfo   see **Adolfo.**
Adalilia   see **Adela.**
Adalina   see **Adela.**
Adalio   see **Adela.**
Adaloida   see **Adelaido.**
Adalona   see **Adela.**
Adalverto   see **Adalberto.**
Adalvida   see **Adela.**
Adamacio   see **Atanasio.**
Adamberto (Ah dahm bare' toe) m.
    EE: Adambert. Comb. of Adán &
    Berto (see both).
Adame (Ah dah' may) m. **EE:** Adam,
    Adamnon. Form of Adamnano? 7th
    cen. Irish S. F. 9/6.
Adán (Ah dahn') m. **EE:** Adam, Edam.
    Heb. "Red earth," substance of
    1st man; "like God." 5 Ss. **Var:**
    Adana, Adanaton.
Adana   see **Adan.**
Adanaton   see **Adan.**
Adanelia (Ah dah nay' lee ah) f.
    EE: Adanelia. Comb. of Adán &
    Helo (see both).
Adaucto (Ah dowk' toe) m. **EE:**
    Adactus, Adauctus. Lat.
    "Adauctus," "increase or
    growth." 4th cen. M. F. 2/7.
    Var: Adausto.
Adausto   see **Adaucto.**
Adbonego   see **Abdenago.**
Addiberto   see **Adalberto.**
Adehleid   see **Adelaido.**
Adela   see **Adelaido.**
Adela (Ah day' lah) f. **EE:** Adela,
    Adele, Adeline. Ger. "Of noble
    lineage." 2 Ss. 7th or 8th cen.
    foundress of monastery at
    Treves. **Dim:** Adi, Adita, Alita,
    Dela, Delio, Lela, Lelito, Lita.
    Var: Adalena, Adalilia, Adalina,
    Adalio, Adalona, Adalvida,
    Adelaina, Adelaisa, Adelam,
    Adelán, Adelea, Adelena,
    Adelesmo, Adeliana, Adelín,
    Adelina, Adelinda, Adelinia,
    Adelins, Adelio, Adeliza,
    Adella, Adelona, Adelonio,
    Adilán, Adilena, Adilín,
    Adilina, Adilio, Adilón, Adlina,
    Adolina, Adolinar, Aodelia,
    Ardelia, Audelino, Audelio,
    Audella, Audilia, Edalia,
    Edelia, Eldelia, Idelita,
    Idelta, Jadelina, Odelina. See
    also Adelaido.
Adelada   see **Adelaido.**
Adeladia   see **Adelaido.**
Adelaidae   see **Adelaido.**

Adelaides   see **Adelaido.**
Adelaido (Ah day lie' doe) m. **EE:**
    Adela, Adelaide, Adele. Ger. "Of
    noble birth." 10th cen. Ger.
    empress. F. 12/16. **Dim:** Chila,
    Lala, Layda, Lela, Lina, Yaya.
    Var: Adaelaida, Adaido,
    Adalaida, Adaloida, Adehleid,
    Adela, Adelada, Adeladia,
    Adelaidae, Adelaides, Adelaita,
    Adelarda, Adelaria, Adelarido,
    Adelaya, Adelayda, Adelayde,
    Adeldoia, Adeledo, Adeleida,
    Adeleide, Adeleita, Adelhaidia,
    Adelheida, Adelhindis, Adeliado,
    Adelicia, Adelido, Adelindo,
    Adeloida, Adialida, Adilaida,
    Adlaida, Ajdelaido, Aleyda,
    Audeida, Delaida, Idelaida,
    Odelaida. See also Adela.
Adelaina   see **Adela.**
Adelaisa   see **Adela.**
Adelaita   see **Adelaido.**
Adelam   see **Adela.**
Adelán   see **Adela.**
Adelarda   see **Adelaido.**
Adelaria   see **Adelaido.**
Adelarido   see **Adelaido.**
Adelaya   see **Adelaido.**
Adelayda   see **Adelaido.**
Adelayde   see **Adelaido.**
Adelberto   see **Adalberto.**
Adeldoia   see **Adelaido.**
Adelea   see **Adela.**
Adeledo   see **Adelaido.**
Adeleida   see **Adelaido.**
Adeleide   see **Adelaido.**
Adeleita   see **Adelaido.**
Adelena   see **Adela.**
Adelesmo   see **Adela.**
Adelfia   see **Adelfo.**
Adelfino   see **Adelfo.**
Adelfo (Ah dell' foe) m. **EE:**
    Adelphe, Adelphius. Gk. "From
    the same form," hence "sister."
    5 Ss. **Var:** Adelfia, Adelfino,
    Adelphino, Adelphuna, Odelfa,
    Odelfia, Odelfina.
Adelhaidia   see **Adelaido.**
Adelheida   see **Adelaido.**
Adelhindis   see **Adelaido.**
Adeliado   see **Adelaido.**
Adeliana   see **Adela.**
Adelicia   see **Adelaido.**
Adelido   see **Adelaido.**
Adelín   see **Adela.**
Adelina   see **Adela.**
Adelinda   see **Adela.**
Adelindo   see **Adelaido.**
Adelinia   see **Adela.**
Adelins   see **Adela.**
Adelio   see **Adela.**
Adeliza   see **Adela.**
Adella   see **Adela.**
Adelman   see **Adelmo.**
Adelmida   see **Adelmo.**
Adelmira   see **Adelmo.**
Adelmo (Ah dell' mo) m. **EE:**
    Adhelm, Aldhelm. Ger. "Noble
    protector." 8th cen. S. of
    England. F. 5/25. **Dim:** Delma,
    Delminda. **Var:** Adelmán,
    Adelmida, Adelmira, Adelnery.
Adelnery   see **Adelmo.**
Adeloida   see **Adelaido.**

Adelona   see **Adela.**
Adelonio   see **Adela.**
Adelphino   see **Adelfo.**
Adelphuna   see **Adelfo.**
Adelsida   see **Ladislao.**
Adelvino   see **Etelvina.**
Ademar (Ah day mar') m. **EE:**
    Ademar. Ger. "Famous in battle."
Adeodato (Ah day oh dah' toe) m.
    EE: Adeodatus. Lat. "One given
    to God." 4 Ss. **Var:** Adeodatum,
    Adiodato.
Adeodatum   see **Adeodato.**
Adeslade   see **Ladislao.**
Adi   see **Adela.**
Adialberto   see **Adalberto.**
Adialida   see **Adelaido.**
Adiana   see **Adrián.**
Adibina (Ah dee bee' nah) f. **EE:**
    Divine. Comb. of Ada & Ludovino
    (see both)?
Adilaida   see **Adelaido.**
Adilán   see **Adela.**
Adilena   see **Adela.**
Adilín   see **Adela.**
Adilina   see **Adela.**
Adilio   see **Adela.**
Adilmira (Ah deel mee' rah) f. **EE:**
    Adelemus. Adelmo, 11th cen. Sp.
    S. who helped restore monastic
    discipline. F. 1/30.
Adilón   see **Adela.**
Adina (Ah dee' nah) f. **EE:** Ada.
    Heb. "Ornament of beauty." Ital.
    diminutive of Ada. 2 x in Bible.
    Wife of Lamech & wife of Esau.
Adiodato   see **Adeodato.**
Adislado   see **Estanislao.**
Adislao   see **Estanislao.**
Adisteo   see **Estanislao.**
Adita   see **Adela.**
Adlaida   see **Adelaido.**
Adlina   see **Adela.**
Admundo   see **Edmundo.**
Adoflo   see **Adolfo.**
Adofo   see **Adolfo.**
Adola   see **Adolfo.**
Adolfo (Ah dole' foe) m. **EE:**
    Adolf, Adolph, Adolphus. Ger.
    "Noble wolf" or "noble hero."
    13th cen. Ger. bishop. F. 2/11.
    Dim: Dolfito, Dolfo, Dolita,
    Edulfo, Fito, Foncho, Fonso,
    Ofo. **Var:** Adalfo, Adoflo, Adofo,
    Adola, Adolfum, Adolofo,
    Adolphou, Adolpo, Adulfo,
    Ataulfo, Ataulfo, Ydolfo.
Adolfum   see **Adolfo.**
Adolgiza (Ah dole hee' sah) f. **EE:**
    Adalgisus, Algisus. Ger. "Of
    noble family." 8th cen. Fr. S.
    F. 6/2.
Adolina   see **Adela.**
Adolinar   see **Adela.**
Adolio   see **Adulio.**
Adolofo   see **Adolfo.**
Adolphou   see **Adolfo.**
Adolpo   see **Adolfo.**
Adón (Ah doan') m. **EE:** Adon,
    Adonais, Adonis. Phoen. "Lord."
    In Heb. may be synonym for God.
    Var: Adonina.
Adona   see **Adonías.**
Adonaicio   see **Atanasio.**
Adonais   see **Adonías.**

Adonaiso   see **Adonías.**
Adonaldo (Ah doe nahl' doe) m. **EE:**
    Adonald. Sp. "Full of ability"?
Adonario (Ah doe nah' ree oh) m.
    EE: Adonario. Lat. "To adore
    oneself"?
Adonías (Ah doe nee' ahs) m. **EE:**
    Adonijah, "Jehovah is Lord."
    David's 4th son who aborted in
    attempt to succeed father. **Var:**
    Adona, Adonais, Adonaiso,
    Adonina, Adonise.
Adonina   see **Adon.**
Adonina   see **Adonías.**
Adonís (Ah doe nees') m. **EE:** Adon,
    Adonais, Adonis. Phoen. "Lord."
    Male of god-like beauty in Gk.
    myth.
Adonise   see **Adonías.**
Adrain   see **Adrián.**
Adrana   see **Adrián.**
Adreana   see **Adrián.**
Adrear   see **Adrián.**
Adreene   see **Adrián.**
Adrés   see **Andrés.**
Adrián (Ah dree ahn') m. **EE:**
    Adrian, Hadrian. Lat. "One from
    Adria." Built great Roman wall
    of Britain. 3 Ss. **Var:** Adiana,
    Adrain, Adrana, Adreana, Adrear,
    Adreene, Adrianna, Adriano,
    Adriento, Adrin, Hadrián.
Adrianna   see **Adrián.**
Adriano   see **Adrián.**
Adriento   see **Adrián.**
Adrín   see **Adrián.**
Adrónico (Ah droe' nee co) m. **EE:**
    Adronicus. Gk. "Conqueror of
    men." 3rd cen. B.C. Roman poet.
    2 Ss.
Adulfo   see **Adolfo.**
Adulio (Ah dew' lee oh) m. **EE:**
    Adulia, Adulio. Lat. "Excessive
    desire to please"? **Var:** Adolio.
Aegidia   see **Agata.**
Aemiliano   see **Emilio.**
Aemilio   see **Emilio.**
Aemilius   see **Emilio.**
Aenulfo   see **Arnulfo.**
Aeofilo   see **Ofelio.**
Afelardo   see **Abelardo.**
Afelio   see **Ofelio.**
Aferino (Ah fay ree' no) m. **EE:**
    Aferino. Sp. "To grasp"? Fig.,
    tenacious one.
Affonso   see **Alfonso.**
Affurso   see **Alfonso.**
Afiliano   see **Afilio.**
Afilín   see **Afilio.**
Afilio (Ah fee' lee oh) m. **EE:**
    Adfilius. Lat. "To recognize as
    son one who is not." Also sug-
    gests to join community. **Var:**
    Afiliano, Afilín.
Afolinar   see **Apolonio.**
Afolonio   see **Apolonio.**
Afrodisio (Ah fro dee' see oh) m.
    EE: Aphrodite. Gk. "Foam." Aph-
    rodite, Gk. goddess of love,
    born of sea.
Agada   see **Agata.**
Agadita   see **Agata.**
Agafrita   see **Agapito.**
Agahita   see **Agapito.**
Agajinto   see **Agapito.**

Agajito   see **Agapito**.
Agajrita   see **Agapito**.
Agapata   see **Agapito**.
Agapeta   see **Agapito**.
Agapifo   see **Agapito**.
Agapilo   see **Agapito**.
Agapina   see **Agapito**.
Agapipo   see **Agapito**.
Agapit   see **Agapito**.
Agapito (Ah gah pee' toe) m. **EE:**
Agape, Agapius. Gk. "Loved one."
In English, meal of fellowship
with prayers, song, & scripture.
Var: Acapito, Agafrita, Agahita,
Agajinto, Agajito, Agajrita,
Agapata, Agapeta, Agapifo,
Agapilo, Agapina, Agapipo,
Agapit, Agapitta, Agapo,
Agappito, Agipeta, Agipito,
Agopetto, Agopito, Agrapito,
Ajapito, Alapito, Algabita,
Algabo, Arapita, Areopajita,
Areopaquita, Argapito, Ariopaca,
Ariopajita, Aripea, Aropagita,
Arropajita, Arupaguita, Ogahita,
Ogapita.
Agapitta   see **Agapito**.
Agapo   see **Agapito**.
Agappito   see **Agapito**.
Agar (Ah gar') f. **EE:** Aagar,
Hagar. Heb. "Forsaken, stranger"
or "to flee" referring to
Hegira, Mohammed's flight from
Medina to Mecca. Biblically,
concubine of Abraham (see) &
mother of Ishmael. **Dim:** Ogarita.
Agaritam   see **Agata**.
Agata (Ah' gah tah) f. **EE:** Agate,
Agatha, Aggie. Gk. "Kind, good."
3rd cen. Sicilian S. F. 2/5.
Var: Aegidia, Agada, Agadita,
Agaritam, Agatha, Ageda,
Agedita, Agedota, Agerita,
Agerora, Agetita (Agueda),
Agida, Agrastina, Agueadita,
Aguedo, Aguenita, Aguida,
Aqueda, Augatia, Ayguda,
Aygueda, Ogueda.
Agatha   see **Agata**.
Agatón (Ah gah tone') m. **EE:**
Agathon. Gk. "Good." Agathon,
Athenian tragedian of 450 B.C. 4
Ss.
Ageda   see **Agata**.
Agedita   see **Agata**.
Agedota   see **Agata**.
Agelila   see **Angel**.
Agelina   see **Angel**.
Agelita   see **Angel**.
Ageo (Ah hay' oh) m. **EE:** Aggaeus,
Aggeus, Haggai. Heb. "Solemn."
Minor Biblical prophet & 2 Ss.
Dim: Agito.
Agerita   see **Agata**.
Agerora   see **Agata**.
Agetita   see **Agata**.
Agida   see **Agata**.
Agilberto (Ah heel bear' toe) m.
EE: Agilbert, Agilbertus. Ger.
"Sword." 3rd cen. S. mart. in
Paris. F. 6/24. **Dim:** Berto.
Agileo (Ah hee lay' oh) m. **EE:**
Agilaeus, Agleus. 4th cen.
African S. mart. in Carthage. F.
10/15.

Aginaldo   see **Aguinaldo**.
Agipeta   see **Agapito**.
Agipito   see **Agapito**.
Agito   see **Ageo**.
Agnatha   see **Inés**.
Agnatia   see **Inés**.
Agneda   see **Inés**.
Agneliano   see **Inés**.
Agnese   see **Inés**.
Agnesita   see **Inés**.
Agnete   see **Inés**.
Agnetem   see **Inés**.
Agnetio   see **Inés**.
Agneto   see **Inés**.
Agnipina   see **Agripino**.
Agobardo (Ah go bar' doe) m. **EE:**
Agobard. Ger. "Gleaming sword."
9th cen. Archbishop of Lyons,
France. F. 6/6. **Var:** Agoberto.
Agoberto   see **Agobardo**.
Agopetto   see **Agapito**.
Agopito   see **Agapito**.
Agostia   see **Agusto**.
Agostin   see **Agusto**.
Agostina   see **Agusto**.
Agraciana (Ah grah see ahn' ah) f.
EE: Agraciana. Sp. "To pardon."
Fig., forgiving person.
Agraciano   see **Graciela**.
Agrafania   see **Agripino**.
Agrapena   see **Agripino**.
Agrapina   see **Agripino**.
Agrapito   see **Agapito**.
Agrastina   see **Agata**.
Agrea   see **Agrícola**.
Agretina (Ah gray tee' nah) f. **EE:**
Agretina. Agreta, plant family
that includes gladiola.
Agria   see **Agrícola**.
Agrícola (Ah gree' co lah) f. **EE:**
Agricola, Agricolus. Lat. "He
who works land." 5 Ss. **Dim:**
Agrea, Agria, Agrola.
Agrifina   see **Agripino**.
Agrigina   see **Agripino**.
Agripa   see **Agripino**.
Agripemia   see **Agripino**.
Agripena   see **Agripino**.
Agripin   see **Agripino**.
Agripinia   see **Agripino**.
Agripino (Ah gree pee' no) m. **EE:**
Agrippa, Agrippinus. Lat. "Born
foot first." 2 Ss. **Dim:** Pine.
Var: Agnipina, Agrafania,
Agrapena, Agrapina, Agrifina,
Agrigina, Agripa, Agripemia,
Agripena, Agripin, Agripinia,
Agripirra, Agrippin, Agrippina,
Agrispina, Agupina.
Agripirra   see **Agripino**.
Agrippin   see **Agripino**.
Agrippina   see **Agripino**.
Agrispina   see **Agripino**.
Agrola   see **Agrícola**.
Agueadita   see **Agata**.
Aguedo   see **Agata**.
Agueleo (Ah whay lay' oh) m? **EE:**
Agueleo. Aguela, sumac type
plant that grows in Peru.
Aguenita   see **Agata**.
Aguida   see **Agata**.
Aguijuna   see **Aquilino**.
Aguilivia   see **Aquilino**.
Aguinaldo (Ah ghee nahl' doe) m.
EE: Aguinald. Teut. "He who

governs with sword." **Var:** Aginaldo.

Agundio   see **Abundio.**
Agundo   see **Abundio.**
Agupina   see **Agripino.**
Agusdín   see **Agusto.**
Agusdro   see **Agusto.**
Agustico   see **Agusto.**
Agustín   see **Agusto.**
Agustinium   see **Agusto.**
Agustino   see **Agusto.**
Agusto (Ah goose' toe) m. **EE:** August, Augustine, Gus. Lat. "Majestic, dignified." Emperor & master of Roman world. 26 x in DS. **Dim:** Asta, Cacho (Agustín), Chucho, Cuxo, Tin (Agustín), Tincho, Tinica (Agustín), Tino, Tinuch (Agustín), Tito, Tuto, Ustín. **Var:** Agostia, Agostín, Agostina, Agusdín, Agusdro, Agustico, Agustín, Agustinium, Agustino, Agustón, Agutín, Augastín, Augostín, Augostino, Augstín, Augusdín, Augustavo, Austén, Augustena, Augustín, Augustina, Augustinea, Augustinus, Augusto, Augustulo, Austeo, Austina, Aygusta.
Agustón   see **Agusto.**
Agutín   see **Agusto.**
Ahbrán   see **Abraham.**
Ahenio   see **Eugenio.**
Ahida   see **Aída.**
Aída (Ah ee' dah) f. **EE:** Aida. Protagonist of 19th cen. opera by Verdi. **Dim:** Ducha. **Var:** Ahida, Ayda.
Airene   see **Irene.**
Aislara (Ay slar' rah) f. **EE:** Aislara. Sp. "To separate." Fig., person given to solitude.
Aixa (Ay' sha) f. **EE:** Aisha, Aishah, Ayesha. Favorite wife of prophet Mohammed. Astute, brilliant, devoted to his teachings.
Ajapito   see **Agapito.**
Ajdelaido   see **Adelaido.**
Alacrio   see **Acario.**
Aladino (Ah lah dee' no) m. **EE:** Aladdin. Ar. "Height of religion." Hero in tale of Arabian Nights.
Alagracia   see **Altagracia.**
Alajandro   see **Alejandro.**
Alalio   see **Eulalio.**
Alalita (Ah lah lee' tah) f. **EE:** Alalita. Stone found in Italy.
Alallo   see **Eulalio.**
Alamar (Ah lah mar') m. **EE:** Alamar. Ar. "An adornment of gold." **Var:** Alamaro.
Alamaro   see **Alamar.**
Alano (Ah lah' no) m. **EE:** Alan, Allen. Celt. "Fair & handsome." 2 British Ss.
Alapito   see **Agapito.**
Alaríco (Ah lah ree' co) m. **EE:** Alaric. Teut. "Ruler of all." Visigothic king who sacked Rome in 400 A.D. **Dim:** Rico.
Alasio   see **Alejandro.**
Alaticia   see **Leticia.**
Alazio   see **Alejandro.**
Albagracia   see **Altagracia.**

Albanasius   see **Albano.**
Albano (Ahl bah' no) m. **EE:** Alban, Albanus. Lat. "White." 4 Ss. 1st M. of Britain. **Var:** Albanasius.
Albar   see **Álbaro.**
Álbaro (Ahl' bah roe) m. **EE:** Alvarus. Ger. "All-prudent." 3 Ss. **Dim:** Alvi, Lalo. **Var:** Albar, Álvaro, Alvarso, Alvarum, Alvera, Alverico, Alverio, Alviria, Alvra, Élvara, Olvaro.
Albarto   see **Alberto.**
Alberdo   see **Alberto.**
Alberico (Ahl bay ree' co) m. **EE:** Alberic. Teut. "King of elves." 6 x in DS.
Albertín   see **Alberto.**
Albertina   see **Alberto.**
Alberto (Ahl bair' toe) m. **EE:** Al, Albert, Bert, etc. Ger. "Noble & bright." 28 x in DS. **Dim:** Aber, Abeto, Albertín, Albertina, Bertunga, Beto, Tico, Titina (Albertina), Tito, Veto. **Var:** Albarto, Alberdo, Albertum, Alertano, Alverto, Elibertam, Eliberto, Hedilberto, Helberto, Heliberto, Laberto.
Albertum   see **Alberto.**
Albetto (Ahl bay' toe) m. **EE:** Albetto. Lat. "White"?
Albienta   see **Albino.**
Albinina   see **Albino.**
Albinita   see **Albino.**
Albino (Ahl bee' no) m. **EE:** Alba, Albion, Aubin, etc. Lat. "White." 17 x in DS. **Dim:** Alvinita. **Var:** Albienta, Albinina, Albinita, Albinus, Aluino, Alunia, Alveena, Alvena, Alvienta, Alvinda, Alvinlum, Alvino, Alvio, Elbina, Elevino.
Albinus   see **Albino.**
Albira   see **Elviro.**
Albundio   see **Abundio.**
Alcadio   see **Arcadio.**
Alcairo   see **Acario.**
Alcalio   see **Arcadio.**
Alcardio   see **Arcadio.**
Alcariae   see **Acario.**
Alcario   see **Acario.**
Alcarius   see **Acario.**
Alcasio   see **Acacio.**
Alcedio   see **Arcadio.**
Alcia   see **Alicio.**
Alcibíades (Ahl see bee' ah days) m. **EE:** Alcibiades. Gk. "Of vigorous life." Athenian statesman & leader during Peloponnesian War of 4th cen. B.C. Fr. M. of 2nd cen.
Alcir (Ahl seer') m. **EE:** Adalcira. Ger. "Noble adornment." **Dim:** Cira, Cirita. **Var:** Alciria.
Alciria   see **Alcir.**
Alcodio   see **Arcadio.**
Aldefonso   see **Ildefonso.**
Aldegundo (Ahl day goon' doe) m. **EE:** Aldegund. Ger. "Battle of nobility." 3rd cen. V. & S. See also Aldonza.
Aldifonsa   see **Ildefonso.**
Aldjandro   see **Alejandro.**
Aldo (Ahl' doe) m. **EE:** Aldo, Aldoud. Ger. "Noble, full of

experience." 2 x in DS. **Var:**
Aldon, Aldora.

Aldon   see **Aldo.**

Aldonza (All doan' sah) f. Ger.
"Battle of nobility." **Dim:**
Loncha.

Aldora   see **Aldo.**

Aleatero (Ah lay ah tay' roe) m.
EE: Aleatero. Aleaterio, Sp.
"dependent upon luck."

Alecio   see **Alejandro.**
Aleco   see **Alejandro.**
Alecta   see **Electra.**
Alectra   see **Electra.**
Aledonia   see **Celedonio.**
Alefandro   see **Alejandro.**
Alefonso   see **Alfonso.**
Alegandro   see **Alejandro.**
Alegario   see **Olegario.**
Alegarius   see **Olegario.**
Alegos   see **Alegra.**

Alegra (Ah lay' grah) f. **EE:**
Happy. Lat. "To make merry."
Var: Alegos, Elegria.

Alehandra   see **Alejandro.**
Aleida   see **Elido.**
Alejadra   see **Alejandro.**
Alejanaro   see **Alejandro.**
Alejanda   see **Alejandro.**
Alejandor   see **Alejandro.**

Alejandro (Ah lay hahn' droe) m.
EE: Alex, Alexander, etc. Gk.
"Defender of men." 1 of greatest
generals of antiquity who con-
quered much of ancient world. 46
x in DS. **Dim:** Alecio, Aleco,
Alejho, Alejo, Alejos, Alejoz,
Alejucho, Alendro, Ales, Alex,
Alhandra, Aljo, Allejos, Alyos,
Asandra, Dejandro, Dina, Drina,
Elejus, Eleseo, Elexis, Ellego,
Gando, Jandino, Jandro, Jando,
Jano, Jeandro, Lejandro,
Llejandro, Sandara, Sandra,
Sandrah, Saundra, Xandra,
Zandra. **Var:** Alajandro, Alasio,
Alazio, Aldjandro, Alefandro,
Alegandro, Alehandra, Alejadra,
Alejanaro, Alejanda, Alejandor,
Alisondro, Alizando, Alizardo,
Alizondo, Allesandro, Alyandro,
Dejandra, Elejandra, Elesandro,
Elijandro, Elinandro, Elisandre,
Elisandro, Elisondro,
Elissandro, Elixandro,
Elixsandro, Elizanda, Elizandro,
Elizondro, Elsandro, Ilisandro.

Alejho   see **Alejandro.**
Alejo   see **Alejandro.**
Alejos   see **Alejandro.**
Alejoz   see **Alejandro.**
Alejucho   see **Alejandro.**
Alelarda   see **Abelardo.**

Alelina (Ah lay lee' nah) f. **EE:**
Alelina. Ar. botanical term.

Alena   see **Elena.**
Alendro   see **Alejandro.**

Alentín (Ah lain teen') m. **EE:**
Alentin, Sp. "To encourage, to
inspire"?

Alertano   see **Alberto.**
Ales   see **Alejandro.**
Alestino   see **Celestino.**
Alesvia   see **Lesbia.**
Alex   see **Alejandro.**

Aleyda   see **Adelaido.**

Alfa (Ahl' fah) f. **EE:** Alpha. 1st
letter of Gk. alphabet. Mentioned with omega, last letter,
signifying beginning & end.
Fig., Jesus Christ.

Alfanso   see **Alfonso.**
Alfedo   see **Alfredo.**

Alfenia (Ahl fay' nee ah) f. **EE:**
Alfenia. Ar. for star Gemini.

Alfenso   see **Alfonso.**
Alferdo   see **Alfredo.**
Alferto   see **Alfredo.**
Alfoncina   see **Alfonso.**
Alfonsín   see **Alfonso.**

Alfonso (Ahl fone' so) m. **EE:**
Alonzo, Alphonse, Lon. Ger.
"Noble & ready." 5 x in DS.
Patron of Palma & Mallorca. F.
10/30. **Dim:** Foncho, Fonso,
Joncho, Loncho, Luncha (Alonsa),
Pocho, Poncho, Ponciano, Ponso.
Var: Affonso, Affurso, Alefonso,
Alfanso, Alfenso, Alfoncina,
Alfonsín, Alfonzo, Alforiso,
Alfronso, Alifanso, Alifondra,
Alifonso, Alifonzao, Alifonzo,
Alinzo, Alionza, Aliphont,
Alonso, Alonzo, Alouso, Alphone,
Alphons, Elifonsi, Elifonso,
Helefonso.

Alfonzo   see **Alfonso.**
Alforiso   see **Alfonso.**
Alfrado   see **Alfredo.**

Alfredo (Ahl fray' doe) m. **EE:** Al,
Alf, Alfred, etc. Ang-Sax.
"Protection of nobility." 4th
cen. S. & bishop in Germany. F.
8/15. **Dim:** Feyo, Fito, Fredi,
Fredo. **Var:** Alfedo, Alferdo,
Alferto, Alfrado, Alfredus,
Alfrido, Elfridio, Elfriede,
Eufredo, Hilfredo, Lafredo.

Alfredus   see **Alfredo.**
Alfrido   see **Alfredo.**
Alfronso   see **Alfonso.**
Algabita   see **Agapito.**
Algabo   see **Agapito.**
Algario   see **Olegario.**
Algora   see **Olegario.**
Alguilana   see **Aquilino.**
Alhandra   see **Alejandro.**
Aliasar   see **Eleazar.**
Alibia   see **Olivo.**
Aliccia   see **Alicio.**
Aliceto   see **Alicio.**

Alicio (Ah lee' see oh) m. **EE:**
Alice, etc. Gk. "Truth." 13th
cen. S. with leprosy & visions.
F. 6/15. **Dim:** Chichi, Chita,
Licha, Lichu, Licia. **Var:** Alcia,
Aliccia, Aliceto, Alis, Alisa,
Aliseo, Alisha, Alisia, Aliza,
Alyas, Alyssa, Elicio, Ellicia,
Lysio, Olicia. See also Elisa.

Alidia   see **Elido.**
Alido   see **Elido.**
Alifanso   see **Alfonso.**
Alifondra   see **Alfonso.**
Alifonso   see **Alfonso.**
Alifonzao   see **Alfonso.**
Alifonzo   see **Alfonso.**
Aligorio   see **Olegario.**

Alindardo (Ah leen dahr' doe) m.
EE: Alindardo. Sp. "To make

beautiful."

Alinzo   see **Alfonso.**
Alionza   see **Alfonso.**
Aliphont   see **Alfonso.**
Alipio (Ah lee' pee oh) m. **EE:**
   Alipius, Alypius, Gk. "He who is
   without sadness." Gk. S. of 7th
   cen. **Var:** Elipio.
Alirio (Ah lee' ree oh) m. **EE:**
   Alirio. S. & bishop of Clermont,
   France in 4th cen.
Alis   see **Alicio.**
Alisa   see **Alicio.**
Aliseo   see **Alicio.**
Alisha   see **Alicio.**
Alisia   see **Alicio.**
Alisondro   see **Alejandro.**
Alita   see **Adela.**
Alitano   see **Atilano.**
Alivia   see **Olivo.**
Aliza   see **Alicio.**
Alizando   see **Alejandro.**
Alizardo   see **Alejandro.**
Alizondo   see **Alejandro.**
Aljimiro (Ahl hee mee' roe) m. Sp.
   "Extremely beautiful"?
Aljo   see **Alejandro.**
Allagracio   see **Altagracia.**
Allejos   see **Alejandro.**
Allesandro   see **Alejandro.**
Alma (Ahl' mah) f. **EE:** Alma. Lat.
   "That which gives life."
Almaiza (Ahl mye' sah) f. **EE:**
   Almaiza. Almaizar or Almaizal,
   gauze veil worn by Moors.
Almando   see **Armando.**
Almaquio (Ahl mock' key oh) m. **EE:**
   Almachius. Roman M. of 4th cen.,
   killed for protesting gladiator
   sports. F. 1/1.
Almarantis   see **Amaranto.**
Almaranto   see **Amaranto.**
Almicar   see **Amilcar.**
Almida   see **Armida.**
Almindro   see **Armida.**
Almira   see **Edelmira.**
Almo   see **Erasmo.**
Alodio   see **Elodio.**
Aloisio (Ah low ee' see oh) m. **EE:**
   Aloysius. Ger. "Glorious in
   combat." Ital. S. of 16th cen.
   who is patron of youth. F. 6/21.
   Var: Aloiza, Alouiso, Aloya,
   Aloyisa, Aloyisious, Aloysa,
   Aluisa. See also Clodoveo,
   Ludivico, Luis.
Aloiza   see **Aloisio.**
Aloma   see **Paloma.**
Alonso   see **Alfonso.**
Alonzo   see **Alfonso.**
Alouiso   see **Aloisio.**
Alouso   see **Alfonso.**
Aloya   see **Aloisio.**
Aloyisa   see **Aloisio.**
Aloyisious   see **Aloisio.**
Aloysa   see **Aloisio.**
Alpedo   see **Elpidio.**
Alphone   see **Alfonso.**
Alphons   see **Alfonso.**
Alpidio   see **Elpidio.**
Alrendia   see **Erendira.**
Alta   see **Altagracia.**
Altagracia (Ahl' tah grah' see ah)
   f. **EE:** Altagracia. Lat. "High
   grace." Blessed V. who is vener-

ated in Dominican Republic. F.
1/6. **Dim:** Alta, Olta, Tatá. **Var:**
Alagracia, Albagracia,
Allagracio, Altagragia,
Altagratia, Altagratiae,
Altagratis, Altagrazia,
Altegracia, Altogracio,
Attagracia, Octagracio.
Altagragia   see **Altagracia.**
Altagratia   see **Altagracia.**
Altagratiae   see **Altagracia.**
Altagratis   see **Altagracia.**
Altagrazia   see **Altagracia.**
Altamasio   see **Atanasio.**
Altamisa   see **Artemio.**
Altanese   see **Atanasio.**
Altegracia   see **Altagracia.**
Altogracio   see **Altagracia.**
Altunasio   see **Atanasio.**
Alturo   see **Arturo.**
Aluino   see **Albino.**
Aluisa   see **Aloisio.**
Alunia   see **Albino.**
Alvanus (Ahl bah' noos) m. **EE:**
   Alvanus. Sp. S. whose remains
   are in Barbastro, Spain. F.
   10/26. Also see Alvino.
Alvaro   see **Albaro.**
Alvarso   see **Albaro.**
Alvarum   see **Albaro.**
Alveena   see **Albino.**
Alvelardo   see **Abelardo.**
Alvena   see **Albino.**
Alvera   see **Albaro.**
Alverico   see **Albaro.**
Alverio   see **Albaro.**
Alverto   see **Alberto.**
Alvi   see **Albaro.**
Alvienta   see **Albino.**
Alvinda   see **Albino.**
Alvinita   see **Albino.**
Alvinlum   see **Albino.**
Alvino   see **Albino.**
Alvio   see **Albino.**
Alviria   see **Albaro.**
Alvirra   see **Elviro.**
Alvirum   see **Elviro.**
Alviso (Ahl bee' so) m. **EE:**
   Alviso. Alvisia, plant belonging
   to orchid family. **Var:** Elbisa.
Alvra   see **Albaro.**
Alyandro   see **Alejandro.**
Alyas   see **Alicio.**
Alyos   see **Alejandro.**
Alyssa   see **Alicio.**
Amabel   see **Amable.**
Amabia   see **Amable.**
Amabilia   see **Amable.**
Amable (Ah mahb' lay) f. **EE:**
   Amabilis, Amable. Lat. "Lov-
   able." 2 x in DS. **Var:** Amabel,
   Amabia, Amabilia.
Amachio   see **Amasio.**
Amacleto   see **Anacleto.**
Amada (Ah mah' dah) f. **EE:** Aimee,
   Amy, etc. Lat. "To love." **Dim:**
   Amadillo. **Var:** Amadar, Amadello,
   Amadia, Amadida, Amadona,
   Amador, Amadre, Amata, Omada.
Amadar   see **Amada.**
Amadello   see **Amada.**
Amadeo (Ah mah day' oh) m. **EE:**
   Amadeus, Amias. Lat. "He who
   loves God." 15th cen. Ital. S.
   F. 3/31. **Var:** Amades, Amdes,

Ameda, Amedes, Amedia, Amesoe.
Amades   see **Amadeo**.
Amadia   see **Amada**.
Amadida   see **Amada**.
Amadillo   see **Amada**.
Amadona   see **Amada**.
Amador   see **Amada**.
Amadre   see **Amada**.
Amaelia   see **Amalio**.
Amalín   see **Amalio**.
Amalio (Ah mah' lee oh) m. **EE:**
   Amelia, Emile. Ger. "Industrious
   one." **Dim:** Amalín, Amelino,
   Lila, Lita, Maya, Mela (Amelia),
   Meli (Amelia), Melita (Amelia),
   Meya (Amelia). **Var:** Amaelia,
   Amelida, Ameline, Amelio, Amila,
   Amilia, Armelia, Emala, Emalia.
   See also Emilio.
Aman   see **Hamión**.
Amancio (Ah mahn' see oh) m. **EE:**
   Amantius. Lat. "Love." 5 x in
   DS. **Var:** Amansio, Anancio,
   Emancio, Eumancia.
Amanda (Ah mahn' dah) f. **EE:**
   Amanda, Mandy, etc. Lat. "Who
   ought to be loved." 14 x in DS.
   Dim: Manda, Mandita, Nanda. **Var:**
   Amano, Amenda, Ammendina,
   Ananda, Emando.
Amano   see **Amanda**.
Amansio   see **Amancio**.
Amapola (Ah mah poe' lah) f. **EE:**
   Amapola. Ar. "Poppy." **Dim:** Pola.
Amara   see **Amaranto**.
Amarande   see **Amaranto**.
Amarante   see **Amaranto**.
Amaranto (Ah mah rahn' toe) m. **EE:**
   Amarantius. Lat. "Imperishable."
   3rd cen. mart. S. F. 11/7. **Dim:**
   Amara, Amario, Amarita,
   Armatina. **Var:**
   Almarantis, Almaranto, Amarande,
   Amarante, Amaritum, Amerardo.
Amarilis (Ah mah ree' lees) f. **EE:**
   Amaryllis, etc. Gk. "Sparkling
   stream." Shepherdess in pastoral
   play by Theocritus. **Var:**
   Amauelis.
Amario   see **Amaranto**.
Amarita   see **Amaranto**.
Amaritum   see **Amaranto**.
Amasio (Ah mah' see oh) m. **EE:**
   Amasius. Lat. "Lover." **Var:**
   Amachio.
Amastasia   see **Anastacio**.
Amata   see **Amada**.
Amauelis   see **Amarilis**.
Ambarosio   see **Ambrosio**.
Amberosio   see **Ambrosio**.
Amboronso   see **Ambrosio**.
Amborsio   see **Ambrosio**.
Ambosio   see **Ambrosio**.
Ambracio   see **Ambrosio**.
Ambrano   see **Ambrosio**.
Ambrasio   see **Ambrosio**.
Ambraso   see **Ambrosio**.
Ambriosio   see **Ambrosio**.
Ambrocian   see **Ambrosio**.
Ambrocio   see **Ambrosio**.
Ambrocto   see **Ambrosio**.
Ambronso   see **Ambrosio**.
Ambros   see **Ambrosio**.
Ambrosa   see **Ambrosio**.
Ambroseno   see **Ambrosio**.

Ambrosio (Ahm broe' see oh) m. **EE:**
   Ambrose, Brush. Gk. "Pertaining
   to gods." 5 x in DS. 1 is father
   of western church. F. 12/7. **Dim:**
   Bocho, Locho, Pocho. **Var:**
   Ambarosio, Amberosio, Amboronso,
   Amborsio, Ambosio, Ambracio,
   Ambrano, Ambrasio, Ambraso,
   Ambriosio, Ambrocian, Ambrocio,
   Ambrocto, Ambronso, Ambros,
   Ambrosa, Ambroseno, Ambrozio,
   Amburosia, Anebrosio, Angrosia,
   Anorocio, Arnbrosio, Embrocio.
Ambrozio   see **Ambrosio**.
Amburosia   see **Ambrosio**.
Amdes   see **Amadeo**.
Ameda   see **Amadeo**.
Amedes   see **Amadeo**.
Amedia   see **Amadeo**.
Amelda   see **Imelda**.
Amelida   see **Amalio**.
Ameline   see **Amalio**.
Amelino   see **Amalio**.
Amelio   see **Amalio**.
Amenda   see **Amanda**.
Amenta   see **Aminta**.
Amerardo   see **Amaranto**.
Américo (Ah may' ree co) m. **EE:**
   Americus. Ger. "Chief or king."
   Namesake of America, Amerigo
   Vespucci. **Dim:** Merco, Mimeco.
   See also Emerico.
Amesoe   see **Amadeo**.
Ameteria   see **Emeterio**.
Amfaro   see **Amparo**.
Amila   see **Amalio**.
Amilcar (Ah meel' cahr) m. **EE:**
   Hamilcar. Phoen. "King of city."
   Carthaginian general of 1st
   Punic War. **Var:** Almicar.
Amilia   see **Amalio**.
Aminda   see **Aminta**.
Aminta (Ah meen' tah) f. **EE:**
   Aminta. Lat. "To protect."
   Popular name for shepherdesses
   in Gk. pastoral poetry. **Var:**
   Amenta, Aminda.
Ammanuela   see **Manuel**.
Ammendina   see **Amanda**.
Amora (Ah mo' rah) f. **EE:** Amora.
   Lat. "Love."
Amorosella (Ah mo' roe sehl' ah)
   f. **EE:** Amorosella. Sp. "One who
   feels love."
Amos (Ah mohs') m. **EE:** Amos. Heb.
   "To be burdened or troubled."
   Biblical prophet & book of Bible
   describing doom of Israel. Men-
   tioned in DS. F. 3/31.
Amparao   see **Amparo**.
Amparo (Ahm pah' roe) f. **EE:**
   Amparo. Sp. "Favor, protection."
   Cult of Blessed V., Nuestra
   Señora de los Desamparados. F.
   5/11. **Var:** Amfaro, Amparao,
   Ampero, Aniparo, Anpero, Emparo.
Ampelio (Ahm pay' lee oh) m. **EE:**
   Ampelius. Gk. "Cultivator of
   vines." African M. of 4th cen.
   F. 2/11.
Ampero   see **Amparo**.
Amselmo   see **Anselmo**.
Amulfo   see **Arnulfo**.
Ana (Ah' nah) f. **EE:** Anita, Anne,
   Hannah. Heb. "Gracious, merci-

ful." Major S. is mother of
Blessed V. F. 7/26. **Dim:** Aneta,
Anetta, Anica, Anilla, Anina,
Anita, Anitta, Nana, Nanita,
Nita, Onita. **Var:** Anissa,
Anitam, Aniteo, Anizia, Anucha.

Anaastasio   see **Anastacio.**
Anabel (Ah' nah behl') f. **EE:**
Annabelle, etc. Comb. of Ana &
Belle (see both). **Var:** Anabelia,
Anabilia, Anarbol, Anavel,
Anavelia, Anival, Anvela.

Anabelia   see **Anabel.**
Anabilia   see **Anabel.**
Anacario (Ah nah cah' ree oh) m.
EE: Anacarius. Gk. "With grace."
Anacasio   see **Anastacio.**
Anacledo   see **Anacleto.**
Anacleto (Ah nah clay' toe) m. **EE:**
Anacletus. Gk. "Called in loud
voice." 2nd cen. pope & M. F.
7/13. **Dim:** Amacleto, Anacledo,
Ancleto, Aniclebo, Naclito. **Var:**
Anacletum, Anacletus, Anaclito,
Anaclitor, Anascleto, Anicleto,
Cleto, Encelata, Enicleto,
Ornacleto. See also Cleto.

Anacletum   see **Anacleto.**
Anacletus   see **Anacleto.**
Anaclito   see **Anacleto.**
Anaclitor   see **Anacleto.**
Analilia (Ah nah lee' lee ah) f.
EE: Analilia. Comb. of Ana &
Lilia (see both).
Analissa (Ah nah lee' sah) f. **EE:**
Annelise, etc. Comb. of Ana &
Lisa (see both).
Anancio   see **Amancio.**
Ananda   see **Amanda.**
Ananias (Ah nah nee' ahs) m. **EE:**
Ananias. Heb. "God is merciful."
Holy Christian of Damascus to
whom God appeared in vision.
Anarbol   see **Anabel.**
Anarosa (Ah nah roe' sah) f. Comb.
of Ana & Rosa (see both).
Anartasia   see **Anastacio.**
Anascleto   see **Anacleto.**
Anaslacio   see **Anastacio.**
Anasolia   see **Anastacio.**
Anassacia   see **Anastacio.**
Anassasio   see **Anastacio.**
Anastaceo   see **Anastacio.**
Anastacio (Ah nahs tah' see oh) m.
EE: Anastasia, Stacy, etc. Gk.
"Of the resurrection." 22 x in
DS. Youngest daughter of Tsar
Nicholas II of Russia, supposed-
ly killed after Revolution. **Dim:**
Anastio, Anasto, Nacho,
Nestacio, Tacha, Tachito, Tasio,
Tato. **Var:** Amastacio,
Anaastasio, Anacasio, Anartasia,
Anaslacio, Anasolia, Anassacia,
Anassasio, Anastaceo,
Anastación, Anastanio, Anastano,
Anastario, Anastas, Anastasa,
Anastasi, Anastasio, Anastasium,
Anastasiz, Anastatia, Anastazio,
Anastecio, Anastesio,
Anasthasio, Anastia, Anastice,
Anastico, Anastisio, Anastonio,
Anastosio, Anastotio, Anastrio,
Anastsio, Anatacio, Anatascia,
Anestacio, Anestania, Anestano,

Anestara, Anestasio, Anistazia,
Annastasia, Anostacio,
Anostasia, Anostosia, Ansansio,
Anstaceo, Ariastacio, Ataniso,
Auastasio, Hanastasio,
Onastacio, Onastasio, Onostisio.

Anastación   see **Anastacio.**
Anastanio   see **Anastacio.**
Anastano   see **Anastacio.**
Anastario   see **Anastacio.**
Anastas   see **Anastacio.**
Anastasa   see **Anastacio.**
Anastasi   see **Anastacio.**
Anastasio   see **Anastacio.**
Anastasium   see **Anastacio.**
Anastasiz   see **Anastacio.**
Anastatia   see **Anastacio.**
Anastazio   see **Anastacio.**
Anastecio   see **Anastacio.**
Anastesio   see **Anastacio.**
Anasthasio   see **Anastacio.**
Anastia   see **Anastacio.**
Anastice   see **Anastacio.**
Anastico   see **Anastacio.**
Anastio   see **Anastacio.**
Anastisio   see **Anastacio.**
Anasto   see **Anastacio.**
Anastolio   see **Anatolio.**
Anastonio   see **Anastacio.**
Anastosio   see **Anastacio.**
Anastotio   see **Anastacio.**
Anastrio   see **Anastacio.**
Anastsio   see **Anastacio.**
Anatacio   see **Anastacio.**
Anatalia   see **Anatolio.**
Anatascia   see **Anastacio.**
Anatolio (Ah nah toe' lee oh) m.
EE: Anatole, Anatoly, etc. Gk.
"One who comes from the East." 4
x in DS. Important philosopher &
mathmatician in Asia Minor. **Var:**
Anastolio, Anatalia, Anlalia,
Anstolia, Antalina, Antolín.

Anavel   see **Anabel.**
Anavelia   see **Anabel.**
Ancelemo   see **Anselmo.**
Ancelia   see **Anselmo.**
Ancelmo   see **Anselmo.**
Ancencia   see **Asunción.**
Ancención   see **Asunción.**
Ancensión   see **Asunción.**
Anchelito   see **Ángel.**
Anciano (Ahn see ah' no) m. **EE:**
Ancient. Lat. "An older person."
Among Jews suggests advanced age
& authority.
Ancilino   see **Acilino.**
Ancirea (Ahn see ray' ah) f. **EE:**
Ancira. Site where baby boys
were mart. Ancyra, in present-
day Turkey. F. 9/23.
Ancleto   see **Anacleto.**
Andalecio   see **Indalecio.**
Andaleno   see **Magdaleno.**
Andalusio   see **Indalecio.**
Andelario   see **Candelario.**
Andelecia   see **Indalecio.**
Andelesio   see **Indalecio.**
Andelio (Ahn day' lee oh) m. **EE:**
Andelius. Form of Andeulus, S. &
M. of Smyrna, Turkey? F. 5/1.
Andero   see **Andrés.**
Andi   see **Andrés.**
Andolesio   see **Indalecio.**
Andón   see **Antonio.**

Andona   see **Antonio.**
Andonia   see **Antonio.**
Andora (Ahn doe' rah) f? **EE:**
Andorra. Independent republic in
Pyrrenees between France &
Spain.
Andream   see **Andrés.**
Andrean   see **Andrés.**
Andreaz   see **Andrés.**
Andreina   see **Andrés.**
Andreita   see **Andrés.**
Andreitta   see **Andrés.**
Andrella   see **Andrés.**
Andrellita   see **Andrés.**
Andreo   see **Andrés.**
Andreolo   see **Andrés.**
Andreón   see **Andrés.**
Andrés (Ahn drays') m. **EE:** Andrew,
Andy. Gk. "Strong, manly." 14 x
in DS. Andrew of Galilee, 1st
apostle summoned by Christ. F.
11/30. **Dim:** Adrés, Andi,
Andresito, Necho, Nesho, Tito.
Var: Andero, Andream, Andrean,
Andreaz, Andreina, Andreita,
Andreitta, Andrella, Andrellita,
Andreo, Andreolo, Andreón,
Andress, Andreto, Andrez,
Andria, Andrianna, Andriceta,
Ondrés.
Andresito   see **Andrés.**
Andress   see **Andrés.**
Andreto   see **Andrés.**
Andrez   see **Andrés.**
Andria   see **Andrés.**
Andrianna   see **Andrés.**
Andriceta   see **Andrés.**
Andrikes   see **Enrique.**
Andrique   see **Enrique.**
Andrónico (Ahn droe' nee co) m.
EE: Andronicus. Gk. "One who
conquers others." 2 x in DS.
Roman poet of 3rd cen. B.C.
Anebrosio   see **Ambrosio.**
Anécimo   see **Onésimo.**
Anelda (Ah nehl' dah) f. **EE:**
Anelda. Comb. of Ana & Nélida
(see both)?
Aneselma   see **Anselmo.**
Anésimo   see **Onésimo.**
Anésino   see **Onésimo.**
Anestacio   see **Anastacio.**
Anestania   see **Anastacio.**
Anestano   see **Anastacio.**
Anestara   see **Anastacio.**
Anestasio   see **Anastacio.**
Anestor   see **Néstor.**
Aneta   see **Ana.**
Anetta   see **Ana.**
Anfanio (Ahn fah' nee oh) m. **EE:**
Anfiano. Form of Anfiano, 3rd
cen. S. of Phoenicia. F. 4/2.
Var: Enfranio.
Anfilo (Ahn fee' low) m. **EE:**
Anfilo. Form of Anfiloquio,
bishop of Cappadocia (Turkey) &
strong enemy of Arians?
Angalina   see **Angel.**
Angalita   see **Angel.**
Angel (Ahn' hehl) m. **EE:** Angel,
Angela, Angelo. Heb. "Messen-
ger." 4 x in DS. Bodiless spirit
is accepted in Jewish, Chris-
tian, & Muslim religions. **Dim:**
Agelina, Agelita, Angalina,

Angalita, Angie, Angilino,
Anhelita, Anjelita, Gelo, Lina,
Lito, Nina, Tita, Tuelis. **Var:**
Agelila, Anchelito, Angelena,
Angeles, Angeliam, Angeliata,
Angélica, Angelida, Angelina,
Angella (Angelmo), Angelmo,
Angelo, Angulo, Anjelo,
Anjileta, Engelita, Ongelita.
See also Evangelina.
Angelena   see **Angel.**
Angeles   see **Angel.**
Angeliam   see **Angel.**
Angeliata   see **Angel.**
Angélica   see **Angel.**
Angelida   see **Angel.**
Angelina   see **Angel.**
Angella   see **Angel.**
Angelmo   see **Angel.**
Angelo   see **Angel.**
Angie   see **Angel.**
Angilberto (Ahn hill bair' toe) m.
EE: Englebert. Comb. of Angel &
Berto (see both).
Angilino   see **Angel.**
Angrosia   see **Ambrosio.**
Angulo   see **Angel.**
Anhelita   see **Angel.**
Aniano (Ah nee ah' no) m. **EE:**
Aniano. Lat. "Consecrated to
Anna," goddess of the year. 3 x
in DS.
Aníbal (Ah nee' bahl) m. **EE:**
Hannibal. Phoen. "Lord is merci-
ful." Carthaginian military
genius who crossed Alps to
attack Romans. **Var:** Hanibal.
Aniberto (Ah nee bair' toe) m. **EE:**
Annabert. Comb. of Ana & Berto
(see both). **Var:** Anoverto.
Anica   see **Ana.**
Anicacio   see **Acacio.**
Anicasio   see **Acacio.**
Aniceto (Ah nee say' toe) m. **EE:**
Anicetus. Gk. "Invincible." 2 x
in DS.
Aniclebo   see **Anacleto.**
Anicleto   see **Anacleto.**
Anilla   see **Ana.**
Anina   see **Ana.**
Aniparo   see **Amparo.**
Anisio (Ah nee' see oh) m. **EE:**
Anisius. Gk. "He who carries out
an obligation." **Var:** Annisia,
Enise.
Anissa   see **Ana.**
Anistazia   see **Anastacio.**
Anita   see **Ana.**
Anitam   see **Ana.**
Aniteo   see **Ana.**
Anitta   see **Ana.**
Anival   see **Anabel.**
Anizia   see **Ana.**
Anjelita   see **Angel.**
Anjelo   see **Angel.**
Anjileta   see **Angel.**
Anlalia   see **Anatolio.**
Annastasia   see **Anastacio.**
Annelmo   see **Anselmo.**
Anniqueta   see **Enrique.**
Annisia   see **Anisio.**
Annuciana   see **Anunciación.**
Annuntitionom   see **Anunciación.**
Anodina (Ah no dee' nah) f. "That
which serves to allay pain."

Anofre   see **Onofre.**
Anofrio   see **Onofre.**
Anorea   see **Anores.**
Anores (Ah no' rays) m. **EE:**
Anoreus. Anoreus, Ethiopian S.
F. 2/12. **Var:** Anorea.
Anorocio   see **Ambrosio.**
Anostacio   see **Anastacio.**
Anostasia   see **Anastacio.**
Anostosia   see **Anastacio.**
Anoverto   see **Aniberto.**
Anpero   see **Amparo.**
Anrelio   see **Aurelio.**
Anreliono   see **Aurelio.**
Anrique   see **Enrique.**
Ansansio   see **Anastacio.**
Ansberto (Ahns bair' toe) m. **EE:**
Ansbert, Austrabert. Ger.
"Splendor of gods." 7th cen.
Archbishop of Rouen, France,
invoked against fevers. F. 2/9.
Var: Esverda, Isverdo.
Anselima   see **Anselmo.**
Anselino   see **Anselmo.**
Anselm   see **Anselmo.**
Anselmo (Ahn sehl' mo) m. **EE:**
Anselm, Selma, etc. Ger. "God &
helmet." 7 x in DS. 10th cen.
scholar who offered proof of
God's existence. F. 4/21. **Dim:**
Chemo, Semo, Yemo. **Var:** Amselmo,
Ancelemo, Ancelia, Ancelmo,
Aneselma, Annelmo, Anselima,
Anselino, Anselm, Anselmus,
Anselono, Ansilmo, Anzelmo,
Aselm, Aselmo, Asnelmo, Auselmo,
Auzelm, Enselmo, Enzelma,
Onselmo, Selmo, Zelmo.
Anselmus   see **Anselmo.**
Anselono   see **Anselmo.**
Ansencio   see **Asunción.**
Ansilmo   see **Anselmo.**
Anstaceo   see **Anastacio.**
Anstolia   see **Anatolio.**
Ancalina   see **Anatolio.**
Antamina   see **Antimio.**
Antania   see **Antonio.**
Antario   see **Antero.**
Antasia   see **Atanasio.**
Antelmo (Ahn tehl' mo) m. **EE:**
Anthelmus, etc. Ger. "Protection
of native country." 12th cen.
Fr. bishop who supported Pope
Alexander III against anti-pope.
F. 6/26.
Antemio   see **Antimio.**
Antenor (Ahn tay nohr') m. **EE:**
Antenorus. Gk. "He who fights
against man." Gk. sculptor of
6th cen. B.C. who executed stat-
ues of Harmodius & Aristigon.
Antero (Ahn tay' roe) m. **EE:**
Antherus, etc. Gk. "Against
love." 3rd cen. pope. F. 1/3.
Dim: Antia. **Var:** Antario,
Anterro, Anthero, Antiro.
Anterro   see **Antero.**
Anthero   see **Antero.**
Antia   see **Antero.**
Antiago   see **Santiago.**
Antilano   see **Atilano.**
Antimio (Ahn tee' mee oh) m. **EE:**
Antimius, Antimus. Gk. "Flower."
10 x in DS. **Var:** Antamina,
Antemio.

Antiocho   see **Antíoco.**
Antíoco (Ahn tee' oh co) m. **EE:**
Antioch, Antiochus. Lat. "One
who opposes or confronts." 13 x
in DS. **Var:** Antiocho.
Antionia   see **Antonio.**
Antipatio (Ahn tee pah' tee oh) m.
EE: Antipater. Gk. "As good as
his father." 2 x in DS. Macedo-
nian general & dynasty in Pales-
tine at time of Christ. **Var:**
Antipatro.
Antipatro   see **Antipatio.**
Antiro   see **Antero.**
Anto   see **Antonio.**
Antoliana   see **Antonio.**
Antolima   see **Antonio.**
Antolín   see **Anatolio.**
Antolin   see **Antonio.**
Antoliona   see **Antonio.**
Antomio   see **Antonio.**
Antón   see **Antonio.**
Antoneo   see **Antonio.**
Antoniae   see **Antonio.**
Antonieto   see **Antonio.**
Antonine   see **Antonio.**
Antonino   see **Antonio.**
Antonio (Ahn toe' nee oh) m. **EE:**
Anthony, Antony, etc. Lat.
"Inestimable." 44 x in DS. Egyp.
hermit who underwent physical &
spiritual temptations. F. 1/17.
Dim: Anto, Antolín, Antón,
Antonieto, Antonino, Antoñito,
Antuco, Antulio, Chantón, Nino,
Nico, Tiffy, Tonche, Toncho,
Toni, Tonico, Tonin, Tonio,
Tono, Tony, Toñico, Toñin, Toño,
Totó, Tuco, Tuncho. **Var:** Andón,
Andona, Andonia, Antania,
Antionia, Antoliana, Antolima,
Antoliona, Antomio, Antoneo,
Antoniae, Antonine, Antonión,
Antonius, Antora, Natonio.
Antonión   see **Antonio.**
Antonius   see **Antonio.**
Antoñito   see **Antonio.**
Antora   see **Antonio.**
Antuco   see **Antonio.**
Antulio   see **Antonio.**
Anucha   see **Ana.**
Anufre   see **Onofre.**
Anulfo   see **Arnulfo.**
Anunciación (Ah noon' see ah see
own') mf. **EE:** Annunciation. Lat.
"To announce." Feast day of
Blessed V. when Gabriel told her
she would be mother of Christ.
F. 3/25. **Dim:** Anuncio, Inuncia.
Var: Annuciana, Annuntitionom,
Anunziata, Nuncio. See also
Nuncio.
Anuncio   see **Anunciación.**
Anunziata   see **Anunciación.**
Anvela   see **Anabel.**
Anzelmo   see **Anselmo.**
Aodelia   see **Adela.**
Aofilia   see **Ofelio.**
Apalaria   see **Apolonio.**
Apalina   see **Apolonio.**
Apalonio   see **Apolonio.**
Aparicio (Ah pah ree' see oh) m.
EE: Apparition. Sp. "Act of
appearing." Refers to Christ's
appearance before apostles after

resurrection. **Var:** Aparición,
Apparicio.
Aparición   see **Aparicio.**
Aphelia   see **Ofelio.**
Aphilia   see **Ofelio.**
Apiano (Ah pee ah' no) m. **EE:**
Apphianus, Appianus. Patronym of
Apio, Roman first name. 6 x in
DS. **Var:** Apriano.
Apifanio   see **Epifanio.**
Apilinar   see **Apolonio.**
Apilinaria   see **Apolonio.**
Aplica (Ah plee' cah) f? **EE:**
Aplica, Lat. "Applicare," "to
apply." Fig., to be outstanding
especially in study.
Aplonio   see **Apolonio.**
Apolanio   see **Apolonio.**
Apolello   see **Apolonio.**
Apolenar   see **Apolonio.**
Apoleonar   see **Apolonio.**
Apoleonio   see **Apolonio.**
Apolesmio   see **Apolonio.**
Apoleyos   see **Apolonio.**
Apolia   see **Apolonio.**
Apolidón   see **Apolonio.**
Apolidori   see **Apolonio.**
Apolifo   see **Apolonio.**
Apolimar   see **Apolonio.**
Apolimio   see **Apolonio.**
Apolina   see **Apolonio.**
Apolinairia   see **Apolonio.**
Apolinania   see **Apolonio.**
Apolinar   see **Apolonio.**
Apolinares   see **Apolonio.**
Apolinario   see **Apolonio.**
Apolines   see **Apolonio.**
Apolinia   see **Apolonio.**
Apolinis   see **Apolonio.**
Apolionio   see **Apolonio.**
Apollania   see **Apolonio.**
Apollinaries   see **Apolonio.**
Apollinaris   see **Apolonio.**
Apollo   see **Apolo.**
Apollonio   see **Apolonio.**
Apolmia   see **Apolonio.**
Apolo (Ah poe' low) m. **EE:** Apollo.
Gk. "Of sun's power." In Gk.
myth., god of light, music,
poetry, prophecy, & pastoral
activities. **Var:** Apollo. See
also Apolonio.
Apolodio   see **Apolonio.**
Apolomio   see **Apolonio.**
Apoloneo   see **Apolonio.**
Apoloniar   see **Apolonio.**
Apolonica   see **Apolonio.**
Apolonio (Ah poe low' nee oh) m.
EE: Apolinar, etc. Gk. "Apollo,"
"light from sun." 27 x in DS.
3rd cen. M. of Alexandria. Teeth
pulled out with pincers & she
became patroness against tooth-
aches, F. 2/9. **Dim:** Apolia,
Appolón, Loño, Palinaria,
Palomia, Pelonia, Pelonoia,
Plalone, Planonia, Polania,
Pole, Polenario, Poley, Poli,
Poliana, Polín, Polinar,
Polinario, Poline, Polinio,
Polo, Polomia, Polonario,
Polonio. **Var:** Abulina, Afolinar,
Afolonio, Apalaria, Apalina,
Apalonio, Apilinar, Apilinaria,
Aplonio, Apolanio, Apolello,

Apolenar, Apoleonar, Apoleonio,
Apolesmio, Apoleyos, Apolidón,
Apolidori, Apolifo, Apolimar,
Apolimio, Apolina, Apolinairia,
Apolinania, Apolinar,
Apolinares, Apolinario,
Apolines, Apolinia, Apolinís,
Apolionio, Apollania,
Apollinaries, Apollinaris,
Apollonio, Apolmia, Apolodio,
Apolomio, Apoloneo, Apoloniar,
Apolonica, Apolonís, Apolono,
Apolonoa, Apolorio, Aponolario,
Appalenia, Appalonio, Appoliano,
Appolinario, Appolinarius,
Appolinina, Appollanio,
Appollonia, Appolloria,
Appolonia, Epelonia, Epolonia,
Epplyonia, Jolonia, Napolinar,
Opalimar, Opalinaria, Papolonia,
Polinarius, Polinarus,
Pollinaria, Polonium, Spolonia,
Upolonia, Ypolario. See also
Apolo.
Apolonís   see **Apolonio.**
Apolono   see **Apolonio.**
Apolonoa   see **Apolonio.**
Apolorio   see **Apolonio.**
Aponolario   see **Apolonio.**
Appalenia   see **Apolonio.**
Appalonio   see **Apolonio.**
Apparicio   see **Aparicio.**
Appoliano   see **Apolonio.**
Appolinario   see **Apolonio.**
Appolinarius   see **Apolonio.**
Appolinina   see **Apolonio.**
Appollanio   see **Apolonio.**
Appollonia   see **Apolonio.**
Appolloria   see **Apolonio.**
Appolón   see **Apolonio.**
Appolonia   see **Apolonio.**
Aprevenido (Ah pray nee' doe)
m. Sp. "To be on guard or to
prevent."
Apriano   see **Apiano.**
Apulego   see **Apuleyo.**
Apuleyo (Ah poo lay' oh) m. **EE:**
Apuleius. Plebian Roman family.
Also, author of "Golden Ass."
Var: Apulego, Apulino.
Apulino   see **Apuleyo.**
Apundia   see **Abundio.**
Aqueda   see **Agata.**
Aquileo   see **Aquiles.**
Aquiles (Ah key' lace) m. **EE:**
Achilles, Achilleus, Gk. "With-
out lips." Hero of "Iliad" of
ancient Greece. **Dim:** Quilo,
Quina. **Var:** Aquileo, Aquilo.
Aquilina   see **Acilino.**
Aquilino (Ah key lee' no) m. **EE:**
Aquilinus. Lat. "Like an eagle."
8 x in DS. **Var:** Aguijuna,
Aguilivia, Alguilana, Aquillina.
Aquillina   see **Aquilino.**
Aquilo   see **Aquiles.**
Arabela (Ah rah bay' lah) f. **EE:**
Arabella, Bella, Belle. Lat.
"Beautiful altar," or Ger.
"eager heroine"? **Dim:** Bela. **Var:**
Arabelia, Arabella, Arabila,
Aravela, Eribel.
Arabelia   see **Arabela.**
Arabella   see **Arabela.**
Arabila   see **Arabela.**

Araceli (Ah rah say' lee) f? Lat.
"Altar of heaven." **Dim:** Chela,
Cheli, Cleli, Cleyo. **Var:**
Aracelis, Aracely, Aranselia,
Araseles, Araselia, Arcedalia,
Arcelida, Arcelio, Arceya,
Archelia, Aregelia, Argelia,
Argelina, Argelisa, Ariselda,
Arizala, Arizela, Arjelia,
Arselia, Arsilia, Aurcelia,
Ercilia, Ercilia, Erciliana,
Haracelia, Harcelo.

Aracelis   see **Araceli.**
Aracely   see **Araceli.**
Aralia   see **Aurelio.**
Aranselia   see **Araceli.**
Arapita   see **Agapito.**
Araseles   see **Araceli.**
Araselia   see **Araceli.**
Arasmo   see **Erasmo.**
Aravela   see **Arabela.**
Arcabio   see **Arcadio.**
Arcadie   see **Arcadio.**
Arcadio (Ahr cah' dee oh) m. **EE:**
Arcadius. Gk. "One born in
Arcadia." Gk. region inhabited
by pastoral people. Fig.,
paradise. 8 x in DS. **Dim:** Cadio,
Minda. **Var:** Acadro, Alcadio,
Alcalio, Alcardio, Alcedio,
Alcodio, Arcabio, Arcadie,
Arcadro, Arcaia, Arcodyo,
Arcordia, Argadio, Arkadi,
Aucauda, Eicadio, Ocadia.
Arcadro   see **Arcadio.**
Arcaia   see **Arcadio.**
Arcano (Ahr cah' no) m. **EE:**
Arcanus. Lat. fig., reserved
person. 2 x in DS.
Arcarcio   see **Acacio.**
Arcario   see **Acacio.**
Arcasio   see **Acacio.**
Arcedalia   see **Araceli.**
Arcelida   see **Araceli.**
Arcelio   see **Araceli.**
Arcenio   see **Arsenio.**
Arceya   see **Araceli.**
Archeláo (Ahr chay lah' oh) m. **EE:**
Archelaus. Archelaus is name of
at least 8 Christian Mm.
Archelia   see **Araceli.**
Archibaldo (Ahr chee bahl' doe) m.
EE: Archibald, Archie. Ger. "No-
bly bold." 7th cen. S. & bishop
of London. F. 4/30. **Dim:** Baldo.
Var: Archivaldo, Ardivaldo.
Archivaldo   see **Archibaldo.**
Arcilin   see **Marcelino.**
Arcodyo   see **Arcadio.**
Arcordia   see **Arcadio.**
Arculano   see **Herculano.**
Ardelia   see **Adela.**
Ardivaldo   see **Archibaldo.**
Arecentio   see **Arsenio.**
Aregelia   see **Araceli.**
Aregina   see **Regina.**
Arelardo   see **Abelardo.**
Arelio   see **Aurelio.**
Arella   see **Aurelio.**
Areopajita   see **Agapito.**
Areopaquita   see **Agapito.**
Aresteo   see **Aristeo.**
Aretimo   see **Artemio.**
Argadio   see **Arcadio.**
Argapito   see **Agapito.**

Argelia   see **Araceli.**
Argelina   see **Araceli.**
Argelisa   see **Araceli.**
Argentina (Ahr hen tee' nah) f.
EE: Argentina. Lat. "Silver."
Term "argentum" used to describe
silver cities of upper Peru &
southern South America. **Dim:**
Tino. **Var:** Arquentina.
Argimino   see **Arquimedis.**
Argimiro   see **Arquimedis.**
Arguimedes   see **Arquimedis.**
Ariano (Ah ree ah' no) m. **EE:**
Arian, Arius. Gk. "Warlike." In
Gk. myth., god of war comparable
to Roman Mars. 2nd cen. priest
who proclaimed Christ was not an
equal of God. **Var:** Arriano,
Arrio.
Ariastacio   see **Anastacio.**
Ariela (Ah ree aay' lah) f. **EE:**
Ariel. Heb. "Lioness of God" or
"hearth of God." Fig., synonym
for Jerusalem.
Ariopaca   see **Agapito.**
Ariopajita   see **Agapito.**
Ariosto (Ah ree ohs' toe) m. **EE:**
Ariosto. 16th cen. Ital. poet
noted for Orlando Furioso,
Roland story in epic form. **Var:**
Arisotos.
Aripea   see **Agapito.**
Ariselda   see **Araceli.**
Arisotos   see **Ariosto.**
Aristedes   see **Aristeo.**
Aristelo   see **Aristeo.**
Aristeo (Ah rees tay' oh) m. **EE:**
Aristide." Gk. "One who is in-
flexible." 2nd cen. philosopher
who stated that only Christians
have true conception of God. F.
8/31. **Var:** Aresteo, Aristedes,
Aristelo, Aristes, Aristides,
Aristio, Aristo, Arysteo,
Eristella, Eristeo.
Aristes   see **Aristeo.**
Aristides   see **Aristeo.**
Aristio   see **Aristeo.**
Aristo   see **Aristeo.**
Aristóteles (Ah rees toe' tay
lays) m. **EE:** Aristotle. Gk.
"Best of thinkers." 4th cen.
B.C. Gk. philosopher who wrote
on science, logic, & poetics.
Arizala   see **Araceli.**
Arizela   see **Araceli.**
Arjelia   see **Araceli.**
Arkadi   see **Arcadio.**
Arlinda   see **Herlindo.**
Armadiana   see **Armando.**
Armadine   see **Armando.**
Armadiwa   see **Armando.**
Armaldo   see **Arnoldo.**
Armalinda   see **Irma.**
Armamdina   see **Armando.**
Armandeina   see **Armando.**
Armandin   see **Armando.**
Armandina   see **Armando.**
Armandira   see **Armando.**
Armandisia   see **Armando.**
Armando (Ahr mahn' doe) m. **EE:**
Armand, Herman. Ger. "Hero of
army." **Dim:** Mando, Mandy. **Var:**
Almando, Armadiana, Armadine,
Armadiwa, Armamdina, Armandeina,

Armandín, Armandina, Armandira,
Armandisia, Armandrina,
Armanona, Armondaria, Armondo,
Armono, Armundira, Armundo,
Aromando, Ermandina, Ermando,
Ermendina, Ermondina, Germán,
Harmando. See also Arminio.
Armandrina   see **Armando.**
Armanona   see **Armando.**
Armardo   see **Arminio.**
Armatina   see **Amaranto.**
Armeda   see **Armida.**
Armedeo   see **Armida.**
Armedina   see **Armida.**
Armelia   see **Amalio.**
Armelina   see **Armida.**
Armelinda   see **Armida.**
Armendina   see **Armida.**
Armendo   see **Armida.**
Armengol   see **Hermenegildo.**
Armenia   see **Arminio.**
Armentina   see **Armida.**
Armida (Ahr mee' dah) f. EE:
Araminda, Arminta. Heb. "Pro-
tection provided by force." Var:
Almida, Almindro, Armeda,
Armedeo, Armedina, Armelina,
Armelinda, Armendina, Armendo,
Armentina, Armilda, Arminda,
Armindina, Arminta, Arnida,
Erminda.
Armilda   see **Armida.**
Arminda   see **Armida.**
Armindina   see **Armida.**
Arminio (Ahr mee' nee oh) m. EE:
Armin, etc. Ger. "Hero of army."
Var: Armardo, Armenia, Herminio.
See also Armando, Herminio.
Arminta   see **Armida.**
Armondaria   see **Armida.**
Armondo   see **Armando.**
Armono   see **Armando.**
Armulio   see **Arnulfo.**
Armundira   see **Armando.**
Armundo   see **Armando.**
Arnaldo   see **Arnoldo.**
Arnbrosio   see **Ambrosio.**
Arnel   see **Arno.**
Arnelia   see **Arno.**
Arnesto   see **Ernesto.**
Arnida   see **Armida.**
Arniflo   see **Arnulfo.**
Arnnulfi   see **Arnulfo.**
Arno (Ahr' no) m. EE: Arno, Arnot,
Arnott. Ger. "Eagle." Ger. M. of
9th cen. F. 6/13. Var: Arnel,
Arnelia.
Arnodo   see **Arnoldo.**
Arnoldo (Ahr nohl' doe) m. EE:
Arnold, etc. Ger. "Strong as an
eagle." 9th cen. Gk. S. noted
for devotion to poor. F. 7/8.
Var: Armaldo, Arnaldo, Arnodo,
Arnolodo, Arnuldo, Aroldo,
Ornaldo.
Arnolodo   see **Arnoldo.**
Arnuldo   see **Arnoldo.**
Arnulf   see **Arnulfo.**
Arnulfo (Ahr nool' foe) m. EE:
Arnulph, Arnulphus. Ger. "Wolf
eagle." 5 x in DS. **Dim:** Nuflo.
Var: Aenulfo, Amulfo, Anulfo,
Armulio, Arniflo, Arnnulfi,
Arnulf, Arnulio, Arnulphi,
Arnulpho, Arrnulfo, Ernolfo.

Arnulio   see **Arnulfo.**
Arnulphi   see **Arnulfo.**
Arnulpho   see **Arnulfo.**
Aroimido   see **Arquimedis.**
Aroldo   see **Arnoldo.**
Aromando   see **Armando.**
Arón   see **Aarón.**
Arona   see **Aarón.**
Aronida   see **Aarón.**
Aropagita   see **Agapito.**
Arquentina   see **Argentina.**
Arquimedes   see **Arquimedis.**
Arquimedis (Ahr key' may dees) m.
EE: Archimedes. Lat. "Arch of
God." 3rd cen. B.C. Gk. mathema-
tician, physicist, & inventor.
Var: Achimedes, Argimino,
Argimiro, Arguimedes, Aroimido,
Arquimedes.
Arrculan   see **Herculano.**
Arrculas   see **Herculano.**
Arrelia   see **Aurelio.**
Arreliano   see **Aurelio.**
Arriano   see **Ariano.**
Arrio   see **Ariano.**
Arrnulfo   see **Arnulfo.**
Arrón   see **Aarón.**
Arropajita   see **Agapito.**
Arrora   see **Aurora.**
Arsanio   see **Arsenio.**
Arselia   see **Araceli.**
Arsemio   see **Arsenio.**
Arsenio (Ahr say' nee oh) m. EE:
Arsenius. Gk. "Masculine &
strong." 14 x in DS. **Var:**
Arcenio, Arecentio, Arsanio,
Arsemio, Arsenisa, Arsinea,
Eresenio.
Arsenisa   see **Arsenio.**
Arsilia   see **Araceli.**
Arsinea   see **Arsenio.**
Artemio (Ahr tay' mee oh) m. EE:
Artemas, Artemis, etc. Gk.
"Whole & perfect." 11 x in DS.
In Gk. myth., Artemis, goddess
of hunt. **Dim:** Artenillo, Micha.
Var: Altamisa, Aretimo,
Artemiro, Artemisa, Artemiza,
Artenio, Artewnia, Artimeo,
Autemia, Ertimio, Hertenia,
Hortemio, Ortemio, Ortermio,
Ortimio, Otemio.
Artemiro   see **Artemio.**
Artemisa   see **Artemio.**
Artemiza   see **Artemio.**
Artencia   see **Hortencia.**
Artenillo   see **Artemio.**
Artenio   see **Artemio.**
Artero   see **Arturo.**
Artewnia   see **Artemio.**
Arthuro   see **Arturo.**
Artimeo   see **Artemio.**
Arturo (Ahr too' roe) m. EE: Art,
Arthur. Welsh, "Noble on high."
Main figure of England's Arthu-
rian legends. **Dim:** Pituro, Turi,
Turin, Turis, Turix, Tuto, Tuyo,
Yayo, Yuyo. **Var:** Alturo, Artero,
Arthuro, Auturo, Orturo.
Arupaguita   see **Agapito.**
Arveliano   see **Aurelio.**
Arvrana   see **Abraham.**
Aryiola (Ah ree oh' lah) f. EE:
Ariolo. Lat. "Fortune teller."
Arysteo   see **Aristeo.**

Asael   see **Acela.**
Asalia   see **Acela.**
Asandra   see **Alejandro.**
Ascanio (Aws cah' nee oh) m. **EE:**
Ascanius. In Roman myth, son of
Aeneas & Creusa. Founder of Alba
Longa, most ancient city of
Latium (Italy).
Ascar   see **Oscar.**
Ascarus   see **Oscar.**
Ascención   see **Asunción.**
Ascenciono   see **Asunción.**
Ascendión   see **Asunción.**
Ascensiana   see **Asunción.**
Ascensiono   see **Asunción.**
Ascenssia   see **Asunción.**
Ascentio   see **Asunción.**
Ascinción   see **Asunción.**
Asción   see **Asunción.**
Asclepíades (Ahs clay pee' ah
days) m. **EE:** Asclepiades. Gk.
"Descendant of Aesculapius," Gk.
god of medicine. 4 x in DS.
Ascunsión   see **Asunción.**
Asdrúbal (Ahs droo' bahl) m. **EE:**
Hasdrubal, etc. Heb. "Help of
Baal." Brother of Hannibal, Car-
thaginian general of antiquity.
Asecenciano   see **Asunción.**
Aseción   see **Asunción.**
Aselina   see **Aselo.**
Aselm   see **Anselmo.**
Aselmo   see **Anselmo.**
Aselo (Ah say' low) m. **EE:** Asella.
Lat. "Asellus," small donkey."
4th cen. Roman V. given to
penance, prayer, & charity. F.
12/6. **Dim:** Aselina, Auselina.
Var: Azela, Azelia.
Asemción   see **Asunción.**
Asencio   see **Asunción.**
Asención   see **Asunción.**
Asendión   see **Asunción.**
Asenet (Ah say net') f. **EE:**
Asenath, etc. Wife of Joseph &
mother of Manases & Efraim.
Mentioned in Apocrypha. Also
called Asenat. **Var:** Acenete,
Aseneth, Aseret, Assenneth,
Azeneth.
Aseneth   see **Asenet.**
Asenión   see **Asunción.**
Asensión   see **Asunción.**
Asensptio   see **Asunción.**
Asentión   see **Asunción.**
Aseret   see **Asenet.**
Ashuca   see **Asunción.**
Asiensión   see **Asunción.**
Asincián   see **Asunción.**
Asislo   see **Acisclo.**
Asnelmo   see **Anselmo.**
Asoltación   see **Exaltación.**
Aspasia (Ahs pah' see ah) f. **EE:**
Aspasia, Aspatia, Spash. Gk.
"Welcome." Mistress of Pericles.
Name is applied to any highly
cultured courtesan. 2 x in DS.
Var: Aspicia.
Aspicia   see **Aspasia.**
Aspiridio   see **Espiridión.**
Assencio   see **Asunción.**
Assención   see **Asunción.**
Asseneth   see **Asenet.**
Assensión   see **Asunción.**
Assentión   see **Asunción.**

Assiano   see **Casiano.**
Assumciones   see **Asunción.**
Assumpción   see **Asunción.**
Assunptionis   see **Asunción.**
Assunta   see **Asunción.**
Assuptia   see **Asunción.**
Asta   see **Agusto.**
Asterina   see **Asterio.**
Asterio (Ahs tay' ree oh) m. **EE:**
Asteria, Asterius, Lat. "That
shines as a star." In myth.,
changed into quail by Zeus. 11 x
in DS. **Dim:** Asterina.
Astevan   see **Esteban.**
Astolfo (Ahs tohl' foe) m. **EE:**
Astolf. Ger. "Eastern wolf."
Var: Estalfo, Estelfo, Estolfo,
Stalfo.
Astrid (Ahs treed') f. **EE:** Asta,
Astrid, etc. Norse, "Strength of
God." Mother of Olaf Trygveson,
king of Norway. Wife of St.
Olaf. **Dim:** Ati. **Var:** Ostrid.
Astrogildo (Ahs troe heel' doe) m.
EE: Astrogild. Lat. "Valorous
star."
Asucena   see **Azusena.**
Asuero (Ah sway' roe) m. **EE:**
Ahasuerus. Pers. "King of pow-
erful eye." 5th cen. B.C. king
who selected Jewess, Esther, as
wife.
Asulema   see **Zulema.**
Asumpción   see **Asunción.**
Asumpsión   see **Asunción.**
Asumptio   see **Asunción.**
Asumsia   see **Asunción.**
Asunción (Ah soon see own') mf.
EE: Assumption. Lat. "Action of
taking or attributing." Refers
to assumption of V. from earth
to heaven following death. F.
8/15. **Dim:** Acencio, Asción,
Asencio, Ashuca, Assencio,
Assunta, Assuptia, Asumptio,
Asumsia, Asunsia, Asunto,
Aucenci, Aucencio, Aucentio,
Auscentia, Azencio, Cención,
Censión, Chencho, Chica, Chón,
Choncha, Chono, Chun, Chuncho,
Oscensio, Sención, Seneción,
Sensión, Sincionite, Sunción.
Var: Acansión, Acencención,
Acención, Acenseón, Acinección,
Acionsión, Ancencia, Ancención,
Ancensión, Ansencio, Ascención,
Ascenciono, Ascendión,
Ascensiana, Ascensiono,
Ascenssia, Ascentio, Ascinción,
Ascunsión, Asecenciano, Aseción,
Asemción, Asención, Asendión,
Asenión, Asensión, Asensptio,
Asentión, Asiensión, Asincián,
Assención, Assensión, Assentión,
Assumciones, Assumpción,
Assunptionis, Asumpción,
Asumpsión, Asunsión, Asusena,
Aucención, Aucenisio,
Auscención, Ausenencio.
Asunsia   see **Asunción.**
Asunsión   see **Asunción.**
Asunto   see **Asunción.**
Asusena   see **Asunción.**
Asusena   see **Azusena.**
Asusino   see **Azusena.**

Asuzena   see **Azusena.**
Aswaldo   see **Osvaldo.**
Atahualpa (Ah tah wahl' pah) m.
  EE: Atahualpa. Quechua, "Happy
  bird of fortune." Last Incan
  ruler of 16th cen. Peru.
  Executed by Spaniards.
Atalasio   see **Atalo.**
Atalo (Ah' tah low) m. **EE:** Atalus,
  Attilus. Lat. "One from city of
  Atalia"? 8 x in DS. **Var:**
  Atalasio, Athala.
Atamanio (Ah tah mah' nee oh) m.
  Ataman is title given to leader
  of Cossacks. Hereditary title
  given to prince of Russia since
  1835.
Atamasio   see **Atanasio.**
Atamicio   see **Atanasio.**
Atanaarcia   see **Atanasio.**
Atanacio   see **Atanasio.**
Atanania   see **Atanasio.**
Atanarii   see **Atanasio.**
Atanaseo   see **Atanasio.**
Atanasil   see **Atanasio.**
Atanasio (Ah tah nah' see oh) m.
  EE: Athanasia, Athanasius. Gk.
  "Without death." 4th cen.
  scholar who opposed Arian
  heresy. F. 5/2. **Dim:** Atancia,
  Atancis, Stanacia, Stanasia,
  Tanacio, Tenasio. **Var:** Adamacio,
  Adonaicio, Altamasio, Altanese,
  Altunasio, Antasia, Atamasio,
  Atamicio, Atanaarcia, Atanacio,
  Atanania, Atanarii, Atanaseo,
  Atanasil, Atanecia, Atanistro,
  Atanocio, Atanosio, Atansio,
  Atatesio, Atenacia, Atencino,
  Athanasio, Athanasius,
  Athanesia, Athonasic, Athonosin,
  Atoanocio, Atonacio, Atonasio,
  Itanasio, Otanasio, Tunacia.
Atancia   see **Atanasio.**
Atancis   see **Atanasio.**
Atanecia   see **Atanasio.**
Atanislado   see **Estanislao.**
Ataniso   see **Anastacio.**
Atanistro   see **Atanasio.**
Atanocio   see **Atanasio.**
Atanosio   see **Atanasio.**
Atansio   see **Atanasio.**
Atarina   see **Catalina.**
Atatesio   see **Atanasio.**
Ataulfo   see **Adolfo.**
Atelano   see **Atilano.**
Atelita   see **Atilano.**
Atenacia   see **Atanasio.**
Atencino   see **Atanasio.**
Atenógenes (Ah tay no' hay nays)
  m. **EE:** Athenogenes. Gk. "Of race
  of Athena," goddess of war &
  wisdom. 2 x in DS. **Dim:** Atenor.
  Var: Atenójenas, Atenójenos,
  Atenóquenes.
Atenójenas   see **Atenógenes.**
Atenójenos   see **Atenógenes.**
Atenóquenes   see **Atenógenes.**
Atenor   see **Atenógenes.**
Ateslano   see **Atilano.**
Athala   see **Atalo.**
Athanasio   see **Atanasio.**
Athanasius   see **Atanasio.**
Athanesia   see **Atanasio.**
Athonasic   see **Atanasio.**

Athonosin   see **Atanasio.**
Ati   see **Astrid.**
Atilano (Ah tee lah' no) m. **EE:**
  Attila. Lat. "He who walks with
  difficulty." 4th cen. leader of
  Huns who attacked crumbling
  Roman Empire. **Dim:** Atelita,
  Atolina, Tilán, Tilano, Tiliana,
  Tilita. **Var:** Alitano, Antilano,
  Atelano, Atelano, Atilina,
  Atilona, Atinano, Atitana,
  Atlino, Atolenia, Attelano,
  Attilajo, Attilio, Attilono,
  Attotilia, Etilano.
Atilina   see **Atilano.**
Atilona   see **Atilano.**
Atinano   see **Atilano.**
Atitana   see **Atilano.**
Atlino   see **Atilano.**
Atoanocio   see **Atanasio.**
Atocha (Ah toe' cha) f. Sp.
  "Feather grass." Image of V.
  brought by apostle of Antioch to
  Madrid & placed in area seeded
  with "atocheles."
Atolenia   see **Atilano.**
Atolina   see **Atilano.**
Atonacio   see **Atanasio.**
Atonasio   see **Atanasio.**
Atreo (Ah tray' oh) m. **EE:** Atreus.
  In Gk. legend Atreus was ruling
  family of Mycenae whose tragic
  fate served as theme for many
  Gk. tragedies.
Attagracia   see **Altagracia.**
Attaviani   see **Octavio.**
Attelano   see **Atilano.**
Attilajo   see **Atilano.**
Attilio   see **Atilano.**
Attilono   see **Atilano.**
Attotilia   see **Atilano.**
Atullfo   see **Adolfo.**
Atzael   see **Azael.**
Aualia   see **Eulalio.**
Auastasio   see **Anastacio.**
Aucauda   see **Arcadio.**
Aucenci   see **Asunción.**
Aucencio   see **Asunción.**
Aucención   see **Asunción.**
Aucenisio   see **Asunción.**
Aucentio   see **Asunción.**
Audeida   see **Adelaido.**
Audelino   see **Adela.**
Audelio   see **Adela.**
Audella   see **Adela.**
Audemia   see **Audomero.**
Audemiro   see **Audomero.**
Audencio (Ow dayn' see oh) m. **EE:**
  Audentius. 5th cen. S. of Milan,
  Italy. Also, 4th cen. bishop of
  Toledo. **Var:** Audensio.
Audenia (Ow dayn' ee ah) f. **EE:**
  Audentius. Feminine form of
  Audentius (see Audencio)?
Audensio   see **Audencio.**
Audifas   see **Audifaz.**
Audifaz (Ow dee' fahz) m. **EE:**
  Audifax. Lat. "He who causes
  attack." 2nd cen. M. put to
  death for gathering remains of
  other Mm. F. 1/19. **Var:** Audifas.
Audilia   see **Adela.**
Audomar   see **Audomero.**
Audomero (Ow doe may' roe) m. **EE:**
  Audomar. Ger. "Famous for its

riches." 7th cen. bishop of
France. F. 9/9. **Var:** Audemia,
Audemiro, Audomar.
Audona (Ow doe' nah) f. **EE:**
Audoenus. Bishop of Rouen,
France. F. 8/24.

Auelrelo	see	**Aurelio.**
Augastín	see	**Agusto.**
Augatia	see	**Agata.**
Augostín	see	**Agusto.**
Augostino	see	**Agusto.**
Augrelio	see	**Aurelio.**
Augstín	see	**Agusto.**
Augundio	see	**Abundio.**

Augurio (Ow goo' ree oh) m. **EE:**
Augurius. Lat. "Favorable sign."
3rd cen. deacon mart. in
Tarragona, Spain. F. 1/21.

Augusdín	see	**Agusto.**
Augustavo	see	**Agusto.**
Augustén	see	**Agusto.**
Augustena	see	**Agusto.**
Augustín	see	**Agusto.**
Augustina	see	**Agusto.**
Augustinea	see	**Agusto.**
Augustinus	see	**Agusto.**
Augusto	see	**Agusto.**
Augustulo	see	**Agusto.**
Aulelio	see	**Aurelio.**
Aundio	see	**Abundio.**

Aura (Ow' rah) f. **EE:** Aura, Aural.
Gk. "Of air." See also Oriol.

Auralia	see	**Aurelio.**
Auraliano	see	**Aurelio.**
Aurara	see	**Aurora.**
Aurcelia	see	**Araceli.**
Aureal	see	**Aureo.**
Aureana	see	**Aurelio.**
Aurebia	see	**Aurelio.**
Aurelaino	see	**Aurelio.**
Aureleo	see	**Aurelio.**
Aureliano	see	**Aurelio.**
Aurelinano	see	**Aurelio.**

Aurelio (Ow ray' lee oh) m. **EE:**
Aurelius. Ora, Orel. Lat.
"Gold." Roman goddess of dawn. 3
x in DS. **Dim:** Guello
(Aureliano), Lelio, Lelo, Orel,
Yeyo (Aureliano). **Var:** Abeliano,
Anrelio, Anreliono, Aralia,
Arelio, Arella, Arrelia,
Arreliano, Arveliano, Auelrelo,
Augrelio, Aulelio, Auralia,
Auraliano, Aureana, Aurebia,
Aurelaino, Aureleo, Aureliano,
Aurelinano, Aurelios, Aurelismo,
Aurelma, Aurgelio, Aurielia,
Aurlia, Aurrelio, Dorelia,
Herailano, Roralia, Ureula. See
also Aureo, Aurora.

Aurelios	see	**Aurelio.**
Aurelismo	see	**Aurelio.**
Aurelma	see	**Aurelio.**

Aureo (Ow ray' oh) m. **EE:** Aureus.
Lat. "Gold." 6 x in DS. 9th cen.
Moslem denounced by parents for
abandoning Islam. F. 7/19. **Var:**
Aureal, Oria. See also Aurelio,
Aurora.

Aurgelio	see	**Aurelio.**
Aurielia	see	**Aurelio.**
Auriora	see	**Aurora.**
Aurlia	see	**Aurelio.**
Auroa	see	**Aurora.**
Aurolia	see	**Aurora.**

Aurora (Ow roe' rah) f. **EE:**
Aurora. Lat. goddess of dawn.
Dim: Lola, Yoya. **Var:** Arrora,
Aurara, Auriora, Auroa, Aurolia,
Auroria, Aurrera, Aurrora,
Hurora, Rory. See also Aurelio,
Aureo.

Auroria	see	**Aurora.**
Aurrelio	see	**Aurelio.**
Aurrera	see	**Aurora.**
Aurrora	see	**Aurora.**

Ausalia (Ow sah' lee ah) f. **EE:**
Ausalia. Could be form of
Ausilo, 5th cen. bishop of
Frejius, France. F. 1/26.

Auscena	see	**Azusena.**
Auscención	see	**Asunción.**
Auscentia	see	**Asunción.**
Auselina	see	**Aselo.**
Auselmo	see	**Anselmo.**

Ausencio (Ow sehn' see oh) m. **EE:**
Auxentius. Lat. "To grow." 8 x
in DS. **Var:** Ausensio, Ausio,
Autencio, Auxencio.

Ausenencio	see	**Asunción.**
Ausensio	see	**Ausencio.**
Ausio	see	**Ausencio.**
Austeo	see	**Agusto.**
Austina	see	**Agusto.**
Austrebertha	see	**Austreberto.**

Austreberto (Ows tray bair' toe)
m. **EE:** Ansbert, Austrebert. Ger.
"Brilliance of the East." 3 x in
DS. **Var:** Austrebertha,
Austrobertha, Austruberto.

Austrobertha	see	**Austreberto.**
Austruberto	see	**Austreberto.**

Autario (Ow tah' ree oh) m. **EE:**
Autharius. Commander of Gallic
mercenaries in Carthaginian army
in 2nd cen. B.C.

Autemia	see	**Artemio.**
Autemia	see	**Eutimia.**
Autencio	see	**Ausencio.**
Autenia	see	**Eutimia.**

Autonia (Ow toe' nee ah) f. **EE:**
Autonoe. Autonoe appears in Gk.
myth. at least 5 x.

Auturo	see	**Arturo.**
Auxcilia	see	**Auxilio.**
Auxencio	see	**Ausencio.**

Auxilio (Owks ee' lee oh) m? **EE:**
Auxilia, Auxilius. Lat. "Aid,
protection." 1 of names of V.
Mary, María Auxiliadora. F.
5/24. 3 x in DS. **Var:** Auxcilia,
Euxilia, Exillo, Ocsilia,
Osilio, Ossiliae, Sausisla.

Auyela	see	**Eulalio.**
Auzelm	see	**Anselmo.**
Ava	see	**Eva.**

Avaceli (Ah' bah say' lee) f. **EE:**
Avaceli. Comb. of Eva & Celia
(see both).

Availia	see	**Ovelia.**

Avalberto (Ah' bahl bair' toe) m.
Comb. of Abel & Berto (see
both).

Avalino	see	**Abelino.**
Avangelino	see	**Evangelina.**
Avaristo	see	**Abaristo.**
Avarsito	see	**Abaristo.**
Avel	see	**Abel.**
Avelarde	see	**Abelardo.**
Avelardo	see	**Abelardo.**

Aveleno   see **Abelino**.
Avelia   see **Abelino**.
Avelimo   see **Abelino**.
Avelín   see **Abelino**.
Avelinda   see **Abelino**.
Avelino   see **Abelino**.
Avellino   see **Abelino**.
Avendio   see **Abdenago**.
Avenicio   see **Abenicio**.
Avenista (Ah bay nees' tah) f?
  Lat. "Ad" & "venire" meaning "to
  reconcile"?
Avento (Ah bane' toe) m. **EE**:
  Aventinus. Form of Aventinus, 3
  Ss. of Christian calendar?
Averando   see **Eberardo**.
Averisto   see **Evaristo**.
Averlino   see **Abelino**.
Avertano   see **Abertano**.
Avideo   see **Ovidio**.
Aviel   see **Abil**.
Avigail   see **Abegail**.
Avilio   see **Abil**.
Avito (Ah bee' toe) m. **EE**: Avitus.
  Lat. "Inherited from grandpar-
  ent." 7 x in DS.
Aviyiano   see **Viviano**.
Avrán   see **Abraham**.
Avundio   see **Abundio**.
Ayalia   see **Eulalio**.

Ayda   see **Aída**.
Ayetano   see **Cayetano**.
Ayguda   see **Agata**.
Aygueda   see **Agata**.
Aygusta   see **Agusto**.
Ayulo   see **Eulalio**.
Azael (Ah zah ehl') m. **EE**: Azael.
  Heb. "Made of God." Brother of
  Joab & member of tribe of
  Simeon. **Var**: Atzael.
Azalea   see **Azalia**.
Azalia (Ah zah' lee ah) f. **EE**:
  Azalea. Gk. "Dry." Flower that
  grows best in dry soil. **Var**:
  Azalea, Zaelia.
Azarel (Ah zah rehl') m. **EE**:
  Azrael, etc. Heb. "God hath
  helped." In Judaism & Islam,
  angel of death who took souls
  from body.
Azela   see **Aselo**.
Azelia   see **Aselo**.
Azencio   see **Asunción**.
Azeneth   see **Asenet**.
Azusena (Ah zoo say' nah) f. **EE**:
  Azusena. Ar. "Lily." **Var**:
  Asucena, Asusena, Asusino,
  Asuzena, Auscena, Azuzena.
Azuzena   see **Azusena**.

B

Bábara   see **Bárbara**.
Bábarra   see **Bárbara**.
Babil (Bah beel') m. **EE**: Babylas.
  Sp. "Babilas," "Babylonian." 6 x
  in DS.
Bacha   see **Beatriz**.
Bacho   see **Bacilio**.
Bacidio   see **Bacilio**.
Bacilin   see **Bacilio**.
Bacilio (Bah see' lee oh) m. **EE**:
  Basil, Vasily. Gk. "King" or
  "sovereign." 7 x in DS. St.
  Basil the Great, of Asia Minor,
  known as great scholar. F. 6/14.
  Dim: Bacho, Bacilin, Chilo,
  Silia. **Var**: Bacidio, Bacilisa,
  Bacillio, Bacilo, Barcelio,
  Basalio, Baselico, Baselio,
  Baselisa, Basibio, Basicilliana,
  Basilcus, Basileo, Basiliam,
  Basiliana, Basilicio, Basilidis,
  Basiligio, Basilio, Basilisa,
  Basiliza, Basilliana, Basillio,
  Basilo, Basilso, Basitio,
  Bassilleo, Bassillio, Bastilla,
  Bazilio, Bisilia, Bosilia,
  Bosilisa, Bracilia, Bracillo,
  Vacilio, Vacilla, Vasilio,
  Vasilisa.
Bacilisa   see **Bacilio**.
Bacillio   see **Bacilio**.
Bacilo   see **Bacilio**.
Baduel   see **Baudilio**.
Baetriz   see **Beatriz**.
Bailjo   see **Bailón**.
Bailón (Bie loan') m. **EE**: Baylon.
  16th cen. Sp. S. declared patron

of eucharistic conferences. **Var**:
  Bailio.
Balante   see **Valente**.
Balbarita   see **Bárbara**.
Balbin   see **Balbina**.
Balbina (Bahl bee' nah) f. **EE**:
  Balbina, Balbinus. Lat. "Stut-
  terer." Roman maiden of early
  Christian years & daughter of
  St. Quirinus. F. 3/31. **Dim**:
  Balbio. **Var**: Balbin, Balvena,
  Balvin, Balvino, Bolbina,
  Palbino, Valbina, Valvino.
Balbio   see **Balbina**.
Balbumero   see **Baldomero**.
Baldamar   see **Baldomero**.
Baldamero   see **Baldomero**.
Baldamiro   see **Baldomero**.
Baldarmena   see **Baldomero**.
Baldazar   see **Baltasar**.
Balde   see **Baldomero**.
Baldema   see **Baldomero**.
Baldemar   see **Baldomero**.
Baldemares   see **Baldomero**.
Baldemas   see **Baldomero**.
Baldemero   see **Baldomero**.
Baldenar   see **Baldomero**.
Baldermar   see **Baldomero**.
Baldimar   see **Baldomero**.
Baldimero   see **Baldomero**.
Baldo   see **Archibaldo**.
Baldoemeno   see **Baldomero**.
Baldomeno   see **Baldomero**.
Baldomer   see **Baldomero**.
Baldomero (Bahl doe may' roe) m.
  EE: Vladimir, Waldemar. Ger.
  "Famous fighter." 11th cen.

Russian S., Duke of Muscovy,
helped to convert Russians to
Gk. Orthodoxy. F. 7/15. **Dim:**
Balde, Valde, Valdera, Valdo.
Var: Balbumero, Baldamar,
Baldamero, Baldamiro,
Baldarmena, Baldema, Baldemar,
Baldemares, Baldemas, Baldemero,
Baldenar, Baldermar, Baldimar,
Baldimero, Baldoemeno,
Baldomeno, Baldomer, Baldomiera,
Baldomino, Baldonero, Baltamar,
Baltimero, Baltomero, Bladimiro,
Boldemar, Paidomero, Paldomero,
Valdamar, Valdamero, Valdemar,
Valdemares, Valdemaro,
Valdemena, Valdemero, Valdemor,
Valdenar, Valderis, Valderma,
Valdermar, Valdimar, Valdino,
Valdmar, Valdomao, Valdomar,
Valdomiro, Valgamero, Valgumero,
Voldemar, Waldemar, Waldemero,
Waldenor, Waldomero.

Baldomiera	see **Baldomero.**
Baldomino	see **Baldomero.**
Baldonero	see **Baldomero.**
Balente	see **Valente.**
Balentin	see **Valente.**
Balentine	see **Valente.**
Balentino	see **Valente.**
Balento	see **Valente.**
Baleriano	see **Valerio.**
Balerio	see **Valerio.**
Baleromo	see **Belarmino.**
Balinda	see **Belinda.**
Balintin	see **Valente.**
Ballazar	see **Baltasar.**
Balmino	see **Belarmino.**
Balo	see **Wilebaldo.**
Balta	see **Bartolomé.**
Baltamar	see **Baldomero.**
Baltaras	see **Baltasar.**
Baltarsar	see **Baltasar.**
Baltasam	see **Baltasar.**

Baltasar (Bahl tah sahr') m. **EE:**
Balthasar, Balthazar. Sem. "God
protects your life." 1 of 3 wise
men to visit Christ after His
birth. Became bishop & died
while celebrating Mass. F. 1/11.
Dim: Balticu, Balto. **Var:**
Baldazar, Ballazar, Baltaras,
Baltarsar, Baltasam, Baltasor,
Baltassar, Baltazán, Baltazar,
Baltazo, Baltazor, Baltegas,
Baltesar, Baltezar, Balthasar,
Balthazar, Baltizar, Baltogar,
Baltosar, Baltozar, Baltozas,
Balzar, Beltezar, Belthasar,
Beltizar, Boltizar, Valtazar,
Valtesar.

Baltasor	see **Baltasar.**
Baltassar	see **Baltasar.**
Baltazán	see **Baltasar.**
Baltazar	see **Baltasar.**
Baltazo	see **Baltasar.**
Baltazor	see **Baltasar.**
Baltegas	see **Baltasar.**
Baltesar	see **Baltasar.**
Baltezar	see **Baltasar.**
Balthasar	see **Baltasar.**
Balthazar	see **Baltasar.**
Balticu	see **Baldomero.**
Baltimero	see **Baldomero.**
Baltizar	see **Baltasar.**
Balto	see **Baltasar.**
Balto	see **Gualterio.**
Baltogar	see **Baltasar.**
Baltomero	see **Baldomero.**
Baltosar	see **Baltasar.**
Baltozar	see **Baltasar.**
Baltozas	see **Baltasar.**
Balvena	see **Balbina.**
Balvín	see **Balbina.**
Balvino	see **Balbina.**
Balzar	see **Baltasar.**
Bandelia	see **Vandelia.**
Banifacio	see **Bonifacio.**
Baptisto	see **Bautista.**
Bar	see **Bárbara.**
Bara	see **Bárbara.**
Barbalo	see **Bárbara.**

Bárbara (Bar' bah rah) f. **EE:**
Babette, Barbara, etc. Gk.
"Strange" or "foreign." St.
Barbara was locked in tower &
killed by father for being a
Christian. She is invoked
against lightning & fire. F.
12/4. **Dim:** Bar, Bara, Barbarina,
Barbaritta, Barberita, Barbina,
Barvarito. **Var:** Bábara, Bábarra,
Balbarita, Barbalo, Barbarda,
Barbato, Bárbera, Barbiano,
Barbola, Barbra, Bárrbaro,
Bárvara, Beryabe, Várvara,
Várvera.

Barbarda	see **Bárbara.**
Barbarina	see **Bárbara.**
Barbaritta	see **Bárbara.**
Barbato	see **Bárbara.**
Bárbera	see **Bárbara.**
Barberita	see **Bárbara.**
Barbiano	see **Bárbara.**
Barbina	see **Bárbara.**
Barbola	see **Bárbara.**

Barbosa (Bar bo' sah) m. **EE:**
Barbosa. Lat. "Bearded one."

Barbra	see **Bárbara.**
Barcelio	see **Bacilio.**
Bardmiano	see **Bardomiano.**
Bardomano	see **Bardomiano.**

Bardomiano (Bar doe mee ahn' no)
m. **EE:** Bardomianus. Lat. "Son by
adoption." Bardomianus & 26 com-
panions mart. in Asia. F. 9/25.
Var: Bardmiano, Bardomano,
Bardominao, Bardomino,
Bardonciana, Bardonious,
Berdomiano, Bordoniamo.

Bardominao	see **Bardomiano.**
Bardomino	see **Bardomiano.**
Bardonciana	see **Bardomiano.**
Bardonious	see **Bardomiano.**
Barilio	see **Berilo.**
Barnaba	see **Bernabé.**
Barnabus	see **Bernabé.**
Bárrbaro	see **Bárbara.**
Bartalo	see **Bartolomé.**
Bartato	see **Bartolomé.**
Bartelo	see **Bartolomé.**
Bartelomeo	see **Bartolomé.**
Bartha	see **Bartolomé.**
Barthel	see **Bartolomé.**
Bartholo	see **Bartolomé.**
Bartilo	see **Bartolomé.**
Bartloviana	see **Bartolomé.**
Barto	see **Bartolomé.**
Bartol	see **Bartolomé.**
Bartolamé	see **Bartolomé.**

Bartolata   see Bartolomé.
Bartoli   see Bartolomé.
Bartolita   see Bartolomé.
Bartollo   see Bartolomé.
Bartolo   see Bartolomé.
Bartolomé (Bar toe low may') m.
    EE: Bart, Bartholomew. Heb.
    "Abounding in furrows." 8 x in
    DS. Apostle of Christ also
    called Nathaniel. F. 8/24. Dim:
    Balta, Bartha, Barto, Tola,
    Toli. Var: Bartalo, Bartato,
    Bartelo, Bartelomeo, Barthel,
    Bartholo, Bartilo, Bartloviana,
    Bartol, Bartolamé, Bartolata,
    Bartoli, Bartolita, Bartollo,
    Bartolo, Bartolomea, Bartolomí,
    Bartoloneo, Bartomea, Bartoro,
    Bartulo, Batalolo, Batolo,
    Borthala, Bortolo, Vartolo.
Bartolomea   see Bartolomé.
Bartolomí   see Bartolomé.
Bartoloneo   see Bartolomé.
Bartomea   see Bartolomé.
Bartoro   see Bartolomé.
Bartulo   see Bartolomé.
Bárvara   see Bárbara.
Barvarito   see Bárbara.
Basalio   see Bacilio.
Baselico   see Bacilio.
Baselio   see Bacilio.
Baselisa   see Bacilio.
Basibio   see Bacilio.
Basicilliana   see Bacilio.
Basilcus   see Bacilio.
Basileo   see Bacilio.
Basiliam   see Bacilio.
Basiliana   see Bacilio.
Basilicio   see Bacilio.
Basilidis   see Bacilio.
Basiligio   see Bacilio.
Basilio   see Bacilio.
Basilisa   see Bacilio.
Basiliza   see Bacilio.
Basilliana   see Bacilio.
Basillio   see Bacilio.
Basilo   see Bacilio.
Basilso   see Bacilio.
Basitio   see Bacilio.
Bassilleo   see Bacilio.
Bassillio   see Bacilio.
Bastián   see Sebastián.
Bastiana   see Sebastián.
Bastilla   see Bacilio.
Batalolo   see Bartolomé.
Batolo   see Bartolomé.
Batrice   see Beatriz.
Battista   see Bautista.
Baucha   see Bautista.
Baudelio   see Baudilio.
Baudello   see Baudilio.
Baudencio (Bough dane' see oh) m.
    EE: Baudencio. Comb. of Baudilio
    & Gaudencio (see both).
Baudilio (Bough dee' lee oh) m.
    EE: Baudelius. Celt. "Victory."
    3rd or 4th cen. S. helped spread
    Christianity in France. About
    400 churches dedicated to him in
    Spain & France. F. 5/20. Dim:
    Lilo. Var: Baduel, Baudelio,
    Baudello, Baudilión, Baudillo,
    Vaudelio.
Baudilión   see Baudilio.
Baudillo   see Baudilio.

Baulio   see Braulia.
Bautesto   see Bautista.
Bautista (Bough tees' tah) m. EE:
    Babtist, Baptist. Gk. "One who
    baptizes." John the Baptist,
    Christ's precursor, sent to
    prepare way for Him. 4 x in DS.
    Dim: Baucha. Var: Baptisto,
    Battista, Bautesto, Boutisto,
    Vautista.
Bazilio   see Bacilio.
Beactrice   see Beatriz.
Beadriz   see Beatriz.
Beariz   see Beatriz.
Bearriz   see Beatriz.
Beato (Bay ah' toe) m? EE: Beata,
    Beatus. Lat. "To make happy."
    Sp. V. M. beheaded with brother
    Sanctianus. F. 9/6. 6 x in DS.
    Var: Beatura. See also Beatriz.
Beatrex   see Beatriz.
Beatrez   see Beatriz.
Beatrica   see Beatriz.
Beatricem   see Beatriz.
Beatricia   see Beatriz.
Beatricis   see Beatriz.
Beatrie   see Beatriz.
Beatris   see Beatriz.
Beatrise   see Beatriz.
Beatrix   see Beatriz.
Beatriz (Bay ah trees') f. EE:
    Beatrice, Beatrix, etc. Lat.
    "Bringer of joy, she who bless-
    es." 9 x in DS. Lord appeared &
    pierced heart with fiery dart.
    F. 7/29. Dim: Bacha, Beti,
    Biachis, Biche, Bicho, Bita,
    Ticha, Tichi, Tis, Tix. Var:
    Baetriz, Batrice, Beactrice,
    Beadriz, Beariz, Bearriz,
    Beatrex, Beatrez, Beatrica,
    Beatricem, Beatricia, Beatricis,
    Beatrie, Beatris, Beatrise,
    Beatrix, Beatrize, Beatruce,
    Beautriz, Bertice, Bertrice,
    Bertriz, Bestris, Betriz,
    Beztrix, Biatrés, Biatris,
    Biatriz, Veatrés, Veatris,
    Veatriz, Viatrice, Viatricia,
    Viatrix. See also Beato.
Beatrize   see Beatriz.
Beatruce   see Beatriz.
Beatura   see Beato.
Beautriz   see Beatriz.
Bebián   see Viviano.
Bebiano   see Viviano.
Becentia   see Vicente.
Becha   see Betsabé.
Beda (Bay' dah) f. EE: Bede. Ger.
    "He who obliges or demands."
    Doctor, theologian, & historian
    of 8th cen. British church. F.
    10/29. Var: Bedila, Bedio, Veda.
Bedal   see Vidal.
Bedila   see Beda.
Bedio   see Beda.
Befania (Bay fah' nee ah) f. EE:
    Befania. Befana is Ital. fairy,
    brings gifts to well-behaved
    children on Christmas Eve & on
    Eve of the 3 Kings.
Begina   see Benigno.
Beginia   see Benigno.
Begninio   see Benigno.
Begonia (Bay go' nee ah) f. EE:

Begonia. Plant with succulent stems & leaves & richly colored petals.

Beinta   see **Benito.**
Bejamín   see **Benjamín.**
Bejanín   see **Benjamín.**
Bel   see **Gabriel.**
Bela   see **Arabela.**
Belán   see **Belén.**
Belarminio   see **Belarmino.**
Belarmino (Bay lahr mee' no) m. **EE:** Bellarmine. Related to Guillermo (see). 16th cen. church scholar who studied problem of spiritual & temporal powers of pope? **Dim:** Beluch. **Var:** Baleromo, Balmino, Belarminio, Beleriniono, Belormino.
Belda (Bell' dah) f. **EE:** Belda. Sp, "Beauty"?
Beleén   see **Belén.**
Belén (Bay lehn') f. **EE:** Bethelem. Heb. "House of bread." Christ's birthplace. **Dim:** Belencita. **Var:** Belán, Beleén, Belena, Belenly, Bellén, Bethlehén, Valén.
Belena   see **Belén.**
Belencita   see **Belén.**
Belenda   see **Belinda.**
Belenly   see **Belén.**
Beleriniono   see **Belarmino.**
Belia (Bay' lee ah) f. **EE:** Bella, Belle, Belva. Sp. "Beautiful." **Var:** Beliano.
Beliano   see **Belia.**
Beliarosa (Bay' lee ah roe' sah) f. **EE:** Beliarosa. Comb. of Belia & Rosa (see both).
Belica   see **Isabel.**
Beliche   see **Belisario.**
Belicia   see **Isabel.**
Belín   see **Belinda.**
Belinda (Bay leen' dah) f. **EE:** Belinda. Possibly Ger. "Shield of bear." **Var:** Balinda, Belenda, Belín, Berlinda, Valenda, Valinda, Velinda.
Belino (Bay lee' no) m. **EE:** Bellina, Bellinus. Lat. "Pretty, handsome, charming." Bellinus, 12th cen. bishop who opposed simony & was assasinated. F. 11/26. **Var:** Velino, Vellino.
Belisandro   see **Belisario.**
Belisario (Bay lee sah' ree oh) m. **EE:** Belisarius. Gk. "Arrow" or "bowman." Belisarius, 6th cen. Byzantine general, defeated Vandals in Africa. Belisario Domínguez, M. of Mexican Revolution. **Dim:** Beliche, Beluch, Chayo. **Var:** Belisandro, Beliserio, Belizario, Bellanina, Berisario, Bilisario, Bliza.
Beliserio   see **Belisario.**
Belita   see **Isabel.**
Belizario   see **Belisario.**
Bellanina   see **Belisario.**
Bellén   see **Belén.**
Belormino   see **Belarmino.**
Belotta (Bay low' tah) f. **EE:** Belota. Belocia, flowering plant.
Belsabé   see **Betsabé.**
Beltezar   see **Baltasar.**

Belthasar   see **Baltasar.**
Beltizar   see **Baltasar.**
Beltrán (Bell trahn') m. **EE:** Bert, Bertram, Bertrand. Ger. "Bertram," "bright raven." 6 x in DS.
Beluch   see **Abelardo.**
Beluch   see **Belarmino.**
Beluch   see **Belisario.**
Belzabé   see **Betsabé.**
Bemigno   see **Benigno.**
Bemina   see **Benjamín.**
Bemito   see **Benito.**
Benadita   see **Benito.**
Benalado   see **Venceslao.**
Benancio   see **Venancio.**
Benansio   see **Venancio.**
Benantia   see **Venancio.**
Benanza   see **Venancio.**
Benanzio   see **Venancio.**
Benaranda   see **Veneranda.**
Benardo   see **Bernal.**
Benarencia   see **Venancio.**
Benaslado   see **Venceslao.**
Benato   see **Benito.**
Bences   see **Venceslao.**
Benceslado   see **Venceslao.**
Benceslao   see **Venceslao.**
Benche   see **Venceslao.**
Bencia   see **Benicio.**
Bendito   see **Benedicto.**
Benecio   see **Benicio.**
Benecio (Bay nay' see oh) m. **EE:** Benecio. Possibly related to Benito or Benedicto (see both).
Beneda   see **Benito.**
Benedetto   see **Benedicto.**
Benedictae   see **Benedicto.**
Benedicto (Bay' nay deek' toe) m. **EE:** Bendix, Benedict, etc. Lat. "Blessed." 33 x in DS. Founded Benedictine order. F. 3/21. **Dim:** Beni, Bento, Dicta. **Var:** Bendito, Benedetto, Benedictae, Benedictra, Benedictum, Benedimas, Benedito, Benictna, Benito, Benneo, Bennina. See also Benicio, Benito.
Benedictra   see **Benedicto.**
Benedictum   see **Benedicto.**
Benedimas   see **Benedicto.**
Benedito   see **Benedicto.**
Benefacita   see **Bonifacio.**
Benegno   see **Benigno.**
Benentio   see **Benito.**
Beneranda   see **Veneranda.**
Benerita (Bay nay nay' tah) f. **EE:** Benerita. Lat. "Worthy of honor."
Benerito   see **Benito.**
Benessio   see **Benicio.**
Beneto   see **Benito.**
Bengamín   see **Benjamín.**
Bengino   see **Benigno.**
Beni   see **Benedicto.**
Beniamín   see **Benjamín.**
Benica   see **Benito.**
Benicio (Bay nee' see oh) m. Could be related to Benito & Benedicto (see both). **Var:** Bencia, Benecio, Benessio, Benisa, Benisia, Benizio, Benocio, Venecio, Venicio, Venisio.
Benictna   see **Benedicto.**
Benidi   see **Benito.**

Benifocio   see **Bonifacio.**
Beniggna   see **Benigno.**
Benigina   see **Benigno.**
Benignae   see **Benigno.**
Benignana   see **Benigno.**
Benigno (Bay neeg' no) m. **EE:**
Beni, Benigna, Benignus. Lat.
"Beneficent." 20 x in DS.
Benignus of Dijon spread faith
in Central France. **Dim:** Nina.
Var: Begina, Beginia, Begninio,
Bemigno, Benegno, Bengino,
Beniggna, Benigina, Benignae,
Benignana, Benigra, Benigrio,
Benigua, Benigue, Benijna,
Beningna, Benino, Beniqua,
Binino, Venigno, Veningna,
Venino.
Benigra   see **Benigno.**
Benigrio   see **Benigno.**
Benigua   see **Benigno.**
Benigue   see **Benigno.**
Benijna   see **Benigno.**
Benilbe   see **Benilde.**
Benilda   see **Benilde.**
Benilde (Bay neel' day) f? **EE:**
Benildis, Ger. "Battle" or
"combat." 9th cen. M. beheaded
in Cordova, Spain, for defiling
name of Mohammed. F. 6/15. **Dim:**
Nilda. **Var:** Benilbe, Benilda,
Benind, Brenilda, Venilde.
Benind   see **Benilde.**
Benind   see **Benito.**
Beningna   see **Benigno.**
Benino   see **Benigno.**
Beniqua   see **Benigno.**
Benisa   see **Benicio.**
Benisia   see **Benicio.**
Benitario   see **Benito.**
Benitin   see **Benito.**
Benitio   see **Benito.**
Benitium   see **Benito.**
Benito   see **Benedicto.**
Benito (Bay nee' toe) m. **EE:** Ben,
Benedicta. Lat. "To speak well
of someone." 4th cen. M. be-
headed in France. F. 10/8. **Dim:**
Benerito, Benitin, Nito. **Var:**
Beinta, Bemito, Benadita,
Benato, Beneda, Benentio,
Beneto, Benica, Benidi, Benind,
Benitario, Benitio, Benitium,
Benitto, Bennito, Bentio,
Bienino, Bineto, Binito, Venito.
See also Benedicto.
Benitto   see **Benito.**
Benizio   see **Benicio.**
Benja   see **Benjamin.**
Benjamé   see **Benjamin.**
Benjamin (Ben ha mean') m. **EE:**
Ben, Benjamin, Benny. Heb.
"Favorite son" or "son of right
hand." Biblically, youngest son
of Jacob & founder of 1 of 12
tribes. 11 x in DS. **Dim:** Benja,
Chelin, Chemin, Min, Mincho,
Mino. **Var:** Bejamín, Bejanin,
Bemina, Bengamin, Beniamin,
Benjamé, Benjaminin, Benjammén,
Benjamo, Benjemín, Venjamin.
Benjaminin   see **Benjamin.**
Benjammén   see **Benjamin.**
Benjamo   see **Benjamin.**
Benjemin   see **Benjamin.**

Bennaventa   see **Bonavento.**
Benneo   see **Benedicto.**
Bennina   see **Benedicto.**
Bennito   see **Benito.**
Bennotiano   see **Venustiano.**
Bennstriano   see **Venustiano.**
Benoabé   see **Bernabé.**
Benobé   see **Bernabé.**
Benocio   see **Benicio.**
Benostiano   see **Venustiano.**
Bensala   see **Venceslao.**
Bensclado   see **Venceslao.**
Benselado   see **Venceslao.**
Benselaso   see **Venceslao.**
Benses   see **Venceslao.**
Bensilao   see **Venceslao.**
Bensis   see **Venceslao.**
Bentio   see **Benito.**
Bento   see **Benedicto.**
Benturo   see **Venturo.**
Benus   see **Venus.**
Benusteana   see **Venustiano.**
Benustiano   see **Venustiano.**
Benustriano   see **Venustiano.**
Benvenido (Bain bay nee' doe) m.
EE: Bonaventure. Ital. "Beve-
nuto," "welcome." 4 x in DS.
Benvenuto   see **Bonavento.**
Benzalao   see **Venceslao.**
Benzelada   see **Venceslao.**
Beño   see **Bernal.**
Bequi   see **Rebeca.**
Bequita   see **Rebeca.**
Berabé   see **Bernabé.**
Beranda   see **Veneranda.**
Berardo   see **Bernal.**
Bercare   see **Bercario.**
Bercario (Bare cah' ree oh) m. **EE:**
Bercharius. Ger. "Army of the
ruler." 7th cen. Fr. M. F.
10/16. **Var:** Bercare.
Berdo   see **Berta.**
Berdomiano   see **Bardomiano.**
Bere   see **Bernicia.**
Beremundo   see **Bermudo.**
Berené   see **Bernicia.**
Berenguela (Bay' ren gay' lah) f?
EE: Berengario. Ger. "Beren-
gario," "protective lance." 2 x
in DS. 1 monk near Toulouse,
France. F. 5/26. **Var:**
Verenguela.
Bergelio   see **Virgilio.**
Berginia   see **Virginia.**
Berilo (Bay ree' low) m. **EE:**
Beryl, Beryle, Berylee. Lat.
"Beryl," sea-green stone. **Var:**
Barilio.
Berisario   see **Belisario.**
Berlinda   see **Belinda.**
Bermada   see **Bermudo.**
Bermadino   see **Bernal.**
Bermardena   see **Bernal.**
Bermardina   see **Bernal.**
Bermardo   see **Bernal.**
Bermo   see **Bermudo.**
Bermobé   see **Bernabé.**
Bermorda   see **Bernal.**
Bermudo (Bare moo' doe) m. **EE:**
Veremond. Ger. "Protection."
Dim: Bermo. **Var:** Beremundo,
Bermada.
Bernaal   see **Bernal.**
Bernabé (Bare nah bay') m. **EE:**
Barnabas, Barnaby. Heb. "Son of

exhortation or consolation."
Apostle, missionary & companion
of Paul & Mark. F. 6/11. **Var:**
Barnaba, Barnabus, Benoabé,
Benobé, Berabé, Bermobé,
Bernabel, Bernada, Bernardé,
Bernavé, Bernavel, Bernaver,
Bernavetilana, Bernavil,
Vernavela.

Bernabel   see **Bernabé.**
Bernada   see **Bernabé.**
Bernadiono   see **Bernal.**
Bernaidas   see **Bernal.**
Bernal (Bare nahl') m. **EE:**
Bernald, Bernard, Ger. "Govern-
ing, ordering." 29 x in DS. St.
Bernard founded 68 Cistercian
monasteries in 12th cen. **Dim:**
Beño (Bernardo), Berno, Dino
(Bernardo), Nado (Bernardo),
Nardo (Bernardo), Nayo
(Bernardo), Nino (Bernardo),
Tato (Bernardo). **Var:** Benardo,
Berardo, Bermadino, Bermardena,
Bermardina, Bermardo, Bermorda,
Bernaal, Bernadiono, Bernaidas,
Bernaldino, Bernaldnia,
Bernaldo, Bernalino, Bernanda,
Bernandino, Bernardedo,
Bernardel, Bernardina,
Bernardinium, Bernardinos,
Bernardo, Bernardus, Bernarfo,
Bernarlino, Bernarva, Bernavil,
Bernidito, Venardo, Veralda,
Verardo, Vernadine, Vernado,
Vernaldo, Vernardino, Vinardo.

Bernaldino   see **Bernal.**
Bernaldnia   see **Bernal.**
Bernaldo   see **Bernal.**
Bernalino   see **Bernal.**
Bernanda   see **Bernal.**
Bernandino   see **Bernal.**
Bernardé   see **Bernabé.**
Bernardedo   see **Bernal.**
Bernardel   see **Bernal.**
Bernardina   see **Bernal.**
Bernardinium   see **Bernal.**
Bernardinos   see **Bernal.**
Bernardo   see **Bernal.**
Bernardus   see **Bernal.**
Bernarfo   see **Bernal.**
Bernarlino   see **Bernal.**
Bernarva   see **Bernal.**
Bernavé   see **Bernabé.**
Bernavel   see **Bernabé.**
Bernaver   see **Bernabé.**
Bernavetilana see **Bernabé.**
Bernavil   see **Bernabé.**
Bernavil   see **Bernal.**
Bernia   see **Bernicia.**
Bernicia (Bare nee' see ah) f. **EE:**
Berenice, Bernice. Gk. "Bringer
of victory." **Dim:** Bere. **Var:**
Berené, Bernia, Berniz, Beronis,
Vericio.

Bernidito   see **Bernal.**
Berniz   see **Bernicia.**
Berno   see **Bernal.**
Berónico   see **Verónico.**
Beronis   see **Bernicia.**
Berrita   see **Berta.**
Bersabá   see **Betsabé.**
Bersabé   see **Betsabé.**
Bersabie   see **Betsabé.**
Bersadá   see **Betsabé.**

Bersahí   see **Betsabé.**
Bersaida   see **Betsabé.**
Berta (Bare' tah) f. **EE:** Bertha,
Bertie, Bettina. Ger. "Bright."
Bertha of the Big Feet, mother
of Charlemagne. 4 x in DS. **Dim:**
Bertuca, Beta, Beti, Tuca. **Var:**
Berdo, Berrita, Bertalea,
Bertea, Bertha, Berthia,
Bertilda, Bertilla, Bertín,
Bertoldino, Bertolin, Bierta,
Birtha, Verta. See also
Bertoldo.

Bertalea   see **Berta.**
Bertea   see **Berta.**
Berterbo   see **Viterbo.**
Bertha   see **Berta.**
Berthia   see **Berta.**
Bertholdo   see **Bertoldo.**
Bertice   see **Beatriz.**
Bertilda   see **Berta.**
Bertilla   see **Berta.**
Bertín   see **Berta.**
Berto   see **Agilberto.**
Berto   see **Humberto.**
Berto   see **Roberto.**
Bertoldino   see **Berta.**
Bertoldino   see **Bertoldo.**
Bertoldo (Bare tole' doe) m. **EE:**
Berthold, Bertold. Ger. "Bright,
resplendent." 7 x in DS. **Dim:**
Bertoldino. **Var:** Bertholdo,
Bertolo. See also Berta.
Bertolin   see **Berta.**
Bertolo   see **Bertoldo.**
Bertrán (Bare trahn') m. **EE:** Bert,
Bertram, Bertrand. Ger. "Bright
raven." 6 x in DS.
Bertrice   see **Beatriz.**
Bertriz   see **Beatriz.**
Bertuca   see **Berta.**
Bertunga   see **Alberto.**
Bertunga   see **Roberto.**
Beryabe   see **Bárbara.**
Besabela   see **Betsabé.**
Besente   see **Vicente.**
Besento   see **Vicente.**
Besi   see **Elisabeth.**
Besnardo (Base nar' doe) m. **EE:**
Besnardis. Besnardis, Fr. sur-
name.
Bessbi   see **Betsabé.**
Besta   see **Vesta.**
Bestrís   see **Beatriz.**
Beta   see **Berta.**
Betariana   see **Betario.**
Betario (Bay tah' ree oh) m. **EE:**
Betario. 7th cen. S. & bishop of
Chartres, France. **Var:**
Betariana.
Bethania (Bay tah nee' ah) f. **EE:**
Bethany. Heb. "Place of unripe
figs." City where resurrected
Lazarus lived.
Bethlehén   see **Belén.**
Bethsabeé   see **Betsabé.**
Bethsaida   see **Betsabé.**
Bethzabé   see **Betsabé.**
Beti   see **Beatriz.**
Beti   see **Berta.**
Beti   see **Elisabeth.**
Beto   see **Adalberto.**
Beto   see **Alberto.**
Beto   see **Gilberto.**
Beto   see **Humberto.**

Beto   see **Norberto.**
Beto   see **Roberto.**
Betra   see **Pedro.**
Betriz   see **Beatriz.**
Betsabé (Bate sah bay') f. **EE:**
  Bathsheba. Heb. "Daughter of
  oath." Wife of Uriah & then
  David. **Dim:** Becha, Bessbi,
  Betsy. **Var:** Belsabé, Belzabé,
  Bersabé, Bersabé, Bersabie,
  Bersadá, Bersahi, Bersaida,
  Besabela, Bethsabeé, Bethsaida,
  Bethzabé, Betzabé, Betzabel.
Betsi   see **Elisabeth.**
Betsy   see **Betsabé.**
Betulia (Bay too' lee ah) f. **EE:**
  Bethulia. Biblical city in
  Palestine. Apocryphal book of
  Judith takes place there.
Betzabé   see **Betsabé.**
Betzabel   see **Betsabé.**
Beva   see **Genoveva.**
Bevelina (Bay bay lee' nah) f. **EE:**
  Beverly. Place in historical
  Macedonia. **Var:** Bevina.
Bevina   see **Bevelina.**
Beztrix   see **Beatriz.**
Biachis   see **Beatriz.**
Biana   see **Bibiano.**
Bianilla   see **Bibiano.**
Biatres   see **Beatriz.**
Biatris   see **Beatriz.**
Biatriz   see **Beatriz.**
Bibaldo   see **Wilebaldo.**
Bibano   see **Viviano.**
Bibeanela (Bee bay' ah nay' lah)
  f. **EE:** Bibeanela. Comb. of
  Bibiano & Nelo (see both)?
Bibi   see **Bibiano.**
Bibi   see **Viviano.**
Bibia   see **Bibiano.**
Bibián   see **Viviano.**
Bibiana   see **Viviano.**
Bibiani   see **Viviano.**
Bibianna   see **Viviano.**
Bibiano (Bee bee ah' no) m. **EE:**
  Vivianus. Lat. "Alive, living."
  5 x in DS. **Dim:** Biana, Bianilla,
  Bibi, Bibia, Viana. **Var:**
  Bibrana, Bribiano, Veviana,
  Vibiano, Vibiena, Vibrano.
Bibino   see **Viviano.**
Bibrana   see **Bibiano.**
Bibrano   see **Viviano.**
Bicenta   see **Vicente.**
Bicente   see **Vicente.**
Bicha   see **Lauro.**
Biche   see **Beatriz.**
Bicho   see **Beatriz.**
Bicho   see **Luis.**
Bicinthia   see **Vicente.**
Bictar   see **Víctor.**
Bictor   see **Víctor.**
Bictoria   see **Víctor.**
Bidad   see **Vidal.**
Bidal   see **Vidal.**
Bidala   see **Vidal.**
Bidalda   see **Vidal.**
Bidar   see **Vidal.**
Bidio   see **Ovidio.**
Bienino   see **Benito.**
Bierta   see **Berta.**
Bígida   see **Brígido.**
Bígita   see **Brígido.**
Bilebalbo   see **Wilebaldo.**

Biliad (Bee lee odd') m. **EE:**
  Bildad. Heb. "Bel has loved." In
  Bible comforts Job but is most
  violent in criticism of Job &
  children.
Bilar (Bee lahr') f. **EE:** Pilar.
  Settlement in Bohol Province,
  Phillipines. Form of Pilar?
  (See).
Bildá (Beel dah') f. **EE:** Bildad.
  Heb. "Beloved." Bildad argued
  with Job over nature of his
  affliction.
Bilisario   see **Belisario.**
Bineto   see **Benito.**
Binino   see **Benigno.**
Binito   see **Benito.**
Biocento   see **Vicente.**
Biocinto   see **Pioquinto.**
Biola   see **Viola.**
Biolanda   see **Viola.**
Bique   see **Víctor.**
Bircilinia   see **Prisciliano.**
Birgida   see **Brígido.**
Birgidio   see **Brígido.**
Birgilio   see **Virgilio.**
Birginio   see **Virginia.**
Birgitta   see **Brígido.**
Birgitti   see **Brígido.**
Birtha   see **Berta.**
Birtudes   see **Virtudes.**
Biscente   see **Vicente.**
Bisenta   see **Vicente.**
Bisente   see **Vicente.**
Bisentes   see **Vicente.**
Bisenti   see **Vicente.**
Bisilia   see **Bacilio.**
Bisitación   see **Visitación.**
Bita   see **Beatriz.**
Bitalia   see **Vidal.**
Bitaria   see **Víctor.**
Biterbo   see **Viterbo.**
Bitervo   see **Viterbo.**
Bito   see **Víctor.**
Bito   see **Vidal.**
Bitor   see **Vidal.**
Bitoria   see **Víctor.**
Bitoriano   see **Víctor.**
Bitriana   see **Víctor.**
Bitulo   see **Víctor.**
Bivián   see **Viviano.**
Biviana   see **Viviano.**
Biye   see **Guillermo.**
Bizenta   see **Vicente.**
Blácida   see **Plácido.**
Bladimiro   see **Baldomero.**
Blanca (Blahn' cah) f. **EE:** Blanch,
  Blanche. Ger. "White, bril-
  liant." 12th & 13th cen. S.
  queen of France, daughter of
  Alfonso IX of Castile, wife of
  Louis VIII, & mother of St.
  Louis of France. **Dim:** Cuca,
  Quita. **Var:** Blanch,
  Blanchariano, Bleanca, Vianca.
Blanch   see **Blanca.**
Blanchariano   see **Blanca.**
Blandina (Blahn dee' nah) f. **EE:**
  Blandina. Lat. "Flattering,
  fondling, caressing." In DS as 1
  of 48 Mm. of Lyons, France.
Blas (Blahs') m. **EE:** Blase, Blaze.
  Lat. "Stuttering." 1 of most
  venerated Mm. of church. 4th
  cen. physician & patron of all

physicians & diseases of throat.
F. 2/3. **Var:** Blasae, Blascida,
Blase, Blasido, Blasima, Blasin,
Blasio, Blasius, Blass, Blassio,
Blaz, Vlas.

Blasae	see **Blas.**
Blascida	see **Blas.**
Blase	see **Blas.**
Blasido	see **Blas.**
Blasima	see **Blas.**
Blasin	see **Blas.**
Blasio	see **Blas.**
Blasius	see **Blas.**
Blass	see **Blas.**
Blassio	see **Blas.**
Blaz	see **Blas.**
Bleanca	see **Blanca.**
Bliza	see **Belisario.**
Bobby	see **Roberto.**
Bocho	see **Ambrosio.**
Bocho	see **Sinforoso.**
Bohifacia	see **Bonifacio.**
Bolbina	see **Balbina.**
Boldemar	see **Baldomero.**

Bolivar (Bo lee' bar) m. **EE:**
Bolivar. Sp. last name used as
1st name. Bolivar, 19th cen.
South American hero, led revolution against Spain. **Dim:** Bolo.

Bolo	see **Bolivar.**
Boltizar	see **Baltasar.**
Bomfacio	see **Bonifacio.**

Bona (Bo' nah) f. **EE:** Bonnie. Lat.
"Bona dea" means "good goddess."
Deity of fertility & Roman
women. **Dim:** Bonito.

Bonaciano	see **Bonifacio.**
Bonafacao	see **Bonifacio.**
Bonafatio	see **Bonifacio.**
Bonafecio	see **Bonifacio.**
Bonaficio	see **Bonifacio.**

Bonajunta (Bo nah hoon' tah) f.
EE: Bonajunta. Ital. "Good ar-
rival." 13th cen. Ital. S. & 1
of founders of Servite order. F.
8/31.

Bonavendura   see **Bonavento.**
Bonavento (Bo nah bane' toe) m.
EE: Bonaventure. Lat. "Bonus" &
"ventus" mean "good wind or
auger." 7 x in DS. **Dim:** Ventura,
Venturino, Venturita. **Var:**
Bennaventa, Benvenuto,
Bonavendura, Bonaventura,
Bonaventurae, Bonoventura, Buena
(Bentura), Buenaventura,
Buenaventuria, Buenoventuro,
Buenventura, Vuena (Ventura).

Bonaventura	see **Bonavento.**
Bonaventurae	see **Bonavento.**
Bonefacio	see **Bonifacio.**
Bonefaco	see **Bonifacio.**
Bonefasio	see **Bonifacio.**
Boneficio	see **Bonifacio.**
Bonfacio	see **Bonifacio.**
Bonfanio	see **Bonifacio.**
Bonfaucio	see **Bonifacio.**

Bonfilio (Bone fee' lee oh) m. **EE:**
Bonfilius. Ital. "Good son." 2 x
in DS.

Boni	see **Bonifacio.**
Boniface	see **Bonifacio.**

Bonifacio (Bo nee fah' see oh) m.
EE: Boniface. Lat. "Well-doer"
or "of good fate." 26 x in DS. 1

helped to convert pagan Germany.
F. 6/5. **Dim:** Boni, Chacha,
Facha, Facino, Guacho, Juacho,
Moñi, Pacho. **Var:** Banifacio,
Benefacita, Benifocio,
Bohifacia, Bomfacio, Bonaciano,
Bonafacao, Bonafatio, Bonafecio,
Bonaficio, Bonefacio, Bonefaco,
Bonefasio, Boneficio, Bonfacio,
Bonfanio, Bonfaucio, Boniface,
Bonifacium, Bonifacius,
Bonifasio, Bonifatio,
Bonifatius, Bonifazio,
Bonificio, Bonifocio, Bonifucio,
Bonofacio, Bunifacia, Vanifacia,
Vonifacio, Vonifaisa.

Bonifacium	see **Bonifacio.**
Bonifacius	see **Bonifacio.**
Bonifasio	see **Bonifacio.**
Bonifatio	see **Bonifacio.**
Bonifatius	see **Bonifacio.**
Bonifazio	see **Bonifacio.**
Bonificio	see **Bonifacio.**
Bonifocio	see **Bonifacio.**
Bonifucio	see **Bonifacio.**
Bonito	see **Bona.**
Bonofacio	see **Bonifacio.**
Bonoventura	see **Bonavento.**
Bonsolabio	see **Bronislava.**
Bordoniamo	see **Bardomiano.**

Borgita (Bore hee' tah) f. **EE:**
Borgita. Diminutive of Borja or
Borgia, Sp.-Ital. Renaissance
noblemen?

Boris (Bo' rees) m. **EE:** Boris.
Slav. "A fighter." Boris
Godunov, 16th cen. Russian tsar
& eponymous hero of Mussorgsky's
opera. 2 x in DS. 1, son of St.
Vladimir.

Borromeo (Bo roe may' oh) m. **EE:**
Borromeo. Lat. "Bonus," "good" &
Sp. "romeo" refers to pilgrim-
age. Hence "Good pilgrim."

Borthala	see **Bartolomé.**
Bortolo	see **Bartolomé.**
Bosilia	see **Bacilio.**
Bosilisa	see **Bacilio.**
Boytisto	see **Baytista.**
Brácedis	see **Práxedes.**
Brácida	see **Plácido.**
Bracilia	see **Bacilio.**
Bracillo	see **Bacilio.**
Bráhedez	see **Práxedes.**
Brájedes	see **Práxedes.**
Brájeres	see **Práxedes.**
Bralilio	see **Braulia.**
Brancho	see **Abraham.**
Brand	see **Brandio.**

Brandio (Brahn' dee oh) m. **EE:**
Brand, Brendan. Teut. "Fire-
brand" or "sword." In DS, 5th
cen. Irish S. patron of sailors.
Var: Brand, Brenda, Brinda,
Prenda.

Branla (Brahn' lah) f. **EE:** Branla.
Musical term referring to 16th &
17th cen. Fr. dances.

Braula	see **Braulia.**
Brauleo	see **Braulia.**
Brauli	see **Braulia.**

Braulia (Brow' lee ah) f. **EE:**
Braulio. Ger. "Sword." 7th cen.
Sp. bishop who labored with St.
Isidore. F. 3/26. **Dim:** Baulio,

Braulina, Lalo. **Var:** Bralilio,
  Braula, Brauleo, Brauli,
  Braulin, Braullio, Brolio,
  Obraulio, Obravlio.
Braulín   see **Braulia.**
Braulina   see **Braulia.**
Braullio   see **Braulia.**
Brecida   see **Briseida.**
Brégido   see **Brígido.**
Brenda   see **Brandio.**
Brenilda   see **Benilde.**
Bresiliano   see **Prisciliano.**
Bribiano   see **Bibiano.**
Bríchida   see **Brígido.**
Bricio (Bree' see oh) m. **EE:**
  Brice, Brictius, Bryce. Lat.
  "Force"? 3 x in DS. Most impor-
  tant, 5th cen. Archbishop of
  Tours, France. F. 11/14. **Var:**
  Briscia, Brisio, Brislio.
Brígado   see **Brígido.**
Brigda   see **Brígido.**
Brígedo   see **Brígido.**
Briget   see **Brígido.**
Brigetta   see **Brígido.**
Brighido   see **Brígido.**
Brigidio   see **Brígido.**
Brígido (Bree' hee doe) m. **EE:**
  Bridget, Brigid. Celt.
  "Strength." 15 x in DS. Most
  famous is patroness of Ireland.
  F. 2/1. **Dim:** Gidita. **Var:**
  Bigida, Bigita, Birgida,
  Birgidio, Birgitta, Birgitti,
  Brégido, Bríchida, Brígado,
  Brigda, Brígedo, Briget,
  Brigetta, Brighido, Brigidio,
  Brigigta, Brigilo, Brigindo,
  Brigio, Brigitha, Brigito,
  Brigitta, Brigittores, Brijeda,
  Brijiblo, Brijido, Brixida,
  Bryida, Prígido, Vígido,
  Vrígido, Vrijeda.
Brigigta   see **Brígido.**
Brigilo   see **Brígido.**
Brigindo   see **Brígido.**
Brigio   see **Brígido.**
Brigitha   see **Brígido.**
Brigito   see **Brígido.**
Brigitta   see **Brígido.**
Brigittores   see **Brígido.**
Brijeda   see **Brígido.**
Brijiblo   see **Brígido.**
Brijido   see **Brígido.**
Brinda   see **Brandio.**
Briscia   see **Bricio.**
Brisciliana   see **Prisciliano.**

Briseida (Bree say ee' dah) f. **EE:**
  Briseis. Maiden in Homer's
  "Iliad" who was concubine of
  Achilles. Taken by Agamemnon &
  is pivotal to entire plot. **Var:**
  Brecida, Briselda, Brisida,
  Brizida.
Briselda   see **Briseida.**
Brisida   see **Briseida.**
Brisiliana   see **Prisciliano.**
Brisio   see **Bricio.**
Brislio   see **Bricio.**
Brixida   see **Brígido.**
Brizida   see **Briseida.**
Brolio   see **Braulia.**
Bronislava (Broe nee slah' bah) f.
  EE: Bronislava. Slav. "Weapon of
  glory." Polish V. invoked
  against pestilence & cholera. F.
  8/30. **Var:** Bonsolabio.
Bruena   see **Bruno.**
Brumilda   see **Brunilda.**
Brunela   see **Bruno.**
Bruni   see **Brunilda.**
Brunilda (Broo neel' dah) f. **EE:**
  Brunhilda, Brunhilde. Ger. "She
  who fights with courage." Female
  warrior in "Nibelungelied." **Var:**
  Brumilda, Bruni.
Bruno (Broo' no) m. **EE:** Bruno.
  Ger. "Brown." 8 x in DS. 1
  founded Carthusians in 11th cen.
  Germany. **Var:** Bruena, Brunela.
Bruto (Broo' toe) m. **EE:** Bruto,
  Brutus. Lat. "Heavy, immovable,
  insensible." 1 of main assassins
  of Caesar.
Bryida   see **Brígido.**
Bucho   see **Tiberio.**
Buena   see **Bonavento.**
Buenaventura   see **Bonavento.**
Buenaventuria see **Bonavento.**
Buenoventuro   see **Bonavento.**
Buenventura   see **Bonavento.**
Bula (Boo' lah) f. **EE:** Beula,
  Beulah. Heb. "Married." Name
  given to Palestine, restored
  land of Jews after exile.
Bulfrano   see **Wulfrano.**
Bulmano (Bool mah' roe) m. **EE:**
  Bulmar. Ger. "Wolf," or fig.
  "famous warrior." **Var:** Bulmero,
  Bulnaro.
Bulmero   see **Bulmaro.**
Bulnaro   see **Bulmaro.**
Bunifacia   see **Bonifacio.**
Burcilla   see **Tiburcio.**

C

Cabalina (Cah bah lee' nah) f. **EE:**
  Caballinus. Lat. "Belonging to a
  horse."
Cabino   see **Gabino.**
Cacha   see **Caridad.**
Cachi   see **Casimiro.**
Cachita   see **Caridad.**
Cachito   see **Jacinto.**
Cacho   see **Agusto.**
Cacho   see **Jacinto.**

Caciana   see **Casiano.**
Cacianna   see **Casiano.**
Cacilda   see **Casildo.**
Cacilde   see **Casildo.**
Cacimiro   see **Casimiro.**
Caco   see **Isaac.**
Cadelario   see **Candelario.**
Cadelia   see **Cordilio.**
Cadio   see **Arcadio.**
Caecelii   see **Cecilio.**

Caecilio   see Cecilio.
Caesarita   see César.
Caesarria   see César.
Caetana   see Cayetano.
Caetastina   see Cayetano.
Cafeatano   see Cayetano.
Cafirio (Cah fee' ree oh) m. EE:
  Cafirio. Cafareo was promontory
  in Eubea, Gk. island where Gk.
  armada was destroyed after Troy.
Cagetacio   see Cayetano.
Cagetano   see Cayetano.
Cagetavo   see Cayetano.
Cahatino   see Cayetano.
Caietano   see Cayetano.
Cailas   see Miguel.
Cailletano   see Cayetano.
Caitano   see Cayetano.
Caiteno   see Cayetano.
Cajatano   see Cayetano.
Cajatona   see Cayetano.
Cajentano   see Cayetano.
Cajerana   see Cayetano.
Cajetán   see Cayetano.
Cajetanam   see Cayetano.
Cajetania   see Cayetano.
Cajetanis   see Cayetano.
Cajetano   see Cayetano.
Cajetanus   see Cayetano.
Cajetaro   see Cayetano.
Cajetemo   see Cayetano.
Cajetón   see Cayetano.
Cajetún   see Cayetano.
Cajetura   see Cayetano.
Cajitano   see Cayetano.
Calala   see Candelario.
Caledonió   see Celedonio.
Calendonio   see Celedonio.
Calestino   see Celestino.
Calesto   see Calixto.
Calestor   see Calixto.
Caletana   see Cayetano.
Calexto   see Calixto.
Cali   see Calixto.
Calicho   see Carlos.
Calin   see Carlos.
Calina   see Catalina.
Caliopa (Cah lee oh' pah) f. EE:
  Calliope, Kelliopi. Gk. "Beau-
  tiful" or "of beautiful voice."
  In Gk. myth., most important of
  Muses as patroness of epic
  poetry & mother of Orpheus.
Calistaro   see Calixto.
Calistia   see Calixto.
Calisto   see Calixto.
Calistro   see Calixto.
Calistus   see Calixto.
Calixto (Cah leeks' toe) m. EE:
  Calixtus, Callista, etc. Gk.
  "Most beautiful." 8 x in DS.
  Dim: Cali. Var: Calesto,
  Calestor, Calexto, Calistaro,
  Calistia, Calisto, Calistro,
  Calistus, Calixtro, Calizto,
  Callestro, Callisto, Callistro,
  Callixto, Celixto, Chalixto,
  Colistro, Colizto, Galisto,
  Galistra.
Calixtro   see Calixto.
Calizto   see Calixto.
Caljetano   see Cayetano.
Callatano   see Cayetano.
Callatina   see Cayetano.
Calleetana   see Cayetano.

Callelano   see Cayetano.
Callentana   see Cayetano.
Callestro   see Calixto.
Calleta   see Cayetano.
Calletano   see Cayetano.
Calletava   see Cayetano.
Calletino   see Cayetano.
Callisto   see Calixto.
Callistro   see Calixto.
Callixto   see Calixto.
Calma (Cahl' mah) f. EE: Calma.
  Lat. "Calm." Fig., peace &
  tranquility.
Calo   see Carlos.
Caltetana   see Cayetano.
Calvino (Cahl bee' no) m. EE:
  Calvin. Lat. "Bald." 16th cen.
  Fr. Protestant responsible for
  Calvinist doctrines.
Camelea   see Camelia.
Camelia (Cah may' lee ah) f. EE:
  Camilla, Camille, etc. Nymph who
  attended Diana in Roman myth.
  13th cen. M. drowned to preserve
  virginity. F. 9/17. Var:
  Camelea, Camelina.
Camelina   see Camelia.
Camen   see Carmen.
Camerino (Cah may ree' no) m. EE:
  Cameron. Lat. "One from Cameria
  (ancient Sabine city)."
Camileta   see Camilo.
Camillo   see Camilo.
Camilo (Cah mee' low) m. EE:
  Camilla, Camille, etc. Lat.
  "Child of free & noble birth."
  Founder of order of Camellians
  of Fathers of Good Death. F.
  7/14. Dim: Camileta, Camito,
  Milico, Milo. Var: Camillo,
  Camireno, Canila, Comilo.
Camireno   see Camilo.
Camiria (Cah mee' ree ah) f. EE:
  Camiria. Camirio refers to type
  of tree.
Camito   see Camilo.
Campia   see Caralampio.
Camucha   see Carmen.
Canacho   see Encarnación.
Cancho   see Carmen.
Cancio (Cahn' see oh) m. EE:
  Cantius. Lat. "Chant, spell."
  3rd cen. Roman M. F. 5/31. Var:
  Cansio.
Canda   see Candelario.
Canda   see Candido.
Candalanio   see Candelario.
Candalano   see Candelario.
Candalario   see Candelario.
Candaleria   see Candelario.
Candalonio   see Candelario.
Candario   see Candelario.
Candeda   see Candelario.
Candeladio   see Candelario.
Candelairo   see Candelario.
Candelano   see Candelario.
Candelar   see Candelario.
Candelareo   see Candelario.
Candelario (Cahn day lah' ree oh)
  mf. EE: Candelario. Lat. "Cad-
  dela," "wax candle." Catholic
  feast day for "La purificación
  de Nuestra Señora." Numerous
  candles commemorate holy fami-
  ly's visit to temple. F. 2/2.

Dim: Calala, Canda, Candeda, Candelas, Candelina, Canducha, Cayaya. **Var:** Andelario, Cadelario, Candalanio, Candalano, Candalario, Candaleria, Candalonio, Candario, Candeladio, Candelairo, Candelano, Candelar, Candelareo, Candelaris, Candelavia, Candeleno, Candelerio, Candeleva, Candelona, Candeloria, Candeloris, Candeluria, Canderlio, Candilano, Candilario, Candlario, Candolario, Caneloris, Cantalario, Cantelario, Condalario, Condelario, Condelaro, Escandelario, Gardelia, Kandelaria.

Candelaris	see	**Candelario.**
Candelas	see	**Candelario.**
Candelavia	see	**Candelario.**
Candeleno	see	**Candelario.**
Candelerio	see	**Candelario.**
Candeleva	see	**Candelario.**
Candelina	see	**Candelario.**
Candelona	see	**Candelario.**
Candeloria	see	**Candelario.**
Candeloris	see	**Candelario.**
Candeluria	see	**Candelario.**
Canderlio	see	**Candelario.**
Candi	see	**Candido.**
Candidas	see	**Candido.**

Candido (Cahn dee' doe) m. **EE:** Candide. Lat. "Glowing white." Famous satire of Voltaire. 16 x in DS. 4th cen. V. M. F. 9/20. **Dim:** Canda, Candi, Candito, Canducha. **Var:** Candidas, Condido.

Candilano	see	**Candelario.**
Candilario	see	**Candelario.**
Candito	see	**Candido.**
Candlario	see	**Candelario.**
Candolario	see	**Candelario.**

Candor (Cahn dohr') m. **EE:** Candor. Lat. Fig. indicates sincerity & purity of soul.

Canducha	see	**Candelario.**
Canducha	see	**Candido.**
Caneloris	see	**Candelario.**

Caniacián (Cah nee' ah see ahn') m? **EE:** Caniacian. Form of Canice, patron S. of Kilkenny, Ireland? F. 10/11.

Canila	see	**Camilo.**
Canoto	see	**Canuto.**
Canrado	see	**Conrado.**
Canroda	see	**Conrado.**
Cansio	see	**Cancio.**
Cansuelo	see	**Consuelo.**
Cantalario	see	**Candelario.**
Cantelario	see	**Candelario.**

Canuto (Cah noo' toe) m. **EE:** Canute, Knute. King of England, Norway, & Denmark in 11th cen. Kinsman of St. Canute who advanced teachings of church in Denmark. F. 1/19. **Var:** Canoto, Canutu, Kanuto.

Canutu	see	**Canuto.**
Caña	see	**Encarnación.**
Caoncha	see	**Concepción.**

Caparina (Cah pah ree' nah) f. **EE:** Caparina. Type of butterfly.

Caporino (Cah poe ree' no) m. **EE:** Caporino. Caporo refers to 1 of Celtic tribes that inhabited Spain.

Carácala (Cah rah' cah lah) f. **EE:** Caracalla. Lat. "Caracalla," type of cape. Marcus Aurelius Antonino received name for use of cape.

Caraino   see **Carino.**

Caralampio (Cah rah lahm' pee oh) m. **EE:** Charalampus. Gk. "Rejoicing." 3 x in DS. Gk. bishop mart. for preaching. F. 9/17. **Var:** Campia, Caralanspio, Caralumpio, Carolampio.

Caralanspio	see	**Caralampio.**
Caralino	see	**Carolina.**
Caralumpio	see	**Caralampio.**
Carcóforo	see	**Carpóforo.**
Cardelia	see	**Cordilio.**

Cardina (Cahr dee' nah) f. **EE:** Cardina. Cardo is administrative unit in Spain.

Cardo	see	**Ricardo.**
Cardulo	see	**Catulo.**
Cari	see	**Caridad.**
Cariana	see	**Carino.**

Caridad (Cah ree dahd') f. **EE:** Carissa, Charity, etc. Lat. "Dear." 1 of 3 daughters of St. Sophia, all mart. in 2nd cen. F. 8/1. **Dim:** Cacha, Cachita, Cari, Caro, Carucha.

Carima	see	**Carino.**
Carimen	see	**Carino.**
Carimila	see	**Carmen.**
Carimira	see	**Carino.**
Carimisa	see	**Carino.**

Carino (Cah ree' no) m. **EE:** Carina. Lat. "Charinus," "funny." Carina mart. under Julian the Apostate. F. 11/7. **Var:** Caraino, Cariana, Carima, Carimen, Carimira, Carimisa, Carión, Garina, Garrina, Kerina.

Carión   see **Carino.**

Carisa (Cah ree' sah) f. **EE:** Carissa. Gk. "Beautiful, graceful." 1 of Mm. of order of St. Ursula (see). F. 8/22. **Var:** Carissima.

Carissima	see	**Carisa.**
Caritana	see	**Cayetano.**
Caritina	see	**Catalina.**

Caritina (Cah ree tee' nah) f. **EE:** Charitina. Gk. "Funny." 2 x in DS. 4th cen. M. with feet & hands cut off & teeth knocked out. F. 10/4.

Carito	see	**Carolina.**
Carlangas	see	**Carlos.**
Carlata	see	**Carlos.**
Carlina	see	**Carlos.**
Carlitin	see	**Carlos.**
Carlito	see	**Carlos.**
Carlitos	see	**Carlos.**
Carloda	see	**Carlos.**
Carlomagno	see	**Carlos.**
Carlona	see	**Carlos.**
Carlonina	see	**Carlos.**

Carlos (Cahr' lohs) m. **EE:** Carl, Charles, Chuck. Ger. "Strong, manly." 8 x in DS. Most famous was Charlemagne, 1st Holy Roman Emperor. F. 1/28. **Dim:** Calicho, Calin, Calo, Carlangas, Carlina, Carlitín, Carlito, Carlitos, Carlucho, Chale, Chalín, Charli, Checho, Cota, Lina (Carolina), Lito, Litos, Lota, Loti, Tito, Tota. **Var:** Carlata, Carloda, Carlomagno, Carlona, Carlonina, Carlota, Carlotta, Carlottae, Carlottia, Carluta, Carolata, Carolota, Carrlota, Corlata, Corolus, Karloz.

Carlota   see **Carlos.**
Carlotta   see **Carlos.**
Carlottae   see **Carlos.**
Carlottia   see **Carlos.**
Carlucho   see **Carlos.**
Carluta   see **Carlos.**
Carma   see **Carmen.**
Carmación   see **Encarnación.**
Carmal   see **Carmen.**
Carmalo   see **Carmen.**
Carman   see **Carmen.**
Carmele   see **Carmen.**
Carmelina   see **Carmen.**
Carmelinda   see **Carmen.**
Carmelita   see **Carmen.**
Carmello   see **Carmen.**
Carmelo   see **Carmen.**
Carmeloria   see **Carmen.**

Carmen (Cahr' mehn) mf. **EE:** Carmel, Carmen. Heb. "Carmel," "fruitful field, garden park." Our Lady of Mt. Carmel, recipient of special devotion. F. 7/16. **Dim:** Camucha, Cancho, Carmelita, Carmencha, Carmenchita, Carmenchu, Carmita, Carmitica, Chita, Cita, Cuca, Lita, Mela, Melita, Mocha, Nana. **Var:** Camen, Carimila, Carma, Carmal, Carmalo, Carman, Carmele, Carmelina, Carmelinda, Carmello, Carmelo, Carmeloria, Carmena, Carmencido, Carmenia, Carmenza, Carmeta, Carmiela, Carmil, Carmildo, Carmile, Carmilino, Carmilio, Carmilla, Carmilo, Carmilum, Carmino, Carmirigida, Carmiro, Carmona, Cormel, Garmea.

Carmena   see **Carmen.**
Carmencha   see **Carmen.**
Carmenchita   see **Carmen.**
Carmenchu   see **Carmen.**
Carmencido   see **Carmen.**
Carmenia   see **Carmen.**
Carmenza   see **Carmen.**
Carmeta   see **Carmen.**
Carmiela   see **Carmen.**
Carmil   see **Carmen.**
Carmildo   see **Carmen.**
Carmile   see **Carmen.**
Carmilino   see **Carmen.**
Carmilio   see **Carmen.**
Carmilla   see **Carmen.**
Carmilo   see **Carmen.**
Carmilum   see **Carmen.**
Carmino   see **Carmen.**
Carmirigida   see **Carmen.**
Carmiro   see **Carmen.**
Carmita   see **Carmen.**
Carmitica   see **Carmen.**
Carmona   see **Carmen.**

Carnación   see **Encarnación.**
Carnelia   see **Cornelio.**
Carnilia   see **Cornelio.**
Caro   see **Caridad.**
Caro   see **Carolina.**
Carolampio   see **Caralampio.**
Carolata   see **Carlos.**
Caroliana   see **Carolina.**

Carolina (Cah roe lee' nah) f. **EE:** Carol, Caroline, Carrie. Ger. "Strong" or "manly." 8 x in DS. **Dim:** Carito, Caro, Carolo, Carrola, Cayoya, Ina. **Var:** Caralino, Caroliana, Corolina.

Carolo   see **Carlos.**
Carolota   see **Carlos.**

Carparem (Cahr pah' rehm) m? **EE:** Carparem. Capernaum, city in Galilee mentioned in life of Christ.

Carpio (Cahr' pee oh) m. **EE:** Carpus. Gk. "Fruit." 4 x in DS. **Var:** Carpo, Carpyo.

Carpo   see **Carpio.**

Carpóforo (Cahr poe' foe roe) m. **EE:** Carphorus. Gk. "He who carries fruits." 7 x in DS. Roman physician mart. under Diocletian. F. 8/27. **Var:** Carcóforo, Corpofora.

Carpyo   see **Carpio.**
Carrlota   see **Carlos.**
Carrola   see **Carolina.**
Carucha   see **Caridad.**
Casamira   see **Casimiro.**

Casandra (Cah sahn' drah) f. **EE:** Cassandra, Cassie. In Gk. legend, had power of prophecy but no believers. **Var:** Cassander, Cassandra, Cassaudra, Kasandra.

Casanio   see **Casiano.**
Casanira   see **Casimiro.**
Casarea   see **César.**
Cascina   see **Casiano.**
Casemida   see **Casimiro.**
Casemiera   see **Casimiro.**
Casemiro   see **Casimiro.**
Cashi   see **Casimiro.**

Casiano (Cah see ah' no) m. **EE:** Cassianus. Lat. "Helmet of steel." 21 x in DS. 4th cen. teacher tormented to death by pagan pupils. F. 8/13. **Dim:** Chano. **Var:** Assiano, Caciana, Cacianna, Casanio, Cascina, Casin, Casinero, Casiono, Cassiana, Cassinta, Gasino, Quesino.

Casidlo   see **Casildo.**

Casildo (Cah seel' doe) m. **EE:** Casilda. Ger. "Battler." 11th cen. Sp. S., daughter of Moorish prince of Toledo. F. 4/9. **Var:** Cacilda, Cacilde, Casidlo.

Casimaro   see **Casimiro.**
Casimeiro   see **Casimiro.**
Casimere   see **Casimiro.**
Casimeria   see **Casimiro.**
Casimero   see **Casimiro.**
Casimerus   see **Casimiro.**
Casimico   see **Casimiro.**
Casimida   see **Casimiro.**
Casimiera   see **Casimiro.**
Casimina   see **Casimiro.**
Casimio   see **Casimiro.**

Casimir   see Casimiro.
Casimiro (Cah see mee' roe) m. EE:
  Casimir, Cass, Castimer, Slav.
  "Proclamation of peace." 15th
  cen. patron S. of Poland &
  Lithuania. F. 3/4. Dim: Cachi,
  Cashi. Var: Cacimiro, Casamira,
  Casanira, Casemida, Casemiera,
  Casemiro, Casimaro, Casimeiro,
  Casimere, Casimeria, Casimero,
  Casimerus, Casimico, Casimida,
  Casimiera, Casimina, Casimio,
  Casimir, Casimirus, Casimis,
  Casimiso, Casimor, Casimoro,
  Casimra, Casinero, Casininro,
  Casiniro, Casiro, Casmario,
  Casmir, Casmirino, Cassimira,
  Castimiro, Cazmiro, Cosimiro,
  Cosimora, Cucimiro, Garcimiro.
Casimirus   see Casimiro.
Casimis   see Casimiro.
Casimiso   see Casimiro.
Casimor   see Casimiro.
Casimoro   see Casimiro.
Casimra   see Casimiro.
Casin   see Casiano.
Casinao (Cah see nah' oh) m. EE:
  Casinao. Form of Casiano (see)?
Casinciro (Cah seen see' roe) m.
  EE: Casinciro. Form of Casine,
  S. mart. in Galatia, Turkey?
Casinero   see Casiano.
Casinero   see Casimiro.
Casininro   see Casimiro.
Casiniro   see Casimiro.
Casio (Cah' see oh) m. EE:
  Cassius. Lat. "Cassius," Roman
  family. Refers to helmet of
  metal. 8 x in DS.
Casiono   see Casiano.
Casiro   see Casimiro.
Casisno (Cah sees' no) m. EE:
  Casisno. Casis is valley in
  Palestine.
Casmario   see Casimiro.
Casmas   see Cosme.
Casmir   see Casimiro.
Casmirino   see Casimiro.
Casmo   see Cosme.
Caspar   see Gaspar.
Casparo   see Gaspar.
Casparus   see Gaspar.
Caspio   see Gaspar.
Cassander   see Casandra.
Cassandra   see Casandra.
Cassaudra   see Casandra.
Cassiana   see Casiano.
Cassimira   see Casiano.
Cassinta   see Casiano.
Castalia (Cahs tah' lee ah) f. EE:
  Castalia. Gk. "Pure fountain"?
  Spring on Mt. Parnassus in
  central Greece sacred to Apollo
  & Muses. Var: Castrala.
Castana   see Casto.
Castarina   see Casto.
Castillón   see Casto.
Castimiro   see Casimiro.
Castina   see Casto.
Casto (Cahs' toe) m. EE: Castus,
  Chastina. Lat. "Pure," 17 x in
  DS. 3rd cen. M. F. 5/22. Dim:
  Castina, Castullo, Castulo,
  Costolo, Costulo, Gastulo,
  Zastolo. Var: Castana,

Castarina, Castillón, Kasto.
Cástoro (Cahs' toe roe) m. EE:
  Castor. Brightest star of Gemini
  twins. In Gk. legend, Castor &
  Pollux were twins of Leda. 8 x
  in DS. 4th cen. patron S. of
  Coblenz, Germany. F. 2/13.
Castrala   see Castalia.
Castullo   see Casto.
Castulo   see Casto.
Cata   see Catalina.
Catalina (Cah tah lee' nah) f. EE:
  Catherine, Cathy, Kay. Gk.
  "Pure." 15 x in DS. Most impor-
  tant, Catherine of Siena, Italy,
  of 14th cen., wrote great mysti-
  cal work "Dialogue." F. 4/30.
  Dim: Calina, Cata, Catina,
  Catita, Catocha, Catuca,
  Catucha, Catuja, Catunga, Rina
  (Catarina), Trina, Trini. Var:
  Atarina, Caritina, Catana,
  Catania, Catarano, Catarcis,
  Catareno, Catariana, Catarino,
  Catarión, Cataro, Catarrine,
  Catelena, Catelina, Caterín,
  Caterino, Caternia, Caterona,
  Catetino, Cathalina, Catharina,
  Cathelina, Catherina, Cathrina,
  Catilina, Catorino, Catracinia,
  Catraina, Catrino, Cotarima,
  Cotorino, Katalina, Kathorina,
  Katriona.
Catana   see Catalina.
Catania   see Catalina.
Catanin   see Catón.
Catanio (Cah tah' nee oh) m.
  Catanus mart. at Salona in
  Dalmatia (Yugoslavia). F. 4/11.
Catarano   see Catalina.
Catarcis   see Catalina.
Catareno   see Catalina.
Catariana   see Catalina.
Catarino   see Catalina.
Catarión   see Catalina.
Cataro   see Catalina.
Catarrine   see Catalina.
Cátedra (Cah' tay drah) mf? EE:
  Catedra. Gk. "Seat on high."
  Fig., pontified dignity.
Catelena   see Catalina.
Catelia (Cah tay' lee ah) f. EE:
  Catelia. Lat. "Catello" refers
  to chain of gold.
Catelina   see Catalina.
Caterín   see Catalina.
Caterino   see Catalina.
Caternia   see Catalina.
Caterona   see Catalina.
Catetino   see Catalina.
Cathalina   see Catalina.
Catharina   see Catalina.
Cathelina   see Catalina.
Catherina   see Catalina.
Cathrina   see Catalina.
Catilina   see Catalina.
Catina   see Catalina.
Catita   see Catalina.
Catocha   see Catalina.
Catón (Cah tohn') m. EE: Cato.
  Lat. "Penetrating or subtle." S.
  mart. in Africa in 3rd cen.
  Also, 2nd cen. B.C. Roman
  writer, statesman, & general.
  Var: Catanin, Catonina.

Catonina   see **Catón.**
Catorino   see **Catalina.**
Catracinia   see **Catalina.**
Catraina   see **Catalina.**
Catrino   see **Catalina.**
Catuca   see **Catalina.**
Catucha   see **Catalina.**
Catuja   see **Catalina.**
Catulo (Cah too' low) m. EE:
  Catalus. Lat. "Subtle, saga-
  cious." Catalus was family of
  ancient Rome. Also S. mart. in
  Africa. F. 3/24. **Var:** Cardulo.
Catunga   see **Catalina.**
Caudencio   see **Gaudencio.**
Cautelario (Cow' tay lah' ree oh)
  m. From Sp. "cautelar,"
  "prevent, be on guard"?
Cavetano   see **Cayetano.**
Cayaya   see **Candelario.**
Cayelano   see **Cayetano.**
Cayetamo   see **Cayetano.**
Cayetanae   see **Cayetano.**
Cayetano (Cai' yay tah' no) m. EE:
  Cajetan, Gaetan. Lat. "Caieta-
  nus," "one from Caieta" (Italy).
  Noted 15th cen. scholar & S.,
  great force in Counter-Reforma-
  tion. F. 8/7. **Dim:** Caetastina,
  Callatina, Cryetina, Tano. **Var:**
  Ayetano, Caetana, Cafeatano,
  Cagetacio, Cagetano, Cagetavo,
  Cahatino, Caietano, Cailletano,
  Caitano, Caiteno, Cajatano,
  Cajatona, Cajentano, Cajerana,
  Cajetán, Cajetanam, Cajetania,
  Cajetanis, Cajetano, Cajetanus,
  Cajetaro, Cajetemo, Cajetón,
  Cajetún, Cajetura, Cajitano,
  Caletana, Caljetano, Callatano,
  Calleetana, Callelano,
  Callentana, Calleta, Calletano,
  Calletava, Calletino, Caltetana,
  Caritana, Cavetano, Cayelano,
  Cayetamo, Cayetanae, Cayetans,
  Cayetarco, Cayetarro, Cayetava,
  Cayetoano, Cayetura, Cayitán,
  Cayitano, Cayotón, Caytno,
  Cazetano, Cejetana, Cietana,
  Coatano, Cogetano, Cojetán,
  Cojetano, Cryetano, Cuyetana,
  Cyetanae, Gaetán, Gaetano,
  Gaetono, Gaietana, Gajetán,
  Gajetano, Gayetano, Quetano,
  Quietano, Tayetano.
Cayetans   see **Cayetano.**
Cayetarco   see **Cayetano.**
Cayetarro   see **Cayetano.**
Cayetava   see **Cayetano.**
Cayetoano   see **Cayetano.**
Cayetura   see **Cayetano.**
Cayitán   see **Cayetano.**
Cayitano   see **Cayetano.**
Cayo   see **Ricardo.**
Cayo (Cah' yo) m. EE: "Caius,
  Cajus. Lat. "Gaius," "magpie."
  30 x in DS. 4th cen. Spaniard
  mart. under Diocletian. F. 4/16.
  Var: Gayo.
Cayotón   see **Cayetano.**
Cayoya   see **Carolina.**
Caytno   see **Cayetano.**
Cazaria   see **César.**
Cazetano   see **Cayetano.**
Cazmiro   see **Casimiro.**

Ceasaria   see **César.**
Ceasrio   see **César.**
Cebastián   see **Sebastián.**
Cebastiana   see **Sebastián.**
Cebera   see **Severo.**
Ceberiano   see **Severo.**
Ceberita   see **Severo.**
Ceboenao   see **Severo.**
Cecario   see **César.**
Ceceilia   see **Cecilio.**
Ceceilo   see **Cecilio.**
Ceceleo   see **Cecilio.**
Cecelio   see **Cecilio.**
Cecerio   see **César.**
Ceciela   see **Cecilio.**
Cecilias   see **Cecilio.**
Cecilio (Say see' lee oh) m. EE:
  Cecil, Cecyl, Cissie. Lat.
  "Blind." 11 x in DS. Patron of
  poets & musicians. F. 11/22.
  Dim: Cecy, Celio, Cellia, Chela,
  Chichilo, Chila, Cilio, Sielia.
  Var: Caecelii, Caecilio,
  Ceceilia, Ceceilo, Ceceleo,
  Cecelio, Ceciela, Cecilias,
  Cecilius, Cecilo, Cecilus,
  Celicia, Celilia, Cesilio,
  Cesilium, Cicilio, Ciselo,
  Cisilia, Secelio, Secilia,
  Sesililo, Sesilium, Sicilio,
  Sisilia.
Cecilius   see **Cecilio.**
Cecilo   see **Cecilio.**
Cecilus   see **Cecilio.**
Cecundina   see **Segundino.**
Cecy   see **Cecilio.**
Cedelia (Say day' lee ah) f.
  Cedalion was Gk. cyclops. **Var:**
  Cedelya.
Cedelya   see **Cedelia.**
Cederino (Say' day ree' no) m.
  Cedar, son of Ishmael in Bible.
Cedia (Say dee ah) f. Could be
  form of Ceidio, 2 Ss. of Chris-
  tian calendar.
Cediaco (Say dee ah' co) m. In Gk.
  myth., Cedico was warrior in
  Messinia.
Cedonia   see **Celedonio.**
Cedro   see **Isidoro.**
Cedromio (Say dro' mee oh) m.
  Could be form of Cedron, valley
  in Palestine between Jerusalem &
  Mount of Olives.
Cefariana   see **Ceferino.**
Cefelina (Say fay lee' na) f. From
  Cepheus, constellation between
  Cygnus & North Pole. In Gk.
  myth., father of Andromeda &
  placed among stars after death.
Cefemina   see **Ceferino.**
Cefenino   see **Ceferino.**
Cefenro   see **Ceferino.**
Cefeonia   see **Ceferino.**
Cefeorina   see **Ceferino.**
Ceferin   see **Ceferino.**
Ceferino (Say fay ree' no) m. EE:
  Zephyr, Zephyrin. Lat. "Gentle
  breeze." Zephyr is Gk. personi-
  fication of wind. Zephyrin, 3rd
  cen. pope, defended divinity of
  Christ. F. 8/26. **Dim:** Cefero,
  Ceffo, Chefino, Fino, Sef,
  Sefia, Sera. **Var:** Cefariana,
  Cefemina, Cefenino, Cefenro,

Cefeonia, Cefeorina, Ceferín,
Cefernia, Cefismo, Geferina,
Safarena, Saferina, Safira,
Safirio, Salfarino, Salforino,
Sapherino, Sarafina, Scrafina,
Sebarino, Sefahrina, Sefariano,
Sefarino, Sefelina, Seferana,
Seferenio, Sefereno, Seferfino,
Seferiano, Seferim, Seferima,
Seferin, Seferino, Sefernio,
Seferrino, Sefevino, Seffano,
Sefirano, Sefireno, Seforina,
Sefrenia, Sefriana, Sefrinia,
Sefrino, Semphoriana, Separina,
Seperino, Sephania, Sepharina,
Sephario, Sepherino, Sepherinus,
Sephirino, Serafana, Serafén,
Serafena, Serafina, Serapheina,
Seraphima, Seraphino, Serefino,
Serifin, Sferino, Siferino,
Silferiana, Soferino, Sofero,
Sofiria, Sofirina, Solferino,
Sypherina, Teferiano, Teferino,
Zaferina, Zefarana, Zefarino,
Zefenira, Zeferimo, Zeferín,
Zeferino, Zeferinus, Zeferna,
Zefernio, Zefirima, Zefirino,
Zefreno, Zefrino, Zelafina,
Zeperino, Zepheayea, Zepherena,
Zepherino, Zepheryna, Zephimno,
Zephoino, Zephyrinae, Zephyrino,
Zephyrinum, Zephyrinus, Zeprina,
Zerafin, Zerapina, Zerofria,
Ziferina.
Cefernia   see **Ceferino.**
Cefero   see **Ceferino.**
Ceffo   see **Ceferino.**
Cefismo   see **Ceferino.**
Cejetana   see **Cayetano.**
Cela   see **Celedonio.**
Celadina   see **Celedonio.**
Celadomo   see **Celedonio.**
Celadonio   see **Celedonio.**
Celares (Say lah' raise) mf? Lat.
"To be vigilant."
Celarina   see **Celerino.**
Celaronio   see **Celerino.**
Celdonio   see **Celedonio.**
Celedanio   see **Celedonio.**
Celedario   see **Celedonio.**
Celedenio   see **Celedonio.**
Celedino   see **Celedonio.**
Celedomia   see **Celedonio.**
Celedón   see **Celedonio.**
Celedonio (Say lay doe' nee oh) m.
EE: Celedonus. Gk. "A swallow"
(bird). Celedonus mart. in Rome.
F. 9/29. **Dim:** Cela, **Var:**
Aledonia, Caledonio, Calendonio,
Cedonia, Celadina, Celadomo,
Celadonio, Celdonio, Celedanio,
Celedario, Celedenio, Celedino,
Celedomia, Celedón, Celedonius,
Celedono, Celedoria, Celedornia,
Celedorno, Celedrín, Celida,
Celidonio, Celodonio, Celondio,
Cledonio, Coledonio, Eledona,
Ludonio, Saladono, Salatonia,
Saledonio, Salradón, Seldona,
Seldonio, Seledino, Seledomia,
Seledón, Seledonio, Seledonis,
Selidón, Selidonio, Selodona,
Silidonia, Slaltonia, Soledonio,
Solodonio, Zeladomio, Zeledonia.
Celedonius   see **Celedonio.**

Celedono   see **Celedonio.**
Celedoria   see **Celedonio.**
Celedornia   see **Celedonio.**
Celedorno   see **Celedonio.**
Celedrín   see **Celedonio.**
Celefora (Say lay foe' rah) f.
Comb. of Celestino or Celedonio
& Telesfora (see all).
Celemancia   see **Clemente.**
Celena   see **Celina.**
Celenio   see **Celina.**
Celentino   see **Celina.**
Celeolorio (Say layo low' ree oh)
m. Celeo in myth. learned art of
agriculture from Ceres.
Celerino (Say lay ree' no) m. EE:
Celerina, Celerinus. Lat. "Rap-
id, fast." 4 x in DS. 1 impli-
cated in church schism. F. 2/3.
Var: Celarina, Celaronio,
Celrina, Salerino, Salerna,
Selerino.
Celésforo (Say lace' foe roe) m.
Comb. of Celestino & Telesforo
(see both).
Celesimo   see **Celestino.**
Celesrina (Say lace ree' na) f.
Comb. of Celesrino & Celestino
(see both).
Celestilo   see **Celestino.**
Celestimo   see **Celestino.**
Celestín   see **Celestino.**
Celestinade   see **Celestino.**
Celestine   see **Celestino.**
Celestineo   see **Celestino.**
Celestino (Say lace tee' no) m.
EE: Celestine, Coelestius. Lat.
"Belonging to heaven." 11 x in
DS. Great antagonist of doctrine
that man is born without origi-
nal sin. F. 4/6. **Dim:** Celia.
Var: Alestino, Calestino,
Celesimo, Celestilo, Celestimo,
Celestín, Celestinade,
Celestine, Celestineo,
Celestivo, Celesto, Celestria,
Celestyna, Celetino, Celistino,
Clestino, Coelestino, Colestino,
Salastina, Selestena, Selestine,
Selestino, Selistino.
Celestivo   see **Celestino.**
Celesto   see **Celestino.**
Celestria   see **Celestino.**
Celestyna   see **Celestino.**
Celetino   see **Celestino.**
Celia   see **Celestino.**
Celia (Say' lee ah) f. EE:
Celestine. St. Celia was friend
of St. Ursula & beheaded by Huns
in 4th cen. F. 10/21.
Celiaco (Say lee ah' co) m. His-
panized version of Cellach, 9th
cen. archbishop & S. of Armagh,
Ireland. 33 Celtic Ss.
Celica   see **Celio.**
Celicia   see **Cecilio.**
Celida   see **Celedonio.**
Celidonio   see **Celedonio.**
Celies   see **Celina.**
Celilia   see **Cecilio.**
Celín   see **Celio.**
Celina (Say lee' na) f. EE: Celia,
Selena. Gk. "Selene, light,
splendor" referring to moon. 6th
cen. V. from Meaux, France. F.

10/21. **Dim:** Lina, Nina, Selicita, Slena. **Var:** Celena, Celenio, Celentino, Celies, Celinda, Celisse, Salena, Salima, Salino, Selena, Selenia, Seles, Seliam, Selice, Selilia, Selina, Selinda, Selita, Sylina. See also Celio.

Celinda	see **Celina.**
Celio	see **Cecilio.**

Celio (Say' lee oh) m. Lat. Caelus, name of Roman family. Could mean "September" or possibly comes from "coela" meaning "heaven." **Dim:** Celín, Celita, Chelo, Lina. **Var:** Celica, Selia, Zelia. See also Celina.

Celisse	see **Celina.**
Celistino	see **Celestino.**
Celita	see **Celio.**
Celixto	see **Calixto.**
Celiza	see **Celso.**
Cellia	see **Cecilio.**
Celodonio	see **Celedonio.**
Celondio	see **Celedonio.**
Celrina	see **Celerino.**
Celsae	see **Celso.**
Celsco	see **Celso.**
Celsi	see **Celso.**
Celsio	see **Celso.**
Celsium	see **Celso.**

Celso (Sell' so) m. **EE:** Celsus. Lat. "Elevated, sublime." 12 x in DS. Archbishop of Armagh, Ireland. F. 4/6. **Var:** Celiza, Celsae, Celsco, Celsi, Celsio, Celsium, Celsum, Celsur, Celsus, Celzo, Salso, Selso, Selzo, Zelsa. See also Ecelso.

Celsum	see **Celso.**
Celsur	see **Celso.**
Celsus	see **Celso.**

Celto (Sell' toe) m. In myth., son of Hercules & Celtino. Father of Celts.

Celvia	see **Silvio.**
Celzo	see **Celso.**

Cemla (Sem' la) f. Thessalian woman turned into diamond for swearing that Jupiter was mortal.

Cemona	see **Zenón.**
Cenabio	see **Zenobio.**
Cenaida	see **Zenaido.**
Cenaide	see **Zenaido.**
Cenanida	see **Zenaido.**
Cenario	see **Génaro.**
Cenavia	see **Zenobio.**
Cenaydo	see **Zenaido.**
Cenbio	see **Zenobio.**
Cención	see **Asunción.**
Cenenobia	see **Zenobio.**
Cenerino	see **Senorina.**
Cenia	see **Eugenio.**
Cenida	see **Zenaido.**
Cenita	see **Zenón.**

Cenizeros (Say' nee say' rose) m? In Bible, Cenicero, place where ashes thrown.

Cenobiae	see **Zenobio.**
Cenobii	see **Zenobio.**
Cenobil	see **Zenobio.**
Cenobio	see **Zenobio.**
Cenón	see **Zenón.**

Cenona	see **Zenón.**
Cenorina	see **Senorina.**
Cenorio	see **Senorina.**

Cenorius (Say no' ree us) m. Form of Censorianus, mart. in Africa.

Cenoveva	see **Genoveva.**
Cenovina	see **Zenobio.**
Cenovio	see **Zenobio.**
Censión	see **Asunción.**
Censoria	see **Censurio.**

Censurio (Sane soo' ree oh) m. **EE:** Censurius. Lat. "He who censures." Bishop of Auxene, France. F. 6/10. **Var:** Censoria.

Cenvio	see **Zenobio.**
Cepherina	see **Serafín.**
Cepriano	see **Cipriano.**
Cerafino	see **Serafín.**
Ceragoza	see **Zaragoza.**
Cerapio	see **Serapio.**
Cerasio	see **Servacio.**
Cerbando	see **Servando.**

Cerbonio (Sair bo' nee oh) m. **EE:** Cerbonius. 3 x in DS. 1, 6th cen. bishop of Piombino, sheltered Roman soldier & was condemned to death. F. 10/10.

Cerefino	see **Serafín.**
Cererino	see **Serafín.**

Ceres (Say' race) f. **EE:** Ceres. Lat. goddess of agriculture. Worship included fertility & death rites.

Ceresfín	see **Serafín.**
Cergio	see **Sergio.**
Cerilio	see **Cirilo.**
Cerilo	see **Cirilo.**
Cerino	see **Cirenia.**
Cerio	see **Ciro.**
Cerispín	see **Crespín.**
Cerobio	see **Zenobio.**
Cerrovio	see **Zenobio.**
Cervacio	see **Servacio.**
Cervardo	see **Servando.**
Cervero	see **Severo.**
Cervilia	see **Servilio.**
Cerville	see **Servilio.**

César (Say' sar) m. **EE:** Caesar. Lat. "Having abundant hair." Most famous Julius Caesar. 5 x in DS. **Dim:** Caesaria, Chayo, Checha, Sarito. **Var:** Caesarria, Casarea, Cazaria, Ceasaria, Ceasrio, Cecario, Cecerio, Cesareo, Cesares, Cesarial, Cesarina, Cesario, Cesarno, Cesaro, Cesarria, Cesorio, Cessarias, Cézar, Cezario, Cezerio, Císar, Cisario, Cizario, Gesaria, Sasaria, Sazaro, Seasaro, Sesadio, Sésar, Sesareo, Sesario, Seserino, Sessaria, Sezario, Sezaro, Sizaris, Xesaria, Zesaria, Zezaria.

Cesareo	see **César.**
Cesares	see **César.**
Cesarial	see **César.**
Cesarina	see **César.**
Cesario	see **César.**
Cesarno	see **César.**
Cesaro	see **César.**
Cesarria	see **César.**
Cesilio	see **Cecilio.**
Cesilium	see **Cecilio.**

Cesorio	see César.	Charli	see Carlos.
Cessarias	see César.	Charo	see Rosa.
Cetoninia	see Saturnino.	Charo	see Rosario.
Ceturnino	see Saturnino.	Charrita	see Sara.
Cevaida	see Zobeida.	Chatta (Cha' tah) f. Lat. "Flat."	
Ceverina	see Severo.	Nickname for one with prominent	
Cevero	see Severo.	& flat nose.	
Cevobia	see Zenobio.	Chaura	see Isauro.
Cézar	see César.	Chava	see Isabel.
Cezario	see César.	Chavel	see Isabel.
Cezerio	see César.	Chavelle	see Isabel.
Chaba	see Isabel.	Chavelo	see Isabel.
Chaba	see Rosa.	Chavo	see Gustavo.
Chaba	see Rosalba.	Chavo	see Salvador.
Chaba	see Salvador.	Chayito	see Rosario.
Chabalito	see Salvador.	Chayo	see Belisario.
Chabel	see Isabel.	Chayo	see César.
Chabelo	see Isabel.	Chayo	see Rosa.
Chabi	see Isabel.	Chayo	see Rosario.
Chabica	see Isabel.	Che	see José.
Chabo	see Sebastián.	Chebita	see José.
Chabuca	see Isabel.	Chebo	see Eusebio.
Chacha	see Bonifacio.	Chebo	see Sebastián.
Chachín	see Joaquín.	Checha	see César.
Chachona	see Encarnación.	Checha	see Crescencio.
Chaco	see Ezequiel.	Cheche	see José.
Chael	see Misael.	Cheche	see Moisés.
Chaga	see Isauro.	Checho	see Carlos.
Chaga	see Rosauro.	Checho	see Consuelo.
Chago	see Jacobo.	Checho	see Sergio.
Chago	see Jaime.	Checo	see Ezequías.
Chago	see Santiago.	Checo	see Ezequiel.
Chagua	see Isauro.	Checo	see Sergio.
Chaguita	see Rosa.	Chefa	see José.
Chaguo	see Rosauro.	Chefi	see Sofío.
Chahua	see Isauro.	Chefina	see José.
Chala	see Rosalío.	Chefino	see Ceferino.
Chalba	see Rosalba.	Chela	see Araceli.
Chale	see Carlos.	Chela	see Cecilio.
Chalelo	see Desiderio.	Chela	see Gabriel.
Chali	see Rosalío.	Chela	see Griselda.
Chalín	see Carlos.	Chela	see Isabel.
Chalina	see Rosa.	Chelago	see Estanislao.
Chalina	see Rosalindo.	Chelago	see Venceslao.
Chalina	see Rosalío.	Chelao	see Venceslao.
Chalío	see Rosalío.	Cheli	see Araceli.
Chalixto	see Calixto.	Chelín	see Benjamín.
Challo	see Rosa.	Chelín	see José.
Challo	see Rosario.	Chelino	see Marcelino.
Chalo	see Gonzalo.	Chelita	see Graciela.
Chalo	see Rosario.	Chelito	see Consuelo.
Chamico	see Temístocles.	Chelo	see Celio.
Chan	see Juan.	Chelo	see Consuelo.
Chando	see Lisandro.	Chelo	see Graciela.
Chango	see Jaime.	Chelo	see Marcelino.
Chango	see Santiago.	Chelo	see Mercedes.
Chano	see Casiano.	Chelo	see Venceslao.
Chano	see Cipriano.	Chema	see Demetrio.
Chano	see Donaciano.	Chema	see Emma.
Chano	see Félix.	Chema	see Manuel.
Chano	see Juan.	Chemín	see Benjamín.
Chano	see Lucas.	Chemo	see Anselmo.
Chano	see Lucía.	Chemo	see Telma.
Chano	see Ponciano.	Chencha	see Hortencia.
Chano	see Prisciliano.	Chenche	see Vicente.
Chano	see Santiago.	Chencho	see Asunción.
Chano	see Sebastián.	Chencho	see Crescencio.
Chano	see Susano.	Chencho	see Fulgencio.
Chanta	see Crisanto.	Chencho	see Inocencio.
Chanti	see Jaime.	Chencho	see Lorenzo.
Chantón	see Antonio.	Chendo	see Rosendo.
Chapica	see Isabel.	Chenelio	see Crescencio.
Chara	see Sara.	Cheno	see Eugenio.
Charita	see Sara.	Cheno	see Nepomuceno.
Charito	see Rosario.	Chenta	see Vicente.

Chente	see Inocencio.		Chiva	see Silvio.
Chente	see Vicente.		Chivete	see Silvestre.
Chentillo	see Vicente.		Chiveto	see Silvestre.
Cheo	see Eliseo.		Chivi	see Silvio.
Cheo	see José.		Chiviz	see Silvio.
Chepa	see José.		Chiyo	see Isidoro.
Chepa	see María.		Chlotilde	see Clotilde.
Chepe	see José.		Chocha	see Eloiso.
Chepillo	see José.		Chocha	see Jorge.
Chepín	see José.		Chocha	see Rosa.
Chepina	see José.		Choche	see Jorge.
Chepís	see José.		Choco	see Socorro.
Chepita	see José.		Chofa	see José.
Chepito	see José.		Chofa	see Sofío.
Chepo	see José.		Chofi	see Sofío.
Cheque	see Ezequiel.		Choforo	see Sinforoso.
Chequel	see Ezequiel.		Chola	see Soledad.
Chequelo	see Ezequiel.		Chola	see Zoilo.
Chequil	see Ezequiel.		Chole	see Isolina.
Chevo	see Eusebio.		Chole	see Soledad.
Cheya	see Graciela.		Cholita	see Soledad.
Cheyo	see Eliseo.		Chololo	see Isidoro.
Chia	see Lucía.		Chombo	see Jerónimo.
Chiano	see Prisciliano.		Chomín	see Domingo.
Chica	see Asunción.		Chomo	see Jerónimo.
Chicha	see Marcia.		Chon	see Asunción,
Chichi	see Alicio.		Chon	see Concepción,
Chichi	see José.		Chon	see Presentación.
Chichicha	see Francisco.		Chon	see Purificación.
Chichilo	see Cecilio.		Chona	see Concepción.
Chicho	see Francisco.		Chona	see Sonio.
Chicho	see Narciso.		Choncha	see Asunción,
Chicho	see Rudesinda.		Choncha	see Concepción.
Chicho	see Vicente.		Chonchita	see Concepción.
Chico	see Hesiquio.		Chonelo	see Encarnación.
Chico	see Narciso.		Chonicho	see Dionisio,
Chidro	see Isidoro.		Chonita	see Concepción.
Chigo	see Isidoro.		Chonita	see Encarnación.
Chila	see Adelaido.		Chono	see Asunción.
Chila	see Cecilio.		Chono	see Encarnación.
Chila	see Hersilia.		Choto	see Crisóstomo.
Chila	see Lucía.		Chrestina	see Cristián.
Chilano	see Maximiliano.		Chris	see Cristóbal.
Chilelo	see Desiderio.		Chrisanda	see Crisanto.
Chillo	see Isidoro.		Chrisástamos	see Crisóstomo.
Chilo	see Bacilio.		Chrisela	see Griselda.
Chilo	see Francisco.		Chriselda	see Griselda.
Chilo	see Isidoro.		Chrisógono	see Crisógono.
Chilolo	see Isidoro.		Chrisóstom	see Crisóstomo.
Chimino	see Máximo.		Chrispena	see Crespín.
Chimón	see Simón.		Chrispin	see Crespín.
Chimona	see Simón.		Chrispino	see Crespín.
Chimone	see Simón,		Christával	see Cristóbal.
China	see Joaquín.		Christela	see Cristo.
Chincha	see Cinta.		Christella	see Cristo.
Chinda	see Lucía.		Christerpher	see Cristóbal.
Chinda	see Rosendo.		Christianto	see Crisanto.
Chindo	see Gumersindo.		Christila	see Cristo.
Chindo	see Rudesinda.		Christinea	see Cristián.
Chinto	see Jacinto.		Christino	see Cristián.
Chintu	see Jacinto.		Christóbal	see Cristóbal.
Chipa	see José.		Christobalina	see Cristóbal.
Chipi	see José.		Christóban	see Cristóbal.
Chiro	see Isidoro.		Christóphor	see Cristóbal.
Chisco	see Francisco.		Christophoro	see Cristóbal.
Chita	see Alicio.		Christorero	see Cristóbal.
Chita	see Carmen.		Christos	see Cristo.
Chita	see Ester.		Christov	see Cristo.
Chita	see Graciela.		Christóval	see Cristóbal.
Chita	see Jesús.		Chritina	see Cristián.
Chita	see Luz.		Chrizantio	see Crisanto.
Chita	see Rosa.		Chronita (Crow nee' tah) f. EE:
Chito	see Félix.		Chronita. Chronides 3 x in DS.
Chito	see Francisco.		Chrysanta	see Crisanto.
Chito	see Juan.		Chrysóphora	see Cristóbal.

Chrysostonio   see **Crisóstomo.**
Chu   see **Jesús.**
Chuchi   see **Jesús.**
Chuchín   see **Jesús.**
Chuchita   see **Jesús.**
Chucho   see **Agusto.**
Chucho   see **Jesús.**
Chuco   see **Francisco.**
Chuey   see **Jesús.**
Chula   see **Julio.**
Chulia   see **María.**
Chumbo   see **Jerónimo.**
Chumín   see **Domingo.**
Chumina   see **Isolina.**
Chumingo   see **Domingo.**
Chumo   see **Domingo.**
Chumo   see **Tomás.**
Chun   see **Asunción.**
Chuncho   see **Asunción.**
Chundo   see **Segundino.**
Chus   see **Jesús.**
Chusita   see **Jesús.**
Chuy   see **Jesús.**
Cibilo   see **Sibilo.**
Cicerón (See say rhone') m. **EE:**
Cicero. Lat. "Vetch," type of
seed. Roman orator & writer.
Cicilio   see **Cecilio.**
Ciderio   see **Isidoro.**
Cidriano   see **Isidoro.**
Cidro   see **Isidoro.**
Cidronea   see **Sidronio.**
Cidronis   see **Sidronio.**
Cietana   see **Cayetano.**
Cifernio   see **Sinforiano.**
Cifirina   see **Sinforiano.**
Ciforiano   see **Sinforiano.**
Cifrana   see **Sinforiano.**
Cifredo   see **Sigfrido.**
Cifriano   see **Cipriano.**
Cigifredo   see **Sigfrido.**
Cigripino   see **Cipriano.**
Cilio   see **Cecilio.**
Cilvestra   see **Silvestre.**
Cilvestre   see **Silvestre.**
Cilviano   see **Silvino.**
Cima   see **Simón.**
Cimitrio   see **Simitrio.**
Cimona   see **Simón.**
Cimplicio   see **Simplicio.**
Cinforiano   see **Sinforiano.**
Cinivio   see **Zenobio.**
Cinnia   see **Zinnia.**
Cinnonia   see **Zenobio.**
Cinobia   see **Zenobio.**
Cinta (Seen' ta) f. **EE:** Cynth,
Cynthia, Cynthie. Goddess
Artemis born on Mt. Cynthus in
Delos, Greece. Image of V.
honored in Tortosa, Spain. F.
2nd Sunday in October. **Dim:**
Chincha. **Var:** Cintha, Cintia,
Cyntia, Cyntjia, Scynthia,
Synthia.
Cintha   see **Cinta.**
Cintia   see **Cinta.**
Cip   see **Cipriano.**
Ciparriano   see **Cipriano.**
Ciperiano   see **Cipriano.**
Cipfrijedo   see **Cipriano.**
Cipiano   see **Cipriano.**
Cipilano   see **Cipriano.**
Cipilo   see **Cipriano.**
Cippiano   see **Cipriano.**
Cippie   see **Cipriano.**

Cippinano   see **Cipriano.**
Cippy   see **Cipriano.**
Ciprano   see **Cipriano.**
Ciprayano   see **Cipriano.**
Cipriams   see **Cipriano.**
Ciprián   see **Cipriano.**
Ciprianita   see **Cipriano.**
Cipriano (See pree ah' no) m. **EE:**
Ciprian, Cyprian, etc. Lat. "One
from Cyprus." Bishop of Carthage
important in development of
Christian thought. F. 9/16. **Dim:**
Chano, Cip, Cippie, Cippy,
Ciprillo, Piano, Sipio, Yano.
Var: Cepriano, Cifriano,
Cigripino, Ciparriano,
Ciperiano, Cipfrijedo, Cipiano,
Cipilano, Cipilo, Cippiano,
Cippinano, Ciprano, Ciprayano,
Cipriams, Ciprián, Ciprianita,
Ciprians, Cipricano, Ciprinio,
Ciprino, Ciprinse, Cipriona,
Cripiano, Cripriana, Cypianas,
Cyprana, Cyprianiam, Cypriano,
Eipriana, Sapriano, Sepreano,
Seprián, Sepriano, Sibrián,
Siplano, Siprano, Siprián,
Siprianita, Sipriano, Siprino,
Syprián, Zipriana, Ziprianes,
Zyprianns.
Ciprians   see **Cipriano.**
Cipricano   see **Cipriano.**
Ciprillo   see **Cipriano.**
Ciprinio   see **Cipriano.**
Ciprino   see **Cipriano.**
Ciprinse   see **Cipriano.**
Cipriona   see **Cipriano.**
Cira   see **Alcir.**
Cirapio   see **Serapio.**
Circumcidión   see **Circuncisión.**
Circumdio   see **Circuncisión.**
Circuncisión (Seer coon see see
own') m. Lat. "Act of cutting
foreskin." Christ circumcised 8
days after birth, celebrated in
Jan. **Var:** Circumcidión,
Circumdio.
Cirenia (See ray' nee ah) f. **EE:**
Cyrenia. Lat. "Cyrenaeus," "one
from Cyrene, Africa." S. mart.
in Tarsus. F. 11/4. **Dim:** Cyro.
Var: Cerino, Ciriano, Ciriño,
Cyrino.
Cirja   see **Ciro.**
Ciriaco (See ree' ah co) m. **EE:**
Cyriaca, Cyriacus. Gk. "Belong-
ing to the Lord." 12 x in DS.
Dim: Siria, Syria, Yaco. **Var:**
Ciriako, Ciriaquo, Ciriceo,
Cirido, Cirioco, Cirtiaco,
Cyriaco, Quirico, Siraco,
Siriaco, Siriago, Siricio,
Syriaco.
Ciriako   see **Ciriaco.**
Ciriano   see **Cirenia.**
Ciriaquo   see **Ciriaco.**
Ciriceo   see **Ciriaco.**
Cirido   see **Ciriaco.**
Cirildo   see **Cirilo.**
Cirileo   see **Cirilo.**
Cirilia   see **Cirilo.**
Cirillum   see **Cirilo.**
Cirilo (See ree' low) m. **EE:**
Cyril, Cyrilla, etc. Diminutive
of Ciro meaning "lord." 9 x in

DS. 2 important doctors of 4th cen. **Dim:** Cirio, Ciro, Lilo. **Var:** Cerilio, Cerilo, Cirildo, Cirileo, Cirilia, Cirillum, Cyrila, Cyrildo, Cyrillo, Siralio, Sirido, Sirila, Sirildo, Sirilio, Srylo.
Cirino   see **Cirenia.**
Cirio   see **Cirilo.**
Ciríoco   see **Ciríaco.**
Cirita   see **Alcir.**
Cirito   see **Ciro.**
Ciro   see **Cirilo.**
Ciro (See' ro) m. **EE:** Cy, Cyrus. Pers. "Sun." Cyrus the Great, king of Persia, created empire in 6th cen. B.C. 8 x in DS. **Dim:** Cirito. **Var:** Cerio, Ciria, Cyrión, Sirio, Siro.
Cirriano   see **Quirino.**
Cirtiaco   see **Ciríaco.**
Cirz (Sirce) f? **EE:** Circe. Celebrated witch in Gk. myth.
Císar   see **César.**
Cisario   see **César.**
Cisco   see **Francisco.**
Ciselo   see **Cecilio.**
Cisilia   see **Cecilio.**
Cisterna   see **Sixto.**
Cisto   see **Sixto.**
Cita   see **Carmen.**
Citali (See tah' lee) ? Aztec, "Star."
Cito   see **Luz.**
Civilo   see **Sibilo.**
Cizario   see **César.**
Cladio   see **Claudio.**
Clara (Clah' rah) f. **EE:** Clair, Clara, Clare, etc. Lat. "Bright." 14 x in DS. Clare of Assis, Italy, founded Poor Clares in 13th cen. F. 8/12. **Dim:** Clarita. **Var:** Clarencio, Claria, Clarisa, Clarisia, Clarivel, Clarra, Clarrisa, Glara.
Clarencio   see **Clara.**
Claria   see **Clara.**
Clarisa   see **Clara.**
Clarisia   see **Clara.**
Clarita   see **Clara.**
Clarra   see **Clara.**
Clarrisa   see **Clara.**
Clatilda   see **Clotilde.**
Clatilde   see **Clotilde.**
Claudelario (Clough day lah' ree oh) m. **EE:** Claudelario. Comb. of 2 popular names, Claudio & Candelario (see both).
Claudicio   see **Claudio.**
Claudinia   see **Claudio.**
Claudino   see **Claudio.**
Claudio (Clough' dee oh) m. **EE:** Claude, Claudius, etc. Lat. "Lame." With variants, 44 x in DS. **Dim:** Claudinia, Claudino, Clod, Clodita, Cloyo, Cludina, Glaudina. **Var:** Cladio, Claudicio, Clavio, Clodia, Glaudio.
Clavio   see **Claudio.**
Cleafás   see **Cleofás.**
Cleandro (Clay ahn' dro) m. **EE:** Cleander, Cleatus, etc. Gk.

"Glory." **Var:** Cleanto.
Cleanto   see **Cleandro.**
Cleatilda   see **Clotilde.**
Cleatilde   see **Clotilde.**
Cledia   see **Clelia.**
Cledis   see **Cleto.**
Cledonio   see **Celedonio.**
Cleemente   see **Clemente.**
Clefás   see **Cleofás.**
Cleito   see **Cleto.**
Cleitón   see **Cleto.**
Cleli   see **Araceli.**
Clelia (Clay' lee ah) f. **EE:** Clelia, Cloelia, etc. Lat. "Client" or fig., "one protected." Roman maiden who saved virtue by swimming Tiber. **Var:** Cledia.
Clema   see **Clemente.**
Clemaencia see **Clemente.**
Clemcia   see **Clemente.**
Cleme   see **Clemente.**
Clemecencia see **Clemente.**
Clemen   see **Clemente.**
Clemenchita see **Clemente.**
Clemenia   see **Clemente.**
Clemenisa   see **Clemente.**
Clemenkia   see **Clemente.**
Clemenlia   see **Clemente.**
Clemente (Clay men' tay) m. **EE:** Clem, Clemens, Clement. Lat. "Mild, merciful." 45 x in DS. 6 popes. **Dim:** Clema (Clementina), Cleme, Clemenchita, Clemetino, Lencha (Clemencia), Mencha (Clemencia), Mente, Te, Tente, Tina (Clementino). **Var:** Celemancia, Cleemente, Clemaencia, Clemcia, Clemecencia, Clemen, Clemenia, Clemenisa, Clemenkia, Clemenlia, Clementiana, Clementiaro, Clementio, Clemento, Clementria, Clementris, Clementro, Clemenza, Clemenzia, Clemess, Clemete, Clemincia, Cleminto, Clemnesia, Clemons, Clemte, Cleniente, Climente, Cremencia.
Clementiana see **Clemente.**
Clementiaro see **Clemente.**
Clementio   see **Clemente.**
Clemento   see **Clemente.**
Clementria see **Clemente.**
Clementris see **Clemente.**
Clementro   see **Clemente.**
Clemenza   see **Clemente.**
Clemenzia   see **Clemente.**
Clemess   see **Clemente.**
Clemete   see **Clemente.**
Clemetino   see **Clemente.**
Clemincia   see **Clemente.**
Cleminto   see **Clemente.**
Clemnesia   see **Clemente.**
Clemons   see **Clemente.**
Clemte   see **Clemente.**
Cleniente   see **Clemente.**
Cleo   see **Cleofás.**
Cleo   see **Clotilde.**
Cleofá   see **Cleofás.**
Cleofar   see **Cleofás.**
Cleofás (Clay oh fahs') m. **EE:** Cleophas. Related to "Cleopatra" meaning "glory of father." At Cleopes' wedding, Christ worked 1st miracle. F. 9/25. **Dim:** Cleo,

Cleofitas, Cleotino. **Var:**
Cleafás, Clefás, Cleofá,
Cleofar, Cleofasa, Cleofasteram,
Cleofaz, Cleofe, Cleofelda,
Cleofés, Cleofhás, Cleofilda,
Cleofús, Cleopás, Cleopaz,
Cleophás, Cleopho, Cleophós,
Cleophosa, Cleova, Clepha,
Clerofás, Clifés, Cliofar,
Cliofás, Cliopás, Clofás,
Clofés, Clofez, Clofía,
Cloforio, Clophás, Creafás,
Heofás, Kleofás, Liofás. See
also Cleopatra.

Cleofasa	see **Cleofás.**
Cleofasteram	see **Cleofás.**
Cleofaz	see **Cleofás.**
Cleofe	see **Cleofás.**
Cleofelda	see **Cleofás.**
Cleofés	see **Cleofás.**
Cleofhás	see **Cleofás.**
Cleofilda	see **Cleofás.**
Cleofitas	see **Cleofás.**
Cleofús	see **Cleofás.**
Cleopás	see **Cleofás.**

Cleopatra (Clay oh pah' tra) f.
EE: Cleo, Cleopatra. Gk. "Glory
of father." Queen of Egypt &
mistress of Julius Caesar. See
also Cleofas.

Cleopaz	see **Cleofás.**
Cleophás	see **Cleofás.**

Cleophilda (Clay oh feel' da) f.
Comb. of Cleofás & Hermenegildo
(see both).

Cleopho	see **Cleofás.**
Cleophós	see **Cleofás.**
Cleophosa	see **Cleofás.**
Cleothilda	see **Clotilde.**
Cleothilde	see **Clotilde.**
Cleotildae	see **Clotilde.**
Cleotilde	see **Clotilde.**
Cleotilo	see **Clotilde.**
Cleotino	see **Cleofás.**
Cleotiola	see **Clotilde.**
Cleova	see **Cleofás.**
Clepha	see **Cleofás.**
Clerofás	see **Cleofás.**

Clesa (Clay' sa) f. Cleso in Gk.
myth. was daughter of Cleson.

Clestilde	see **Clotilde.**
Clestino	see **Celestino.**
Clete	see **Cleto.**
Cletilde	see **Clotilde.**
Cleto	see **Anacleto.**

Cleto (Clay' toe) m. EE: Cletus.
Gk. "Illustrious." 2nd successor
of St. Peter. F. 4/26, **Var:**
Cledis, Cleito, Cleitón, Clete,
Cletus, Cleyto, Clita. See also
Anacleto.

Cletus	see **Cleto.**
Cleyo	see **Araceli.**
Cleyto	see **Cleto.**
Clicerio	see **Cliserio.**
Clifés	see **Cleofás.**
Clímacho	see **Clímaco.**

Clímaco (Clee' mah co) m. Gk.
"Climax." Author of theological
work describing steps necessary
for perfection. **Var:** Clímacho,
Clímaso.

Clímaso	see **Clímaco.**
Clemente	see **Clemente.**

Clinia (Clee' nee ah) f. Clinus

was Gk. S. who died in Aquino,
Italy. F. 2/30.
Clioberta (Clee oh bear' tah) f.
Comb. of Cleofás & Berta (see
both).

Cliofar	see **Cleofás.**
Cliofás	see **Cleofás.**
Cliopás	see **Cleofás.**
Cliotilde	see **Clotilde.**
Clisanto	see **Crisanto.**

Cliserio (Clee say' ree oh) m.
Form of Clicerius, 5th cen. S. &
Archbishop of Milan. F. 2/20.
Var: Clicerio.

Clita	see **Cleto.**
Clobilde	see **Clotilde.**
Clod	see **Claudio.**
Clodia	see **Claudio.**
Clodilda	see **Clotilde.**
Clodilde	see **Clotilde.**

Clodimiro (Cloe dee mee' roe) m.
Ger. "Great in fame." **Dim:**
Clodina, Clodita. **Var:**
Clodomiro.

Clodina	see **Clodimiro.**
Clodita	see **Claudio.**
Clodita	see **Clodimiro.**
Clodomiro	see **Clodimiro.**

Clodoveo (Cloe doe bay' oh) m.
Ger. "Glorious combat." **Var:**
Clovias, Glova. See also
Aloisia, Ludovico, Luis.

Cloetilda	see **Clotilde.**
Clofás	see **Cleofás.**
Clofés	see **Cleofás.**
Clofez	see **Cleofás.**
Clofía	see **Cleofás.**
Clofilde	see **Clotilde.**
Cloforio	see **Cleofás.**
Clolide	see **Clotilde.**
Clophás	see **Cleofás.**

Clorinda (Cloe reen' dah) f. Gk.
"Green herbs." **Dim:** Clory.

Clory	see **Clorinda.**
Clota	see **Clotilde.**

Clotario (Cloe tah' ree oh) m. EE:
Clotaire, Clotarius. Ger. "Glory
of army." Several Frankish kings
of 6th & 7th cen.

Clotelde	see **Clotilde.**
Clothilda	see **Clotilde.**
Clothildes	see **Clotilde.**
Clotido	see **Clotilde.**

Clotilde (Cloe til' day) f. EE:
Clothildis, Clotildis. Ger.
"Loud battle." 6th cen. S. &
queen of France who helped in
conversion of King Clovis. F.
6/3. **Dim:** Cleo, Clota, Coti,
Cotila, Coty, Tila, Tilda,
Tilde. **Var:** Chlotilde, Clatilda,
Clatilde, Cleatilda, Cleatilde,
Cleothilda, Cleothilde,
Cleotildae, Cleotilde, Cleotilo,
Cleotiola, Clestilde, Cletilde,
Cliotilde, Clobilde, Clodilda,
Clodilde, Cloetilda, Clofilde,
Clolide, Clotelde, Clothilda,
Clothildes, Clotido, Clotildea,
Clotilila, Clotilla, Clutilde,
Cotilde, Cutilde, Gleotilda,
Guiotilda, Guiotilde, Queotilde,
Quetilda, Quiotilde.

Clotildea	see **Clotilde.**
Clotilila	see **Clotilde.**

Clotilla   see **Clotilde.**
Clovias   see **Clodoveo.**
Clovio (Cloe' bee oh) m. **EE:**
Clovis. Ger. "Glorious battle."
Frankish king who converted most
of Gaul & SW Germany. Converted
to Christianity by St. Clotilde.
Var: Clovis. See also Luis.
Clovis   see **Clovio.**
Cloyo   see **Claudio.**
Cludina   see **Claudio.**
Cluterio   see **Lotario.**
Clutilde   see **Clotilde.**
Coatano   see **Cayetano.**
Coca   see **Jorge.**
Coca   see **Olga.**
Coche   see **José.**
Cochiche   see **Mercedes.**
Cocó   see **Jorge.**
Cocó   see **Socorro.**
Cocoy   see **Jorge.**
Cocoy   see **Leonor.**
Coelestino   see **Celestino.**
Coesencio (Co aye sen' see oh) m.
Lat. "Cum" & "essencio" meaning
"coessential." Concept of con-
substantiality: Father, Son &
Holy Spirit are single, divine
substance.
Cogetano   see **Cayetano.**
Cointa (Coy een' tah) f. Lat.
"Fifth" or "fifth born." 3rd
cen. S. mart. in Alexandria,
Egypt when dragged to death by
horse. F. 2/8. See also Quinto.
Cojetán   see **Cayetano.**
Cojetano   see **Cayetano.**
Cola   see **Nicolás.**
Colacho   see **Escolástica.**
Colacho   see **Nicolás.**
Colaco   see **Escolástica.**
Colás   see **Nicolás.**
Colástica   see **Escolástica.**
Coledonio   see **Celedonio.**
Colestino   see **Celestino.**
Coleta   see **Nicolás.**
Coleta (Co lay' tah) f. **EE:**
Colette, Collette. Fr. "Co-
lette." Diminutive of Nicolás
(see). 14th cen. S. who aided in
reform of Poor Clares. F. 3/6.
Var: Colleta. See also Nicolás.
Colistro   see **Calixto.**
Colizto   see **Calixto.**
Colleta   see **Coleta.**
Coloca   see **Escolástica.**
Colón (Co loan') m. **EE:** Columbus.
Lat. "Columbo," "pigeon, dove."
21 x in DS. See also Columba.
Columba (Co loom' ba) f. **EE:**
Columba, Columbus, etc. Lat.
"Pigeon." 21 x in DS. Greatest
S. of Celtic church after St.
Patrick. F. 6/9. **Var:** Columia,
Columinia. See also Colón.
Columia   see **Columba.**
Columinia   see **Columba.**
Comada (Co mah' dah) f. Form of
Comatus, mart. in Mesopotamia.
Comcepción   see **Concepción.**
Comilo   see **Camilo.**
Cómodo (Co' mo doe) m. **EE:**
Commodus, Lat. "He who has tem-
perance." Vain Roman emperor of
2nd cen.

Composa   see **Compostela.**
Composta   see **Compostela.**
Compostela (Comb po stay' lah) mf.
Lat. "Campis stellae" referring
to 9th cen. miraculous discovery
of St. James' tomb in NW Spain.
Dim: Composa, Composta.
Comrado   see **Conrado.**
Conce   see **Concepción.**
Conceción   see **Concepción.**
Concecpción   see **Concepción.**
Concención   see **Concepción.**
Concensión   see **Concepción.**
Concento   see **Concepción.**
Concepció   see **Concepción.**
Concepción (Cone sape see own')
mf. **EE:** Conception. Lat. "Con-
ception." Refers to sinlessness
of Blessed V. from 1st moment of
conception. F. 12/8. **Dim:**
Caoncha, Chón, Chona, Choncha,
Chonchita, Chonita, Conce,
Concha, Conchita, Cota, Cotita,
Cuncha, Cunshi. **Var:** Comcepción,
Conceción, Concecpción,
Concención, Concensión,
Concento, Concepció,
Concepciono, Concephió,
Concepián, Concepsión,
Conceptió, Conceptionis,
Concesión, Concetta, Concipció,
Concipción, Concisión,
Concsepsión, Conepzión,
Consascián, Consasción,
Conscenciana, Consepción,
Consepsión, Consepción,
Consesión, Consisión, Consomptá,
Consumpción.
Concepciono   see **Concepción.**
Concephió   see **Concepción.**
Concepián   see **Concepción.**
Concepsión   see **Concepción.**
Conceptió   see **Concepción.**
Conceptionis   see **Concepción.**
Concesión   see **Concepción.**
Concetta   see **Concepción.**
Concha   see **Concepción.**
Conchita   see **Concepción.**
Concipció   see **Concepción.**
Concipción   see **Concepción.**
Concisión   see **Concepción.**
Concondio (Cone cone' dee oh) m.
Concordio (see), 9 Sp. Ss.
Concordio (Cone cor' dee oh) m.
EE: Concordio, Concordius, Lat.
"Of same heart." 9 x in DS.
Concsepsión   see **Concepción.**
Condalario   see **Candelario.**
Condelario   see **Candelario.**
Condelaro   see **Candelario.**
Condelonio (Cone day low' nee oh)
m. Comb. of Candelario &
Celedonio (see both).
Condido   see **Candido.**
Cóndora (Cone' doe rah) f. Femi-
nine form of "condor," large
American vulture?
Conegunda   see **Cunegunda.**
Conepzión   see **Concepción.**
Conferina (Cone fay ree' na) f.
Comb. of "con" & "ferina"
meaning "with fierceness or
relating to strong person."
Confesor (Cone fay sor') m. Lat.
referring to one who accepts

Christ & is willing to die for Him.

Conocelo   see **Consuelo.**
Conradino   see **Conrado.**
Conradio   see **Conrado.**
Conrado (Cone rah' doe) m. **EE:** Con., Conrad. Ger. "Bold counsel." 11 x in DS. Patron against hernias. F. 2/19. **Dim:** Conradino. **Var:** Canrado, Canroda, Comrado, Conradio, Conredo, Conrod, Conrodo, Conrrado.
Conredo   see **Conrado.**
Conrod   see **Conrado.**
Conrodo   see **Conrado.**
Conrrado   see **Conrado.**
Consalsción   see **Consolación.**
Consanción   see **Constancio.**
Consantión   see **Constancio.**
Consascián   see **Concepción.**
Consasción   see **Concepción.**
Conscenciana   see **Concepción.**
Conse   see **Constancio.**
Conseja (Cone say' ha) f. Lat. "Counsel." Refers to V. Mary, "Nuestra Señora del Buen Consejo," or "Our Lady of Good Counsel." F. 4/26.
Conselo   see **Consuelo.**
Consepción   see **Concepción.**
Consepsión   see **Concepción.**
Conseptión   see **Concepción.**
Consesión   see **Concepción.**
Consisión   see **Concepción.**
Conso   see **Constancio.**
Consolación (Cone so lah see own') f. **EE:** Consuela, Consuelo. Lat. "Consolation," mystical name. **Var:** Consalsción.
Consolita   see **Consuelo.**
Consolo   see **Consuelo.**
Consomptá   see **Concepción.**
Consorica (Cone so ree' cah) f. Form of Consortia, S. of 5th cen. France.
Constancio (Cone stawn' see oh) m. **EE:** Connie, Constantine, etc. Lat. "Constancy." 41 x in DS. Constantine the Great (288?-337) converted to Christianity & convened Council of Nicea to combat Arianism. F. 5/21. **Dim:** Conse, Conso, Stancio, Stanzo, Tancha, Tino (Constantino). **Var:** Consanción, Consantión, Constansió, Constante, Constantia, Constantino, Constantrio, Constanz, Constanzo, Constinta, Costancio, Costanza, Coustantino, Konstadinos.
Constansió   see **Constancio.**
Constante   see **Constancio.**
Constantia   see **Constancio.**
Constantino   see **Constancio.**
Constantrio   see **Constancio.**
Constanz   see **Constancio.**
Constanzo   see **Constancio.**
Constinta   see **Constancio.**
Consualo   see **Consuelo.**
Consueda   see **Consuelo.**
Consueles   see **Consuelo.**
Consuello   see **Consuelo.**
Consuelo (Cone sway' low) m. **EE:** Connie, Consuelo, etc. Lat. "Consolation." **Dim:** Checho, Chelito, Chelo, Consolita, Elo, Suelito, Suelo. **Var:** Cansuelo, Conocelo, Conselo, Consolo, Consualo, Consueda, Consueles, Consuello, Consuelz, Consulación, Consulla, Consulo, Conusuelo, Conxuela, Conzuelo, Cosuelo.
Consuelz   see **Consuelo.**
Consulación   see **Consuelo.**
Consulla   see **Consuelo.**
Consulo   see **Consuelo.**
Consumción   see **Consunción.**
Consumpción   see **Concepción.**
Consunción (Cone soon see own') mf. Comb. of Concepción & Asunción (see both). **Var:** Consumción.
Conusuelo   see **Consuelo.**
Conxuela   see **Consuelo.**
Conzuelo   see **Consuelo.**
Copo   see **Procopio.**
Copriano (Co pree ah' no) m. Could be form of Coprius, 6th cen. S. F. 9/24.
Coque   see **Jorge.**
Coquis   see **Jorge.**
Coral (Co rawl') f. **EE:** Coral, Coraline, etc. Lat. "Stone." Coral from Red Sea used to protect bearer. **Var:** Coralia.
Coralia   see **Coral.**
Corazón (Co rah sone') mf. Sp. "Heart," probably derived from Catholic organization "Corazón de María," or "Corazón de Jesús."
Corcinio (Core see' nee oh) m. In myth. Corcino was wet nurse of Ariadne.
Cordilio (Core dee' lee oh) m. **EE:** Cordelia, Delia, etc. Welsh "Sea jewel." Youngest daughter of Shakespeare's King Lear. **Dim:** Dilia. **Var:** Cadelia, Cardelia, Gardelia.
Corida (Co ree' dah) f. Coridon, Gk. giant, son of Tartaro & Earth in Gk. myth.
Corina (Co ree' nah) f. **EE:** Cora, Corine, etc. Lat. "Corinna," "maiden." Kore in Gk. myth. another name for Persephone, goddess of fertility. **Var:** Corinna, Corrina.
Corinna   see **Corina.**
Corlata   see **Carlos.**
Cormel   see **Carmen.**
Cornelio (Core nay' lee oh) m. **EE:** Cornel, Cornelius, etc. Gk. "Cornel tree," vegetation sacred to Apollo. 19 x in DS. **Dim:** Melio, Nelo. **Var:** Carnelia, Carnilia, Cornelio, Cornilio.
Cornello   see **Cornelio.**
Cornilio   see **Cornelio.**
Corolina   see **Carolina.**
Corolus   see **Carlos.**
Corona (Co roe' nah) f. Lat. "Ring of flowers surrounding head." 2nd cen. M. **Var:** Corondo.
Corondo   see **Corona.**
Corpofora   see **Carpóforo.**

Corrina   see **Corina**.
Corsini (Core see' nee) m. Surname
used as baptismal name. Andrew
Corsini converted in 13th cen. &
became Carmelite charitable to
poor. F. 2/4. **Var**: Corsinio,
Corsino.
Corsinio   see **Corsini**.
Corsino   see **Corsini**.
Cosimiro   see **Casimiro**.
Cosimora   see **Casimiro**.
Cosmas   see **Cosme**.
Cosmaso (Coze mah' so) m. Cosmos,
6th cen. monk of Alexandria, was
geographer, traveler, & writer.
Cosme (Coze' may) m. **EE**: Cosimo,
Cosmas, Cosmo. Gk. "Order." 18 x
in DS. Cosmas & Damian were twin
physicians in Cilicia in 3rd
cen. Accepted no fees & convert-
ed many to Christianity. F.
9/27. **Dim**: Cosmosita. **Var**:
Casmas, Casmo, Cosmas, Cosmer,
Cosmo, Gosmi, Josmia.
Cosmer   see **Cosme**.
Cosmo   see **Cosme**.
Cosmosita   see **Cosme**.
Costancio   see **Constancio**.
Costanza   see **Constancio**.
Costolo   see **Casto**.
Costulo   see **Casto**.
Cosuelo   see **Consuelo**.
Cota   see **Carlos**.
Cota   see **Concepción**.
Cotarima   see **Catalina**.
Coti   see **Clotilde**.
Cotila   see **Clotilde**.
Cotilde   see **Clotilde**.
Cotita   see **Concepción**.
Cotorino   see **Catalina**.
Coty   see **Clotilde**.
Coustantino   see **Constancio**.
Coya   see **Florencio**.
Coya   see **Maclovio**.
Coyo   see **Glorio**.
Coyo   see **Socorro**.
Crasino (Crah see' no) m. Craso,
famous Roman lawyer & orator
before Christ.
Crauhtémoc   see **Cuauhtémoc**.
Creacencio   see **Crescencio**.
Creafás   see **Cleofás**.
Crecenciana   see **Crescencio**.
Crecencio   see **Crescencio**.
Crecensio   see **Crescencio**.
Crecentiana   see **Crescencio**.
Crecentio   see **Crescencio**.
Crecicin   see **Crescencio**.
Crecinciano   see **Crescencio**.
Crecinciao   see **Crescencio**.
Crecincio   see **Crescencio**.
Credenciana (Cray den see ah' nah)
f. **EE**: Credence. Lat. "To have
faith in."
Crederina (Cray day ree' nah) f.
Lat. "To believe." Bearer be-
lieves in truths revealed by God
& church.
Crelensia   see **Crescencio**.
Cremencia   see **Clemente**.
Crencencio   see **Crescencio**.
Crencenciones see **Crescencio**.
Crencico   see **Crescencio**.
Crencio   see **Crescencio**.
Crenice (Cray nee' say) f. In

myth., Crenis was Nereid, 1 of
daughters of Neru & Diri.
Crensencio   see **Crescencio**.
Crepino (Cray pee' no) m. **EE**:
Crispian, Crispin, etc. 3rd cen.
S. mart. under Diocletian. Pa-
tron of shoemakers. F. 10/25.
Also known as Crispino. See also
Crespin.
Cres   see **Crescencio**.
Cres   see **Crespin**.
Cresáforo   see **Crisóforo**.
Cresancia   see **Crescencio**.
Cresanto   see **Crescencio**.
Cresanto   see **Crisanto**.
Cresatiana   see **Crescencio**.
Crescecia   see **Crescencio**.
Crescenciano see **Crescencio**.
Crescencio (Cray sen' see oh) m.
EE: Crescentianus, etc. Lat. "To
grow." 54 x in DS. **Dim**: Checha,
Chencho, Chenelio, Cres. **Var**:
Creacencio, Crecenciana,
Crecencio, Crecensio,
Crecentiana, Crecentio,
Crecicin, Crecinciano,
Crecinciao, Crecincio,
Crelensia, Crencencio,
Crencenciones, Crencico,
Crencio, Crensencio, Cresancia,
Cresanto, Cresatiana, Crescecia,
Crescenciano, Crescenciono,
Crescenda, Crescendia,
Crescenio, Crescensia,
Crescensiana, Crescensión,
Crescentiano, Crescentino,
Crescentio, Crescentión,
Crescentium, Crescenzio,
Crescincia, Crescinia,
Cresecenciana, Cresencia,
Cresenciano, Cresendo,
Cresenico, Cresenio,
Cresensiana, Cresensio,
Cresentino, Cresentio,
Cresentius, Cresenzio,
Cresincio, Cressentio,
Cresunzia, Crezeniano,
Cricentio, Criescencio,
Criscentio, Criscento,
Crisencio, Crosencia, Grecencio,
Grecensiano, Grencenio.
Crescenciono see **Crescencio**.
Crescenda   see **Crescencio**.
Crescendia   see **Crescencio**.
Crescenio   see **Crescencio**.
Crescensia   see **Crescencio**.
Crescensiana see **Crescencio**.
Crescensión   see **Crescencio**.
Crescentiano see **Crescencio**.
Crescentino   see **Crescencio**.
Crescentio   see **Crescencio**.
Crescentión   see **Crescencio**.
Crescentium   see **Crescencio**.
Crescenzio   see **Crescencio**.
Crescincia   see **Crescencio**.
Crescinia   see **Crescencio**.
Cresecenciana see **Crescencio**.
Cresencia   see **Crescencio**.
Cresenciano   see **Crescencio**.
Cresendo   see **Crescencio**.
Cresenico   see **Crescencio**.
Cresenio   see **Crescencio**.
Cresensiana   see **Crescencio**.
Cresensio   see **Crescencio**.
Cresentino   see **Crescencio**.

Cresentio   see **Crescencio.**
Cresentius   see **Crescencio.**
Cresenzio   see **Crescencio.**
Cresincio   see **Crescencio.**
Cresinta   see **Crisanto.**
Cresóstimo   see **Crisóstomo.**
Crespiliano   see **Crespín.**
Crespín (Crays peen') m. **EE:**
Crispian, Crispin, etc. Lat.
"Curly hair." 18 x in DS.
Crispinus & Crispinianus made
shoes for poor. Patrons of shoe-
makers. F. 10/25. **Dim:** Cres,
Pino. **Var:** Cerispín, Chrispena,
Chrispin, Chrispino,
Crespiliano, Crespio, Crezpín,
Cripin, Crisbín, Crisfín,
Crisín, Crispén, Crispián,
Crispiana, Crispín, Crispinan,
Crispiniana, Crispínn, Crispino,
Crispinoe, Crispio, Crispo,
Crispolo, Crisprín, Crispulo,
Crisuelo, Cryspi, Cryspin,
Cryspino. See also Crepino.
Crespio   see **Crespín.**
Cressentio   see **Crescencio.**
Crestela (Crays tay' lah) f. Form
of Cresto, bishop of Syracuse.
F. 7/3.
Crestena   see **Cristián.**
Cresterna   see **Cristián.**
Crestín (Crays teen') m. Could be
form of Cresto, bishop of
Syracuse. F. 7/3.
Crestino   see **Cristián.**
Crestóval   see **Cristóbal.**
Cresunzia   see **Crescencio.**
Cresusa (Cray sue' sah) f. **EE:**
Creusa. Appears several x in Gk.
myth. 1, beloved of Jason, died
of convulsions when Medea,
Jason's wife, sent her magic
robe.
Crezeniano   see **Crescencio.**
Crezpín   see **Crespín.**
Cricentio   see **Crescencio.**
Criescencio   see **Crescencio.**
Cripiano   see **Cipriano.**
Cripín   see **Crespín.**
Cripriana   see **Cipriano.**
Cris   see **Cristóbal.**
Crisálago   see **Crisólogo.**
Crisalde   see **Griselda.**
Crisalto   see **Crisanto.**
Crisalva (Cree sahl' ba) f. Comb.
of Cristóbal & Salvador (see
both).
Crisando   see **Crisanto.**
Crisanna   see **Crisanto.**
Crisantio   see **Crisanto.**
Crisanto (Cree san' toe) m. **EE:**
Chrysantus. Gk. "Flower of
gold." 8 x in DS. 1 buried alive
for helping to spread Christian-
ity. F. 10/25. **Dim:** Chanta,
Criz. **Var:** Chrisanda,
Christianto, Chrizantio,
Chrysanta, Clisanto, Cresanto,
Cresinta, Crisalto, Crisando,
Crisanna, Crisantio, Crisento,
Crissanta, Crizanto, Crysanto,
Grisanta.
Crisástomo   see **Crisóstomo.**
Crisbín   see **Crespín.**
Criscentio   see **Crescencio.**

Criscento   see **Crescencio.**
Criselado   see **Griselda.**
Criselda   see **Griselda.**
Criselta   see **Griselda.**
Crisencio   see **Crescencio.**
Crisento   see **Crisanto.**
Crisfín   see **Crespín.**
Crisgono   see **Crisógono.**
Crisín   see **Crespín.**
Crisófano   see **Crisóforo.**
Crisófero   see **Crisóforo.**
Crisóforo   see **Cristóbal.**
Crisóforo (Cree so' foe roe) m.
EE: Christophorus. Gk. "He who
carries gold." 4th cen. M. con-
nected with legend of St.
George. F. 4/19. **Var:** Cresáforo,
Crisófano, Crisófero, Crisolfo.
Crisógono (Cree so' go no) m. **EE:**
Chrysogonus. Gk. "Gold-born."
5th cen. M. & spiritual advisor
of St. Anastasia. F. 11/24. **Var:**
Chrisogono, Crisgono.
Crisolfo   see **Crisóforo.**
Crisólogo (Cree so' low go) m. **EE:**
Chrysologus, etc. Gk. "His words
are like gold." **Var:** Crisálago.
Crisóstome   see **Crisóstomo.**
Crisóstomo (Cree soes' toe mo) m.
EE: Chysostom. Gk. "Golden
mouth." 5th cen. S. with persua-
sive powers. 1 of greatest of
Gk. church. F. 1/27. **Dim:** Choto.
Var: Chrisástamos, Chrisóstom,
Chrysostonio, Cresóstimo,
Crisástomo, Crisóstome,
Crisostonio, Cristono,
Cristóstamo.
Crisostonio   see **Crisóstomo.**
Crispén   see **Crespín.**
Crispián   see **Crespín.**
Crispiana   see **Crespín.**
Crispín   see **Crespín.**
Crispinan   see **Crespín.**
Crispiniana   see **Crespín.**
Crispínn   see **Crespín.**
Crispino   see **Crespín.**
Crispinoe   see **Crespín.**
Crispio   see **Crespín.**
Crispo   see **Crespín.**
Crispolo   see **Crespín.**
Crispridión (Crees pree' dee own')
m. **EE:** Crispridion. Comb. of
Crispin & Spiridión (see both).
Crisprin   see **Crespín.**
Crispulo   see **Crespín.**
Crissanta   see **Crisanto.**
Crisselda   see **Griselda.**
Cristábal   see **Cristóbal.**
Cristábel   see **Cristóbal.**
Cristabo   see **Cristóbal.**
Cristante   see **Cristóbal.**
Cristébol   see **Cristóbal.**
Cristelia   see **Cristo.**
Cristella   see **Cristo.**
Cristelo   see **Cristo.**
Cristián (Crees tee ahn') m. **EE:**
Christian. Lat. "Belonging to
the religion of Jesus Christ."
25 x in DS. **Dim:** Ina (Cristina),
Khris, Nina (Cristina), Tina
(Cristina), Tita (Cristina),
Titina (Cristina). **Var:**
Chrestina, Christinea,
Christino, Chritina, Crestena,

Cresterna, Crestino, Cristiano, Cristila, Cristín, Cristino, Cristma, Cristy, Kristina. See also Cristo.

Cristiano   see **Cristián.**
Cristila   see **Cristián.**
Cristín   see **Cristián.**
Cristino   see **Cristián.**
Cristíval   see **Cristóbal.**
Cristma   see **Cristián.**
Cristo (Crees' toe) m. **EE:** Christ. Gk. "Useful, of service." 2nd source claims from same language but meaning "Anointed one." **Var:** Christela, Christella, Christila, Christos, Christov, Cristelia, Cristella, Cristelo, Cristón. See also Cristián.
Cristóbal (Crees toe' bahl) m. **EE:** Chris, Christopher, Kit. Gk. "One who carries Christ." Ferryman who carried Christ across ford & sank under weight. F. 7/25. **Dim:** Chris, Cris, Tobal, Tobalito. **Var:** Christával, Christerpher, Christóbal, Christobalina, Christóban, Christóphor, Christophoro, Christorero, Christóval, Chrysóphora, Crestóval, Crisóforo, Cristábal, Cristábel, Cristabo, Cristante, Cristébol, Cristíval, Cristódal, Cristófano, Cristófel, Cristófer, Cristófero, Cristófor, Cristol, Cristóval, Cristovella, Cristovo, Crystóbal, Crystóval, Grisóforo, Kristóvolis, Xcristóbal, Xotábel, Xptóbal, Xptobalina.
Cristódal   see **Cristóbal.**
Cristófano   see **Cristóbal.**
Cristófel   see **Cristóbal.**
Cristófer   see **Cristóbal.**
Cristófero   see **Cristóbal.**
Cristófor   see **Cristóbal.**
Cristol   see **Cristóbal.**
Cristón   see **Cristo.**
Cristono   see **Crisóstomo.**
Cristóstamo   see **Crisóstomo.**
Cristóval   see **Cristóbal.**
Cristovella   see **Cristóbal.**
Cristovo   see **Cristóbal.**
Cristy   see **Cristián.**
Crisuelo   see **Crespín.**
Criszelda   see **Griselda.**
Criz   see **Crisanto.**
Crizanto   see **Crisanto.**
Crizelda   see **Griselda.**
Crosencia   see **Crescencio.**
Cruce   see **Cruz.**
Crucida   see **Cruz.**
Crucila   see **Cruz.**
Crucio   see **Cruz.**
Crucis   see **Cruz.**
Crus   see **Cruz.**
Cruse   see **Cruz.**
Crusita   see **Cruz.**
Crux   see **Cruz.**
Cruz (Cruce) mf. **EE:** Crux, Cruz. Lat. "Crux" refers to Roman instrument of torture. Symbol of Christ. **Dim:** Crucila, Crusita, Cruzesita, Cucha. **Var:** Cruce, Crucida, Crucio, Crucis, Crus,

Cruse, Crux, Cruza, Cruzelia, Cruzie.
Cruza   see **Cruz.**
Cruzelia   see **Cruz.**
Cruzesita   see **Cruz.**
Cruzie   see **Cruz.**
Cryetano   see **Cayetano.**
Cryetina   see **Cayetano.**
Crysanto   see **Crisanto.**
Cryselda   see **Griselda.**
Cryspi   see **Crespín.**
Cryspín   see **Crespín.**
Cryspino   see **Crespín.**
Crystóbal   see **Cristóbal.**
Crystóval   see **Cristóbal.**
Cuantémor   see **Cuauhtémoc.**
Cuauhtémoc (Cwao tay' moke) m. **EE:** Cuauhtemoc. Nahuatl, "Eagle that falls." Great Aztec warrior & emperor. **Var:** Crauhtémoc, Cuantémor, Cuautémoc, Guauatémoc, Huatimocin.
Cuautémoc   see **Cuauhtémoc.**
Cuberto   see **Cutberto.**
Cuca   see **Blanca.**
Cuca   see **Carmen.**
Cucha   see **Cruz.**
Cucimiro   see **Casimiro.**
Cuco   see **Hebacuc.**
Cuco   see **Refugio.**
Cudverto   see **Cutberto.**
Cuilmas   see **Quilmes.**
Culacho   see **Nicolás.**
Culasa   see **Nicolás.**
Culaza   see **Nicolás.**
Culberto   see **Cutberto.**
Culose   see **Nicolás.**
Culsa   see **Nicolás.**
Culusa   see **Nicolás.**
Cumecinda   see **Gumersindo.**
Cumesindo   see **Gumersindo.**
Cuncarnación   see **Encarnación.**
Cuncha   see **Concepción.**
Cunegunda (Coo nay goon' dah) f. **EE:** Cunigundis. Ger. "Battle of the races." 6 x in DS. V. wife of Holy Roman Emperor, St. Henry II. **Var:** Conegunda.
Cunshi   see **Concepción.**
Cupriano (Coo pree ah' no) m. **EE:** Cuprian. Cupra, in Gk. & Roman myth., name by which Juno was worshipped. Protectress of honest housewives.
Cuquito   see **Refugio.**
Curcio (Coor' see oh) m. **EE:** Curt, Curtis. Lat. "Short."
Currito   see **Francisco.**
Curro   see **Francisco.**
Custaquio   see **Eustaquio.**
Custodia (Coo stoe' dee ah) mf? Lat. "To guard, to watch." Refers to Catholic feast day of guardian angels. F. 10/2. **Dim:** Toya.
Cutberto (Coot behr' toe) m. **EE:** Bert, Cuthbert. Ger. "Famous & bright." 3 x in DS. 7th cen. English S. known as "wonderworker" of Britain. F. 3/20. **Var:** Cuberto, Cudverto, Culberto, Cuthberto, Ucuberto.
Cuthberto   see **Cutberto.**
Cutilde   see **Clotilde.**
Cuxo   see **Agusto.**

Cuyetana   see **Cayetano.**
Cybil   see **Sibilo.**
Cyetanae   see **Cayetano.**
Cynilo (See nee' low) m. EE:
  Cynllo, 5th cen. S. from Wales.
  F. 7/17.
Cyntia   see **Cinta.**
Cyntjia   see **Cinta.**
Cypianas   see **Cipriano.**
Cyprana   see **Cipriano.**
Cyprianiam   see **Cipriano.**
Cypriano   see **Cipriano.**
Cyriaco   see **Ciriaco.**

Cyriano (See ree ah' no) m. EE:
  Cyrian. Form of Cyria, 3 Ss. on
  Christian calendar?
Cyrila   see **Cirilo.**
Cyrildo   see **Cirilo.**
Cyrillo   see **Cirilo.**
Cyrino   see **Cirenia.**
Cyrión   see **Ciro.**
Cyro   see **Cirenia.**
Cysta   see **Sixto.**
Cystine   see **Sixto.**
Cyvia   see **Silvio.**

D

Dabid   see **David.**
Dacio (Dah' see oh) m. EE: Dacius.
  Lat. "Inhabitant of Dacia
  (Rumania)."
Dadillo (Dah dee' yo) m. EE:
  Datum. Lat. "Gift or donation."
Dagalberto   see **Dagoberto.**
Dagaverto   see **Dagoberto.**
Dagoberto (Dah' go bare' toe) m.
  EE: Dagobert. Ger. "Clarity."
  7th cen. king & M. of Austrasia.
  F. 12/23. **Var:** Dagalberto,
  Dagaverto, Daguberto.
Daguberto   see **Dagoberto.**
Dahlia   see **Dalia.**
Daimantesa   see **Diamantina.**
Daimintina   see **Diamantina.**
Daina   see **Dina.**
Dalfina   see **Delfino.**
Dalia (Dah' lee ah) f. EE: Dahlia.
  Mexican flower named after
  Swedish botanist Dahl. **Var:**
  Dahlia, Dilala.
Dalio   see **Darío.**
Dalmacio (Dahl mah' see oh) m. EE:
  Dalmatius, Dalmatus. Lat. "One
  from Dalmatia (Yugoslavia)." 4 x
  in DS. 1 in solitary for 48
  years. **Var:** Dalmatia.
Dalmatia   see **Dalmacio.**
Dalores   see **Dolores.**
Daly   see **Edelmira.**
Damacio   see **Dámaso.**
Damaclo   see **Democles.**
Damario (Dah mah' ree oh) m. EE:
  Damaris. Possibly from Damaris,
  Gk. matron who believed St.
  Paul's teachings. **Var:** Damaro.
Damaro   see **Damario.**
Damas   see **Dámaso.**
Damasia   see **Dámaso.**
Damasiano   see **Dámaso.**
Damasico   see **Dámaso.**
Dámaso (Dah' mah so) m. EE:
  Damasus. Gk. "One who tames."
  4th cen. pope & doctor of
  church. F. 12/11. **Var:** Damacio,
  Damas, Damasia, Damasiano,
  Damasico, Damasse, Damatia,
  Damatiano, Damazco, Dámazo,
  Damecia, Damicio, Damisio,
  Demasio, Demecio, Dememcio,
  Dimsia, Domacio, Domasio,
  Dómaso, Domentia, Domonia.

Damasse   see **Dámaso.**
Damatia   see **Dámaso.**
Damatiano   see **Dámaso.**
Damatra   see **Demetrio.**
Damazco   see **Dámaso.**
Dámazo   see **Dámaso.**
Damecia   see **Dámaso.**
Damentina   see **Diamantina.**
Dametrio   see **Demetrio.**
Damián (Dah mee ahn') m. EE:
  Damien, Damon, etc. Gk. "One who
  tames." Damianus & Cosmas prac-
  ticed medicine without payment
  in 3rd cen. F. 9/27. **Var:**
  Damiano, Damina, Domiana.
Damiano   see **Damián.**
Damicio   see **Dámaso.**
Damiel   see **Daniel.**
Damina   see **Damián.**
Damisio   see **Dámaso.**
Danaciano   see **Donaciano.**
Danacio   see **Donaciano.**
Danación   see **Donaciano.**
Danaciono   see **Donaciano.**
Danahiano   see **Donaciano.**
Dananciano   see **Donaciano.**
Danatiano   see **Donaciano.**
Dandolo   see **Dante.**
Danelya   see **Daniel.**
Danésimo   see **Onésimo.**
Dani   see **Daniel.**
Danialo   see **Daniel.**
Daniel (Don yell') m. EE: Daniel,
  Danielle, etc. Heb. "The Lord is
  my judge." Biblical prophet,
  famous for escape from lions'
  den. F. 7/21. 35 x in DS. **Dim:**
  Dani, Nelo (Danilo), Nilo. **Var:**
  Damiel, Danelya, Danialo,
  Danielis, Danilo, Danniela,
  Donelia, Donelo, Donilia.
Danielis   see **Daniel.**
Danilo   see **Daniel.**
Danniela   see **Daniel.**
Dansiana   see **Donaciano.**
Dante (Don' tay) m. EE: Dante,
  Dantus, Duran. Ital. "To en-
  dure." Author of "Divine Comedy"
  (1265-1321). African M. F.
  12/11. **Var:** Dandolo, Dantel.
Dantel   see **Dante.**
Daréo   see **Darío.**
Darí   see **Darío.**
Darigildo (Dah ree heel' doe) m.

EE: Darigildo. Comb. of Darío & Gildo (see both).
Darío (Dah ree' oh) m. **EE:** Darian, Darius, etc. Pers. "Repressor." 9 x in DS. **Dim:** Darí, Dayo, Lalo. **Var:** Dalio, Daréo.
Darotea   see **Doroteo.**
Dativa (Dah tee' bah) f. **EE:** Dativa, Dativus. Lat. "Belonging to the one who gives." 10 x in DS. 1 mart. by Vandals in Africa in 5th cen. F. 12/6.
Daviana   see **David.**
David (Dah beed') m. **EE:** Dave, David, Davy. Heb. "Beloved." King of Israel, harp player, & slayer of Goliath. 26 x in DS. **Var:** Dabid, Daviana, Davida.
Davida   see **David.**
Davigen   see **Eduvigis.**
Davigildo (Dah bee heel' doe) m. **EE:** Davigildo. Comb. of David & Hermenesgildo (see both).
Davina   see **Ludovino.**
Dayamanti   see **Diamantina.**
Dayo   see **Darío.**
Deamantina   see **Diamantina.**
Deanamtina   see **Diamantina.**
Débara   see **Débora.**
Débarah   see **Débora.**
Débbora   see **Débora.**
Debby   see **Débora.**
Débora (Day' bo rah) f. **EE:** Debbie, Deborah, etc. Heb. "Swarm of bees." Nurse of Rebekah & prophetess-judge who led revolt against Canaanite kings. **Dim:** Debby. **Var:** Débara, Débarah, Débbora, Deboricia, Déborrah, Debrah, Debrina, Diborah.
Deboricia   see **Débora.**
Déborrah   see **Débora.**
Debrah   see **Débora.**
Debrina   see **Débora.**
Decederia   see **Desiderio.**
Decediro   see **Desiderio.**
Decideriadela   see **Desiderio.**
Deciderio   see **Desiderio.**
Decidoro   see **Desiderio.**
Decio (Day' see oh) m. **EE:** Decius. Lat. "Tenth or tenth son." Roman emperor (201-251) who persecuted Christians.
Decisderio   see **Desiderio.**
Defilia   see **Delfino.**
Defino   see **Delfino.**
Dejandra   see **Alejandro.**
Dejandro   see **Alejandro.**
Dejiderio   see **Desiderio.**
Dela   see **Adela.**
Delaida   see **Adelaido.**
Delbina   see **Ludovino.**
Delferio   see **Delfino.**
Delfhina   see **Delfino.**
Delfido   see **Delfino.**
Delfido (Dell fee' doe) m. **EE:** Delfidio. Delfidio was famous Roman poet of 4th cen.
Delfidotory   see **Delfino.**
Delfino (Dell fee' no) m. **EE:** Delfina, Delphinus, etc. Lat. "Dolphin." St. Delfina of 13th cen. France maintained virginity even after marriage. F. 11/26.

Dim: Delfy, Finita, Fino, Pina. **Var:** Dalfina, Defilia, Defino, Delferio, Delfhina, Delfido, Delfidotory, Delfno, Delfurio, Delphia, Delphino, Delphono, Delpino, Dilfina, Dolphina, Edelfino.
Delfno   see **Delfino.**
Delfurio   see **Delfino.**
Delfy   see **Delfino.**
Delgadino (Dell gah dee' no) m. **EE:** Delgadino. Sp. "Smooth, delicate, fine."
Delicia (Day lee' see ah) f. **EE:** Delicia, Delizea, etc. Lat. "That which causes pleasure." **Var:** Deliciano, Delisa, Delissa, Delyssa.
Deliciano   see **Delicia.**
Delida (Day lee' dah) f. **EE:** Deliada. Deliada in Gk. myth. was priestess of Apollo's temple at Delos.
Delina   see **Teodolinda.**
Delio   see **Adela.**
Delisa   see **Delicia.**
Delisario (Day le sah' ree oh) m. Appears to be comb. of Delicia & Belisario (see both).
Delissa   see **Delicia.**
Dellanira   see **Deyanira.**
Delma   see **Adelmo.**
Delmantina   see **Diamantina.**
Delmetrio   see **Demetrio.**
Delminda   see **Adelmo.**
Delmira   see **Edelmira.**
Delores   see **Dolores.**
Delorida   see **Dolores.**
Deloris   see **Dolores.**
Delorites   see **Dolores.**
Delphia   see **Delfino.**
Delphino   see **Delfino.**
Delphono   see **Delfino.**
Delpino   see **Delfino.**
Delubina   see **Ludovino.**
Deluvín   see **Ludovino.**
Delyssa   see **Delicia.**
Demantina   see **Diamantina.**
Demasio   see **Dámaso.**
Dematra   see **Demetrio.**
Demecio   see **Dámaso.**
Demecio   see **Nemesio.**
Demeltrio   see **Demetrio.**
Dememcio   see **Dámaso.**
Dementio   see **Demetrio.**
Dementria   see **Demetrio.**
Demesio   see **Nemesio.**
Demestrio   see **Demetrio.**
Demeterio   see **Demetrio.**
Demetino (Day may tee' no) m. **EE:** Demeter. Form of Demetriano, S. mart. on Cyprus? F. 6/23.
Demetira   see **Demetrio.**
Demetre   see **Demetrio.**
Demetreo   see **Demetrio.**
Demetres   see **Demetrio.**
Demetrin   see **Demetrio.**
Demetrina   see **Demetrio.**
Demetrio (Day may' tree oh) m. **EE:** Demeter, Demetrius. Gk. "Belonging to Demeter," earth goddess in Gk. legend. 53 x in DS. **Dim:** Chema, Mecho. **Var:** Damatra, Dametrio, Delmetrio, Dematra, Demeltrio, Dementio, Dementria,

Demestrio, Demeterio, Demetira,
Demetre, Demetreo, Demetres,
Demetrin, Demetrina, Demetro,
Demietro, Demiterio, Demitia,
Demitita, Demitla, Demitre,
Demitria, Demstrio, Denetrio,
Denetrius, Dernetrio, Diametria,
Dimertio, Dimetrio, Dimetrium,
Dimitreo, Dimitrio, Dimitrius,
Domitrio, Donetrio.

Demetro	see **Demetrio**.
Demietro	see **Demetrio**.
Demiterio	see **Demetrio**.
Demitia	see **Demetrio**.
Demitita	see **Demetrio**.
Demitla	see **Demetrio**.
Demitre	see **Demetrio**.
Demitria	see **Demetrio**.

Democles (Day mo' clays) m. **EE:**
Democles. Gk. "Glory of his
people." Attended banquet where
he saw sword suspended above his
head. **Var:** Damaclo.

Demofilo (Day mo' fee low) m. **EE:**
Demophilus. Gk. "Friend of the
people."

Demóstenes (Day mose' tay nays) m.
EE: Demosthenes. Gk. "Force of
the people." Among greatest of
Gk. orators & famous for
Philippics. **Var:** Demóstines.

Demóstines	see **Demóstenes**.
Demstrio	see **Demetrio**.
Denaciano	see **Donaciano**.
Denanira	see **Deyanira**.
Denderia	see **Deyanira**.
Denetrio	see **Demetrio**.
Denetrius	see **Demetrio**.
Denisa	see **Dionisio**.
Denisio	see **Dionisio**.
Denizo	see **Dionisio**.

Deodato (Day oh dah' toe) m. **EE:**
Deodatus. Lat. "He who has given
himself to God." 7 x in DS. **Var:**
Diosdado.

Deodoro	see **Teodoro**.

Deogracias (Day oh grah' see ahs)
m. **EE:** Deogratias. Lat. "Thanks
to God." 5th cen. bishop of
Carthage who nursed prisoners
sold as slaves in Africa after
sack of Rome. F. 3/22. **Var:**
Deogracio, Deogracios,
Deogratias, Diogracias,
Diogratio.

Deogracio	see **Deogracias**.
Deogracios	see **Deogracias**.
Deogratias	see **Deogracias**.
Deolinda	see **Teodolinda**.
Deomides	see **Diomedes**.
Deonicio	see **Dionisio**.
Deonisio	see **Dionisio**.
Deonisius	see **Dionisio**.
Deonysio	see **Dionisio**.
Dernetrio	see **Demetrio**.
Derotea	see **Doroteo**.
Derotio	see **Doroteo**.
Desadero	see **Desiderio**.
Desedenio	see **Desiderio**.
Desederio	see **Desiderio**.
Desi	see **Desiderio**.
Desidaro	see **Desiderio**.
Desidenio	see **Desiderio**.
Desideno	see **Desiderio**.
Desidera	see **Desiderio**.
Desidercia	see **Desiderio**.
Desiderco	see **Desiderio**.
Desidereo	see **Desiderio**.

Desiderio (Day see day' ree oh) m.
EE: Desiderius. Lat. "Yearning"
or "grief for an absent person."
11 x in DS. **Dim:** Chalelo,
Chilelo, Desi, Dessie, Gery,
Sidero, Yeyo. **Var:** Decederia,
Decediro, Decideriadela,
Deciderio, Decidoro, Decisderio,
Dejiderio, Desadero, Desedenio,
Desederio, Desidaro, Desidenio,
Desideno, Desidera, Desidercia,
Desiderco, Desidereo,
Desiderium, Desiderous,
Desidevia, Desidina, Desidirio,
Desidorio, Desidoro, Desierio,
Desitirio, Desuderio, Dicidora,
Disideno, Disiderio, Disidoro,
Disidorum, Disidro, Dissidoro,
Dissidro, Dixidora.

Desiderium	see **Desiderio**.
Desiderous	see **Desiderio**.
Desidevia	see **Desiderio**.
Desidina	see **Desiderio**.
Desidirio	see **Desiderio**.
Desidorio	see **Desiderio**.
Desidoro	see **Desiderio**.
Desierio	see **Desiderio**.
Desitirio	see **Desiderio**.
Dessie	see **Desiderio**.

Destina (Days tee' na) f. **EE:**
Destiny. Destiny or predeter-
mined course of events. 1 of 3
Fates.

Desuderio	see **Desiderio**.
Deudoria	see **Teodoro**.
Devorcio	see **Tiburcio**.
Devorsia	see **Tiburcio**.
Deyamira	see **Deyanira**.

Deyanira (Day yah nee' rah) f. **EE:**
Deianira, Dejanira. Gk. "He who
kills forcefully." Wife of Hera-
cles who unwittingly caused his
death in trying to win back his
love. **Var:** Dellanira, Denanira,
Denderia, Deyamira, Diamira,
Dianira.

Diamanina	see **Diamantina**.

Diamantina (Dee' ah mahn tee' nah)
f. **EE:** Diamanta. Gk. "Indomita-
ble one." **Var:** Daimantesa,
Daimintina, Damentina,
Dayamanti, Deamantina,
Deanamtina, Delmantina,
Demantina, Diamanina,
Diamantine, Diamenina,
Diamentina, Diamontina,
Dimantina, Diomantina,
Diormantina, Doamantiana.

Diamantine	see **Diamantina**.
Diamenina	see **Diamantina**.
Diamentina	see **Diamantina**.
Diametria	see **Demetrio**.
Diamira	see **Deyanira**.
Diamontina	see **Diamantina**.

Diana (Dee ah' na) f. **EE:** Di,
Diana, Diane. Gk. "Divine one."
In Roman myth., goddess of moon,
forest animals, & women in
childbirth. **Var:** Dianida,
Dianna.

Dianicio	see **Dionisio**.
Dianida	see **Diana**.

Dianira   see **Deyanira.**
Dianisia   see **Dionisio.**
Dianna   see **Diana.**
Díborah   see **Débora.**
Diburtio   see **Tiburcio.**
Dicasio (Dee cah' see oh) m. EE:
   Dicasio. Two-parted flower, the
   cyme.
Dicidora   see **Desiderio.**
Dicta   see **Benedicto.**
Didaco   see **Santiago.**
Dideo   see **Didio.**
Didio (Dee' dee oh) m. EE: Didius.
   Lat. "Granted by God." S. mart.
   at Alexandria, Egypt. F. 11/26.
   Var: Dideo, Didión.
Didión   see **Didio.**
Dieco   see **Santiago.**
Diego   see **Jaime.**
Diego   see **Santiago.**
Diegolino   see **Santiago.**
Dieguin   see **Santiago.**
Dieguito   see **Jacobo.**
Dieguito   see **Jaime.**
Dieguito   see **Santiago.**
Digna (Deeg' nah) f. EE: Digna,
   Dignus. Lat. "One who merits
   respect." 8 x in DS. 1, of 9th
   cen. Spain, beheaded. F. 6/14.
Digo   see **Jacobo.**
Dilala   see **Dalia.**
Dilario   see **Hilario.**
Dilfina   see **Delfino.**
Dilia   see **Cordilio.**
Diluvina   see **Ludovino.**
Dimantina   see **Diamantina.**
Dimás (Dee mahs') m. EE: Dismas.
   Good thief of Bible to whom
   Christ said, "Today you shall be
   with me in Paradise." F. 3/25.
   Var: Dimós.
Dimaso (Dee mah' so) m. EE: Dimas.
   St. Dimas, of 18th cen., mart.
   at Smyrna, Turkey, for refusing
   to become a Moslem. F. 4/10.
Dimecia (Dee may' see ah) f. EE:
   Dimecio. St. Dimecio mart. in
   Cesena, Italy. Mentioned in
   Jeronomite Martyrology. F. 7/21.
   Var: Dimensia, Dimisio.
Dimensia   see **Dimecia.**
Dimertio   see **Demetrio.**
Dimetrio   see **Demetrio.**
Dimetrium   see **Demetrio.**
Dimisio   see **Dimecia.**
Dimitreo   see **Demetrio.**
Dimitrio   see **Demetrio.**
Dimitrius   see **Demetrio.**
Dimós   see **Dimás.**
Dimpna (Deemp' nah) f. EE: Dympna,
   Dymphna. Irish V. pursued by
   lecherous father. Patroness of
   insane. F. 5/15.
Dimsia   see **Dámaso.**
Dina   see **Alejandro.**
Dina (Dee' nah) f. EE: Di, Dina,
   Dinah, etc. Heb. "Judgement."
   Biblically, daughter of Jacob &
   Leah. Outraged by Shechem, she
   precipitated a massacre. **Var:**
   Daina, Dinobra, Dinohra,
   Dinorah, Dinorha.
Dinicio   see **Dionisio.**
Dinisio   see **Dionisio.**
Dinnisia   see **Dionisio.**

Dino   see **Bernal.**
Dino   see **Leopoldo.**
Dinobra   see **Dina.**
Dinohra   see **Dina.**
Dinorah   see **Dina.**
Dinorha   see **Dina.**
Diocina   see **Dionisio.**
Diodoro (Dee oh doe' roe) m. EE:
   Diodorus. Gk. "Gift of Zeus," 13
   x in DS. 3rd cen. S. mart. by
   suffocation. F. 12/1.
Diogenes (Dee oh' hay naze) m. EE:
   Diogenes. Gk. "Born." Gk. philo-
   sopher who believed in simple
   life & lived in tub. 6 x in DS.
Diogolino   see **Jacobo.**
Diogracias   see **Deogracias.**
Diogratio   see **Deogracias.**
Diomantina   see **Diamantina.**
Diomar (Dee oh mar') m. EE:
   Diodemaro. Diodemaro was 11th
   cen. Bavarian S. F. 9/28.
Diomedes (Dee oh may' days) m. EE:
   Diomede, Diomedes. Gk. "Thought,
   plan." 1 of Epigoni prominent in
   Trojan War. 15 x in DS. 1, of
   3rd cen., called "Fee-less" for
   practicing medicine free of
   charge. F. 8/16. **Var:** Deomides,
   Diomedo, Diomides, Dionedes,
   Dionides, Dionidez, Dionidio,
   Dionidis, Dionijio.
Diomedo   see **Diomedes.**
Diomides   see **Diomedes.**
Diomina (Dee oh mee' nah) f.
   Diomma was S. of Limerick,
   Ireland. F. 2/12. **Var:** Dionima.
Diomira   see **Teodomiro.**
Diomisio   see **Dionisio.**
Dione (Dee oh' nay) f. EE: Dion.
   Possibly Gk. "of God." In Gk.
   myth. mother of Venus. 3 x in
   DS. **Var:** Dionel, Dionilio.
Dionecio   see **Dionisio.**
Dionedes   see **Diomedes.**
Dionel   see **Dione.**
Dionesio   see **Dionisio.**
Dioniccia   see **Dionisio.**
Dionicid   see **Dionisio.**
Dionicio   see **Dionisio.**
Dioniciol   see **Dionisio.**
Dionicis   see **Dionisio.**
Dionico   see **Dionisio.**
Dionides   see **Diomedes.**
Dionidez   see **Diomedes.**
Dionidio   see **Diomedes.**
Dionidis   see **Diomedes.**
Dionijio   see **Diomedes.**
Dionilio   see **Dione.**
Dionima   see **Diomina.**
Dionires   see **Teodomiro.**
Dionis   see **Dionisio.**
Dionisa   see **Dionisio.**
Dionisea   see **Dionisio.**
Dionisio (Dee oh nee' see oh) m.
   EE: Dennis, Dionysius. Gk.
   "Consecrated to Dionysius," god
   of fertility & wine. 68 x in DS.
   Dim: Chonicho, Nicho. **Var:**
   Denisa, Denisio, Denizo,
   Deonicio, Deonisio, Deonisius,
   Deonysio, Dianicio, Dianisia,
   Dinicio, Dinisio, Dinnisia,
   Diocina, Diomisio, Dionecio,
   Dionesio, Dioniccia, Dionicid,

Dionicio, Dioniciol, Dionicis,
Dionico, Dionis, Dionisa,
Dionisea, Dionisis, Dionisnio,
Dioniteo, Dionizio, Dionizsia,
Dionsio, Dionsisio, Dionyno,
Dionysio, Diosisio, Dioysia,
Disnisio, Domosio, Domysio,
Dyanisio, Dyinisio, Dynisio,
Dyonicia, Dyonisio.

Dionisis   see **Dionisio.**
Dionisnio   see **Dionisio.**
Dioniteo   see **Dionisio.**
Dionizio   see **Dionisio.**
Dionizsia   see **Dionisio.**
Dionora (Dee oh no' rah) f. **EE:**
Dianora, Dina, Dinorah. Aramaic,
"Causing light." Eponymous her-
oine of Myerbeer's 1859 opera.
Dianora is character in
Bacaccio's Decameron.
Dionsio   see **Dionisio.**
Dionsisio   see **Dionisio.**
Dionyno   see **Dionisio.**
Dionysio   see **Dionisio.**
Diormantina   see **Diamantina.**
Diosa (Dee oh' sah) f. Lat.
"Goddess."
Dióscoro (Dee ohs' co roe) m. **EE:**
Dioscuri, Dioscurus. Gk. "Son of
Jupiter." Twin heroes, Castor &
Pollux, transformed into con-
stellation Gemini. 15 x in DS.
Diosdado   see **Deodato.**
Diosisio   see **Dionisio.**
Dioysia   see **Dionisio.**
Disideno   see **Desiderio.**
Disiderio   see **Desiderio.**
Disidoro   see **Desiderio.**
Disidorum   see **Desiderio.**
Disidro   see **Desiderio.**
Disnisio   see **Dionisio.**
Dissidora   see **Isidoro.**
Dissidoro   see **Desiderio.**
Dissidro   see **Desiderio.**
Dita   see **Edita.**
Divertio   see **Tiburcio.**
Divia   see **Divino.**
Divinda   see **Divino.**
Divinisio (Dee bee nee' see oh) m.
Lat. "Relating to God"? Fig.,
excellence or perfection.
Divino (Dee bee' no) m. **EE:**
Devine, Divine. Sp. "Belonging
to God, divine." **Var:** Divia,
Divinda.
Divisio (Dee bee' see oh) m. **EE:**
Divitianus. Possibly form of
Divitianus, 4th cen. S. of
Soissons, France. F. 10/5.
Divorsia   see **Tiburcio.**
Divortio   see **Tiburcio.**
Divortis   see **Tiburcio.**
Divurecia   see **Tiburcio.**
Divursio   see **Tiburcio.**
Dixidora   see **Desiderio.**
Dlores   see **Dolores.**
Doamantiana   see **Diamantina.**
Doda   see **Dolores.**
Dolarez   see **Dolores.**
Dolarum   see **Dolores.**
Doleres   see **Dolores.**
Doleriana   see **Dolores.**
Dolfito   see **Adolfo.**
Dolfo   see **Adolfo.**
Dolita   see **Adolfo.**

Dolora   see **Dolores.**
Dolorcita   see **Dolores.**
Dolorcitas   see **Dolores.**
Dolores (Doe low' raise) mf. **EE:**
Deloris, Dolores. Lat. "Suffer-
ing." Refers to 7 sorrows of
Mary in relationship with
Christ. F. 9/15. **Dim:** Doda,
Dolorcita, Dolorcitas, Dolorita,
Doloritas, Doloritta, Lalo,
Lola, Loli, Lolica, Lolicia,
Lolis, Lolita, Loltie. **Var:**
Dalores, Delores, Delorida,
Deloris, Delorites, Dlores,
Dolarez, Dolarum, Doleres,
Doleriana, Dolora, Doloress,
Doloris, Doloros, Dolors,
Dolorum, Dolres, Dorlores,
Dulores.
Doloress   see **Dolores.**
Doloris   see **Dolores.**
Dolorita   see **Dolores.**
Doloritas   see **Dolores.**
Doloritta   see **Dolores.**
Doloros   see **Dolores.**
Dolors   see **Dolores.**
Dolorum   see **Dolores.**
Dolphina   see **Delfino.**
Dolres   see **Dolores.**
Domaciamo   see **Donaciano.**
Domaciano   see **Donaciano.**
Domacio   see **Dámaso.**
Domasio   see **Dámaso.**
Dómaso   see **Dámaso.**
Domatida   see **Domitilo.**
Domatila   see **Domitilo.**
Domecia (Doe may' see ah) f. **EE:**
Dometian, Dometius. Form of
Dometius, 15 Ss. on Christian
calendar?
Domecinda   see **Domitilo.**
Domenga   see **Domingo.**
Domenico   see **Domingo.**
Domenja   see **Domitilo.**
Domentia   see **Dámaso.**
Dometela   see **Domitilo.**
Dometilea   see **Domitilo.**
Dometillo   see **Domitilo.**
Domiana   see **Damián.**
Domicella   see **Domitilo.**
Domicio   see **Domingo.**
Domifila   see **Domitilo.**
Domilila   see **Domitilo.**
Domilio   see **Domitilo.**
Dominciano   see **Domingo.**
Dominego   see **Domingo.**
Domingan   see **Domingo.**
Domingas   see **Domingo.**
Domingila   see **Domingo.**
Domingo (Doe mean' go) m. **EE:**
Dominic, Dominick. Lat. "Belong-
ing to the Lord." 36 x in DS.
Spaniard Dominic Guzmán, founded
Dominican order in 13th cen. F.
8/4. **Dim:** Chomin, Chumin,
Chumingo, Chumo, Mingo, Minguín.
Var: Domenga, Domenico, Domicio,
Dominciano, Dominego, Domingan,
Domingas, Domingila, Domingue,
Dominica, Dominiciae, Dominicum,
Dominiga, Domnega. See also
Domnino.
Domingue   see **Domingo.**
Dominia   see **Domnino.**
Dominica   see **Domingo.**

Dominiciae   see **Domingo**.
Dominicum   see **Domingo**.
Dominiga   see **Domingo**.
Domino   see **Domnino**.
Domis (Doe' mees) m. **EE**: Dominius.
  Could be form of Dominius, 6th
  cen. Fr. S.
Domitelo   see **Domitilo**.
Domitiala   see **Domitilo**.
Domitida   see **Domitilo**.
Domitilda   see **Domitilo**.
Domitilo (Doe mee tee' low) m. **EE**:
  Dometius. Lat. "To tame, to
  subjugate." 14 x in DS. 1, a
  Pers. ascetic & wonder-worker
  walled up and left to die of
  hunger. F. 9/24. **Dim**: Tilo. **Var**:
  Domatila, Domatila, Domecinda,
  Domenja, Dometela, Dometilea,
  Dometillo, Domicella, Domifila,
  Domilila, Domilio, Domitelo,
  Domitiala, Domitida, Domitilda,
  Domitla, Dommitillo, Domolia,
  Donatila, Donitilia, Donitilo,
  Dormitila, Endomitila.
Domitla   see **Domitilo**.
Domitrio   see **Demetrio**.
Dommitillo   see **Domitilo**.
Domnega   see **Domingo**.
Domnino (Dome nee' no) m. **EE**:
  Domino, Dona, Donna. Lat. "Lord,
  master." Also gives Sp. title of
  respect for woman, "dona." 36 x
  in DS. **Var**: Dominia, Domino. See
  also Domingo.
Domolia   see **Domitilo**.
Domonia   see **Dámaso**.
Domosio   see **Dionisio**.
Domysio   see **Dionisio**.
Donaceno   see **Donaciano**.
Donacho   see **Donaciano**.
Donaciano (Doe nah see ah' no) m.
  EE: Donatus. Lat. "Gift, dona-
  tion." 75 x in DS. 1, 4th cen.
  bishop of Arezzo, Italy, mart.
  under Julian the Apostate. F.
  8/7. **Dim**: Chano. **Var**: Danaciano,
  Danacio, Danación, Danaciono,
  Danahiano, Dananciano,
  Danatiano, Dansiana, Denaciano,
  Domaciamo, Domaciano, Donaceno,
  Donacho, Donacio, Donación,
  Donaciono, Donaciuno, Donafiana,
  Donasiano, Donatiano,
  Donatianum, Donaziano,
  Donazians, Donerciana, Donicio,
  Donnasiano, Donocano, Donoclano,
  Donotiano. See also Donato.
Donacio   see **Donaciano**.
Donación   see **Donaciano**.
Donaciono   see **Donaciano**.
Donaciuno   see **Donaciano**.
Donafiana   see **Donaciano**.
Donaldo (Doe nahl' doe) m. **EE**:
  Don, Donald. Gaelic, "Prince of
  the universe." Scotland's 1st
  Christian king. Had 9 daughters,
  but still lived religious life.
  F. 7/15. **Var**: Donaldonio.
Donaldonio   see **Donaldo**.
Donariana   see **Donato**.
Donasiano   see **Donaciano**.
Donatia   see **Donato**.
Donatiano   see **Donaciano**.
Donatianum   see **Donaciano**.

Donatila   see **Domitilo**.
Donatino   see **Donato**.
Donato (Doe nah' toe) m. **EE**:
  Donatus. Lat. "Gift or given."
  75 x in DS. **Var**: Donariana,
  Donatia, Donatino. See also
  Donaciano.
Donaziano   see **Donaciano**.
Donazians   see **Donaciano**.
Donécimo   see **Onésimo**.
Donelia   see **Daniel**.
Donelo   see **Daniel**.
Donerciana   see **Donaciano**.
Donésimo   see **Onésimo**.
Donetrio   see **Demetrio**.
Donicio   see **Donaciano**.
Donilia   see **Daniel**.
Donitilia   see **Domitilo**.
Donitilo   see **Domitilo**.
Donnasiano   see **Donaciano**.
Donocano   see **Donaciano**.
Donoclano   see **Donaciano**.
Donorato   see **Honoria**.
Donoriano   see **Honoria**.
Donotiano   see **Donaciano**.
Dora   see **Doroteo**.
Doralisa   see **Doroteo**.
Doraliza (Doe rah lee' sah) f. **EE**:
  Doralice. Doralice is nymph in
  Porcel's "Adonis."
Doralva (Doe rahl' bah) f. **EE**:
  Doralva. Comb. of Doroteo (see)
  & "alba" Sp. "white"?
Dorasio (Doe rah' see oh) m. **EE**:
  Dorceo. Dorceo, of Gk. legend,
  was son of Hipocoin revered in
  Sparta.
Dorata   see **Doroteo**.
Dorateo   see **Doroteo**.
Doratheo   see **Doroteo**.
Doratio   see **Doroteo**.
Doratreo   see **Aurelio**.
Dorelia   see **Doroteo**.
Dorelia   see **Orencio**.
Dorenz   see **Doroteo**.
Dores   see **Doroteo**.
Dores   see **Teodoro**.
Doreta   see **Doroteo**.
Doretea   see **Doroteo**.
Doretha   see **Doroteo**.
Doretra   see **Doroteo**.
Dorfelia   see **Ofelio**.
Dori   see **Doroteo**.
Doria   see **Doroteo**.
Doribeo   see **Toribio**.
Doriciana   see **Doroteo**.
Dorila   see **Doroteo**.
Dorina   see **Doroteo**.
Dorina   see **Isidoro**.
Dorita   see **Doroteo**.
Dorivia   see **Toribio**.
Dorlinda   see **Doroteo**.
Dorlisa   see **Doroteo**.
Dorlores   see **Dolores**.
Dormitila   see **Domitilo**.
Doro   see **Doroteo**.
Doro   see **Heliodoro**.
Doro   see **Isidoro**.
Doro   see **Teodoro**.
Dorodeo   see **Doroteo**.
Dorofelia (Doe roe fay' lee ah) f.
  EE: Dorofelia. Comb. of Doroteo
  & Ofelio (see both).
Dorolinda (Doe roe lean' dah) f.
  EE: Dorolinda. Comb. of Doroteo

(see) & "linda" Sp. "pretty."
Dorote   see **Doroteo.**
Doroteio   see **Doroteo.**
Doroteo (Doe roe tay' oh) m. **EE:**
Dorothea, Dorothy, Dot. Gk.
"Gift of God." 18 x in DS. **Dim:**
Dori, Dorita, Doro, Doti, Lola,
Teo, Teya. **Var:** Darotea,
Derotea, Derotio, Dora,
Doralisa, Dorata, Dorateo,
Doratheo, Doratio, Doratreo,
Dorelia, Dores, Doreta, Doretea,
Doretha, Doretra, Doria,
Doriciana, Dorila, Dorina,
Dorlinda, Dorlisa, Dorodeo,
Dorote, Doroteio, Doroteous,
Dorotes, Dorotez, Dorotheo,
Doroti, Dorotia, Dorotiana,
Doroto, Dorotoro, Dorotreo,
Dorsilo, Dorteo, Dortheus.
Doroteous   see **Doroteo.**
Dorotes   see **Doroteo.**
Dorotez   see **Doroteo.**
Dorotheo   see **Doroteo.**
Doroti   see **Doroteo.**
Dorotia   see **Doroteo.**
Dorotiana   see **Doroteo.**
Doroto   see **Doroteo.**
Dorotoro   see **Doroteo.**
Dorotreo   see **Doroteo.**
Dorsilo   see **Doroteo.**
Dorteo   see **Doroteo.**
Dortheus   see **Doroteo.**
Dositeo (Doe' see tay' oh) m. **EE:**
Dositheus. Gk. "Gift from God."
Monk who served as page to army
officer. After life of sensual-
ity, converted to Christianity
in Jerusalem upon seeing picture
of torments of hell. F. 2/23.
Doti   see **Doroteo.**
Doveja   see **Eduvigis.**
Doya   see **Teodoro.**
Dramona   see **Ramón.**
Drina   see **Alejandro.**
Drucilla   see **Drusila.**
Drusila (Drew see' lah) f. **EE:**
Drucilla, Drusilla. Lat. "The
strong." Youngest daughter of
Herod Agrippa I. Defied Jewish

law & married foreigner & idola-
tor. **Var:** Drucilla, Durcilla.
Duardo   see **Eduardo.**
Dubijen   see **Eduvigis.**
Dubijes   see **Eduvigis.**
Ducha   see **Aida.**
Duella (Dway' lah) f. **EE:** Duella.
Lat. "Affliction or sorrow."
Dula   see **Dulas.**
Dulalio (Doo law' lee oh) m. **EE:**
Dulalio. Comb. of Dula, S. mart.
in Nicomedia for trying to save
chastity, & Eulalia (see).
Dulas (Doo' lahs) m. **EE:** Dula,
Dulas. Gk. "Servant or slave." 4
x in DS. 4th cen. M. in persecu-
tion of Diocletian. F. 6/15.
Var: Dula, Dules.
Dulce (Dool' say) f. **EE:** Dulcia,
Dulcina, Dulcy. Lat. "Agree-
able." Refers to "dulce nombre
de María," "Sweet Name of Mary."
F. 9/12. **Var:** Dulcenio, Dulcie,
Dulcina, Dulcinea, Dulcinia.
Dulcenio   see **Dulce.**
Dulcie   see **Dulce.**
Dulcina   see **Dulce.**
Dulcinea   see **Dulce.**
Dulcinia   see **Dulce.**
Dules   see **Dulas.**
Dulores   see **Dolores.**
Dunstano (Doon stah' no) m. **EE:**
Dunstan. Ger. "Stone on hill."
10th cen. Ang-Sax. S. Reformed
English church & is overshadowed
only by St. Thomas.
Durcilla   see **Drusila.**
Duva   see **Eduvigis.**
Duvencio   see **Juvencio.**
Duvigen   see **Eduvigis.**
Duvijen   see **Eduvigis.**
Duvijes   see **Eduvigis.**
Duvijos   see **Eduvigis.**
Duvirgin   see **Eduvigis.**
Dyanisio   see **Dionisio.**
Dyinisio   see **Dionisio.**
Dynisio   see **Dionisio.**
Dyonicia   see **Dionisio.**
Dyonisio   see **Dionisio.**

E

Eabaristo   see **Evaristo.**
Eastacio   see **Eustacio.**
Ebangelina   see **Evangelina.**
Ebaristo   see **Evaristo.**
Ebelardo   see **Abelardo.**
Ebelino   see **Evelio.**
Ebelio   see **Evelio.**
Ebenezer (Aay bay nay sair') m.
EE: Ebbie, Eben, Ebenezer. Scene
of Israelites' defeat by Philis-
tines.
Eberardo (Aay bay rahr' doe) m.
EE: Everard, Everett, etc. Ger.
"Strong as a boar." 3 x in DS.
1, Englishman converted from
Protestantism & executed. **Var:**
Averando, Eberedo.

Eberedo   see **Eberardo.**
Eberto   see **Edberto.**
Ebilia   see **Evelio.**
Ebita   see **Eva.**
Ebodeo   see **Evodio.**
Ecarnación   see **Encarnación.**
Ecasio   see **Acacio.**
Ecedro   see **Isidoro.**
Ecelso (Aay sehl' so) m. **EE:**
Ecelso. Lat. "Eminent, high,
lofty." Fig., excellence of
bearer. See also Celso.
Ecequiel   see **Ezequiel.**
Ecequiela   see **Ezequiel.**
Ecidro   see **Isidoro.**
Eciguel   see **Ezequiel.**
Eciqinio   see **Hesiquio.**

Eciquio   see **Hesiquio.**
Eclestina   see **Escolástica.**
Ecliserio   see **Glicerio.**
Ecmundo   see **Edmundo.**
Ecolástica   see **Escolástica.**
Econina (Aay co nee' nah) f. EE:
  Econina. 1 of 50 sons of Prince
  Egypt & husband of Acamantis.
Ectavio   see **Octavio.**
Ector   see **Héctor.**
Eda (Aay' dah) f. EE: Edda, Hedda,
  Hedwig, Ger. "Hedwig," "strife &
  fight." 2 x in DS. 7th cen,
  bishop of West Saxony. F. 7/7.
Edalecio   see **Indalecio.**
Edalia   see **Adela.**
Edberto (Aid bare' toe) m. EE:
  Edbert. Ger. "Nice & bright."
  Successor of Cuthbert of 7th
  cen. Britain & noted for charity
  to poor. F. 5/6. **Var:** Eberto,
  Eddieberto, Ediberto.
Eddieberto   see **Edberto.**
Eddifonsa   see **Ildefonso.**
Eddy   see **Eduardo.**
Edelburga (Aay dehl boor' gah) f.
  EE: Ethelburge. Ang-Sax. "Of
  noble race." Daughter of 7th
  cen. Anglo king. F. 7/7. **Var:**
  Edilburga.
Edelfino   see **Delfino.**
Edelfraida   see **Edelfrida.**
Edelfrida (Aay dehl free' dah) f.
  EE: Edelfrida. Elements of
  Edelmiro & Alfredo (see both).
  Var: Edelfraida.
Edelia   see **Adela.**
Edelmera   see **Edelmira.**
Edelmida   see **Edelmira.**
Edelmina   see **Edelmira.**
Edelmir   see **Edelmira.**
Edelmira (Aay dehl mee' rah) f.
  EE: Adelmar. Ger. form of
  "adelmaro," "of noble race." 1
  S. F. 3/24. **Dim:** Daly, Mima,
  Mimi, Mimia, Mimiya, Miro. **Var:**
  Almira, Delmira, Edelmera,
  Edelmida, Edelmina, Edelmir,
  Edelmmo, Edelniro, Edelvira,
  Edmiro, Edmirro, Eldimira,
  Elmiro, Elnira, Ermirio, Ermrio,
  Idmiro, Odelmirra.
Edelmmo   see **Edelmira.**
Edelniro   see **Edelmira.**
Edelvira   see **Edelmira.**
Edenia (Aay day' nee ah) f. EE:
  Edenia. Heb. "Eden," "garden."
Ederardo   see **Eduardo.**
Edesio (Aay day' see oh) m. EE:
  Aedesius, Edesius. Aedesius
  mart. in Alexandria (Egypt) in
  4th cen. when thrown into sea.
  F. 4/8.
Edevegen   see **Eduvigis.**
Edevergin   see **Eduvigis.**
Edeviges   see **Eduvigis.**
Edgardo (Ayd gahr' doe) m. EE: Ed,
  Eddie, Edgar. Ang-Sax. "Spear or
  javelin." 10th cen. Ang-Sax.
  king. F. 7/8. **Dim:** Lalo. **Var:**
  Edgrado, Jedegardo.
Edgrado   see **Edgardo.**
Edi   see **Eduardo.**
Ediberto   see **Edberto.**
Edicación (Aay dee cah see own')

mf? EE: Edicacion. Sp. "Edifi-
  cación," "build up" (in a moral
  sense).
Edifanio   see **Epifanio.**
Edilberto   see **Adalberto.**
Edilburga   see **Edelburga.**
Edilio (Aay dee' lee oh) m. EE:
  Edilio. Gk. "She who is like a
  statue."
Edissa (Aay dee' sah) f. EE:
  Edissa. Could be form of
  Edistio, S. mart. in Ravenna,
  Italy, in 4th cen. F. 10/12.
Edisteo (Aay dees tay' oh) m. EE:
  Edisteo. Could be form of
  Edistio, mart. under Diocletian
  in 4th cen. in Ravenna, Italy.
  F. 10/12.
Edita (Aay dee' tah) f. EE: Dita,
  Edith, Edythe. Ang-Sax. "Rich,
  prosperous." 6 x in DS. 1,
  daughter of King Edgar of 10th
  cen. England, spent life in
  convent. F. 9/16. **Var:** Dita,
  Edith, Editha.
Edith   see **Edita.**
Editha   see **Edita.**
Ediviges   see **Eduvigis.**
Edme   see **Edmundo.**
Edmendo   see **Edmundo.**
Edmida   see **Edmundo.**
Edmiro   see **Edelmira.**
Edmirro   see **Edelmira.**
Edmundo (Ayd moon' doe) m. EE:
  Edmund. Ang-Sax. "Protection of
  property." 4 x in DS. 1, of 12th
  cen. England, Archbishop of
  Canterbury. F. 11/16. **Dim:** Edme,
  Mundo. **Var:** Admundo, Ecmundo,
  Edmendo, Edmida.
Edna (Ayd' nah) f. EE: Edna. Heb.
  "Rejuvenation."
Edolina (Aay doe lee' nah) f. EE:
  Edolina. St. Edo, 6th cen.
  Benedictine monk, bishop of
  Ireland. F. 2/28.
Edonila (Aay doe nee' lah) f. EE:
  Edonila. In myth., Edon another
  name for Minerva.
Edoviga   see **Eduvigis.**
Edoviges   see **Eduvigis.**
Edovijas   see **Eduvigis.**
Edovina   see **Etelvina.**
Edowicea   see **Eduvigis.**
Edowiga   see **Eduvigis.**
Edowigin   see **Eduvigis.**
Edpifania   see **Epifanio.**
Edrardo   see **Eduardo.**
Edrivigen   see **Eduvigis.**
Eduardo (Aay dwahr' doe) m. EE:
  Eddie, Edward, Ned, etc. Ang-
  Sax. "Rich guard." 3 x in DS. 1,
  of 10th cen. England, killed
  unjustly but not mart., S. F.
  3/18. **Dim:** Duardo, Eddy, Edi,
  Edy, Guayo, Huadin, Huayo, Lalo,
  Quiro, Tato, Varito, Yayo. **Var:**
  Ederardo, Edrardo, Eduardus,
  Eduarelo, Eduavida, Eduarada,
  Edwardo, Esduardo, Eudardo,
  Euduarda.
Eduardus   see **Eduardo.**
Eduarelo   see **Eduardo.**
Eduavida   see **Eduardo.**
Eduaviges   see **Eduvigis.**

Edubeahes	see **Eduvigis.**
Edubeges	see **Eduvigis.**
Edubegez	see **Eduvigis.**
Edubehen	see **Eduvigis.**
Edubejon	see **Eduvigis.**
Edubices	see **Eduvigis.**
Edubigen	see **Eduvigis.**
Edubiges	see **Eduvigis.**
Edubigio	see **Eduvigis.**
Edubija	see **Eduvigis.**
Edubije	see **Eduvigis.**
Edubijen	see **Eduvigis.**
Edubijeo	see **Eduvigis.**
Edubijes	see **Eduvigis.**
Edubijio	see **Eduvigis.**
Edubijis	see **Eduvigis.**
Edubina	see **Eduvigis.**
Edubina	see **Etelvina.**
Edubipen	see **Eduvigis.**
Edubiquez	see **Eduvigis.**
Edubises	see **Eduvigis.**
Edubyin	see **Eduvigis.**
Eduigen	see **Eduvigis.**
Eduiges	see **Eduvigis.**
Eduijis	see **Eduvigis.**
Edulfo	see **Adolfo.**
Edumigen	see **Eduvigis.**
Edumigis	see **Eduvigis.**
Edunigis	see **Eduvigis.**

Eduplidio (Aay doo plee' dee oh)
m. EE: Eduplidio. Comb. of
Eduvigis & Elpidio (see both).

Edurada	see **Eduardo.**
Eduriges	see **Eduvigis.**
Edurigis	see **Eduvigis.**
Edurviges	see **Eduvigis.**
Edurviha	see **Eduvigis.**
Eduryes	see **Eduvigis.**
Eduvegen	see **Eduvigis.**
Eduveges	see **Eduvigis.**
Eduvego	see **Eduvigis.**
Eduvejes	see **Eduvigis.**
Eduvejetedo	see **Eduvigis.**
Eduvenza	see **Eduvigis.**
Eduvides	see **Eduvigis.**
Eduvies	see **Eduvigis.**
Eduviga	see **Eduvigis.**
Eduvigas	see **Eduvigis.**
Eduvige	see **Eduvigis.**
Eduvigen	see **Eduvigis.**
Eduviges	see **Eduvigis.**
Eduvigies	see **Eduvigis.**
Eduvigilda	see **Eduvigis.**
Eduvigin	see **Eduvigis.**

Eduvigis (Aay doo bee' hees) f.
EE: Heda, Hedwig. Ger. "Fight,
battle." St. Hedwig, 12th cen.
Duchess of Silesia, took vow of
continency after 6 children. F.
10/17. **Dim:** Duva, Vijes. **Var:**
Davigen, Doveja, Dubijen,
Dubijes, Duvigen, Duvijen,
Duvijes, Duvijos, Duvirgin,
Edevegen, Edevergin, Edeviges,
Ediviges, Edoviga, Edoviges,
Edovijas, Edowicea, Edowiga,
Edowigin, Edrivigen, Eduaviges,
Edubeahes, Edubeges, Edubegez,
Edubehen, Edubejon, Edubices,
Edubigen, Edubiges, Edubigio,
Edubija, Edubije, Edubijen,
Edubijeo, Edubijes, Edubijio,
Edubijis, Edubina, Edubipen,
Edubiquez, Edubises, Edubyin,
Eduigen, Eduiges, Eduijis,
Edumigen, Edumigis, Edunigis,
Eduriges, Edurigis, Edurviges,
Edurviha, Eduryes, Eduvegen,
Eduveges, Eduvego, Eduvejes,
Eduvejetedo, Eduvenza, Eduvides,
Eduvies, Eduviga, Eduvigas,
Eduvige, Eduvigen, Eduviges,
Eduvigies, Eduvigilda, Eduvigin,
Eduvigues, Eduvije, Eduvijes,
Eduvijis, Eduvina, Eduvique,
Eduvjetedo, Eduwige, Eduwigen,
Eduwiges, Eduwigio, Eduwigis,
Eduwijis, Edviges, Edvinges,
Edwifen, Edwige, Edwiger,
Edwiges, Edwigies, Edwigio,
Edwigis, Edwijen, Edwirge,
Edwirges, Edwugen, Eldubigen,
Erubijes, Eruvigen, Eudavigen,
Eudaviges, Eudbigis, Eudivio,
Eudovigen, Eudowiges, Eudubiges,
Euduvigas, Evebejes, Heduvige,
Heduvigen, Heduviges, Heduvigis,
Hedvigen, Hedviges, Hedwigen,
Hedwiges, Hedwigis, Hedwigo,
Hiduviges, Idovigan, Idubigen,
Idubijen, Iduvigen, Ydubiges,
Ydubijes, Yelubiges.

Eduvigues	see **Eduvigis.**
Eduvije	see **Eduvigis.**
Eduvijes	see **Eduvigis.**
Eduvijis	see **Eduvigis.**
Eduvina	see **Eduvigis.**
Eduvique	see **Eduvigis.**
Eduvjetedo	see **Eduvigis.**
Eduwige	see **Eduvigis.**
Eduwigen	see **Eduvigis.**
Eduwiges	see **Eduvigis.**
Eduwigio	see **Eduvigis.**
Eduwigis	see **Eduvigis.**
Eduwijis	see **Eduvigis.**
Edviges	see **Eduvigis.**
Edvina	see **Etelvina.**
Edvinges	see **Eduvigis.**
Edwardo	see **Eduardo.**
Edwifen	see **Eduvigis.**
Edwige	see **Eduvigis.**
Edwiger	see **Eduvigis.**
Edwiges	see **Eduvigis.**
Edwigies	see **Eduvigis.**
Edwigio	see **Eduvigis.**
Edwigis	see **Eduvigis.**
Edwijen	see **Eduvigis.**
Edwirge	see **Eduvigis.**
Edwirges	see **Eduvigis.**
Edwugen	see **Eduvigis.**
Edy	see **Eduardo.**
Eester	see **Ester.**
Efaim	see **Efraín.**
Efanio	see **Epifanio.**
Efelia	see **Ofelio.**
Efenia	see **Ifigenia.**

Eferino (Aay fay ree' no) m. EE:
Eferino. Lat. "Efferus" means
"fierce."

Efern	see **Efraín.**
Effa	see **Ifigenia.**
Effigenia	see **Ifigenia.**
Efibiana	see **Ifigenia.**
Efifania	see **Ifigenia.**
Efigencia	see **Ifigenia.**
Efigeneia	see **Ifigenia.**
Efigenia	see **Ifigenia.**
Efigmenio	see **Epigmenio.**
Efignia	see **Ifigenia.**
Efigonia	see **Ifigenia.**

Efilia   see **Ofelio.**
Efimenia   see **Epigmenio.**
Efizenio   see **Ifigenia.**
Efra   see **Efraín.**
Efraém   see **Efraín.**
Efraén   see **Efraín.**
Efraín (Aay frah een') m. **EE:**
  Ephraem, Ephraim, etc. Heb.
  "Double fruitfulness." Younger
  son of Joseph & founder of
  Ephraemites. 14 x in DS. **Dim:**
  Efra, Juincho, Juncho. **Var;**
  Efaim, Efern, Efraém, Efraén,
  Efraine, Efrallín, Efreín,
  Efrém, Efrén, Efrín, Ephraín,
  Ifraín.
Efraine   see **Efraín.**
Efrallín   see **Efraín.**
Efreín   see **Efraín.**
Efrém   see **Efraín.**
Efrén   see **Efraín.**
Efrín   see **Efraín.**
Efumercio   see **Eufemia.**
Egalantina   see **Eglantina.**
Egedita   see **Egidio.**
Egenia   see **Eugenio.**
Egesipo   see **Egipciacas.**
Egidio (Aay hee' dee oh) m. **EE:**
  Egidius. Lat. "Aegidius," de-
  fender." Patron S. of cripples,
  beggars, & blacksmiths. **Dim:**
  Egedita, Gil.
Eginio   see **Eugenio.**
Eginio   see **Higinio.**
Eginito   see **Eugenio.**
Egino   see **Eugenio.**
Egino   see **Higinio.**
Egipciaca   see **Egipciacas.**
Egipciacas (Aay heep see ah' cahs)
  f? **EE:** Egipciacas. Religious
  order dedicated to Santa María
  Egipciaca. 1 of 2 women who
  refused to obey Pharoah's order
  to strangle all male infants.
  Var: Egesipo, Egipciaca,
  Egipsiaca.
Egipsiaca   see **Egipciacas.**
Eglantina (Aay glahn tee' nah) f.
  EE: Eglantina, Eglantine. Lat.
  "Needle." Mentioned from Chaucer
  to Shakespeare in English poet-
  ry. **Dim:** Eglena. **Var:**
  Egalantina, Eglastina, Eglatina,
  Eglentina, Englantina,
  Englentina, Higlentina,
  Inglantina.
Eglastina   see **Eglantina.**
Eglatina   see **Eglantina.**
Eglena   see **Eglantina.**
Eglentina   see **Eglantina.**
Egnacio   see **Ignacio.**
Ehemia   see **Eufemia.**
Eicadio   see **Arcadio.**
Eifracia   see **Eufracio.**
Einés   see **Inés.**
Eipriana   see **Cipriano.**
Eirasema   see **Iracema.**
Eizabetta   see **Elisabeth.**
Ejelvina   see **Etelvina.**
Ejénaro   see **Génaro.**
Ejinio   see **Eugenio.**
Ejinio   see **Higinio.**
Ejnacia   see **Ignacio.**
Ela (Aay' lah) f? **EE:** Ela.
  Biblically, Ela or Elah, is

valley in which Israelites
camped in war with Philistines.
Elactio (Aay lahk' tee oh) m. **EE:**
  Elactio. In myth., feast cele-
  brated in honor of Elactos, fa-
  vorite of Hercules.
Eladia   see **Heladio.**
Eladis   see **Heladio.**
Elado   see **Heladio.**
Elaina   see **Elena.**
Elaisa   see **Eloiso.**
Elaiso   see **Eleázar.**
Elaiza   see **Eleázar.**
Elaizar   see **Eleázar.**
Elajio   see **Eligio.**
Elalio   see **Eulalio.**
Elanor   see **Eleonor.**
Elario (Aay lah' ree oh) m. **EE:**
  Elario. In myth., Elara mistress
  of Jupiter & mother of Titan.
Elásar   see **Eleázar.**
Elauterio   see **Eleuterio.**
Elázar   see **Eleázar.**
Elba (Ehl' bah) f. **EE:** Elba, Ger.
  "elf"? Island of Napoleon's
  exile.
Elberia   see **Elviro.**
Elbiera   see **Elviro.**
Elbina   see **Albino.**
Elbirio   see **Elviro.**
Elbiro   see **Elviro.**
Elbisa   see **Alviso.**
Elchio   see **Eligio.**
Eldefonso   see **Ildefonso.**
Eldelia   see **Adela.**
Eldifonso   see **Ildefonso.**
Eldiforzo   see **Ildefonso.**
Eldimira   see **Edelmira.**
Eldora   see **Heliodoro.**
Eldubigen   see **Eduvigis.**
Eleadora   see **Heliodoro.**
Eleanore   see **Eleonor.**
Eleanoro   see **Eleonor.**
Eleas   see **Eleázar.**
Eleásar   see **Eleázar.**
Eleázar (Aay lee ah' zahr) m. **EE:**
  Eleazar, Lazarus, etc. Heb. "God
  hath helped." Son of Aaron who
  appears frequently in Talmud.
  Hellenized form is Lazarus. 9 x
  in DS. **Var:** Aliásar, Elaiso,
  Elaiza, Elaízar, Elásar, Elázar,
  Eleas, Eleásar, Eleázor, Eleiso,
  Elénzar, Eleózar, Eleózor,
  Elézar, Elgázar, Eliácer,
  Eliásar, Eliazar, Eliazas,
  Elicerio, Eliécer, Eliéser,
  Eliézar, Eliézer, Eliózar,
  Elisair, Elizar, Elizario,
  Elízer, Elizor, Elizordo,
  Elizur, Elusario, Iliázar. See
  also Lázaro.
Eleázor   see **Eleázar.**
Elebonia (Aay lay bo' nee ah) f.
  EE: Elebonia. Elebouban, mother
  of St. Gonen. Venerated in
  Brittany.
Eleceo   see **Eliseo.**
Electa (Aay lake' tah) f. **EE:**
  Electa, Electus, Elita." Lat.
  "The selected one." V. killed by
  prince madly in love with her.
  F. 8/1.
Electra (Aay lake' trah) f. **EE:**
  Electra. Gk. "The millionth."

Sister of Orestes in Gk. tragedy. Helped him avenge murder of
father by their mother. **Var:**
Alecta, Alectra.

Eledona see **Celedonio.**
Eledoro see **Heliodoro.**
Elegio see **Eligio.**
Elegius see **Eligio.**
Elegria see **Alegra.**
Elehia see **Eligio.**
Elehonor see **Eleonor.**
Eleiso see **Eleázar.**
Elejandra see **Alejandro.**
Elejio see **Eligio.**
Elejo see **Eligio.**
Elejus see **Alejandro.**
Elementro (Aay lay mayn' troe) m.
EE: Elementro. Probably from Sp.
adjective "elemental" meaning
"fundamental or primordial."
Elena (Aay lay' nah) f. **EE:** Ellen,
Helen, etc. Gk. "Brilliant,
resplendent." In Gk. myth. Helen
caused Trojan War. **Dim:** Lena,
Leni, Nélida, Nelly, Nena. **Var:**
Alena, Elaina, Elenina, Elina,
Elleno, Helen, Heleno, Helina,
Hella, Helleno, Hilana, Hileana,
Ileana, Ilene, Iliana. See also
Eleonor, Leonor.
Elenina see **Elena.**
Eleno see **Magdaleno.**
Elenpherio see **Eleuterio.**
Elentaro see **Eleuterio.**
Elentera see **Eleuterio.**
Elenterio see **Eleuterio.**
Elentnio see **Eleuterio.**
Elentoriz see **Eleuterio.**
Elentueria see **Eleuterio.**
Elenzar see **Eleázar.**
Eleocaida see **Leocadia.**
Eleodoro see **Heliodoro.**
Eleonara see **Eleonor.**
Eleonor (Aay lay oh nor') f. **EE:**
Eleonor, Leonor. Gk. "Brilliant,
resplendent." **Dim:** Nora. **Var:**
Elanor, Eleanore, Eleanoro,
Elehonor, Eleonara, Eleonora,
Elianora, Elonor. See also
Elena, Leonor.
Eleonora see **Eleonor.**
Eleosa see **Eloiso.**
Eleozar see **Eleázar.**
Eleozor see **Eleázar.**
Elerio see **Eliberto.**
Eleriterio see **Eleuterio.**
Elesandro see **Alejandro.**
Eleseo see **Alejandro.**
Elesforo see **Telesforo.**
Elesia see **Elisabeth.**
Elesio see **Eliseo.**
Elesteria see **Eleuterio.**
Elestheria see **Eleuterio.**
Elestreria see **Eleuterio.**
Eleterio see **Eleuterio.**
Eleticia see **Leticia.**
Eletisia see **Leticia.**
Eletrerio see **Eleuterio.**
Eleucadio see **Leocadia.**
Eleudero see **Eleuterio.**
Eleutena see **Eleuterio.**
Eleuterio (Aay lay ooh tay' ree
oh) m. **EE:** Eleutherius. Gk.
"Free." 24 x in DS. 1 fought
against Montanism, heresy that

expected the immediate coming of
Judgement Day. **Dim:** Elut, Telio,
Tella, Teyo, Xlut. **Var:**
Elauterio, Elenpherio, Elentaro,
Elentera, Elenterio, Elentnio,
Elentoriz, Elentueria,
Eleriterio, Elesteria,
Elestheria, Elestreria,
Eleterio, Eletrerio, Eleudero,
Eleutena, Eleuterius, Eleuthera,
Eleutherio, Eleutherius,
Eleuthesia, Eleutina, Eleutnera,
Eleutrerio, Eleutrerius,
Eleutresia, Ellusteria,
Eloteria, Elouterio, Elucteria,
Elutario, Elutena, Eluterio,
Elutero, Elutherio, Elutiro,
Elutorio, Elutrerio, Elutrio,
Elutterio, Enluderia, Enluteria,
Eueterio, Eulateria, Eulenteria,
Eulesteria, Euleterio,
Euluterio, Eulutherio.
Eleuterius see **Eleuterio.**
Eleuthera see **Eleuterio.**
Eleutherio see **Eleuterio.**
Eleutherius see **Eleuterio.**
Eleuthesia see **Eleuterio.**
Eleutina see **Eleuterio.**
Eleutnera see **Eleuterio.**
Eleutrerio see **Eleuterio.**
Eleutrerius see **Eleuterio.**
Eleutresia see **Eleuterio.**
Eleveo (Aay lay bay' oh) m. **EE:**
Eleveo. Lat. "Elevare," "to put
one in position of honor."
Eleverio (Aay lay bay' ree oh) m.
EE: Eleverio. Elevaria, 3rd cen.
Fr. S.
Eleverto see **Herberto.**
Elevino see **Albino.**
Elevira see **Elviro.**
Elexis see **Alejandro.**
Elezabeth see **Elisabeth.**
Elezar see **Eleázar.**
Elfego (Ehl fay' go) m. **EE:**
Alphege, Elphege. Ger. "Tall
elf." 2 x in DS. 1, of 10th cen.
England, was tortured & axed by
Danes. F. 4/19. **Dim:** Fego. **Var:**
Elfigo.
Elfido (Ehl fee' doe) m. **EE:**
Elfido. Ger. "From the race of
elves."
Elfigo see **Elfego.**
Elfina (Ehl fee' nah) f. **EE:**
Elfina. In myth., wife of an
elf.
Elfrida (Ehl free' dah) f. **EE:**
Elfrida. Teut. "Edelfrido," "he
who obtains a noble peace." V. &
M. F. 12/8. **Var:** Eliofredo.
Elfridio see **Alfredo.**
Elfriede see **Alfredo.**
Elga see **Helga.**
Elgario see **Olegario.**
Elgazar see **Eleázar.**
Eliácer see **Eleázar.**
Eliácim (Aay lee ah' seem) m. **EE:**
Eliakim. Heb. "God establishes."
5 x in Bible, 1 an ancestor of
Christ. **Var:** Eliáscim, Eliázim.
Eliadora see **Heliodoro.**
Elianora see **Eleonor.**
Elías (Aay lee' ahs) m. **EE:**
Elijah. Heb. "My name is

Yahweh." OT prophet. 36 x in DS. 1 lived in cave for 70 years. F. 1/18. **Dim:** Lincha. **Var:** Eliaz.

Eliásar   see **Eleázar.**
Eliáscim   see **Eliácim.**
Eliaz   see **Elías.**
Eliazar   see **Eleázar.**
Eliazas   see **Eleázar.**
Eliázim   see **Eliácim.**
Elibaria   see **Olivo.**
Eliberio   see **Olivo.**
Elibertam   see **Alberto.**
Eliberto   see **Alberto.**
Eliberto   see **Herberto.**
Eliberto (Aay lee behr' toe) m.
   EE: Eliberto. Comb. of any name
   beginning with "Eli" & "Berto"
   (see). **Var:** Elerio.
Elibrada   see **Liberato.**
Eliceo   see **Eliseo.**
Elicerio   see **Eleázar.**
Elichio   see **Eligio.**
Elicio   see **Alicio.**
Elidam (Aay lee' dam) m. **EE:**
   Elidam, Patron of Welch church.
   F. 2/16.
Elide   see **Elido.**
Elidio   see **Elido.**
Elido (Aay lee' doe) m. **EE:** Elido.
   Region in Peloponnesus. **Var:**
   Aleida, Alidia, Alido, Elide,
   Elidio, Elita, Elydia, Helida,
   Helidio, Helita.
Elidor   see **Heliodoro.**
Elidoro   see **Heliodoro.**
Elidubina   see **Ludovino.**
Eliécer   see **Eleázar.**
Eliedoro   see **Heliodoro.**
Eliegio   see **Eligio.**
Eliéser   see **Eleázar.**
Eliézar   see **Eleázar.**
Eliézer   see **Eleázar.**
Elifaz (Aay lee' faz) m. **EE:**
   Eliphaz. Heb. "God is strong."
   Son of Esau, by Adah.
Elifonsi   see **Alfonso.**
Elifonso   see **Alfonso.**
Eligeo   see **Eligio.**
Eligeria   see **Eligio.**
Eliginus   see **Eligio.**
Eligio (Aay lee' hee oh) m. **EE:**
   Eligius, Eloi. Lat. "The elect."
   3 x in DS. 1 of most popular Ss.
   of France, 7th cen. minter &
   goldsmith. F. 12/1. **Var:** Elajio,
   Elchio, Elegio, Elegius, Elehia,
   Elejio, Elejo, Elichio, Eliegio,
   Eligeo, Eligeria, Eliginus,
   Eliguio, Elijao, Elijio, Elijo,
   Elique, Eliquio, Elixio, Elohim,
   Elohima, Eloi, Eloy, Eloya,
   Eloyae. See also Eloina.
Eliguio   see **Eligio.**
Elijabeth   see **Elisabeth.**
Elijandro   see **Alejandro.**
Elijao   see **Eligio.**
Elijio   see **Eligio.**
Elijo   see **Eligio.**
Eliloria   see **Heliodoro.**
Elina   see **Elena.**
Elinandro   see **Alejandro.**
Elio   see **Helio.**
Eliodoria   see **Heliodoro.**
Eliodoro   see **Heliodoro.**
Eliofredo   see **Elfrida.**

Eliózar   see **Eleázar.**
Elpidio   see **Elpidio.**
Elipio   see **Alipio.**
Elipio (Aay lee' pee oh) m. **EE:**
   Elipio, Eliphius, 4th cen. Fr.
   M. F. 10/16.
Elique   see **Eligio.**
Eliquio   see **Eligio.**
Elisabel   see **Elisabeth.**
Elisabel   see **Isabel.**
Elisabertha   see **Elisabeth.**
Elisabet   see **Elisabeth.**
Elisabeth (Aay lee sah bet') f.
   EE: Betty, Elizabeth, etc. Heb.
   "Consecrated to God." 17 x in
   DS. 1, 12th cen. Ger. mystic,
   had visions & suffered cheer-
   fully for entire life. F. 6/18.
   Dim: Besi, Beti, Betsi, Elesia,
   Elisas (Elisa), Eliso, Elissa,
   Elizio, Elliza, Elsa, Elsi, Isa,
   Lezith, Licha, Lisa, Lisbet,
   Liseta, Lisias, Liza, Nena. **Var:**
   Eizabetta, Elezabeth, Elijabeth,
   Elisabel, Elisabertha, Elisabet,
   Elisitha, Elixabet, Elixabeth,
   Elizabé, Elizaberta, Elizabet,
   Elizabetha, Elsabet, Erlisa,
   Lizebeth. See also Isabel.
Elisaeo   see **Eliseo.**
Elisaeus   see **Eliseo.**
Elisair   see **Eleázar.**
Elisandre   see **Alejandro.**
Elisandro   see **Alejandro.**
Elisas   see **Elisabeth.**
Elisaso   see **Eliseo.**
Eliseo (Aay lee say' oh) m. **EE:**
   Elisha, Ellis, etc. Heb. "God is
   my health or salvation." Ap-
   pointed by God to succeed
   Elijah. 9 x in DS. **Dim:** Cheo,
   Cheyo, Licha. **Var:** Eleceo,
   Elesio, Eliceo, Elisaeo,
   Elisaeus, Elisaso, Eliseus,
   Elisino, Elisio, Elisius,
   Elizeo, Elsaeo, Elseo, Elysiuio,
   Heliceo.
Eliserio   see **Glicerio.**
Eliseus   see **Eliseo.**
Elisino   see **Eliseo.**
Elisio   see **Eliseo.**
Elisitha   see **Elisabeth.**
Elisius   see **Eliseo.**
Eliso   see **Elisabeth.**
Elisodoro (Aay lee so doe' roe) m.
   EE: Elisodoro. Comb. of Eliseo &
   Isodoro (see both)?
Elisondro   see **Alejandro.**
Elissa   see **Elisabeth.**
Elissa   see **Isabel.**
Elissandro   see **Alejandro.**
Elistasia   see **Eustacio.**
Elita   see **Elido.**
Eliud (Aay lee ood') m. **EE:** Eliud.
   In Scan. myth., Palace of Mis-
   ery, abode of Hela. **Var:** Eliuhd.
Eliuhd   see **Eliud.**
Elivara   see **Olivo.**
Elivera   see **Olivo.**
Eliverio   see **Olivo.**
Elivia   see **Olivo.**
Elivo   see **Olivo.**
Elixabet   see **Elisabeth.**
Elixabeth   see **Elisabeth.**
Elixandro   see **Alejandro.**

Elixio	see **Eligio.**
Elixsandro	see **Alejandro.**
Elizabé	see **Elisabeth.**
Elizabé	see **Isabel.**
Elizaberta	see **Elisabeth.**
Elizabet	see **Elisabeth.**
Elizabetha	see **Elisabeth.**
Elizanda	see **Alejandro.**
Elizandro	see **Alejandro.**
Elizar	see **Eleázar.**
Elizario	see **Eleázar.**
Elizeo	see **Eliseo.**
Elizer	see **Eleázar.**
Elizio	see **Elisabeth.**
Elizondro	see **Alejandro.**
Elizor	see **Eleázar.**
Elizordo	see **Eleázar.**
Elizur	see **Eleázar.**
Elladoro	see **Heliodoro.**
Ellego	see **Alejandro.**
Elleno	see **Elena.**
Ellicia	see **Alicio.**
Elliza	see **Elisabeth.**
Ellusteria	see **Eleuterio.**
Elmar	see **Erasmo.**
Elmiro	see **Edelmira.**
Elmo	see **Erasmo.**
Elnira	see **Edelmira.**
Elo	see **Consuelo.**
Elocadia	see **Leocadia.**
Elocario	see **Eucario.**
Elochio	see **Eulogio.**
Elocio	see **Eloiso.**
Elodea	see **Elodio.**
Elodina	see **Elodio.**

Elodio (Aay low' dee oh) m. **EE:** Elodie. Gk. "Shore, plain, marsh." **Dim:** Lodia. **Var:** Alodio, Elodea, Elodina, Elopia, Erodio.

Eloesa	see **Eloiso.**
Elofonsa	see **Ildefonso.**
Elogario	see **Olegario.**
Elogio	see **Eulogio.**
Elogium	see **Eulogio.**
Elogonia	see **Eulogio.**
Elohia	see **Eulogio.**
Elohim	see **Eligio.**
Elohima	see **Eligio.**
Eloi	see **Eligio.**

Eloina (Aay low ee' nah) f. **EE:** Eloine. From Eloy, "selected one." See also Eligio.

Eloisal	see **Eloiso.**
Eloisca	see **Eloiso.**

Eloiso (Aay low ee' so) m. **EE:** Eloise, Heloise, etc. Ger. "Hale, complete." Lover of Abelard, 12th cen. Fr. scholar, castrated by Heloise's uncle. **Dim:** Chocha, Guichi, Licha, Locha, Lochi, Lucha. **Var:** Elaisa, Eleosa, Elocio, Eloesa, Eloisal, Eloisca, Eloiza, Elosa, Elosio, Eloysa, Eloysae, Eloyza, Elozio, Eluisio, Eluysa, Elysa, Heloisa, Hilosia. See also Luis.

Eloiza	see **Eloiso.**
Elojio	see **Eulogio.**
Elonides	see **Leonides.**
Elonor	see **Eleonor.**
Elopia	see **Elodio.**
Elopoldo	see **Leopoldo.**
Eloquio	see **Eulogio.**
Elosa	see **Eloiso.**
Elosio	see **Eloiso.**

Eloteria	see **Eleuterio.**
Elouterio	see **Eleuterio.**
Eloy	see **Eligio.**
Eloya	see **Eligio.**
Eloyadio	see **Heladio.**
Eloyae	see **Eligio.**
Eloysa	see **Eloiso.**
Eloysae	see **Eloiso.**
Eloyza	see **Eloiso.**
Elozio	see **Eloiso.**
Elpavio	see **Elpidio.**
Elpedeo	see **Elpidio.**
Elpedio	see **Elpidio.**
Elpedro	see **Elpidio.**
Elpichia	see **Elpidio.**
Elpideo	see **Elpidio.**

Elpidio (Ehl pee' dee oh) m. **EE:** Elpidius. Gk. "Hope." 15 x in DS. 1 dragged by wild horse & burned at stake in 4th cen. F. 11/15. **Var:** Alpedo, Alpidio, Elipidio, Elpavio, Elpedeo, Elpedio, Elpedro, Elpichia, Elpideo, Elpido, Elpidro, Elpigia, Elpio, Elpiodea, Elpitio, Elpodio, Epedia, Epidia, Epidión, Opidio, Upidio.

Elpido	see **Elpidio.**
Elpidro	see **Elpidio.**
Elpigia	see **Elpidio.**
Elpio	see **Elpidio.**
Elpiodea	see **Elpidio.**
Elpitio	see **Elpidio.**
Elpodio	see **Elpidio.**
Elsa	see **Elisabeth.**
Elsa	see **Isabel.**
Elsabet	see **Elisabeth.**
Elsaeo	see **Eliseo.**
Elsandro	see **Alejandro.**
Elseo	see **Eliseo.**
Elsi	see **Elisabeth.**
Eluadio	see **Eulalio.**

Eluanita (Aay loo ah nee' tah) f. **EE:** Lugidianus. Eluane, disciple of Joseph of Arimathea in 2nd cen. Palestine.

Elucteria	see **Eleuterio.**
Elud	see **Eludio.**

Eludio (Aay loo' dee oh) m. **EE:** Eludio. Lat. "Eludere," "to flee from difficulty." **Var:** Elud, Eluid.

Elugarda	see **Ludgarda.**
Elugio	see **Eulogio.**
Eluid	see **Eludio.**
Eluisio	see **Eloiso.**
Elulalia	see **Eulalio.**

Elura (Aay loo' rah) f. **EE:** Elura. Eluro, Egyp. divinity depicted as cat.

Elusario	see **Eleázar.**
Elustacia	see **Eustacio.**
Elut	see **Eleuterio.**
Elutario	see **Eleuterio.**
Elutena	see **Eleuterio.**
Eluterio	see **Eleuterio.**
Elutero	see **Eleuterio.**
Elutherio	see **Eleuterio.**
Elutiro	see **Eleuterio.**
Elutorio	see **Eleuterio.**
Elutrerio	see **Eleuterio.**
Elutrio	see **Eleuterio.**
Elutterio	see **Eleuterio.**
Eluvidina	see **Ludovino.**
Eluvina	see **Ludovino.**

Eluysa   see **Eloiso.**
Elvanelia   see **Evangelina.**
Elvara   see **Albaro.**
Elveira   see **Elviro.**
Elvenia (Ehl bay' nee ah) f. **EE:**
Elvenia. Elvina in Gk. myth. was
1 of epithets of Ceres.
Elvera   see **Elviro.**
Elveria   see **Elviro.**
Elvia (Ehl' bee ah) f. **EE:** Elvas,
Elvia. Lat. "Helvia." "variety
of yellow." Teut. "Elf"? **Var:**
Elvias.
Elvias   see **Elvia.**
Elvire   see **Elviro.**
Elvirea   see **Elviro.**
Elviri   see **Elviro.**
Elviria   see **Elviro.**
Elviro (Ehl bee' roe) m. **EE:**
Albinia, Alva, Elvira, Ger.
"Amiable, friendly." Lat.
"Albus," "white"? **Dim:** Evia,
Vila, Virucha, Vivita. **Var:**
Albira, Alvirra, Alvirum,
Elberia, Elbiera, Elbirio,
Elbiro, Elevira, Elveira,
Elvera, Elveria, Elvire,
Elvirea, Elviri, Elviria,
Elvirra, Evira, Ilvira.
Elvirra   see **Elviro.**
Elvisa (Ehl bee' sah) f. **EE:**
Elvisa. Beatified 11th cen.
benefactress of church. **Var:**
Elviza. See also Eloisa.
Elviza   see **Elvisa.**
Elydia   see **Elido.**
Elysa   see **Eloiso.**
Elysiuio   see **Eliseo.**
Ema   see **Emma.**
Emala   see **Amalio.**
Emalia   see **Amalio.**
Emalinda   see **Emma.**
Emalo   see **Emma.**
Emana (Aay mah' nah) f. **EE:** Emana.
Probably Lat. "emanere" meaning
"to come forth, to radiate."
Emancio   see **Amancio.**
Emancipación (Aay mahn' see pah
see own') f. **EE:** Emancipation.
Lat. "Act or process of setting
free."
Emando   see **Amanda.**
Emannela   see **Manuel.**
Emanuel   see **Manuel.**
Emanuelem   see **Manuel.**
Emanuelis   see **Manuel.**
Emanuelo   see **Manuel.**
Emaro   see **Amaranto.**
Emasa (Aay mah' sah) f. **EE:** Emasa.
Emasia, S. & M. F. 7/17.
Ematario   see **Emeterio.**
Embrocio   see **Ambrosio.**
Emedalio   see **Imelda.**
Emedina   see **Henedina.**
Emegirio   see **Hermenegildo.**
Emeldo   see **Imelda.**
Emelerio   see **Emereo.**
Emelesio   see **Emerenciana.**
Emeliano   see **Emma.**
Emelie   see **Emilio.**
Emelina   see **Emilio.**
Emelinda   see **Emilio.**
Emelinda   see **Emma.**
Emelino   see **Emma.**
Emelio   see **Emilio.**

Emelizio   see **Emilio.**
Emelo   see **Emilio.**
Emenchilda   see **Hermenegildo.**
Emencio   see **Emerenciana.**
Emenecia   see **Emerenciana.**
Emenegildo   see **Hermenegildo.**
Emenesio   see **Emerenciana.**
Emengeldo   see **Hermenegildo.**
Emensio   see **Emerenciana.**
Emenziana   see **Emerenciana.**
Emerado   see **Esmeralda.**
Emeraldo   see **Esmeralda.**
Emeranbiana (Aay may rahn bee ah'
nah) f. **EE:** Emeranbiana. St.
Emerano of 7th cen. mart. in
Rome. F. 9/22.
Emerenciana   see **Emerenciana.**
Emercio   see **Emerenciana.**
Emerdina   see **Emereo.**
Emeregilde   see **Hermenegildo.**
Emeregildo   see **Hermenegildo.**
Emereida   see **Emereo.**
Emerejildo   see **Hermenegildo.**
Emerenciana (Aay may rehn see ah'
nah) f. **EE:** Merrit, Merritt.
Lat. "Emerentius," "worthy of
merit." 2 x in DS. 1, foster
sister of St. Agnes, stoned to
death while praying. F. 1/23.
Var: Emelesio, Emencio,
Emenecia, Emenesio, Emensio,
Emenziana, Emeranciana, Emercio,
Emerentiannae, Emerio,
Emeronsia, Eminencio,
Emrenciona, Encemencia,
Enerenciana, Enimencio,
Enomencio, Eremencio, Ermencia,
Esmerenciana, Merenciano,
Merensiana, Merenza. See also
Emereo.
Emerentiannae see **Emerenciana.**
Emereo (Aay may' ray oh) m. **EE:**
Emerito, Merritt, etc. Lat.
"Worthy of merit." 13 x in DS.
1, sister of St. Digna & M. of
3rd cen. Rome, hanged by hair &
then torched. F. 9/22. **Var:**
Emelerio, Emerdina, Emereida,
Emerita, Enerito, Hemerio,
Hemero. See also Emerenciana.
Emergildo   see **Hermenegildo.**
Emerico (Aay may ree' co) m. **EE:**
Emerio. Goth. "Powerful for his
cattle." Son of St. Stephen, of
11th cen. Hungary, led a pure
life. F. 11/4. See also Américo.
Emerio   see **Emerenciana.**
Emerita   see **Emereo.**
Emeritano   see **Emeterio.**
Emeronsia   see **Emerenciana.**
Emesias   see **Nemesio.**
Emestina (Aay may stee' nah) f.
EE: Emestina. Emesa, city in
Phoenicia (Lebanon) where many
Christian women were mart. by
Arabs.
Emetario   see **Emeterio.**
Emetena   see **Emeterio.**
Emetercio   see **Emeterio.**
Emeterico   see **Emeterio.**
Emeterio (Aay may tay' ree oh) m.
EE: Emeterius, Emetherius. Lat.
"Half-fierce." 2 x in DS. Both
beheaded in Spain in 5th cen. F.
3/3. **Dim:** Teyo. **Var:** Ameteria,

Ematario, Emeritano, Emetario,
Emetena, Emetercio, Emeterico,
Emetia, Emetirio, Emetrio,
Emetterio, Emiferia, Emisteria,
Emitaria, Emiterial, Emiterio,
Emitezio, Eniterio, Eniterius,
Hemeterio, Hemiterio, Meterio,
Miterica, Miterio, Ometerio,
Omiterio.

Emetia	see Emeterio.
Emetirio	see Emeterio.
Emetrio	see Emeterio.
Emetterio	see Emeterio.
Emictio	see Emigdio.
Emidio	see Emigdio.
Emielo	see Emilio.
Emifanio	see Eufemia.
Emiferia	see Emeterio.

Emigdio (Aay meeg' dee oh) m. EE:
Emygdius. 4th cen. bishop of
Ascoli, Italy. F. 8/5. **Var:**
Emictio, Emidio, Emizdo, Emylid,
Enigdio, Ermidio.

Emileo	see Emilio.
Emilerio	see Emilio.
Emiliano	see Emilio.

Emilio (Aay mee' lee oh) m. EE:
Emil, Emile, etc. Lat. "Aemili-
us" Roman family name. 3 differ-
ent sources claim it means
"amiable," "swollen," or "indus-
trious." **Dim:** Emelina, Lila
(Amelia), Llillo, Melo, Mili,
Miliquis, Milo, Mimila, Miyo.
Var: Aemiliano, Aemilio,
Aemilius, Emelie, Emelinda,
Emelio, Emelizio, Emelo, Emielo,
Emileo, Emilerio, Emiliano,
Emilium, Emilla, Emilono,
Emolio, Eniliano, Hemelia,
Hemilio, Hemilo, Imelio,
Imilina, Milana, Miliana,
Millan. See also Amalio,
Maximiliano.

Emilium	see Emilio.
Emilla	see Emilio.
Emilono	see Emilio.
Eminencio	see Emerenciana.
Emiquita	see Emma.
Emirito	see Emma.
Emisteria	see Emeterio.
Emitaria	see Emeterio.
Emiterial	see Emeterio.
Emiterio	see Emeterio.
Emitezio	see Emeterio.
Emitia	see Emma.
Emizdo	see Emigdio.

Emma (Aay' mah) f. EE: Emma. Teut.
"Grandmother." 2 x in DS. **Dim:**
Chema, Emiquita, Linda, Mema,
Mita, Neneca, Nuela. **Var:** Ema,
Emalinda, Emalo, Emeliano,
Emelinda, Emelino, Emirito,
Emitia, Emmaline.

Emmaline	see Emma.
Emmanuel	see Manuel.
Emmanuela	see Manuel.
Emmanuelae	see Manuel.
Emmanuelem	see Manuel.
Emmanuelis	see Manuel.
Emolio	see Emilio.
Emoreigilda	see Hermenegildo.

Emosita (Aay mo see' tah) f? EE:
Emosita. In myth. Emo was son
of Boreas, changed into mountain
for taking name Jupiter.

Emparo	see Amparo.
Empiria	see Imperio.
Emrenciona	see Emerenciana.
Emriliddo	see Hermenegildo.
Emylid	see Emigdio.
Enacasio	see Acacio.
Enacio	see Ignacio.
Enangelina	see Evangelina.
Enaro	see Genaro.
Enascia	see Ignacio.
Enass	see Inés.
Encamacijer	see Encarnación.
Encamacin	see Encarnación.
Encamación	see Encarnación.
Encanación	see Encarnación.
Encaña	see Encarnación.
Encaración	see Encarnación.
Encaranción	see Encarnación.
Encarción	see Encarnación.
Encarencia	see Encarnación.
Encarmación	see Encarnación.
Encarnaci	see Encarnación.
Encarnació	see Encarnación.

Encarnación (Ehn cahr nah' see
own') f. EE: Incarnate. Mystical
name meaning "Word became
flesh." Union of 2nd person of
Trinity with human nature, i.e.,
Christ. F. 3/25. **Dim:** Canacho,
Caña, Chachona, Chonelo,
Chonita, Chono, Encaña, Tonsa.
Var: Carmación, Carnación,
Cuncarnación, Ecarnación,
Encamacijer, Encamacin,
Encamación, Encanación,
Encaración, Encaranción,
Encarción, Encarencia,
Encarmación, Encarnaci,
Encarnació, Encarnadión,
Encarnasión, Encarnción,
Encarnsción, Encarnsión,
Encernación, Encranción,
Incanción, Incarción,
Incarnacién, Incarnació,
Incarnación, Incarnatió,
Incarnationis, Incarnazión,
Incarnoció, Inccarnación,
Incornación, Yncarnación.

Encarnadión	see Encarnación.
Encarnasión	see Encarnación.
Encarnción	see Encarnación.
Encarnsción	see Encarnación.
Encarnsión	see Encarnación.
Encelata	see Anacleto.
Encemencia	see Emerenciana.
Encernación	see Encarnación.
Encranción	see Encarnación.
Endalesio	see Indalecio.
Endelencia	see Indalecio.
Endelesio	see Indalecio.
Endina	see Enedina.
Endomitila	see Domitilo.

Endoro (Ehn doe' roe) m. EE:
Endor, Endora. In myth. Endora
was 1 of Hiadas, daughters of
Atlas & Ethra.

Endovico (Ehn doe bee' co) m. EE:
Endovico. Endovelico, 1 of 13
indigenous Iberian gods.

| Endrigueta | see Enrique. |
| Endriqueta | see Enrique. |

Eneas (Aay nay' ahs) m. EE:
Aeneas. Possibly "praised one."
Trojan prince who went from Troy

to Carthage & met Dido.
Adventures comprise "Aeneid."
Descendants founded Rome. See
also Eneida.

Eneco   see **Ignacio.**
Enedelio (Aay nay day' lee oh) m.
    Comb. of Ana & Adela (see both).
Enedena   see **Enedina.**
Enedia   see **Enedina.**
Enedida   see **Enedina.**
Enedina (Aay nay dee' nah) f. EE:
    Heneldina. Gk. "To be agree-
    able." M. & patroness of Sta.
    Giusta (Sardinia). F. 5/14. **Var:**
    Endina, Enedena, Enedia,
    Enedida, Enediora, Enedria,
    Inedina.
Enediora   see **Enedina.**
Enedria   see **Enedina.**
Eneida (Aay nay' dah) f. EE:
    Eneida. From "Eneas" (see),
    eponymous hero of "Aeneid." His
    descendants founded Rome. **Var:**
    Enereida, Enerida, Enerieda. See
    also Eneas.
Enelda   see **Imelda.**
Enemacia   see **Nemesio.**
Enemancio   see **Nemesio.**
Enemario   see **Nemesio.**
Enemartius   see **Nemesio.**
Enemcencio   see **Nemesio.**
Enemecio   see **Nemesio.**
Enememcio   see **Nemesio.**
Enemencio   see **Nemesio.**
Enemención   see **Nemesio.**
Enemenia   see **Nemesio.**
Enemensio   see **Nemesio.**
Enemenso   see **Nemesio.**
Enementio   see **Nemesio.**
Enemenzia   see **Nemesio.**
Enemesis   see **Nemesio.**
Enemica   see **Nemesio.**
Enemicia   see **Nemesio.**
Enemincio   see **Nemesio.**
Enemisio   see **Nemesio.**
Enemorio   see **Nemesio.**
Enemsio   see **Nemesio.**
Enenencia   see **Nemesio.**
Enenesio   see **Nemesio.**
Enequia   see **Ignacio.**
Enera   see **Genaro.**
Enereida   see **Eneida.**
Enerenciana   see **Emerenciana.**
Enereo   see **Genaro.**
Enerida   see **Eneida.**
Enerieda   see **Eneida.**
Enerina (Aay nay ree' nah) f. EE:
    Enerina. Enero, Sicilian M. F.
    10/11.
Enerito   see **Emereo.**
Enés   see **Inés.**
Enesenico   see **Inocencio.**
Enester   see **Néstor.**
Enez   see **Inés.**
Enezz   see **Inés.**
Enfiania (Ehn fee ah' nee ah) f.
    EE: Enfiania. Lat. "En" & "fian"
    meaning "have faith in someone."
Enfranio   see **Anfanio.**
Engelina   see **Evangelina.**
Engelita   see **Angel.**
Engemia   see **Engenio.**
Engenio (Ehn hay' nee oh) m. EE:
    Ingenious. Lat. "Ingenio,"
    "ability to discover or invent

with facility." **Var:** Engemia,
Engenirmo, Eugenimo.

Engenirmo   see **Engenio.**
Englantina   see **Eglantina.**
Englentina   see **Eglantina.**
Engracia (Ehn grah' see ah) f. EE:
    Grace, Gracienne, etc. Lat. "In
    gratia," "one who is in the
    Lord's grace." **Dim:** Gacho, Ique,
    Quico, Quicolín, Quique. **Var:**
    Engrahia, Eugracia, Gracia. See
    also Graciela.
Engrahia   see **Engracia.**
Enicasio   see **Nicasio.**
Enicencio   see **Inocencio.**
Enicleto   see **Anacleto.**
Enidena (Aay nee day' nah) f. EE:
    Enidena. Could be form of St.
    Enedina, 2nd cen. M. of Cerdena,
    Italy. **Var:** Ennedín.
Enigdio   see **Emigdio.**
Eniguetta   see **Enrique.**
Eniliano   see **Emilio.**
Enimencio   see **Emerenciana.**
Enise   see **Anisio.**
Eniterio   see **Emeterio.**
Eniterius   see **Emeterio.**
Enlogio   see **Eulogio.**
Enluderia   see **Eleuterio.**
Enluteria   see **Eleuterio.**
Ennedín   see **Enidena.**
Enoc (Aay noke') m. EE: Enoch,
    Hanoch. Heb. "The dedicated."
    Biblically, progenitor of Methu-
    selah. Also, 1st cen. monk of
    Mt. Carmel. F. 7/7. **Var:** Enox,
    Henoch.
Enocencio   see **Inocencio.**
Enocente   see **Inocencio.**
Enoelia   see **Onelia.**
Enoema   see **Noemí.**
Enomencio   see **Emerenciana.**
Enosencia   see **Inocencio.**
Enova   see **Genoveva.**
Enoveva   see **Genoveva.**
Enox   see **Enoc.**
Enregueta   see **Enrique.**
Enrequeta   see **Enrique.**
Enrequette   see **Enrique.**
Enrerita   see **Enrique.**
Enrica   see **Enrique.**
Enricelta   see **Enrique.**
Enriceta   see **Enrique.**
Enricetta   see **Enrique.**
Enrichera   see **Enrique.**
Enrigque   see **Enrique.**
Enrigua   see **Enrique.**
Enrigue   see **Enrique.**
Enrigueta   see **Enrique.**
Enriguetta   see **Enrique.**
Enriprieta   see **Enrique.**
Enriqua   see **Enrique.**
Enrique (Ehn ree' kay) m. EE:
    Hank, Harry, Henry, etc. Ger.
    "Ruler of private property." 16
    x in DS. 1, Ger. king & Holy
    Roman Emperor of 10th cen. F.
    7/15. **Dim:** Ico, Kiki, Kiko,
    Queta (Enriqueta), Quetita
    (Enriqueta), Quico, Quinto,
    Quique, Quiqui, Riqueta
    (Enriqueta). **Var:** Andrikes,
    Andrique, Anniqueta, Anrique,
    Endrigueta, Endriqueta,
    Eniguetta, Enregueta, Enrequeta,

Enrequette, Enrerita, Enrica,
Enricelta, Enriceta, Enricetta,
Enrichera, Enrigque, Enrigua,
Enrigue, Enriguela, Enriguetta,
Enriprieta, Enriqua, Enriquel,
Enriquela, Enriquerta, Enriques,
Enriqueta, Enriquete,
Enriquetta, Enriquita,
Enriqurta, Enriteria, Enrrique,
Erreka, Eurique, Euriqueta,
Henerequeta, Henrequeta,
Henrequetta, Henrice, Henrico,
Henricum, Henricus, Henriella,
Henrieta, Henrignetta,
Henrigueta, Henriko, Henriqua,
Henriquetta, Herarique,
Inriques.

Enriquel	see **Enrique.**
Enriquela	see **Enrique.**
Enriquerta	see **Enrique.**
Enriques	see **Enrique.**
Enriqueta	see **Enrique.**
Enriquete	see **Enrique.**
Enriquetta	see **Enrique.**
Enriquita	see **Enrique.**
Enriqurta	see **Enrique.**
Enriteria	see **Enrique.**
Enrrique	see **Enrique.**
Ensebino	see **Eusebio.**
Ensebins	see **Eusebio.**
Ensebio	see **Eusebio.**
Enselao	see **Venceslao.**
Enselmo	see **Anselmo.**
Enseve	see **Eusebio.**
Entimio	see **Eutimia.**
Entiquia	see **Eutiquio.**

Enula (Aay noo' lah) f. **EE:** Enula.
Vivid plant. **Var:** Enuleo,
Enuliana.

Enuleo	see **Enula.**
Enuliana	see **Enula.**

Enviso (En bee' so) m. **EE:** Enviso.
Lat. "En" & "visus" meaning
"sagacious or astute."

Enzelma	see **Anselmo.**
Eoclorio	see **Euclides.**
Eodelia	see **Odilia.**
Eofelia	see **Ofelio.**
Eofilia	see **Ofelio.**
Eofracio	see **Eufracio.**
Eolivia	see **Olivo.**
Eololio	see **Eulalio.**
Eostacio	see **Eustacio.**
Eotavio	see **Octavio.**
Epatisio	see **Epitacio.**
Epectación	see **Expectación.**
Epedia	see **Elpidio.**
Epefanio	see **Epifanio.**
Epefina	see **Epifanio.**
Epegmenio	see **Epigmenio.**
Epeigmenio	see **Epigmenio.**

Epelmiro (Aay pehl mee' roe) m.
EE: Epelmiro. Comb. of Epimencia
& Adelmiro (see both).

Epelonia	see **Apolonio.**
Epemencio	see **Epigmenio.**
Epeminio	see **Epigmenio.**
Epephania	see **Epifanio.**
Epetación	see **Epitacio.**
Epfanio	see **Epifanio.**
Epfifaria	see **Epifanio.**
Epfinio	see **Epifanio.**
Ephefania	see **Epifanio.**
Ephenio	see **Epifanio.**
Ephepania	see **Epifanio.**

Ephiamia	see **Epifanio.**
Ephifanio	see **Epifanio.**
Ephilia	see **Ofelio.**
Ephiphania	see **Epifanio.**
Ephrain	see **Efrain.**
Epi	see **Epifanio.**
Epi	see **Epigmenio.**
Epi	see **Epimaco.**
Epi	see **Epitacio.**
Epicinencio	see **Epigmenio.**
Epicmenio	see **Epigmenio.**

Epidano (Aay pee dah' no) m. **EE:**
Epidano. In myth. Epidamnio,
father of nymph of Venus' court.

Epidasio	see **Epitacio.**
Epidia	see **Elpidio.**
Epidion	see **Elpidio.**

Epidus (Aay pee' doos) m? **EE:**
Epidus. Could be from "Oedipus,"
son & husband of Jocasta in
Sophocles' "Oedipus Rex."

Epifabio	see **Epifanio.**
Epifacina	see **Epifanio.**
Epifacio	see **Epitacio.**
Epifaima	see **Epifanio.**
Epifaina	see **Epifanio.**
Epifamin	see **Epifanio.**
Epifamio	see **Epifanio.**
Epifán	see **Epifanio.**
Epifancio	see **Epifanio.**
Epifanco	see **Epifanio.**
Epifaneo	see **Epifanio.**
Epifanessio	see **Epifanio.**
Epifani	see **Epifanio.**

Epifanio (Aay pee fah' nee oh) m.
EE: Epiphanius, Tiffany. Gk.
"Manifestation." Relates to
Epiphany, Christian feast that
commemorates 3 events: visit of
3 wise men, baptism of Jesus, &
miracle at Cana. F. 1/6. 11 x in
DS. **Dim:** Pifania, Pifano. **Var:**
Apifanio, Edifanio, Edpifania,
Efanio, Epefanio, Epefina,
Epephania, Epfanio, Epfifania,
Epfinio, Ephefania, Ephenio,
Ephepania, Ephiamia, Ephifanio,
Ephiphania, Epi, Epifabio,
Epifacina, Epifaima, Epifaina,
Epifamin, Epifamio, Epifán,
Epifancio, Epifanco, Epifaneo,
Epifanessio, Epifani, Epifanis,
Epifano, Epifario, Epifarus,
Epifasio, Epifhanio, Epifia,
Epifina, Epifinia, Epifmenio,
Epifona, Epifonio, Epifornio,
Epifphanio, Epifronis, Epihanio,
Epijanio, Epinafio, Epipanio,
Epiphamia, Epiphamo, Epiphani,
Epiphanio, Epiphanro, Epipharío,
Epiplania, Epiplanis, Epivanio,
Epofanio, Eprifania, Epsifanio,
Epufanio, Esefana, Esifania,
Espefán, Espefanita, Espifania,
Espifiano, Espimemio, Espín,
Espincina, Essifana, Hephani,
Spifamia.

Epifanis	see **Epifanio.**
Epifano	see **Epifanio.**
Epifario	see **Epifanio.**
Epifarus	see **Epifanio.**
Epifasio	see **Epifanio.**
Epifhanio	see **Epifanio.**
Epifia	see **Epifanio.**
Epifina	see **Epifanio.**

Epifinia   see Epifanio.
Epifmenio   see Epifanio.
Epifona   see Epifanio.
Epifonio   see Epifanio.
Epifornio   see Epifanio.
Epifphanio   see Epifanio.
Epifronis   see Epifanio.
Epiganio   see Epigmenio.
Epigencio (Aay pee hayn' see oh)
  m. Comb. of Epigmenio & Incencio
  (see both).
Epigenia   see Ifigenia.
Epigmencio   see Epigmenio.
Epigmenio (Aay peeg may' nee oh)
  m. EE: Epigmenius, Pigmenius.
  Gk. "To desire deeply." 4th cen.
  Roman M. F. 3/24. Dim: Epi. Var:
  Efigmenio, Efimenia, Epegmenio,
  Epeigmenio, Epemencio, Epeminio,
  Epicinencio, Epicmenio,
  Epiganio, Epigmencio, Epigmia,
  Epignenio, Epignsenio,
  Epigonienio, Epigucino,
  Epimania, Epimeana, Epimeina,
  Epimena, Epimenio, Epimeniun,
  Epimenius, Epizmenio, Epmenio,
  Epugemio, Espimenia, Hepimenia,
  Ipenemio, Opimenio, Pimeneo,
  Pimenio, Pimeno, Pimimenio,
  Spigmenio.
Epigmia   see Epigmenio.
Epignenio   see Epigmenio.
Epignsenio   see Epigmenio.
Epigonienio   see Epigmenio.
Epigucino   see Epigmenio.
Epihanio   see Epifanio.
Epijanio   see Epifanio.
Epilacio   see Epitacio.
Epilatio   see Epitacio.
Epimaco (Aay pee' mah co) m. EE:
  Epimachus. Gk. "Easy to attack."
  7 x in DS. 1, M. of Alexandria,
  suffered exquisite torture &
  finally burnt alive. F. 5/10.
  Dim: Epi.
Epimania   see Epigmenio.
Epimanuel (Aay pee mahn wehl') m.
  EE: Epimanuel. Comb. of
  Epigmenio & Manuel (see both).
Epimeana   see Epigmenio.
Epimeina   see Epigmenio.
Epimelio   see Epimeno.
Epimena   see Epigmenio.
Epimencio (Aay pee mayn' see oh)
  m. EE: Epimencio. Roman S. de-
  capitated by Diocletian. F.
  3/24. Var: Epimenco, Epimensio.
Epimenco   see Epimencio.
Epimeneo   see Epimeno.
Epimenio   see Epigmenio.
Epimeniun   see Epigmenio.
Epimenius   see Epigmenio.
Epimeno (Aay pee may' no) m. EE:
  Epimenus, Epimeneo, Ital. S.
  from Lombardy. F. 2/18. Var:
  Epimelio, Epimeneo, Epimera,
  Epimerio, Epimernia, Epiminia,
  Epimminio, Epiminia, Epinamio,
  Epinenia, Epinero.
Epimensio   see Epimencio.
Epimera   see Epimeno.
Epimerio   see Epimeno.
Epimernia   see Epimeno.
Epiminia   see Epimeno.
Epimminio   see Epimeno.

Epimonia   see Epimeno.
Epimoseno   see Nepomuceno.
Epinafio   see Epifanio.
Epinamio   see Epimeno.
Epinenia   see Epimeno.
Epinero   see Epimeno.
Epinicina (Aay pee nee see' nah)
  f. EE: Epinicina. Lat.
  "Epinicion," "sons of victory."
Epipanio   see Epifanio.
Epiphamia   see Epifanio.
Epiphamo   see Epifanio.
Epiphani   see Epifanio.
Epiphanio   see Epifanio.
Epiphanro   see Epifanio.
Epiphario   see Epifanio.
Epiplania   see Epifanio.
Epiplanis   see Epifanio.
Episidión   see Espiridión.
Epistema (Aay peese tay' mah) m?
  EE: Episteme. Apocryphal S.
  married to St. Galaction. Per-
  suaded her to lead virginal
  life. Both beheaded. F. 11/5.
Epitachio   see Epitacio.
Epitacio (Aay pee tah' see oh) m.
  EE: Epitatius. Gk. "Ready for
  battle." 2 x in DS. 1, 1st
  bishop of Tuy, Spain. Mart.
  under Nero. F. 5/23. Dim: Epi.
  Var: Epatisio, Epetación,
  Epidasio, Epifacio, Epilacio,
  Epilatio, Epitachio, Epitafio,
  Epitania, Epitario, Epitarvol,
  Epitasio, Epitatio, Epitato,
  Epitavia, Epitayio, Epitosio,
  Epitsia, Epritasio, Epstasia,
  Eptacio, Espataso, Ezpitasia,
  Petacea, Petasho, Petasio,
  Pitacio, Pitasio, Pitazio.
Epitafio   see Epitacio.
Epitania   see Epitacio.
Epitario   see Epitacio.
Epitarvol   see Epitacio.
Epitasio   see Epitacio.
Epitatio   see Epitacio.
Epitato   see Epitacio.
Epitavia   see Epitacio.
Epitayio   see Epitacio.
Epitosio   see Epitacio.
Epitsia   see Epitacio.
Epivanio   see Epifanio.
Epizmenio   see Epigmenio.
Epmenio   see Epigmenio.
Epofanio   see Epifanio.
Epólito   see Hipólito.
Epolonia   see Apolonio.
Epomosena   see Nepomuceno.
Epomuceno   see Nepomuceno.
Eponunceno   see Nepomuceno.
Epplyonia   see Apolonio.
Eprifania   see Epifanio.
Epritasio   see Epitacio.
Epsifanio   see Epifanio.
Epstasia   see Epitacio.
Eptacio   see Epitacio.
Epufanio   see Epifanio.
Epugemio   see Epigmenio.
Equiterio   see Equitoria.
Equitoria (Aay key toe' ree ah) f?
  EE: Equitoria. Could be a form
  of Equtius, 6th cen. S. of
  present-day Italy. F. 8/11. Var:
  Equiterio.
Erácleo   see Heráclio.

Eracles   see Heráclio.
Eraclio   see Heráclio.
Eradio (Aay rah' dee oh) m. EE:
  Erhard. 2 Ss. 1 mart. in Noyon,
  France; other in Alexandria,
  Egypt.
Erainio   see Irene.
Eraldina   see Geraldo.
Eralia   see Eulalio.
Eralije   see Eulalio.
Erangelina   see Evangelina.
Eraquio   see Heráclio.
Erasino   see Erasmo.
Erasmo (Aay rahs' mo) m. EE:
  Asmus, Erasmus, Rasmus. Gk.
  "Worthy of love, lovely." Dutch
  scholar (1469-1536), broadest of
  humanists. Var: Almo, Arasmo,
  Elmar, Elmo, Erasino, Erasmun,
  Erasumus, Eraymo, Erazmo,
  Erazmun, Eresmo, Erosmo, Erusmo,
  Helmo, Irasmo, Irasmus. See also
  Erasto.
Erasmun   see Erasmo.
Erasto (Aay rahs' toe) m. EE:
  Erastus. Gk. "Beloved, lovely."
  Biblically, ministered to Paul.
  Appears in DS. F. 6/26. Var:
  Erastro, Herasto. See also
  Erasmo.
Erastro   see Erasto.
Erasumus   see Erasmo.
Eraymo   see Erasmo.
Erazmo   see Erasmo.
Erazmun   see Erasmo.
Ercelia   see Araceli.
Ercilia   see Araceli.
Ercilia   see Hersilia.
Erciliana   see Araceli.
Erculano   see Herculano.
Ereberto   see Herberto.
Ereclio   see Heráclio.
Eredina (Aay ray dee' nah) f. EE:
  Eredius, Eredio, 3rd or 4th cen.
  S. F. 2/3.
Eregenia   see Regina.
Eregorio   see Gregorio.
Eremehilda   see Hermenegildo.
Eremencio   see Emerenciana.
Eremia (Aay ray' mee ah) f. EE:
  Eremia. Could be form of St.
  Herenia, African M.
Ereminia   see Herminio.
Eremita (Aay ray mee' tah) f. EE:
  Eremita. Lat. "Eremite," "de-
  sert." Refers to persons who go
  into solitude in order to lead
  religious life.
Erendina   see Eréndira.
Eréndira (Aay rayn' dee rah) f.
  EE: Erendira. Aztec, "The one
  who smiles." Princess of Mexico.
  Var: Alrendia, Erendina,
  Hirendina, Iridira.
Erene   see Irene.
Ereneo   see Irene.
Erenio   see Irene.
Eresenio   see Arsenio.
Eresmo   see Erasmo.
Eresnita   see Ernesto.
Erestina   see Ernesto.
Erestine   see Ernesto.
Erestorgio   see Eustorgio.
Ergástulo (Ehr gahs' too low) m.
  EE: Ergastulo. Lat. "Servant who

is held prisoner."
Erginio   see Higinio.
Erianio   see Irene.
Eribel   see Arabela.
Eriberio   see Herberto.
Eriberto   see Herberto.
Eriginio   see Higinio.
Erilerto   see Herberto.
Erineo   see Irene.
Erinesto   see Ernesto.
Erineu   see Irene.
Erinia   see Irene.
Erinimia   see Herminio.
Erinma   see Herminio.
Erinmia   see Herminio.
Eristella   see Aristeo.
Eristeo   see Aristeo.
Eriverto   see Herberto.
Erlalia   see Eulalio.
Erlenda   see Herlindo.
Erlina   see Herlindo.
Erlindo   see Herlindo.
Erlinga   see Herlindo.
Erlisa   see Elisabeth.
Ermandina   see Armando.
Ermando   see Armando.
Ermania   see Herman.
Ermanisfilda   see Hermenegildo.
Ermanogilda   see Hermenegildo.
Ermegie   see Esmeregildo.
Ermelando   see Hermelinda.
Ermelina   see Hermelinda.
Ermelinda   see Hermelinda.
Ermelo   see Hermelinda.
Ermelrejilda   see Hermenegildo.
Ermemio   see Herminio.
Ermencia   see Emerenciana.
Ermendina   see Armando.
Ermenegild   see Hermenegildo.
Ermenegildo   see Hermenegildo.
Ermenehildo   see Hermenegildo.
Ermenejilda   see Hermenegildo.
Ermenezildo   see Hermenegildo.
Ermengildo   see Hermenegildo.
Ermengildus   see Hermenegildo.
Ermenia   see Herman.
Ermenia   see Herminio.
Ermenigilda   see Hermenegildo.
Ermenijildo   see Hermenegildo.
Ermeregildo   see Hermenegildo.
Ermergildo   see Hermenegildo.
Ermergilla   see Hermenegildo.
Ermidio   see Emigdio.
Ermigildo   see Hermenegildo.
Ermilinda   see Hermelinda.
Ermilo   see Hermenegildo.
Erminda   see Armida.
Erminio   see Herminio.
Erminlana   see Herminio.
Erminni   see Herminio.
Ermirio   see Edelmira.
Ermma   see Irma.
Ermminia   see Herminio.
Ermna   see Herminio.
Ermógenes   see Hermógenes.
Ermondina   see Armando.
Ermrio   see Edelmira.
Ermunia (Ehr moo' nee ah) f. EE:
  Ermunia. Lat. "Ermunius," "im-
  mune or exempt, one free from
  tribute."
Erna   see Ernesto.
Ernán   see Hernanda.
Ernehilda   see Esmeregildo.
Ernelde   see Imelda.

Ernessina   see Ernesto.
Ernesterio   see Ernesto.
Ernestesio   see Ernesto.
Ernestia   see Ernesto.
Ernestica   see Ernesto.
Ernestino   see Ernesto.
Ernesto (Ehr nay' stoe) m. EE:
    Ernest, Ernie, etc. Ger.
    "Earnest." 12th cen. abbot of
    Zwiefalten, tortured to death at
    Mecca during 1 of Crusades. F.
    11/7. Dim: Erna, Ernio, Ina,
    Irnes, Irnia, Necho, Tina,
    Titina. Var: Arnesto, Eresnita,
    Erestina, Erestine, Erinesto,
    Ernessina, Ernesterio,
    Ernestesio, Ernestia, Ernestica,
    Ernestino, Ernestor, Ernestora,
    Ernestus, Ernestyna, Erneterio,
    Ernigria, Ernilia, Ernilo,
    Ernistina, Hernesta, Hernestina,
    Hernistina, Irnestina.
Ernestor   see Ernesto.
Ernestora   see Ernesto.
Ernestus   see Ernesto.
Ernestyna   see Ernesto.
Erneterio   see Ernesto.
Ernigria   see Ernesto.
Ernilia   see Ernesto.
Ernilo   see Ernesto.
Ernimia   see Herminio.
Erninio   see Herminio.
Ernio   see Ernesto.
Ernistina   see Ernesto.
Ernolfo   see Arnulfo.
Erodio   see Elodio.
Erón   see Aarón.
Erosmo   see Erasmo.
Erreka   see Enrique.
Ersila   see Hersilia.
Ersilisa (Ehr see lee' sah) f. EE:
    Ersilisa. Ersilia, wife of Romu-
    lus, legendary founder of Rome.
Erster   see Ester.
Ertimio   see Artemio.
Erubijes   see Eduvigis.
Erudo (Aay roo' doe) m. EE: Erudo.
    Lat. "Learned."
Erulalia   see Eulalio.
Erulia (Aay roo' lee ah) f. EE:
    Erulia. South American Indian of
    Tucano tribe.
Erusmo   see Erasmo.
Eruvigen   see Eduvigis.
Eruvin   see Ervino.
Ervinia   see Ervino.
Ervino (Ehr bee' no) m. EE: Irvin,
    Marvin, Mervin. Ger. "Friend of
    honor." Var: Eruvin, Ervinia.
Erwinia   see Herwin.
Erzelia   see Hersilia.
Erzilia   see Hersilia.
Esabel   see Isabel.
Esabela   see Isabel.
Esabella   see Isabel.
Esaltación   see Exaltación.
Esanislao   see Estanislao.
Esaquina   see Hesiquio.
Esaú (Aay sah ooh') m. EE: Esau.
    Heb. "Covered with hair." Bib-
    lically, son of Rebekah & Isaac
    who sold birthright to brother
    Jacob. Var: Esaul, Esaulo, Esaw.
Esaul   see Esaú.
Esaulo   see Esaú.

Esavel   see Isabel.
Esaw   see Esaú.
Escalastic   see Escolástica.
Escalástica   see Escolástica.
Escalentaria (Aays cah layn tah'
    ree ah) f. EE: Escalentaria. Sp.
    "Escalentar," "to foment or pro-
    mote."
Escandelario   see Candelario.
Escepulo   see Esquipulas.
Escholástico   see Escolástica.
Escilia (Aay see' lee ah) f. EE:
    Escilia. Variant of Escilea from
    Lat. "scylla", water nymph.
Escipión (Aay see pee own') m. EE:
    Scipio. Lat. "Cane or support."
    Patrician family of Rome noted
    for learning & warfare. Var:
    Scipio.
Escipula   see Esquipulas.
Esciquio   see Hesiquio.
Escobástica   see Escolástica.
Escolástica (Aays co lahs' tee
    cah) f. EE: Scholastica. Lat.
    "Belonging to school." 4 x in
    DS. 1, sister of St. Benedict,
    was 5th cen. V. F. 2/10. Dim:
    Colacho, Colaco, Colástica,
    Coloca. Var: Eclestina,
    Ecolástica, Escalastic,
    Escalástica, Escholástico,
    Escobástica, Escolastice,
    Escolastina, Escolastrio,
    Escolóstico, Schalástica,
    Scholastice, Scleastiana,
    Scolástica, Scolóstico,
    Seolasticus.
Escolastice   see Escolástica.
Escolastina   see Escolástica.
Escolastrio   see Escolástica.
Escolóstico   see Escolástica.
Escquiel   see Ezequiel.
Escuipula   see Esquipulas.
Escupulo   see Esquipulas.
Esdra   see Esdras.
Esdras (Aays' drahs) m. EE: Esdra,
    Ezra, Ezrah. Heb. "Help." Bibli-
    cally, leader of Jews after
    destruction of 1st temple.
    Mentioned in DS. F. 7/13. Var:
    Esdra.
Esduardo   see Eduardo.
Esebella   see Isabel.
Esebio   see Eusebio.
Esechio   see Hesiquio.
Esecial   see Ezequiel.
Eseciel   see Ezequiel.
Esefana   see Epifanio.
Eseguiel   see Ezequiel.
Eseguiela   see Ezequiel.
Esekiel   see Ezequiel.
Esekiela   see Ezequiel.
Esenia (Aay say' nee ah) f. EE:
    Esenia. Lat. "Esseni," "one
    belonging to Essenes," monastic
    brotherhood among Jews.
Eseqnio   see Hesiquio.
Esequeil   see Ezequiel.
Esequel   see Ezequiel.
Esequela   see Ezequiel.
Esequi   see Hesiquio.
Esequial   see Ezequiel.
Esequiel   see Ezequiel.
Esequiela   see Ezequiel.
Esequiele   see Ezequiel.

Esequíez   see Ezequías.
Esequil   see Ezequiel.
Esequild   see Ezequiel.
Esequio   see Hesiquio.
Esequivel   see Ezequiel.
Esequiz   see Ezequías.
Esevan   see Esteban.
Esevio   see Eusebio.
Esfamislado   see Estanislao.
Esfernanza   see Esperanza.
Esfrael   see Israel.
Esías   see Isaías.
Esibell   see Isabel.
Esibella   see Isabel.
Esica   see Hesiquio.
Esichio   see Hesiquio.
Esidera   see Isidoro.
Esido   see Isidoro.
Esidor   see Isidoro.
Esidore   see Isidoro.
Esidoro   see Isidoro.
Esidro   see Isidoro.
Esifania   see Epifanio.
Esiginel   see Ezequiel.
Esike   see Hesiquio.
Esikia   see Hesiquio.
Esilio   see Hersilia.
Esiqia   see Hesiquio.
Esiqmio   see Hesiquio.
Esiqnio   see Hesiquio.
Esique   see Hesiquio.
Esiquiel   see Ezequiel.
Esiquiela   see Ezequiel.
Esiquio   see Hesiquio.
Esiqura   see Hesiquio.
Esisiaca   see Hesiquio.
Esita   see Isaí.
Esladislao   see Estanislao.
Eslalislada   see Estanislao.
Esleban   see Esteban.
Eslefano   see Esteban.
Esmael   see Ismael.
Esmal   see Ismael.
Esmanuela   see Manuel.
Esmarada   see Esmeralda.
Esmaragdo   see Esmeralda.
Esmaragilda   see Esmeregildo.
Esmarejilda   see Esmeregildo.
Esmariahilda   see Esmeregildo.
Esmarihilda   see Esmeregildo.
Esmarilda   see Esmeregildo.
Esmealda   see Esmeregildo.
Esmebelda   see Esmeregildo.
Esmegildo   see Esmeregildo.
Esmeiro   see Esmero.
Esmela   see Ismael.
Esmerada   see Esmeralda.
Esmeralda (Aays may rahl' dah) f.
  EE: Emerald, Esmeralda. Sp.
  "Emerald." Var: Emerado,
  Emeraldo, Esmarada, Esmaragdo,
  Esmerada, Esmeraldina,
  Esmeranda, Esmerelda, Esmerildo,
  Esmerlada, Esmerlda, Esmerlinda,
  Esmerolda, Esmiraldo, Esmoralda,
  Eumeraldo, Ezmeralda,
  Ismaerelda, Ismaralda,
  Ismeralda, Meraldo.
Esmeraldina   see Esmeralda.
Esmeranda   see Esmeralda.
Esmerechilda   see Hermenegildo.
Esmeregildo (Aays may ray heel'
  doe) m. EE: Esmeregildo. Appears
  to be comb. of Esmeralda,
  Mechilda, & Hermenegildo (see

all). Var: Ermegie, Ernehilda,
Esmaragilda, Esmarejilda,
Esmariahilda, Esmarihilda,
Esmarilda, Esmealda, Esmebelda,
Esmegildo, Esmerehildo,
Esmerejildo, Esmerelildo,
Esmergildo, Esmerigeldo,
Esmerigildo, Esmerijildo,
Esmerjildo, Esmerngilda,
Esmerogildo, Esmirgildo,
Esmirigilao, Esomergildo,
Exmeregildo, Hesmeregildo,
Hesmerigilda, Ismerio,
Marajilda, Maregilda, Margeldia,
Marigilda, Marihilda, Marijildo,
Melejieda.
Esmerehildo   see Esmeregildo.
Esmerejildo   see Esmeregildo.
Esmerelda   see Esmeralda.
Esmerelildo   see Esmeregildo.
Esmerenciana   see Emerenciana.
Esmergildo   see Esmeregildo.
Esmerigeldo   see Esmeregildo.
Esmerigildo   see Esmeregildo.
Esmerijildo   see Esmeregildo.
Esmerildo   see Esmeralda.
Esmerjildo   see Esmeregildo.
Esmerlada   see Esmeralda.
Esmerlda   see Esmeralda.
Esmerlinda   see Esmeralda.
Esmerngilda   see Esmeregildo.
Esmero (Aays may' roe) m. EE:
  Esmero. Lat. "Ismirus," "with
  much care in order to achieve
  perfection." Var: Esmeiro.
Esmerogildo   see Esmeregildo.
Esmerolda   see Esmeralda.
Esmiraldo   see Esmeralda.
Esmirgildo   see Esmeregildo.
Esmirigilao   see Esmeregildo.
Esmoel   see Ismael.
Esmondo   see Osmundo.
Esmoralda   see Esmeralda.
Esmyrna (Aays meer' nah) f. EE:
  Esmirna. Daughter of Cinyras &
  mother of Adonis.
Esobel   see Isabel.
Esomergildo   see Esmeregildo.
Espanislado   see Estanislao.
Esparansa   see Esperanza.
Esparanza   see Esperanza.
Esparaza   see Esperanza.
Espareza   see Esperanza.
Esparidión   see Espiridión.
Espataso   see Epitacio.
Espadedión   see Espiridión.
Espedia   see Espiridión.
Espedión   see Espiridión.
Espediono   see Espiridión.
Espedjria   see Espiridión.
Espefán   see Epifanio.
Espefanita   see Epifanio.
Espeirión   see Espiridión.
Espenaza   see Esperanza.
Esperance   see Esperanza.
Esperansa   see Esperanza.
Esperanta   see Esperanza.
Esperanza (Aays pay rahn' zah) f.
  EE: Hope. Lat. "Spes," "hope." [1]
  of 3 theological virtues re-
  sulting from God's grace. 1 of
  daughters of St. Sophia. F. 8/1.
  Dim: Lancha, Pela, Pelancha,
  Pelanchita, Pera, Perita. Var:
  Esfernanza, Esparansa,

Esparanza, Esparaza, Espareza,
Espenaza, Esperance, Esperansa,
Esperanta, Esperanze, Esperarza,
Esperaza, Esperdanza, Esperensa,
Esperenza, Espernaza, Espernza,
Esperonza, Espiranda, Espiranza,
Espransa, Espranza, Isperonza,
Sperancia, Speranza.

Esperanze	see **Esperanza.**
Esperarza	see **Esperanza.**
Esperaza	see **Esperanza.**
Esperdanza	see **Esperanza.**
Esperedión	see **Espiridión.**
Esperensa	see **Esperanza.**
Esperenza	see **Esperanza.**
Espererión	see **Espiridión.**
Espererona	see **Espiridión.**
Esperguill	see **Espiridión.**
Esperia	see **Espiridión.**
Espericento	see **Espiridión.**
Esperidián	see **Espiridión.**
Esperido	see **Espiridión.**
Esperidona	see **Espiridión.**
Esperión	see **Espiridión.**
Esperirina	see **Espiridión.**
Espernaza	see **Esperanza.**
Espernza	see **Esperanza.**
Esperonza	see **Esperanza.**
Espetación	see **Expectación.**
Espetatio	see **Expectación.**
Espetatión	see **Expectación.**
Espidanio	see **Espiridión.**
Espideón	see **Espiridión.**
Espides	see **Espiridión.**
Espidián	see **Espiridión.**
Espididión	see **Espiridión.**
Espidio	see **Espiridión.**
Espidión	see **Espiridión.**
Espidirión	see **Espiridión.**
Espidro	see **Espiridión.**
Espidrón	see **Espiridión.**
Espifania	see **Epifanio.**
Espifiano	see **Epifanio.**
Espimemio	see **Epifanio.**
Espimenia	see **Epigmenio.**
Espin	see **Epifanio.**
Espincina	see **Epifanio.**
Espindión	see **Espiridión.**
Espinidión	see **Espiridión.**
Espinidiona	see **Espiridión.**
Espinidrón	see **Espiridión.**
Espinindio	see **Espiridión.**
Espiranda	see **Esperanza.**
Espiranza	see **Esperanza.**
Espire	see **Espiridión.**
Espiredión	see **Espiridión.**
Espireno	see **Espiridión.**
Espirian	see **Espiridión.**
Espiridán	see **Espiridión.**
Espirideón	see **Espiridión.**
Espiridián	see **Espiridión.**
Espiridiocio	see **Espiridión.**

Espiridión (Aays spee ree dee own´) m. EE: Spiridion. Gk. "Basketmaker." 3 x in DS. 1, 4th cen. Archbishop of Tremithus (Cyprus), blinded, mutilated and sent into mines. F. 12/14. **Dim:** Sperión, Spiridio, Spriana. **Var:** Aspiridio, Episidión, Esparidión, Espededión, Espedia, Espedión, Espediono, Espediria, Espeirión, Esperedión, Espererión, Espererona, Esperguill, Esperia,

Espericento, Esperidián,
Esperido, Esperidona, Esperión,
Esperirina, Espidanio, Espideón,
Espides, Espidián, Espididión,
Espidio, Espidión, Espidirión,
Espidro, Espidrón, Espindión,
Espinidión, Espinidiona,
Espinidrón, Espinindio, Espire,
Espiredión, Espireno, Espirian,
Espiridán, Espirideón,
Espiridián, Espiridiocio,
Espiridiosa, Espirido,
Espiridon, Espiridoric,
Espirillio, Espirindión,
Espirinon, Espirio, Espirión,
Espiriona, Espiririona,
Espirisión, Espirition,
Espirordión, Esporidión,
Espridón, Espuridión,
Expiridón, Spiridine,
Spiridión, Spiridione,
Spiridionis, Spiridionus,
Spiridón, Spiridonio, Spiridrán,
Spiriona, Sprindión.

Espiridiosa	see **Espiridión.**
Espirido	see **Espiridión.**
Espiridon	see **Espiridión.**
Espiridoric	see **Espiridión.**
Espirillio	see **Espiridión.**
Espirindión	see **Espiridión.**
Espirinon	see **Espiridión.**
Espirio	see **Espiridión.**
Espirión	see **Espiridión.**
Espiriona	see **Espiridión.**
Espiririona	see **Espiridión.**
Espirisión	see **Espiridión.**
Espirition	see **Espiridión.**

Espirmenia (Aays peer may´ nee ah) f? EE: Espirmenia. Appears to be combined form of Espiridión & Epigmenio (see both).

Espirordión	see **Espiridión.**
Esporidión	see **Espiridión.**
Espransa	see **Esperanza.**
Espranza	see **Esperanza.**
Espridón	see **Espiridión.**
Espuridión	see **Espiridión.**
Esquepola	see **Esquipulas.**
Esquepula	see **Esquipulas.**
Esquevil	see **Ezequiel.**
Esquiel	see **Ezequiel.**
Esquiela	see **Ezequiel.**
Esquil	see **Ezequiel.**

Esquilo (Aays key low´) m. EE: Aeschill, Aeschylus, etc. Gk. "Modesty." Aeschylus, Gk. poet of tragedy (525–456 B.C.). In 11th cen., Eskill accompanied St. Sigfried to Sweden to help with evangelization. F. 6/12.

Esquio	see **Hesiquio.**
Esquipula	see **Esquipulas.**

Esquipulas (Aays key poo´ lahs) m. EE: Esquipulas. Shrine venerated in Esquipulas, Guatemala with famous image of crucifixion. In 1805 this cult arrived in New Mexico where oratory was built near Chimayo. **Var:** Escepulo, Escipula, Escuipula, Escupulo, Esquepola, Esquepula, Esquipula, Esquipulla, Estepula, Estipula.

Esquipulla	see **Esquipulas.**
Esquivel	see **Ezequiel.**
Esseban	see **Esteban.**

Essifana   see Epifanio.
Essiqnio   see Hesiquio.
Essiquia   see Hesiquio.
Estabón   see Esteban.
Estacho   see Eustacio.
Estacita (Aays tah see' tah) f?
  EE: Estacita. St. Estacto mart.
  in Rome. F. 9/28.
Estaer   see Ester.
Estafana   see Esteban.
Estafania   see Esteban.
Estafina   see Esteban.
Estagio   see Eustacio.
Estaguo   see Eustacio.
Estainaldo   see Estanislao.
Estalfo   see Astolfo.
Estalislada   see Estanislao.
Estallada   see Estanislao.
Estameslao   see Estanislao.
Estamislado   see Estanislao.
Estamislao   see Estanislao.
Estamlado   see Estanislao.
Estaneslado   see Estanislao.
Estanidado   see Estanislao.
Estanilao   see Estanislao.
Estanilar   see Estanislao.
Estanislad   see Estanislao.
Estanislado   see Estanislao.
Estanislano   see Estanislao.
Estanislao (Aays tah' nee slah'
  oh) m. EE: Estanislaus, Stan,
  etc. Slav. "Glory of Slavs."
  Several Polish kings. 3 x in DS.
  1, 11th cen. Polish bishop, had
  head split open for opposing
  king. F. 5/7. Dim: Chelago,
  Islada, Lalo, Lao, Tadislao,
  Tanas, Taneslado, Tani, Tanis,
  Tanisla, Tanislado, Tanislodo,
  Tanix, Tano, Tansilado,
  Tenalado, Teneslardo, Tilo,
  Tranislao. Var: Adislado,
  Adislao, Adisteo, Atanislado,
  Esanislao, Esfamislado,
  Esladislao, Eslalislada,
  Espanislado, Estainaldo,
  Estalislada, Estallada,
  Estameslao, Estamislado,
  Estamislao, Estamlado,
  Estanislado, Estanidado,
  Estanilao, Estanilar,
  Estanislad, Estanislado,
  Estanislano, Estanislar,
  Estanisleda, Estanislo,
  Estanislos, Estanistav,
  Estanito, Estansilo, Estarilado,
  Estarislada, Estarislao,
  Estavislada, Estemslada,
  Estenislao, Estnislado,
  Estonislado, Estonislar,
  Estonislas, Estonisloda,
  Estorislado, Estraneslada,
  Estumislado, Instanislado,
  Sadislao, Sadislas, Sanisildo,
  Staneslaus, Stanidlado,
  Stanilada, Stanisla, Stanislace,
  Stanislado, Stanislao,
  Stanislaus, Stanislav,
  Stanislava, Stanislio,
  Stanisloa, Stanislor, Stnaisloo.
Estanislar   see Estanislao.
Estanisleda   see Estanislao.
Estanislo   see Estanislao.
Estanislos   see Estanislao.
Estanistav   see Estanislao.

Estanito   see Estanislao.
Estansilo   see Estanislao.
Estaquio   see Eustaquio.
Estar   see Ester.
Estarilado   see Estanislao.
Estarislada   see Estanislao.
Estarislao   see Estanislao.
Estasia   see Eustacio.
Estauquia   see Eustaquio.
Estaván   see Esteban.
Estavcia   see Esteban.
Estavén   see Esteban.
Estavislada   see Estanislao.
Estebam   see Esteban.
Esteban (Aays tay' bahn) m. EE:
  Stephen, Steven, etc. Gk.
  "Crown." 82 x in DS. 1, priest-
  martyr, stoned to death outside
  gates of Jerusalem. F. 12/26.
  Dim: Estefanita, Fana, Fani,
  Stefa, Teb. Var: Astevan,
  Esevan, Esleban, Eslefano,
  Esseban, Estabón, Estafana,
  Estafania, Estafina, Estaván,
  Estavcia, Estavén, Estebam,
  Estebana, Estebanna, Estebe,
  Esteben, Estebena, Estebo,
  Estebón, Estebún, Estedana,
  Estefa, Estefanas, Estefania,
  Estefano, Estefara, Estefarea,
  Estefaria, Estefaza, Estefena,
  Estefin, Estefino, Estefon,
  Estefora, Estegana, Estemfam,
  Estepenita, Estephano, Estervan,
  Estevan, Estevar, Estevava,
  Estevon, Estiban, Estifan,
  Estifano, Estifonam, Estiphana,
  Estivan, Estivida, Estofana,
  Estovan, Istevan, Sefano,
  Steban, Stefana, Steperina,
  Stephano, Stephona, Stifana.
Estebana   see Esteban.
Estebanna   see Esteban.
Estebe   see Esteban.
Esteben   see Esteban.
Estebena   see Esteban.
Estebo   see Esteban.
Estebón   see Esteban.
Estebún   see Esteban.
Estedana   see Esteban.
Estefa   see Esteban.
Estefanas   see Esteban.
Estefania   see Esteban.
Estefanita   see Esteban.
Estefano   see Esteban.
Estefara   see Esteban.
Estefarea   see Esteban.
Estefaria   see Esteban.
Estefaza   see Esteban.
Estefena   see Esteban.
Estefin   see Esteban.
Estefino   see Esteban.
Estefon   see Esteban.
Estefora   see Esteban.
Estegana   see Esteban.
Estela (Aays tay' lah) f. EE:
  Eustella, Stella. Lat. "Stella,"
  "star." Eustella appears in DS,
  V. M. tortured & killed by order
  of her brothers. F. 5/3. Dim:
  Estelita, Neta, Tela, Telita,
  Teté. Var: Estelae, Estelbina,
  Estell, Estellia, Estello,
  Esthela, Estilan, Estilla,
  Estles, Estrell, Lita. See also

Ester.

Estelae   see **Estela.**
Estelbina   see **Estela.**
Estelfo   see **Astolfo.**
Estelita   see **Estela.**
Estell   see **Estela.**
Estellia   see **Estela.**
Estello   see **Estela.**
Estema (Aays tay' mah) f? **EE:**
Estema. From Lat. "stigma," "a
mark"? Stigmatization considered
visible sign of participation in
passion of Christ.
Estemfam   see **Esteban.**
Estemslada   see **Estanislao.**
Estenislao   see **Estanislao.**
Estepenita   see **Esteban.**
Estephano   see **Esteban.**
Estepula   see **Esquipulas.**
Ester (Aays tehr') f. **EE:** Essie,
Esther, Hester. Pers. "Star."
Biblically, defended Jews
against slaughter contrived by
Haman. In DS. F. 12/20. **Dim:**
Chita, Estercita, Esterlita,
Teche, Teté, Tey. **Var:** Eester,
Erster, Estaer, Estar, Esteran,
Esteranza, Esterlisa, Esterna,
Estero, Esterón, Esterra,
Esthergilda, Estoria. See also
Estela.
Esteran   see **Ester.**
Esteranza   see **Ester.**
Estercita   see **Ester.**
Esterlisa   see **Ester.**
Esterlita   see **Ester.**
Esterna   see **Ester.**
Estero   see **Ester.**
Esterón   see **Ester.**
Esterra   see **Ester.**
Estervan   see **Esteban.**
Estevan   see **Esteban.**
Estevar   see **Esteban.**
Estevava   see **Esteban.**
Estevon   see **Esteban.**
Esthela   see **Estela.**
Esthergilda   see **Ester.**
Estiban   see **Esteban.**
Estifan   see **Esteban.**
Estifano   see **Esteban.**
Estifonam   see **Esteban.**
Estilan   see **Estela.**
Estilla   see **Estela.**
Estimio (Aays tee' mee oh) m. **EE:**
Estimio. Lat. "Estimer," "to
appreciate."
Estiphana   see **Esteban.**
Estipula   see **Esquipulas.**
Estirgio   see **Eustorgio.**
Estivan   see **Esteban.**
Estivida   see **Esteban.**
Estles   see **Estela.**
Estnislado   see **Estanislao.**
Estofana   see **Esteban.**
Estolfo   see **Astolfo.**
Estolio   see **Eustalio.**
Estón (Aays tohn') m. **EE:** Eston.
Biblically, descendant of tribe
of Judah. Also place name.
Estonislado   see **Estanislao.**
Estonislar   see **Estanislao.**
Estonislas   see **Estanislao.**
Estonisloda   see **Estanislao.**
Estorcio   see **Eustorgio.**
Estorgio   see **Eustorgio.**

Estoria   see **Ester.**
Estorislado   see **Estanislao.**
Estorjio   see **Eustorgio.**
Estovan   see **Esteban.**
Estraberto (Aays trah behr' toe)
m. **EE:** Estraberto. Comb. of
Ester & Berta (see both)? **Var:**
Estroberto, Estuberta.
Estrabón (Aays trah bohn') m. **EE:**
Strabo. Strabo was 1st cen. B.C.
Gk. geographer. Writings are
richest source on ancient world.
Estradivario (Aay strah dee bah'
ree oh) m. **EE:** Stradivarius. Sp.
equivalent of Stradivarius,
famous Ital. violin maker of
17th cen.
Estraneslada see **Estanislao.**
Estrell   see **Estela.**
Estroberto   see **Estraberto.**
Estuardo (Aay stoo ahr' doe) m.
EE: Stuart. Royal dynasty of
England & Scotland.
Estuberta   see **Estraberto.**
Estumislado   see **Estanislao.**
Esverda   see **Ansberto.**
Etelano   see **Etelvina.**
Etelina   see **Etelvina.**
Etelmira   see **Etelvina.**
Etelvina (Aay tehl bee' nah) f.
EE: Etheluin. Ang-Sax. "Of noble
race." Etheluin appears in DS as
2nd bishop of Lindsey, England.
F. 5/3. **Dim:** Telvina, Tolvino,
Vina. **Var:** Adelvino, Edovina,
Edubina, Edvina, Ejelvina,
Etelano, Etelina, Etelmira,
Etelvira, Ethelvina, Eudilvina,
Udelbina, Udelvina.
Etelvira   see **Etelvina.**
Ethelvina   see **Etelvina.**
Etilano   see **Atilano.**
Etminia   see **Eutimia.**
Eto   see **Héctor.**
Etrudes   see **Gertrudis.**
Eubaldo   see **Ubaldo.**
Eubedio   see **Evelio.**
Eubelia   see **Evelio.**
Eubence   see **Juvencio.**
Eubencio   see **Juvencio.**
Eubense   see **Juvencio.**
Eubio (Aay ooh' bee oh) m? **EE:**
Eubio. Eubea, daughter of Aesop,
6th cen. B.C. Gk. author of
fables.
Eucadio   see **Eucardio.**
Eucardio (Aay ooh cahr' dee oh) m.
EE: Eucardio. Gk. "Of good
heart." **Var:** Eucadio.
Eucario (Aay ooh cah' ree oh) m.
EE: Eucharius. Gk. "Good chari-
ty, hospitable." 8 x in DS. 1,
8th cen. bishop of Orleans
opposed Charles Martel's confis-
cation of church property to
fight Saracens. F. 2/20. **Var:**
Elocario, Lucaria, Lucaro.
Eucebio   see **Eusebio.**
Eucencia   see **Inocencio.**
Eucevia   see **Eusebio.**
Euclides (Aay ooh clee' days) m.
EE: Euclid. Gk. "Glorious one."
Gk. mathematician of 300 B.C.
whose theorems laid basis for
geometry. **Var:** Eoclorio,

Oclides.

Euclorio (Aay ooh cloe' ree oh) m.
EE: Euclorio. Euclorito is type
of hard mineral.

Eudaldo (Aay ooh dahl' doe) m. **EE:**
Euald, Evald. Teut. "He who
governs according to law." In
DS, 2 brothers of Northumbria,
mart. trying to Christianize
peasantry in Saxony. F. 10/3.

Eudalesio   see **Indalecio.**
Eudalia   see **Odilia.**
Eudardo   see **Eduardo.**
Eudavigen   see **Eduvigis.**
Eudaviges   see **Eduvigis.**
Eudbigis   see **Eduvigis.**
Eudehia   see **Odilia.**
Eudelio   see **Odilia.**
Eudella   see **Odilia.**
Eudemia   see **Eutimia.**
Eudenia   see **Eutimia.**
Eudilvina   see **Etelvina.**

Eudina (Aay ooh dee' nah) f. **EE:**
Eudo, Odo. Diminutive form of
Eudo. 7th cen. Swiss abbot. F.
11/20.

Eudivio   see **Eduvigis.**
Eudlia   see **Odilia.**

Eudocio (Aay ooh doe' see oh) m.
EE: Eudocio, Eudoxa, etc. Gk.
"Good will." 11 x in DS. 1, a
harlot, lived in Egypt in 2nd
cen. Converted & gave money to
poor. F. 3/1. **Var:** Eudosio,
Eudox, Eudoxio.

Eudolia   see **Odilia.**

Eudonia (Aay ooh doe' nee ah) f?
EE: Eudonia. Eudon, 7th cen. S.,
established monastery in
Cambrai, France.

Eudoro (Aay ooh doe' roe) m. **EE:**
Eudoro. Gk. "Good."

Eudosio   see **Eudocio.**
Eudovica   see **Ludovico.**
Eudovigen   see **Eduvigis.**
Eudowiges   see **Eduvigis.**
Eudox   see **Eudocio.**
Eudoxio   see **Eudocio.**
Euduarda   see **Eduardo.**
Eudubiges   see **Eduvigis.**
Euduvigas   see **Eduvigis.**
Euedelia   see **Odilia.**
Euelio   see **Eulalio.**
Euelogio   see **Eulogio.**
Euesebio   see **Eusebio.**
Euestorgio   see **Eustorgio.**
Eueterio   see **Eleuterio.**
Eufacia   see **Eufracio.**
Eufamia   see **Eufemia.**
Eufancio   see **Eufracio.**
Eufario   see **Eufracio.**
Eufasia   see **Eufracio.**
Eufelia   see **Ofelio.**

Eufemia (Aay ooh fay' mee ah) f.
EE: Effe, Euphemia. Gk. "Of good
report." 16 x in DS. 1, famous
M. of Greek church. F. 9/16.
Dim: Femia, Uxa. **Var:** Efumercio,
Ehemia, Emifanio, Eufamia,
Eufemiade, Eufencia, Eufenia,
Eufenir, Eufermia, Eufernio,
Eufimia, Eufinia, Euphania,
Euphem, Euphemius, Euphenia,
Euphenria, Euphensia, Euphimia,
Frenea, Frenia, Ofemia, Ofimia,
Rufemio, Ufemia, Ufenia.

Eufemiade   see **Eufemia.**
Eufencia   see **Eufemia.**
Eufenia   see **Eufemia.**
Eufenir   see **Eufemia.**
Eufermia   see **Eufemia.**
Eufernio   see **Eufemia.**
Eufigenia   see **Ifigenia.**
Eufilio   see **Ofelio.**
Eufimia   see **Eufemia.**
Eufinia   see **Eufemia.**
Euforina   see **Eufracio.**
Eufra   see **Eufracio.**

Eufracio (Aay ooh frah' see oh) m.
EE: Euphrasic, Eupraxic, etc.
Gk. "Full of joy." 15 x in DS.
1, of Constantinople, became nun
at age of 7. F. 3/13. **Dim:**
Eufra, Fracia, Frecha, Fresia,
Pacha. **Var:** Eifracia, Eofracio,
Eufacia, Eufancio, Eufario,
Eufasia, Euforina, Eufradia,
Eufragia, Eufragina, Eufrania,
Eufraria, Eufrasia, Eufrasina,
Eufrasium, Eufrazia, Eufrecenia,
Eufresinla, Euofrasio, Eupasia,
Euphrasio, Euphresia, Euprasia,
Ofracia, Ofrasia, Ofrecia,
Ofrecino, Ofrocinia, Rufrosia,
Ufascia, Ufracia, Ufrasia,
Ufrosia.

Eufradia   see **Eufracio.**
Eufragia   see **Eufracio.**
Eufragina   see **Eufracio.**
Eufrania   see **Eufracio.**
Eufraria   see **Eufracio.**
Eufrasia   see **Eufracio.**
Eufrasina   see **Eufracio.**
Eufrasium   see **Eufracio.**
Eufrazia   see **Eufracio.**
Eufrecenia   see **Eufracio.**
Eufredo   see **Alfredo.**
Eufresinla   see **Eufracio.**
Eufricia   see **Eufrosina.**
Eufrocia   see **Eufrosina.**
Eufrocino   see **Eufrosina.**
Eufrosima   see **Eufrosina.**

Eufrosina (Aay ooh froe see' nah)
f. **EE:** Euphrosyne. Gk. "Joyous."
14 x in DS. 1, 5th cen. Gk. V.,
lived in monastery for 38 years
in order to escape marriage. F.
1/1. **Var:** Eufricia, Eufrocia,
Eufrocino, Eufrosima,
Eufrosinio, Eufrosma,
Eufrotocián, Euphorasia,
Euphronsio, Euphrosio,
Euprocina, Euprosia, Eusrocina,
Ufricina.

Eufrosinio   see **Eufrosina.**
Eufrosma   see **Eufrosina.**
Eufrotocián   see **Eufrosina.**
Eugemio   see **Eugenio.**
Eugemo   see **Eugenio.**
Eugenimo   see **Eugenio.**

Eugenio (Aay ooh hay' nee oh) m.
EE: Eugene, Eugenia, Gene. Gk.
"Well born." 54 x in DS. Eugenia
lived in Alexandria, donned male
clothing, & joined monastery. F.
12/25. **Dim:** Cenia, Cheno,
Gencho, Genio, Geñi, Geño,
Queña, Uxo. **Var:** Ahenio, Egenia,
Eginio, Eginito, Egino, Ejinio,
Eugemio, Eugemo, Eugercio,

Eugerina, Eugina, Euginio,
Eujenio, Eujina, Eujinio,
Oginia, Ojenio, Uegenio, Ugenio,
Uhenio.

Eugercio	see	Eugenio.
Eugerina	see	Eugenio.
Eugina	see	Eugenio.
Euginio	see	Eugenio.
Euglogia	see	Eulogio.
Eugolio	see	Eulogio.
Eugracia	see	Engracia.
Euidelia	see	Odilia.
Euilio	see	Eulalio.
Euisitemio	see	Eutimia.
Eujenio	see	Eugenio.
Eujina	see	Eugenio.
Eujinio	see	Eugenio.
Eulabio	see	Eulalio.
Eulacia	see	Eulalio.
Euladia	see	Eulalio.
Eulado	see	Eulalio.
Eulagio	see	Eulalio.
Eulahia	see	Eulalio.
Eulaho	see	Eulalio.
Eulaia	see	Eulalio.
Eulaley	see	Eulalio.
Eulali	see	Eulalio.
Eulaliam	see	Eulalio.
Eulalias	see	Eulalio.
Eulalin	see	Eulalio.
Eulalins	see	Eulalio.

Eulalio (Aay ooh lah' lee oh) m.
EE: Eulalia, Eulalius, etc. Gk.
"He who speaks well." 7 x in DS.
Most celebrated, Sp. V. & M.,
Eulalia at 13 refused to give up
faith & was burned. F. 12/10.
Dim: Eulia, Lali, Lalia, Lalie,
Lalo, Laya, Layita, Lulalio,
Ula, Ulia, Yayo. **Var:** Alalio,
Alallo, Aualia, Auyela, Ayalia,
Ayulo, Elalio, Eluadio,
Elulalia, Eololio, Eralia,
Eralije, Erlalia, Erulalia,
Euelio, Euilio, Eulabio,
Eulacia, Euladia, Eulado,
Eulagio, Eulahia, Eulaho,
Eulaia, Eulaley, Eulali,
Eulaliam, Eulalias, Eulalin,
Eulalins, Eulalios, Eulalis,
Eulalium, Eulatio, Eulelio,
Eulila, Eulileo, Eulilia,
Eulimia, Eullagia, Eulolio,
Eululio, Evlalia, Holalla,
Holayo, Hollala, Hulala,
Hulalia, Julalio, Ohalia,
Olagia, Olaia, Olallo, Olaya,
Oloia, Oloya, Uelalia, Ulalio,
Ularia, Ulelea, Ullallio,
Ululio, Wulalia, Ylalio.

Eulalios	see	Eulalio.
Eulalis	see	Eulalio.
Eulalium	see	Eulalio.
Eulanda	see	Yolanda.
Eulateria	see	Eleuterio.
Eulatio	see	Eulogio.
Eulelio	see	Eulalio.
Eulenteria	see	Eleuterio.
Eulesteria	see	Eleuterio.
Euleterio	see	Eleuterio.

Eulgencio (Aay oohl hayn' see oh)
m. EE: Eulgencio. Comb. of
Eulogio & Fulgencio (see both).

Eulia	see	Eulalio.

Euligio	see	Eulogio.
Eulila	see	Eulalio.
Eulileo	see	Eulalio.
Eulilia	see	Eulalio.
Eulimia	see	Eulalio.
Euliogio	see	Eulogio.
Eullagia	see	Eulalio.
Eulobio	see	Eulogio.
Eulochio	see	Eulogio.
Eulochius	see	Eulogio.
Eulocia	see	Eulogio.
Eulodiso	see	Eulogio.
Euloggio	see	Eulogio.
Eulogies	see	Eulogio.
Eulogilo	see	Eulogio.

Eulogio (Aay ooh low' hee oh) m.
EE: Eulogius. Gk. "He who is
great orator." 13 x in DS. 1,
Archbishop of Toledo, executed
for protecting Sarcen maiden who
converted. F. 3/11. **Dim:** Locho,
Logio, Lolo. **Var:** Elochio,
Elogio, Elogium, Elogonia,
Elohia, Elojio, Eloquio, Elugio,
Enlogio, Euelogio, Euglogia,
Eugolio, Eulegio, Euligio,
Euliogio, Eulobio, Eulochio,
Eulochius, Eulocia, Eulodiso,
Euloggio, Eulogies, Eulogilo,
Eulogis, Eulogium, Eulogua,
Eulohia, Eulojio, Eulugio,
Olijio, Ologio, Oloija, Olojio,
Ulogia, Ulojio.

Eulogis	see	Eulogio.
Eulogium	see	Eulogio.
Eulogua	see	Eulogio.
Eulohia	see	Eulogio.
Eulojio	see	Eulogio.
Eulolio	see	Eulalio.
Eulugio	see	Eulogio.
Eululio	see	Eulalio.
Euluterio	see	Eleuterio.
Eulutherio	see	Eleuterio.
Eumancia	see	Amancio.

Eumelia (Aay ooh may' lee ah) f.
EE: Eumelia. Gk. "She who sings
well." **Var:** Ulemia.
Eumenia (Aay ooh may' nee ah) f.
EE: Eumenius. Gk. "Well dis-
posed." 5 x in DS. 1, bishop of
Gortyna (Crete), exiled for
combatting monothelitism, belief
that Christ had only 1 will. F.
9/16.
Eumenzio (Aay ooh mayn' zee oh) m.
EE: Eumenzio. Could be form of
Eumenius, 4 Ss. of Christian
calendar.

Eumeraldo	see	Esmeralda.

Eumicia (Aay ooh mee' see ah) f.
EE: Eumicia. Could be form of
Eunice (see), 3 Christian Mm.

Eunecia	see	Eunice.

Eunice (Aay ooh nee' say) f. EE:
Eunice. Gk. "Happy victory." 3 x
in DS. **Var:** Eunecia, Euniza,
Eunizia.

Euniza	see	Eunice.
Eunizia	see	Eunice.
Euofrasio	see	Eufracio.
Eupasia	see	Eufracio.
Euphania	see	Eufemia.
Euphelia	see	Ofelio.
Euphem	see	Eufemia.
Euphemius	see	Eufemia.

Euphenia   see **Eufemia.**
Euphenria   see **Eufemia.**
Euphensia   see **Eufemia.**
Euphimia   see **Eufemia.**
Euphorasia   see **Eufrosina.**
Euphorio (Aay ooh foe´ ree oh) m.
  EE: Euphorio. Gk. "Fertility or
  abundance."
Euphrasio   see **Eufracio.**
Euphresia   see **Eufracio.**
Euphronsio   see **Eufrosina.**
Euphrosio   see **Eufrosina.**
Euprasia   see **Eufracio.**
Euprocina   see **Eufrosina.**
Euprosia   see **Eufrosina.**
Euralia   see **Eurialo.**
Euraul   see **Eurialo.**
Eurbana   see **Urbano.**
Eurelina   see **Eurialo.**
Eurelio   see **Eurialo.**
Eurialo (Aay ooh ree´ ah low) m.
  EE: Euryalus. Gk. "Vast, ample."
  Euryalus went with Aeneas to
  Italy where they perished in
  attack on Rutulian camp. **Var:**
  Euralia, Euraul, Eurelina,
  Eurelio, Eurilia.
Eurico (Aay ooh ree´ co) m. **EE:**
  Eric. Ger. "Kingly." Euric,
  Visigothic king who initiated
  conquest of Spain in 5th cen. &
  codified Visigothic law. **Var:**
  Eurique.
Euridice (Aay ooh ree´ dee say) f.
  EE: Eurydice. Gk. "Of double
  delight." In Gk. legend, brought
  from Hades by husband Orpheus.
  Var: Viche.
Eurilia   see **Eurialo.**
Eurique   see **Enrique.**
Eurique   see **Eurico.**
Euriqueta   see **Enrique.**
Eursa   see **Úrsula.**
Eurtochia   see **Eustorgio.**
Eurvana   see **Urbano.**
Eusabea   see **Eusebio.**
Eusabec   see **Eusebio.**
Eusabio   see **Eusebio.**
Eusachio   see **Eustacio.**
Eusavia   see **Eusebio.**
Eusbaldo   see **Ubaldo.**
Eusbio   see **Eusebio.**
Euschio   see **Eustacio.**
Eusebiam   see **Eusebio.**
Eusebii   see **Eusebio.**
Eusebines   see **Eusebio.**
Eusebio (Aay ooh say´ bee oh) m.
  EE: Eusebic, Eusebius. Gk. "Pi-
  ous one." 72 x in DS. 1, bishop
  of Vercelli, Italy, champion
  against Arianism in 3rd cen. F.
  12/15. **Dim:** Chebo, Chevo, Shebo.
  Var: Ensebino, Ensebins,
  Ensebio, Enseve, Esebio, Esevio,
  Eucebio, Eucevia, Euesebio,
  Eusabea, Eusabec, Eusabio,
  Eusavia, Eusbio, Eusebiam,
  Eusebii, Eusebines, Eusebius,
  Eusebria, Eusebro, Eusebuim,
  Eusedia, Eusefio, Euselbio,
  Euseleia, Euselvio, Eusephia,
  Eusetia, Euseva, Eusevio,
  Eusibio, Euzebio, Iusebio,
  Lusebia, Ocevia, Osevia, Usavia,
  Usebio, Usevio, Usibio, Ysevio.

Eusebius   see **Eusebio.**
Eusebria   see **Eusebio.**
Eusebro   see **Eusebio.**
Eusebuim   see **Eusebio.**
Eusedia   see **Eusebio.**
Eusefio   see **Eusebio.**
Euselbio   see **Eusebio.**
Euseleia   see **Eusebio.**
Euselica   see **Eustalio.**
Euselio   see **Eustalio.**
Euselvio   see **Eusebio.**
Eusephia   see **Eusebio.**
Eusequia   see **Hesiquio.**
Eusetia   see **Eusebio.**
Euseva   see **Eusebio.**
Eusevio   see **Eusebio.**
Eusibio   see **Eusebio.**
Eusicio   see **Eutiquio.**
Euslolia   see **Eustalio.**
Eusolio   see **Eustalio.**
Eusraquio   see **Eustaquio.**
Eusrocina   see **Eufrosina.**
Eussolio   see **Eustalio.**
Eustabio   see **Eustavio.**
Eustace   see **Eustacio.**
Eustach   see **Eustacio.**
Eustachio   see **Eustacio.**
Eustachius   see **Eustacio.**
Eustacio (Aay ooh stah´ see oh) m.
  EE: Eustace, Eustis, Stacy. Gk.
  "Firm, constant." 10 x in DS. 1
  converted to Christianity upon
  seeing apparition of Chirst
  between antlers of stag. F.
  9/20. **Var:** Eastacio, Elistasia,
  Elustacia, Eostacio, Estacho,
  Estagio, Estaguo, Estasia,
  Eusachio, Euschio, Eustace,
  Eustach, Eustachio, Eustachius,
  Eustactria, Eustagino, Eustagio,
  Eustajio, Eustargio, Eustasiae,
  Eustasio, Eustaslia, Eustathia,
  Eustecia, Eustorchio, Eustosia,
  Eustotia, Eutasio, Ustacia,
  Ustasio.
Eustactria   see **Eustacio.**
Eustadio (Aay ooh stah´ dee oh) m.
  EE: Eustadio. Eustadius, 6th
  cen. abbot & S. of Dijon,
  France. F. 2/3.
Eustagino   see **Eustacio.**
Eustagio   see **Eustacio.**
Eustajio   see **Eustacio.**
Eustalio (Aay ooh stah´ lee oh) m.
  EE: Eustolia, Eustoilus. Gk.
  "Well prepared." 2 x in DS.
  Roman V. who helped found monas-
  tery in Constantinople. F. 11/9.
  Var: Estolio, Euselica, Euselio,
  Euslolia, Eusolio, Eussolio,
  Eustallia, Eustelia, Eustilia,
  Eustoleo, Eustolina, Eustolio,
  Eustonia, Istolia, Ustalia,
  Ustolia.
Eustallia   see **Eustalio.**
Eustaquino   see **Eustaquio.**
Eustaquio (Aay ooh stah´ key oh)
  m. **EE:** Eustachius, Eustacia. Gk.
  "He who is fruitful." 3rd cen.
  Christian mart. in Asia Minor.
  F. 11/20. **Dim:** Taco. **Var:**
  Custaquio, Estaquio, Estauquia,
  Eusraquio, Eustaquino,
  Eustiquio, Eustoquia, Euszaqio,
  Eutequeo, Euztaquia, Ustaque,

Ustaquio, Ustiquio, Ustochia.

Eustargio see **Eustacio.**
Eustasiae see **Eustacio.**
Eustasio see **Eustacio.**
Eustaslia see **Eustacio.**
Eustathia see **Eustacio.**
Eustavio (Aay ooh stah' bee oh) m.
EE: Eustavio. Comb. of Eustacio,
Eusebio, Eustaquio, or Gustavo
(see all)? **Var:** Eustabio.
Eustecia see **Eustacio.**
Eustefa (Aay ooh stay' fah) f. **EE:**
Eustefa. Eustefia, type of
flower.
Eustelia see **Eustalio.**
Eustilia see **Eustalio.**
Eustiorgio see **Eustorgio.**
Eustiquio see **Eustaquio.**
Eustojio see **Eustorgio.**
Eustoleo see **Eustalio.**
Eustolina see **Eustalio.**
Eustolio see **Eustalio.**
Eustonia see **Eustalio.**
Eustoquia see **Eustaquio.**
Eustoquio (Aay ooh stoe' key oh)
m. **EE:** Eustochium, Eustochius.
Gk. "Sharply intelligent." 8 x
in DS. 1, 4th cen. Roman V. F.
9/28. **Var:** Eustoquito.
Eustoquito see **Eustoquio.**
Eustorchio see **Eustacio.**
Eustorchio see **Eustorgio.**
Eustorgio (Aay ooh stohr' hee oh)
m. **EE:** Eustrogius. Gk. "Well-
loved." 5 x in DS. 1, 1st Arch-
bishop of Milan, Italy in 4th
cen. Wrote against Arians. F.
9/18. **Var:** Erestorgio, Estirgio,
Estorcio, Estorgio, Estorjio,
Euestorgio, Eurtochia,
Eustiorgio, Eustojio,
Eustorchio, Eustorica,
Eustorijo, Eustorjeo, Eustorjio,
Eustrojia, Eutorgea, Hestoigia,
Jostorgo, Ostogio, Ustorgio,
Ustoria.
Eustorica see **Eustorgio.**
Eustorijo see **Eustorgio.**
Eustorjeo see **Eustorgio.**
Eustorjio see **Eustorgio.**
Eustosia see **Eustacio.**
Eustotia see **Eustacio.**
Eustrojia see **Eustorgio.**
Euszaqio see **Eustaquio.**
Eutalia (Aay ooh tah' lee ah) f.
EE: Euthalia. Lat. "Flourish-
ing." Sicilian V. converted by
mother. Her brother upon discov-
ering this, killed her. F. 8/27.
Var: Eutelia.
Eutasio see **Eustacio.**
Eutelia see **Eutalia.**
Eutemio see **Eutimia.**
Eutenio see **Eutimia.**
Eutequeo see **Eustaquio.**
Eutequio see **Eutiquio.**
Euthimiae see **Eutimia.**
Euthymio see **Eutimia.**
Euticio see **Eutiquio.**
Eutiemia see **Eutimia.**
Eutiguio see **Eutiquio.**
Eutigun see **Eutiquio.**
Eutimeo see **Eutimia.**
Eutimia (Aay ooh tee' mee ah) f.
EE: Euthymia, Euthymius. Gk.

"One who enjoys great honor." 19
x in DS. 1, abbot of Palestine,
lived in desert & founded mon-
astery. F. 1/20. **Var:** Autemia,
Autenia, Entimio, Etminia,
Eudemia, Eudenia, Euisitemio,
Eutemio, Eutenio, Euthimiae,
Euthymio, Eutiemia, Eutimeo,
Eutinio, Eutinnio, Eutirmio,
Eutrimiae, Eutrimio, Eutrinio,
Eutrymio, Eutyminus, Eutymio,
Odimia, Otimio, Otinio, Ottimia,
Utenio, Utimio, Utumio.
Eutinio see **Eutimia.**
Eutinnio see **Eutimia.**
Eutiquin see **Eutiquio.**
Eutiquio (Aay ooh tee' key oh) m.
EE: Euticius, Eutychius, etc.
Gk. "Fortunate one." 52 x in DS.
1, Patriarch of Constantinople
in 6th cen. F. 4/6. **Dim:** Tico,
Tiquio. **Var:** Entiquia, Eusicio,
Eutequio, Euticio, Eutiguio,
Eutigun, Eutiquin, Eutisio,
Eytiquio, Uticio, Utikio.
Eutirmio see **Eutimia.**
Eutisio see **Eutiquio.**
Eutorgea see **Eustorgio.**
Eutrimiae see **Eutimia.**
Eutrimio see **Eutimia.**
Eutrinio see **Eutimia.**
Eutropia (Aay ooh troe' pee ah) f.
EE: Eutropia, Eutropius. Gk. "Of
good spirit." 21 x in DS. 1, 1st
bishop of Saintes of 3rd cen.
Mart. with head split by pagans.
F. 4/30.
Eutrymio see **Eutimia.**
Eutyminus see **Eutimia.**
Eutymio see **Eutimia.**
Euvence see **Juvencio.**
Euvencio see **Juvencio.**
Euxilia see **Auxilio.**
Euzebio see **Eusebio.**
Euztaquia see **Eustaquio.**
Euzuquia see **Hesiquio.**
Eva (Aay' bah) f. **EE:** Eva, Eve,
Eveline, etc. Heb. "Life." 1st
woman & wife of Adam. 4 x in DS.
Other Eves recluses. **Dim:** Evita,
Jevita, Velia. **Var:** Ava, Ebita,
Evadina, Evalina, Evelino,
Eveltina, Evenlina, Evila,
Ibelina.
Evadina see **Eva.**
Evagelina see **Evangelina.**
Evaginlina see **Evangelina.**
Evalardo see **Abelardo.**
Evalina see **Eva.**
Evanagelina see **Evangelina.**
Evangela see **Evangelina.**
Evangelina (Aay bahn hay lee' nah)
f. **EE:** Evangeline. Gk. "Bearer
of good tidings." Refers to
Matthew, Mark, Luke, & John,
evangelists in primitive church.
Var: Abangelina, Avangelino,
Ebangelina, Elvanelia,
Enangelina, Engelina,
Erangelina, Evagelina,
Evaginlina, Evanagelina,
Evangela, Evangeline,
Evangelintina, Evangelista,
Evangenlina, Evangilia,
Evangulina, Evanjelina,

Evanjeline, Evengelina,
Ivangelina, Vangelina. See also
Ángel.

Evangeline   see **Evangelina.**
Evangelintina   see **Evangelina.**
Evangelista   see **Evangelina.**
Evangenlina   see **Evangelina.**
Evangilia   see **Evangelina.**
Evangulina   see **Evangelina.**
Evanisto   see **Evaristo.**
Evanjelina   see **Evangelina.**
Evanjeline   see **Evangelina.**
Evarisdo   see **Evaristo.**
Evaristo (Aay bah ree' stoe) m.
EE: Evaristo. Gk. "Well, good."
4 x in DS. 1, 4th successor of
St. Peter, divided Rome into
parishes & deaconries. F. 10/26.
Var: Averisto, Eabaristo,
Ebaristo, Evanisto, Evarisdo,
Everisto, Eversita, Eviristo,
Evirsto, Evoristo.
Evebejes   see **Eduvigis.**
Eveio   see **Evelio.**
Evelalia   see **Evelio.**
Evelardo   see **Everardo.**
Eveliar   see **Evelio.**
Evelino   see **Eva.**
Evelio (Aay bay' lee oh) m. EE:
Evellius. Gk. "Well, good." M.
of 1st cen. Rome. **Var:** Ebelino,
Ebelio, Ebilia, Eubedio,
Eubelia, Eveio, Evelalia,
Eveliar, Evellia, Evilio.
Evellia   see **Evelio.**
Eveltina   see **Eva.**
Evencio (Aay bayn' see oh) m. EE:
Eventius. Lat. "To be success-
ful." 2 x in DS. 1 mart. under
Diocletian in Saragossa, Spain.
F. 4/16. **Var:** Eventino, Ibencas.
See also Juvencio.
Evengelina   see **Evangelina.**
Evenlina   see **Eva.**
Eveno (Aay bay' no) m. EE: Eveno.
In Gk. myth., river god of
Atolia.
Eventino   see **Evencio.**
Everado   see **Everardo.**
Everaldo   see **Everardo.**
Everando   see **Everardo.**
Everardo (Aay bay rahr' doe) m.
EE: Everett, Everhard, etc. Ger.
"Strong as wild boar." 3 x in
DS. 1, 16th cen. Protestant
minister, converted to Catholi-
cism. F. 10/2. Dim: Lalo. **Var:**
Evelardo, Everado, Everaldo,
Everando, Everdo.
Everdo   see **Everardo.**
Everisto   see **Evaristo.**
Eversita   see **Evaristo.**
Evia   see **Elviro.**
Evidio (Aay bee' dee oh) m. EE:
Evidio. S. & M. of 10th cen.
Gerona, Spain. F. 6/13. See also
Ovidio.
Evila   see **Eva.**
Evilardo   see **Abelardo.**
Evilio   see **Evelio.**
Evira   see **Elviro.**
Eviristo   see **Evaristo.**
Evirsto   see **Evaristo.**
Evita   see **Eva.**
Evlalia   see **Eulalio.**

Evodig   see **Evodio.**
Evodio (Aay bo' dee oh) m. EE:
Evodius, Evodus, Evotius. Lat.
"He who prospers." 11 x in DS.
1, 1st bishop of Antioch,
thought to have coined word
"Christian." F. 5/6. **Var:**
Ebodeo, Evodig, Evodis.
Evodis   see **Evodio.**
Evoristo   see **Evaristo.**
Exaltación (Aayks ahl tah see
own') f. EE: Exultation. Lat.
"To glorify." Refers to feast,
Exaltación de la Santa Cruz
commemorating holy cross
miraculously immovable from
Jerusalem. F. 9/14. **Dim:** Salto.
Var: Asoltación, Esaltación,
Eximenio.
Exasiaca   see **Hesiquio.**
Exciquio   see **Hesiquio.**
Exequia   see **Hesiquio.**
Exequial   see **Ezequiel.**
Exiciara   see **Hesiquio.**
Exignio   see **Higinio.**
Exillo   see **Auxilio.**
Eximenio   see **Exaltación.**
Eximenio (Aay hee may' nee oh) m.
EE: Eximenio. Form of "eximio"
meaning "very excellent"?
Exiquiel   see **Ezequiel.**
Exiquio   see **Hesiquio.**
Exiquius   see **Ezequias.**
Exisicia   see **Hesiquio.**
Exissaca   see **Hesiquio.**
Exmeregildo   see **Esmeregildo.**
Expectacia   see **Expectación.**
Expectación (Aayks payk' tah see
own') f. EE: Expectation. Lat.
"Expectatio," "intention with
which one awaits." Refers to
feast day of expectation, also
known as Annunciation, announce-
ment of Jesus' birth to Mary. F.
3/25. **Var:** Epectación,
Espetación, Espetatio,
Espetatión, Expectacia,
Expectatione.
Expectatione   see **Expectación.**
Expedito (Aayks pay dee' toe) m.
EE: Expeditus. Lat. "Free from
obstacles." In DS, Expeditus is
apocryphal. Venerated in desper-
ate cases. F. 4/19. **Var:**
Expidus.
Expidus   see **Expedito.**
Expiridión   see **Espiridión.**
Exsiquio   see **Hesiquio.**
Exssicia   see **Hesiquio.**
Exzekiel   see **Ezequiel.**
Exzequiel   see **Ezequiel.**
Eytiquio   see **Eutiquio.**
Ezcquio   see **Hesiquio.**
Ezeakiel   see **Ezequiel.**
Ezechial   see **Ezequiel.**
Ezechiel   see **Ezequiel.**
Ezechielio   see **Ezequiel.**
Ezechielis   see **Ezequiel.**
Ezechielo   see **Ezequiel.**
Ezechill   see **Ezequiel.**
Ezechina   see **Hesiquio.**
Ezechio   see **Hesiquio.**
Ezechria   see **Hesiquio.**
Ezeciel   see **Ezequiel.**
Ezecliela   see **Ezequiel.**

Ezeclieo	see **Ezequiel.**
Ezegio	see **Hesiquio.**
Ezeguil	see **Ezequiel.**
Ezeihiel	see **Ezequiel.**
Ezekiel	see **Ezequiel.**
Ezekil	see **Ezequiel.**
Ezekio	see **Hesiquio.**
Ezenia	see **Zinnia.**
Ezeqkiel	see **Ezequiel.**
Ezeqniel	see **Ezequiel.**
Ezequel	see **Ezequiel.**

Ezequías (Aay zay key' ahs) m. **EE:**
Ezechias, Hezekiah, etc. Gk.
"Strength from God." Biblically,
king of Judah noted for capacity
to govern. 21 x in DS. **Dim:**
Checo. **Var:** Esequiez, Esequiz,
Exiquius, Ezequíos.

Ezequiel (Aay zay key ehl') m. **EE:**
Ezekiah, Ezekial, Zeke. Heb.
"God will strengthen." 1 of
better known of OT prophets.
Foretold capture of Jerusalem,
judgement against nations, &
restoration of Jerusalem.
Mentioned in DS. **Dim:** Chaco,
Checo, Cheque, Chequel,
Chequelo, Chequil, Quelo, Quiel,
Sequel, Sequiel, Ziek. **Var:**
Ecequiel, Ecequiela, Eciguel,
Escquiel, Esecial, Eseciel,
Eseguiel, Eseguiela, Esekiel,
Esekiela, Esequeil, Esequel,
Esequela, Esequial, Esequiel,
Esequiela, Esequiele, Esequil,
Esequild, Esequivel, Esiginel,
Esiquiel, Esiquiela, Esguevil,
Esquiel, Esquiela, Esquil,
Esquivel, Exequial, Exiquiel,
Exzekiel, Exzequiel, Ezeakiel,
Ezechial, Ezechiel, Ezechielio,
Ezechielis, Ezechielo, Ezechill,

Ezeciel, Ezecliela, Ezeclieo,
Ezeguil, Ezeihiel, Ezekiel,
Ezekil, Ezeqkiel, Ezeqniel,
Ezequel, Ezequiela, Ezequiele,
Ezequil, Ezequill, Ezequiuel,
Ezequivel, Ezichiel, Eziekel,
Eziglia, Ezikiel, Eziqiel,
Ezochiel, Ezquivel, Ezrekiel,
Ezuquiel, Ezyquiel, Hesequiel,
Isequiel, Isiquiel, Izechiel.

Ezequiela	see **Ezequiel.**
Ezequiele	see **Ezequiel.**
Ezequil	see **Ezequiel.**
Ezequill	see **Ezequiel.**
Ezequio	see **Hesiquio.**
Ezequíos	see **Ezequías.**
Ezequiuel	see **Ezequiel.**
Ezequivel	see **Ezequiel.**
Ezichiel	see **Ezequiel.**
Ezicio	see **Hesiquio.**
Eziekel	see **Ezequiel.**
Eziglia	see **Ezequiel.**
Ezikia	see **Hesiquio.**
Ezikiel	see **Ezequiel.**
Eziqiel	see **Ezequiel.**
Eziqnio	see **Hesiquio.**
Eziquino	see **Hesiquio.**
Eziquio	see **Hesiquio.**
Eziquisa	see **Hesiquio.**
Eziso	see **Hesiquio.**
Ezmeralda	see **Esmeralda.**
Ezmundo	see **Osmundo.**
Ezochiel	see **Ezequiel.**
Ezpitasia	see **Epitacio.**
Ezquio	see **Hesiquio.**
Ezquivel	see **Ezequiel.**
Ezrekiel	see **Ezequiel.**
Ezuquia	see **Hesiquio.**
Ezuquiel	see **Ezequiel.**
Ezychio	see **Hesiquio.**
Ezyquiel	see **Ezequiel.**

F

Fabeán	see **Fabián.**
Fabella	see **Fabián.**
Fabialio	see **Fabián.**

Fabián (Fah bee ahn') m. **EE:**
Fabian, etc. Lat. "Belonging to
Fabius." Name of several Roman
emperors. 16 x in DS. **Var:**
Fabeán, Fabella, Fabialio,
Fabiano, Fabién, Fabio, Fabiola,
Fabiona, Favana, Favián,
Faviana, Faviola, Febián. See
also Fabiola.

Fabiano	see **Fabián.**
Fabién	see **Fabián.**
Fabio	see **Fabián.**
Fabiola	see **Fabián.**

Fabiola (Fah bee oh' lah) f. **EE:**
Fabiola. Lat. "Fabius," Roman
family name. In DS as Roman
matron devoted to ascetism. Gave
property to poor & founded
hospice. F. 12/27. **Var:** Fabola,
Faby. See also Fabián.

Fabiona	see **Fabián.**
Fabola	see **Fabiola.**

Fabriano	see **Fabriciano.**

Fabriciano (Fah bree see ah' no)
m. **EE:** Fabricianus. Lat. "Fab-
ricius," "one who works with
hard objects." 2 x in DS. **Var:**
Fabriano.

Faby	see **Fabiola.**
Facha	see **Bonifacio.**
Facindo	see **Facundo.**
Facino	see **Bonifacio.**
Faconda	see **Facundo.**

Facundo (Fah coon' doe) m. **EE:**
Facundus. Lat. "He who speaks
with ease." Major character in
"Life in the Argentine Republic"
written by Sarmiento in 1845.
Sp. M. under Diocletian. F.
11/27. **Var:** Facindo, Faconda,
Fecundo, Vacunda.

Fadrique	see **Federico.**
Fafa	see **Rafael.**
Fafa	see **Raul.**
Falconaire	see **Falconia.**

Falconia (Fahl co' nee ah) f. **EE:**
Falconia. Lat. "Falconaria,"

"falconry." Falconer, one who works with hawks. **Var:** Falconaire.

Fallo   see **Rafael.**
Fallo   see **Raul.**
Falo   see **Rafael.**
Falo   see **Raul.**
Falvio   see **Flavio.**
Famoso (Fah mo' so) m. **EE:** Famoso. Lat. "Reknowned." Famosa in DS is V. M. who accompanied St. Achatius of Byzance. F. 5/8.
Fana   see **Esteban.**
Fanasa (Fah nah' sa) f. **EE:** Fanasa. Fanas was one of gods included among nymphs.
Fani   see **Esteban.**
Fanita (Fah nee' tah) f. **EE:** Fanita. Fannia was Roman woman who lived in 1st cen. B.C.
Fanstina   see **Faustino.**
Fara (Fah' rah) f. **EE:** Farrah. Fara (St. Burgundo), lived in 7th cen. Meaux, France. Cures sore eyes. F. 2/3.
Faragón (Fah rah goan') m. **EE:** Faragon. Farag, 2nd son of Ismail, king of Granada.
Faraón (Fah rah own') m. **EE:** Pharoah. Heb. & Egyp. "Great house". Kings of Egypt out of reverence called Pharoah instead of name. **Var:** Farohán, Farón.
Fariamo (Fah ree ah' mo) m. **EE:** Fariamo. Form of Famiano, S, who visited shrine of Santiago & stayed in Spain for 35 years? F. 11/28.
Farid (Fah reed') m. **EE:** Farid. Ar. "Unequaled." **Var:** Farida.
Farida   see **Farid.**
Faro   see **Rafael.**
Faro   see **Raul,**
Farohán   see **Faraón.**
Farón   see **Faraón.**
Farrucho   see **Francisco.**
Farruco   see **Francisco.**
Fastino   see **Faustino.**
Fata   see **Faustino.**
Faurstino   see **Faustino.**
Faustano   see **Faustino.**
Faustautino   see **Faustino.**
Fausteno   see **Faustino.**
Faustia   see **Faustino.**
Faustín   see **Faustino.**
Faustiniano   see **Faustino.**
Faustino (Faos tee' no) m. **EE:** Faust, Faustina, etc. Lat. "Faustus," "bringing good luck." 87 x in DS. 1 burned alive in Cordova, Spain in 4th cen. F. 10/13. **Dim:** Fata (Fausta), Faz, Tino. **Var:** Fanstina, Fastino, Faurstino, Faustano, Faustautino, Fausteno, Faustia, Faustín, Faustiniano, Faustinus, Faustivo, Fausto, Faustulo, Fautino, Fauztino, Fostín, Fostona, Frausta, Fraustro, Frustino, Fustino, Fusto. See also Festo.
Faustinus   see **Faustino.**
Faustivo   see **Faustino.**
Fausto   see **Faustino.**
Faustulo   see **Faustino.**

Fautino   see **Faustino.**
Fauztino   see **Faustino.**
Favana   see **Fabián.**
Favián   see **Fabián.**
Faviana   see **Fabián.**
Faviola   see **Fabián.**
Fay   see **Rafael.**
Faz   see **Faustino.**
Fe (Fay) mf? **EE:** Faith. Lat. "Fides," "belief, trust." 1 of 3 Virtues. Fides, age 12, beaten, thrown into molten pitch, & beheaded. Sisters suffered similar fate. F. 8/1.
Febe (Fay' bee) f. **EE:** Phoebe, etc. Gk. "The bright." Gk. personification of moon. Mentioned in Bible & DS. F. 9/3. **Var:** Phebe, Phoebe.
Feberico   see **Febronio.**
Febián   see **Fabián.**
Febranio   see **Febronio.**
Febronio (Fay broe' nee oh) m. **EE:** Febronius. Related to February & refers to purification. In DS, 20-year-old nun in Assyria in 4th cen. Subjected to ghastly tortures before beheading. F. 6/25. **Var:** Feberico, Febranio, Feburcio, Frebrico.
Feburcio   see **Febronio.**
Fecundo   see **Facundo.**
Feda   see **Fedro.**
Fede   see **Federico.**
Fedel   see **Fidel.**
Fedela   see **Fidel.**
Fedelio   see **Fidel.**
Fedelis   see **Fidel.**
Fedencio   see **Fidencio.**
Fedenco   see **Fidel.**
Fedenico   see **Fidel.**
Fedensio   see **Fidencio.**
Fedenzio   see **Fidencio.**
Federico (Fay day ree' co) m. **EE:** Frederick, etc. Ger. "Powerful, peace, rich." 8 x in DS. 1, Augustinian lay brother, associated with miracles. F. 11/29. **Dim:** Fede, Federquito, Fico, Fredi, Ikoy, Lico. **Var:** Fadrique, Federiel, Federigo, Federio, Fiderico, Fredercio, Fredericlo, Fredico, Fredrico, Friderico, Quico.
Federiel   see **Federico.**
Federigo   see **Federico.**
Federio   see **Federico.**
Federquito   see **Federico.**
Fedil   see **Fidel.**
Fedila   see **Fidel.**
Fedlia   see **Fidel.**
Fedo   see **Rafael.**
Fedro (Fay' droe) m. **EE:** Phoedra, etc. Lat. "Brilliant." In Gk. legend, wife of Theseus whose advances were rejected by his son. Immortalized by Euripides, Seneca, & Racine. Mentioned in DS as M. boiled in pitch. F. 11/29. **Dim:** Feda.
Fefa   see **José.**
Fefita   see **José.**
Feginia   see **Ifigenia.**
Fego   see **Elfego.**
Fela   see **Ofelio.**

Felcienza	see **Félix.**
Feleberta	see **Filiberto.**
Felecia	see **Félix.**
Feleciano	see **Félix.**
Felecidad	see **Félix.**
Felecidas	see **Félix.**
Felecita	see **Félix.**
Felemena	see **Filemón.**
Felemón	see **Filemón.**
Felemono	see **Filemón.**
Felepe	see **Felipo.**
Felepita	see **Felipo.**
Feles	see **Félix.**
Felesitas	see **Félix.**
Félex	see **Félix.**
Félez	see **Félix.**
Felia	see **Félix.**
Feliberto	see **Filiberto.**
Felica	see **Félix.**
Felicanna	see **Félix.**
Felice	see **Félix.**
Feliceario	see **Félix.**
Felicem	see **Félix.**
Felices	see **Félix.**
Felicetas	see **Félix.**
Felicetos	see **Félix.**
Felicha	see **Félix.**
Felichi	see **Felipo.**
Felichi	see **Félix.**
Feliciaeno	see **Félix.**
Feliciania	see **Félix.**
Feliciano	see **Félix.**
Felicibas	see **Félix.**
Felicidá	see **Félix.**
Felicidad	see **Félix.**
Felicidadas	see **Félix.**
Felicilas	see **Félix.**
Felicina	see **Félix.**
Felicio	see **Félix.**
Felición	see **Félix.**
Felicione	see **Félix.**
Felicious	see **Félix.**
Felicismo	see **Félix.**
Felicistas	see **Félix.**
Felicitas	see **Félix.**
Felicitate	see **Félix.**
Felicítaz	see **Félix.**
Felicitus	see **Félix.**
Felides	see **Félix.**
Felidis	see **Félix.**
Feliditas	see **Félix.**
Feliferto	see **Filiberto.**
Felije	see **Félix.**
Felijita	see **Félix.**
Felimón	see **Filemón.**
Felino	see **Félix.**
Felio	see **Rafael.**
Felip	see **Felipo.**
Felipe	see **Felipo.**
Felipha	see **Felipo.**
Felipia	see **Felipo.**
Felipino	see **Felipo.**

Felipo (Fay lee' poe) m. **EE:** Phil, Philip, Philippa. Gk. "Lover of horses." Alexander the Great's father & also several Sp. kings. 55 x in DS. Most important, Philip the Apostle. F. 5/1. **Dim:** Felepita, Felichi, Felo, Lipe, Lipo, Pil, Pipe, Xpil. **Var:** Felepe, Felip, Felipe, Felipha, Felipia, Felipino, Felippe, Felippo, Felopa, Felupe, Filip, Filipe, Filipento, Filipino, Filipo, Filippa, Filippe, Filliphe, Fillippus, Phaleppa, Phelipa, Phelipe, Philipa, Philippa, Phillipa, Phillippe, Phillippo.

Felippe	see **Felipo.**
Felippo	see **Felipo.**
Felis	see **Félix.**
Felisa	see **Félix.**
Felisano	see **Félix.**
Felisario	see **Félix.**
Felisbaldo	see **Félix.**
Felise	see **Félix.**
Felisianno	see **Félix.**
Felisiano	see **Félix.**
Felisitas	see **Félix.**
Felissísimo	see **Félix.**
Felista	see **Félix.**
Felistate	see **Félix.**
Felitas	see **Félix.**
Felitiana	see **Félix.**
Feliverto	see **Filiberto.**

Félix (Fay' leeks) m. **EE:** Felicia, Felix. Lat. "Happy." Roman procurator in Palestine to whom St. Paul spoke about justice to come. 230 x in DS. **Dim:** Chano (Feliciano), Chito (Felicito), Felecita, Felesitas, Felicha (Felisa), Felichi (Feliciano), Felijita, Felisitas, Felizitas, Felizsita, Filesitos, Filiceta, Filícita, Licho (Felicito), Pitín, Pito, Zita. **Var:** Felcienza, Felecia, Feleciano, Felecidad, Felecidas, Feles, Félex, Félez, Felia, Felica, Felicanna, Felice, Feliceario, Felicem, Felices, Felicetas, Felicetos, Feliciaeno, Feliciania, Feliciano, Felicibas, Felicidá, Felicidad, Felicidadas, Felicilas, Felicina, Felicio, Felición, Felicione, Felicious, Felicismo, Felicistas, Felicitas, Felicitate, Felicítaz, Felicitus, Felides, Felidis, Feliditas, Felije, Felino, Felis, Felisa, Felisano, Felisario, Felisbaldo, Felise, Felisianno, Felisiano, Felissísimo, Felista, Felistate, Felitas, Felitiana, Felixa, Felixe, Felixia, Felixiano, Felixta, Felizandro, Felizano, Felizardo, Felizia, Feliziano, Felizo, Felo, Felux, Felysa, Filex, Filiz, Fliez, Phelia, Phelis, Phelisiana, Philysa.

Felixa	see **Félix.**
Felixe	see **Félix.**
Felixia	see **Félix.**
Felixiano	see **Félix.**
Felixta	see **Félix.**
Felizandro	see **Félix.**
Felizano	see **Félix.**
Felizardo	see **Félix.**
Felizia	see **Félix.**
Feliziano	see **Félix.**
Felizitas	see **Félix.**
Felizo	see **Félix.**
Felizsita	see **Félix.**
Felma	see **Filomeno.**
Felmina	see **Filomeno.**
Felo	see **Felipo.**

Felo   see **Félix**.
Felo   see **Raul**.
Felomela   see **Filomeno**.
Felomeno   see **Filomeno**.
Feloneno   see **Filomeno**.
Feloniz   see **Filomeno**.
Felopa   see **Felipo**.
Felorencio   see **Florencio**.
Felupe   see **Felipo**.
Felux   see **Félix**.
Felysa   see **Félix**.
Femia   see **Eufemia**.
Fencho   see **Fulgencio**.
Fenis   see **Fénix**.
Fénix (Fay' neeks) m. **EE**: Phoenix.
Lat. "Phoenix." Fig., what is
marvelous &/or unique. Refers to
mythological Ar. bird that lives
for 500 years, burned to death &
reborn. **Var**: Fenis.
Feomina   see **Filomeno**.
Ferando   see **Fernando**.
Ferdenanda   see **Fernando**.
Ferdi   see **Fernando**.
Ferdino   see **Fernando**.
Ferdoro (Fare doe' roe) m. Comb.
of Fernando & Teodoro (see
both).
Ferdynando   see **Fernando**.
Ferendo   see **Fernando**.
Fereso (Fay ray' so) m. **EE**:
Pheres. In Gk. myth. Pheres was
son of Jason & Medea.
Ferima   see **Fermín**.
Ferimino   see **Fermín**.
Fermán   see **Fermín**.
Fermen   see **Fermín**.
Fermena   see **Fermín**.
Fermi   see **Fermín**.
Fermilia   see **Fermín**.
Fermín (Fare meen') m. **EE**:
Firmian, etc. Lat. "Firmus,"
"firm, constant." 30 x in DS. 1,
1st bishop of Amiens in 3rd cen,
decapitated. F. 9/25. **Dim**:
Fermi, Min, Mincho. **Var**: Ferima,
Ferimino, Fermán, Fermén,
Fermena, Fermilia, Ferminila,
Ferminio, Fermino, Fermón,
Fernime, Firmia, Firmín,
Firminio, Firmino, Firminus,
Firmo, Frema, Fremios,
Ferminila   see **Fermín**.
Ferminio   see **Fermín**.
Fermino   see **Fermín**.
Fermón   see **Fermín**.
Fernada   see **Fernando**.
Fernandeo   see **Fernando**.
Fernandino   see **Fernando**.
Fernando (Fare nahn' doe) m. **EE**:
Ferdinand, etc. Ger. "To make
peace, to be bold." Popular
among Sp. kings. **Dim**: Ferdi,
Fernandino, Ferni, Nando, Nano.
Var: Ferando, Ferdenanda,
Ferdino, Ferdynando, Ferendo,
Fernada, Fernandeo, Fernania.
See also Hernando.
Fernania   see **Fernando**.
Ferni   see **Fernando**.
Fernime   see **Fermín**.
Feronio   see **Jerónimo**.
Ferrer (Fay rare') m. **EE**: Ferrer.
Sp. surname. Lat. "Ferrarius,"
"relating to iron." Vincent

Ferrer, 14th cen. proselytizer,
converted 33,000. F. 4/5.
Festilo   see **Festo**.
Festividad (Fays' tee bee dahd')
f? **EE**: Festivity. Day set apart
& celebrated in Catholic church
in honor of God, Christ, Ss.,
angels or sacred mysteries &
events. Feast day in English.
Festo (Fay' stoe) m. **EE**: Festus.
Lat. "Faustus," "happy." Roman
procurator of Judea under Nero.
Gave St. Paul fair hearing. 7 x
in DS. **Var**: Festilo. See also
Faustino.
Fexenia   see **Ifigenia**.
Feyo   see **Alfredo**.
Fhilomena   see **Filomeno**.
Fia   see **Sofío**.
Fiacro (Fee ah' croe) m. **EE**:
Fiacre. Lat. "One who fights."
7th cen. Irish S. Patron of
gardeners & Fr. cab drivers. F.
8/30.
Fico   see **Federico**.
Fico   see **Francisco**.
Fico   see **Teófilo**.
Fidal   see **Fidel**.
Fide   see **Fidel**.
Fideila   see **Fidel**.
Fidel (Fee dehl') m. **EE**: Fidel,
etc. Lat. "Faithful, loyal." 9 x
in DS. 1, 17th cen. Capuchin
preacher, so successful that was
murdered by Zwinglian competi-
tion. F. 4/24. **Dim**: Fido,
Fidolo, Lela (Fidelia). **Var**:
Fedel, Fedela, Fedelio, Fedelis,
Fedenco, Fedenico, Fedil,
Fedila, Fedlia, Fidal, Fide,
Fideila, Fidela, Fidelcio,
Fidelfa, Fidelice, Fidelino,
Fidelio, Fidélix, Fidello,
Fiderria, Fidilia, Filelia.
Fidela   see **Fidel**.
Fidelcio   see **Fidel**.
Fidelfa   see **Fidel**.
Fidelice   see **Fidel**.
Fidelino   see **Fidel**.
Fidelio   see **Fidel**.
Fidélix   see **Fidel**.
Fidello   see **Fidel**.
Fidemencia   see **Fidencio**.
Fidenancio   see **Fidencio**.
Fidencio (Fee dayn' see oh) m. **EE**:
Fidentius. Lat. "Confidence,
boldness." 6 x in DS. **Var**:
Fedencio, Fedensio, Fedenzio,
Fidemencia, Fidenancio,
Fidencium, Fidenio, Fideniso,
Fidensio, Fidentiae, Fidentio,
Fidentis, Fidenziana, Fidenzio,
Fidiancio, Fidincio, Firdencio,
Fredencio, Fudencio, Phidencia.
Fidencium   see **Fidencio**.
Fidenio   see **Fidencio**.
Fideniso   see **Fidencio**.
Fidensio   see **Fidencio**.
Fidentiae   see **Fidencio**.
Fidentio   see **Fidencio**.
Fidentis   see **Fidencio**.
Fidenziana   see **Fidencio**.
Fidenzio   see **Fidencio**.
Fiderico   see **Federico**.
Fiderria   see **Fidel**.

Fidiancio   see **Fidencio.**
Fidilia   see **Fidel.**
Fidincio   see **Fidencio.**
Fido   see **Fidel.**
Fidolo   see **Fidel.**
Fifi   see **José.**
Fifi   see **Sofío.**
Figenia   see **Ifigenia.**
Filadelfio   see **Filadelfo.**
Filadelfo (Fee lah dehl' foe) m.
  EE: Philadelphus. Gk. "Brotherly
  love." 4 x in DS. **Var:**
  Filadelfio, Filadelphio.
Filadelphio   see **Filadelfo.**
Filamena   see **Filomeno.**
Filamino   see **Filomeno.**
Filaneno   see **Filomeno.**
Filbert   see **Filiberto.**
Filberta   see **Filiberto.**
Filbertha   see **Filiberto.**
Filborto   see **Filiberto.**
Filderto   see **Filiberto.**
Fileberto   see **Filiberto.**
Filelja   see **Fidel.**
Filemán   see **Filemón.**
Filemeno   see **Filomeno.**
Fileminio   see **Filomeno.**
Filemna   see **Filomeno.**
Filemo   see **Filomeno.**
Filemón (Fee lay mohn') m. **EE:**
  Philemon, Gk. "Loving, affec-
  tionate." In Gk. legend Philemon
  & Baucis only ones to offer
  shelter to Zeus & Hermes. Immor-
  talized as trees. 9 x in DS.
  Var: Felemena, Felemón,
  Felemono, Felimón, Filemán,
  Flaymón.
Filemono   see **Filomeno.**
Filesitos   see **Félix.**
Filex   see **Félix.**
Filiberto (Fee' lee bare' toe) m.
  EE: Philbert, etc. Teut. "Bright
  of will." In DS as 7th cen.
  abbot of Gascony, France. **Dim:**
  Filis. **Var:** Feleberta,
  Feliberta, Feliferto, Feliverto,
  Filbert, Filberta, Filbertha,
  Filborto, Filderto, Fileberto,
  Filverto, Philberto, Philiberta,
  Philibertus.
Filiceta   see **Félix.**
Filicita   see **Félix.**
Filigonio   see **Filogonio.**
Filimeno   see **Filomeno.**
Filimón   see **Filomeno.**
Filip   see **Felipo.**
Filipe   see **Felipo.**
Filipento   see **Felipo.**
Filipino   see **Felipo.**
Filipo   see **Felipo.**
Filippa   see **Felipo.**
Filippe   see **Felipo.**
Filis   see **Filiberto.**
Filiz   see **Félix.**
Filliphe   see **Felipo.**
Fillippus   see **Felipo.**
Filmeno   see **Filomeno.**
Filmín   see **Filomeno.**
Filo   see **Filomeno.**
Filo   see **Porfirio.**
Filo   see **Teófilo.**
Filogonio (Fee low go' nee oh) m.
  EE: Philagonia. Gk. "Friend of
  his race." Ital. M. whose exis-

tence is dubious. F. 3/6. **Var:**
  Filigonio.
Filomana   see **Filomeno.**
Filomenio   see **Filomeno.**
Filomeno (Fee' low may' no) m. **EE:**
  Philomela, Philomeno. Gk. "Of
  loving mind." Ital. S. of un-
  known date with relics discov-
  ered in 1802. F. 8/10. **Dim:**
  Felma, Filo, Filunga, Mena,
  Menalia. **Var:** Felmina, Felomela,
  Felomeno, Feloneno, Feloniz,
  Feomina, Fhilomena, Filamena,
  Filamino, Filaneno, Filemeno,
  Fileminio, Filemna, Filemo,
  Filomeno, Filimeno, Filimón,
  Filmeno, Filmín, Filomana,
  Filomenio, Filomero, Filomerro,
  Filomino, Filomono, Filonena,
  Filoniz, Fiomara, Fiomín, Flema,
  Flomeno, Flomentín, Flomentino,
  Gilomena, Hilomena, Ilomeno,
  Jelomena, Jilomena, Philemona,
  Philemone, Philimena, Philomén,
  Philomeno, Philumena.
Filomero   see **Filomeno.**
Filomerro   see **Filomeno.**
Filomino   see **Filomeno.**
Filomono   see **Filomeno.**
Filonena   see **Filomeno.**
Filoniz   see **Filomeno.**
Filorentino   see **Florencio.**
Filucho   see **Lucía.**
Filunga   see **Filomeno.**
Filverto   see **Filiberto.**
Fina   see **José.**
Fineas (Fee nay' ahs) m. **EE:**
  Phineas. Egyp. "Dark-complex-
  ioned." Grandson of Aaron
  rewarded with everlasting
  priesthood for combatting
  idolatry. 2 x in DS. **Var:** Fines.
Fines   see **Fineas.**
Finita   see **Delfino.**
Fino   see **Ceferino.**
Fino   see **Delfino.**
Fiomara   see **Filomeno.**
Fiomín   see **Filomeno.**
Firdencio   see **Fidencio.**
Firenzio   see **Florencio.**
Firmia   see **Fermín.**
Firmín   see **Fermín.**
Firminio   see **Fermín.**
Firmino   see **Fermín.**
Firminus   see **Fermín.**
Firmo   see **Fermín.**
Firo   see **Porfirio.**
Firtunato   see **Fortunato.**
Fita   see **Sofío.**
Fito   see **Adolfo.**
Fito   see **Alfredo.**
Fito   see **Rodolfo.**
Flabia   see **Flavio.**
Flabiola   see **Flavio.**
Flamantino   see **Flaminio.**
Flaminio (Flah mee' nee oh) m. **EE:**
  Flaminia. Lat. "Belonging to
  priestly caste." Flaminia mart.
  under Diocletian. F. 5/2. **Var:**
  Flamantino, Flamino, Flamintina.
Flamino   see **Flaminio.**
Flamintina   see **Flaminio.**
Flarencio   see **Florencio.**
Flarintino   see **Florencio.**
Flaviano   see **Flavio.**

Flavio (Flah' bee oh) m. **EE:**
Flavia, Flavius. Lat. "Yellow or
blond." 3 Roman emperors. 38 x
in DS. 1, 5th cen. Patriarch of
Constantinople. F. 2/18. **Var:**
Falvio, Flabia, Flabiola,
Flaviano, Flavis, Flivio.

Flavis	see	**Flavio.**
Flaymón	see	**Filemón.**
Flema	see	**Filomeno.**
Flerida	see	**Florencio.**
Fliez	see	**Félix.**
Flivio	see	**Flavio.**
Floentina	see	**Florencio.**
Flomeno	see	**Filomeno.**
Flomentín	see	**Filomeno.**
Flomentino	see	**Filomeno.**
Flonencia	see	**Florencio.**
Floracio	see	**Florencio.**
Floralia	see	**Florencio.**
Floralva	see	**Florencio.**
Florancio	see	**Florencio.**
Florante	see	**Florencio.**
Floranzio	see	**Florencio.**
Florcinda	see	**Florencio.**
Florde	see	**Florencio.**
Flore	see	**Florencio.**
Floreciano	see	**Florencio.**
Floreinda	see	**Florencio.**
Florenca	see	**Florencio.**

Florencio (Flow rehn' see oh) m.
EE: Flo, Flora, Florence, etc.
Lat. "Blooming." 66 x in DS.
Dim: Coya (Flora), Florencita,
Florita (Flora), Lencho, Linda
(Florinda), Poncho, Tino
(Florentino). **Var:** Felorencio,
Filorentino, Firenzio,
Flarencio, Flarintino, Flerida,
Floentina, Flonencia, Floracio,
Floralia, Floralva, Florancio,
Florante, Floranzio, Florcinda,
Florde, Flore, Floreciano,
Floreinda, Florenca, Florencis,
Florenda, Florendia, Florenezia,
Florenio, Florensia, Florenso,
Florenteno, Florentia,
Florentián, Florentías,
Florentinio, Florentino,
Florentión, Florentius,
Florenzio, Florenzo, Floresio,
Floreta, Floretino, Floria,
Florián, Florida, Florifes,
Florincia, Florinda, Florine,
Florino, Florinto, Floripe,
Floripes, Florisa, Florium,
Florival, Flornia, Flornida,
Floro, Flotentina, Forencia.

Florencis	see	**Florencio.**
Florencita	see	**Florencio.**
Florenda	see	**Florencio.**
Florendia	see	**Florencio.**
Florenezia	see	**Florencio.**
Florenio	see	**Florencio.**
Florensia	see	**Florencio.**
Florenso	see	**Florencio.**
Florenteno	see	**Florencio.**
Florentia	see	**Florencio.**
Florentián	see	**Florencio.**
Florentías	see	**Florencio.**
Florentinio	see	**Florencio.**
Florentino	see	**Florencio.**
Florentión	see	**Florencio.**
Florentius	see	**Florencio.**
Florenzio	see	**Florencio.**
Florenzo	see	**Florencio.**
Floresio	see	**Florencio.**
Floreta	see	**Florencio.**
Floretino	see	**Florencio.**
Floria	see	**Florencio.**
Florián	see	**Florencio.**

Floriberto (Flow' ree bare' toe)
m. **EE:** Floribert, etc. Teut.
"Wise & splendid."

Florida	see	**Florencio.**
Florifes	see	**Florencio.**
Florincia	see	**Florencio.**
Florinda	see	**Florencio.**
Florine	see	**Florencio.**
Florino	see	**Florencio.**
Florinto	see	**Florencio.**
Floripe	see	**Florencio.**
Floripes	see	**Florencio.**
Florisa	see	**Florencio.**
Florita	see	**Florencio.**
Florium	see	**Florencio.**
Florival	see	**Florencio.**

Flormenegilda (Flore may nay heel'
dah) f. **EE:** Flormenegilda. Comb.
of Florencio & Hermenegildo (see
both).

Flornia	see	**Florencio.**
Flornida	see	**Florencio.**
Floro	see	**Florencio.**
Flotentina	see	**Florencio.**
Flovia	see	**Fulvio.**
Flugencio	see	**Fulgencio.**
Flugentia	see	**Fulgencio.**
Flumencio	see	**Frumencio.**
Flumentio	see	**Frumencio.**
Flutoso	see	**Fulgencio.**
Fluvia	see	**Fulvio.**
Fluxenia	see	**Fulgencio.**

Focas (Foe' cahs) m. **EE:** Phocas.
Gk. "Seal." 9 x in DS. 1, of 3rd
cen., invoked against poisonous
snakes. F. 4/5.

Fofo	see	**Rodolfo.**
Foncho	see	**Adolfo.**
Foncho	see	**Alfonso.**
Fonctioso	see	**Fructuoso.**
Fonso	see	**Adolfo.**
Fonso	see	**Alfonso.**
Fontisano	see	**Fuensanta.**
Forencia	see	**Florencio.**

Fornasa (Fore nah' sah) f. **EE:**
Fornasa. Lat. "Fornacea," "large
fireplace." One who loves home.

Foro	see	**Sinforoso.**
Fortimio	see	**Fortunato.**

Fortino (Fore tee' no) m. **EE:**
Fortune. Related to Fortuno &
Fortunato (see).

Fortumato	see	**Fortunato.**
Fortunado	see	**Fortunato.**

Fortunato (Fore too nah' toe) m.
EE: Fortunatus, etc. Lat. "For-
tunate, lucky." 69 x in DS. In
legend, had limitless funds &
magic cap to transport him. **Var:**
Firtunato, Fortimio, Fortumato,
Fortunado, Frotunato, Furtanato.
See also Fortino, Fortuno.

Fortunio   see **Fortuno.**

Fortuno (Fore too' no) m. **EE:**
Fortune, etc. Lat. "Fortune."
Goddess of luck & chance who
gave out poverty, riches, mis-
fortunes, & pain. 5 x in DS.
Dim: Tino, Tuni. **Var:** Fortunio.

See also Fortino, Fortunato.

Fostín	see	**Faustino.**
Fostona	see	**Faustino.**
Fracia	see	**Eufracio.**
Fractuoso	see	**Fructuoso.**
Frailama	see	**Froilán.**
Frailano	see	**Froilán.**
Franasca	see	**Francisco.**
Francasca	see	**Francisco.**
Francesco	see	**Francisco.**
Francesia	see	**Francisco.**
Francho	see	**Francisco.**
Francica	see	**Francisco.**
Francis	see	**Francisco.**
Franciscis	see	**Francisco.**

Francisco (Frahn sees' co) m. **EE:**
Fran, Francis, Frank, Ger.
"Free." 48 x in DS. Both Francis
of Assisi & Francis Xavier great
Ss. **Dim:** Chichicha, Chicho,
Chilo, Chisco, Chito, Chuco,
Cisco, Currito, Curro, Farrucho,
Farruco, Fico, Francho,
Francisquito, Frasco, Frascuelo,
Frasquillo, Frasquito, Frisco,
Pacheco, Pachico, Pachín, Pacho,
Pachu, Paco, Pacurro, Paíto,
Pajito, Panchio, Panchito,
Pancho, Pancholo, Panchy, Panzo,
Paquillo, Paquín, Paquito,
Payito, Quico, Quito. **Var:**
Franasca, Francasca, Francesco,
Francesia, Francica, Francis,
Franciscis, Franciscoa,
Franciskita, Francisko,
Franciszka, Francixa, Franco,
Franedis, Frangina, Franicisca,
Franina, Franisca, Franqubino,
Franquiline, Fransheska,
Fransico, Fransisco, Fransito,
Frantisca, Franxisca, Franzico,
Franzisko, Francisco, Frencisia.

Franciscoa	see	**Francisco.**
Franciskita	see	**Francisco.**
Francisko	see	**Francisco.**
Francisquito	see	**Francisco.**
Franciszka	see	**Francisco.**
Francixa	see	**Francisco.**
Franco	see	**Francisco.**
Franedis	see	**Francisco.**
Frangina	see	**Francisco.**
Franicisca	see	**Francisco.**
Franina	see	**Francisco.**
Franisca	see	**Francisco.**
Franqubino	see	**Francisco.**
Franquiline	see	**Francisco.**
Fransheska	see	**Francisco.**
Fransico	see	**Francisco.**
Fransisco	see	**Francisco.**
Fransito	see	**Francisco.**
Frantisca	see	**Francisco.**
Franxisca	see	**Francisco.**
Franzico	see	**Francisco.**
Franzisko	see	**Francisco.**
Frasco	see	**Francisco.**
Frascuelo	see	**Francisco.**
Frasquillo	see	**Francisco.**
Frasquito	see	**Francisco.**
Frausta	see	**Faustino.**
Fraustro	see	**Faustino.**
Fraylán	see	**Froilán.**
Fraylano	see	**Froilán.**
Frebrico	see	**Febronio.**
Frecha	see	**Eufracio.**
Fredencio	see	**Fidencio.**

Fredercio	see	**Federico.**
Fredericlo	see	**Federico.**
Fredi	see	**Alfredo.**
Fredi	see	**Federico.**
Fredico	see	**Federico.**

Fredisberto (Fray dees bare' toe)
m. Comb. of Federico & Berto
(see both).

Fredo	see	**Alfredo.**
Fredrico	see	**Federico.**
Frema	see	**Fermín.**
Fremencio	see	**Frumencio.**
Fremios	see	**Fermín.**
Frencisco	see	**Francisco.**
Frencisia	see	**Francisco.**
Frenea	see	**Eufemia.**
Frenia	see	**Eufemia.**
Fresia	see	**Eufracio.**
Friderico	see	**Federico.**

Fridolín (Free doe leen') m. Ger.
"Protection, security, lover of
peace." Native of 6th cen. Ire-
land, did missionary work in
Germany. F. 3/6. **Var:** Fridolino,
Fruida.

Fridolino	see	**Fridolín.**

Frigio (Free' hee oh) m. **EE:**
Frigidius. Lat. "Cold." 2 x in
DS.

Frilán	see	**Froilán.**

Fringustina (Freen hoos tee' nah)
f. **EE:** Fringustina. Comb. of
Francisco & Agusto (see both)?

Frisco	see	**Francisco.**

Froilán (Froy lahn') m. **EE:**
Froylan. Teut. "Lord." In DS,
9th cen. Archbishop of Leon,
Spain. Built many monasteries.
F. 10/5. **Var:** Frailama,
Frailano, Fraylán, Fraylano,
Frilán, Froilón, Fruela.

Froilón	see	**Froilán.**
Fromunciano	see	**Frumencio.**

Fronintino (Froe neen tee' no) m.
EE: Fronintino. Form of Frontin-
ianus, 4th cen. Fr. S. & M? F.
4/27.

Frotunato	see	**Fortunato.**
Fructaroso	see	**Fructuoso.**
Fructo	see	**Fructuoso.**
Fructoso	see	**Fructuoso.**
Fructuo	see	**Fructuoso.**

Fructuoso (Frook too oh' so) m.
EE: Fructuosus, etc. Lat.
"Fruitful, fertile." 7 x in DS.
1, 3rd cen. bishop of Tarragona,
Spain, burnt at stake. F. 1/21.
Var: Fonctioso, Fractuoso,
Fructaroso, Fructo, Fructoso,
Fructuo, Frudoso, Fruetoso,
Fruitoso, Frukturosa, Frustoso,
Frustuoso, Frutios, Frutoro,
Frutos, Frutoso, Frutozo,
Frutuoso, Frutuoza.

Frudoso	see	**Fructuoso.**
Fruela	see	**Froilán.**
Fruetoso	see	**Fructuoso.**
Fruida	see	**Fridolín.**
Fruitoso	see	**Fructuoso.**
Frukturosa	see	**Fructuoso.**

Frumencio (Froo mane' see oh) m.
EE: Frumentius. Lat. "Frumentius," "he who supplies grain." 2
x in DS. 1 considered apostle of
Abyssinia, Ethiopia. F. 10/27.

Var: Flumencio, Flumentio, Fremencio, Fromunciano, Frumentio, Frumintio.

Frumentio	see **Frumencio.**
Frumintio	see **Frumencio.**
Frustino	see **Faustino.**
Frustoso	see **Fructuoso.**
Frustuoso	see **Fructuoso.**
Frutios	see **Fructuoso.**
Frutoro	see **Fructuoso.**
Frutos	see **Fructuoso.**
Frutoso	see **Fructuoso.**
Frutozo	see **Fructuoso.**
Frutuoso	see **Fructuoso.**
Frutuoza	see **Fructuoso.**
Fucho	see **Refugio.**
Fudencio	see **Fidencio.**

Fuensanta (Fwehn sahn' tah) f. Lat. "Fons" & "sanctus" meaning "holy fount." Nuestra Señora de la Fuensanta (Our Lady of the Holy Fount) venerated in Murcia, Spain. Weedgatherer found statue in thermal waters & miracles began. **Dim:** Fuenta. **Var:** Fontisano.

Fuenta	see **Fuensanta.**
Fujo	see **Refugio.**
Fule	see **Rafael.**
Fulgancia	see **Fulgencio.**

Fulgencio (Fool hehn' see oh) m.

EE: Fulgentius. Lat. "Brilliant, resplendent." 7 x in DS. 1, 4th cen. African bishop, fought Arian heresy. F. 1/1. **Dim:** Chencho, Fencho, Gencho. **Var:** Flugencio, Flugentia, Flutoso, Fluxenia, Fulgancia, Fulgenio, Fulgentio, Fuljensio, Furjencio.

Fulgenio	see **Fulgencio.**
Fulgentio	see **Fulgencio.**
Fuljensio	see **Fulgencio.**

Fulvio (Fool' bee oh) m. **EE:** Fulvia, Fulvius. Lat. "Red root." "Fulvia pierced Cicero's tongue because he attacked her in "Phillipics." Ethopian S. **Var:** Flovia, Fluvia.

Fura	see **Furius.**

Furius (Foo' ree oohs) m. **EE:** Furius. Lat. family name meaning "furious", probably relates to military qualities. **Var:** Fura.

Furjencio	see **Fulgencio.**
Furtanato	see **Fortunato.**

Fusciano (Foo see ah' no) m. **EE:** Fuscianus. 3rd cen. Fr. M. considered apostle of France. F. 2/11.

Fustino	see **Faustino.**
Fusto	see **Faustino.**

G

Gabe	see **Gabriel.**
Gabel	see **Gabriel.**
Gabella	see **Gabriel.**
Gabi	see **Gabriel.**
Gabián	see **Gabriel.**
Gabicho	see **Gabriel.**
Gabicu	see **Gabriel.**
Gabiel	see **Gabriel.**

Gabino (Gah bee' no) m. **EE:** Gabinius, Gabinus, Lat. "Inhabitant of Gabio." 2 x in DS. 1, brother of Pope Cajus, imprisoned when daughter refused to marry 3rd cen. Caesar. F. 2/19. **Var:** Cabino, Gabinum, Gabinus, Gabrino, Galveno, Galvino, Garvino, Gaveno, Gavini, Gavino, Gavinos, Girbina, Gubino, Guvino, Jabino.

Gabinum	see **Gabino.**
Gabinus	see **Gabino.**
Gabirel	see **Gabriel.**
Gabreil	see **Gabriel.**
Gabrela	see **Gabriel.**
Gabrial	see **Gabriel.**
Gabrido	see **Gabriel.**
Gabrieala	see **Gabriel.**

Gabriel (Gah bree ehl') m. **EE:** Gabe, Gabriel, Gabriella. Heb. "Man of God." Biblical archangel of God. 24 x in DS. Will blow trumpet on last day. F. 3/24. **Dim:** Bel, Chela, Gabi, Gabicho, Gabicu, Gabuch, Gaby, Lelo, Lucho, Riel. **Var:** Abrielo, Gabe, Gabel, Gabella, Gabián, Gabiel, Gabirel, Gabreil, Gabrela, Gabrial, Gabrido, Gabrieala, Gabrielam, Gabrieles, Gabrielo, Gabril, Gabrill, Galiriela, Garela, Garrabiel, Gavriel, Gebriela, Goraviela, Grabel, Grabide, Grabiel, Grabilita, Gravael, Gravel, Gravelita, Graviel, Graviella, Gravil, Graviola, Gravoll.

Gabrielam	see **Gabriel.**
Gabrieles	see **Gabriel.**
Gabrielo	see **Gabriel.**
Gabril	see **Gabriel.**
Gabrill	see **Gabriel.**
Gabrino	see **Gabino.**
Gabuch	see **Gabriel.**
Gaby	see **Gabriel.**
Gach	see **Graciela.**
Gache	see **Graciela.**
Gacho	see **Engracia.**
Gacinta	see **Jacinto.**
Gaetán	see **Cayetano.**
Gaetano	see **Cayetano.**
Gaetono	see **Cayetano.**
Gaietana	see **Cayetano.**
Gajetán	see **Cayetano.**
Gajetano	see **Cayetano.**

Galación (Gah lah see own') m? **EE:** Galaction. Gk. "Native of Galacia (Turkey)." 4 x in DS. 1, possibly apocryphal, persuaded wife to lead virginal life. Both beheaded in Phoenicia. F. 11/5.

Galdeno	see **Ubaldo.**
Galdino	see **Ubaldo.**

Galdro　　　see **Ubaldo.**
Galeno (Gah lay' no) m. **EE:** Galen.
Lat. "Sea clam." Gk. physician
whose writings managed to retard
medicine for almost 14 cens.
Galieno (Gah lee aay' no) m. **EE:**
Galenus, Gallienus. Lat.
"Galenus," "joyful, tranquil."
In DS, 1 of 10,000 crucified Mm.
of Mt. Ararat (Turkey). F. 6/22.
Var: Gallieno.
Galiriela　　see **Gabriel.**
Galisto　　　see **Calixto.**
Galistra　　see **Calixto.**
Galli　　　　see **Galo.**
Gallieno　　see **Galieno.**
Gallus　　　see **Galo.**
Galo (Gah' low) m. **EE:** Gall,
Gallus. Lat. "Gallus," "one from
Gaul." 9 x in DS, 1, 6th cen.
Irishman, 1 of 12 disciples of
St. Columban. F. 10/16. **Var:**
Galli, Gallus.
Galveno　　　see **Gabino.**
Galvino　　　see **Gabino.**
Gamabiel　　see **Gamaliel.**
Gamacinda　　see **Gumersindo.**
Gamacinto　　see **Gumersindo.**
Gamaliel (Gah mah lee ehl') m. **EE:**
Gamaliel. Heb. "God's reward."
Biblical law doctor, who cau-
tioned against persecuting
Christians. F. 8/3. **Var:**
Gamabiel.
Gamecinda　　see **Gumersindo.**
Gando　　　　see **Alejandro.**
Gandolyn　　see **Genoveva.**
Garagoza　　see **Zaragoza.**
García (Gahr see' ah) m. **EE:**
Garcia. 1 of few Sp. surnames
used as 1st name. Could be of
pre-Roman origin meaning "fox."
Var: Garcisa.
Garcimiro　　see **Casimiro.**
Garcisa　　　see **García.**
Gardelia　　see **Candelario.**
Gardelia　　see **Cordilio.**
Garela　　　see **Gabriel.**
Garganio　　see **Gorgonio.**
Gargario　　see **Gorgonio.**
Gargonio　　see **Gorgonio.**
Garibaldi　　see **Garibaldo.**
Garibaldo (Gah ree bahl' doe) m.
EE: Garibald, etc. Teut. "Bold
with his lance." 19th cen. Ital.
patriot who fought in South
American wars. In DS, 8th cen.
bishop. F. 9/7. **Var:** Garibaldi,
Giribaldo.
Garina　　　see **Carino.**
Garmea　　　see **Carmen.**
Garrabiel　　see **Gabriel.**
Garrina　　　see **Carino.**
Garvino　　　see **Gabino.**
Gasino　　　see **Casiano.**
Gaspar (Gahs pahr') m. **EE:** Gaspar,
Jasper, etc. Pers. "Treasure
holder." Biblically, 1 of 3
kings who visited Christ child.
8 x in DS. 1, Japanese Jesuit of
16th cen, buried alive in
Nagasaki. F. 6/20. **Var:** Caspar,
Casparo, Casparus, Caspio,
Gaspor, Gazpar, Gospar.
Gaspor　　　see **Gaspar.**

Gastón (Gahs tone') m. **EE:** Gascon,
Gaston, Teut. "Hospitable."
Literally, native of Gascony,
France. In DS, Vedastus, 6th
cen. co-worker of St. Remisio,
who helped convert Franks. F.
2/6.
Gastulo　　　see **Casto.**
Gaudalupe　　see **Guadalupe.**
Gaudencio (Gao dane' see oh) m.
EE: Gaudentia, Gaudentius. Lat.
"One who is happy." 16 x in DS.
1, 4th cen. bishop of Rimini,
Italy, put to death by Arians.
F. 10/14. **Dim:** Gaudio. **Var:**
Caudencio.
Gaudio　　　see **Gaudencio.**
Gavdalupe　　see **Guadalupe.**
Gaveno　　　see **Gabino.**
Gavini　　　see **Gabino.**
Gavino　　　see **Gabino.**
Gavinos　　　see **Gabino.**
Gavriel　　　see **Gabriel.**
Gayetano　　see **Cayetano.**
Gayo　　　　see **Cayo.**
Gazpar　　　see **Gaspar.**
Gebardo　　　see **Gebhardo.**
Gebhardo (Habe hahr' doe) m. **EE:**
Gebhardt. Teut. "Determined
giver." 2 x in DS. 1, 10th cen.
bishop of Constance, Germany. F.
8/27. **Var:** Gebardo.
Gebriela　　see **Gabriel.**
Gedeón (Hay day own') m. **EE:**
Gideon. Heb. "Hewer of trees." 3
x in DS. Received favorable omen
regarding sheep's fleece, went
into battle & freed Israel from
Midianites. Gideon Society gives
free Bibles.
Geferina　　see **Ceferino.**
Gehardo　　　see **Gerardo.**
Gela　　　　see **Rogelio.**
Gelasio (Hay lah' see oh) m. **EE:**
Gellaseo, Gellasio. Gk. "Laugh-
ter." 14 x in DS. 1, son of
Afro-Roman parents, 5th cen.
pope noted for writings & fight-
ing schisms. F. 11/21. **Var:**
Gellaseo, Gellasio.
Gelberto　　see **Gilberto.**
Geliberto　　see **Gilberto.**
Gellaseo　　see **Gelasio.**
Gellasio　　see **Gelasio.**
Gellermina　　see **Guillermo.**
Gellrudis　　see **Gertrudis.**
Gelo　　　　see **Angel.**
Geltrudis　　see **Gertrudis.**
Gemecindo　　see **Gumersindo.**
Gemen　　　　see **Germán.**
Gemerlindo　　see **Hermelinda.**
Geminiano　　see **Gemino.**
Gemino (Hay mee' no) m. **EE:**
Geminianus, etc. Lat. "Twins."
Another name for Janus, Roman
god with 2 faces that looked in
opposite directions. 3rd sign of
zodiac referring to twins Castor
& Pollux. 16 x in DS. **Var:**
Geminiano.
Genaida (Hay nigh' dah) f. **EE:**
Genaida. Gk. "Noble of birth."
Patriarch of Constantinople in
5th cen. Genaides in Gk. myth.
were gods worshiped in Focea in

Asia Minor.

Genareo   see **Génaro**.
Génaro (Hay' nah roe) m. EE:
Janarius, etc. Lat. "Ianuarius,"
"consecrated to God." Refers to
Janus, 2-headed Roman god. 62 x
in DS. 1, 10th cen. bishop of
Beneventum, Italy, whose pre-
served blood liquifies annually.
F. 9/19. **Dim:** Yenerita. **Var:**
Cenario, Ejénaro, Énaro, Enera,
Enereo, Genareo, Génarro,
Géniro, Génnaro, Génnora, Genro,
Ginaro, Hénaro, Jenardo, Jénaro,
Jenarrio, Jenerio, Jénero,
Jénora, Sénaro, Xenar, Zénora,
Zénore. See also Genessio,
Ienero, Jano.
Génarro   see **Génaro**.
Genavera   see **Genoveva**.
Genaveva   see **Genoveva**.
Genaviva   see **Genoveva**.
Genavo   see **Genoveva**.
Gencho   see **Eugenio**.
Gencho   see **Fulgencio**.
Genebra   see **Genoveva**.
Genefefo   see **Genoveva**.
Genefeva   see **Genoveva**.
Genefora   see **Genoveva**.
Geneo   see **Genoveva**.
Generaso   see **Generosa**.
Generosa (Hay nay roe' sah) f. EE:
Generosa. Lat. "Noble by birth."
5 x in DS. 1 has relics en-
shrined in cathedral of Tivoli,
Italy. F. 7/17. **Var:** Generaso,
Generozo.
Generozo   see **Generosa**.
Genervieve   see **Genoveva**.
Genessio (Hay nays' see oh) m. EE:
Genessee. Lat. "Genus," "birth,
origin, descent." Genesia was V.
M. of Turin, Italy invoked
against drought. F. 6/8. **Var:**
Gines. See also Génaro.
Genevafa   see **Genoveva**.
Genevevam   see **Genoveva**.
Genevie   see **Genoveva**.
Genevine   see **Genoveva**.
Geneviro   see **Genoveva**.
Geneviva   see **Genoveva**.
Genevive   see **Genoveva**.
Genieve   see **Eugenio**.
Genio   see **Eugenio**.
Genio (Hay' nee oh) m. EE: Genio.
Lat. "Extraordinary intellectual
powers." **Var:** Genito.
Géniro   see **Génaro**.
Genito   see **Genio**.
Geniva   see **Genoveva**.
Genive   see **Genoveva**.
Genivefam   see **Genoveva**.
Geniveve   see **Genoveva**.
Génnaro   see **Génaro**.
Génnora   see **Génaro**.
Genobaba   see **Genoveva**.
Genobeba   see **Genoveva**.
Genobelio   see **Genoveva**.
Genofefa   see **Genoveva**.
Genofera   see **Genoveva**.
Genofeva   see **Genoveva**.
Genola   see **Genoveva**.
Genón   see **Genoveva**.
Genona   see **Genoveva**.
Genora   see **Genoveva**.

Genorefa   see **Genoveva**.
Genorena   see **Genoveva**.
Genorero   see **Genoveva**.
Genorevo   see **Genoveva**.
Genosefa   see **Genoveva**.
Genova   see **Genoveva**.
Genovava   see **Genoveva**.
Genovave   see **Genoveva**.
Genovea   see **Genoveva**.
Genoveava   see **Genoveva**.
Genovebo   see **Genoveva**.
Genoveda   see **Genoveva**.
Genovefa   see **Genoveva**.
Genovefae   see **Genoveva**.
Genovefam   see **Genoveva**.
Genovefi   see **Genoveva**.
Genovelo   see **Genoveva**.
Genovena   see **Genoveva**.
Genoveón   see **Genoveva**.
Genovero   see **Genoveva**.
Genovesa   see **Genoveva**.
Genoveva (Hay no bay' bah) f. EE:
Genevieve, Jennifer, etc. Celt.
"White." 1 of richest names in
Sp. for variants. Patroness of
Paris whose prayers stopped
Attila the Hun. F. 1/3. **Dim:**
Beva, Geneo, Genola, Genón,
Genona, Genora, Genovita, Geva,
Hanovia, Veva, Xenov. **Var:**
Cenoveva, Enova, Enoveva,
Gandolyn, Genavera, Genaveva,
Genaviva, Genavo, Genebra,
Genefefo, Genefeva, Genefora,
Genervieve, Genevafa, Genevevam,
Genevie, Genevine, Geneviro,
Geneviva, Genevive, Genieve,
Geniva, Genive, Genivefam,
Geniveve, Genobaba, Genobeba,
Genobelio, Genofefa, Genofera,
Genofeva, Genorefa, Genorena,
Genorero, Genorevo, Genosefa,
Genova, Genovava, Genovave,
Genovea, Genoveava, Genovebo,
Genoveda, Genovefa, Genovefae,
Genovefam, Genovefi, Genovelo,
Genovena, Genoveón, Genovero,
Genovesa, Genovevam, Genovia,
Genoviera, Genoviva, Genovova,
Genoweva, Genufia, Genvevo,
Genvipham, Geovanino, Geriobeba,
Gernveva, Ginabebo, Ginabeva,
Ginavefa, Ginobedo, Ginobelo,
Ginobevo, Ginoveva, Guendolina,
Guineveva, Henoveva, Hinovana,
Hinovava, Hinovevo, Jannovena,
Januveva, Jeaneva, Jenefeva,
Jeneiveves, Jeneva, Jenevava,
Jeneveba, Jenevieve, Jenivio,
Jenobeba, Jenoveba, Jenovefa,
Jenoveffa, Jenoveva, Jeovana,
Jinobeba, Jinoveva, Jinvevo,
Jonabeba, Senivina, Senovina,
Xenobio, Xenovio, Yenobio,
Yenobis. See also Ginebra.
Genovevam   see **Genoveva**.
Genovia   see **Genoveva**.
Genoviera   see **Genoveva**.
Genovita   see **Genoveva**.
Genoviva   see **Genoveva**.
Genovova   see **Genoveva**.
Genoweva   see **Genoveva**.
Genro   see **Génaro**.
Gensérico (Hane say' ree co) m.
EE: Gaiseric. King of Vandals of

5th cen. & 1 of most successful barbarian invaders of Rome.

Genufia   see **Genoveva**.
Genvevo   see **Genoveva**.
Genvipham   see **Genoveva**.
Geñi   see **Eugenio**.
Geño   see **Eugenio**.
Geofreda   see **Godofredo**.
Geogoria   see **Jorge**.
Georgina   see **Jorge**.
Georgorio   see **Jorge**.
Georja   see **Jorge**.
Geornita   see **Jorge**.
Geovanino   see **Genoveva**.
Gerado   see **Geraldo**.
Geraldinea   see **Gerardo**.
Geraldino   see **Geraldo**.
Geraldita   see **Geraldo**.
Geraldo (Hay rahl' doe) m. **EE:** Gerald, Jerry. Ger. "Spear-wielder or ruler." 8 x in DS. 1, 9th cen. count of Aurillac, France, led life of contemplation & charity. F. 10/13. **Dim:** Geraldino, Geraldita, Gerda. **Var:** Eraldina, Gerado, Giralda, Guerarda, Herrado, Jerado, Jeraldo. See also Gerardo.
Geramina   see **Guillermo**.
Geraminio   see **Jerónimo**.
Gerando   see **Gerardo**.
Gerardina   see **Gerardo**.
Gerardo (Hay rahr' doe) m. **EE:** Gerard, Gerry, Jerry. Ger. "Strong with spear." 16 x in DS. Gerard Majella, 18th cen. Redemptorist favored by God with ecstasies, prophecy, discernment of heart, & bilocation. F. 10/16. **Var:** Gehardo, Geraldinea, Gerando, Gerardina, Gerardus, Gerildo, Gernado, Gerrado, Gevardo, Herardo, Jerado, Xerardo. See also Geraldo.
Gerardus   see **Gervasio**.
Gerasia   see **Gervasio**.
Gerbacio   see **Gervasio**.
Gerbasco   see **Gervasio**.
Gerculano   see **Herculano**.
Gerda   see **Geraldo**.
Geremías   see **Jeremías**.
Gereón (Hay ray own') m. **EE:** Gereon. 13th cen. S. mart. with 600 others in Cologne, Germany. F. 10/10.
Gerfrudio   see **Gertrudis**.
Gerildo   see **Gerardo**.
Gerínimo   see **Jerónimo**.
Gerino (Hay ree' no) m. **EE:** Gerino. Gerin or Girinus of Aureillan, France, S. beheaded by Visigoths in 5th cen. F. 10/12.
Geriobeba   see **Genoveva**.
Germán   see **Armando**.
Germán (Hare mahn') m. **EE:** Armon, Herman, etc. Teut. "Man of spear." 6 x in DS. 1, 12th cen. mystic, wrote valuable treatises on mystical prayer. F. 4/7. **Dim:** Manche. **Var:** Gemen, Germanico, Germanva, Germinal, Germindo, Germinia, Germo, Germudio, Jermaine, Jermana.
Germanico   see **Germán**.

Germanva   see **Germán**.
Germinal   see **Germán**.
Germinal (Hare mee nahl') m. **EE:** Germinal. Lat. "In earliest stage of development." 7th month of Fr. revolutionary calendar. Var: Jerminal.
Germindo   see **Germán**.
Germinia   see **Germán**.
Germo   see **Germán**.
Germudio   see **Germán**.
Gernado   see **Gerardo**.
Gernveva   see **Genoveva**.
Gerofina (Hay roe fee' nah) f. **EE:** Gerofina. Comb. of Jerónimo & Josefina (see both)?
Gerolmina   see **Guillermo**.
Gerómima   see **Jerónimo**.
Gerominina   see **Jerónimo**.
Gerómino   see **Jerónimo**.
Gerómnimo   see **Jerónimo**.
Geromo   see **Jerónimo**.
Geronemo   see **Jerónimo**.
Geronicio (Hay roe nee' see oh) m. **EE:** Gerontius, Geruntius. Gk. "Old one." 12 x in DS. 1, 5th cen. Archbishop of Milan, Italy. F. 5/5.
Gerónimo   see **Jerónimo**.
Geroninio   see **Jerónimo**.
Geronino   see **Jerónimo**.
Geronivino   see **Jerónimo**.
Gerónivo   see **Jerónimo**.
Gerónomo   see **Jerónimo**.
Gerrado   see **Gerardo**.
Gertendis   see **Gertrudis**.
Gertrado   see **Gertrudis**.
Gertredes   see **Gertrudis**.
Gertridis   see **Gertrudis**.
Gertruda   see **Gertrudis**.
Gertrude   see **Gertrudis**.
Gertruden   see **Gertrudis**.
Gertrudes   see **Gertrudis**.
Gertrudez   see **Gertrudis**.
Gertrudia   see **Gertrudis**.
Gertrudies   see **Gertrudis**.
Gertrudis (Hare troo' dees) m. **EE:** Gert, Gertrude, Trudy. Ger. "Spear-loved maiden." In Norse legend 1 of Valkyries. 8 x in DS. 1, 13th cen. Cistercian nun, excellent writer on mystic theology. F. 11/15. **Dim:** Jecho, Toolis, Trudel, Tule, Tules, Tulez, Tulia, Tulis, Tulitas, Tuliz, Tulles, Tulo, Tuly, Tuto, Tutu. **Var:** Etrudes, Gellrudis, Geltrudis, Gerfrudio, Gertendis, Gertrado, Gertredes, Gertridis, Gertruda, Gertrude, Gertruden, Gertrudes, Gertrudez, Gertrudia, Gertrudies, Gertrudix, Gertrudiz, Gertruedis, Gertruidis, Gertruzed, Gertudes, Gertudio, Gertudis, Gerturdes, Gerturdis, Getiludas, Getredes, Getruda, Getrudio, Getrudis, Gretrodis, Gutrudas, Hertuda, Hetrudes, Jertrudes, Jertrudis, Jetrudes, Jetrudis, Xertrudez, Yertrudis. See also Tulio.
Gertrudix   see **Gertrudis**.
Gertrudiz   see **Gertrudis**.
Gertruedis   see **Gertrudis**.
Gertruidis   see **Gertrudis**.

Gertruzed   see Gertrudis.
Gertudes   see Gertrudis.
Gertudio   see Gertrudis.
Gertudis   see Gertrudis.
Gerturdes   see Gertrudis.
Gerturdis   see Gervasio.
Gervacio   see Gervasio.
Gervaldina (Hare bahl dee' nah) f.
   EE: Gervaldina. Comb. & confu-
   sion of Gervasio (see) &
   Geraldina (see Geraldo).
Gervasio (Hare bah' see oh) m. EE:
   Jarvis, etc. Teut. "Sharp
   spear." 6 x in DS. 1, priest-
   martyr of 2nd cen. Milan, beaten
   to death with leaden whips. F.
   6/19. Var: Gerasia, Gerbacio,
   Gerbasco, Gervacio, Gervasius,
   Gurasio, Herbacio, Jervaso.
Gervasius   see Gervasio.
Gery   see Desiderio.
Gesaria   see César.
Getiludas   see Gertrudis.
Getredes   see Gertrudis.
Getruda   see Gertrudis.
Getrudio   see Gertrudis.
Getrudis   see Gertrudis.
Geva   see Genoveva.
Gevardo   see Gerardo.
Gevaro (Hay bah' roe) m. EE:
   Gevaro. In Scan. myth. Gevar 1
   of names of Neff, father of Nann
   & father-in-law of Balder. Var:
   Gevero.
Gevero   see Gevaro.
Geyo   see Rogelio.
Gicelia   see Gisela.
Gidita   see Brígido.
Giefreda   see Godofredo.
Giermo   see Guillermo.
Gigermo   see Guillermo.
Gigifredo   see Godofredo.
Gigo   see Rodrigo.
Gijermo   see Guillermo.
Gil   see Egidio.
Gil   see Gilberto.
Gila   see Gilberto.
Gilardo   see Gildardo.
Gilberda   see Gilberto.
Gilbero   see Gilberto.
Gilberso   see Gilberto.
Gilberto (Heel bare' toe) m. EE:
   Bert, Gilbert. Ger. "Bright of
   will." 7 x in DS. 1 founded Gil-
   bertines, only English monastic
   order. F. 2/4. Dim: Beto, Gil,
   Gila, Gilito, Gillio, Xil. Var:
   Gelberto, Geliberto, Gilberda,
   Gilbero, Gilberso, Gilbertum,
   Gilbirto, Gilverto, Guiberto,
   Guilberta, Hilberto, Hilbertus,
   Hileleborto, Hillberto,
   Hilverto, Ilberto, Jiberto,
   Jilberto, Jilverto.
Gilbertum   see Gilberto.
Gilbirto   see Gilberto.
Gildardo (Heel dahr' doe) m. EE:
   Gildard. Ger. "Bold invader." 2
   x in DS. 1, 6th cen. bishop of
   Rouen, France. F. 6/8. Var:
   Gilardo.
Gildo   see Hermenegildo.
Gilevaldo   see Wilebaldo.
Gilibaldo   see Wilebaldo.
Gilito   see Gilberto.

Gilivaldo   see Wilebaldo.
Gillermina   see Guillermo.
Gillermo   see Guillermo.
Gillio   see Gilberto.
Gillirmo   see Guillermo.
Gilma   see Guillermo.
Gilo   see Virgilio.
Gilomena   see Filomeno.
Gilverto   see Gilberto.
Gimecindo   see Gumersindo.
Gina   see Jorge.
Gina   see Regina.
Gina   see Virginia.
Ginabebo   see Genoveva.
Ginabeva   see Genoveva.
Ginaro   see Genaro.
Ginavefa   see Genoveva.
Ginebra (Hee nay' brah) f. EE:
   Guinevere, etc. Celt. "White
   one, beautiful one." Wife of
   hero of Arthurian legend, had
   illicit affair with Sir Lan-
   celot. Var: Ginerva. See also
   Genoveva.
Ginerva   see Ginebra.
Gines   see Genessio.
Ginia   see Virginia.
Ginio   see Higinio.
Ginita   see Virginia.
Ginobedo   see Genoveva.
Ginobelo   see Genoveva.
Ginobevo   see Genoveva.
Ginoveva   see Genoveva.
Giolia (Hee oh' lee ah) f. EE:
   Giolia. 2 x in DS. 1, 12th cen.
   bishop; other, 12th cen. Irish
   archbishop.
Giomar   see Guiomar.
Giordano   see Gordiano.
Giorgio   see Jorge.
Giralda   see Geraldo.
Girbina   see Gabino.
Giribaldo   see Garibaldo.
Girónimo   see Jerónimo.
Giruncho   see Jerónimo.
Gisela (Hee say' lah) f. EE:
   Giselle, etc. Teut. "Hostage." 3
   x in DS. 1, 11th cen. queen of
   Hungary, helped with conversion
   of Magyars. Var: Gicelia,
   Giselda, Hissela, Icela, Icelda,
   Incelda, Iscela, Isela, Isella,
   Izela, Izelda.
Giselda   see Gisela.
Gittermo   see Guillermo.
Giyermo   see Guillermo.
Gláfiro (Glah' fee roe) m. EE:
   Glaphyra, Gk. "Polished, fine,
   elegant." V. M. who tried to
   save chastity by fleeing from
   Emperor Licinius. F. 1/13.
Glara   see Clara.
Glaudina   see Claudio.
Glaudio   see Claudio.
Glegario   see Gregorio.
Gleotilda   see Clotilde.
Glicerio (Glee say' ree oh) m. EE:
   Glycera, etc. Gk. "Sweet, amia-
   ble." 11 x in DS. 1, V. M. of
   Rome, broke statue of Zeus & was
   thrown to wild beasts. F. 5/13.
   Var: Ecliserio, Eliserio,
   Glicina, Licerio, Liserio.
Glicina   see Glicerio.
Gliselda   see Griselda.

Glorea   see **Glorio.**
Glori   see **Glorio.**
Glorinda   see **Glorio.**
Glorio (Glow' ree oh) m. EE:
  Gloria, etc. Lat. "Fame, glory,
  reknown." Has religious value in
  Sp. for reference to heaven.
  Dim: Coyo, Glori, Glorinda,
  Goya, Poya, Yoya. **Var:** Glorea.
Glova   see **Clodoveo.**
Gnosancio   see **Inocencio.**
Gobita   see **Joviano.**
Godeleva   see **Godeliva.**
Godelia   see **Gudelio.**
Godeliva (Goe day lee' bah) f. EE:
  Godiva, etc. Ger. "Beloved of
  God." 11th cen. Saxon maiden who
  rode through streets naked to
  protest taxation. **Var:** Godeleva,
  Godelva, Goldevia.
Godelva   see **Godeliva.**
Godfreda   see **Godofredo.**
Godislao (Goe dee slah' oh) m. EE:
  Godislav. Slav. "He who looks
  for glory." Could relate to
  Gonzalo (see). **Var:** Gondisalvi,
  Gondisalvo.
Godofredo (Goe doe fray' doe) m.
  EE: Godfrey, Jeff, Jeffrey.
  Teut. "He who enjoys peace of
  God." 5 x in DS. 1, 11th cen.
  bishop of Amiens, France. F.
  11/8. **Var:** Geofreda, Giefreda,
  Gigifredo, Godfreda, Gofredo.
Gofredo   see **Godofredo.**
Goldevia   see **Godeliva.**
Golia   see **Goliat.**
Goliat (Goe lee aht') m. EE:
  Goliath. Heb. "An exile." Giant
  slain by David in Bible. **Var:**
  Golia.
Gollita   see **Gregorio.**
Gollo   see **Gregorio.**
Golo   see **Gregorio.**
Gomacinda   see **Gumersindo.**
Gomacinto   see **Gumersindo.**
Gomasinto   see **Gumersindo.**
Gombert   see **Gumbertus.**
Gomecinde   see **Gumersindo.**
Gomecinda   see **Gumersindo.**
Gomecinto   see **Gumersindo.**
Gomecunda   see **Gumersindo.**
Gomercundo see **Gumersindo.**
Gomesina   see **Gumersindo.**
Gomesinto   see **Gumersindo.**
Gomezindo   see **Gumersindo.**
Gomicindo   see **Gumersindo.**
Gominsindo see **Gumersindo.**
Gomisinda   see **Gumersindo.**
Gomisio   see **Gumersindo.**
Goncecinda see **Gumersindo.**
Gondisalvi see **Godislao.**
Gondisalvo see **Godislao.**
Gonicindo   see **Gumersindo.**
Gonocindo   see **Gumersindo.**
Gonsalo   see **Gonzalo.**
Gontrán (Gone trahn') m. EE:
  Gontran, etc. Teut. "Bird of
  war." King of Franks in 6th cen.
  F. 3/28.
Gonzago (Gone zah' go) m. EE:
  Gonzago. Ger. "Fighter, war-
  rior." Ital. princely house that
  ruled Mantua from 14th to 18th
  cen.

Gonzal   see **Gonzalo.**
Gonzaleo   see **Gonzalo.**
Gonzales   see **Gonzalo.**
Gonzalo (Gone zah' low) m. EE:
  Gundisalvus, etc. Ger. "Fight,
  combat." 5 x in DS. 1, 13th cen.
  Portuguese priest. F. 1/10. From
  Gonzalo is formed patronymic
  Gonzales, popular Sp. surname.
  Dim: Chalo, Gonzi. **Var:** Gonsalo,
  Gonzal, Gonzaleo, Gonzales,
  Gonzoyo, Gozalo.
Gonzi   see **Gonzalo.**
Gonzoyo   see **Gonzalo.**
Goraviela   see **Gabriel.**
Gordiano (Gore dee ah' no) m. EE:
  Gordius, etc. Patronymic of Lat.
  "gordius." Central figure of
  legend of Gordian knot. 7 x in
  DS. 4th cen. M. F. 1/3. **Var:**
  Giordano.
Gorge   see **Jorge.**
Gorgina   see **Jorge.**
Gorgio   see **Jorge.**
Gorgomio   see **Gorgonio.**
Gorgomo   see **Gorgonio.**
Gorgonio (Gore go' nee oh) m. EE:
  Gorgonius, etc. Gk. "Violent,
  tempestuous." In myth. Gorgons,
  3 monsters whose hideousness
  turned men to stone. 7 x in DS.
  1, 3rd cen. M. under Diocletian.
  F. 9/9. **Var:** Garganio, Gargario,
  Gargonio, Gorgomio, Gorgomo,
  Gorgonius, Gorgorio, Gurgonio.
Gorgonius   see **Gorgonio.**
Gorgorio   see **Gorgonio.**
Gorio   see **Gregorio.**
Gormescinta see **Gumersindo.**
Gornecindo see **Gumersindo.**
Gosefina   see **José.**
Gosmi   see **Cosme.**
Gospar   see **Gaspar.**
Gova   see **Joviano.**
Govita   see **Joviano.**
Goya   see **Glorio.**
Goyitico   see **Gregorio.**
Goyito   see **Gregorio.**
Goyo   see **Gregorio.**
Gozalo   see **Gonzalo.**
Grabel   see **Gabriel.**
Grabide   see **Gabriel.**
Grabiel   see **Gabriel.**
Grabilita   see **Gabriel.**
Graceile   see **Graciela.**
Gracela   see **Graciela.**
Gracella   see **Graciela.**
Gracen   see **Graciela.**
Gracensia   see **Graciela.**
Gracia   see **Engracia.**
Graciano   see **Graciela.**
Graciela (Grah see aay' lah) f.
  EE: Grace, Gratia, etc. Lat.
  "Gratia," "agreeableness,
  pleasantness." Refers to
  religious concept of grace,
  unmerited gift bestowed on
  rational creatures by God for
  their salvation. 16 x in DS.
  Dim: Chelita, Chelo, Cheya,
  Chita, Gach, Gache. **Var:**
  Agraciano, Graceile, Gracela,
  Gracella, Gracen, Gracensia,
  Graciano, Gracielia, Graciella,
  Gracielle, Gracila, Gracilla,

Graciniano, Gracino, Graseano,
Grasiela, Gratiano, Grationo,
Graziana, Graziela, Graziella,
Greciana, Greciela, Grecillano.
See also Engracia, Grata.

Gracielia   see Graciela.
Graciella   see Graciela.
Gracielle   see Graciela.
Gracila   see Graciela.
Gracilla   see Graciela.
Graciniano   see Graciela.
Gracino   see Graciela.
Graco   see Grata.
Gragoria   see Gregorio.
Gramecia (Grah may' see ah) f. EE:
Gramecia. Probably form of
Grammatiusa, bishop of Salerno,
Italy.
Grania (Grah' nee ah) f. EE:
Grania. Could be feminine form
of Roman surname "Granio,"
family with many members in
Senate at time of republic.
Graseano   see Graciela.
Grasiela   see Graciela.
Grata (Grah' tah) f. EE: Gratiana.
Lat. "Gratus," "pleasing." In
DS, native of Bergamo, Italy,
converted parents from paganism.
F. 5/1. Var: Graco, Grati,
Gratia. See also Graciela.
Grati   see Grata.
Gratia   see Grata.
Gratiano   see Graciela.
Grationo   see Graciela.
Gravael   see Gabriel.
Gravel   see Gabriel.
Gravelita   see Gabriel.
Graviel   see Gabriel.
Graviella   see Gabriel.
Gravil   see Gabriel.
Graviola   see Gabriel.
Gravoll   see Gabriel.
Graziana   see Graciela.
Graziela   see Graciela.
Graziella   see Graciela.
Grecencio   see Crescencio.
Grecensiano   see Crescencio.
Greciana   see Graciela.
Greciela   see Graciela.
Grecillano   see Graciela.
Gredeleo   see Gudelio.
Greforia   see Gregorio.
Grega   see Gregorio.
Gregerio   see Gregorio.
Gregino (Gray hee' no) m. EE:
Gregino. Comb. of Gregorio &
Regina (see both).
Gregorica   see Gregorio.
Gregorio (Gray go' ree oh) m. EE:
Greg, Gregory. Gk. "To awaken."
5 Ss. & 17 popes. Pope St. Greg-
ory the Great noted for enforce-
ment of papal supremacy. F.
3/12. Dim: Gollita, Gollo, Golo,
Gorio, Goyitico, Goyito, Goyo,
Grega, Gregorito, Gugu. Var:
Eregorio, Glegario, Gragoria,
Greforia, Gregerio, Gregorica,
Gregorria, Gregrio, Grejoria,
Grezoria, Gridoro, Gugorio.
Gregorito   see Gregorio.
Gregorria   see Gregorio.
Gregrio   see Gregorio.
Grejoria   see Gregorio.

Gremersindo   see Gumersindo.
Grencenio   see Crescencio.
Greseldo   see Griselda.
Greta   see Margarito.
Gretrodis   see Gertrudis.
Grevea (Gray bay' ah) f. EE:
Grevea. Type of flower.
Grezoria   see Gregorio.
Gricelda   see Griselda.
Gridoro   see Gregorio.
Grieseda   see Griselda.
Grifonio (Gree foe' nee oh) m. EE:
Grifonio. Grifonia refers to
rose family.
Grimalda (Gree mahl' dah) f. EE:
Grimald, etc. Teut. "Powerful
guardian." In DS, 12th cen.
British priest who built cathe-
dral in Pontecorvo, Italy, com-
memorating apparition of John
the Baptist. F 9/29.
Grisalda   see Griselda.
Grisanta   see Crisanto.
Griscelda   see Griselda.
Griselda (Gree sehl' dah) f. EE:
Griselda, etc. Lat. & Ger. "Gray
battle-maid." Medieval heroine
whose husband tested her devo-
tion through numerous trials.
Popularized by Chaucer & Boccac-
cio. Dim: Chela. Var: Chrisela,
Chriselda, Crisalde, Criselado,
Criselda, Criselta, Crisselda,
Criszelda, Crizelda, Cryselda,
Gliselda, Greseldo, Gricelda,
Grieseda, Grisalda, Griscelda,
Gristela, Grizelda.
Grisóforo   see Cristóbal.
Gristela   see Griselda.
Grizelda   see Griselda.
Grumacinda   see Gumersindo.
Guacho   see Bonifacio.
Guacho   see Washington.
Guada   see Guadalupe.
Guadalipe   see Guadalupe.
Guadaloupe   see Guadalupe.
Guadalup   see Guadalupe.
Guadalupa   see Guadalupe.
Guadalupana   see Guadalupe.
Guadalupe (Gwah dah loo' pay) mf.
EE: Guadalupe. Arab. "Valley of
wolf." Mexico's Our Lady of
Guadalupe, most venerated in all
Christendom. F. 12/12. Dim:
Guada, Lopita, Loupe, Lupe,
Lupeta, Lupie, Lupina, Lupita,
Lupo, Luppe, Lupy, Quadal, Upa,
Upe, Ylupe. Var: Gaudalupe,
Gavdalupe, Guadalipe,
Guadaloupe, Guadalup, Guadalupa,
Guadalupana, Guadalupem,
Guadalupi, Guadaluppe,
Guadalupum, Guaddalupe,
Guadelupe, Guadelupi,
Guadelupe, Guadilupa, Guadlupe,
Guadolupa, Guadolupe, Guadulup,
Guadulupa, Guadulupe, Gudalupe,
Juadalupe, Quadalupe, Quadelupe,
Quadupe, Zaudalupe.
Guadalupem   see Guadalupe.
Guadalupi   see Guadalupe.
Guadaluppe   see Guadalupe.
Guadalupum   see Guadalupe.
Guaddelupe   see Guadalupe.
Guadelupe   see Guadalupe.

Guadelupi   see **Guadalupe**.
Guadeluppe   see **Guadalupe**.
Guadilupa   see **Guadalupe**.
Guadlupe   see **Guadalupe**.
Guadolupa   see **Guadalupe**.
Guadolupe   see **Guadalupe**.
Guadulup   see **Guadalupe**.
Guadulupa   see **Guadalupe**.
Guadulupe   see **Guadalupe**.
Guakín   see **Joaquín**.
Gualberto (Wahl bare' toe) m. **EE**:
  Galbert. Teut. "He who is re-
  splendent in power."
Gualdina   see **Ubaldo**.
Guallermo   see **Guillermo**.
Gualterio (Wahl tay' ree oh) m.
  EE: Walter, etc. Ger. "Ruling
  host." 7 x in DS. 1, 5th cen.
  abbot of Pontoise. F. 4/8. **Dim**:
  Balto. **Var**: Gutierre, Waterio.
Guanita   see **Juan**.
Guarino (Wah ree' no) m. **EE**:
  Guarian, etc. Teut. "Gold de-
  fender." 12th cen. bishop of
  Palestrina, Italy. F. 2/6. **Var**:
  Guerrina.
Guasho,   see **Washington**.
Guauatémoc   see **Cuauhtémoc**.
Guayo   see **Eduardo**.
Gubino   see **Gabino**.
Gudalupe   see **Guadalupe**.
Gudelio (Goo day' lee oh) m. **EE**:
  Gudelio. Ger. "Battle." V. M. of
  Persia scalped & nailed to tree.
  F. 9/29. **Var**: Godelia, Gredeleo,
  Gudilia, Gudolia, Gutelio.
Gudemero   see **Gumaro**.
Gudemilia (Goo day mee' lee ah) f.
  EE: Gudemilia. Comb. of Gudelio
  & Ludemila (see both).
Gudilia   see **Gudelio**.
Gudolia   see **Gudelio**.
Gudran (Goo' drahn) f. **EE**: Gudrun,
  etc. Norse, "Divine wisdom."
  Heroine of Icelandic Volsunga-
  saga. marries Attila the Hun &
  kills him & their sons.
Guello   see **Aurelio**.
Guences   see **Venceslao**.
Guendolina   see **Genoveva**.
Guenseslado   see **Venceslao**.
Guerarda   see **Geraldo**.
Guerma   see **Guillermo**.
Guermillo   see **Guillermo**.
Guerrina   see **Guarino**.
Gugorio   see **Gregorio**.
Gugu   see **Gregorio**.
Guibebaldo   see **Wilebaldo**.
Guiberto   see **Gilberto**.
Guichi   see **Eloiso**.
Guicho   see **Luis**.
Guicho   see **Mauricio**.
Guico   see **Guillermo**.
Guido (Ghee' doe) m. **EE**: Guy,
  Guyon, Wyatt. Teut. "Well-known
  guide." 10 x in DS. 1 made pil-
  grimage from Belgium to Rome in
  12th cen. F. 9/12.
Guielderma   see **Guillermo**.
Guiermo   see **Guillermo**.
Guiffredo   see **Wilfrido**.
Guilberta   see **Gilberto**.
Guilde   see **Wilebaldo**.
Guilebaldo   see **Wilebaldo**.
Guilelmus   see **Guillermo**.

Guilermina   see **Guillermo**.
Guilermón   see **Guillermo**.
Guilevaldo   see **Wilebaldo**.
Guilfredo   see **Wilfrido**.
Guilhelmo   see **Guillermo**.
Guilibaldo   see **Wilebaldo**.
Guilibardo   see **Wilebaldo**.
Guilla   see **Guillermo**.
Guillarmío   see **Guillermo**.
Guillarmo   see **Guillermo**.
Guille   see **Guillermo**.
Guilleano   see **Julio**.
Guillelmo   see **Guillermo**.
Guillemo   see **Guillermo**.
Guillén   see **Guillermo**.
Guilleno   see **Guillermo**.
Guillerano   see **Guillermo**.
Guilleriminia   see **Guillermo**.
Guillermino   see **Guillermo**.
Guillermo (Ghee yare' mo) m. **EE**:
  Bill, Will, William, etc. Teut.
  "Defender with strong will." 1
  of most popular names of Chris-
  tian world. 50 x in DS. **Dim**:
  Biye, Guico, Guilla
  (Guillermina), Guille, Guillo,
  Ilma (Guillermina), Llermo,
  Memo, Mina (Guillermina), Minita
  (Guillermina), Mito, Nina
  (Guillermina), Vilma
  (Guillermina). **Var**: Gellermina,
  Geramina, Gerolmina, Giermo,
  Gigermo, Gijermo, Gillermina,
  Gillermo, Gillirmo, Gilma,
  Gittermo, Giyermo, Guallermo,
  Guerma, Guermillo, Guielderma,
  Guiermo, Guilelmus, Guilermina,
  Guilermón, Guilhelmo,
  Guillarmío, Guillarmo,
  Guillelmo, Guillemo, Guillén,
  Guilleno, Guillerano,
  Guilleriminia, Guillermino,
  Guillermunio, Guillernío,
  Guillerno, Guirmo, Gullermo,
  Gumermina, Gurmo, Hiermo,
  Inermo, Quillermo, Wilhelmio,
  Wilhelmo. See also Wilma.
Guillermunio   see **Guillermo**.
Guillernío   see **Guillermo**.
Guillerno   see **Guillermo**.
Guillia   see **Julio**.
Guillibaldo   see **Wilebaldo**.
Guillo   see **Guillermo**.
Guilo   see **Virgilio**.
Guimenindo   see **Gumersindo**.
Guinesindo   see **Gumersindo**.
Guineveva   see **Genoveva**.
Guiomar (Ghee oh mar') f. **EE**:
  Guiomar. Teut. "Glory of for-
  est." Also "famous in battle."
  Var: Giomar, Xiomara.
Guiotilda   see **Clotilde**.
Guiotilde   see **Clotilde**.
Guirmo   see **Guillermo**.
Guita   see **Olga**.
Guiteria   see **Quiterio**.
Guiterria   see **Quiterio**.
Guka   see **Refugio**.
Gulema   see **Julio**.
Gulianno   see **Julio**.
Gullermo   see **Guillermo**.
Gumacindo   see **Gumersindo**.
Gumar   see **Gumaro**.
Gumaro (Goo mah' roe) m. **EE**:
  Gummar. Teut. "Man of army." 8th

cen. knight helped found monastery at Lierre, Belgium. F. 10/11. **Var:** Gudemero, Gumar.

Gumasindo   see **Gumersindo.**

Gumbertus (Goom bare' toose) m. EE: Gumbert, etc. Ger. "Splendid fighter." 2 x in DS. 1, 8th cen. Benedictine abbot, gave possessions to church, built church & monastery in Ansbach, Germany. F. 7/15. **Var:** Gombert.

Gume	see **Gumersindo.**
Gumecinde	see **Gumersindo.**
Gumecindo	see **Gumersindo.**
Gumecino	see **Gumersindo.**
Gumecirdo	see **Gumersindo.**
Gumeciuder	see **Gumersindo.**
Gumegindo	see **Gumersindo.**
Gumelsindo	see **Gumersindo.**
Gumencindo	see **Gumersindo.**
Gumendinda	see **Gumersindo.**
Gumenindo	see **Gumersindo.**
Gumensido	see **Gumersindo.**
Gumensinda	see **Gumersindo.**
Gumerando	see **Gumersindo.**
Gumerciando	see **Gumersindo.**
Gumercina	see **Gumersindo.**
Gumercindo	see **Gumersindo.**
Gumercinto	see **Gumersindo.**
Gumerindo	see **Gumersindo.**
Gumerino	see **Gumersindo.**
Gumermina	see **Guillermo.**
Gumerninda	see **Gumersindo.**
Gumernudo	see **Gumersindo.**
Gumerrindo	see **Gumersindo.**
Gumersando	see **Gumersindo.**
Gumersido	see **Gumersindo.**

Gumersindo (Goo mare seen' doe) m. EE: Gumersind. Ger. "Road of war." 9th cen. Spaniard beheaded by Moors at Cordoba, Spain. F. 1/13. **Dim:** Chindo, Gomisio, Gume. **Var:** Cumecinda, Cumesindo, Gamacinda, Gamacinto, Gamecinda, Gemecindo, Gimecindo, Gomacinda, Gomacinto, Gomasinto, Gomecinde, Gomecindo, Gomecinto, Gomecunda, Gomercundo, Gomesina, Gomesinto, Gomezindo, Gomicindo, Gominsindo, Gomisinda, Goncecinda, Gonicindo, Gonocindo, Gormescinta, Gornecindo, Gremersindo, Grumacinda, Guimenindo, Guinesindo, Gumacindo, Gumasindo, Gumecinde, Gumecindo, Gumecino, Gumecirdo, Gumeciuder, Gumegindo, Gumelsindo, Gumencindo, Gumendinda, Gumenindo, Gumensido, Gumensinda, Gumerando, Gumerciando, Gumercina, Gumercindo, Gumercinto, Gumerindo, Gumerino, Gumerninda, Gumernudo, Gumerrindo, Gumersando, Gumersindo, Gumersundo, Gumersurdo, Gumerzindo, Gumescindo, Gumesendo, Gumesinco, Gumesind, Gumesindae, Gumesindo, Gumesinta, Gumessindo, Gumezienda, Gumezindo, Gumiersinda, Gumisundo, Gummisendo, Gumnsindo, Gunecinde, Gunecindo, Gunescindo, Gurmecindo, Gurnscindo, Gurracindo, Guversinda, Homesindo, Humecindo, Humexindo, Jermosinda, Jumesindo, Omesindo, Qumensindo, Qumisindo, Sumerando, Sumersindo, Umasenda, Umecindae, Umecindi, Umesindo, Umesinta, Umicindae, Umicindi, Umocinda, Zumersindo.

Gumersundo	see **Gumersindo.**
Gumersurdo	see **Gumersindo.**
Gumerzindo	see **Gumersindo.**
Gumescindo	see **Gumersindo.**
Gumesendo	see **Gumersindo.**
Gumesinco	see **Gumersindo.**
Gumesind	see **Gumersindo.**
Gumesindae	see **Gumersindo.**
Gumesindo	see **Gumersindo.**
Gumesinta	see **Gumersindo.**
Gumessindo	see **Gumersindo.**
Gumezienda	see **Gumersindo.**
Gumezindo	see **Gumersindo.**
Gumiersinda	see **Gumersindo.**
Gumisundo	see **Gumersindo.**
Gummisendo	see **Gumersindo.**
Gumnsindo	see **Gumersindo.**
Gunecinde	see **Gumersindo.**
Gunecindo	see **Gumersindo.**
Gunescindo	see **Gumersindo.**
Gurasio	see **Gervasio.**
Gurgonio	see **Gorgonio.**
Gurmecindo	see **Gumersindo.**
Gurmo	see **Guillermo.**
Gurnscindo	see **Gumersindo.**
Gurracindo	see **Gumersindo.**
Gusta	see **Gustavo.**
Gustablo	see **Gustavo.**
Gustabo	see **Gustavo.**
Gustacio	see **Gustavo.**
Gustado	see **Gustavo.**
Gustav	see **Gustavo.**

Gustavo (Goo stah' bo) m. EE: Gus, Gustav. Teut. "With sceptre of king." 3 famous Swedish monarchs. **Dim:** Chavo, Gusta, Guti, Tabo, Tavin, Tavito, Tavo. **Var:** Gustablo, Gustabo, Gustacio, Gustado, Gustav, Gustivo, Gustovo, Gutavo, Justavo.

Gustia	see **Justino.**
Gustiano	see **Justino.**
Gustin	see **Justino.**
Gustino	see **Justino.**
Gustivo	see **Gustavo.**
Gusto	see **Justino.**
Gustosia	see **Justino.**
Gustovo	see **Gustavo.**
Gutavo	see **Gustavo.**
Gutelio	see **Gudelio.**
Guti	see **Gustavo.**
Gutierre	see **Gualterio.**
Gutrudas	see **Gertrudis.**
Guversinda	see **Gumersindo.**
Guvino	see **Gabino.**

Guzmán (Gooz mahn') m. EE: Guzman. Goth. "Ready for arms." Formerly baptismal name but now mainly surname. Refers to nobleman who formerly served as cadet in army.

Gynatia   see **Ignacio.**

H

Habier   see **Javier**.
Habrán   see **Abraham**.
Hacindo   see **Jacinto**.
Hacintho   see **Jacinto**.
Hacinto   see **Jacinto**.
Hacoba   see **Jacobo**.
Hacora   see **Jacobo**.
Hacyntho   see **Jacinto**.
Hadio   see **Heladio**.
Hadrián   see **Adrián**.
Haggeo (Ah hay' oh) m. **EE**: Ageo. Form of Ageo, Heb. for 1 of prophets.
Haidee (Aay' day) f. **EE**: Haidee, etc. Gk. "Calm." In Byron's version of "Don Juan" Gk. girl who rescues hero from death. **Var**: Jaide.
Haime   see **Jaime**.
Hamero   see **Homero**.
Hamión (Ah mee own') m. **EE**: Hamon. Commanded slaughter of Jews. Esther interceded & Hamon was hanged. **Var**: Aman.
Hanastasio   see **Anastacio**.
Hancytho   see **Jacinto**.
Hanibal   see **Aníbal**.
Hanora   see **Honoria**.
Hanovia   see **Genoveva**.
Hanquilino   see **Tranquilino**.
Haracelia   see **Araceli**.
Haracia   see **Horacio**.
Harcelo   see **Araceli**.
Hario (Ah' ree oh) m. **EE**: Hario. Ancient Germanic tribe cited by Tacitus.
Harmando   see **Armando**.
Harmenegildo   see **Hermenegildo**.
Haroldo (Ah rohl' doe) m. **EE**: Hal, Harold, Harry, etc. Ger. "One in command of army." In DS, infant killed by Gloucester Jews. F. 3/17. **Var**: Heraldia, Heraldo, Heroldo.
Hartencia   see **Hortencia**.
Hartense   see **Hortencia**.
Hartensia   see **Hortencia**.
Hartessia   see **Hortencia**.
Hartinsia   see **Hortencia**.
Hasael   see **Hazael**.
Hascinto   see **Jacinto**.
Haviana   see **Javier**.
Hazael (Ah zah ehl') m. **EE**: Hazael. Heb. "God hath seen." King of Damascus who took all Jewish possessions east of Jordan River. **Var**: Hasael, Jazael.
Heacinto   see **Jacinto**.
Hebacuc (Aay bah cook') m. **EE**: Hebacuc. Heb. "Embrace." Also garden plant. Minor prophet & author of book of Bible, listed in DS. F. 1/15. **Dim**: Cuco.
Heberto   see **Herberto**.
Hecktor   see **Héctor**.
Heco   see **Héctor**.
Héctor (Eck' tore) m. **EE**: Heck,

Héctor. Gk. "To hold fast." In "Iliad," leader of Trojan army & famous for courage. **Dim**: Eto, Heco, Tito, Tocho. **Var**: Ector, Hecktor, Jector.
Hedilberto   see **Alberto**.
Heduvige   see **Eduvigis**.
Heduvigen   see **Eduvigis**.
Heduviges   see **Eduvigis**.
Heduvigis   see **Eduvigis**.
Hedvigen   see **Eduvigis**.
Hedviges   see **Eduvigis**.
Hedwigen   see **Eduvigis**.
Hedwiges   see **Eduvigis**.
Hedwigis   see **Eduvigis**.
Hedwigo   see **Eduvigis**.
Hefenia   see **Ifigenia**.
Hegesipo (Ay hay see' poe) m. **EE**: Hegesippus. Gk. "He who drives horses." Listed in DS as convert from Judaism & reputedly father of church history. F. 4/7.
Heginio   see **Higinio**.
Heirberto   see **Herberto**.
Hejinia   see **Higinio**.
Heladio (Ay lah' dee oh) m. **EE**: Eladius. Gk. "The Greek." Christian mart. with 18 companions at Nice in Bithynia, Turkey. F. 6/8. **Var**: Eladia, Eladis, Elado, Eloyadio, Hadio, Hiladio, Iladio.
Helario   see **Hilario**.
Helarión   see **Hilario**.
Helberto   see **Alberto**.
Helda   see **Hildo**.
Heledoro   see **Heliodoro**.
Helefonso   see **Alfonso**.
Helen   see **Elena**.
Heleno   see **Elena**.
Heleodoro   see **Heliodoro**.
Helga (El' gah) f. **EE**: Helga. Scan. "The holy." **Var**: Elga.
Heliadaro   see **Heliodoro**.
Heliberto   see **Alberto**.
Heliceo   see **Eliseo**.
Helida   see **Elido**.
Helidio   see **Elido**.
Helina   see **Elena**.
Helio (Aay' lee oh) m. Gk. "Sun." **Var**: Elio.
Heliodoro (Aay lee oh doe' roe) m. **EE**: Heliodorus. Gk. "Gift of sun." 10 x in DS. 1, beheaded at Magious in Pamphylia, Turkey, converted his executioners. F. 11/21. **Dim**: Doro, Lolo. **Var**: Eldora, Eleadora, Eledoro, Eleodoro, Eliadora, Elidor, Elidoro, Eliedoro, Eliloria, Eliodoria, Eliodoro, Elladoro, Heledoro, Heleodoro, Heliadaro, Hiliodoro, Hilodoro.
Helita   see **Elido**.
Hella   see **Elena**.
Helleno   see **Elena**.
Helmo   see **Erasmo**.

Heloisa	see Eloiso.
Hemberto	see Humberto.
Hemecia	see Nemesio.
Hemelia	see Emilio.
Hemenegilas	see Hermenegildo.
Hemenegild	see Hermenegildo.
Hemenyildo	see Hermenegildo.
Hemerio	see Emereo.
Hemero	see Emereo.
Hemeterio	see Emeterio.

Hemico (Aay mee' co) m. **EE:** Hemico. Related to blood.

Hemilio	see Emilio.
Hemilo	see Emilio.
Hemiterio	see Emeterio.
Hemunegilda	see Hermenegildo.
Hénaro	see Génaro.

Henedina (Aay nay dee' nah) f. **EE:** Henedina. Probably Gk. "to be complacent." Mentioned in DS as Ital. M. F. 5/14. **Var:** Emedina.

Henemencio	see Nemesio.
Henemensio	see Nemesio.
Henerequeta	see Enrique.

Heniverto (Aay nee bare' toe) m. Comb. of Enrique & Berto (see both).

Henoch	see Enoc.
Henoveva	see Genoveva.
Henrequeta	see Enrique.
Henrequetta	see Enrique.
Henrice	see Enrique.
Henrico	see Enrique.
Henricum	see Enrique.
Henricus	see Enrique.
Henriella	see Enrique.
Henrieta	see Enrique.
Henrignetta	see Enrique.
Henrigueta	see Enrique.
Henriko	see Enrique.
Henriqua	see Enrique.
Henriquetta	see Enrique.
Heofás	see Cleofás.
Hephani	see Epifanio.
Hepimenia	see Epigmenio.
Heplito	see Hipólito.
Hepólito	see Hipólito.
Heracle	see Heráclio.
Heraclea	see Heráclio.
Heraclides	see Heráclito.

Heráclio (Aay rah' clee oh) m. **EE:** Hercules, etc. Gk. "Glory of Hera." In Gk. & Roman legend, Hercules famous for strength. 3 x in DS. **Var:** Erácleo, Eracles, Eraclio, Eraquio, Ereclio, Heracle, Heraclea, Herclio, Heroclio, Oracleto. See also Herculano.

Heráclito (Aay rah' clee toe) m. **EE:** Heraclitus, etc. Gk. "He who wishes to do sacred things." Gk. philosopher (c. 540-475 B.C.) with major work "On Nature." Has idea of universality of change. 3 x in DS. **Var:** Heraclides.

Herailano	see Aurelio.
Heraldia	see Haroldo.
Heraldo	see Haroldo.
Herardo	see Gerardo.
Herarique	see Enrique.
Herasto	see Erasto.
Herbacio	see Gervasio.

Herberto (Ehr bare' toe) m. **EE:** Bert, Herbert, etc. Ang-Sax.

"Bright warrior." 2 x in DS. 1, disciple of St. Cuthbert. F. 3/20. **Dim:** Heri. **Var:** Eleverto, Eliberto, Ereberto, Eriberio, Eriberto, Erilerto, Eriverto, Heberto, Heirberto, Heriberio, Heriberto, Heribeto, Heriverda, Herliberto, Herriberto, Hervert, Hibberto, Hiberto, Hiriberto, Jiriberto, Urberto.

Hercilia	see Hersilia.
Herclio	see Heráclio.

Herculano (Ehr coo lah' no) m. **EE:** Herculanus, etc. Lat. "Belonging to Hercules." 11 x in DS. 1, bishop of Perugia, flayed & beheaded by Goths. F. 3/1. **Var:** Arculano, Arrculan, Arrculas, Erculano, Gerculano, Herculario, Herculasa, Herculaud, Herculeno, Hércules, Herculese, Hericulona, Herjulano, Urcula. See also Heraclio.

Herculario	see Herculano.
Herculasa	see Herculano.
Herculaud	see Herculano.
Herculeno	see Herculano.
Hércules	see Herculano.
Herculese	see Herculano.
Heregildo	see Hermenegildo.
Herenelinda	see Hermenegildo.
Heri	see Herberto.
Heriberio	see Herberto.
Heriberto	see Herberto.
Heribeto	see Herberto.
Hericulona	see Herculano.
Herimia	see Herminio.
Heriverda	see Herberto.
Herjulano	see Herculano.
Herliberto	see Herberto.
Herlina	see Herlindo.

Herlindo (Ehr leen' doe) m. **EE:** Erland, etc. Ger. "Shield of army." 8th cen. Belgian nun. F. 3/22. **Var:** Arlinda, Erlenda, Erlina, Erlindo, Erlinga, Herlina.

Hermainio	see Herminio.
Hermalinda	see Hermelinda.

Hermán (Ehr mahn') m. **EE:** Herman, etc. Ger. "Army man." 6 x in DS. 1, 12th cen. mystic of Cologne, Germany. F. 4/7. **Var:** Ermania, Ermenia. See also Herminio.

Hermandiva	see Hermelinda.
Hermanegildo	see Hermenegildo.
Hermanejelda	see Hermenegildo.
Hermangildo	see Hermenegildo.
Hermberto	see Humberto.
Hermegildo	see Hermenegildo.
Hermegildo	see Hermenegildo.
Hermegillo	see Hermenegildo.
Hermeguildo	see Hermenegildo.
Hermelenda	see Hermelinda.
Hermelina	see Hermelinda.

Hermelinda (Ehr may leen' dah) f. **EE:** Ermelindis. Ger. "Shield of power." 6th cen. recluse of Brabant, Belgium. F. 10/29. **Dim:** Mela, Meli. **Var:** Ermelando, Ermelina, Ermelinda, Ermelo, Ermilinda, Gemerlindo, Hermalinda, Hermandiva, Hermelenda, Hermelina, Hermelinga, Hermerlinda,

Hermilinda.
Hermelindo   see **Hermenegildo.**
Hermelinga   see **Hermelinda.**
Hermelo (Ehr may' low) m. **EE:**
Hermelo. Could be form of
Hermilo, S. of Belgrade, Yugo-
slavia, mart. when thrown into
Danube in 315. F. 1/13.
Hermena   see **Herminio.**
Hermenecildo   see **Hermenegildo.**
Hermenegila   see **Hermenegildo.**
Hermenegilde   see **Hermenegildo.**
Hermenegildo (Ehr may nay heel'
doe) m. **EE:** Hermengild. Teut.
"He who offers sacrifice to
gods." 6th cen. Visigothic king
of Spain who preferred to die
rather than deny his Catholic
faith. F. 4/13. **Dim:** Ermilo,
Gildo, Hermilo, Jildo, Merejo,
Umelda. **Var:** Armengol, Emegirio,
Emenchilda, Emenegilda,
Emengeldo, Emeregilde,
Emeregildo, Emerejildo,
Emergildo, Emoreigilda,
Emriliddo, Eremehilda,
Ermanisfilda, Ermanogilda,
Ermelrejilda, Ermenegild,
Ermenegildo, Ermenehildo,
Ermenejilda, Ermenezildo,
Ermengildo, Ermengildus,
Ermenigilda, Ermenijildo,
Ermeregildo, Ermergildo,
Ermergilla, Ermigildo,
Esmerechilda, Harmenegildo,
Hemenegilas, Hemenegild,
Hemenyildo, Hemunegilda,
Heregildo, Herenelinda,
Hermanegildo, Hermanejelda,
Hermangildo, Hermedildo,
Hermegildo, Hermegillo,
Hermeguildo, Hermelindo,
Hermenecildo, Hermenegila,
Hermenegilde, Hermenegilds,
Hermenegilvo, Hermeneguildo,
Hermenehilda, Hermeneilda,
Hermenejild, Hermenergildo,
Hermenezildo, Hermengalde,
Hermengelida, Hermenghildo,
Hermengild, Hermengildo,
Hermenigildo, Hermenildo,
Hermenjeldo, Hermenzildo,
Hermeregildo, Hermerejeldo,
Hermerejildo, Hermerigilda,
Hermerinda, Hermerlinda,
Hermerregildo, Hermesinda,
Hermeugeldo, Hermilnegildo,
Herminegildo, Herminigildo,
Hermolinda, Hermonegilda,
Hernelinda, Hernenegilda,
Hernengildo, Humemejildo,
Margilda, Medejildo, Melegilda,
Menejildo, Menjildo, Merajildo,
Merefilda, Meregildo, Merejilde,
Merejildo, Merejiledo,
Mereyildo, Merezildo, Mergildo,
Merhelda, Merhilda, Merigilda,
Merihildo, Merijildo, Meriyilda,
Merjildo, Mermenegildo,
Merrchilda, Merrfildo,
Merygilda, Mirajilda, Mirejilda.
Hermenegilds   see **Hermenegildo.**
Hermenegilvo   see **Hermenegildo.**
Hermeneguildo   see **Hermenegildo.**
Hermenehilda   see **Hermenegildo.**

Hermeneilda   see **Hermenegildo.**
Hermenejild   see **Hermenegildo.**
Hermenergildo   see **Hermenegildo.**
Hermenes   see **Hermes.**
Hermenezildo   see **Hermenegildo.**
Hermengalde   see **Hermenegildo.**
Hermengelida   see **Hermenegildo.**
Hermenghildo   see **Hermenegildo.**
Hermengild   see **Hermenegildo.**
Hermengildo   see **Hermenegildo.**
Hermenia   see **Herminio.**
Hermenigildo   see **Hermenegildo.**
Hermenildo   see **Hermenegildo.**
Hermenjeldo   see **Hermenegildo.**
Hermensia   see **Herminio.**
Hermenzildo   see **Hermenegildo.**
Hermeregildo   see **Hermenegildo.**
Hermerejeldo   see **Hermenegildo.**
Hermerejildo   see **Hermenegildo.**
Hermerigilda   see **Hermenegildo.**
Hermerinda   see **Hermenegildo.**
Hermerlinda   see **Hermelinda.**
Hermerlinda   see **Hermenegildo.**
Hermerregildo   see **Hermenegildo.**
Hermes (Ehr' mays) m. **EE:** Hermes.
Gk. "Messenger." Gk. god with 3
duties: gods' messenger, fertil-
izer of flocks, carrier of souls
to Hades. 18 x in DS. 1 mart.
under Hadrian. F. 8/28. **Var:**
Hermenes.
Hermesinda   see **Hermenegildo.**
Hermeugeldo   see **Hermenegildo.**
Hermi   see **Herminio.**
Hermichaela (Ehr mee cah aay' lah)
f. Comb. of Hermenegildo &
Miguel (see both).
Hermil   see **Herminio.**
Hermilina   see **Herminio.**
Hermilinda   see **Hermelinda.**
Hermilio   see **Herminio.**
Hermilnegildo   see **Hermenegildo.**
Hermilo   see **Hermenegildo.**
Hermilo   see **Herminio.**
Hermincio   see **Herminio.**
Herminea   see **Herminio.**
Herminegildo   see **Hermenegildo.**
Herminiam   see **Herminio.**
Herminigildo   see **Hermenegildo.**
Herminin   see **Herminio.**
Herminio   see **Arminio.**
Herminio (Ehr mee' nee oh) m. **EE:**
Armina, Herman, Irma, etc. Ger.
"Army man." 2nd cen. S. of Eph-
esus (Turkey) who ministered to
sick. F. 9/4. **Dim:** Hermi,
Hermita, Mimi, Mina, Minita,
Nina, Nini. **Var:** Ereminia,
Erinmia, Erinma, Erinmia,
Ermemio, Ermenia, Erminio,
Erminlana, Erminni, Ermminia,
Ermna, Ernimia, Erninio,
Herimia, Hermainio, Hermena,
Hermenia, Hermensia, Hermil,
Hermilina, Hermilio, Hermilo,
Hermincio, Herminea, Herminiam,
Herminin, Herminis, Herminnia,
Hermino, Hermio, Hermma,
Hernimia, Herninia, Irimeo,
Merminia. See also Arminio,
Herman, Irma.
Herminis   see **Herminio.**
Herminnia   see **Herminio.**
Hermino   see **Herminio.**
Hermio   see **Herminio.**

Hermita   see **Herminio**.
Hermina   see **Herminio**.
Hermógenes (Ehr mo' hay nays) m.
   EE: Hermogenes. Gk. "Descendant
   of Hermes." Biblical character
   who turned away from St. Paul.
   18 x in DS. 1 accompanied body
   of St. James from Spain to Pal-
   estine in legend. F. 9/2. **Var:**
   Ermógenes.
Hermolinda   see **Hermenegildo**.
Hermonegilda   see **Hermenegildo**.
Hermonica (Ehr mo nee' cah) f.
   Hermon is ancient mountain in
   Palestine.
Hernanda (Ehr nahn' dah) f. **EE:**
   Ferdinand, etc. Ger. "To make
   peace." Same as Fernando (see).
   Dim: Nando, Nano, Nanon. **Var:**
   Ernán, Hernander. See also
   Fernando.
Hernander   see **Hernanda**.
Hernelinda   see **Hermenegildo**.
Hernenegilda   see **Hermenegildo**.
Hernengildo   see **Hermenegildo**.
Hernesta   see **Ernesto**.
Hernestina   see **Ernesto**.
Hernimia   see **Herminio**.
Herninia   see **Herminio**.
Hernistina   see **Ernesto**.
Heroclio   see **Heráclio**.
Herodes (Aay roe' days) m. **EE:**
   Herod. Heb. "Dragon of fire."
   Rulers of Palestine at time of
   Christ. 1 famous for massacre of
   innocents.
Herodoto (Aay roe doe' toe) m. **EE:**
   Herodotus. Gk. "Holy gift." 5th
   cen. Gk. historian who wrote
   about conflict between Greece &
   Persia.
Heroldo   see **Haroldo**.
Herónimo   see **Jerónimo**.
Herón (Aay roan') m. **EE:** Heron.
   Gk. "Valiant in war." Famous Gk.
   mathematician & mechanic. Noted
   for formula for area of triangle
   in terms of its sides. 2 x in
   DS.
Herónimo   see **Jerónimo**.
Herónomo   see **Jerónimo**.
Herrado   see **Geraldo**.
Herriberto   see **Herberto**.
Hersilia (Ehr see' lee ah) f. **EE:**
   Hersilia. Gk. "Tender, deli-
   cate." Beautiful Sabine woman
   carried off by Romulus, mythical
   founder of Rome. **Dim:** Chila.
   Var: Ercilia, Ersila, Erzelia,
   Erzilia, Esilio, Hercilia,
   Irsilia.
Hertenia   see **Artemio**.
Hertense   see **Hortencia**.
Hertensia   see **Hortencia**.
Hertuda   see **Gertrudis**.
Hervert   see **Herberto**.
Herwin (Air' win) m. **EE:** Erwin,
   Herwin. Teut. "War friend." **Var:**
   Erwinia.
Hesequia   see **Hesiquio**.
Hesequiel   see **Ezequiel**.
Hesichio   see **Hesiquio**.
Hesiguio   see **Hesiquio**.
Hesiodo (Aay see' oh doe) m. **EE:**
   Hesiod. Gk. poet of 8th or 9th
   cen. B.C. Some doubt existence.
Hesiqio   see **Hesiquio**.
Hesiqnio   see **Hesiquio**.
Hesique   see **Hesiquio**.
Hesiquio (Aay see' key oh) m. **EE:**
   Ezechiel, Hezekiah, Zeke. Heb.
   "Strong in God." Biblical king
   of Judah for 29 years. Reign
   marked by presence of prophet
   Isaiah. 21 x in DS. **Dim:** Chico.
   Var: Eciqinio, Eciquio,
   Esaquina, Esciquio, Esechio,
   Eseqnio, Esequi, Esequio, Esica,
   Esichio, Esike, Esikia, Esiqia,
   Esiqmio, Esiqnio, Esique,
   Esiquio, Esiqura, Esisiaca,
   Esquio, Essiqnio, Essiquia,
   Eusequia, Euzuquia, Exasiaca,
   Exciquio, Exequia, Exiciara,
   Exiquio, Exisicia, Exissaca,
   Exsiquio, Exssicia, Ezcquio,
   Ezechina, Ezechio, Ezechria,
   Ezegio, Ezekio, Ezequio, Ezicio,
   Ezikia, Eziqnio, Eziquino,
   Eziquio, Eziquisa, Eziso,
   Ezquio, Ezuquia, Ezychio,
   Hesequia, Hesichio, Hesiguio,
   Hesiqio, Hesiqnio, Hesique,
   Hesiquioj, Hesychia, Hexiquio,
   Hezichii, Isiquio, Issichia.
Hesiquioj   see **Hesiquio**.
Hesmeregildo   see **Esmeregildo**.
Hesmerigilda   see **Esmeregildo**.
Hestoigia   see **Eustorgio**.
Hesús   see **Jesús**.
Hesuth   see **Jesús**.
Hesychia   see **Hesiquio**.
Hetrudes   see **Gertrudis**.
Hexiquio   see **Hesiquio**.
Hezichii   see **Hesiquio**.
Hiacintho   see **Jacinto**.
Hiacyntho   see **Jacinto**.
Hiacynto   see **Jacinto**.
Hiancinta   see **Jacinto**.
Hibaria   see **Iberia**.
Hibberto   see **Herberto**.
Hiberto   see **Herberto**.
Hicario   see **Icario**.
Hicidoro   see **Isidoro**.
Hicinio   see **Higinio**.
Hidalia   see **Idalia**.
Hidefonso   see **Ildefonso**.
Hidolina   see **Idolina**.
Hidora   see **Isidoro**.
Hiduyiges   see **Eduvigis**.
Hieránimo   see **Jerónimo**.
Hiermo   see **Guillermo**.
Hiernymum   see **Jerónimo**.
Hierónimo   see **Jerónimo**.
Hierónina   see **Jerónimo**.
Hieroninso   see **Jerónimo**.
Hieronym   see **Jerónimo**.
Hierónymo   see **Jerónimo**.
Hieronymum   see **Jerónimo**.
Hierónymus   see **Jerónimo**.
Hierónynio   see **Jerónimo**.
Hierónzmo   see **Jerónimo**.
Higenia   see **Higinio**.
Higimio   see **Higinio**.
Higines   see **Higinio**.
Higinid   see **Higinio**.
Higinio (Ee hee' nee oh) m. **EE:**
   Hygieia, Hyginius. Gk. "He who
   has health." In Gk. myth., per-
   sonification of health. 2 x in

DS. 1, 2nd cen. pope. F. 1/11.
Dim: Ginio, Hino. **Var:** Eginio,
Egino, Ejinio, Erginio,
Eriginio, Exignio, Heginio,
Hejinia, Hicinio, Higenia,
Higimio, Higines, Higinid,
Higino, Higiuio, Hijinio,
Hijino, Hygimio, Hygin, Hyginio,
Igenio, Iginio, Iginnio, Igino,
Ijinio, Niginio, Ygenio, Yginio,
Yigenia.

Higino	see **Higinio.**
Higiuio	see **Higinio.**
Higlentina	see **Eglantina.**
Hignacio	see **Ignacio.**

Higuria (Ee goo' ree ah) f.
Higuera in Roman myth. fig tree
sacred to Mercury.

Hijinio	see **Higinio.**
Hijino	see **Higinio.**
Hiladio	see **Heladio.**
Hilana	see **Elena.**
Hilarida	see **Hilario.**
Hilarino	see **Hilario.**

Hilario (Ee lah' ree oh) m. **EE:**
Hilary, etc. Gk. "Cheerful." 35
x in DS. 1, 4th cen. doctor of
church who fought Arianism.
Patron against snakes. F. 1/13.
Dim: Lalo. **Var:** Dilario,
Helario, Helarión, Hilarida,
Hilarino, Hilarión, Hilaritta,
Hilarius, Hilarrio, Hilarto,
Hilirii, Hiloriano, Hilorio,
Hylario, Ilarea, Ilario, Ilaris,
Ilaro, Illario, Illeria, Ularia,
Ylario.

Hilarión	see **Hilario.**
Hilaritta	see **Hilario.**
Hilarius	see **Hilario.**
Hilarrio	see **Hilario.**
Hilarto	see **Hilario.**
Hilberto	see **Gilberto.**
Hilbertus	see **Gilberto.**
Hildafonsa	see **Ildefonso.**

Hildeberto (Eel day bare' toe) m.
EE: Hildebert. Teut. "He who is
outstanding in combat." 5 x in
DS. 1, bishop of Meaux, France,
raised dead boy to life. Venerated as cure for epilepsy. F.
5/29.

Hildebrando (Eel day brahn' doe)
m. **EE:** Hildebrand. Teut. "Flame
of battle." 3 x in DS. **Var:**
Hilderbrand, Ildebrando.

Hildefonso	see **Ildefonso.**
Hildefunto	see **Ildefonso.**
Hildegardis	see **Hildigardo.**
Hildejardo	see **Hildigardo.**
Hilderbrand	see **Hildebrando.**
Hildifanso	see **Ildefonso.**

Hildigardo (Eel dee gahr' doe) m.
EE: Hildegard, etc. Teut. "She
who watches over combat." 12th
cen. mystic & prophetess of
Germany. Major work "Scivia,"
series of visions, apocalyptic
in nature. F. 9/17. **Var:**
Hildegardis, Hildejardo.

Hildo (Il' doe) m. **EE:** Hild,
Hilda, etc. Teut. "Battle."
Famous 7th cen. English abbess
who became greatest figure in
church of Northern England. F.

11/17. **Dim:** Hilito. **Var:** Helda,
Ilda, Yilda.

Hileana	see **Elena.**
Hileleborto	see **Gilberto.**
Hilfredo	see **Alfredo.**
Hiliodoro	see **Heliodoro.**
Hilirii	see **Hilario.**
Hilito	see **Hildo.**
Hillberto	see **Gilberto.**

Hilma (Eel' mah) f. **EE:** Helma,
Hilma. Ger. "War protection."
Var: Ilma.

Hilmelda	see **Imelda.**
Hilodoro	see **Heliodoro.**
Hilomena	see **Filomeno.**
Hiloriano	see **Hilario.**
Hilorio	see **Hilario.**
Hilosia	see **Eloiso.**
Hilverto	see **Gilberto.**
Himelda	see **Imelda.**
Hinberto	see **Humberto.**
Hinnocencia	see **Inocencio.**
Hino	see **Higinio.**
Hinofrio	see **Onofre.**
Hinosencia	see **Inocencio.**
Hinovana	see **Genoveva.**
Hinovava	see **Genoveva.**
Hinovevo	see **Genoveva.**
Hipalito	see **Hipólito.**
Hipilito	see **Hipólito.**
Hipilota	see **Hipólito.**
Hiplito	see **Hipólito.**

Hipócrates (Ee poe' crah tays) m.
EE: Hippocrates. Gk. "Invincible
with his horses." Gk. physician
(c. 460-370 B.C.) considered to
be father of medicine. Wanted
medicine on scientific basis.

Hipoleto	see **Hipólito.**
Hipolifa	see **Hipólito.**
Hipolite	see **Hipólito.**

Hipólito (Ee poe' lee toe) m. **EE:**
Hippolytus. Gk. "He loosens his
horses." Son of Theseus & se-
duced by stepmother Phaedra. 16
x in DS. 1, 3rd cen. Roman bish-
op. F. 8/22. **Dim:** Poli, Polin,
Polina, Polito, Polo, Polyta.
Var: Epólito, Heplito, Hepólito,
Hipalito, Hipilito, Hipilota,
Hiplito, Hipoleto, Hipolifa,
Hipólite, Hipólitus, Hipóloto,
Hipotito, Hipplytus, Hippólito,
Hippólitus, Hippoloto, Hopilita,
Hypólitor, Ipalito, Ipolio,
Ipólito, Ippólito, Ypolito,
Ypóloto.

Hipólitus	see **Hipólito.**
Hipóloto	see **Hipólito.**
Hipotito	see **Hipólito.**
Hipplytus	see **Hipólito.**
Hippólito	see **Hipólito.**
Hippólitus	see **Hipólito.**
Hippoloto	see **Hipólito.**
Hiram	see **Hirán.**

Hirán (Ee rahn') m. **EE:** Hiram, Hy.
Heb. "Noble born." Biblical king
of Tyre (Lebanon) & friend of
Solomon & David. **Var:** Hiram.

Hirena	see **Irene.**
Hirendina	see **Eréndira.**
Hiriberto	see **Herberto.**
Hirma	see **Irma.**
Hirónima	see **Jerónimo.**
Hisidro	see **Isidoro.**

Hissela   see **Gisela.**
Histo (Ee' stoe) m. EE: Histo, Hixta, Hyxta. Hixta or Hyxta, V. daughter of St. Notburga of Jestetten, Germany. F. 1/26. **Var:** Hitolito.
Hitolito   see **Histo.**
Hiveria   see **Iberia.**
Hocinto   see **Jacinto.**
Hocowa   see **Jacobo.**
Hoisia   see **Josué.**
Holalla   see **Eulalio.**
Holayo   see **Eulalio.**
Holda (Ohl' dah) f. EE: Huldah, etc. Heb. "Weasel." Biblical prophetess lived during reign of Josiah & predicted destruction of Jerusalem. In DS. F. 4/10. **Var:** Ulda.
Holegaria   see **Olegario.**
Holivia   see **Olivo.**
Hollala   see **Eulalio.**
Hombono (Ohm bo' no) m. EE: Goodman, Homobonus. Lat. "Good man." Listed in DS as honest, pious merchant of Cremona, Italy of 14th cen. F. 11/13. **Var:** Homobano, Homoboni, Homovono, Nomobono.
Homero (Oh may' roe) m. EE: Homer. Gk. "Blind." Gk. poet of c. 900 B.C. & author of "Iliad" & "Odyssey." **Var:** Hamero, Humero, Omero.
Homesindo   see **Gumersindo.**
Homobano   see **Hombono.**
Homoboni   see **Hombono.**
Homovono   see **Hombono.**
Honafre   see **Onofre.**
Honésimo   see **Onésimo.**
Honesto (Oh nays' toe) m. EE: Honestus. Lat. "Honorable, reputable." 2 x in DS. 1, 3rd cen. priest, preached gospel in Navarre & was mart. in Pamplona. F. 2/16. **Var:** Onesto.
Honorato   see **Honoria.**
Honoria (Oh no' ree ah) f. EE: Honor, Honora, Nora. Lat. "Honor." 51 x in DS. 1, bishop of Arles, France. Great man of 5th cen. F. 1/16. **Dim:** Honorino, Onerina. **Var:** Donorato, Donoriano, Hanora, Honorato, Onora, Onorato, Onorio.
Honorino   see **Honoria.**
Hopilita   see **Hipólito.**
Horacio (Oh rah' see oh) m. EE: Horace, Horatio. Lat. "Of the hours." 1 of 2 greatest Lat. lyrical poets, shortly before Christ. **Dim:** Lacho, Racho. **Var:** Haracia, Horatio, Horentino, Horis, Horsecinto, Hracio, Oracio, Orasio, Oratia.
Horatio   see **Horacio.**
Horentino   see **Horacio.**
Horetesia   see **Hortencia.**
Horis   see **Horacio.**
Hormisdas (Ohr mees' dahs) m. EE: Hormisdas. Pers. "Ahura mazdah" means "all-knowing one." In Zoroastrianism, personified good principle. 6 x in DS. 1, 4th cen. Pers., degraded for faith.

F. 8/8.
Horsecinto   see **Horacio.**
Hortecia   see **Hortencia.**
Hortemio   see **Artemio.**
Hortence   see **Hortencia.**
Hortencia (Ohr tain' see ah) f. EE: Hortense. Lat. "Hortus, "garden." Thus "hortencia" could be "gardener." Famous Roman lawyer & orator. **Dim:** Chencha, Tencha, Tenche, Tenchi. **Var:** Artencia, Hartencia, Hartense, Hartensia, Hartessia, Hartinsia, Hertense, Hertensia, Horetesia, Hortecia, Hortence, Hortencin, Hortenia, Hortensio, Hortentio, Hortenxia, Hortinzia, Hortnecia, Hurtensia, Jortensia, Ortencia, Ortense, Ortensia, Ortensión, Ortenza, Ortesia.
Hortencin   see **Hortencia.**
Hortenia   see **Hortencia.**
Hortensio   see **Hortencia.**
Hortentio   see **Hortencia.**
Hortenxia   see **Hortencia.**
Hortilia   see **Odilia.**
Hortinzia   see **Hortencia.**
Hortnecia   see **Hortencia.**
Hosé   see **José.**
Hoseá   see **Josué.**
Hosefina   see **José.**
Hosephine   see **José.**
Hospicio (Oh spee' see oh) m. EE: Hospitius. Lat. "Hospitium," "hospitality." 6th cen. hermit of Nice, France. Foretold invasion of Lombards. F. 5/21. **Var:** Ospicio.
Hovita   see **Joviano.**
Hracio   see **Horacio.**
Hrosita   see **Rosa.**
Huach   see **Joaquín.**
Huachina   see **Joaquín.**
Huacho   see **Joaquín.**
Huadin   see **Eduardo.**
Huanita   see **Juan.**
Huatimocín   see **Cuauhtémoc.**
Huayo   see **Eduardo.**
Hubaldo   see **Ubaldo.**
Hubertina   see **Humberto.**
Huberto   see **Humberto.**
Hubi   see **Humberto.**
Hudelia   see **Odilia.**
Huelo   see **Manuel.**
Huenche   see **Venceslao.**
Hugo (Ooh' go) m. EE: Huey, Hugh, etc. Teut. "He who has spirit & intelligence." 22 x in DS. 1, Hugh the Great of 11th cen. **Var:** Hugolino, Hugón, Ugón.
Hugolino   see **Hugo.**
Hugón   see **Hugo.**
Huicho   see **Luis.**
Hulala   see **Eulalio.**
Hulalia   see **Eulalio.**
Huliana   see **Julio.**
Humbelina   see **Umberlina.**
Humberto (Oom bare' toe) m. EE: Humbert, etc. Teut. "Of great fame & splendor." 6 x in DS. 1 founded Mariolles monastery at Cambra, France in 7th cen. F. 3/25. **Dim:** Berto, Beto, Hubi, Tito. **Var:** Hemberto, Hermberto, Hinberto, Hubertina, Huberto,

Huverto, Uberto, Umberto,
Unberto, Uneberto, Univerto.

Humecindo	see **Gumersindo.**
Humemejildo	see **Hermenegildo.**
Humero	see **Homero.**
Humexindo	see **Gumersindo.**
Humfredo	see **Onofre.**
Hunfredo	see **Onofre.**
Huróniomo	see **Jerónimo.**
Hurora	see **Aurora.**
Hurtensia	see **Hortencia.**
Hustina	see **Justino.**
Husto	see **Justino.**

Huventino	see **Juventino.**
Huverto	see **Humberto.**
Hyacintho	see **Jacinto.**
Hyacinto	see **Jacinto.**
Hyascintho	see **Jacinto.**
Hycedra	see **Isidoro.**
Hygimio	see **Higinio.**
Hygin	see **Higinio.**
Hyginio	see **Higinio.**
Hylario	see **Hilario.**
Hypólitor	see **Hipólito.**
Hyrómino	see **Jerónimo.**
Hysabel	see **Isabel.**

I

Ibaria	see **Iberia.**
Ibelina	see **Eva.**
Ibencas	see **Evencio.**
Iberania	see **Iberia.**

Iberia (Ee bay' ree ah) f?. **EE:**
Iberia. Lat. "Hiberes," "inhabitant of Spain." **Var:**
Hibaria, Hiveria, Ibaria,
Iberania.

Ibiginio	see **Ifigenia.**
Ibrahim	see **Abraham.**
Ibrain	see **Abraham.**

Icario (Ee cah' ree oh) m. **EE:**
Icarus. Lat. "Icarus" son of
Daedalus used artificial wings
to fly too high & sun melted wax
causing fall. **Var:** Hicario,
Ycario, Ycarrio.

Icela	see **Gisela.**
Icelda	see **Gisela.**
Icha	see **Isabel.**
Icidora	see **Isidoro.**
Icidro	see **Isidoro.**
Icira	see **Isauro.**
Icnacio	see **Ignacio.**
Ico	see **Enrique.**

Ida (Ee' dah) f. **EE:** Ida, Idella.
Teut. "Diligent." 9 x in DS. Ida
of Hertzfeld, Germany, led life
of piety & founded nunnery in
9th cen. F. 9/4. **Var:** Yda.

Idal	see **Idalia.**
Idalea	see **Idalia.**
Idalecio	see **Indalecio.**

Idalia (Ee dah' lee ah) f. **EE:**
Idalia. Gk. "I see the sun."
Place consecrated to Venus,
goddess of love. **Var:** Hidalia,
Idal, Idalea, Idalina, Idelio,
Ihdalia, Ydalia, Ydelia.

Idalina	see **Idalia.**
Idelaida	see **Adelaido.**
Idelfina	see **Ildefonso.**
Idelfonso	see **Ildefonso.**
Idelio	see **Idalia.**
Idelisa	see **Indalecio.**
Idelita	see **Adela.**
Idelta	see **Adela.**

Idemia (Ee day' mee ah) f. **EE:**
Idemia. Idumaea from Gk. word
"belonging to Edom," Biblical
place in Palestine given to Esau
& descendants.

Idephonsa	see **Ildefonso.**

Idiana	see **Indiana.**
Idicidro	see **Isidoro.**

Idilio (Ee dee' lee oh) m. **EE:**
Idyll. Lat. "Idyllium" or idyll,
poem dealing with rural life,
hence pleasing or simple.

Idmiro	see **Edelmira.**

Idolina (Ee doe lee' nah) f. **EE:**
Idolina. Lat. "Idolum," "image,
likeness." Statue representing
S. **Var:** Hidolina, Idolio,
Indolina, Ydolina.

Idolio	see **Idolina.**

Idonia (Ee doe' nee ah) f. **EE:**
Idonia. Lat. "Idoneus," "good
disposition."

Idovigan	see **Eduvigis.**
Idubigen	see **Eduvigis.**
Idubijen	see **Eduvigis.**
Iduvigen	see **Eduvigis.**

Ienero (Ee aay nay' roe) m. **EE:**
Ienero. Sp, "Enero," "January."
See also Genaro, Jano.

Iesideria	see **Isidoro.**
Ifela	see **Ofelio.**

Ifigenia (Ee fee hay' nee ah) f.
EE: Iphigene, Iphigenia. Gk.
"Royal birth." Daughter of
Agamemnon intended for sacrifice
for his crime. Subject of 2
plays by Euripides. Once in DS
as Ethiopian king's daughter. F.
9/21. **Dim:** Effa, Jinio. **Var:**
Efenia, Effigenia, Efibiana,
Efifania, Efigencia, Efigeneia,
Efigenia, Efignia, Efigonia,
Efizenio, Epigenia, Eufigenia,
Feginia, Fexenia, Figenia,
Hefenia, Ibiginio, Ifigiano,
Iphigenia, Iphygenia.

Ifigiano	see **Ifigenia.**
Ifrain	see **Efrain.**
Igacio	see **Ignacio.**
Igancio	see **Ignacio.**
Iganicio	see **Ignacio.**
Igantio	see **Ignacio.**
Igencia	see **Inocencio.**
Igenio	see **Higinio.**
Iginio	see **Higinio.**
Iginnio	see **Higinio.**
Igino	see **Higinio.**
Ignace	see **Ignacio.**

Ignacio (Eeg nah' see oh) m. **EE:**
Ignace, Ignatius, etc. Lat. "Ar-

dent, flaming." 15 x in DS. Most famous, St. Ignatius Loyola, founder of Society of Jesus & leader of Catholic Reformation. F. 6/31. **Dim:** Eneco, Enequia, Nachito, Nacho, Nas, Ygnacito. **Var:** Egnacio, Ejnacia, Enacio, Enascia, Gynatia, Hignacio, Icnacio, Igacio, Igancio, Iganicio, Igantio, Ignace, Ignacis, Ignacito, Ignacius, Ignadia, Ignafia, Ignas, Ignasio, Ignatae, Ignatio, Ignatión, Ignatz, Ignazio, Ignecia, Igneo, Ignes, Ignesa, Ignez, Ignicia, Ignocio, Ignofio, Ijnasio, Inacio, Inagcius, Inasia, Ingancio, Ingnacio, Innacio, Iñigo, Isnacia, Ugnacio, Ygancio, Ygnacio, Ygnacus, Ygnaico, Ygnasio, Ygnés, Ygnocio, Ynación, Ynaiso, Yñacio.

Ignacis   see **Ignacio.**
Ignacito   see **Ignacio.**
Ignacius   see **Ignacio.**
Ignadia   see **Ignacio.**
Ignafia   see **Ignacio.**
Ignas   see **Ignacio.**
Ignasio   see **Ignacio.**
Ignatae   see **Ignacio.**
Ignatio   see **Ignacio.**
Ignatión   see **Ignacio.**
Ignatz   see **Ignacio.**
Ignazio   see **Ignacio.**
Ignecia   see **Ignacio.**
Igneo   see **Ignacio.**
Ignes   see **Ignacio.**
Ignesa   see **Ignacio.**
Ignestacco   see **Ignestacio.**
Ignestacio (Eeg ness tah' see oh) m. EE: Ignestacio. Comb. of Ignacio & Eustacio (see both). **Var:** Ignestacco, Inestacio.

Ignez   see **Ignacio.**
Ignicia   see **Ignacio.**
Ignocio   see **Ignacio.**
Ignofio   see **Ignacio.**
Igo   see **Rodrigo.**
Ihdalia   see **Idalia.**
Ijinio   see **Higinio.**
Ijnasio   see **Ignacio.**
Ikoy   see **Federico.**
Iladio   see **Heladio.**
Ilarea   see **Hilario.**
Ilario   see **Hilario.**
Ilaris   see **Hilario.**
Ilaro   see **Hilario.**
Ilberto   see **Gilberto.**
Ilda   see **Hildo.**
Ildalesio   see **Indalecio.**
Ildebrando   see **Hildebrando.**
Ildefanra   see **Ildefonso.**
Ildefanso   see **Ildefonso.**
Ildefanzo   see **Ildefonso.**
Ildefonra   see **Ildefonso.**
Ildefons   see **Ildefonso.**
Ildefonso (Eel day fohn' so) m. EE: Ildephonsus. Teut. "Agile, ready for combat." 7th cen. Archbishop of Toledo. St. Leocadia resurrected to thank him for defense of Mary's virginity. F. 1/23. **Dim:** Joncho, Ponso. **Var:** Aldefonso,

Aldifonsa, Eddifonsa, Eldefonso, Eldifonso, Eldiforzo, Elofonsa, Hidefonso, Hildafonsa, Hildefonso, Hildefunto, Hildifanso, Idelfina, Idelfonso, Idephonsa, Ildefanra, Ildefanso, Ildefanzo, Ildefonra, Ildefons, Ildefora, Ildeforino, Ildefrisa, Ildelisa, Ildifanso, Ildifonso, Ilefonzo, Ilifonso, Udelfonsa, Yldafonso, Yldaphonzo, Yldefonzo, Yldefonzo, Yldephonsa, Yldephoso, Yldifonza, Yledefonso, Ylefonsa.
Ildefora   see **Ildefonso.**
Ildeforino   see **Ildefonso.**
Ildefrisa   see **Ildefonso.**
Ildelisa   see **Ildefonso.**
Ildifanso   see **Ildefonso.**
Ildifonso   see **Ildefonso.**
Ileana   see **Elena.**
Ilefonzo   see **Ildefonso.**
Ilene   see **Elena.**
Iliana   see **Elena.**
Iliazar   see **Eleázar.**
Ilifonso   see **Ildefonso.**
Ilisandro   see **Alejandro.**
Illario   see **Hilario.**
Illeria   see **Hilario.**
Ilma   see **Guillermo.**
Ilma   see **Hilma.**
Ilomeno   see **Filomeno.**
Ilona (Ee low' nah) f. EE: Ilona. Hungarian name.
Iluminado (Ee loo mee nah' doe) m. EE: Iluminado. Lat. "Illuminated or clarified." 4 x in DS. 1, accused of being Christian, saved from prison by a miracle. F. 11/28.
Ilustre (Ee loos' tray) m. EE: Illustrious. Lat. "Distinguished."
Ilvira   see **Elviro.**
Imaelde   see **Imelda.**
Imdalesio   see **Indalecio.**
Imela   see **Imelda.**
Imelda (Ee mehl' dah) f. EE: Imelda, Imelde. Teut. "Powerful fighter." 14th cen. S. of Bologna received 1st communion in miraculous manner. F. 5/12. **Dim:** Mela. **Var:** Amelda, Emedalio, Emeldo, Enelda, Ernelde, Hilmelda, Himelda, Imaelde, Imela, Imelde, Inelda, Ismelda, Jmelda, Melda, Ymelda.
Imelde   see **Imelda.**
Imelio   see **Emilio.**
Imenia   see **Jimeno.**
Imilina   see **Emilio.**
Immocencio   see **Inocencio.**
Immocentio   see **Inocencio.**
Imocencia   see **Inocencio.**
Imperio (Eem pay' ree oh) m. EE: Imperio. Lat. "Order, command, mastery." V. from Poitiers, France. F. 9/6. **Var:** Empiria.
Ina   see **Carolina.**
Ina   see **Cristián.**
Ina   see **Ernesto.**
Ina   see **Marino.**
Inacancia   see **Inocencio.**
Inacencio   see **Inocencio.**
Inacio   see **Ignacio.**

Inagcius   see **Ignacio.**
Inasia   see **Ignacio.**
Incanción   see **Encarnación.**
Incarción   see **Encarnación.**
Incarnacién   see **Encarnación.**
Incarnació   see **Encarnación.**
Incarnación   see **Encarnación.**
Incarnatió   see **Encarnación.**
Incarnationis   see **Encarnación.**
Incarnazión   see **Encarnación.**
Incarnoció   see **Encarnación.**
Inccarnación   see **Encarnación.**
Incelda   see **Gisela.**
Incelda   see **Iselda.**
Incencio   see **Inocencio.**
Incención   see **Inocencio.**
Incentia   see **Inocencio.**
Incentii   see **Inocencio.**
Incentius   see **Inocencio.**
Incete   see **Inocencio.**
Inciano   see **Inocencio.**
Incornación   see **Encarnación.**
Indalasio   see **Indalecio.**
Indalcio   see **Indalecio.**
Indalecio (Een dah lay' see oh) m.
EE: Indaletius, etc. Gk. "He who
is like a teacher." Bishop of
Almería, Spain. Invoked against
drought. F. 5/5. **Dim:** Lecho.
Var: Andalecio, Andalusio,
Andelecia, Andelesio, Andolesio,
Edalecio, Endalesio, Endelencia,
Endelesio, Eudalesio, Idalecio,
Idelisa, Ildalesio, Imdalesio,
Indalasio, Indalcio, Indalecis,
Indalencio, Indaleno,
Indalensio, Indalerio, Indalés,
Indalesio, Indalesis, Indaletio,
Indalicio, Indalino, Indalisio,
Indalizio, Indalsio, Indanacio,
Indelacio, Indelecio, Indelesio,
Indelicio, Indilesio, Indolecio,
Indolesio, Indolicio, Ingalesio,
Ingelacio, Iudallsio, Judalecio,
Judalencio, Judalesio,
Yadelicio, Yldalecio, Yndalecio,
Yndalicio, Yndalisio, Yndalisio,
Yndelacio, Yndelecio,
Ynslalesio, Ysidalesio,
Yudalecio.
Indalecis   see **Indalecio.**
Indalencio   see **Indalecio.**
Indaleno   see **Indalecio.**
Indalensio   see **Indalecio.**
Indalerio   see **Indalecio.**
Indalés   see **Indalecio.**
Indalesio   see **Indalecio.**
Indalesis   see **Indalecio.**
Indaletio   see **Indalecio.**
Indalicio   see **Indalecio.**
Indalino   see **Indalecio.**
Indalisio   see **Indalecio.**
Indalizio   see **Indalecio.**
Indalsio   see **Indalecio.**
Indanacio   see **Indalecio.**
Indelacio   see **Indalecio.**
Indelecio   see **Indalecio.**
Indelesio   see **Indalecio.**
Indelicio   see **Indalecio.**
Indiana (Een dee ah' nah) f. EE:
Indiana. "Belonging to Indies."
From "india" meaning "hind."
Var: Idiana.
Indilesio   see **Indalecio.**
Indolecio   see **Indalecio.**

Indolesio   see **Indalecio.**
Indolicio   see **Indalecio.**
Indolina   see **Idolina.**
Inebel (Ee nay behl') f. EE:
Inebel. Comb. of Inés & Isabel
(see both).
Inedina   see **Enedina.**
Inelda   see **Imelda.**
Inermo   see **Guillermo.**
Inés (Ee nays') f. EE: Agnes,
Ines. Gk. "Pure one." 13 x in
DS. 1, 3rd cen. 12-year-old M.,
patroness of gardeners & young
girls. F. 1/21. **Dim:** Agnesita,
Neches, Nechi, Nechin, Necho,
Nex, Niche. **Var:** Agnatha,
Agnatia, Agneda, Agneliano,
Agnese, Agnete, Agnetem,
Agnetio, Agneto, Einés, Enass,
Enés, Enez, Enezz, Inez, Innez,
Uness, Ynéss, Ynez.
Inestacio   see **Ignestacio.**
Inez   see **Inés.**
Infinio (Een fee' nee oh) m. EE:
Infinity, Lat. "Infinite, un-
bounded." Could be attribute of
God in sense of perfection.
Ingalesio   see **Indalecio.**
Ingancio   see **Ignacio.**
Ingelacio   see **Indalecio.**
Inglantina   see **Eglantina.**
Ingnacio   see **Ignacio.**
Ingres (Een' grays) m. EE: Ingres.
Fr. "Maingre," "thin, without
flesh."
Inicancio   see **Inocencio.**
Iniciano (Ee nee see ah' no) m.
EE: Iniciano. Lat. "To instruct
in abstract things."
Inmocenio   see **Inocencio.**
Innacio   see **Ignacio.**
Innez   see **Inés.**
Innocencio   see **Inocencio.**
Innocención   see **Inocencio.**
Innocensio   see **Inocencio.**
Innocentii   see **Inocencio.**
Innocentio   see **Inocencio.**
Innocentius   see **Inocencio.**
Innocita   see **Inocencio.**
Innoncencio   see **Inocencio.**
Innoscensia   see **Inocencio.**
Innscentia   see **Inocencio.**
Innumerbilio (Ee noo mehr bee' lee
oh) m. EE: Innumerable. Lat.
"Numerabiles" means "that can be
counted." Prefix "in" renders
"numberless."
Inocante   see **Inocencio.**
Inocencino   see **Inocencio.**
Inocencio (Ee no sayn' see oh) m.
EE: Innocent, Kenneth. Lat.
"Inoffensive, harmless." 27 x in
DS. Refers to slaughter of male
children by order of Herod. F.
12/28. **Dim:** Chencho, Chente,
Inza, Inzana, Sencio. **Var:**
Enesenico, Enicencio, Enocencio,
Enocente, Enosencia, Eucencia,
Gnosancio, Hinnocencia,
Hinosencia, Igencia, Immocencio,
Immocentio, Imocencia,
Inacancia, Inacencio, Incencio,
Incención, Incentia, Incentii,
Incentius, Incete, Inciano,
Inicancio, Inmocenio,

Innocencio, Innocención,
Innocensio, Innocentii,
Innocentio, Innocentius,
Innocita, Innoncencio,
Innoscensia, Innscentia,
Inocante, Inocencino,
Inocención, Inocenia, Inoceniro,
Inocensia, Inocente, Inocentes,
Inocentino, Inocentins,
Inocentio, Inocento, Inocenzio,
Inocercio, Inocete, Inocicio,
Inocincio, Inocinsio,
Inoecencia, Inoncencio,
Inonentio, Inosceno, Inoscentia,
Inosencio, Inosente, Inosentio,
Inscencio, Inscente, Insiensio,
Insocensia, Inucente,
Invecencia, Invencia, Isencio,
Nocencio, Ygnacencio,
Ygnocencio, Ynacencio,
Ynnocente, Ynocencio, Ynocensio,
Ynocente, Ynoscencio, Ynoscente,
Ynosencio, Yonocencia.

Inocención	see **Inocencio.**
Inocenia	see **Inocencio.**
Inoceniro	see **Inocencio.**
Inocensia	see **Inocencio.**
Inocente	see **Inocencio.**
Inocentes	see **Inocencio.**
Inocentino	see **Inocencio.**
Inocentins	see **Inocencio.**
Inocentio	see **Inocencio.**
Inocento	see **Inocencio.**
Inocenzio	see **Inocencio.**
Inocercio	see **Inocencio.**
Inocete	see **Inocencio.**
Inocicio	see **Inocencio.**
Inocincio	see **Inocencio.**
Inocinsio	see **Inocencio.**
Inoecencia	see **Inocencio.**
Inoncencio	see **Inocencio.**
Inonentio	see **Inocencio.**
Inosceno	see **Inocencio.**
Inoscentia	see **Inocencio.**
Inosencio	see **Inocencio.**
Inosente	see **Inocencio.**
Inosentio	see **Inocencio.**
Inriques	see **Enrique.**
Inscencio	see **Inocencio.**
Inscente	see **Inocencio.**
Insiensio	see **Inocencio.**
Insocensia	see **Inocencio.**
Instanislado	see **Estanislao.**
Inucente	see **Inocencio.**
Inuncia	see **Anunciación.**
Invecencia	see **Inocencio.**
Invencia	see **Inocencio.**
Inza	see **Inocencio.**
Inzana	see **Inocencio.**
Iñigo	see **Ignacio.**
Ioachino	see **Joaquín.**
Iolanda	see **Yolanda.**
Ipálito	see **Hipólito.**
Ipenemio	see **Epigmenio.**
Iphigenia	see **Ifigenia.**
Iphygenia	see **Ifigenia.**
Ipolio	see **Hipólito.**
Ipólito	see **Hipólito.**
Ippolito	see **Hipólito.**
Ique	see **Engracia.**

Ira (Ee' rah) m. **EE:** Ira, Irah.
Heb. "Watchful." Chief priest to
King David.
Iracema (Ee rah say' mah) f. **EE:**
Iracema. Tupi, "Coming from

Hong." Indian heroine of roman-
tic novel of same name by Jose
Martinian de Alencar. **Var:**
Eirasema, Irasema, Irasena,
Irazema.
Iram (Ee rahm') m. **EE:** Hiram, Hy.
Heb. "Watchful." Leader of Edom
in time of Jacob. **Var:** Irame.

Irame	see **Iram.**
Irasema	see **Iracema.**
Irasena	see **Iracema.**
Irasmo	see **Erasmo.**
Irasmus	see **Erasmo.**
Irazema	see **Iracema.**
Ireane	see **Irene.**
Irema	see **Irene.**
Iremea	see **Irene.**
Irén	see **Irene.**

Irene (Ee ray' nay) f. **EE:** Irene,
etc. Gk. "Lover of peace." 21 x
in DS. 1, 7th cen. nun killed by
infatuated nobleman. F. 10/20.
Dim: Nea, Renica, Reniquita.
Var: Airene, Erainio, Erene,
Ereneo, Erenio, Erianio, Erineo,
Erineu, Erinia, Hirena, Ireane,
Irema, Iremea, Irén, Irenello,
Ireneo, Irenia, Ireniz, Ireña,
Irina, Irineo, Irines, Irinia,
Iririno, Jreneo, Xrenio, Yrena,
Yrene, Yreneo, Yrenia, Yrinea.

Irenello	see **Irene.**
Ireneo	see **Irene.**
Irenia	see **Irene.**
Ireniz	see **Irene.**
Ireña	see **Irene.**
Iridira	see **Eréndira.**
Irimeo	see **Herminio.**
Irina	see **Irene.**
Irineo	see **Irene.**
Irines	see **Irene.**
Irinia	see **Irene.**
Iririno	see **Irene.**

Iris (Ee' rees) f. **EE:** Iris. Gk.
"Rainbow." Goddess of rainbow.
Irma (Eer' mah) f. **EE:** Armina,
Hermine, Irma. Ger. "Force." In
DS, 7th cen. Austrian who lived
in convent. F. 12/24. **Var:**
Armalinda, Ermma, Hirma,
Irmaida, Irmalenda, Irmina,
Irminia. See also Herminio.

Irmaida	see **Irma.**
Irmalenda	see **Irma.**
Irmina	see **Irma.**
Irminia	see **Irma.**
Irnes	see **Ernesto.**
Irnestina	see **Ernesto.**
Irnia	see **Ernesto.**
Irsilia	see **Hersilia.**
Isa	see **Elisabeth.**
Isa	see **Isabel.**
Isa	see **Luis.**

Isaac (Ee sahk') m. **EE:** Ike,
Isaac, etc. Heb. "Laughing one."
Abraham ordered by God to sacri-
fice son Isaac as test of faith.
48 x in DS. **Dim:** Caco. **Var:**
Isaaca, Isaak, Isac, Isacc,
Isaciosia, Isaco, Isahac, Izaac,
Ysaax, Ysaax, Ysac, Yssaach,
Yssac.

Isaaca	see **Isaac.**
Isaak	see **Isaac.**
Isaballo	see **Isabel.**

Isabeall   see **Isabel**.
Isabel (Ee sah behl') f. **EE:**
Bella, Belle, Isabel, etc. Heb.
"God is my affirmation." 4 x in
DS. 1, daughter of King Louis
VIII of France, became nun
rather than marry Emperor
Frederic's son. F. 8/31. **Dim:**
Belica, Belicia, Belita, Chaba,
Chabel, Chabelo, Chabi, Chabica,
Chabuca, Chapica, Chava, Chavel,
Chavelle, Chavelo, Chela, Icha,
Isa, Ishacu, Isobelita, Issa,
Ita, Iza, Licha, Lisa, Lito,
Liza, Mabel, Nibia, Nivia, Yssa,
Yza. **Var:** Elisabel, Elissa,
Elizabe, Elsa, Esabel, Esabela,
Esabella, Esavel, Esebella,
Esibell, Esibella, Esobel,
Hysabel, Isaballo, Isabeall,
Isabela, Isabelam, Isabelito,
Isabell, Isabelle, Isabello,
Isable, Isaebel, Isambel,
Isavel, Isbel, Isbell, Isebel,
Isebela, Isibal, Isobel, Isovel,
Issabel, Issabela, Issabelle,
Izabel, Izabela, Sabela, Sbella,
Ysabel, Ysavel, Yzabel, Yzabela.
See also Elisabeth.
Isabela   see **Isabel**.
Isabelam   see **Isabel**.
Isabelito   see **Isabel**.
Isabell   see **Isabel**.
Isabelle   see **Isabel**.
Isabello   see **Isabel**.
Isable   see **Isabel**.
Isac   see **Isaac**.
Isacc   see **Isaac**.
Isachar (Ee' sah cahr) m. **EE:**
Issachar. Heb. "There is time."
Son of Jacob & Leah & founder of
1 of 12 tribes.
Isaciosia   see **Isaac**.
Isaco   see **Isaac**.
Isadare   see **Isidoro**.
Isadario   see **Isidoro**.
Isadel (Ee sah dehl') f. Comb. of
Isabel & Adele (see both).
Isadero   see **Isidoro**.
Isadro   see **Isidoro**.
Isaebel   see **Isabel**.
Isael   see **Israel**.
Isahac   see **Isaac**.
Isai (Ee sah ee') m. **EE:** Jess,
Jesse. Heb. "God's grace."
Descendant of Boaz & Ruth,
father of David. Genealogy of
Christ represented as beginning
with Jesse. Mentioned in DS. as
6th cen. Syrian apostle. F.
12/2. **Dim:** Jesina. **Var:** Esita,
Issae, Jesé, Jesica, Ysay.
Isaías (Ee sah ee' ahs) m. **EE:**
Isa, Isaiah, etc. Heb. "Salva-
tion of the Lord." 1st of 4
major prophets. 15 x in DS. **Var:**
Esías, Isáis, Isaisa, Ysaís.
Isaidra   see **Isidoro**.
Isáis   see **Isaías**.
Isaisa   see **Isaías**.
Isambel   see **Isabel**.
Isamel   see **Ismael**.
Isamela   see **Ismael**.
Isandro (Ee sahn' droe) m. **EE:**
Isander, Lysander. In Gk. myth,

son of Bellerophon. Killed by
god Mars.
Isareal   see **Israel**.
Isauas   see **Isauro**.
Isaugro   see **Isauro**.
Isauro (Ee sough' roe) m. **EE:**
Isaurus. Gk. "Native of
Isauria," wild region in Asia
Minor inhabited by predatory
bands. M. from Athens. F. 6/17.
Dim: Chaga, Chagua, Chahua,
Chaura, Izaurina. **Var:** Icira,
Isauas, Isaugro, Isaver, Isawro,
Izaura, Sauro, Ysaure, Ysauro.
Isavel   see **Isabel**.
Isaver   see **Isauro**.
Isawro   see **Isauro**.
Isbel   see **Isabel**.
Isbell   see **Isabel**.
Iscela   see **Gisela**.
Iscidro   see **Isidoro**.
Isdra   see **Isidoro**.
Isebel   see **Isabel**.
Isebela   see **Isabel**.
Isedera   see **Isidoro**.
Isederio   see **Isidoro**.
Isedor   see **Isidoro**.
Isedora   see **Isidoro**.
Isedore   see **Isidoro**.
Isedro   see **Isidoro**.
Isela   see **Gisela**.
Iselda (Ee sehl' dah) f. **EE:**
Giselle, etc. Teut. "Pledge of
fidelity." 2 x in DS. 1, 10th
cen. queen of Hungary, worked to
convert Magyars. **Var:** Incelda,
Izela, Izelda.
Isella   see **Gisela**.
Isencio   see **Inocencio**.
Isequiel   see **Ezequiel**.
Iseratiam (Ee say rah' tee ahm')
m. **EE:** Iseratiam. Isertia, type
of flower like gardenia.
Ishacu   see **Isabel**.
Ishico   see **Isidoro**.
Ishmael   see **Ismael**.
Isibal   see **Isabel**.
Isidaro   see **Isidoro**.
Isideo   see **Isidoro**.
Isiderio   see **Isidoro**.
Isidero   see **Isidoro**.
Isidio   see **Isidoro**.
Isidore   see **Isidoro**.
Isidori   see **Isidoro**.
Isidoria   see **Isidoro**.
Isidoro (Ee see doe' roe) m. **EE:**
Isidore, Izzy. Gk. "Gift of
Isis," Egyp. goddess. 31 x in
DS. 1, laborer & plowman of 11th
cen. Spain. Patron of Madrid.
Dim: Cedro, Chidro, Chigo,
Chillo, Chilo, Chilolo, Chiro,
Chiyo, Chololo, Cidro, Dorina,
Doro, Ishico, Ixhico, Sidro,
Ysa. **Var:** Ciderio, Cidriano,
Dissidora, Ecedro, Ecidro,
Esidera, Esido, Esidor, Esidore,
Esidoro, Esidro, Hicidoro,
Hidora, Hisidro, Hycedra,
Icidora, Icidro, Idicidro,
Iesideria, Isadare, Isadario,
Isadero, Isadro, Isaidra,
Iscidro, Isdra, Isedera,
Isederio, Isedor, Isedora,
Isedore, Isedro, Isidaro,

Isideo, Isiderio, Isidero,
Isidio, Isidore, Isidori,
Isidoria, Isidorum, Isidorus,
Isidro, Isidrro, Isidru, Isitro,
Isodoro, Isodro, Issidra,
Isydro, Izedro, Izidero, Izidro,
Sididoro, Usidoro, Usidro,
Ycidro, Ygidroro, Yisadore,
Yisdero, Ysadora, Ysedora,
Ysedro, Ysidero, Ysidor,
Ysidoro, Ysidro.
Isidorum   see **Isidoro.**
Isidorus   see **Isidoro.**
Isidro   see **Isidoro.**
Isidrro   see **Isidoro.**
Isidru   see **Isidoro.**
Isiquiel   see **Ezequiel.**
Isiquio   see **Hesiquio.**
Isis (Ee' sees) f. EE: Isis. Egyp.
  Could mean "earth" or "throne."
  Egyptian goddess of nature. Cult
  l of antagonistic forces to
  Christianity.
Isitro   see **Isidoro.**
Islada   see **Estanislao.**
Ismael (Ees mah ehl') m. EE:
  Ishmael, Ismael. Heb. "God
  hears." Son of Abraham & Hagar &
  patron of Arabs. 2 unimportant
  Ss. **Dim:** Melito. **Var:** Esmael,
  Esmal, Esmela, Esmoel, Isamel,
  Isamela, Ishmael, Ismaele,
  Ismala, Ismale, Ismall, Ismeal,
  Ismel, Ismell, Yismael, Ysamrel,
  Ysmael, Ysmaela.
Ismaele   see **Ismael.**
Ismaerelda   see **Esmeralda.**
Ismala   see **Ismael.**
Ismale   see **Ismael.**
Ismall   see **Ismael.**
Ismaralda   see **Esmeralda.**
Ismeal   see **Ismael.**
Ismel   see **Ismael.**
Ismelda   see **Imelda.**
Ismell   see **Ismael.**
Ismeme (Ees may' may) f. EE:
  Ismene. In Gk myth, daughter of
  Oedipus & Jocasta.
Ismeralda   see **Esmeralda.**
Ismerio   see **Esmeregildo.**
Isnacia   see **Ignacio.**
Isobel   see **Isabel.**
Isobelita   see **Isabel.**
Isodoro   see **Isidoro.**
Isodro   see **Isidoro.**
Isolina (Ee so lee' nah) f. EE:
  Isolde, etc. Teut. "One who
  rules with fist of iron." Medi-
  eval romantic heroine & part of
  Arthurian legend. **Dim:** Chole,
  Chumina.
Isovel   see **Isabel.**
Isperonza   see **Esperanza.**
Isra   see **Israel.**
Israel (Ees rah ehl') m. EE:
  Israel, Izzy. Heb. "Prevailing
  with God." Jacob became Israel
  after wrestling with archangel
  Michael. Northern Hebrew kingdom
  became Israel; southern, Judah.

10th cen. Fr. S. F. 12/31. **Dim:**
Isra, Israh. **Var:** Esfrael,
Isael, Isareal, Israil, Isreal,
Isrrel, Ysrael, Ysrrael.
Israh   see **Israel.**
Israil   see **Israel.**
Isreal   see **Israel.**
Isrrel   see **Israel.**
Issa   see **Isabel.**
Issabel   see **Isabel.**
Issabela   see **Isabel.**
Issabelle   see **Isabel.**
Issae   see **Isaí.**
Issichia   see **Hesiquio.**
Issidra   see **Isidoro.**
Istevan   see **Esteban.**
Istolia   see **Eustalio.**
Isverdo   see **Ansberto.**
Isydro   see **Isidoro.**
Ita   see **Isabel.**
Ita   see **Margarito.**
Ita (Ee' tah) f. EE: Itha, Ytha.
  Patroness of Killeedy, Ireland,
  refused to marry & became nun.
  F. 1/15.
Itaciona (Ee tah see oh' nah) f.
  EE: Itaciona. Native of Ithaca.
Itanasio   see **Atanasio.**
Itiancinta   see **Jacinto.**
Itinarino (Ee tee nah ree' no) m.
  EE: Itinarino. Lat. "Belonging
  to the road." Could refer to Sp.
  "Itinerario," book of prayer or
  medieval book of travel.
Itzá (Eet zah') f. EE: Itza.
  Central American Indian tribe of
  Maya family. Probably founders
  of Chichén Itzá.
Iudallsio   see **Indalecio.**
Iusebio   see **Eusebio.**
Ivangelina   see **Evangelina.**
Ivara (Ee bah' rah) f. EE: Ivara.
  Ivaro, ancient Celtic for
  Salzach River in Austria.
Ivé   see **Ivés.**
Ivés (Ee bays') f. EE: Yvette,
  etc. 2 x in DS. **Var:** Ivé,
  Ivette, Iviz, Ivo, Ivonna,
  Ybette, Ybona, Yevette, Yvés,
  Yvesette, Yvette, Yvone, Yvonne,
  Yvonny.
Ivette   see **Ivés.**
Iviz   see **Ivés.**
Ivo   see **Ivés.**
Ivonna   see **Ivés.**
Ixhico   see **Isidoro.**
Iza   see **Isabel.**
Izaac   see **Isaac.**
Izabel   see **Isabel.**
Izabela   see **Isabel.**
Izaura   see **Isauro.**
Izaurina   see **Isauro.**
Izechiel   see **Ezequiel.**
Izedro   see **Isidoro.**
Izela   see **Gisela.**
Izela   see **Iselda.**
Izelda   see **Gisela.**
Izelda   see **Iselda.**
Izidero   see **Isidoro.**
Izidro   see **Isidoro.**

J

Jabino   see **Gabino.**
Jacabo   see **Jacobo.**
Jacaranda (Hah cah rahn' dah) f.
EE: Jacaranda, Tupi-Guarani,
"Strong odor." Tropical American
tree of fragrant wood & showy
blue flowers.
Jacava   see **Jacobo.**
Jaccinto   see **Jacinto.**
Jacento   see **Jacinto.**
Jacián (Hah see ahn') m. EE:
Jason. Form of Jason, leader of
Argonauts of Gk. myth.
Jaciento   see **Jacinto.**
Jacindo   see **Jacinto.**
Jacinto (Hah seen' toe) m. EE:
Hyacinth, Jacinth, Jack, Gk.
"Beautiful as Hyacinth." In Gk.
legend, beautiful youth, beloved
of Apollo. When killed flower
sprang from blood. 18 x in DS.
Dim: Cachito, Cacho, Chinto,
Chintu, Jas. **Var:** Gacinta,
Hacindo, Hacintho, Hacinto,
Hacyntho, Hancytho, Hascinto,
Heacinto, Hiacintho, Hiacynto,
Hiacynto, Hiancinta, Hocinto,
Hyacintho, Hyacinto, Hyascintho,
Itiancinta, Jaccinto, Jacento,
Jaciento, Jacindo, Jancinta,
Jascinto, Jasclino, Jasenia,
Jasenta, Jasinto, Jaxinto,
Jecenta, Jesento, Jocinto,
Xacino, Xasinto, Xintu.
Jacob   see **Jacobo.**
Jacobaita   see **Jacobo.**
Jacobeth   see **Jacobo.**
Jacobina   see **Jacobo.**
Jacobita   see **Jacobo.**
Jacobo (Hah co' bo) m. EE: Jacob,
Jacobina, James. Heb. "Supplant-
er." 3rd of Heb. patriarchs;
Rebekah's favorite; eponymous
ancestor of tribe of Israel. 87
x in DS. **Dim:** Chago, Dieguito,
Digo, Diogolino. **Var:** Hacoba,
Hacora, Hocowa, Jacabo, Jacava,
Jacob, Jacobaita, Jacobeth,
Jacobina, Jacobita, Jacobus,
Jacogo, Jacolea, Jacovo,
Jacqunine, Jakoba, Jaquelina,
Jaqueline, Jocob, Jocobo,
Jokabel, Xacoba, Yacobia,
Zacobia. See also Jaime,
Santiago.
Jacobus   see **Jacobo.**
Jacogo   see **Jacobo.**
Jacolea   see **Jacobo.**
Jacondo   see **Jucundo.**
Jacovo   see **Jacobo.**
Jacqunine   see **Jacobo.**
Jacundo   see **Jucundo.**
Jadelina   see **Adela.**
Jafet (Hah feht') m. EE: Japhet,
Japheth, etc. Heb. "Beauty," or
"let him enlarge." Noah's son
whose descendants were given

lands near Mediterranean.
Jaide   see **Haidee.**
Jaime (Hai' may) m. EE: Jaime,
James, etc. Heb. "Supplanter."
Dim: Chago, Chango, Chanti,
Diego, Dieguito, Jaimito, Jimmy,
Mito, Yimi. **Var:** Haime, Xaime.
See also Jacobo, Santiago.
Jaimitio   see **Santiago.**
Jaimito   see **Jaime.**
Jaimito   see **Santiago.**
Jairo (Hai' roe) m. EE: Jair,
Jairus. Heb. "He enlightens." 4
men in Bible: judge of Israel,
descendant of Manasseh, father
of Mordecai, & father of
Elhanar.
Jakoba   see **Jacobo.**
Jancinta   see **Jacinto.**
Jandino   see **Alejandro.**
Jandito   see **Alejandro.**
Jando   see **Alejandro.**
Janin   see **Juan.**
Janina   see **Juan.**
Janitzia (Hah neet' zee ah) f.
Pre-Columbian Mexican, "dry
corn, corn flower." Janitzio is
island near Pátzcuaro, Mexico.
Janno   see **Jano.**
Jannovena   see **Genoveva.**
Jano   see **Alejandro.**
Jano (Hah' no) m. EE: Januarius,
Janus. Gk. "Brilliant as sun."
In Roman religion, had two faces
that looked in opposite direc-
tions. Guardian of door & name-
sake of January. **Var:** Janno,
Januaria, Xano, Yano, Yanuario.
See also Génaro, Jenero.
Jansenio (Hahn sehn' ee oh) m. EE:
Jansen, Jansenius. Probably
variant of Juan (see). Dutch
theologian. Father of Jansenism.
Jantiago   see **Santiago.**
Januaria   see **Jano.**
Januveva   see **Genoveva.**
Jaquelina   see **Jacobo.**
Jaqueline   see **Jacobo.**
Jas   see **Jacinto.**
Jascinto   see **Jacinto.**
Jasclino   see **Jacinto.**
Jasenia   see **Jacinto.**
Jasenta   see **Jacinto.**
Jasinto   see **Jacinto.**
Jasús   see **Jesús.**
Jasusa   see **Jesús.**
Javeir   see **Javier.**
Javiel   see **Javier.**
Javiela   see **Javier.**
Javier (Hah bee air') m. EE:
Javier, Xavier. Basque, "New
house." Francis Xavier, 1 of
founders of Society of Jesus &
apostle of India. F. 12/3. **Dim:**
Ve. **Var:** Habier, Haviana,
Javeir, Javiel, Javiela,
Javiera, Javieria, Javiez,

Javis, Jevier, Xabiel, Xabier, Xabiera, Xaverio, Xavier, Xavior, Zavier.

Javiera	see **Javier.**
Javieria	see **Javier.**
Javiez	see **Javier.**
Javis	see **Javier.**
Javita	see **Joviano.**
Jaxinto	see **Jacinto.**
Jazael	see **Hazael.**

Jazmín (Hahs meen') f. Sp. "Gema," Jasmine, Jessamyn, etc. Pers. fragrant flower. **Var:** Yazmín.

Jeandro	see **Alejandro.**
Jeaneva	see **Genoveva.**
Jecenta	see **Jacinto.**
Jecho	see **Gertrudis.**
Jecho	see **Jesús.**
Jechú	see **Jesús.**
Jéctor	see **Héctor.**
Jedegardo	see **Edgardo.**
Jelomena	see **Filomena.**

Jemsa (Hem' sah) f. Sp. "Gema," precious stone.

Jemuel (Hem yoo ehl') m. EE: Jemuel, Nemuel. Heb. possibly "warmth or desire of God." Son of Simeon.

Jenadio (Hay nah' dee oh) m. Gk. "Noble of birth."

Jenardo	see **Génaro.**
Jenaro	see **Génaro.**
Jenarrio	see **Génaro.**
Jenefeva	see **Genoveva.**
Jeneiveves	see **Genoveva.**
Jenerio	see **Génaro.**
Jénero	see **Génaro.**
Jeneva	see **Genoveva.**
Jenevava	see **Genoveva.**
Jeneveba	see **Genoveva.**
Jenevieve	see **Genoveva.**
Jenivio	see **Genoveva.**
Jenobeba	see **Genoveva.**

Jenofonte (Hay no fohn' tay) m. EE: Xenophon. Gk. "He who is brilliant in front of stran- gers," Gk. historian (c. 430 B.C.). 2 x in DS.

Jenoma	see **Jerónimo.**
Jenona	see **Jerónimo.**
Jénora	see **Génaro.**
Jenoveba	see **Genoveva.**
Jenovefa	see **Genoveva.**
Jenoveffa	see **Genoveva.**
Jenoveva	see **Genoveva.**
Jeorge	see **Jorge.**
Jeorgia	see **Jorge.**
Jeorje	see **Jorge.**
Jeovana	see **Genoveva.**
Jerado	see **Geraldo.**
Jerado	see **Gerardo.**
Jeraldo	see **Geraldo.**
Jerámino	see **Jerónimo.**
Jeránimo	see **Jerónimo.**
Jerebio	see **Jeroboam.**

Jeremías (Hay ray mee' ahs) m. EE: Jeremiah, Jeremy, Jerry. Heb. "Jehovah doth establish." 1 of greatest figures of OT who constantly held unpopular opinions. F. 5/1. 6 x in DS. **Var:** Geremías, Jeremio.

Jeremio   see **Jeremías.**

Jericó (Hay ree co') m. EE: Jericho. Heb. "Fragrant," or

"city of moon god." Destroyed by Joshua. Also, 18th cen. Sp. church scholar.

Jerímino	see **Jerónimo.**
Jermaine	see **Germán.**
Jermana	see **Germán.**
Jermina	see **Jerónimo.**
Jerminal	see **Germinal.**
Jermosinda	see **Gumersindo.**
Jernimo	see **Jerónimo.**
Jerniomo	see **Jerónimo.**

Jeroboam (Hay roe bo ahm') m. EE: Jeroboam. Heb. "He who has many subjects." King of northern kingdom of Israel who plotted against Solomon & fostered idolatry. **Var:** Jerebio.

Jerometo	see **Jerónimo.**
Jeromina	see **Jerónimo.**
Jeromio	see **Jerónimo.**
Jeromo	see **Jerónimo.**
Jeronemo	see **Jerónimo.**
Jeronimino	see **Jerónimo.**

Jerónimo (Hay roe' nee mo) m. EE: Jerome, Jeronimo, Jerry. Gk. "Holy name." 1 of greatest of early Christian scholars. F. 9/30. 15 x in DS. **Dim:** Chombo, Chomo, Chumbo, Geraminio, Giruncho, Jenona, Nono, Xerón. **Var:** Feronio, Gerínimo, Gerómima, Gerominina, Gerómino, Gerómnimo, Geromo, Gerónemo, Gerónimo, Geroninio, Geronino, Geronivino, Gerónivo, Gerónomo, Girónimo, Herómimo, Herónimo, Herónomo, Hieránimo, Hiernymum, Hierónimo, Hierónina, Hieroninso, Hieronym, Hierónymo, Hieronymum, Hierónymus, Hierónynio, Hierónzmo, Hirónima, Huróniomo, Hyrónimo, Jenoma, Jerámino, Jeránimo, Jerimino, Jermina, Jernimo, Jerniomo, Jerometo, Jeromina, Jeromio, Jeromo, Jerónemo, Jeronimino, Jeroninica, Jerónino, Jeronous, Jeronumo, Jerónyma, Jerrónimo, Jerruino, Jierónima, Jieroninia, Jirónimo, Xerónima.

Jeroninica	see **Jerónimo.**
Jerónino	see **Jerónimo.**
Jeronous	see **Jerónimo.**
Jeronumo	see **Jerónimo.**
Jerónyma	see **Jerónimo.**
Jerrónimo	see **Jerónimo.**
Jerruino	see **Jerónimo.**
Jertrudes	see **Gertrudis.**
Jertrudis	see **Gertrudis.**

Jerusa (Hay roo' sah) f. EE: Jerusha, Jerushah. Heb. "Pos- session." Wife of King Uzziah of Judah & mother of Jotham.

Jervaso	see **Gervasio.**
Jesasita	see **Isaí.**
Jesé	see **Isaí.**
Jesento	see **Jacinto.**
Jesica	see **Isaí.**

Jesifredo (Hay see fray' doe) m. Comb. of Isaí & Alfredo (see both).

Jesina	see **Isaí.**
Jesito	see **Jesús.**
Jessesa	see **Jesús.**
Jessí	see **Jesús.**

Jessical   see **Jesús.**
Jessús   see **Jesús.**
Jessusita   see **Jesús.**
Jesú   see **Jesús.**
Jesucita   see **Jesús.**
Jesum   see **Jesús.**
Jesús (Hay soos') m. **EE:** Jesus.
Gk. for Heb. "Joshua," "savior."
In orthodox theology, God became
man & 2nd person of Holy Trini-
ty. **Dim:** Chita, Chu, Chuchi,
Chuchín, Chuchita, Chucho,
Chuey, Chus, Chusita, Chuy,
Jecho, Jessusita, Jesucita,
Jesusetta, Jesusito. **Var:** Resús,
Hesuth, Jasús, Jasusa, Jechú,
Jesasita, Jesito, Jessesa,
Jessí, Jessical, Jessús, Jesú,
Jesum, Jesusia, Jesuso, Jesussa,
Jesusta, Jezús.
Jesusetta   see **Jesús.**
Jesusia   see **Jesús.**
Jesusito   see **Jesús.**
Jesuso   see **Jesús.**
Jesussa   see **Jesús.**
Jesusta   see **Jesús.**
Jetrudes   see **Gertrudis.**
Jetrudis   see **Gertrudis.**
Jeventina   see **Juventino.**
Jevier   see **Javier.**
Jevita   see **Eva.**
Jezús   see **Jesús.**
Jiberto   see **Gilberto.**
Jierónima   see **Jerónimo.**
Jieroninia   see **Jerónimo.**
Jilberto   see **Gilberto.**
Jildo   see **Hermenegildo.**
Jilomena   see **Filomeno.**
Jilverto   see **Gilberto.**
Jimenia   see **Jimeno.**
Jimeno (Hee may' no) m. **EE:** Si,
Simeón, Simon, etc. Form of
Simeón. **Var:** Imenia, Jimenia,
Ximena. See also Simeón.
Jimmy   see **Jaime.**
Jinio   see **Ifigenia.**
Jinobeba   see **Genoveva.**
Jinoveva   see **Genoveva.**
Jinvevo   see **Genoveva.**
Jiorgianna   see **Jorge.**
Jiriberto   see **Herberto.**
Jirónimo   see **Jerónimo.**
Jivencio   see **Juventino.**
Jmelda   see **Imelda.**
Joabel (Hoe ah behl') m. Form of
Joab, 3 Biblical personages.
Joachim   see **Joaquín.**
Joachima   see **Joaquín.**
Joachimar   see **Joaquín.**
Joachimas   see **Joaquín.**
Joachin   see **Joaquín.**
Joachino   see **Joaquín.**
Joachius   see **Joaquín.**
Joackinia   see **Joaquín.**
Joakim   see **Joaquín.**
Joakin   see **Joaquín.**
Joanita   see **Juan.**
Joaquén   see **Joaquín.**
Joaquim   see **Joaquín.**
Joaquín (Hwa keen') m, **EE:**
Joachim, etc. Heb. "God gives
strength." In Apocrypha, husband
of St. Anne & father of V. F,
3/20. 10 x in DS. **Dim:** Chachín,
China, Guakín, Huach, Huacho,

Juacho, Juaco, Juaquinillo,
Pina, Quin, Quincho, Quino. **Var:**
Huachina, Ioachino, Joachim,
Joachima, Joachimar, Joachimas,
Joachin, Joachino, Joachius,
Joackinia, Joakim, Joakín,
Joaquén, Joaquim, Joaquinna,
Jochinae, Jocquín, Joequín,
Joquina, Jougoin, Juachín,
Juakín, Juaqín, Juaquín,
Juaquino, Quaquín, Wakín,
Yoaquín.
Joaquinna   see **Joaquín.**
Job (Hohb) m. **EE:** Job. Heb.
"Afflicted." Biblical personage
whose biography questions
suffering of just. F. 5/10. 4 x
in DS. **Var:** Joba, Jobieta,
Jobita, Jovila, Jovilia.
Joba   see **Job.**
Jobieta   see **Job.**
Jobita   see **Job.**
Jobo   see **José.**
Jochinae   see **Joaquín.**
Jocifa   see **José.**
Jocinto   see **Jacinto.**
Jocob   see **Jacobo.**
Jocobo   see **Jacobo.**
Jocorro   see **Socorro.**
Jocquín   see **Joaquín.**
Jocundo   see **Jucundo.**
Joel (Hoe ehl') m. **EE:** Joel. Heb.
"God is God." Heb. prophet whose
book suggests desolation after
Judgement. F. 7/14. **Var:** Joelda.
Joelda   see **Joel.**
Joequín   see **Joaquín.**
Jokabel   see **Jacobo.**
Jolanda   see **Yolanda.**
Jolina   see **Yolanda.**
Jolinda   see **Yolanda.**
Jolonia   see **Apolonio.**
Jonabeba   see **Genoveva.**
Jonaphán   see **Jonatán.**
Jonás (Hoe nahs') m, **EE:** Jonah,
Jonas, etc. Heb. "Gentle as a
dove." Prophet swallowed by
whale. F. 9/21. 18 x in DS.
Jonatán (Hoe nah tahn') m. **EE:**
Jonathan, etc. Heb. "Gift of
God." 16 x in Bible. **Var:**
Jonaphán, Jonatás.
Jonatás   see **Jonatán.**
Joncho   see **Alfonso.**
Joncho   see **Ildefonso.**
Joquina   see **Joaquín.**
Joram (Hoe rahm') m. **EE:** Hedora,
Jehoram, Joram. Heb. "Jehovah is
high." 5 x in OT. **Var:** Joramin.
Joramin   see **Joram.**
Jordán (Hohr dahn') m. **EE:** Jordan.
Heb. "Descender." River of Pal-
estine where Christ was bap-
tized. 5 x in DS. 1, of 13th
cen., 2nd general of Dominicans.
F. 2/15.
Jorejina   see **Jorge.**
Jorge (Hohr' hay) m. **EE:** George,
Georgia, Gk. "He who works
fields," 48 x in DS. Most fa-
mous, 4th cen. dragon slayer. F.
4/23. **Dim:** Chocha (Georgina),
Choche, Coca (Georgina), Cocó,
Cocoy, Coque, Coquis, Gina
(Georgina), Jorgelina, Jorrín,

Orito, Yoya (Georgina), Yoyi,
Yoyo. **Var:** Geogoria, Georgina,
Georgorio, Georja, Geornita,
Giorgio, Gorge, Gorgina, Gorgio,
Jeorge, Jeorgia, Jeorje,
Jiorgianna, Jorejina, Jorgina,
Jorja, Jorje, Jorji, Xorge.
Jorgelina   see Jorge.
Jorgina   see Jorge.
Jorja   see Jorge.
Jorje   see Jorge.
Jorji   see Jorge.
Jorlanda   see Yolanda.
Jorrin   see Jorge.
Jortensia   see Hortencia.
Josafa   see Josefat.
Josafata   see Josefat.
Josafina   see José.
Josaphina   see José.
José (Hoe say') m. **EE:** Jo, Joe,
Joseph, etc. Heb. "God will
add." Favored son of Jacob &
Rachel, sold into slavery by
brothers. Also, husband of V.
Mary. F. 2/19. 60 x in DS. **Dim:**
Che, Chebita (Josefa), Cheche,
Chefa (Josefa), Chefina
(Josefina), Chelin, Cheo, Chepa
(Josefa), Chepe, Chepillo,
Chepin, Chepina (Josefina),
Chepis (Josefina), Chepita
(Josefa), Chepito, Chepo,
Chichi, Chipa, Chipi (Josefa),
Chofa (Josefa), Coche, Fefa
(Josefa), Fefita (Josefa), Fifi
(Josefa), Fina (Josefina), Jobo,
Josecho, Josecito, Josefita
(Josefa), Joselillo, Joselin,
Joselito, Josenina, Josesito,
Josilla, Jota, Pepa (Josefa),
Pepe, Pepillo, Pepin, Pepina
(Josefa), Pepito, Pepón, Pina
(Josefina), Pipina (Josefina),
Pipo, Pita (Josefa), Sefa
(Josefa). **Var:** Gosefina, Hosé,
Hosefina, Hosephine, Jocifa,
Josafina, Josaphina, Joseán,
Joseardo, Josefa, Josefana,
Josefat, Josefenia, Josefenna,
Josefeno, Josefián, Josefiba,
Josefin, Josefina, Josefine,
Josefredo, Josefus, Josega,
Josehine, Joseifa, Joseja,
Josepa, Joseph, Josepha,
Josephae, Josephfa, Josephin,
Josephina, Josephita, Joseptito,
Joserja, Joseva, Josevia,
Josifina, Josiph, Jozefa,
Jozefina, Jusefa.
Joseán   see José.
Joseardo   see José.
Josecho   see José.
Josecito   see José.
Josefa   see José.
Josefana   see José.
Josefat   see José.
Josefat (Hoe say faht') m. **EE:**
Jehoshaphat, etc. Heb. "He who
has God as judge." 4th king of
Judah. Valley of Jehoshaphat
considered to be place of
judgement. 2 x in DS. **Var:**
Josafa, Josafata, Josepeta.
Josefenia   see José.
Josefenna   see José.

Josefeno   see José.
Josefián   see José.
Josefiba   see José.
Josefin   see José.
Josefina   see José.
Josefine   see José.
Josefita   see José.
Josefredo   see José.
Josefus   see José.
Josega   see José.
Josehine   see José.
Joseifa   see José.
Joseja   see José.
Joselillo   see José.
Joselin   see José.
Joselito   see José.
Josenina   see José.
Josepa   see José.
Josepeta   see Josefat.
Joseph   see José.
Josepha   see José.
Josephae   see José.
Josephfa   see José.
Josephin   see José.
Josephina   see José.
Josephita   see José.
Joseptito   see José.
Joserja   see José.
Josesito   see José.
Joseva   see José.
Josevia   see José.
Josias (Hoe see' ahs) m. **EE:**
Josiah. "Jehovah healeth." Son
of Amon. King of Judah at age 8.
Josifina   see José.
Josilla   see José.
Josiph   see José.
Josmia   see Cosme.
Jostorgo   see Eustorgio.
Josué (Hoe soo aay') m. **EE:** Josh,
Joshua, etc. Heb. "God is salva-
tion." As successor of Moses,
led Jews into promised land. F.
9/1. **Var:** Hoisiá, Hoseá, Oseás,
Osseá.
Jota   see José.
Jotero (Hoe tay' roe) m. Dancer of
the jota.
Jouqoín   see Joaquín.
Jovana   see Joviano.
Jovanas   see Joviano.
Jovatino   see Juventino.
Joveita   see Joviano.
Jovencio   see Juvencio.
Jovenia   see Joviano.
Joventanio   see Juventino.
Joventino   see Juventino.
Joviano (Hoe bee ah' no) m. **EE:**
Jovian, etc. Patronymic of Jove,
Roman god who conquered Gk.
Zeus. 4th cen. Roman emperor who
aided Christianity with freedom
of worship. 20 x in DS. **Dim:**
Gobita (Jovita), Gova, Govita
(Jovita). **Var:** Hovita, Javita,
Jovana, Jovanas, Joveita,
Jovenia, Joviniano, Jovino,
Jovita, Jovitar, Jovitta,
Juvanio, Juvita.
Jovila   see Job.
Jovilia   see Job.
Joviniano   see Joviano.
Jovino   see Joviano.
Jovita   see Joviano.
Jovitar   see Joviano.

Jovitta	see **Joviano.**
Jozefa	see **José.**
Jozefina	see **José.**
Jreneo	see **Irene.**
Jsipora	see **Sippora.**
Juachín	see **Joaquín.**
Juacho	see **Bonifacio.**
Juacho	see **Joaquín.**
Juaco	see **Joaquín.**
Juadalupe	see **Guadalupe.**
Juakín	see **Joaquín.**

Juan (Hwahn) m. **EE:** Jack, John. Heb. "Full of grace of God." 1 of 12 disciples & Gospel author. F. 12/27. 418 x in DS. **Dim:** Chan, Chano, Chito, Janín, Janina, Joanita, Juanch, Juancho, Juancito, Juanelo, Juanillo, Juanito, Juanitocho, Juanitto, Nano, Nito, Yoni. **Var:** Guanita, Huanita, Juann, Juanna, Jwanita, Quanita, Wanita, Yohanmes, Yovanna, Yuana, Yuanita. See also Jansenio.

Juanch	see **Juan.**
Juancho	see **Juan.**
Juancito	see **Juan.**
Juanelo	see **Juan.**
Juanillo	see **Juan.**
Juanito	see **Juan.**
Juanitocho	see **Juan.**
Juanitto	see **Juan.**
Juann	see **Juan.**
Juanna	see **Juan.**
Juaqín	see **Joaquín.**
Juaquín	see **Joaquín.**
Juaquinillo	see **Joaquín.**
Juaquino	see **Joaquín.**

Jubal (Hoo bahl') m. **EE:** Junal, etc. Heb. "Filled with jubilation." Son of Lamech & Ada & father of all who play harp & pipes.

Jubena	see **Juvenal.**
Jubenal	see **Juvenal.**
Jubencio	see **Juvencio.**
Jubentia	see **Juvencio.**
Jubentino	see **Juventino.**
Jubenzio	see **Juvencio.**
Jubesio	see **Juvencio.**

Jucundo (Hoo coon' doe) m. **EE:** Jucunda, Jucundus, Lat. "He who gives pleasure." 24 x in DS. 5th cen. S. & bishop of Bologna. F. 5/14. **Var:** Jacondo, Jacundo, Jocundo, Yacundo, Yocundo.

Judalecio	see **Indalecio.**
Judalencio	see **Indalecio.**
Judalesio	see **Indalecio.**

Judalsio (Hoo dahl' see oh) m. Judacilio, 1st cen. B.C. Roman.

Judas (Hoo' dahs) m. **EE:** Judas, Jude, etc. Heb. "Praise of God." Youngest son of Jacob & Leah & founder of 1 of 12 tribes of Israel. Another, disciple & betrayer of Christ. See also Judit.

Judelia	see **Odilia.**

Judit (Hoo deet') f. **EE:** Judith, etc. Heb. "Praise of God." 1 of Esau's wives & heroine of 1 of books of Apocrypha. Beheaded Holofernes to save her city, Bethulia. **Dim:** Yudi. **Var:**

Judith. See also Judas.

Judith	see **Judit.**
Juelio	see **Julio.**
Juincho	see **Efraín.**
Jula	see **Julio.**
Julalio	see **Eulalio.**
Julán	see **Julio.**
Julea	see **Julio.**
Juleán	see **Julio.**
Juleana	see **Julio.**
Julencio	see **Julio.**
Juli	see **Julio.**
Julián	see **Julio.**
Julianis	see **Julio.**
Julianita	see **Julio.**
Juliano	see **Julio.**
Julianum	see **Julio.**
Juliau	see **Julio.**
Juliena	see **Julio.**
Julieta	see **Julio.**
Julina	see **Julio.**
Julineta	see **Julio.**

Julio (Hoo' lee oh) m. **EE:** Jill, Julie, Julius, etc. Lat. "Jupiter," "God, the Father." 1, 1st Caesar, murdered by triumvirate. 198 x in DS. **Dim:** Chula, Juli, Julianita, Julieta, Julina, Julito, Lián, Liana, Lyana, Pacheco, Ulián, Ulio, Yuyo, Yuyu. **Var:** Guilleano, Guillia, Gulema, Gulianno, Huliana, Juelio, Jula, Julán, Julea, Juleán, Juleana, Julencio, Julián, Julianis, Juliano, Julianum, Juliau, Juliena, Julineta, Julissa, Yulius, Yulos.

Julissa	see **Julio.**
Julito	see **Julio.**
Jumesindo	see **Gumersindo.**
Juncho	see **Efraín.**
Jurelia	see **Uriel.**
Jusdina	see **Justino.**
Jusefa	see **José.**
Justano	see **Justino.**
Justavo	see **Gustavo.**
Justeno	see **Justino.**
Justia	see **Justino.**
Justianio	see **Justino.**
Justinia	see **Justino.**
Justiniano	see **Justino.**

Justino (Hoos tee' no) m. **EE:** Justin, Justina, Justus. Lat. "Justus," "upright, impartial." 6th cen. Roman emperor who codified Roman law. Also, 2nd cen. S. called Justin the Philosopher. F. 4/14. **Dim:** Tino, Tuto. **Var:** Gustia, Gustiano, Gustin, Gustino, Gusto, Gustosia, Hustina, Husto, Jusdina, Justano, Justeno, Justia, Justianio, Justinia, Justiniano, Justita, Justivo, Justo, Justus, Juztina.

Justita	see **Justino.**
Justivo	see **Justino.**
Justo	see **Justino.**
Justus	see **Justino.**
Juto	see **Jutta.**

Jutta (Hoo' tah) f. **EE:** Ute. Ger. "Gudula," "fight." 4 x in DS. **Var:** Juto.

Juvancia	see **Juvencio.**

Juvanio   see Joviano.
Juven   see Juventino.
Juvenal (Hoo bay nahl') m. EE:
   Juvenal, Juvenalis. Lat. "He who
   is young." Roman satirist. 8 x
   in DS. I, Patriarch of Jerusalem
   in 5th cen. F. 5/3. Var: Jubena,
   Jubenal, Juveral.
Juvenceslas   see Venceslao.
Juvenciana   see Juvencio.
Juvencio (Hoo bayn', see oh) m. EE:
   Juventius. Lat. "Iuventius,"
   "youth." 6 x in DS. 1, 2nd cen.
   bishop of Pavia, Italy. F. 2/8.
   Var: Duvencio, Eubence,
   Eubense, Eubense, Euvence,
   Euvencio, Jovencio, Jubencio,
   Jubentia, Jubenzio, Jubesio,
   Juvancia, Juvenciana, Juvenio,
   Juvensio, Juventio, Juvento,
   Juviancio, Ovencio, Ubence,
   Ubencio, Ubense, Ubensi, Uvence,
   Uvencio, Ybencio, Yubencio,

Yuvencio. See also Evencio,
   Juventino.
Juvenio   see Juvencio.
Juvensio   see Juvencio.
Juventeno   see Juventino.
Juventin   see Juventino.
Juventino (Hoo bayn tee' no) m.
   Lat. "Youth." 6 x in DS. Var:
   Huventino, Jeventina, Jivencio,
   Jovatino, Joventanio, Joventino,
   Jubentino, Juven, Juventeno,
   Juventin, Juventurio, Juventuro.
   See also Juvencio.
Juventio   see Juvencio.
Juvento   see Juvencio.
Juventurio   see Juventino.
Juventuro   see Juventino.
Juveral   see Juvenal.
Juviancio   see Juvencio.
Juvita   see Joviano.
Juztina   see Justino.
Jwanita   see Juan.

K

Kandelaria   see Candelario.
Kanuto   see Canuto.
Karloz   see Carlos.
Kasandra   see Casandra.
Kasto   see Casto.
Katalina   see Catalina.
Kathorina   see Catalina.
Katriona   see Catalina.
Kerina   see Carino.
Khris   see Cristián.

Kiki   see Enrique.
Kiko   see Enrique.
Kilina   see Tranquilino.
Kilmes   see Quilmes.
Kilo   see Tranquilino.
Kleofás   see Cleofás.
Konstadinos   see Constancio.
Kristina   see Cristián.
Kristovolis   see Cristóbal.

L

Labán (Lah baan') m. EE: Laban.
   Heb. "White." In Bible, father
   of Jacob's wives, Rachel & Leah.
   Var: Labiano, Labino, Lablo,
   Labo, Laceta.
Laberto   see Alberto.
Labiano   see Labán.
Labina   see Lavinia.
Labino   see Labán.
Lablo   see Labán.
Labo   see Labán.
Labrencio   see Lauro.
Lacadia   see Leocadia.
Laceta   see Labán.
Lacho   see Horacio.
Lacho   see Lázaro.
Lacho   see Nicolás.
Lacticia   see Leticia.
Ladae   see Leda.
Ladaslao   see Ladislao.
Ladeslao   see Ladislao.
Ladiclas   see Ladislao.
Ladilada   see Ladislao.
Ladis   see Ladislao.
Ladislad   see Ladislao.
Ladislado   see Ladislao.

Ladislao (Law deese law' oh) m.
   EE: Leslie, etc. Slav. "He who
   governs with glory." 30 Hun-
   garian kings. 3 x in DS. 1, 11th
   cen. S. Conquered Croatia. F.
   6/27. Dim: Ladis, Lalo, Ula.
   Var: Adelsida, Adeslade,
   Ladaslao, Ladeslao, Ladiclas,
   Ladilada, Ladislad, Ladislado,
   Ladislau, Ladislaus, Ladislav,
   Ladislo, Ladisloa, Ladislos,
   Ladistro, Laisladoltona,
   Laolislado, Lavuslalo, Ledelada,
   Ledislado, Ledislao, Vladislav.
Ladislau   see Ladislao.
Ladislaus   see Ladislao.
Ladislav   see Ladislao.
Ladislo   see Ladislao.
Ladisloa   see Ladislao.
Ladislos   see Ladislao.
Ladistro   see Ladislao.
Laercio (Lah air' see oh) m. EE:
   Laertes. Gk. "Lifter of rocks."
   Gk. hero with Argonauts in quest
   for Golden Fleece.
Laeticia   see Leticia.

Lafa	see Rafael.	Lássaro	see Lázaro.
Lafredo	see Alfredo.	Laszio	see Lázaro.
Lagaria	see Lucaria.	Laterio	see Lautaro.
Lagaro	see Lucaria.	Latheria	see Lautaro.
Laida	see Leda.	Laticia	see Leticia.
Laila	see Leila.	Laticie	see Leticia.
Laisladoltona	see Ladislao.	Laturmina	see Lautaro.
Laititia	see Leticia.	Latvina	see Lavinia.
Laizar	see Lázaro.	Lauceano	see Lorenzo.

Laudelina (Lah ooh day lee' nah) f. EE: Landelin. Ger. "Country, land." 2 x in DS. 1, 7th cen. abbot of Crespin, France, a converted robber. F. 6/15.

Laizaro	see Lázaro.
Lala	see Adelaido.
Lali	see Eulalio.
Lalia	see Eulalio.
Lalie	see Eulalio.
Lalo	see Abelardo.
Lalo	see Albaro.

Laudes (Lah ooh' dehs) m. Lat. "Laus, laudis," "to praise."

Lalo	see Braulia.	Laugrencio	see Lorenzo.
Lalo	see Darío.	Laurantina	see Lauro.
Lalo	see Dolores.	Laureán	see Lauro.
Lalo	see Edgardo.	Laureana	see Lauro.
Lalo	see Eduardo.	Laureanabea	see Lauro.
Lalo	see Estanislao.	Laureano	see Lorenzo.
Lalo	see Eulalio.	Laurela	see Lauro.
Lalo	see Everardo.	Laurencio	see Lorenzo.
Lalo	see Hilario.	Laureno	see Lauro.
Lalo	see Ladislao.	Laurentena	see Lorenzo.

Lamberto (Lahm bear' toe) m. EE: Lambert, etc. Ger. "His country's glory." 11 x in DS. 1, bishop of Maestricht in 7th cen. Noted for vigorous leadership. F. 9/19.

Laurentia	see Lorenzo.
Laurentino	see Lorenzo.
Laurento	see Lorenzo.
Laurenzo	see Lorenzo.
Lauriniano	see Lorenzo.
Laurino	see Lauro.

Lamentius (Lah main' tee us) m. Lat. "Lamentarius," "mournful." Similar to Dolores or Angustias (see both). Could also be Lamentations, book in Bible.

Lamiro (Lah mee' roe) m. Lat. leader killed by Nero.

Lauro (Lah ooh' roe) m. EE: Laura, Laurel, etc. Lat. "Laurel." 9th cen. matron of Cordova, Spain. Became nun & was boiled in pitch by Moors. F. 10/19. **Dim:** Bicha (Lauriza), Laryssa, Laurino, Lorita. **Var:** Labrencio, Laoriano, Larara, Larela, Lareo, Lareto, Laro, Laurantina, Laureán, Laureana, Laureanabea, Laurela, Laureno, Lautos, Lora, Loraida, Lorelo, Lori, Louria, Lowrada.

Lancha	see Esperanza.
Lando	see Roldán.
Landra	see Landrada.

Landrada (Lahn drah' dah) f. EE: Landrada. Ger. "He who counsels his country." In DS, 7th cen. V. of Bilsen, Belgium, who led ascetic life & built convent. F. 4/17. **Var:** Landra.

Lautaro (Lah ooh tah' roe) m. Araucanian, "Daring & enterprising." Hero of Ercilla's epic poem of Chile, "La Araucana." In 16th cen. defeated Spaniards & killed Pedro de Valdivia. **Var:** Laterio, Latheria, Laturmina.

Langino	see Longinos.
Lao	see Estanislao.
Laolislado	see Ladislao.
Laoriano	see Lauro.
Lapo	see Serapio.
Laragosa	see Zaragoza.
Larara	see Lauro.
Larela	see Lauro.

Lautos	see Lauro.
Laviano	see Lavinia.

Lavinia (Lah bee' nee ah) f. EE: Lavinia, etc. Lat. king's daughter who married Aeneas, hero of Virgil's epic "The Aeneid." **Var:** Labina, Latvina, Laviano, Lavino, Levina, Levinio, Livinia, Luvena, Luvenia.

Larensa	see Lorenzo.
Larenzo	see Lorenzo.
Lareo	see Lauro.
Lareto	see Lauro.
Largardo	see Ludgarda.
Larina	see Larrina.

Larios (Lah' ree ohs) m. Form of Larius, Roman M. F. 4/15.

Laro	see Lauro.

Larrina (Lah ree' na) f. Larino in Roman myth. followed Camilo to all battles. **Var:** Larina.

Lavino	see Lavinia.
Lavuslalo	see Ladislao.
Lawentia	see Lorenzo.
Lawrencio	see Lorenzo.
Lawrenzis	see Lorenzo.
Laya	see Eulalio.
Layda	see Adelaido.
Layda	see Leda.
Layita	see Eulalio.
Layla	see Leila.

Laryssa	see Lauro.
Lasario	see Lázaro.
Lásaro	see Lázaro.
Lásero	see Lázaro.
Láserow	see Lázaro.
Láserus	see Lázaro.
Lásora	see Lázaro.

Lazarda	see Lázaro.
Lazaria	see Lázaro.

Lázaro (Lah' zah roe) m. EE:

Eleazar, Lazar, Lazarus. Heb.
"God has helped." Mary &
Martha's brother resurrected by
Christ. F. 12/17. 5 x in DS.
Dim: Lacho. **Var:** Laizar,
Laizaro, Lasario, Lásaro,
Lásero, Láserow, Láserus,
Lásora, Lássaro, Laszio,
Lazarda, Lazaria, Lázarra,
Lázaru, Lázero, Lazro, Lázuro,
Lazzari, Lessario. See also
Eleazar.

Lázarra	see **Lázaro.**
Lázaru	see **Lázaro.**
Lázero	see **Lázaro.**
Lazro	see **Lázaro.**
Lázuro	see **Lázaro.**
Lazzari	see **Lázaro.**

Lea (Lay' ah) f. EE: Lea, Leah,
Lee. Heb. "Weary." Less at-
tractive daughter of Laban who,
through trickery, became Jacob's
bride. **Var:** Leah, Lia.

Leabardo	see **Leopardo.**
Leadegario	see **Leodegario.**
Leadrin	see **Leandro.**
Leah	see **Lea.**
Leanard	see **Leonardo.**
Leanardo	see **Leonardo.**
Leandera	see **Leandro.**
Leandes	see **Leandro.**
Leando	see **Leandro.**
Leandria	see **Leandro.**

Leandro (Lay ahn' droe) m. EE:
Andy, Leander, Lee. Gk. "Lion
man." In myth., swam Hellespont
each evening to meet Hero,
priestess of Aphrodite. 4 x in
DS. 1, 6th cen. bishop of
Seville. F. 2/27. **Var:** Leadrín,
Leandera, Leandes, Leando,
Leandria, Leandrón, Lendro,
Leoandra, Leodro, Leondro,
Liandro.

Leandrón	see **Leandro.**
Leanides	see **Leonides.**
Leanoro	see **Leonor.**
Leapaldo	see **Leopoldo.**
Leatitia	see **Leticia.**
Leatrice	see **Leticia.**
Leberato	see **Liberato.**
Lebrado	see **Liberato.**
Lecadio	see **Leocadia.**
Lecardia	see **Leocadia.**
Lecha	see **Lorenzo.**
Lechita	see **Lorenzo.**
Lecho	see **Indalecio.**
Lecodio	see **Leocadia.**

Leda (Lay' dah) f. EE: Leda. In
Gk. legend mother of Helen,
Castor & Pollux, & Clytemnestra.
Zeus appeared to her as swan.
Var: Ladae, Laida, Layda, Ledia,
Lediana, Leeta, Leida, Leidia,
Loida, Lyda.

Ledelada	see **Ladislao.**
Ledia	see **Leda.**
Lediana	see **Leda.**
Ledislado	see **Ladislao.**
Ledislao	see **Ladislao.**
Ledivina	see **Ludovino.**
Ledovico	see **Ludovico.**
Ledovina	see **Ludovino.**
Leduvina	see **Ludovino.**
Ledy	see **Leticia.**

Leeta	see **Leda.**
Legoria	see **Leodegario.**

Lehi (Lay' he) m. EE: Lehi. Heb.
"Cheek, jawbone." Here Samson
met Philistines.

Leida	see **Leda.**
Leidia	see **Leda.**

Leila (Lay ee' lah) f. EE: Leila,
etc. Gk. & Ar. "Night." 1 x in
DS. F. 8/11. **Var:** Laila, Layla,
Leilani, Leillia, Lella, Leyla.

Leilani	see **Leila.**
Leillia	see **Leila.**
Leinardo	see **Leonardo.**
Leionysio	see **Leoncio.**
Lejandro	see **Alejandro.**
Lela	see **Adela.**
Lela	see **Adelaido.**
Lela	see **Fidel.**
Lelio	see **Aurelio.**
Lelito	see **Adela.**
Lella	see **Leila.**
Lelo	see **Aurelio.**
Lelo	see **Gabriel.**
Lena	see **Elena.**
Lena	see **Magdaleno.**
Lena	see **Natalio.**
Lenadra	see **Leonardo.**
Lenaida	see **Leonides.**
Lenardo	see **Leonardo.**
Lenayda	see **Leonides.**
Lencha	see **Clemente.**
Lencho	see **Florencio.**
Lencho	see **Lorenzo.**
Lencia	see **Leoncio.**
Lendro	see **Leandro.**
Lenecio	see **Leoncio.**
Leni	see **Elena.**
Leniro	see **Leonor.**
Lenoiele	see **León.**
Lenor	see **Leonor.**
Lenorda	see **Leonardo.**
Lenorina	see **Leonor.**
Leo	see **León.**
Leoadio	see **Leocadia.**
Leoandra	see **Leandro.**

Leoba (Lay oh' bah) f. Form of
Lioba (Liobgitha) 8th cen. Ang-
Sax. nun of present-day Germany.

Leobardo	see **Leopardo.**
Leobegilda	see **Leovigildo.**

Leocadia (Lay oh cah' dee ah) f.
EE: Leocadius, etc. Gk. "Splen-
did whiteness." 2nd cen. V. M.
of Spain supposed to have risen
from tomb to defend virginity of
Blessed V. F. 12/9. **Dim:** Paya.
Var: Eleocaida, Eleucadio,
Elocadia, Lacadia, Lecadio,
Lecardia, Lecodio, Leoadio,
Leocadra, Leocalio, Leocardio,
Leocario, Leocordio, Leokadia,
Leucadio, Liocadia, Locadio,
Locordia, Loricadia, Lucadio.

Leocadra	see **Leocadia.**
Leocalio	see **Leocadia.**
Leocardio	see **Leocadia.**
Leocario	see **Leocadia.**
Leocordio	see **Leocadia.**

Leodegario (Lay' oh day gah' ree
oh) m. EE: Leodegar, etc. Teut.
"He who defends his people with
lance." 4 x in DS. 1, 7th cen.
bishop of Autun, France, mart.
by beheading. F. 10/2. **Var:**

Leadegario, Legoria, Leogardo,
Leogario, Leudegerio. See also
Ludgarda.
Leodro   see **Leandro**.
Leofila   see **Leofilia**.
Leofilia (Lay oh fee' lee ah) f.
Comb. of Leopoldo & Ofelia (see
both). **Var:** Leofila.
Leofredo   see **Leofrido**.
Leofrido (Lay oh free' doe) m.
Teut. "He who brings peace to
his people." **Var:** Leofredo.
Leogardo   see **Leodegario**.
Leogario   see **Leodegario**.
Leoides   see **Leonides**.
Leojeldo   see **Leovigildo**.
Leokadia   see **Leocadia**.
León (Lay own') m. EE: Leon,
Lionel. Lat. "Valiant as lion."
48 x in DS. 1, 5th cen. pope,
2nd greatest among popes. F.
4/11. **Dim:** Lenoiele, Leonel,
Leonelo, Leonetta, Leoniel,
Leonil, Leonila, Leonilla. **Var:**
Leo, Leonijildo, Leonires,
Leonírez, Leonís, Leonise,
Leoniso, Leonista, Leonives,
Leoniz, Leonjina, Leonon,
Lionzo, Loenona, Loenosa. See
also Leoncio, Leonildes.
Leona   see **Leonildes**.
Leonada   see **Leonardo**.
Leonadez   see **Leonardo**.
Leonadra   see **Leonardo**.
Leonaida   see **Leonardo**.
Leonal   see **Leoncio**.
Leonar   see **Leonor**.
Leonara   see **Leonor**.
Leonardae   see **Leonardo**.
Leonardida   see **Leonardo**.
Leonardo (Lay oh nar' doe) m. EE:
Len, Leonard, etc. Lat. "Strong
& brave as a lion." 10 x in DS.
1, of 6th cen. Limoges, France,
patron of insane & domestic
animals. F. 11/6. **Dim:** Nado,
Nayito, Nayo. **Var:** Leanard,
Leanardo, Leinardo, Lenadra,
Lenardo, Lenorda, Leonada,
Leonadez, Leonadra, Leonaida,
Leonardae, Leonardida, Leonarel,
Leondez, Leondida, Leonorda,
Leornarda, Lernado, Lernando,
Lionardo.
Leonarel   see **Leonardo**.
Leoncinio   see **Leoncio**.
Leoncio (Lay own' see oh) m. Lat.
"Lion." **Dim:** Loncha. **Var:**
Leionysio, Lencia, Lenecio,
Leonal, Leoncinio, Leonicio,
Leonisia, Leonso, Leonysio,
Leonzo, Lianicia, Lionesio,
Lionises, Lionisio, Loncia,
Lonicia, Lonisio, Lonseo,
Lyonisia. See also León,
Leontina.
Leonda   see **Leonides**.
Leondes   see **Leonides**.
Leondez   see **Leonardo**.
Leondida   see **Leonardo**.
Leondro   see **Leandro**.
Leoneda   see **Leonides**.
Leonedes   see **Leonides**.
Leonel   see **León**.
Leoneldes   see **Leonides**.

Leoneldo   see **Leonides**.
Leonelo   see **León**.
Leonetta   see **León**.
Leongilia   see **Leovigildo**.
Leoni   see **Leonor**.
Leonicio   see **Leoncio**.
Leonidas   see **Leonides**.
Leonide   see **Leonides**.
Leonideas   see **Leonides**.
Leonideo   see **Leonides**.
Leonides (Lay oh nee' days) m. EE:
Leonides. Gk. "Fights like a
lion." 4th cen. B.C. Spartan
king fought Xerxes' armies at
Thermopylae. 13 x in DS. **Var:**
Elonides, Leanides, Lenaida,
Lenayda, Leoides, Leonda,
Leondes, Leoneda, Leonedes,
Leoneldes, Leoneldo, Leonidas,
Leonide, Leonideas, Leonideo,
Leonidez, Leonidino, Leonidis,
Leonido, Leonidos, Lionaido,
Lionides, Lionidez, Lionidos,
Lonidas.
Leonidez   see **Leonides**.
Leonidino   see **Leonides**.
Leonidis   see **Leonides**.
Leonido   see **Leonides**.
Leonidos   see **Leonides**.
Leoniel   see **León**.
Leonijildo   see **León**.
Leonil   see **León**.
Leonila   see **León**.
Leonildes (Lay oh neel' days) m.
Ger. & Lat. "He who fights like
a lion." **Dim:** Leona, Nildo. See
also León.
Leonilla   see **León**.
Leonires   see **León**.
Leonírez   see **León**.
Leonís   see **León**.
Leonís   see **Leonor**.
Leonise   see **León**.
Leonisia   see **Leoncio**.
Leoniso   see **León**.
Leonista   see **León**.
Leonives   see **León**.
Leoniz   see **León**.
Leonjina   see **León**.
Leonon   see **León**.
Leonor (Lay oh nore') f. EE:
Leonor, etc. Ger. "Compassion-
ate, humane." 6th cen. S. of
Brittany, France. F. 7/1. **Dim:**
Cocoy, Lenorina, Leoni, Leonís,
Leonorcita, Nélida, Nol, Nola,
Nono, Nonor, Nony, Nora, Norita,
Nosha, Noy, Noya. **Var:** Leanoro,
Leniro, Lenor, Leonar, Leonara,
Leonorilda, Leonres, Leornora,
Linor, Lionar, Lioner, Lionor,
Lionora, Lioria, Loniro. See
also Elena, Eleanor.
Leonorcita   see **Leonor**.
Leonorda   see **Leonardo**.
Leonorilda   see **Leonor**.
Leonres   see **Leonor**.
Leonso   see **Leoncio**.
Leontia (Lay own' tee ah) f. In
Gk. myth. Leontiade, son of
Hercules & Augea.
Leontina (Lay own tee' nah) f. EE:
Leontine, etc. Lat. "Lion-like."
Dim: Tina, Titina. See also
Leoncio.

Leonysio   see **Leoncio**.
Leonzo   see **Leoncio**.
Leopaldo   see **Leopoldo**.
Leopardo (Lay oh par' doe) m. **EE:** Leopardus, etc. Lat. "Leopard." 4 x in DS. **Var:** Leabardo, Leobardo, Leovaldo, Leovardo, Leovrado, Liovardo, Lobardo.
Leopoldas   see **Leopoldo**.
Leopoldino   see **Leopoldo**.
Leopoldo (Lay oh pole' doe) m. **EE:** Leopold. Ger. "Bold for people." 2 x in DS. 1, 11th cen. margrave. Patron of Archduchy of Austria. F. 11/14. **Dim:** Dino, Lupa (Leopoldina), Polda, Poldi, Polin, Polo. **Var:** Elopoldo, Leapaldo, Leopaldo, Leopoldas, Leopolvo, Leopott, Leoquinto, Liopold, Loepolt, Loepolus.
Leopolvo   see **Leopoldo**.
Leopott   see **Leopoldo**.
Leoquinto   see **Leopoldo**.
Leornarda   see **Leonardo**.
Leornora   see **Leonor**.
Leovaldo   see **Leopardo**.
Leovardo   see **Leopardo**.
Leovegildo   see **Leovigildo**.
Leovigildo (Lay oh heel' doe) m. **EE:** Leovigild. Teut. "Worthy to be loved by his people." 6th cen. Visigothic king of Spain put son to death for accepting Catholicism instead of Arianism. **Var:** Leobegilda, Leojeldo, Leongilia, Leovegildo, Leovijilda, Leovino, Lesvigilda, Liojildo, Liorigildo, Luigildo.
Leovijilda   see **Leovigildo**.
Leovino   see **Leovigildo**.
Leovrado   see **Leopardo**.
Lernado   see **Leonardo**.
Lernando   see **Leonardo**.
Lesandro   see **Lisandro**.
Lesbia (Lays' bee ah) f. **EE:** Lesbia. Gk. "Native of Lesbos" (Gk. island). Home of Sappho, lyrical poetess who supposedly wrote verses for female lover. **Dim:** Lesvita. **Var:** Alesvia, Lessavia, Lesvia.
Lessario   see **Lázaro**.
Lessavia   see **Lesbia**.
Lesvia   see **Lesbia**.
Lesvigilda   see **Leovigildo**.
Lesvita   see **Lesbia**.
Letecea   see **Leticia**.
Letecia   see **Leticia**.
Leteica   see **Leticia**.
Leti   see **Leticia**.
Leticia (Lay tee' see ah) f. **EE:** Leticia, Letty, Tish, etc. Lat. "She who brings joy & happiness." **Dim:** Ledy, Leti, Leto, Lettie, Lety, Licha, Ticha. **Var:** Alaticia, Eleticia, Eletisia, Lacticia, Laeticia, Laititia, Laticia, Laticie, Leatitia, Leatrice, Letecea, Letecia, Leteica, Letisia, Letizia, Lettcia, Letticia, Liticia, Luticia, Lydice.
Letisia   see **Leticia**.
Letizia   see **Leticia**.

Leto   see **Leticia**.
Lettcia   see **Leticia**.
Letticia   see **Leticia**.
Lettie   see **Leticia**.
Lety   see **Leticia**.
Leucadio   see **Leocadia**.
Leudegerio   see **Leodegario**.
Leudovico   see **Ludovico**.
Leuterio   see **Lutero**.
Levia (Lay' bee ah) f. Lat. "Left-handed," or "unlucky one." Levio, Lat. poet of 1st cen.
Levina   see **Lavinia**.
Levinio   see **Lavinia**.
Lewisa   see **Luis**.
Leydia   see **Lidio**.
Leyla   see **Leila**.
Lezith   see **Elisabeth**.
Lía   see **Lea**.
Lía   see **Rosalío**.
Lián   see **Julio**.
Liana   see **Julio**.
Liandro   see **Leandro**.
Lianicia   see **Leoncio**.
Libardo   see **Liberato**.
Libe   see **Liberato**.
Libera   see **Liberato**.
Liberada   see **Liberato**.
Liberale   see **Liberato**.
Liberao   see **Liberato**.
Liberasta   see **Liberato**.
Liberato (Lee bay rah' toe) m. **EE:** Liberatus, etc. Lat. "He who has been liberated." 16 x in DS. 1, mystical S. of Portugal, grew beard to maintain her vow of virginity. F. 7/20. **Dim:** Libe, Libertina, Libra, Libranita, Livra. **Var:** Elibrada, Leberato, Lebrado, Libardo, Libera, Liberada, Liberale, Liberao, Liberasta, Liberda, Libertae, Liberto, Libirada, Librad, Libradita, Librado, Librao, Librara, Libravo, Liebrado, Lirata, Liverato, Livrada. See also Liberio.
Liberda   see **Liberato**.
Liberio (Lee bay' ree oh) m. **EE:** Liberius. Lat. "Free from slavery." 9 x in DS. 1, 4th cen. pope involved in Arianism. F. 9/23. **Var:** Liberius, Liberuim. See also Liberato.
Liberius   see **Liberio**.
Libertae   see **Liberato**.
Libertina   see **Liberato**.
Liberto   see **Liberato**.
Liberuim   see **Liberio**.
Libia (Lee' bee ah) f. Lat. "Born in Libya." Mart. at Palmyra under Diocletian in 4th cen. F. 6/15. **Var:** Livia, Lylvia, Lyvia.
Libirada   see **Liberato**.
Libozio (Lee bo' zee oh) m. St. Liboso mart. in Africa.
Libra   see **Liberato**.
Librad   see **Liberato**.
Libradita   see **Liberato**.
Librado   see **Liberato**.
Libranita   see **Liberato**.
Librao   see **Liberato**.
Librara   see **Liberato**.
Libravo   see **Liberato**.
Librocio (Lee broe' see oh) m.

Could be form of Libosa, S.
mart. in Nicomedia, Turkey. F.
2/22.

Lica   see **Lucrecio.**
Lica (Lee' cah) f. EE: Lycas. Gk.
"Light." **Var:** Licco.
Licaldo   see **Ricardo.**
Licalo   see **Ricardo.**
Licco   see **Lica.**
Licerio   see **Glicerio.**
Lich   see **Luis.**
Licha   see **Alicio.**
Licha   see **Elisabeth.**
Licha   see **Eliseo.**
Licha   see **Eloiso.**
Licha   see **Isabel.**
Licha   see **Leticia.**
Licho   see **Félix.**
Licho   see **Lisandro.**
Licho   see **Luis.**
Licho   see **Ulises.**
Lichu   see **Alicio.**
Licia   see **Alicio.**
Liciano   see **Licinio.**
Licilio (Lee see' lee oh) m. Gk.
"Licia," "native of Lycia (Asia
Minor),"
Licinio (Lee see' nee oh) m. EE:
Licinius. Lat. "Licinius," Roman
family name. 1, S. struck with
leprosy on eve of wedding. Cured
by miracle, he became monk. F.
2/13. **Var:** Liciano.
Lico   see **Federico.**
Lico   see **Manuel.**
Lico   see **Ricardo.**
Licurgo (Lee coor' go) m. EE:
Lycurgus. Gk. "He who puts
wolves to flight." Spartan
reformer of 7th cen. B.C. who
gave city martial image. See
also Lupercio.
Lida   see **Lidio.**
Lidda   see **Lidio.**
Lidiam   see **Lidio.**
Lidio (Lee' dee oh) m. EE: Liddy,
Lydell, Lydia. Gk. "Born in
Lydia," ancient kingdom in Asia
Minor. 2 x in DS. 1, Jewess, 1st
European convert of St. Paul. F.
8/3. **Var:** Leydia, Lida, Lidda,
Lidiam, Litia, Lydio.
Lidubina   see **Liduvino.**
Liduvino (Lee doo bee' no) m. EE:
Love, Luvenia, etc. Teut. "Leo-
bino," "loyal friend." **Var:**
Lidubina, Lidvina.
Lidvina   see **Liduvino.**
Liebrado   see **Liberato.**
Liela   see **Lilia.**
Lifrado (Lee frah' doe) m. Form of
Lifard or Pietphard, 7th cen.
English S. F. 2/4.
Ligario (Lee gah' ree oh) m. Could
be variant of Logaria, Lugoria,
or Ligorio (see all).
Ligia (Lee' hee ah) f. Gk. "Of
clear, sharp sound." Christian
heroine of "Quo Vadis" (1897).
Var: Lijio.
Ligorio (Lee go' ree oh) m. EE:
Ligorius. Lat. "Native of
Liguria," region of Italy now
comprising Genoa, Savona, &
Spezia. Gk. chemist killed by

pagan hunters. F. 9/13. **Var:**
Locario, Locoro, Logaria,
Logoria, Lokario.

Lijio   see **Ligia.**
Lila   see **Amalio.**
Lila   see **Emilio.**
Lili   see **Lilia.**
Lilia (Lee' lee ah) f. EE:
Lillian, etc. Lat. "Lilium,"
"lily," symbol of purity & inno-
cence & predominant botanical
symbol of V. Mary. **Var:** Liela,
Lili, Liliana, Lilianna.
Liliana   see **Lilia.**
Lilianna   see **Lilia.**
Liliosa (Lee lee oh' sah) f. S.
mart. by Moslems in Cordova,
Spain. F. 7/27.
Lilo   see **Baudilio.**
Lilo   see **Cirilo.**
Lilo   see **Virgilio.**
Liloesia (Lee low ay' see ah) f.
Could be form of Liliosa (see).
Limbania (Leem bah' ne ah) f. 13th
cen. Genoan V. & S. who lived in
cave for austere life. F. 8/16.
Limeo   see **Limneo.**
Limneo (Leem' nay oh) m. Limnea is
surname for Diana or Artemis.
Also Linnaeus (Linneo), Swedish
founder of systematic botany.
Var: Limeo, Limnes, Linao,
Linneo, Linoe.
Limnes   see **Limneo.**
Limona (Lee mo' nah) f. In Gk.
myth., daughter of Hipomenes.
For adultery, imprisoned &
devoured by wild horse.
Lina   see **Abelino.**
Lina   see **Adelaido.**
Lina   see **Angel.**
Lina   see **Carlos.**
Lina   see **Celina.**
Lina   see **Celio.**
Lina   see **Natalio.**
Lina   see **Rosalindo.**
Lina   see **Víctor.**
Linao   see **Limneo.**
Lincha   see **Elías.**
Linda   see **Emma.**
Linda   see **Florencio.**
Linda   see **Teodolinda.**
Lingina   see **Longinos.**
Linneo   see **Limneo.**
Lino   see **Marcelino.**
Lino   see **Paulo.**
Lino (Lee' no) m. EE: Linus. Gk.
son of Apollo who taught music
to Hercules & Orpheus. Linus
also mentioned in NT & DS. 1st
bishop of Rome after apostles.
F. 9/23. **Var:** Linus.
Linoe   see **Limneo.**
Linor   see **Leonor.**
Linus   see **Lino.**
Lioba (Lee oh' bah) f. EE: Lioba.
Ger. "Lovable." 8th cen. Ang-
Sax. nun. Held in high esteem by
Charlemagne & Pepin. F. 9/26.
Var: Liova.
Liocadia   see **Leocadia.**
Liofás   see **Cleofás.**
Liojildo   see **Leovigildo.**
Lionaido   see **Leonides.**
Lionar   see **Leonor.**

Lionardo   see Leonardo.
Lioner   see Leonor.
Lionesio   see Leoncio.
Lionides   see Leonides.
Lionidez   see Leonides.
Lionidos   see Leonides.
Lionises   see Leoncio.
Lionisio   see Leoncio.
Lionor   see Leonor.
Lionora   see Leonor.
Lionzo   see León.
Liopold   see Leopoldo.
Lioria   see Leonor.
Liorigildo   see Leovigildo.
Liova   see Lioba.
Liovardo   see Leopardo.
Lipe   see Felipo.
Lipo   see Felipo.
Lirata   see Liberato.
Lisa   see Elisabeth.
Lisa   see Isabel.
Lisandro (Lee sawn' droe) m. EE: Lysander. Gk. "Liberator." Spartan naval hero in war with Athens. Dim: Chando, Licho. Var: Lesandro, Lisandrum, Lisandrus, Luisandra.
Lisandrum   see Lisandro.
Lisandrus   see Lisandro.
Lisbet   see Elisabeth.
Liselota   see Luis.
Liserio   see Glicerio.
Liseta   see Elisabeth.
Lisgarda   see Ludgarda.
Lisias   see Elisabeth.
Lita   see Adela.
Lita   see Amalio.
Lita   see Carmen.
Lita   see Estela.
Litia   see Lidio.
Liticia   see Leticia.
Lito   see Angel.
Lito   see Carlos.
Lito   see Isabel.
Lito   see Luis.
Lito   see Miguel.
Lito   see Rafael.
Litos   see Carlos.
Liverato   see Liberato.
Livia   see Libia.
Livinia   see Lavinia.
Livra   see Liberato.
Livrada   see Liberato.
Liza   see Elisabeth.
Liza   see Isabel.
Lizaro (Lee sah' roe) m. Lizarra, term for heather.
Lizebeth   see Elisabeth.
Llejandro   see Alejandro.
Llermo   see Guillermo.
Llillo   see Emilio.
Llolanda   see Yolanda.
Lobardo   see Leopardo.
Loberto   see Oberto.
Lobiano   see Lobo.
Lobita   see Lobo.
Lobo (Lo' bo) m. Lat. "Wolf." Remembered today mainly in patronymic López. Lupus, 16 x in DS. 1, 6th cen. bishop of Sens, France. F. 9/1. Dim: Lobita. Var: Lobiano.
Locadio   see Leocadia.
Locario   see Ligorio.
Locha   see Eloiso.

Lochi   see Eloiso.
Locho   see Ambrosio.
Locho   see Eulogio.
Locinda   see Lucinda.
Locordia   see Leocadia.
Locoro   see Ligorio.
Lodia   see Elodio.
Lodovina   see Ludovino.
Loenona   see León.
Loenosa   see León.
Loenza   see Lorenzo.
Loepolt   see Leopoldo.
Loepolus   see Leopoldo.
Logaria   see Ligorio.
Logio   see Eulogio.
Logoria   see Ligorio.
Loguita   see Olga.
Loida   see Leda.
Lojenio   see Longinos.
Lojinio   see Longinos.
Lojino   see Longinos.
Lojio   see Longinos.
Lokario   see Ligorio.
Lol   see Lorenzo.
Lola   see Aurora.
Lola   see Dolores.
Lola   see Doroteo.
Loledonia (Low lay doe' nee ah) f. Comb. of Lola & Celedonia (see both).
Loli   see Dolores.
Lolica   see Dolores.
Lolicia   see Dolores.
Lolis   see Dolores.
Lolita   see Dolores.
Lolo   see Eulogio.
Lolo   see Heliodoro.
Lolo   see Lorenzo.
Loltie   see Dolores.
Lomgino   see Longinos.
Lomosa   see Luminosa.
Loncha   see Aldonza.
Loncha   see Leoncio.
Loncho   see Alfonso.
Loncia   see Leoncio.
Lonenza   see Lorenzo.
Lonenzia   see Lorenzo.
Longheno   see Longinos.
Longima   see Longinos.
Longindo   see Longinos.
Longino   see Longinos.
Longinos (Loan hee' noes) m. EE: Longinus. Gk. "Carries lance." Apocryphal soldier who pierced Christ's side. 15 x in DS. F. 3/15. Var: Langino, Lingina, Lojenio, Lojinio, Lojino, Lojio, Lomgino, Longheno, Longima, Longindo, Longino, Longmio, Longnia, Longono, Lonjinana, Lonjino, Lunjino.
Longira   see Longirón.
Longirio   see Longirón.
Longirón (Loan he roan') m. 7th cen. Fr. S. Var: Longira, Longirio, Longiros.
Longiros   see Longirón.
Longmio   see Longinos.
Longnia   see Longinos.
Longono   see Longinos.
Lonicia   see Leoncio.
Lonidas   see Leonides.
Loniro   see Leonor.
Lonisio   see Leoncio.
Lonjinana   see Longinos.

Lonjino   see **Longinos.**
Lonseo   see **Leoncio.**
Loño   see **Apolonio.**
Lopita   see **Guadalupe.**
Lora   see **Lauro.**
Loraida   see **Lauro.**
Loranzio   see **Lorenzo.**
Lorcenda   see **Lucinda.**
Lordes   see **Lourdes.**
Lorelo   see **Lauro.**
Loren   see **Lorenzo.**
Lorena (Low ray' nah) f. EE:
Lorraine, etc. Fr. "From
Lorraine," or Lothair's Terri-
tory, kingdom created as realm
of Lothair I. F. 6/15. **Var:**
Lorenya. See also Lotario.
Lorenjio   see **Lorenzo.**
Lorenjo   see **Lorenzo.**
Lorenso   see **Lorenzo.**
Lorenya   see **Lorena.**
Lorenzino   see **Lorenzo.**
Lorenzio   see **Lorenzo.**
Lorenzita   see **Lorenzo.**
Lorenzo (Low ren' zo) m. EE:
Lawrence, etc. Lat. "Crowned
with laurel." 32 x in DS. 1,
asked to bring forth treasure of
church & brought forth the poor.
F. 8/10. **Dim:** Chencho, Lecha,
Lechita, Lencho, Lol, Lolo,
Loren, Lorenzino, Lori. **Var:**
Larensa, Larenzo, Lauceano,
Laugrencio, Laureano, Laurencio,
Laurentena, Laurentia,
Laurentino, Laurento, Laurenzo,
Lauriniano, Lawentia, Lawrencio,
Lawrenzis, Loenza, Lonenza,
Lonenzia, Loranzio, Lorenjio,
Lorenjo, Lorenso, Lorenzio,
Lorenzita, Lorezo, Lorezza,
Lorneza, Lornzo.
Loretha   see **Loreto.**
Loreto (Low ray' toe) m. EE:
Loreta. Lat. "Beautiful as a
laurel forest." Residence of
image of V. supposedly borne
through air by angels in 13th
cen. Patroness of aviators. **Var:**
Loretha.
Lorezo   see **Lorenzo.**
Lorezza   see **Lorenzo.**
Lori   see **Lauro.**
Lori   see **Lorenzo.**
Loricadia   see **Leocadia.**
Lorita   see **Lauro.**
Lorneza   see **Lorenzo.**
Lornzo   see **Lorenzo.**
Lota   see **Carlos.**
Lotario (Low tah' ree oh) m. EE:
Lothair, Lothar, Teut. "Illus-
trious warrior." 8th cen. emper-
or given territory of Lotharin-
gia (France & Germany). Also 8th
cen. bishop of Seez, France, who
led hermitic life. F. 6/15. **Var:**
Cluterio, Lotera. See also
Lorena, Lutero.
Lotera   see **Lotario.**
Loti   see **Carlos.**
Louesa   see **Luis.**
Lougarda   see **Ludgarda.**
Louisildo   see **Luis.**
Louiso   see **Luis.**
Loupe   see **Guadalupe.**

Lourdes (Lure' days) f. Basque
toponym means "craggy slope."
Town in SW France where V. Mary
appeared to St. Bernadette in
1858. F. 2/11. **Var:** Lordes,
Lourdez, Lurdes.
Lourdez   see **Lourdes.**
Louria   see **Lauro.**
Lovelia   see **Ovelia.**
Lowrada   see **Lauro.**
Loyola (Low yo' lah) m. Lat. "Wolf
on shield." Village of St.
Ignatius (see Ignacio).
Lozano (Low zah' no) m. Refers to
area of luxurious green. More
often surname than 1st name.
Lubina   see **Ludovino.**
Lubinia   see **Ludovino.**
Luca   see **Lucas.**
Luca   see **Lucrecio.**
Lucadio   see **Leocadia.**
Lucano (Loo cah' no) m. EE:
Lucian, etc. Lat. "Native of
Lucania," region in Italy.
Lucan, 1st cen. Lat. poet of
Cordoba, Spain.
Lucaria   see **Eucario.**
Lucaria (Loo cah' ree ah) f. Lat.
"Guardian of forests." Grove
festival celebrated in Rome.
Var: Lagaria, Lagaro.
Lucaro   see **Eucario.**
Lucas (Loo' cahs) m. EE: Lucius,
Luke. Probably abbreviation of
Lat. "lucarus," Lucarian native.
25 x in DS. Author of Gospel
bearing his name in Bible. F.
10/18. **Dim:** Chano, Lucho. **Var:**
Luca, Luciano, Lucidio,
Luciliano, Lucilo, Lucindo,
Lucinio, Lucino, Lucio, Luciolo.
Luceano   see **Lucia.**
Lucecita   see **Lucia.**
Lucecita   see **Luz.**
Lucelida   see **Luz.**
Lucelva   see **Luz.**
Lucenda   see **Lucinda.**
Lucendo   see **Lucia.**
Luceo   see **Lucia.**
Luceria   see **Lucero.**
Lucero (Loo say' roe) m. Lat.
"Lux," "light." **Var:** Luceria.
See also Lucia, Lucifer,
Lucinda, Lucino, Luz.
Lucha   see **Eloiso.**
Lucha   see **Luz.**
Luchi   see **Lucia.**
Luchi   see **Luis.**
Luchin   see **Lucia.**
Lucho   see **Gabriel.**
Lucho   see **Lucas.**
Lucho   see **Lucia.**
Lucho   see **Luis.**
Lucho   see **Rafael.**
Luci   see **Lucia.**
Lucia (Loo see' ah) f. EE: Lucia,
Lucille, Lulu, etc. Lat. "Lux,"
"light." 18 x in DS. 1, 2nd cen.
M. who caused miracle. F. 9/16.
Dim: Chano (Luciano), Chia
(Lucila), Chila, Chinda
(Lucinda), Filucho, Luceano,
Lucecita (Luz), Lucendo, Luceo,
Luchi, Luchin, Lucho, Luisita.
Var: Luci, Luciano, Lucibia,

Lucidio, Lucila, Lucilda,
Lucimbre, Lucy, Lurciano,
Luscilo, Lusiano, Lusila,
Luzelidea. See also Lucero,
Lucifer, Lucinda, Lucinio, Luz.

Luciano   see Lucas.
Luciano   see Lucia.
Lucibia   see Lucia.
Lucidio   see Lucas.
Lucidio   see Lucia.
Lucienda   see Lucinda.
Lucifer (Loo see fair') m. EE:
  Lucifer. Lat. "Lux" & "ferr"
  meaning "he who gives light."
  Planet Venus as Morning Star. By
  mistake, refers to Satan. Var:
  Lufero. See also Lucero, Lucia,
  Lucinda, Lucinio, Luz.

Lucila   see Lucia.
Lucila   see Luz.
Lucilda   see Lucia.
Luciliano   see Lucas.
Lucilo   see Lucas.
Lucimbre   see Lucia.
Lucina   see Luz.
Lucinda (Loo seen' dah) f. EE:
  Lucinda. Variant of Lucia
  meaning "light." Var: Locinda,
  Lorcenda, Lucenda, Lucienda,
  Lucinida, Lucinto, Luscienda,
  Lusinda, Luslinda. See also
  Lucero, Lucia, Lucifer, Lucinio,
  Luz.

Lucindo   see Lucas.
Lucinida   see Lucinda.
Lucinio   see Lucas.
Lucinio (Loo see' nee oh) m. Lat.
  "Belonging to Lucina," Roman
  goddess of birth, or "one who
  gives light." Var: Lucirio,
  Lucrina. See also Lucero, Lucia,
  Lucifer, Lucinda, Luz.

Lucino   see Lucas.
Lucinto   see Lucinda.
Lucio   see Lucas.
Luciolo   see Lucas.
Lucirio   see Lucinio.
Lucito   see Luz.
Lucos   see Luz.
Lucrecio (Loo cray' see oh) m. EE:
  Lucrece, Lucretia. Lat. "To gain
  riches." Roman matron committed
  suicide after rape. Dim: Lica,
  Luca, Lulu, Quecha. Var:
  Lucresio, Lucretiae, Lucricio.

Lucresio   see Lucrecio.
Lucretiae   see Lucrecio.
Lucricio   see Lucrecio.
Lucrina   see Lucinio.
Lucy   see Lucia.
Ludalecio (Loo dah lay' see oh) m.
  Comb. of Ludovico & Indalecio
  (see both).

Ludelia   see Odilia.
Ludevina   see Ludovino.
Ludgarda (Lood gar' dah) f. EE:
  Leodagar, Lutgard. Ger. "Dwell-
  ing place of people." 2 x in DS.
  1, Cistercian mystic of 13th
  cen. Flanders, Belgium. F. 6/16.
  Var: Elugarda, Largardo,
  Lisgarda, Lougarda, Ludgarido,
  Ludgrada, Lugarda, Lugurda,
  Lujardo, Lukgarda, Lurgarda,
  Lusgarda, Lutgarda, Lutharda,

Luzgardo, Luzgolda, Luzzarda.
  See also Leodegario.
Ludgarido   see Ludgarda.
Ludgrada   see Ludgarda.
Ludila   see Odilia.
Ludivino   see Ludovino.
Ludmila (Lood mee' lah) f. EE:
  Ludmilla, etc. Slav. "Beloved by
  people." "Russla & Ludmilla,"
  5-act opera by Glinke (1842). In
  DS, wife of 1st Christian duke
  of Bohemia (Czechoslovakia). F.
  9/16.

Ludo   see Luis.
Ludonica   see Ludovico.
Ludonio   see Celedonio.
Ludoreica   see Ludovico.
Ludoric   see Ludovico.
Ludorica   see Ludovico.
Ludoricus   see Ludovico.
Ludoviano   see Ludovino.
Ludovic   see Ludovico.
Ludovicae   see Ludovico.
Ludovice   see Ludovico.
Ludovico (Loo doe bee' co) m. EE:
  Ludwig, etc. Teut. "Famous war-
  rior." Var: Eudovica, Ledovico,
  Leudovico, Ludonica, Ludoreica,
  Ludoric, Ludorica, Ludoricus,
  Ludovic, Ludovicae, Ludovice,
  Ludovicum, Ludovicus, Ludovio,
  Ludvigen, Ludwig. See also
  Aloisia, Clodoveo, Luis.
Ludovicum   see Ludovico.
Ludovicus   see Ludovico.
Ludovino (Loo doe bee' no) m. Ger.
  "Friend of people." Dim: Davina.
  Var: Delbina, Delubina, Deluvin,
  Diluvina, Elidubina, Eluvidina,
  Eluvina, Ledivina, Ledovina,
  Leduvina, Lodovina, Lubina,
  Lubinia, Ludevina, Ludivino,
  Ludoviano, Ludovio, Ludvina,
  Ludwina, Lusdivina, Luvin,
  Luvina, Luz (Divina), Luzdibina.
Ludovio   see Ludovico.
Ludovio   see Ludovino.
Ludrina (Loo dree' nah) f. Could
  be form of Ludre or Lysor, S. of
  Bourges, France. F. 2/10.
Ludvigen   see Ludovico.
Ludvina   see Ludovino.
Ludwig   see Ludovico.
Ludwina   see Ludovino.
Lues   see Luis.
Lufero   see Lucifer.
Lugarda   see Ludgarda.
Lugurda   see Ludgarda.
Luieta   see Luis.
Luigildo   see Leovigildo.
Luis (Loo eece') m. EE: Lewis,
  Louis, etc. Ger. "Famous war-
  rior." 28 x in DS. 1, Louis II
  of France, noted for piety,
  justice, & asceticism. F. 8/25.
  Dim: Bicho, Guicho, Huicho, Isa
  (Luisa), Lewisa (Luisa), Lich,
  Licho, Liselota (Luisa), Lito,
  Louesa, Luchi (Luisa), Lucho,
  Ludo, Lues, Luieta (Luisa), Lulu
  (Luisa), Wichi, Wicho. Var:
  Louisildo, Louiso, Luisano,
  Luisiana, Luisiro, Luiza,
  Luoisa. See also Aloisio,
  Clodoveo, Clovio, Eloisa,

Ludovico.

Luisandra	see **Lisandro.**
Luisano	see **Luis.**
Luisiana	see **Luis.**
Luisiro	see **Luis.**
Luisita	see **Lucia.**
Luiza	see **Luis.**
Lujardo	see **Ludgarda.**
Lukgarda	see **Ludgarda.**
Lula	see **Luz.**
Lula	see **Obdulio.**
Lulalio	see **Eulalio.**
Lulito	see **Raul.**
Lulito	see **Rodolfo.**

Lulo (Loo' low) m. Archbishop of Bavaria, Germany. F. 12/1.

Lulu	see **Lucrecio.**
Lulu	see **Luis.**
Lumina	see **Luminosa.**

Luminosa (Loo mee no' sah) f. Lat. "Brilliant, resplendent." **Var:** Lomosa, Lumina.

Luncha	see **Alfonso.**
Lunjino	see **Longinos.**
Luolsa	see **Luis.**
Lupa	see **Leopoldo.**
Lupe	see **Guadalupe.**

Lupercio (Loo pear' see oh) m. **EE:** Luperculus, Lupercus. Lat. "Luperco," "he who puts wolves to flight." Lupercalia, ancient Roman feast honoring pastoral deity. 3 x in DS. M. of 4th cen. Saragossa, Spain. F. 4/16. **Var:** Luperio. See also Licurgo.

Luperio   see **Lupercio.**

Luperto (Loo pear' toe) m. Probably from St. Luperio, bishop of Verona in 8th cen. F. 11/15.

Lupeta	see **Guadalupe.**
Lupie	see **Guadalupe.**
Lupina	see **Guadalupe.**
Lupita	see **Guadalupe.**
Lupo	see **Guadalupe.**
Luppe	see **Guadalupe.**
Lupy	see **Guadalupe.**
Lurciano	see **Lucia.**
Lurdes	see **Lourdes.**
Lurgarda	see **Ludgarda.**
Lus	see **Luz.**
Lusa	see **Luz.**
Luscilo	see **Lucia.**
Luscinda	see **Lucinda.**
Lusdivina	see **Ludovino.**
Luse	see **Luz.**
Lusebia	see **Eusebio.**

Luselva (Loo sell' bah) f. Comb. of Luz & Alba. (see both). **Var:** Luzelba.

Lusgarda	see **Ludgarda.**
Lusiano	see **Lucia.**
Lusila	see **Lucia.**
Lusinda	see **Lucinda.**

Lusitanus (Loo see tah' noose) m.

Lat. "Native of Lusitania," Roman name for Portugal.

Luslinda   see **Lucinda.**

Lustriano (Loose tree ah' no) m. Lat. "To be bright or splendid."

Luta	see **Lutero.**
Luterga	see **Lutero.**
Luteria	see **Lutero.**
Luteris	see **Lutero.**

Lutero (Loo tay' roe) m. **EE:** Luthario, Luther, etc. Ger. "Illustrious warrior." 16th cen. Ger. Augustinian monk who became leader of Protestant Reformation. **Dim:** Luta. **Var:** Leuterio, Luterga, Luteria, Luteris, Lutherio, Lutiria, Luturina. See also Lotario.

Lutgarda	see **Ludgarda.**
Lutharda	see **Ludgarda.**
Lutherio	see **Lutero.**
Luticia	see **Leticia.**
Lutiria	see **Lutero.**
Luturina	see **Lutero.**
Luvena	see **Lavinia.**
Luvenia	see **Lavinia.**
Luvin	see **Ludovino.**
Luvina	see **Ludovino.**
Lux	see **Luz.**
Luxiola	see **Luz.**
Luz	see **Ludovino.**

Luz (Loose) f. **EE:** Lucas, Luke. Lat. "Lux," "light." Special devotion to V. Mary as Nuestra Señora de la Luz, Our Lady of Light. **Dim:** Chita, Cito, Lucecita, Lucha, Lucila, Lucina, Lucito, Lucos, Lula. **Var:** Lucelida, Lucelva, Lus, Lusa, Luse, Lux, Luxiola, Luzano, Luzel, Luziano, Luzo, Luzrano. See also Lucero, Lucia, Lucifer, Lucinda, Lucinio.

Luzano	see **Luz.**
Luzdibina	see **Ludovino.**
Luzel	see **Luz.**
Luzelba	see **Luselva.**
Luzelidea	see **Lucia.**
Luzgardo	see **Ludgarda.**
Luzgolda	see **Ludgarda.**
Luziano	see **Luz.**
Luzo	see **Luz.**
Luzrano	see **Luz.**
Luzzarda	see **Ludgarda.**
Lyana	see **Julio.**
Lyda	see **Leda.**
Lydice	see **Leticia.**
Lydio	see **Lidio.**
Lylvia	see **Libia.**

Lyndia (Leen' de ah) f. Comb. of Linda & Lidia (see both).

Lyonisia	see **Leoncio.**
Lysio	see **Alicio.**
Lyvia	see **Libia.**

M

Maada   see **Magdaleno.**
Mabel   see **Isabel.**
Mabel   see **María.**
Mabelde (Mah bell' day) f. Sp.
  "Amable," "amiable."
Mabicho   see **Mauricio.**
Maca   see **Macarena.**
Macabeo (Mah cah bay' oh) m. EE:
  Maccabee. Heb. "Hammerer." Jew-
  ish family that led revolt & re-
  established independent Jewish
  state. Maccabean Mm. killed at
  Antioch, Turkey, in era of
  revolt. F. 8/1. **Var:** Macabeos.
Macabeos   see **Macabeo.**
Macadonio   see **Macedonio.**
Macaela   see **Miguel.**
Macaliana   see **Miguel.**
Macarena (Mah cah ray' nah) f.
  Possibly Ar. Maybe from Macario
  (see). In Seville, Macarena is
  gypsy area. So-called Virgen de
  la Macarena is la Virgen de la
  Esperanza de la Macarena (Our
  Lady of Hope, shrine in Mac-
  arena). **Dim:** Maca. See also
  Macario.
Macareo   see **Macario.**
Macariam   see **Macario.**
Macario (Mah cah' ree oh) m. EE:
  Macaria, Macarius. Gk. "Fortu-
  nate one." 73 x in DS. 1, of 4th
  cen. Egypt, noted for mysticism.
  F. 1/15. **Var:** Macareo, Macariam,
  Macarisa, Macarria, Macarro,
  Maccario, Mackario, Macorio,
  Marcario, Mecario, Mercario,
  Micario, Nacario.
Macarisa   see **Macario.**
Macarria   see **Macario.**
Macarro   see **Macario.**
Maccario   see **Macario.**
Maccedonio   see **Macedonio.**
Macedanio   see **Macedonio.**
Macedario   see **Macedonio.**
Macedenio   see **Macedonio.**
Macedimio   see **Macedonio.**
Macedins   see **Macedonio.**
Macednia   see **Macedonio.**
Macedón   see **Macedonio.**
Macedone   see **Macedonio.**
Macedonea   see **Macedonio.**
Macedoni   see **Macedonio.**
Macedonio (Mah say doe' nee oh) m.
  EE: Macedonia, Macedonius. Gk.
  "He who is aggrandized through
  triumphs." 8 x in DS. 1, Syrian
  hermit, wandered 40 years. F.
  1/24. **Var:** Acedonio, Macadonio,
  Maccedonio, Macedanio,
  Macedario, Macedenio, Macedimio,
  Macedins, Macednia, Macedón,
  Macedone, Macedonea, Macedoni,
  Macedonis, Macedonius, Magedonia,

Marcedina, Marcedonio,
Marcedovio, Maredonia, Maredono,
Masedonio, Masidona, Mazedona,
Mazedonia, Mecedonia.
Macedonis   see **Macedonio.**
Macedonius   see **Macedonio.**
Macedonna   see **Macedonio.**
Macedor   see **Macedonio.**
Macedorrio   see **Macedonio.**
Macelino   see **Marcelino.**
Macemiana   see **Maximiano.**
Macendonia   see **Macedonio.**
Maceonio   see **Macedonio.**
Macericio   see **Macerio.**
Macerio (Mah say' ree oh) m. Sp.
  "One who bears mace." **Var:**
  Macericio.
Maceronia   see **Macedonio.**
Macglovio   see **Maclovio.**
Machín   see **Martín.**
Machito   see **Narciso.**
Macidenio   see **Macedonio.**
Macidonio   see **Macedonio.**
Macimeano   see **Maximiano.**
Macimeno   see **Maximino.**
Macimiaivo   see **Maximiano.**
Macimiano   see **Maximiano.**
Macisimi   see **Máximo.**
Mackario   see **Macario.**
Maclaudia (Mah clow' dee ah) f.
  Comb. of María & Claudio (see
  both).
Maclavia   see **Maclovio.**
Maclobio   see **Maclovio.**
Maclodio   see **Maclovio.**
Maclonia   see **Maclovio.**
Macloria   see **Maclovio.**
Maclovio (Mah cloe' bee oh) m. EE:
  Maclovius, etc. Gael. "Son of
  love." 6th cen. Welsh S. who
  became bishop of Aleth, France.
  F. 11/15. **Dim:** Coya, Maco. **Var:**
  Macglovio, Maclavia, Maclobio,
  Maclodio, Maclonia, Macloria,
  Macrobio, Maglovio, Malcolva,
  Manclava, Marclovia, Moclovia,
  Monclovio, Naclovia.
Maco   see **Maclovio.**
Maco   see **Magdaleno.**
Maco   see **Mardoqueo.**
Macorio   see **Macario.**
Macrino (Mah cree' no) m. EE:
  Macrinus, etc. Gk. "He who be-
  comes famous." 6 x in DS. In 3rd
  cen. France, Macra mart. by fire
  torture, breasts cut off, &
  rolled on hot coals. F. 1/6.
  Var: Macrio, Magro.
Macrio   see **Macrino.**
Macrobio   see **Maclovio.**
Madalén   see **Magdaleno.**
Madaleno   see **Magdaleno.**
Madalina   see **Magdaleno.**
Maddeleno   see **Magdaleno.**
Madela   see **Magdaleno.**
Madeleno   see **Magdaleno.**
Madelina   see **Magdaleno.**

Madeline   see **Magdaleno.**
Madelón   see **Magdaleno.**
Madesto   see **Modesto.**
Madina   see **Magdaleno.**
Madline   see **Magdaleno.**
Madril (Mah dreel') mf? Native of
   Madrid.
Madronio (Mah droe' nee oh) m.
   Form of Matrona. 3 x in DS.
Madurano (Mah dew rah' no) m. Lat.
   "Maturus," "one who is wise &
   prudent."
Maecelo   see **Marcelino.**
Maga   see **Magdaleno.**
Magadalena   see **Magdaleno.**
Magadelana   see **Magdaleno.**
Magadleno   see **Magdaleno.**
Magaleno   see **Magdaleno.**
Magallanes (Mah gah yah' nace) m.
   Surname of Portuguese explorer
   who circumnavigated globe in
   16th cen.
Magaly   see **Magdaleno.**
Magarido   see **Margarito.**
Magarito   see **Margarito.**
Magda   see **Magdaleno.**
Magdadlena   see **Magdaleno.**
Magdalán   see **Magdaleno.**
Magdalano   see **Magdaleno.**
Magdalemo   see **Magdaleno.**
Magdalén   see **Magdaleno.**
Magdalend   see **Magdaleno.**
Magdaleno (Mag dah lay' no) m. EE:
   Magadalene, Magdeline. Heb.
   "From Magdala, place of high
   tower." 1 of Biblical Marys,
   reputed harlot, forgiven by
   Christ. 8 x in DS. **Dim:** Eleno,
   Lena, Maada, Maco, Maga, Magaly,
   Male, Malena, Nena. **Var:**
   Andaleno, Madalén, Madaleno,
   Madalina, Maddeleno, Madela,
   Madeleno, Madelina, Madeline,
   Madelón, Madina, Madline,
   Magadalena, Magadelana,
   Magadleno, Magaleno, Magda,
   Magdadlena, Magdalán, Magdalano,
   Magdalemo, Magdalén, Magdalend,
   Magdalerio, Magdalina,
   Magdalinam, Magdalma, Magdanelo,
   Magdelana, Magdeleno, Magdlena,
   Magdoleno, Magdolino, Magola,
   Malaleno, Mandelino, Maydaleno,
   Maydlena, Maydoleno, Medeline,
   Megdolina, Modaleno, Neogdalena.
   See also Migdalia.
Magdalerio   see **Magdaleno.**
Magdalina   see **Magdaleno.**
Magdalinam   see **Magdaleno.**
Magdalma   see **Magdaleno.**
Magdanelo   see **Magdaleno.**
Magdelana   see **Magdaleno.**
Magdeleno   see **Magdaleno.**
Magdlena   see **Magdaleno.**
Magdoleno   see **Magdaleno.**
Magdolino   see **Magdaleno.**
Magedonia   see **Macedonio.**
Magi   see **Margarito.**
Magín (Mah heen') m. Lat.
   "Maginus," "belonging to Magus"
   or "magi, wiseman." Gaspar,
   Melchior, Balthazar brought
   gifts to Jesus. 2 x in DS. **Var:**
   Magina, Majín.
Magina   see **Magín.**

Maglorio (Mah glow' ree oh) m. EE:
   Magloire, Maglorius. Probably
   "My glory." Magloire was 6th cen
   Welsh nobleman. F. 10/24.
Maglovio   see **Maclovio.**
Magno (Mag' no) m. EE: Magnus,
   etc. Lat. "He who is of great
   fame." 2 Scan. monarchs. 25 x in
   DS. **Var:** Mago. See also Máximo,
   Maximiano, Maximiliano,
   Maximino.
Mago   see **Magno.**
Mago   see **Margarito.**
Magola   see **Magdaleno.**
Magóniam (Mah go' nee am) m.
   Magon, founder of Carthaginian
   power (c. 600 B.C.)
Magro   see **Macrino.**
Magueta (Mah gay' tah) f. Straw-
   berry patch.
Magui   see **Margarito.**
Maguis   see **Margarito.**
Maguita   see **Margarito.**
Magurita   see **Margarito.**
Maida   see **María.**
Maik   see **Miguel.**
Maita   see **María.**
Maita   see **Marta.**
Maizes   see **Moisés.**
Majín   see **Magín.**
Malachia   see **Malaquías.**
Malachinas   see **Malaquías.**
Malacia   see **Melesio.**
Malagia   see **Malaquías.**
Malaleno   see **Magdaleno.**
Malano   see **Melanio.**
Malaquía   see **Malaquías.**
Malaquías (Mah lah key' ahs) m.
   EE: Malachi, Malachy. Heb.
   "Messenger of the gods." Minor
   prophet who denounced Jews for
   laxity regarding sacrifices.
   Var: Malachia, Malachinas,
   Malagia, Malaquía, Malaquica,
   Maloquías.
Malaquica   see **Malaquías.**
Malba   see **Melba.**
Malchíades   see **Melquíades.**
Malchor   see **Melchor.**
Malco (Mall' co) m. EE: Malchus.
   Heb. "Like the king." Peter cut
   off Malchus' ear & Christ healed
   him. 9 x in DS.
Malcolva   see **Maclovio.**
Malcor   see **Melchor.**
Male   see **Magdaleno.**
Malecio   see **Melesio.**
Malena   see **Magdaleno.**
Malena   see **María.**
Malesio   see **Melesio.**
Malguiades   see **Melquíades.**
Malía   see **María.**
Malisa   see **María.**
Malisa   see **Melisa.**
Malissa   see **Melisa.**
Malita   see **María.**
Malitón   see **Melito.**
Mallitonia   see **Melito.**
Mallu   see **María.**
Maloquías   see **Malaquías.**
Malquades   see **Melquíades.**
Malquíades   see **Melquíades.**
Malrubio (Mahl roo' bee oh) m. 2
   Catholic Ss.
Malva   see **Malvina.**

Malvina (Mahl bee' nah) f. EE: Malvina, Malvinia. Teut. "Chieftainess." Malvinas, 2nd name for Falkland Islands. **Var:** Malva.

Mamarto   see **Mamerto.**
Mamases   see **Manases.**
Mamela   see **Manuel.**
Mamerto (Mah mare' toe) m. EE: Mamertinus, Mamertus. Lat. "Native of Mamertium, Italy." Archbishop of Vienna, Austria in 5th cen. **Var:** Mamarto, Manerto.
Mamilio (Mah mee' lee oh) m. Form of Mamillas, African M. F. 3/8.
Mamoy   see **Manuel.**
Manaces   see **Manases.**
Manases (Mah nah sace') m. Gk. "Making to forget." Elder son of Joseph & Asenath & brother of Ephraim. **Var:** Mamases, Manaces, Manasio, Monases.
Manasio   see **Manases.**
Manche   see **German.**
Mancho   see **Maximiliano.**
Mancho   see **Roman.**
Manclava   see **Maclovio.**
Manda   see **Amanda.**
Mandelino   see **Magdaleno.**
Mandita   see **Amanda.**
Mando   see **Armando.**
Mandonio (Mahn doe' nee oh) m. 2nd cen. native caudillo of Roman Spain. Revolted against Romans.
Mandy   see **Armando.**
Maneco   see **Manuel.**
Manerto   see **Mamerto.**
Maneto (Mah nay' toe) m. Manetto or Maentius, S. & 1 of founders of Servite order in 13th cen. Italy. F. 8/20.
Manfredo (Mahn fray' doe) m. EE: Fred, Manfred. Teut. "Man of peace." 13th cen. S. of Milan. F. 2/28.
Mango   see **Manuel.**
Manico   see **Mónico.**
Mannela   see **Manuel.**
Mannuel   see **Manuel.**
Manny   see **Manuel.**
Mano   see **Manuel.**
Manola   see **Manuel.**
Manolete   see **Manuel.**
Manolito   see **Manuel.**
Manolo   see **Manuel.**
Manolón   see **Manuel.**
Manos (Mah' nos) m. Mannus in Ger. myth., son of Tuisto & founder of Germanic race.
Mansarrata   see **Montserrat.**
Manucho   see **Manuel.**
Manuda   see **Manuel.**
Manue   see **Manuel.**
Manuel (Mahn well') m. EE: Emanuel, Emmanuel. Heb. "God is with us." Prophet Isaiah gave name to Jesus. 6 x in DS. **Dim:** Chema (Manuela), Huelo, Lico, Mamoy, Maneco, Mango, Manny, Mano, Manola (Manuela), Manolete, Manolito, Manolo, Manolón, Manucho, Manuda, Manue, Manuelcho, Manuelito, Manuelitta (Manuela), Manunga, Mel, Melico, Melita (Manuela), Melo, Meme,

Meneque, Minel, Mito, Neli (Manuela), Nelia (Manuela), Nelo, Neneques, Nungo. **Var:** Ammanuela, Emannela, Emanuel, Emanuelem, Emanuelis, Emanuelo, Emmanuel, Emmanuela, Emmanuelae, Emmanuelem, Emmanuelis, Esmanuela, Mamela, Mannela, Mannuel, Manuelem, Manuella, Manuelo, Manuiella, Manula, Manvella, Manwela.
Manuelcho   see **Manuel.**
Manuelem   see **Manuel.**
Manuelito   see **Manuel.**
Manuelitta   see **Manuel.**
Manuella   see **Manuel.**
Manuelo   see **Manuel.**
Manuiella   see **Manuel.**
Manula   see **Manuel.**
Manunga   see **Manuel.**
Manvella   see **Manuel.**
Manwela   see **Manuel.**
Marajilda   see **Esmeregildo.**
Maranela (Mah rah nay' lah) f. Comb. of María & Nelo (see both).
Maravilla (Mah rah bee' yah) f. EE: Marvel. Lat. "Mirabilia," "admirable." **Var:** Marivel, Marvella. See also Milagros, Mira, Miranda.
Marberto (Mar bear' toe) m. Comb. of María & Berto (see both).
Marcalfa   see **Marcolfo.**
Marcanita   see **Marcos.**
Marcanius (Mar cah' nee oose) m. Marcan was Welsh S. who viewed soul of St. Brioc carried to heaven. F. 5/21.
Marcano   see **Marcos.**
Marcardia (Mar car' dee ah) f. Comb. of María & Arcadio (see both).
Marcario   see **Macario.**
Marcas   see **Marcos.**
Marccino   see **Marcelino.**
Marceda   see **Mercedes.**
Marcedera   see **Mercedes.**
Marcedes   see **Mercedes.**
Marcedina   see **Macedonio.**
Marcedonio   see **Macedonio.**
Marcedovio   see **Macedonio.**
Marcehia   see **Marsilio.**
Marceleno   see **Marcelino.**
Marcelfa   see **Marcolfo.**
Marceliano   see **Marcelino.**
Marcelimo   see **Marcelino.**
Marcelino (Mar say lee' no) m. EE: Marcella, etc. Lat. "Marcos," "Mars," Roman god of war. 69 x in DS. 1, 4th cen. pope. F. 1/16. **Dim:** Chelino, Chelo, Lino. **Var:** Arcilín, Macelino, Maecelo, Marccino, Marceleno, Marceliano, Marcelimo, Marcellena, Marcelliana, Marcellino, Marcello, Marcellonia, Marcelluio, Marcelma, Marcelo, Marcelona, Marcelonio, Marcetino, Marcilino, Maresila, Maricana, Maricel, Maricelda, Marsaleno, Marsalina, Marselino, Marselo, Marshildo, Marzelino, Marzello, Marzila, Maselina, Mercelino, Mercelo, Merceo. See

also Marcia, Marcial, Marciano, Marcos, Mario, Marsilio, Martin.

Marcellena   see **Marcelino.**
Marcelliana   see **Marcelino.**
Marcellino   see **Marcelino.**
Marcello   see **Marcelino.**
Marcellonia   see **Marcelino.**
Marcelluio   see **Marcelino.**
Marcelma   see **Marcelino.**
Marcelo   see **Marcelino.**
Marcelona   see **Marcelino.**
Marcelonio   see **Marcelino.**
Marcemiado   see **Maximiano.**
Marcenino   see **Marciana.**
Marcenio   see **Marciana.**
Marcetino   see **Marcelino.**
Marcia (Mar' see ah) f. EE:
Marcia. Lat. "Martius," "belonging to Mars." 12 x in DS. **Dim:** Chicha. **Var:** Marcizo, Marzima, Marzio, Narcio. See also Marcelino, Marcial, Marciana, Marcos, Mario, Marsilio, Martín.
Marciada   see **Marcial.**
Marcial (Mar see ahl') m. EE: Martial, Martialis. Lat. "Martialis," "belonging to Mars." One disposed to war. Famous Roman epigrammatist. 24 x in DS. **Var:** Marciada, Marciala, Marcialia, Marcifia, Martial, Marzial, Mercial, Morcial, Narcial. See also Marcelino, Marcia, Marciana, Marcos, Mario, Marsilio, Martín.
Marciala   see **Marcial.**
Marcialia   see **Marcial.**
Marciana (Mar see ah' nah) f. EE: Marciana, Marcianus. Lat. "Martianus," "son of Marcio," or "one belonging to Mars," Roman god of war. 53 x in DS. Marcian was Roman emperor of East (450-457). **Var:** Marcenino, Marcenio, Marciona, Marinasa, Marsiana, Marziana, Narciana. See also Marcelino, Marcia, Marcial, Marcos, Mario, Marsilio, Martín.
Marcifia   see **Marcial.**
Marcilino   see **Marcelino.**
Marcimiliano   see **Maximiliano.**
Marcimino   see **Maximiano.**
Marciona   see **Marciana.**
Marciosa (Mar see oh' sah) f. Martial music.
Marcisno (Mar sees' no) m. Marciso was S. mart. in Africa. F. 2/19.
Marciso   see **Narciso.**
Marcizo   see **Marcia.**
Marclovia   see **Maclovio.**
Marco   see **Marcos.**
Marcofa   see **Marcolfo.**
Marcofia   see **Marcolfo.**
Marcolfo (Mar coal' foe) m. EE: Marculf. Ger. "Daring warrior." 6th cen. Fr. abbot noted for curing scrofula. F. 5/1. **Var:** Marcalfa, Marcelfa, Marcofa, Marcofia, Mascolfa.
Marcolino   see **Marcos.**
Marcolino (Mar co lee' no) m. 14th cen. Ital. S. who helped reform Dominican order. F. 1/24.
Marcos (Mar' coze) m. EE: March,

Mark, Martin. Lat. "Marcus," "of Mars," god of war." Author of 2nd Gospel of NT. F. 4/25. 66 x in DS. **Dim:** Marcanita, Marcolino, Marquitos. **Var:** Marcano, Marcas, Marco, Marcus, Marko. See also Marcelino, Marcia, Marcial, Marciana, Mario, Marsilio, Martín.
Marcus   see **Marcos.**
Mardarito   see **Margarito.**
Mardonio (Mar doe' nee oh) m. EE: Mardon, Mardonius, etc. Pers. "Warrior." 2 x in DS. 1, 4th cen. M. during persecution of Diocletian. F. 3/12.
Mardoqueo (Mar doe kay' oh) m. EE: Mordecai, etc. Pers. "Warrior." In Bible, helped Esther save Jewish people from Haman. **Dim:** Maco.
Mareano   see **María.**
Maredonia   see **Macedonio.**
Maredono   see **Macedonio.**
Maregilda   see **Esmeregildo.**
Mareno   see **Marino.**
Mareos (Mah ray' os) m. Form of Mareas, 4th cen. S. mart. in Persia (Iran).
Maresila   see **Marcelino.**
Marga   see **Margarito.**
Margaita   see **Margarito.**
Margant   see **Margarito.**
Margareta   see **Margarito.**
Margarete   see **Margarito.**
Margaretha   see **Margarito.**
Margariat   see **Margarito.**
Margarifa   see **Margarito.**
Margariga   see **Margarito.**
Margario   see **Margarito.**
Margarit   see **Margarito.**
Margaritha   see **Margarito.**
Margaritia   see **Margarito.**
Margarito (Mar gah ree' toe) m. EE: Margaret, Margie, Peggy. Lat. "Precious as a pearl." 23 x in DS. 1, 11th cen. queen of Scotland. F. 6/10. **Dim:** Greta (Margareta), Ita (Margarita), Magi (Margarita), Mago (Margarita), Magui (Margarita), Maguis (Margarita), Maguita (Margarita), Margó (Margarita), Margotica (Margarita) Meta (Margarita), Reto (Margarita), Rita (Margarita), Tita (Margarita), Titay (Margarita). **Var:** Magarido, Magarito, Mardarito, Marga, Margaita, Margant, Margareta, Margarete, Margaretha, Margariat, Margarifa, Margariga, Margarío, Margarit, Margaritha, Margaritia, Margaritta, Margariya, Margaro, Margartha, Margarto, Margatito, Margereto, Margerito, Margeta, Margherita, Margirita, Margita, Margorito, Margot, Margret, Margrito, Marguarido, Marguerida, Marguerit, Marguerita, Margurito, Margzrita, Marjarita, Marjartio, Mogarito.
Margaritta   see **Margarito.**

Margariya	see **Margarito**.
Margaro	see **Margarito**.
Margartha	see **Margarito**.
Margarto	see **Margarito**.
Margatito	see **Margarito**.
Margeldia	see **Esmeregildo**.
Margereto	see **Margarito**.
Margerito	see **Margarito**.
Margeta	see **Margarito**.
Margherita	see **Margarito**.
Margil	see **Margila**.

Margila (Mar hee' lah) f. Comb. of María & Julia (see both). **Var:** Margil.

Margildo	see **Hermenegildo**.
Margirita	see **Margarito**.
Margita	see **Margarito**.
Margo	see **Margarito**.
Margorito	see **Margarito**.
Margot	see **Margarito**.
Margotica	see **Margarito**.
Margret	see **Margarito**.
Margrito	see **Margarito**.
Marguarito	see **Margarito**.
Marguerida	see **Margarito**.
Marguerit	see **Margarito**.
Marguerita	see **Margarito**.
Margurito	see **Margarito**.
Margzrita	see **Margarito**.
Mari	see **María**.

María (Mah ree' ah) f. **EE:** Mary, etc. Heb. "Lady, exalted one, bitterness, & star of sea." Most common Christian name. Honors Christ's mother. Has 7 feast days. **Dim:** Chepa, Chulia, Maida, Maita, Malena, Malia, Malisa, Malita, Mallu, Marí, Marica, Marichu, Marilú, Marilucha, Mariquilla, Mariquito, Maritza, Maruca, Maruch, Marucha, Maruja, Marysa, Marusha, Maruxa, Melida, Meri, Milota, Mimi, Nano, Nina (Marina), Nita (Marina), Ría, Rialino, Tani (Marina), Uca, Yana (Marina). **Var:** Mabel, Mareano, Mariad, Mariada, Mariade, Mariae, Marián, Mariano, Omaida. See also Miriam.

Mariad	see **María**.
Mariada	see **María**.
Mariade	see **María**.

Mariadel (Mah ree' ah dell') f. Comb. of María & Adela (see both).

Mariae	see **María**.

Mariaelena (Mah ree' aay lay' nah) f. Comb. of María & Elena (see both).

Marial (Mah ree ahl') ? Books containing prayers to Blessed V.

Mariamo	see **Mariana**.
Marián	see **María**.

Mariana (Mah ree ah' nah) f. **EE:** Marianus. Lat. "Son of Marius." 14 x in DS. **Var:** Mariamo. See also María, Martín.

Mariano	see **María**.

Maribel (Mah ree bell') f. Comb. of María (see) & Belle, Fr. for "beautiful one."

Marica	see **María**.
Maricana	see **Marcelino**.
Marice	see **Mauricio**.

Maricel	see **Marcelino**.
Maricelda	see **Marcelino**.
Marichilda	see **Mechilda**.
Maricho	see **Mauricio**.
Marichu	see **María**.
Maricia	see **Marisa**.
Maricio	see **Mauricio**.
Marigilda	see **Esmeregildo**.
Marigilda	see **Marilda**.
Marihilda	see **Esmeregildo**.
Marijildo	see **Esmeregildo**.

Marilda (Mah reel' dah) f. Ger. "Famous in combat." **Var:** Marigilda.

Marilú	see **María**.
Marilucha	see **María**.
Marima	see **Marino**.
Marinasa	see **Marciana**.

Marino (Mah ree' no) m. **EE:** Marino, Marinus. Lat. "Man of the sea." 37 x in DS. 1, patron of San Marino, Italy. Known as mason & comforter of Christians. F. 9/4. **Dim:** Ina, Mina. **Var:** Mareno, Marima.

Mario (Mah' ree oh) m. **EE:** Marius. Lat. "Descending from Mars, war god." 11 x in DS. 1 mart. in 3rd cen. for burying 260 other Mm. F. 1/19. **Dim:** Mayito, Mayo. See also Marcelino, Marcia, Marcial, Marciana, Marcos, Mariana, Martín.

Mariquilla	see **María**.
Mariquito	see **María**.

Marisa (Mah ree' sah) f. **EE:** Marisa. Comb. of María & Luisa (see both). **Var:** Maricia, Marissa, Mariza, Marricia, Marrisa.

Mariselda	see **Marsilio**.

Marisidra (Mah ree see' drah) f. Comb. of María & Isidro (see both).

Marisio	see **Mauricio**.
Mariso	see **Mauricio**.

Marisol (Mah ree soul') f. Comb. of María & Soledad (see both). **Var:** Marizol.

Marissa	see **Marisa**.

Maristela (Mah ree stay' la) f. Comb. of María & Estela (see both).

Maritza	see **María**.
Marivel	see **Maravilla**.
Mariza	see **Marisa**.
Marizela	see **Marsilio**.
Marizella	see **Marsilio**.
Marizol	see **Marisol**.
Marjarita	see **Margarito**.
Marjartio	see **Margarito**.
Marko	see **Marcos**.
Marquitos	see **Marcos**.

Marrana (Mah rah' nah) f. Possibly from anathema "maran atha" meaning "the Lord comes."

Marricia	see **Marisa**.
Marrisa	see **Marisa**.
Marsaleno	see **Marcelino**.
Marsalina	see **Marcelino**.
Marselino	see **Marcelino**.
Marselo	see **Marcelino**.
Marshildo	see **Marcelino**.
Marsial	see **Marsilio**.
Marsiana	see **Marciana**.

Marsilio (Mar see' lee oh) m. Lat. "Marcilius," "son of Mars, god of war." **Var:** Marcehia, Mariselda, Marizela, Marizella, Marsial. See also Marcelino, Marcia, Marcial, Marciana, Marcos, Martin.

Marta (Mar' tah) f. **EE:** Martha, Marty, Matty. Heb. "Lady of the house." Biblical friend of Jesus & sister of Lazarus. F. 7/29. 17 x in DS. **Dim:** Maita, Martila, Martina, Martuca. **Var:** Martha, Marthina, Marthini, Martia, Mata.

Marteriano	see **Martirio.**
Martha	see **Marta.**
Marthina	see **Marta.**
Marthini	see **Marta.**
Martia	see **Marta.**
Martial	see **Marcial.**
Martiano	see **Martin.**
Martidiano	see **Martin.**
Martila	see **Marta.**
Martiliano	see **Martin.**
Martimiano	see **Martin.**

Martin (Mar teen') m. **EE:** Martin, etc. Lat. "Belonging to Mars." 40 x in DS. 1, Martin of Tours, France, extirpated idolatry. Invoked against drunkeness. F. 11/11. **Dim:** Machin, Marto, Tin, Tina (Martina). **Var:** Martiano, Martidiano, Martiliano, Martimiano, Martincho, Martineano, Martineza, Martiniano, Martiniares, Martinicino, Martinita, Martinnino, Martinum, Martiona, Martirano, Martiriano, Martriano, Martrirana, Matimana, Mertina. See also Marcelino, Marcia, Marcial, Marciana, Marcos, Mariana, Mario, Marsilio.

Martina	see **Marta.**
Martincho	see **Martin.**
Martineano	see **Martin.**
Martineza	see **Martin.**
Martiniano	see **Martin.**
Martiniares	see **Martin.**
Martinicino	see **Martin.**
Martinita	see **Martin.**
Martinnino	see **Martin.**
Martinum	see **Martin.**
Martiona	see **Martin.**
Martirano	see **Martin.**
Martiriano	see **Martin.**

Martirio (Mar tee' ree oh) m. **EE:** Martyrius, etc. Gk. "Witness." One who dies or suffers rather than renounce Christ. 11 x in DS. **Var:** Marteriano.

Marto	see **Martin.**
Martriano	see **Martin.**
Martrirana	see **Martin.**
Martuca	see **Marta.**
Maruca	see **Maria.**
Maruch	see **Maria.**
Marucha	see **Maria.**
Maruja	see **Maria.**
Marusa	see **Maria.**
Marusha	see **Maria.**
Maruxa	see **Maria.**
Marvella	see **Maravilla.**

Marzelino	see **Marcelino.**
Marzello	see **Marcelino.**
Marzial	see **Marcial.**
Marziano	see **Marciana.**
Marzila	see **Marcelino.**
Marzima	see **Marcia.**
Marzio	see **Marcia.**
Masario	see **Nazario.**
Mascimiana	see **Maximiano.**
Mascimilian	see **Maximiliano.**
Mascimiliano	see **Maximiliano.**
Mascimino	see **Maximiano.**
Mascimo	see **Máximo.**
Mascimoliano	see **Maximiliano.**
Mascolfa	see **Marcolfo.**
Masedonio	see **Macedonio.**
Maseima	see **Máximo.**
Maseimina	see **Máximo.**
Maselina	see **Marcelino.**
Mashmiana	see **Maximiano.**
Masial	see **Máximo.**
Masidona	see **Macedonio.**
Masimiano	see **Maximiano.**
Masimino	see **Maximino.**
Masimio	see **Máximo.**
Masimo	see **Máximo.**
Masino	see **Máximo.**
Massema	see **Máximo.**
Massimiana	see **Maximiano.**
Massimiona	see **Maximiano.**

Mastin (Maas teen') ? Lat. "Mansuetinus," "domesticated."

Masumino	see **Maximino.**
Mata	see **Marta.**
Matalia	see **Natalio.**
Matatías	see **Matías.**
Matejo	see **Mateo.**
Matelda	see **Matilde.**
Matelde	see **Matilde.**
Mateldia	see **Matilde.**

Mateo (Mah tay' oh) m. **EE:** Matt, Matthew, etc. Heb. "Gift of Yahweh." 1 of Jesus' disciples & author of 1st Gospel of NT. F. 9/21. 21 x in DS. **Dim:** Matty, Teo. **Var:** Matejo, Matheo, Matteo, Mattheo.

Materno (Mah tair' no) m. **EE:** Materna, etc. Lat. "Belonging to mother." 6 x in DS. 1st bishop of Cologne, Germany. Resurrected by staff of St. Peter. F. 9/13.

Matheo	see **Mateo.**
Mathías	see **Matías.**
Mathilda	see **Matilde.**
Mathilde	see **Matilde.**
Mathildus	see **Matilde.**
Mathios	see **Matías.**
Matia	see **Matías.**

Matías (Mah tee' ahs) m. **EE:** Matthias, etc. Heb. "Gift of Yahweh." Chosen to replace Judas as 1 of 12 apostles. F. 2/24. 12 x in DS. **Var:** Matatías, Mathias, Mathios, Matia, Maties, Matios, Mattaes, Matthías, Mattía, Mattías.

Maties	see **Matías.**
Matil	see **Matilde.**
Matild	see **Matilde.**

Matilde (Mah teel' day) mf. **EE:** Mathilde, Maude, Tilly. Ger. "Battle maid." Wife of William the Conqueror. 4 x in DS. 1, wife of Henry I of Germany in

10th cen. F. 3/14. **Dim**: Matil,
Matild, Matucha, Matusha, Matux,
Matuxa, Mota, Tila, Tilda,
Tilde, Tildita, Tilín, Tita.
Var: Matelda, Matelde, Mateldia,
Mathilda, Mathilde, Mathildus,
Matildo, Metilda, Metilde,
Metyldo, Mitalda, Mitalde. See
also Mechilda.
Matildo   see **Matilde.**
Matimana   see **Martín.**
Matíos   see **Matías.**
Matrona (Mah troe' nah) f. EE:
Marne. Lat. "Married woman." 15
x in DS. 1, servant in Thessa-
lonica, beaten to death for
being Christian. F. 3/15.
Mattáes   see **Matías.**
Matteo   see **Mateo.**
Mattheo   see **Mateo.**
Matthías   see **Matías.**
Mattía   see **Matías.**
Mattías   see **Matías.**
Matty   see **Mateo.**
Matucha   see **Matilde.**
Maturiano (Mah too ree ah' no) m.
EE: Maturin. Lat. "Maturinus,"
"mature." 3 x in DS.
Matusha   see **Matilde.**
Matux   see **Matilde.**
Matuxa   see **Matilde.**
Maunicio   see **Mauricio.**
Maurecio   see **Mauricio.**
Maurelio   see **Maurilio.**
Maureo   see **Mauricio.**
Mauresia   see **Mauricio.**
Mauricio (Mao ree' see oh) m. EE:
Maurice, Morris, etc. Lat.
"Mauritius" means "from Maurus"
(NW Africa). 15 x in DS. 1, head
of legendary army of Christians,
slaughtered in Switzerland. F.
9/22. **Dim**: Guicho, Mabicho,
Maricho, Morich, Moris, Richo.
Var: Marice, Maricio, Marisio,
Mariso, Maunicio, Maurecio,
Maureo, Mauresia, Maurisio,
Mauritio, Maurizio, Maurosio,
Maursio, Maurstio. See also
Maurilio, Mauro.
Maurielita   see **Maurilio.**
Maurilio (Mao ree' lee oh) m. EE:
Maurelius. Lat. "From Mauro" (NW
Africa). 4 x in DS. **Dim**:
Maurielita. **Var**: Maurelio,
Maurillio. See also Mauricio,
Mauro.
Maurillio   see **Maurilio.**
Maurisio   see **Mauricio.**
Mauritio   see **Mauricio.**
Maurizio   see **Mauricio.**
Mauro (Mao' roe) m. EE: Maura,
Maurus. Lat. "From Mauritania,"
Africa. Evolved to "dark-
complected." 9 x in DS. **Var**:
Morin. See also Mauricio,
Maurilio.
Maurosio   see **Mauricio.**
Maursio   see **Mauricio.**
Maurstio   see **Mauricio.**
Max   see **Máximo.**
Max   see **Tomás.**
Máxcimi   see **Máximo.**
Maxcimia   see **Máximo.**
Maxcimiano   see **Maximiano.**

Máxcimo   see **Máximo.**
Máxcina   see **Máximo.**
Maxemino   see **Maximino.**
Maxi   see **Máximo.**
Maxiameano   see **Maximiano.**
Maxicima   see **Máximo.**
Maxico   see **Tomás.**
Maxiliano   see **Maximiliano.**
Maximaina   see **Maximiano.**
Maximdiano   see **Maximiano.**
Maximeliano   see **Maximiano.**
Maximelieno   see **Maximiliano.**
Maximenio   see **Maximiano.**
Maximeno   see **Maximiano.**
Maximiano (Mahx ee mee ah' no) m.
EE: Maxim, Maximianus. Lat. "Son
of Maximus." **Var**: Macemiana,
Macimeano, Macimiaivo,
Macimiano, Marcemiado,
Marcimino, Mascimiana,
Mascimino, Mashmiana, Masimiano,
Massimiana, Massimiona,
Maxcimiano, Maxiameano,
Maximaina, Maximdiano,
Maximeliano, Maximenio,
Maximeno, Maximihano, Maximisia,
Maxiniano, Maxiumiano,
Maxsimiano, Messimino, Miximino.
See also Máximo, Magno,
Maximiliano, Maximino.
Maximihano   see **Maximiano.**
Maximil   see **Maximiliano.**
Maximiliano (Mahx' ee mee lee ah'
no) m. EE: Maximilian. Lat.
"Greatest." Popular among Ger.
emperors. 7 x in DS. **Dim**:
Chilano, Mancho. **Var**:
Marcimiliano, Mascimilián,
Mascimiliano, Máscimoliano,
Maxiliano, Maximelieno, Maximil,
Maximilianus, Maximilla,
Maximillan, Maximillano,
Maxismilla. See also Emilio,
Máximo, Magno, Maximiano,
Maximino.
Maximilianus   see **Maximiliano.**
Maximilla   see **Maximiliano.**
Maximillan   see **Maximiliano.**
Maximillano   see **Maximiliano.**
Maximino (Mahx ee mee' no) m. Lat.
"Greatest." **Var**: Macimeno,
Masimino, Masumino, Maxemino,
Mixinio. See also Máximo, Magno,
Maximiano, Maximiliano.
Maximisia   see **Maximiano.**
Máximo (Mahx' ee mo) m. EE:
Maximus, etc. Lat. "Greatest."
149 x in DS. 1, Gk. theologian,
defended doctrine of Incarna-
tion. F. 8/13. **Dim**: Chimino,
Max, Maxi. **Var**: Macísimi,
Máscimo, Máseima, Maseimina,
Masial, Másimio, Másimo, Másino,
Mássema, Máxcimi, Maxcimia,
Máxcimo, Máxcina, Maxicima,
Maxinio, Máxino, Maxinono,
Méssimo, Méximo, Miscimi,
Miscimo, Míximo. See also Magno,
Maximiano, Maximiliano,
Maximino.
Maxiniano   see **Maximiano.**
Maxinio   see **Máximo.**
Máxino   see **Máximo.**
Maxinono   see **Máximo.**
Maxismilla   see **Maximiliano.**

Maxiumiano   see **Maximiano.**
Maxsimiano   see **Maximiano.**
Maya   see **Amalio.**
Maya (My' yah) f. **EE:** Maia, May.
  Gk. "Mother." In Gk. myth.,
  daughter of Atlas, wife of Zeus,
  & mother of Hermes. May named
  after her. **Dim:** Mayanita. **Var:**
  Mayela.
Mayanita   see **Maya.**
Maydaleno   see **Magdaleno.**
Maydlena   see **Magdaleno.**
Maydoleno   see **Magdaleno.**
Mayela   see **Maya.**
Mayito   see **Mario.**
Mayo   see **Mario.**
Mayolo (Mah yo' low) m. **EE:**
  Maieul, etc. Fr. S. of great
  Cluniac reform of 10th cen. F.
  5/11.
Mazario   see **Nazario.**
Mazedona   see **Macedonio.**
Mazedonia   see **Macedonio.**
Meacla   see **Miguel.**
Mecaela   see **Miguel.**
Mecaila   see **Miguel.**
Mecario   see **Macario.**
Mecedes   see **Mercedes.**
Mecedonia   see **Macedonio.**
Mecenas (May say' nahs) m. **EE:**
  Maecenas. Lat. "Belonging to
  Maecia," Roman family. Roman
  patron of arts.
Mecha   see **Mercedes.**
Meche   see **Mercedes.**
Meches   see **Mercedes.**
Mechilda (May cheel' dah) f. **EE:**
  Mechthild. Form of Mechthildis,
  13th cen. Ger. nun & 1 of 1st to
  propagate devotion to Sacred
  Heart. F. 11/19. **Var:**
  Marichilda, Menechilda.
  Merechilda. See also Matilde.
Mechita   see **Mercedes.**
Mecho   see **Demetrio.**
Mecho   see **Nemesio.**
Mechor   see **Melchor.**
Mechora   see **Melchor.**
Medalla (May dye' ya) f. Lat.
  "Metallum," "metal." Miraculous
  medals relating to apparition of
  V. Mary.
Medardo (May dar' doe) m. **EE:**
  Medard. Ang-Sax. "Worthy of
  great honor." Bishop of Noyon,
  France in 6th cen. F. 6/8. **Var:**
  Medaro, Mederdo, Meinrado,
  Merardo.
Medaro   see **Medardo.**
Medejildo   see **Hermenegildo.**
Medeline   see **Magdaleno.**
Mederdo   see **Medardo.**
Medesto   see **Modesto.**
Medila (May dee' lah) f. Could be
  form of Medilama, Egyp. V. & M.
  F. 9/17.
Medrano (May draw' no) m. **EE:**
  Madron, Medran. 6th cen. Irish
  S. F. 5/17.
Megdolina   see **Magdaleno.**
Megorio (May go' ree oh) m.
  Megara, Megareo, & Megaro,
  deities from Gk. myth.
Meguil   see **Miguel.**
Meinrado   see **Medardo.**

Mel   see **Manuel.**
Mel   see **Samuel.**
Mela   see **Amalio.**
Mela   see **Carmen.**
Mela   see **Hermelinda.**
Mela   see **Imelda.**
Mela   see **Melas.**
Mela   see **Melito.**
Melacio   see **Melesio.**
Melaguias   see **Melquiades.**
Melahiades   see **Melquiades.**
Melanchthon   see **Melantón.**
Melanio (May lah' nee oh) m. **EE:**
  Melanie, etc. Gk. "Dark, black."
  In myth., earth goddess. 2 x in
  DS. 1, of 4th cen., gave all of
  her wealth to poor. F. 12/31.
  Var: Malano. See also Melas.
Melantón (May lahn tone') m. **EE:**
  Melanchthon. Gk. "Black earth."
  After Luther, main personage of
  Protestant Reformation
  (1497-1560). **Var:** Melanchthón.
Melas (May' lahs) m. Gk. "Dark."
  4th cen. bishop of Rhinocolura,
  Egypt. Driven from see by
  Arians. F. 1/16. **Var:** Mela,
  Nelas, Nelaz. See also Melanio.
Melba (Mel' bah) f. **EE:** Melba. Old
  Eng. "From mill stream." Also,
  "handmaiden" in Celtic. **Dim:**
  Melvena. **Var:** Malba, Melva,
  Nelba, Nelva.
Melchar   see **Melchor.**
Melchara   see **Melchor.**
Melchares   see **Melchor.**
Melcharia   see **Melchor.**
Melcher   see **Melchor.**
Melchiades   see **Melquiades.**
Melchiadez   see **Melquiades.**
Melchiadis   see **Melquiades.**
Melchiado   see **Melquiades.**
Melchiales   see **Melquiades.**
Melchiar   see **Melchor.**
Melchiaria   see **Melchor.**
Melchiaries   see **Melquiades.**
Melchiddez   see **Melquiades.**
Melchidis   see **Melquiades.**
Melchiera   see **Melchor.**
Melchilda   see **Melquiades.**
Melchiodes   see **Melchor.**
Melchior   see **Melchor.**
Melchiora   see **Melchor.**
Melchiordez   see **Melchor.**
Melchiorita   see **Melchor.**
Melchiorrae   see **Melchor.**
Melchivades   see **Melchor.**
Melchivera   see **Melchor.**
Melcho   see **Melchor.**
Melchoca   see **Melchor.**
Melchoir   see **Melchor.**
Melchor (Mel chor') m. **EE:**
  Melchior. Heb. "King of light."
  1 of 3 wise men to adore Christ
  child. F. 1/6. **Dim:** Melcho,
  Melchoca. **Var:** Malchor, Malcor,
  Mechor, Mechora, Melchar,
  Melchara, Melchares, Melcharia,
  Melcher, Melchiar, Melchiaria,
  Melchiera, Melchiodes, Melchior,
  Melchiora, Melchiordez,
  Melchiorita, Melchiorrae,
  Melchivades, Melchivera,
  Melchoir, Melchora, Melchoz,
  Melchurris, Melcor, Melquiora.

Melchora   see **Melchor.**
Melchoz   see **Melchor.**
Melchurris   see **Melchor.**
Melciades   see **Melquíades.**
Melcor   see **Melchor.**
Melda   see **Imelda.**
Melda (Mel' dah) f. Possibly from
  "meldar" meaning "to teach."
Melecho   see **Melesio.**
Melecio   see **Melesio.**
Melécium   see **Melesio.**
Melegilda   see **Hermenegildo.**
Meleida (May lay ee' dah) f. Form
  of Meletius. 9 x in DS.
Melejieda   see **Esmeregildo.**
Melesandro   see **Melisendo.**
Melesio (May lay' see oh) m. **EE:**
  Meletius. Gk. "Careful, atten-
  tive." 9 x in DS. 1, 4th cen.
  schismatic bishop of Antioch,
  Turkey. F. 2/12. **Dim:** Melecho,
  Mesio, Messe. **Var:** Malacia,
  Malecio, Malesio, Melacio,
  Melecio, Melécium, Melesios,
  Meletio, Melezio, Melicio,
  Meliesia, Meliseo, Milacio,
  Milecio, Milesio, Nelacio,
  Nelesio.
Melesios   see **Melesio.**
Meletio   see **Melesio.**
Meletón   see **Melito.**
Melezio   see **Melesio.**
Melgiades   see **Melquíades.**
Melginades   see **Melquíades.**
Melgino   see **Melquíades.**
Melgniade   see **Melquíades.**
Melgniades   see **Melquíades.**
Melguiada   see **Melquíades.**
Melguiades   see **Melquíades.**
Melguiar   see **Melquíades.**
Melguides   see **Melquíades.**
Melguinadez   see **Melquíades.**
Meli   see **Amalio.**
Meli   see **Hermelinda.**
Meli   see **Melibea.**
Meli   see **Melito.**
Melibea (May lee bay' ah) f. Gk.
  "To take care of." Heroine of
  Fernando de Rojas' "Celestina,"
  15th cen. Sp. classic. **Dim:**
  Meli.
Melicio   see **Melesio.**
Melico   see **Manuel.**
Melida   see **Maria.**
Melida   see **Melito.**
Melidón   see **Melito.**
Meliesia   see **Melesio.**
Melihiades   see **Melquíades.**
Melina   see **Melinda.**
Melinda (May leen' dah) f. **EE:**
  Melinda, etc. Gk. "Gentle." **Var:**
  Melina, Melinia, Milinda.
Melinia   see **Melinda.**
Melio   see **Cornelio.**
Melisa (May lee' sah) f. **EE:**
  Melissa. Gk. "Honey-sweet
  flower." **Var:** Malisa, Malissa,
  Melissa, Meliza, Melizio,
  Melizza, Milissa.
Melisandro   see **Melisendo.**
Melisendo (May lee sayn' doe) m.
  EE: Melicent, Millicent. Ger.
  "Strong work." **Var:** Melesandro,
  Melisandro, Melisendro,
  Mellisandra.

Melisendro   see **Melisendo.**
Meliseo   see **Melesio.**
Melissa   see **Melisa.**
Melita   see **Amalio.**
Melita   see **Carmen.**
Melita   see **Manuel.**
Melitana   see **Melito.**
Meliterio (May lee tay' ree oh) m.
  Meliteo in Gk. myth., son of
  Jupiter. At birth, hidden in
  forest & fed by bees.
Melithón   see **Melito.**
Melito   see **Ismael.**
Melito (May lee' toe) m. **EE:**
  Mellitus, etc. Gk. "Like honey."
  4 x in DS. Mellitus, 3rd Arch-
  bishop of Canterbury in 7th cen.
  F. 2/24. **Dim:** Mela, Meli. **Var:**
  Malitón, Mallitonia, Meletón,
  Melida, Melidón, Melitana,
  Melithón, Melitoa, Melitón,
  Melitona, Melitone, Mellito,
  Meritón, Miletón.
Melitoa   see **Melito.**
Melitón   see **Melito.**
Melitona   see **Melito.**
Melitone   see **Melito.**
Meliza   see **Melisa.**
Melizio   see **Melisa.**
Melizza   see **Melisa.**
Melkiades   see **Melquíades.**
Mellechiades   see **Melquíades.**
Mellisandra   see **Melisendo.**
Mellito   see **Melito.**
Melo   see **Emilio.**
Melo   see **Manuel.**
Melodio (May low' dee oh) m. **EE:**
  Melody. Lat. "Melos," "music."
Melquade   see **Melquíades.**
Melquades   see **Melquíades.**
Melquares   see **Melquíades.**
Melqueades   see **Melquíades.**
Melquedes   see **Melquíades.**
Melqueleados   see **Melquíades.**
Melquiada   see **Melquíades.**
Melquiadas   see **Melquíades.**
Melquiade   see **Melquíades.**
Melquiader   see **Melquíades.**
Melquíades (Mel key' ah days) m.
  EE: Melchiades, Milkiades. Heb.
  "King of gods." 4th cen. pope
  important in Donatus controver-
  sy. F. 1/10. **Dim:** Mequila. **Var:**
  Malchiades, Malguíades,
  Malquades, Malquíades,
  Melaguias, Melahiades,
  Melchiades, Melchiadez,
  Melchiadis, Melchiado,
  Melchiadis, Melchiaries,
  Melchiddez, Melchidis,
  Melchilda, Melciades, Melgiades,
  Melginades, Melgino, Melgniade,
  Melgniades, Melguiada,
  Melguiades, Melguiar, Melguides,
  Melguinadez, Melihiades,
  Melkiades, Mellechiades,
  Melquade, Melquades, Melquares,
  Melqueades, Melquedes,
  Melqueleados, Melquiada,
  Melquiadas, Melquiade,
  Melquiader, Melquiadez,
  Melquiadis, Melquiales,
  Melquiares, Melquiaves,
  Melquidas, Melquider, Melquides,
  Melquinades, Melquirades,

Melquísades, Merchida,
Merquíades, Milchíades.

Melquíadez	see **Melquíades.**
Melquíadis	see **Melquíades.**
Melquíales	see **Melquíades.**
Melquíares	see **Melquíades.**
Melquíaves	see **Melquíades.**
Melquídas	see **Melquíades.**
Melquíder	see **Melquíades.**
Melquídes	see **Melquíades.**
Melquínades	see **Melquíades.**

Melquíones (Mel key' owe nace) m.
Melquion was 3rd cen. Syrian S.
F. 10/28.

Melquíora	see **Melchor.**
Melquírades	see **Melquíades.**
Melquísades	see **Melquíades.**

Melusina (May loo see' nah) f. Fr.
water fairy happily married
until husband intruded on seclu-
sion. Related to legends of
banshee & mermaid.

Melva	see **Melba.**
Melvena	see **Melba.**
Mema	see **Emma.**
Meme	see **Manuel.**
Memo	see **Guillermo.**

Memorio (May mo' ree oh) m. EE:
Memorianus, etc. Lat. "Ability
to retain past." 3 x in DS. 1 M.
of Troyes, France, beheaded by
Attila the Hun. F. 9/7.

Mena	see **Filomeno.**
Menalia	see **Filomeno.**

Menas (May' nahs) m. EE: Mennas.
Gk. "Strong, valiant." 23 x in
DS. 1, mart. for public declara-
tion of Christianity. F. 11/11.

Mencelado	see **Venceslao.**
Mencha	see **Clemente.**
Menche	see **Mercedes.**

Mencia (Main' see ah) f. Beatified
religious from Portugal.

Menechildo	see **Mechilda.**
Menejildo	see **Hermenegildo.**
Meneque	see **Manuel.**
Menerva	see **Minerva.**
Menjildo	see **Hermenegildo.**
Mente	see **Clemente.**

Meodoro (May oh doe' roe) m. Could
be form of Menodora, 4th cen. S.
of Bithynia (Asia Minor) mart.
during Diocletian's persecution.
F. 9/10.

Mequila	see **Melquíades.**
Merajildo	see **Hermenegildo.**
Meraldo	see **Esmeralda.**
Merardo	see **Medardo.**
Mercario	see **Macario.**
Mercé	see **Mercedes.**
Merced	see **Mercedes.**
Mercedalia	see **Mercedes.**
Mercedas	see **Mercedes.**
Mercede	see **Mercedes.**

Mercedes (Mare say' days) f. EE:
Mercedes, Mercy. Lat. "Pity,
mercy." Special devotion to V.
under name Nuestra Señora de las
Mercedes, or Our Lady of Mercy.
F. 9/24. **Dim:** Aches, Chelo,
Cochiche, Mecha, Meche, Meches,
Mechita, Menche, Merche, Mersi,
Meté, Miche. **Var:** Marceda,
Marcedera, Marcedes, Mecedes,
Mercé, Merced, Mercedalia,

Mercedas, Mercede, Mercedez,
Mercedis, Mercedo, Merceles,
Mercés, Mercese, Mercid,
Mercida, Mercio, Meredes, Mersé,
Mersed, Mersedes, Merzé, Merzed,
Mescedes, Mircedes.

Mercedez	see **Mercedes.**
Mercedis	see **Mercedes.**
Mercedo	see **Mercedes.**
Merceles	see **Mercedes.**
Mercelino	see **Marcelino.**
Mercelo	see **Marcelino.**
Merceo	see **Marcelino.**
Mercés	see **Mercedes.**
Mercese	see **Mercedes.**
Merche	see **Mercedes.**
Merchida	see **Melquíades.**
Mercial	see **Marcial.**
Mercid	see **Mercedes.**
Mercida	see **Mercedes.**
Mercio	see **Mercedes.**
Merco	see **Américo.**

Mercurio (Mare coo' ree oh) m. EE:
Mercury. Lat. "He who takes care
of business." Roman god of commerce. 19 x in DS. 1, Mercurius
of Caesarea, returned 113 years
after death to kill Julian the
Apostate. F. 11/25.

Merechilda	see **Mechilda.**

Merede (May ray' day) m. EE:
Mered. 2nd of 4 sons of Ezra.
Married daughter of Pharoah.

Meredes	see **Mercedes.**
Merefilda	see **Hermenegildo.**
Meregildo	see **Hermenegildo.**
Mereida	see **Nereida.**
Merejilde	see **Hermenegildo.**
Merejildo	see **Hermenegildo.**
Merejiledo	see **Hermenegildo.**
Merejo	see **Hermenegildo.**
Merenciano	see **Emerenciana.**
Merensiana	see **Emerenciana.**
Merenza	see **Emerenciana.**
Mereyildo	see **Hermenegildo.**
Merezildo	see **Hermenegildo.**
Mergildo	see **Hermenegildo.**
Merhelda	see **Hermenegildo.**
Merhilda	see **Hermenegildo.**
Meri	see **María.**

Meridina (May ree dee' nah) f.
From Meridana, native of Mérida,
Mexico.

Merigilda	see **Hermenegildo.**
Merihildo	see **Hermenegildo.**
Merijildo	see **Hermenegildo.**

Merissa (May ree' sah) f. Comb. of
María & Lovisa (see both).

Meritón	see **Melito.**
Meriyilda	see **Hermenegildo.**
Merjildo	see **Hermenegildo.**
Merla	see **Merle.**

Merle (Mare' lay) ? EE: Merle.
Lat. "Merula," "blackbird." **Var:**
Merla.

Merlinda (Mare leen' dah) f. From
Merlin, wizard in Arthurian
legends.

Mermenegildo	see **Hermenegildo.**
Merminia	see **Herminio.**
Merquiades	see **Melquíades.**
Merrchilda	see **Hermenegildo.**
Merrfildo	see **Hermenegildo.**
Mersé	see **Mercedes.**
Mersed	see **Mercedes.**

Mersedes   see **Mercedes.**
Mersera (Mare say' rah) f. Comb.
  of Mercedes & Sara (see both).
Mersi   see **Mercedes.**
Mertina   see **Martín.**
Merygilda   see **Hermenegildo.**
Merze   see **Mercedes.**
Merzed   see **Mercedes.**
Mesalina (May sah lee' nah) f. **EE:**
  Messalina. Ital. S. of 16th cen.
  Also Roman empress.
Mescedes   see **Mercedes.**
Mesio   see **Melesio.**
Messe   see **Melesio.**
Messimino   see **Maximiano.**
Messimo   see **Máximo.**
Mestona (Mace toe' nah) f. Form of
  Mesithon, S. mart. in Granada,
  Spain? F. 2/15.
Mestora   see **Néstor.**
Meta   see **Margarito.**
Mete   see **Mercedes.**
Meterio   see **Emeterio.**
Metilda   see **Matilde.**
Metilde   see **Matilde.**
Metodio (May toe' dee oh) m. **EE:**
  Methodius. Gk. "He who has
  orderly system." 6 x in DS. 1,
  Patriarch of Constantinople in
  9th cen. F. 6/14.
Metro   see **Metrobio.**
Metrobio (May troe' bee oh) m. **EE:**
  Metrobius. Gk. "He who has
  orderly life." 5 x in DS. **Dim:**
  Metro.
Metyldo   see **Matilde.**
Méximo   see **Máximo.**
Meya   see **Amalio.**
Micaala   see **Miguel.**
Micacio (Mee cah' see oh) m.
  "Micaceo," "containing mica."
Micada (Mee cah' dah) f. Feminine
  form of Sp. for Mikado, emperor
  of Japan.
Micaela   see **Miguel.**
Micaella   see **Miguel.**
Micaelma   see **Miguel.**
Micaila   see **Miguel.**
Micalao   see **Miguel.**
Micalda   see **Miguel.**
Micalea   see **Miguel.**
Micalla   see **Miguel.**
Micario   see **Macario.**
Micasio   see **Nicasio.**
Mich   see **Remigio.**
Micha   see **Artemio.**
Michaelo   see **Miguel.**
Miche   see **Mercedes.**
Michea   see **Miqueas.**
Michel   see **Miguel.**
Michelito   see **Miguel.**
Mickella   see **Miguel.**
Mickey   see **Miguel.**
Mico   see **Miguel.**
Midonio (Mee doe' nee oh) m. Midon
  in Gk. myth. was Trojan killed
  by Achilles.
Migael   see **Miguel.**
Migala   see **Migdalia.**
Migdalia (Meeg dah' lee ah) f.
  Migdal is Biblical word "tower."
  Town on Sea of Galilee, suppos-
  edly home of Mary Magdalene.
  Var: Migala, Migdelia, Mygdalia.
  See also Magdaleno.

Migdelia   see **Migdalia.**
Migel   see **Miguel.**
Migela   see **Miguel.**
Migil   see **Miguel.**
Migila   see **Miguel.**
Miguaela   see **Miguel.**
Miguel (Mee ghell') m. **EE:**
  Michael, Michelle, Mike. Heb.
  "Who is like God." Archangel
  important in Jewish, Moslem, &
  Christian tradition. In latter,
  carries sword & conquers Satan.
  F. 9/29. 48 x in DS. **Dim:** Cailas
  (Micaela), Lito, Maik,
  Michelito, Mickey, Mico,
  Miguelino, Miguelón, Migui,
  Miguicho, Miki, Milicho, Mime
  (Micaela), Mique, Miqui, Quela
  (Micaela). **Var:** Macaela,
  Macaliana, Meacla, Mecaela,
  Mecaila, Meguil, Micaala,
  Micaela, Micaella, Micaelma,
  Micaila, Micalao, Micalda,
  Micalea, Micalla, Michaelo,
  Michel, Mickella, Migael, Migel,
  Migela, Migil, Migila, Miguaela,
  Miguela, Migueo, Miguil, Mijuel,
  Mikaela, Miqaela, Miquaela,
  Miquel, Miquela, Miquella,
  Miquila, Nicaela. See also
  Miqueas.
Miguela   see **Miguel.**
Miguelino   see **Miguel.**
Miguelón   see **Miguel.**
Migueo   see **Miguel.**
Migui   see **Miguel.**
Miguicho   see **Miguel.**
Miguil   see **Miguel.**
Mijuel   see **Miguel.**
Mikaela   see **Miguel.**
Miki   see **Miguel.**
Milacio   see **Melesio.**
Milagoros   see **Milagros.**
Milagros (Mee lah' gross) f. Lat.
  "Miraculum," "exciting, aston-
  ishing." Title for Blessed V.,
  Nuestra Señora de los Milagros,
  Our Lady of Miracles. F. 7/9.
  Dim: Mili. **Var:** Milagoros. See
  also Maravilla, Mira, Miranda.
Milana   see **Emilio.**
Milburga (Meel boor' gah) f. **EE:**
  Milburga. Teut. "Friendly pro-
  tector." 8th cen. nun & founder
  of abbey in Shropshire, England.
  F. 2/23.
Milchíades   see **Melquíades.**
Milda (Meel' dah) f. In myth.,
  goddess venerated by ancient
  Italians.
Milecio   see **Melesio.**
Milena (Mee lay' nah) f. Comb. of
  María & Elena (see both).
Milesio   see **Melesio.**
Miletón   see **Melito.**
Mili   see **Emilio.**
Mili   see **Milagros.**
Miliana   see **Emilio.**
Milicho   see **Miguel.**
Milico   see **Camilo.**
Milinda   see **Melinda.**
Miliquis   see **Miguel.**
Milissa   see **Melisa.**
Millan   see **Emilio.**
Milo   see **Camilo.**

Milo   see Emilio.
Milota   see María.
Mima   see Edelmira.
Mime   see Miguel.
Mimeco   see Américo.
Mimi   see Edelmira.
Mimi   see Herminio.
Mimi   see María.
Mimi   see Noemí.
Mimia   see Edelmira.
Mimila   see Emilio.
Mimiya   see Edelmira.
Min   see Benjamín.
Min   see Fermín.
Mina   see Guillermo.
Mina   see Herminio.
Mina   see Marino.
Mincho   see Benjamín.
Mincho   see Fermín.
Minda   see Arcadio.
Minel   see Manuel.
Minerba   see Minerva.
Minerma   see Minerva.
Minerra   see Minerva.
Minerva (Mee nair' bah) f. EE:
  Minerva, Minnie. Lat. "Wisdom,
  force, or purpose." 1 of main
  Roman goddesses, patroness of
  learning & handicrafts. 3 x in
  DS. Var: Menerva, Minerba,
  Minerma, Minerra, Minnerva,
  Ninerva, Numerva.
Minfa   see Ninfa.
Mingo   see Domingo.
Minguín   see Domingo.
Minina   see Abelino.
Minita   see Guillermo.
Minita   see Herminio.
Minnerva   see Minerva.
Mino   see Benjamín.
Minta (Mean' tah) f. Menta in
  myth., mistress of Pluto.
Miqaela   see Miguel.
Miquaela   see Miguel.
Mique   see Miguel.
Miqueas (Mee kay' ahs) m. EE:
  Michah, etc. Heb. "Who is like
  God." 6 x in DS. Var: Michea.
  See also Miguel.
Miquel   see Miguel.
Miquela   see Miguel.
Miquella   see Miguel.
Miqui   see Miguel.
Miquila   see Miguel.
Mira (Mee' rah) f. EE: Myra, etc.
  Lat. "Wonderful." Var: Myria.
  See also Maravilla, Milagros,
  Miranda.
Mirada   see Miranda.
Mirajilda   see Hermenegildo.
Miranda (Mee rahn' dah) f. Lat.
  "Admirable." Var: Mirada,
  Mirindo. See also Maravilla,
  Milagros, Mira.
Mircedes   see Mercedes.
Mirdmon (Meerd' moan) m. Mirmidon
  in Gk. myth., son of Zeus &
  eponymous ancestor of Myrmidons.
Mirejilda   see Hermenegildo.
Mirella   see Mireya.
Mireslava   see Miroslava.
Mireya (Mee ray' yah) f. EE:
  Amariah. Heb. "God has spoken."
  9 x in OT. Var: Mirella, Miriah,
  Mirya.

Miriah   see Mireya.
Miriam (Mee ree' ahm) f. EE:
  Miriam, etc. Heb. "Bitter."
  Prophetess, sister of Moses &
  Aaron; made leper for siding
  with Aaron against Moses. See
  also María.
Mirindo   see Miranda.
Mirma   see Mirna.
Mirna (Meer' nah) f. EE: Myrna,
  etc. Possibly from Morna, "soft
  or gentle." Var: Mirma.
Miro   see Edelmira.
Miroslava (Mee' roe slah' bah) f.
  Slav. "Glorious peace." Var:
  Mireslava.
Mirta (Meer' tah) f. Gk. "Crown of
  beauty." Var: Mirtala, Mirtha,
  Mirtila, Myrathalla, Myrtala,
  Myrthala, Myrthea, Mythala.
Mirtala   see Mirta.
Mirtha   see Mirta.
Mirtila   see Mirta.
Mirya   see Mireya.
Mirza (Meer' zah) f. Pers. title
  "lady" or "princess."
Misael (Mee sah el') m. EE:
  Mishael, etc. Heb. "He who is
  like God." 3 x in Bible. Dim:
  Chael.
Misaís (Mee sah ees') m. Mart. in
  Africa.
Miscimi   see Máximo.
Miscimo   see Máximo.
Mita   see Emma.
Mita   see Telma.
Mitalda   see Matilde.
Mitalde   see Matilde.
Miterica   see Emeterio.
Miterio   see Emeterio.
Mito   see Guillermo.
Mito   see Jaime.
Mito   see Manuel.
Miximino   see Maximiano.
Míximo   see Máximo.
Mixinio   see Maximino.
Miyo   see Emilio.
Mocés   see Moisés.
Mocha   see Carmen.
Moclovia   see Maclovio.
Modaleno   see Magdaleno.
Modestae   see Modesto.
Modesth   see Modesto.
Modesto (Mo dace' toe) m. EE:
  Modestus. Lat. "He who is
  moderate in acts." 20 x in DS.
  Dim: Mota, Motita. Var: Madesto,
  Medesto, Modestae, Modesth,
  Modestus.
Modestus   see Modesto.
Moesés   see Moisés.
Mogarito   see Margarito.
Moicelio   see Moisés.
Moicés   see Moisés.
Moirío (Moy ree' oh) m. EE: Moira,
  etc. Gk. "Merit." 1 of Fates in
  Gk. myth. May be equated with
  death.
Moisá   see Moisés.
Moisés (Moy sace') m. EE: Moe,
  Moses. Heb. "Saved from water,"
  or Egyp. "son, child." Heb. law-
  giver who led his people out of
  Egypt. F. 9/4. 30 x in DS. Dim:
  Cheche, Moisá, Moisetes, Monchi,

Mos, Moy, Totó. **Var:** Maizés, Mocés, Moesés, Moicelio, Moicés, Moisís, Moseos, Mosesto, Mouserato, Mousés, Moysés, Moysís, Mozés.

Moisetes	see **Moisés.**
Moisís	see **Moisés.**
Mon	see **Ramón.**
Mon	see **Salomón.**
Mona	see **Ramón.**
Mónaca	see **Mónico.**
Monases	see **Manases.**
Monceo	see **Montserrat.**
Moncerat	see **Montserrat.**
Moncerrato	see **Montserrat.**
Monces	see **Montserrat.**
Monche	see **Ramón.**
Monchi	see **Moisés.**
Monchi	see **Raimundo.**
Monchi	see **Ramón.**
Monchin	see **Raimundo.**
Moncho	see **Raimundo.**
Moncho	see **Ramón.**
Moncho	see **Simón.**
Monclovio	see **Maclovio.**
Moneco	see **Montserrat.**
Mongo	see **Raimundo.**
Mongo	see **Ramón.**

Mónico (Mo' nee co) m, EE: Mona, Monica. Lat. "Monk," Mother of St. Augustine. F. 5/4, **Var:** Mánico, Mónaca, Monicón, Mónika, Múnico.

Monicón	see **Mónico.**
Mónika	see **Mónico.**
Monona	see **Ramón.**
Monsei	see **Montserrat.**
Monseís	see **Montserrat.**
Monseise	see **Montserrat.**
Monserate	see **Montserrat.**
Monserato	see **Montserrat.**
Monseratta	see **Montserrat.**
Monserrato	see **Montserrat.**
Monsete	see **Ramón.**
Monsita	see **Montserrat.**
Monsorate	see **Montserrat.**

Montserrat (Moant say rhat') f. Lat. "Mons serratus" means "saw-like mountain." Near Barcelona with church with image carved by St. Luke & brought to Spain by St. Peter. **Dim:** Monceo, Monces, Moneco, Monsei, Monseís, Monseise, Monsita. **Var:** Mansarrata, Moncerat, Moncerrato, Monserate, Monserato, Monseratta, Monserrato, Monsorate.

Moñi	see **Bonifacio.**
Moñi	see **Salomón.**
Moño	see **Ramón.**

Moraemia	see **Moraima.**

Moraima (Mo rye' mah) f. Morayma is 1 of best known ballads from Moorish Spain. **Var:** Moraemia, Moriam.

Morcial	see **Marcial.**
Moriam	see **Moraima.**
Morich	see **Mauricio.**
Morida	see **Morta.**
Morin	see **Mauro.**
Morina	see **Morio.**

Morio (Mo' ree oh) m. Moria in Gk. myth. was sacred olive tree given by Minerva in dispute with Neptune over possesion of Attica. **Dim:** Morina.

Moris	see **Mauricio.**

Morta (More' tah) f. In myth., 1 of Parcas that presides over those born prematurely or late. **Var:** Morida.

Mortina (More tee' nah) f. Leaf of myrtle plant. **Var:** Mortinia.

Mortinia	see **Mortina.**
Mos	see **Moisés.**
Moseos	see **Moisés.**
Mosesto	see **Moisés.**
Mota	see **Matilde.**
Mota	see **Modesto.**
Motita	see **Modesto.**
Mouserato	see **Moisés.**
Mousés	see **Moisés.**
Moy	see **Moisés.**
Moysés	see **Moisés.**
Moysis	see **Moisés.**
Mozés	see **Moisés.**

Mucio (Moo' see oh) m. EE: Mucius. Lat. "He who forbears in silence." 3 x in DS. **Dim:** Muselina. **Var:** Musia, Muzio.

Mundo	see **Edmundo.**
Mundo	see **Raimundo.**
Múnico	see **Mónico.**
Muno	see **Segismundo.**

Muñeca (Moon yay' cah) f. Sp. "Doll." **Dim:** Muñequita.

Muñequita	see **Muñeca.**

Murtina (Moor tee' nah) f. Murtillo is Chilean shrub with white flowers.

Muselina	see **Mucio.**
Musia	see **Mucio.**
Muzio	see **Mucio.**
Mygdalia	see **Migdalia.**
Myrathalla	see **Mirta.**
Myria	see **Mira.**
Myrtala	see **Mirta.**
Myrthala	see **Mirta.**
Myrthea	see **Mirta.**
Mythala	see **Mirta.**

N

Nabar	see **Nabor**.
Nabara	see **Nabor**.
Naberta	see **Norberto**.
Nabón	see **Nabor**.

Nabor (Nah bore') m. EE: Nabor.
Heb. "Light of prophet." 6 x in
DS. 1, Moor beheaded for faith
in 4th cen. F. 7/12. **Var:** Nabar,
Nabara, Nabón, Nabora, Naboris,
Nabós, Nabove, Nabur, Narbora,
Navor, Navora, Navorra, Nibor,
Nobar, Nober, Nobor, Novor.

Nabora	see **Nabor**.
Naboris	see **Nabor**.
Nabós	see **Nabor**.
Nabove	see **Nabor**.
Nabur	see **Nabor**.
Nacario	see **Macario**.
Nacerio	see **Nazario**.
Nachito	see **Ignacio**.
Nacho	see **Anastacio**.
Nacho	see **Ignacio**.
Nacho	see **Narciso**.
Nacido	see **Natividad**.
Naclito	see **Anacleto**.
Naclovia	see **Maclovio**.
Nadividada	see **Natividad**.
Nado	see **Bernal**.
Nado	see **Leonardo**.

Nahum (Nah oom') m. EE: Nahum.
Heb. "He who is compassionate."
Prophet & author of book of
Nahum. Gloats over prospect of
destruction of Nineveh. F. 12/1.
2 x in DS.

Naida	see **Zenaida**.
Naiomá	see **Noemí**.
Naiomí	see **Noemí**.
Naldo	see **Reinaldo**.
Namesio	see **Nemesio**.
Nana	see **Ana**.
Nana	see **Carmen**.
Nancho	see **Venancio**.
Nanda	see **Amanda**.

Nandad (Nahn dahd') m. In Indian
myth., Nanda, husband of Yacoda,
saved Krishna.

Nando	see **Fernando**.
Nando	see **Hernanda**.
Nanesio	see **Nemesio**.
Nanita	see **Ana**.
Nano	see **Fernando**.
Nano	see **Hernanda**.
Nano	see **Juan**.
Nano	see **María**.
Nano	see **Viviano**.
Nanon	see **Hernanda**.
Naomí	see **Noemí**.
Napalión	see **Napoleón**.
Napolem	see **Napoleón**.

Napoleón (Nah poe lay own') m. EE:
Nap, Napoleon. Gk. "He who comes
from new city (Naples)." Emperor
of France & remaker of map of
Europe, 1 S. F. 8/15. **Var:**
Napalión, Napolem, Napoleonis,
Napolián, Neapoleón.

Napoleonis	see **Napoleón**.
Napolián	see **Napoleón**.
Napolinar	see **Apolonio**.
Napomesena	see **Nepomuceno**.
Naponceno	see **Nepomuceno**.
Narasio	see **Nazario**.
Narassa	see **Nazario**.
Narberta	see **Norberto**.
Narbora	see **Nabor**.

Narcedalia (Nar say dah' lee ah)
f. Narceo in Gk. myth. was son
of Bacchus & nymph Bascoa.

Narcesia	see **Narciso**.
Narceso	see **Narciso**.
Narcessa	see **Narciso**.
Narcia	see **Narciso**.
Narcial	see **Marcial**.
Narciana	see **Marciana**.
Narcio	see **Marcia**.
Narcio	see **Nazario**.
Narciro	see **Nazario**.
Narcisco	see **Narciso**.
Narcisna	see **Narciso**.

Narciso (Nar see' so) m. EE:
Narcisse, Narcissus. Gk. "To put
to sleep." In myth., youth enam-
ored of own image. 7 x in DS. 1,
3rd cen. bishop of Gerona,
Spain. F. 3/18. **Dim:** Chicho,
Chico, Machito, Nacho, Narcito,
Nareo, Nario, Narissa, Narsi,
Nasio. **Var:** Marciso, Narcesia,
Narceso, Narcessa, Narcia,
Narcisco, Narcisna, Narcisso,
Narcisza, Narcizo, Narjcisa,
Narsirio, Narsisia, Narsiso,
Narsisum, Narsizo, Narziso,
Narzissa, Narziza, Nasaico,
Nascico, Nasisco, Norcissi,
Norcisso.

Narcisso	see **Narciso**.
Narcisza	see **Narciso**.
Narcito	see **Narciso**.
Narcizo	see **Narciso**.
Nardo	see **Bernal**.

Nareda (Nah ray' dah) f. In Indian
myth., Brahma's son dextrous in
art & arms.

Nareo	see **Narciso**.
Nario	see **Narciso**.
Narissa	see **Narciso**.
Narizo	see **Nazario**.
Narjcisa	see **Narciso**.
Narmo	see **Narno**.

Narno (Nar' no) m. EE: Narnius,
Narnus. Lat. "Born in Narnia,
Italy." 2 x in DS. 1, 1st cen.
bishop of Bergamo, Italy. F.
8/27. **Var:** Narmo.

Narsi	see **Narciso**.
Narsirio	see **Narciso**.
Narsisia	see **Narciso**.
Narsiso	see **Narciso**.
Narsisum	see **Narciso**.
Narsizo	see **Narciso**.
Narziso	see **Narciso**.
Narzissa	see **Narciso**.

Narziza   see **Narciso.**
Nas   see **Ignacio.**
Nasaico   see **Narciso.**
Nasareno   see **Nazario.**
Nasareo   see **Nazario.**
Nasario   see **Nazario.**
Nasarrio   see **Nazario.**
Nasavio   see **Nazario.**
Nascico   see **Narciso.**
Nasio   see **Narciso.**
Nasisco   see **Narciso.**
Nassario   see **Nazario.**
Natacho   see **Natalio.**
Natalina   see **Natalio.**
Natalio (Nah tah' lee oh) m. **EE:**
Natalia, Natalie, Nettie. Lat.
"Birthday," Christ's birthday.
F. 12/25. 7 x in DS. 1, succored
husband & 23 fellow prisoners
for 7 days. F. 9/8. **Dim:** Lena,
Lina, Natacho, Nati, Nato, Naty,
Tacho, Talia, Talino, Vivita.
Var: Matalia, Natalina, Natelio,
Nathalia, Natolio. See also
Natividad, Noel.
Natán   see **Nataniel.**
Natanael   see **Nataniel.**
Nataniel (Nah tahn yell') m. **EE:**
Nathan, Nathaniel, etc. Heb.
"Gift of God." Biblical prophet
who rebuked David because of
Bathsheba. 2 x in DS. **Var:**
Natán, Natanael, Nathenail,
Natilio, Natilla.
Natebadad   see **Natividad.**
Natelio   see **Natalio.**
Natevidad   see **Natividad.**
Nathalia   see **Natalio.**
Nathenail   see **Nataniel.**
Nati   see **Natalio.**
Nati   see **Natividad.**
Natibidá   see **Natividad.**
Natibidad   see **Natividad.**
Naticidad   see **Natividad.**
Natidad   see **Natividad.**
Natilio   see **Nataniel.**
Natilla   see **Nataniel.**
Natinidad   see **Natividad.**
Nativadad   see **Natividad.**
Nativado   see **Natividad.**
Natividad   see **Natividad.**
Nativiadad   see **Natividad.**
Natividá   see **Natividad.**
Natividad (Nah tee bee dahd') mf.
Lat. "Birth." Birth of V. Mary.
F. 9/8. **Dim:** Nati. **Var:** Nacido,
Nadividada, Natebadad,
Natevidad, Natibidá, Natibidad,
Naticidad, Natidad, Natinidad,
Nativadad, Nativado, Nativedad,
Nativiadad, Natividá, Natividao,
Natividat, Natividod, Natività,
Nativitas, Nativitat,
Nativitatas, Nativitate, Nativo,
Navidá, Navidad, Navitidad,
Netividad, Nitividad. See also
Natalio, Noel.
Natividao   see **Natividad.**
Natividat   see **Natividad.**
Natividod   see **Natividad.**
Natività   see **Natividad.**
Nativitas   see **Natividad.**
Nativitat   see **Natividad.**
Nativitatas   see **Natividad.**
Nativitate   see **Natividad.**

Nativo   see **Natividad.**
Nato   see **Natalio.**
Natolio   see **Natalio.**
Natonio   see **Antonio.**
Naturio (Nah too' ree oh) m. Sp.
"Native." Possibly variant of
Natalio or Natividad (see both).
Naty   see **Natalio.**
Navidá   see **Natividad.**
Navidad   see **Natividad.**
Navitidad   see **Natividad.**
Navor   see **Nabor.**
Navora   see **Nabor.**
Navorra   see **Nabor.**
Nayito   see **Leonardo.**
Nayo   see **Bernal.**
Nayo   see **Leonardo.**
Nazaia   see **Nazario.**
Nazano   see **Nazario.**
Nazareo   see **Nazario.**
Nazari   see **Nazario.**
Nazariam   see **Nazario.**
Nazario (Nah zah' ree oh) m. **EE:**
Nazarius. Heb. "Offshoot." Could
also mean "consecrated to God."
9 x in DS. 1, Roman of 1st cen.,
preached & was beheaded. F.
7/28. **Dim:** Nazarita, Nazor. **Var:**
Masario, Mazario, Nacerio,
Narasio, Narassa, Narcio,
Narciro, Narizo, Nasareno,
Nasareo, Nasario, Nasarrio,
Nasavio, Nassario, Nazaia,
Nazano, Nazareo, Nazari,
Nazariam, Nazarius, Nazaro,
Nazarro, Nazoria, Nesario,
Nozarea, Nozario.
Nazarita   see **Nazario.**
Nazarius   see **Nazario.**
Nazaro   see **Nazario.**
Nazarro   see **Nazario.**
Nazimovo (Nah zee mo' bo) m.
Nazimova was 19th-20th cen.
Russian actress famous for Ibsen
roles. **Var:** Nizmova.
Nazor   see **Nazario.**
Nazoria   see **Nazario.**
Nea   see **Irene.**
Neapoleón   see **Napoleón.**
Neaves   see **Nieves.**
Necanor   see **Nicanor.**
Necario   see **Nectario.**
Necasio   see **Nicasio.**
Neches   see **Inés.**
Nechi   see **Inés.**
Nechin   see **Inés.**
Necho   see **Andrés.**
Necho   see **Ernesto.**
Necho   see **Inés.**
Necífaro   see **Nicéforo.**
Neco   see **René.**
Necolás   see **Nicolás.**
Necolasa   see **Nicolás.**
Necolousa   see **Nicolás.**
Necomedes   see **Nicomedes.**
Necomedez   see **Nicomedes.**
Necosio   see **Nicasio.**
Nectario (Nake tah' ree oh) m. **EE:**
Nectarius. Gk. "Relating to
nectar." 8 x in DS. 1, 1st
Patriarch of Constantinople in
4th cen. F. 10/11. **Var:** Necario.
Necuesia   see **Nicasio.**
Nefie   see **Neftalí.**
Neftal   see **Neftalí.**

Neftalí (Nafe tah lee') m. EE:
Naphtali. Heb. "God will aid me
in my struggle." Son of Jacob &
Bilhah & founder of 1 of 12
tribes of Israel. **Dim:** Nefie,
Nepo. **Var:** Neftal, Nephtalí,
Nephtalie, Neptaly.

Nehemías (Nay aay mee' ahs) m. EE:
Nehemiah. Heb. "Consoled by
God." In Bible considered with
Ezra to be restorer of his
people.

Neives	see **Nieves.**
Nelas	see **Melas.**
Nelaz	see **Melas.**
Nelba	see **Melba.**
Nelda	see **Reinaldo.**
Nelde	see **Reinaldo.**
Neldina	see **Reinaldo.**
Nelecio	see **Melesio.**

Neleno (Nay lay' no) m. In Gk.
myth. Neleo, son of Neptune.

Nelesio	see **Melesio.**
Neli	see **Manuel.**
Nelia	see **Manuel.**
Nélida	see **Elena.**
Nélida	see **Leonor.**
Nélida	see **Reinaldo.**
Nelly	see **Elena.**
Nelo	see **Cornelio.**
Nelo	see **Daniel.**
Nelo	see **Manuel.**
Nelta	see **Reinaldo.**
Nelva	see **Melba.**
Nemansio	see **Nemesio.**

Nemario (Nay mah' ree oh) m. Lat.
"Nemorio," "he who lives in
forest." F. 9/7.

Nemasio	see **Nemesio.**
Nemecino	see **Nemesio.**
Nemecio	see **Nemesio.**
Nemecsio	see **Nemesio.**
Nemencio	see **Nemesio.**
Nementia	see **Nemesio.**
Nemerco	see **Nemesio.**
Nemescio	see **Nemesio.**
Nemesino	see **Nemesio.**

Nemesio (Nay may' see oh) m. EE:
Nemesius. Gk. "He who gives
justice fairly." 11 x in DS. 1,
mart. in 3rd cen for faith. F.
12/19. **Dim:** Mecho. **Var:** Demecio,
Demesio, Emesias, Enemacia,
Enemancio, Enemario, Enemartius,
Enemcencio, Enemecio, Enememcio,
Enemencio, Enemención, Enemenia,
Enemensio, Enemenso, Enementio,
Enemenzia, Enemesis, Enemica,
Enemica, Enemincio, Enemisio,
Enemorio, Enemsio, Enenencia,
Enenesio, Hemecia, Henemencio,
Henemensio, Namesio, Nanesio,
Nemansio, Nemasio, Nemecino,
Nemecio, Nemecsio, Nemencio,
Nementia, Nemerco, Nemescio,
Nemesian, Nemesino, Nemesmo,
Nemessio, Nemiso, Nencencio,
Nencesio, Nenesio, Neniesia,
Nenmesio, Nermesio, Nimecia,
Nomecio, Nomosio.

Nemesmo	see **Nemesio.**
Nemessio	see **Nemesio.**
Nemiso	see **Nemesio.**
Nemoiro	see **Nemorio.**

Nemoreo	see **Nemorio.**

Nemorio (Nay mo' ree oh) m. EE:
Nemorius. Lat. "He who lives in
forest." Deacon of Troyes,
France, mart. by Attila the Hun
in 5th cen. F. 9/7. **Var:**
Nemoiro, Nemoreo, Neoriono.

Nena	see **Elena.**
Nena	see **Elisabeth.**
Nena	see **Magdaleno.**
Nencencio	see **Nemesio.**
Nencesio	see **Nemesio.**
Neneca	see **Emma.**
Neneques	see **Manuel.**
Nenesio	see **Nemesio.**
Neniesia	see **Nemesio.**

Nenito (Nay nee' toe) m. Nenia in
Roman myth., goddess of funeral
rites.

Nenmesio	see **Nemesio.**
Nenselada	see **Venceslao.**
Neogdalena	see **Magdaleno.**
Neomi	see **Noemi.**

Neón (Nay own') m. EE: Neon. Gk.
"Young one." 11 x in DS. **Dim:**
Neonila.

Neonila	see **Neón.**
Neoriono	see **Nemorio.**
Nepamuceno	see **Nepomuceno.**
Nephtalí	see **Neftalí.**
Nephtalie	see **Neftalí.**
Nepo	see **Neftalí.**
Nepolito	see **Nepomuceno.**
Nepomasano	see **Nepomuceno.**
Nepomceno	see **Nepomuceno.**
Nepomcina	see **Nepomuceno.**
Nepomenco	see **Nepomuceno.**
Nepomeno	see **Nepomuceno.**
Nepomenteno	see **Nepomuceno.**
Nepomesena	see **Nepomuceno.**
Nepomesenia	see **Nepomuceno.**
Nepomesina	see **Nepomuceno.**
Nepomicena	see **Nepomuceno.**
Nepomiseno	see **Nepomuceno.**
Nepomocene	see **Nepomuceno.**
Nepomose	see **Nepomuceno.**
Nepomoseno	see **Nepomuceno.**
Nepomosino	see **Nepomuceno.**
Nepomucanio	see **Nepomuceno.**
Nepomucenae	see **Nepomuceno.**
Nepomucene	see **Nepomuceno.**

Nepomuceno (Nay poe moo say' no)
m. EE: Nepomucene. Slav. "He who
gives his aid." John Nepomucene
of 14th cen. Bohemia mart. for
refusal to violate seal of con-
fession. F. 5/16. **Dim:** Cheno.
Var: Epimoseno, Epomosena,
Epomuceno, Eponunceno,
Napomesena, Naponceno,
Nepamuceno, Nepolito,
Nepomasano, Nepomceno,
Nepomcina, Nepomenco, Nepomeno,
Nepomenteno, Nepomesena,
Nepomesenia, Nepomesina,
Nepomicena, Nepomiseno,
Nepomocene, Nepomose,
Nepomoseno, Nepomosino,
Nepomucanio, Nepomucenae,
Nepomucene, Nepomueno,
Nepomunceno, Nepomunciano,
Nepomuncio, Nepomuseena,
Nepomuseno, Neponuceno,
Neposemo, Neposeno, Nepumeceno,
Nepumenseno, Nepumuceno,

Nepunuceno, Npeomunencio,
Pamosena, Pomacena, Pomesana,
Pomoseno, Pomuceno, Pumesano.
Nepomueno   see **Nepomuceno.**
Nepomunceno   see **Nepomuceno.**
Nepomunciano see **Nepomuceno.**
Nepomuncio   see **Nepomuceno.**
Nepomuseena   see **Nepomuceno.**
Nepomuseno   see **Nepomuceno.**
Neponuceno   see **Nepomuceno.**
Neposemo   see **Nepomuceno.**
Neposeno   see **Nepomuceno.**
Nepote (Nay poe' tay) m. EE:
  Nepos. Lat. "Grandsons." 1 x in
  DS. F. 6/3.
Neptaly   see **Neftalí.**
Nepumeceno   see **Nepomuceno.**
Nepumenseno   see **Nepomuceno.**
Nepumuceno   see **Nepomuceno.**
Nepunuceno   see **Nepomuceno.**
Nerberto   see **Norberto.**
Nereida (Nay ray' dah) f. Gk.
  "Daughter of Nereus." Gk. sea
  god, **Var:** Mereida, Nereyda,
  Nerin, Nireida.
Néreo (Nay' ray oh) m. EE: Nereus.
  Gk. "He who swims in ocean." Gk.
  god of Aegean Sea & father of
  Nereids. 3 x in DS. 1, Roman M.
  F. 5/12. **Var:** Nerero, Nerio.
Nerero   see **Nereo.**
Nereyda   see **Nereida.**
Neri (Nay' ree) m. Ital.
  "Negroes." St. Philip Neri lived
  in 16th cen. Italy & founded
  Congregation of the Oratory. F.
  5/26.
Nerín   see **Nereida.**
Nerio   see **Nereo.**
Nermesio   see **Nemesio.**
Nerón (Nay roan') m. EE: Nero.
  Sabine, "Strong, daring." Cruel
  Roman emperor of 1st cen.
Nersa (Nair' sah) f. Nersas was
  Pers. S. of 4th cen.
Nerverto   see **Norberto.**
Nesario   see **Nazario.**
Nesfora   see **Nicéforo.**
Nesho   see **Andrés.**
Nesta   see **Néstor.**
Nestacio   see **Anastacio.**
Nestara   see **Néstor.**
Nester   see **Néstor.**
Nestera   see **Néstor.**
Nestereo   see **Néstor.**
Nesterio   see **Néstor.**
Néstor (Nace' tore) m. EE: Nestor.
  Gk. "He remembers." In Trojan
  War a counselor because of age.
  Nestorius, Patriarch of Constan-
  tinople & expounder of doctrine
  regarding dual nature of Christ.
  Var: Anestor, Enester, Mestora,
  Nesta, Nestara, Nester, Nestera,
  Nestereo, Nesterio, Nestore,
  Nestorio, Nestorite, Nestoro,
  Nestro, Nistor.
Nestore   see **Néstor.**
Nestorio   see **Néstor.**
Nestorite   see **Néstor.**
Nestoro   see **Néstor.**
Nestova (Nace toe' bah) f. Could
  be form of Nestabus, mart. in
  Gaza in 4th cen.
Nestro   see **Néstor.**

Neta   see **Estela.**
Neteo (Nay tay' oh) m. Sp. "Neto,"
  from Lat. "nitidus" means "clean
  & pure."
Netividad   see **Natividad.**
Nevara (Nay bah' rah) f. Sp.
  "Nevar," "to snow." Indicates
  purity.
Nevio (Nay' bee oh) m. EE: Nevius.
  Naevius, Roman family with fa-
  mous dramatic & epic poet of 3rd
  cen. **Var:** Nevolana, Nevolena,
  Nevolona.
Nevolana   see **Nevio.**
Nevolena   see **Nevio.**
Nevolona   see **Nevio.**
Nex   see **Inés.**
Nianor   see **Nicanor.**
Nibaldo   see **Sinibaldo.**
Nibia   see **Isabel.**
Nibor   see **Nabor.**
Nica   see **Nicasio.**
Nica   see **Nicolás.**
Nicacio   see **Nicasio.**
Nicaela   see **Miguel.**
Nicalás   see **Nicolás.**
Nicalasa   see **Nicolás.**
Nicalosa   see **Nicolás.**
Nicalous   see **Nicolás.**
Nicaloza   see **Nicolás.**
Nicamor   see **Nicanor.**
Nicamora   see **Nicanor.**
Nicanar   see **Nicanor.**
Nicanara   see **Nicanor.**
Nicandreo   see **Nicandro.**
Nicandro (Nee cahn' dro) m. EE:
  Nicander. Gk. "Victory." 9 x in
  DS. 1, 3rd cen. Egyp. physician,
  mart. for comforting Christians.
  F. 3/15. **Var:** Nicandreo,
  Nicanon.
Nicanna   see **Nicanor.**
Nicanon   see **Nicandro.**
Nicanor (Nee cah nore') m. EE:
  Nicanor. Gk. "Victorius conquer-
  or." Biblical personage selected
  to surpress Judean revolt. In
  DS, 1 of 7 deacons of Jerusalem
  church. E. 1/10. **Dim:** Nicar,
  Nicara, Nico. **Var:** Necanor,
  Nianor, Nicamor, Nicamora,
  Nicanar, Nicanara, Nicanna,
  Nicanore, Nicanoria, Nicanoro,
  Nicanos, Nicanova, Nicanro,
  Nicanura, Nicarcio, Nicarcon,
  Nicardies, Nicareno, Nicario,
  Nicarno, Nicarnor, Nicarnora,
  Nicaurora, Nicavar, Nicenora,
  Nichanor, Nicnor, Nicomor,
  Niconara, Niconer, Niconom,
  Niconor, Nicora, Nicornora,
  Nicosnor, Nikanor, Nocanora.
Nicanore   see **Nicanor.**
Nicanoria   see **Nicanor.**
Nicanoro   see **Nicanor.**
Nicanos   see **Nicanor.**
Nicanova   see **Nicanor.**
Nicanro   see **Nicanor.**
Nicanura   see **Nicanor.**
Nicar   see **Nicanor.**
Nicara   see **Nicanor.**
Nicarcio   see **Nicanor.**
Nicarcon   see **Nicanor.**
Nicardies   see **Nicanor.**
Nicareno   see **Nicanor.**

Nicario   see **Nicanor.**
Nicarno   see **Nicanor.**
Nicarnor   see **Nicanor.**
Nicarnora   see **Nicanor.**
Nicasio (Nee cah' see oh) m. EE:
Nicasius. Gk. "Conqueror." 7 x
in DS. 1, 1st Archbishop of
Rheims, France. Killed by Van-
dals in 5th cen. F. 12/14. **Dim:**
Nica. **Var:** Enicasio, Micasio,
Necasio, Necosio, Necuesia,
Nicacio, Nicasor.
Nicasor   see **Nicasio.**
Nicaurora   see **Nicanor.**
Nicavar   see **Nicanor.**
Nicéforo (Nee say' foe roe) m. EE:
Nicephorus, Gk. "He who brings
victory." 22 x in DS. 1, Patri-
arch of Constantinople in 8th
cen. F. 3/13. **Var:** Necífaro,
Nésfora, Niséforo.
Nicenora   see **Nicanor.**
Nicenta (Nee sane' tah) f. Could
be form of Niceo, "native of
Nicea." **Var:** Nicente.
Nicente   see **Nicenta.**
Nicerata (Nee say rah' tah) f. EE:
Niceras. Gk. "Loved for victo-
ry." Devout woman of 5th cen.
Constantinople known for good
works. F. 12/27.
Nicetas   see **Niseto.**
Niceto   see **Niseto.**
Nichanor   see **Nicanor.**
Niche   see **Inés.**
Nicho   see **Dionisio.**
Nicholosa   see **Nicolás.**
Nicki   see **Nicolás.**
Nickolás   see **Nicolás.**
Nickolasa   see **Nicolás.**
Niclolazza   see **Nicolás.**
Niclosa   see **Nicolás.**
Nicnor   see **Nicanor.**
Nicodemus (Nee co day' moose) m.
EE: Nick, Nicodemus. Gk. "Con-
queror of people." In Bible,
member of Sanhedrin who helped
bury Christ. 10 x in DS. **Var:**
Nicudemos, Nikodimas.
Nicola   see **Nicolás.**
Nicolao   see **Nicolás.**
Nicolara   see **Nicolás.**
Nicolás (Nee co loss') m. EE:
Claus, Nicholas, Nick. Gk. "He
who carries his people to victo-
ry." 49 x in DS. Most popular,
4th cen. bishop of Myra, Turkey.
F. 12/6. **Dim:** Cola, Colacho,
Colás, Coleta, Culacho, Culasa,
Culaza, Culose, Culsa, Culusa,
Lacho, Nica, Nicki, Nicotes,
Nico. **Var:** Necolás, Necolasa,
Necolousa, Nicalás, Nicalasa,
Nicalosa, Nicalous, Nicaloza,
Nicholosa, Nickolás, Nickolasa,
Niclolazza, Niclosa, Nicola,
Nicolao, Nicolara, Nicolase,
Nicolaso, Nicolassa, Nicolata,
Nicolaum, Nicolaz, Nicolaza,
Nicolio, Nicolona, Nicolós,
Nicolosa, Nicoloza, Nicolum,
Nicotasa, Nikolás, Nikolaus,
Nocolás, Nocolasa, Nocolaza. See
also Coleta.
Nicolase   see **Nicolás.**

Nicolaso   see **Nicolás.**
Nicolassa   see **Nicolás.**
Nicolata   see **Nicolás.**
Nicolaum   see **Nicolás.**
Nicolaz   see **Nicolás.**
Nicolaza   see **Nicolás.**
Nicolio   see **Nicolás.**
Nicolona   see **Nicolás.**
Nicolós   see **Nicolás.**
Nicolosa   see **Nicolás.**
Nicoloza   see **Nicolás.**
Nicolum   see **Nicolás.**
Nicomede   see **Nicomedes.**
Nicomedeo   see **Nicomedes.**
Nicomedes (Nee co may' days) m.
EE: Nicomedia, etc. Gk. "He who
prepares well his victories."
Nicomedia, Asia Minor city where
Hannibal died. 13 x in DS. 1,
Roman priest, beaten with leaden
whips. F. 9/15. **Dim:** Niconia,
Nico. **Var:** Necomedes, Necomedez,
Nicomede, Nicomedeo, Nicomedis,
Nicomedo, Nicomedum, Niconedes,
Niconiedes, Nocomedo.
Nicomedis   see **Nicomedes.**
Nicomedo   see **Nicomedes.**
Nicomedum   see **Nicomedes.**
Nicomor   see **Nicanor.**
Niconara   see **Nicanor.**
Niconedes   see **Nicomedes.**
Niconer   see **Nicanor.**
Niconia   see **Nicomedes.**
Niconiedes   see **Nicomedes.**
Niconom   see **Nicanor.**
Niconor   see **Nicanor.**
Nicora   see **Nicanor.**
Nicornora   see **Nicanor.**
Nicosnor   see **Nicanor.**
Nicotasa   see **Nicolás.**
Nicotes   see **Nicolás.**
Nicudemos   see **Nicodemus.**
Nidala (Nee dah' lah) f. "Nidal,"
"place of shelter."
Nidia (Nee dee ah) f. EE: Nydia.
Blind girl who saved Glaucus in
Bulwer Lytton's "Last Days of
Pompeii." **Var:** Nidya, Nydia.
Nidya   see **Nidia.**
Niebes   see **Nieves.**
Nievas   see **Nieves.**
Nieve   see **Nieves.**
Nieves (Nee aay' bays) f. Lat.
Nivis, "snow." Title of V.
Mary, Nuestra Señora de las
Nieves (Our Lady of Snows).
Miracle in Rome of unmelted snow
in heat. **Var:** Neaves, Neives,
Niebes, Nievas, Nieve, Nievez,
Nievis, Nives.
Nievez   see **Nieves.**
Nievis   see **Nieves.**
Nifa   see **Ninfa.**
Niginio   see **Higinio.**
Nigorio (Nee go' ree oh) m.
Nigoro, S. mart. in Italy.
Nikanor   see **Nicanor.**
Nikodimas   see **Nicodemus.**
Nikolás   see **Nicolás.**
Nikolaus   see **Nicolás.**
Nilda   see **Benilde.**
Nilda   see **Reinaldo.**
Nildo   see **Leonildes.**
Nilo   see **Daniel.**
Nimecia   see **Nemesio.**

Nimfa	see **Ninfa.**
Nimpha	see **Ninfa.**
Nina	see **Angel.**
Nina	see **Benigno.**
Nina	see **Celina.**
Nina	see **Cristián.**
Nina	see **Guillermo.**
Nina	see **Herminio.**
Nina	see **María.**
Ninerva	see **Minerva.**

Ninfa (Neen' fah) f. EE: Nympha, Nymphas. Gk. "Youth." In Gk. myth. nymphs, associated with natural objects, divinities most like humans. St. Nympha of 4th cen Palermo fled invasion of Goths. F. 11/10. **Var:** Minfa, Nifa, Nimfa, Nimpha, Ninja, Ninpha, Ninphae, Nipha, Nymfa, Nympha, Nynfa.

Nini	see **Herminio.**
Ninja	see **Ninfa.**
Nino	see **Antonio.**
Nino	see **Bernal.**
Nino	see **Saturnino.**

Nino (Nee' no) m. EE: Nino. Chaldaic, "Owner of his palaces." 1 x in DS, Healer from Cappadocia. F. 1/14.

Ninpha	see **Ninfa.**
Ninphae	see **Ninfa.**
Nipha	see **Ninfa.**
Nireida	see **Nereida.**

Niria (Nee' ree ah) f. Nireo, king of Naxos. Most handsome Gk. at Troy after Achilles.

Niséforo	see **Nicéforo.**

Niseto (Nee say' toe) m. EE: Nicetas, etc. Gk. "Victory." 26 x in DS. 1, sent to seduce St. Christopher, was converted. F. 7/24. **Var:** Nicetas, Niceto.

Nistor	see **Néstor.**
Nita	see **Ana.**
Nita	see **María.**

Nitardo (Nee tar' doe) m. EE: Nithard. Teut. "Firm & valiant." Scan. S. killed by pagans for denouncing Thor & Odin. F. 2/3. **Var:** Nitordana.

Nitividad	see **Natividad.**
Nito	see **Benito.**
Nito	see **Juan.**
Nitordana	see **Nitardo.**
Nives	see **Nieves.**
Nivia	see **Isabel.**
Nizmova	see **Nazimovo.**
Noamy	see **Noemí.**
Nobar	see **Nabor.**
Nober	see **Nabor.**
Noberto	see **Norberto.**
Nobor	see **Nabor.**
Noca	see **Oscar.**
Nocanora	see **Nicanor.**
Nocencio	see **Inocencio.**
Nocolás	see **Nicolás.**
Nocolasa	see **Nicolás.**
Nocolaza	see **Nicolás.**
Nocomedo	see **Nicomedes.**

Noé (No ay') m. EE: Noah, Noey. Heb. "Rest." Long-lived ark builder & descendant of Adam & Eve's son Seth. **Var:** Noha, Nohé.

Noehmí	see **Noemí.**

Noel (No ell') m. EE: Newell, Noel, Nowell. Lat. "Natal." Christ's birth. **Var:** Noelia, Noelin. See also Natalio, Natividad.

Noelia	see **Noel.**
Noelin	see **Noel.**
Noemá	see **Noemí.**
Noemé	see **Noemí.**

Noemí (No mee') f. EE: Naomi, Noami. Heb. "Pleasant." In Bible, wife of Elimelech & Ruth's mother-in-law. **Dim:** Mimi, Numa. **Var:** Enoemá, Naiomá, Naiomí, Naomí, Neomí, Noamy, Noehmí, Noemá, Noemé, Noemie, Noemy, Nohemí.

Noemie	see **Noemí.**
Noemy	see **Noemí.**
Nofri	see **Onofre.**
Noha	see **Noé.**
Nohé	see **Noé.**
Nohemí	see **Noemí.**
Nol	see **Leonor.**
Nola	see **Leonor.**

Nolasco (No loss' co) m. St. Peter Nolasco of 13th cen. founded Mercedarians who pledged themselves as hostage to free Christians. F. 1/31.

Nolbertha	see **Norberto.**
Nolberto	see **Norberto.**
Noliverto	see **Norberto.**
Nolverta	see **Norberto.**
Nomecio	see **Nemesio.**
Nomobono	see **Hombono.**
Nomosio	see **Nemesio.**
Nona	see **Abdón.**
Nonato	see **Nono.**
Nono	see **Jerónimo.**
Nono	see **Leonor.**

Nono (No' no) m. EE: Nonnosus, Nonnus. Lat. "Ninth." 5th cen. Syrian bishop who converted actress & dancer Pelagia. F. 12/2. **Dim:** Nonato, Nunila. **Var:** Nunio, Nunis.

Nonor	see **Leonor.**
Nony	see **Eleonor.**
Nora	see **Eleonor.**
Nora	see **Leonor.**
Noraida	see **Zoraida.**
Norbertha	see **Norberto.**

Norberto (Nor bare' toe) m. EE: Bert, Norbert. Teut. "Splendor of North." 12th cen. bishop of Magdeburg & founder of order blending contemplative & active life. F. 6/6. **Dim:** Beto. **Var:** Naberta, Narberta, Nerberto, Nerverto, Noberto, Nolbertha, Nolberto, Noliverto, Nolverta, Norbertha, Norbeto, Norvento, Norverto, Norveto, Nosberta.

Norbeto	see **Norberto.**
Norcissi	see **Narciso.**
Norcisso	see **Narciso.**
Norita	see **Leonor.**

Nortina (Nor tee' nah) f. Nortia, Etruscan goddess of destiny.

Norvento	see **Norberto.**
Norverto	see **Norberto.**
Norveto	see **Norberto.**
Nosberta	see **Norberto.**
Nosha	see **Leonor.**
Novata	see **Novatus.**

Novatus (No bah' toose) m. **EE:**
Novatus. Lat. "New." 2 x in DS.
1, rich Roman layperson, gave
wealth to charity. F. 6/20. **Var:**
Novata.

Novor	see **Nabor.**
Noy	see **Leonor.**
Noya	see **Leonor.**
Nozarea	see **Nazario.**
Nozario	see **Nazario.**
Npeomunencio	see **Nepomuceno.**
Nuela	see **Emma.**
Nuflo	see **Arnulfo.**
Numa	see **Noemi.**
Numerva	see **Minerva.**
Nunciano	see **Nuncio.**
Nuncio	see **Anunciación.**

Nuncio (Noon' see oh) m. Lat. "He
who brings message." **Var:**

Nunciano, Nunzio. See also
Anunciación.

Nunila	see **Nono.**
Nunio	see **Nono.**
Nunis	see **Nono.**
Nunzio	see **Nuncio.**
Nuri	see **Nuria.**

Nuria (Noo' ree ah) f. 11th cen
Catalan shrine, Our Lady of
Nuria. **Dim:** Nuri.

Nydia	see **Nidia.**
Nymfa	see **Ninfa.**
Nympha	see **Ninfa.**
Nynfa	see **Ninfa.**
Nico	see **Antonio.**
Nico	see **Nicanor.**
Nico	see **Nicolás.**
Nico	see **Nicomedes.**
Nungo	see **Manuel.**

O

| Oalo | see **Paulo.** |

Obdulio (Obe doo' lee oh) m. **EE:**
Abdullah. Lat. "He who lessens
pains & sorrows." Obdulia, V. of
Toledo, Spain. **Dim:** Lula. **Var:**
Odulia.

Obed (Oh bade') m. **EE:** Obed. Heb.
"Server, worshipper." In Bible
as son of Boaz & Ruth & ancestor
of Christ. **Var:** Obedalia,
Obelia.

Obedalia	see **Obed.**
Obelia	see **Obed.**
Obelino	see **Abelino.**
Oberino	see **Oberón.**

Oberón (Oh bay roan') m. In myth.,
fairy king & husband of Titania.
Both in Shakespeare's "A Mid-
summer Night's Dream." **Dim:**
Oberino.

Oberto (Oh bare' toe) m. **EE:**
Obert. Ger. "Property, wealth."
2 x in DS. 1, patron of Scotland. F. 12/11. **Var:** Loberto.

| Obidio | see **Ovidio.** |
| Obigilio | see **Ovidio.** |

Obispo (Oh bees' poe) m. Lat.
"Episcopus," "bishop." Head of
diocese in Catholic hierarchy.
Used as component in compound
1st name such as St. Luis
Obispo.

| Obita | see **Ovidio.** |

Oblado (Oh blah' doe) m. Lat.
"Offering, gift." Person who
lives in monastic state & gives
wealth to community.

Obraulio	see **Braulia.**
Obravlio	see **Braulia.**
Ocadia	see **Arcadio.**
Ocevia	see **Eusebio.**
Ocha	see **Rosa.**
Ochaviano	see **Octavio.**
Oclides	see **Euclides.**
Ocsilia	see **Auxilio.**
Octabia	see **Octavio.**
Octabiano	see **Octavio.**
Octabina	see **Octavio.**

Octagracio	see **Altagracia.**
Octairano	see **Octavio.**
Octano	see **Octavio.**
Octar	see **Octavio.**
Octariano	see **Octavio.**
Octarriano	see **Octavio.**
Octaviacia	see **Octavio.**
Octavianno	see **Octavio.**
Octaviano	see **Octavio.**
Octaviario	see **Octavio.**
Octavino	see **Octavio.**

Octavio (Oak tah' bee oh) m. **EE:**
Octavian, Octavius. Lat.
"Eight." 12 x in DS. 1, 5th cen.
African, led solitary life in
elm tree. F. 9/2. **Dim:** Taviano
(Octaviano), Tavio, Tavito,
Tavo. **Var:** Actaniano, Actaviano,
Actavio, Attaviani, Ectavio,
Eotavio, Ochaviano, Octabia,
Octabiano, Octabina, Octairano,
Octano, Octar, Octariano,
Octarriano, Octaviacia,
Octaviano, Octaviano,
Octaviario, Octavino, Octavión,
Octiana, Octimio, Octovano,
Octoveono, Octoviana, Octovio,
Otabia, Otabiano, Otaviano,
Otavio, Otaviono, Otavita,
Ottava, Ottavian, Ottaviana,
Ottaviani.

Octavión	see **Octavio.**
Octiana	see **Octavio.**
Octimio	see **Octavio.**
Octovano	see **Octavio.**
Octoveono	see **Octavio.**
Octoviana	see **Octavio.**
Octovio	see **Octavio.**
Odalia	see **Odilia.**

Odana (Oh dah' nah) f. Could be
form of Oda, 3 Ss. of Christian
calendar.

Odela	see **Odilia.**
Odelaida	see **Adelaido.**
Odelea	see **Odilia.**
Odelfa	see **Adelfo.**
Odelfia	see **Adelfo.**
Odelfina	see **Adelfo.**

Odelia	see **Odilia**.
Odelina	see **Adela**.
Odella	see **Odilia**.
Odelmirra	see **Edelmira**.
Odelón	see **Odilia**.

Odessa (Oh day' sah) f. **EE:**
Odessa. Gk. "Of 'The Odyssey.'"
Ukrainian city founded in 18th
cen. **Var:** Odiseo. See also
Ulises.

Odilán	see **Odilia**.

Odilia (Oh dee' lee ah) f. **EE:**
Odile, Ottilie, etc. Teut.
"Owner of many riches." 5 x in
DS. 1, 7th cen. patroness of
Alsace. F. 12/13. **Dim:** Tila,
Tilde, Tilla. **Var:** Eodelia,
Eudalia, Eudehia, Eudelio,
Eudella, Eudlia, Eudolia,
Euedelia, Euidelia, Hortilia,
Hudelia, Judelia, Ludelia,
Ludila, Odalia, Odea, Odelea,
Odelia, Odella, Odelón, Odilán,
Odilón, Odilone, Odolia,
Ortilia, Ortilla, Ortillia,
Ortilo, Ortino, Ortitia, Otelio,
Otelo, Othelia, Othilia,
Otilano, Otilario, Otilda,
Otilea, Otilio, Otillo, Otilo,
Otilono, Ottilia, Ottiliana,
Ottilla, Ottillia, Otyl, Otylia,
Udelia, Udilia, Udilón, Uidalia,
Utilio, Yudel, Yudelia.

Odilón	see **Odilia**.
Odilone	see **Odilia**.
Odimia	see **Eutimia**.
Odiseo	see **Odessa**.
Odolia	see **Odilia**.
Odom	see **Otón**.
Odón	see **Otón**.
Odonel	see **Otón**.
Odosia	see **Teodosio**.
Odulia	see **Obdulio**.
Ofalia	see **Ofelio**.
Ofalinda	see **Orfalinda**.

Ofelio (Oh fay' lee oh) m. **EE:**
Ophelia, etc. Gk. "Serpent."
Also "Endearing one." Character
in Shakespeare's "Hamlet." **Dim:**
Fela, Pela. **Var:** Aeofilo,
Afelio, Aofilia, Aphelia,
Aphilia, Dorfelia, Efelia,
Efilia, Eofelia, Eofilia,
Ephilia, Eufelia, Eufilio,
Euphelia, Ifela, Ofalia, Ofella,
Offelia, Offilia, Ofhelia,
Ofilio, Olfilia, Ophelio,
Ophilio, Orfelio, Orfila,
Orfilia, Orphile, Orphilia,
Ufelia, Ufilia, Uofilo.

Ofella	see **Ofelio**.
Ofemia	see **Eufemia**.
Offelia	see **Ofelio**.
Offilia	see **Ofelio**.
Ofhelia	see **Ofelio**.
Ofilio	see **Ofelio**.
Ofimia	see **Eufemia**.
Ofo	see **Adolfo**.
Ofracia	see **Eufracio**.
Ofrasia	see **Eufracio**.
Ofrecia	see **Eufracio**.
Ofrecino	see **Eufracio**.
Ofrocinia	see **Eufracio**.
Ogahita	see **Agapito**.
Ogapita	see **Agapito**.

Ogarita	see **Agar**.
Oginia	see **Eugenio**.
Ogueda	see **Agata**.
Ohalia	see **Eulalio**.
Ohtón	see **Otón**.
Ojenio	see **Eugenio**.
Olagia	see **Eulalio**.
Olaia	see **Eulalio**.
Olallo	see **Eulalio**.

Olav (Oh lahb') m. **EE:** Olaf, Olav.
Norse, "Ancestral heritage." 2 x
in DS. Both Scan. kings of 10th
& 11th cen. **Var:** Olaviana.

Olaviana	see **Olav**.
Olaya	see **Eulalio**.
Olcario	see **Olegario**.

Olegario (Oh lay gah' ree oh) m.
EE: Ollegarius. Teut. "He who
rules with lance." Bishop of
Barcelona in 12th cen. F. 3/6.
Dim: Olich. **Var:** Alegario,
Alegarius, Algario, Algora,
Aligorio, Elgario, Elogario,
Holegaria, Olcario, Olegasio,
Olejario, Oleyario, Olezario,
Oligario, Oligarrio, Oligerio,
Ulgario.

Olegasio	see **Olegario**.
Olejario	see **Olegario**.

Olentina (Oh laín tee' nah) f. In
myth., Jupiter's son Oleno
turned into rock for annoying
gods.

Olevia	see **Olivo**.
Oleyario	see **Olegario**.
Olezario	see **Olegario**.
Olfilia	see **Ofelio**.

Olga (Ol' gah) f. **EE:** Olga, etc.
Norse, "Peace." 9th cen. Russian
matron who tried to introduce
Christianity into her country.
F. 7/11. **Dim:** Coca, Guita,
Loguita. See also Olivo.

Oliberio	see **Olivo**.
Olibia	see **Olivo**.
Olich	see **Olegario**.
Olicia	see **Alicio**.
Olida	see **Olivo**.
Olidia	see **Olivo**.
Oligario	see **Olegario**.
Oligarrio	see **Olegario**.
Oligerio	see **Olegario**.
Olijio	see **Eulogio**.

Olimpia (Oh leem' pee ah) f. **EE:**
Olympia. Gk. "Heavenly." Olym-
pus, home of Gk. gods. 2 x in
DS. 1, 4th cen. Turkish matron,
gave riches to poor. F. 12/17.
Var: Olimpo.

Olimpo	see **Olimpia**.

Olinda (Oh lean' dah) f. Lat.
"Native of Olinda." Olindo,
lover of Sophronia in Tasso's
"Jerusalem Delivered." **Dim:**
Olindino. **Var:** Olino, Olinto.

Olindino	see **Olinda**.
Olino	see **Olinda**.
Olinto	see **Olinda**.
Olivama	see **Olivo**.
Oliverio	see **Olivo**.
Oliveros	see **Olivo**.
Olivido	see **Ovidio**.
Olivio	see **Olivo**.

Olivo (Oh lee' bo) m. **EE:** Olga,
Olive, Olivia. Lat. "Olives,"

symbol of peace. 5 x in DS. 1, of 10th cen., beheaded for converting Moors to Christianity. F. 6710. **Var:** Alibia, Alivia, Elibaria, Eliberio, Elivara, Elivera, Eliverio, Elivia, Elivo, Eolivia, Holivia, Olevia, Oliberio, Olibia, Olida, Olidia, Olivama, Oliverio, Oliveros, Olivio, Ollibia, Polivario, Tolivia, Ulibia.

Ollibia	see Olivo.
Olo	see Roldán.
Ologio	see Eulogio.
Oloia	see Eulalio.
Oloija	see Eulogio.
Olojio	see Eulogio.
Oloya	see Eulalio.
Olta	see Altagracia.
Olvaro	see Albaro.
Olvido	see Ovidio.
Omada	see Amada.
Omahár	see Omar.
Omaida	see María.

Omar (Oh mar') m. EE: Omar. Ar. "Builder." 2nd Mohammedan caliph. Made Islam an imperial power. **Var:** Omahár, Omaro.

Omaro	see Omar.

Omega (Oh may' gah) f. EE: Omega. Gk. "Large." Largest & last letter of Gk. alphabet.

Omelia	see Onelia.
Omero	see Homero.
Omesindo	see Gumersindo.
Ometerio	see Emeterio.
Omfala	see Onfalia.
Omiterio	see Emeterio.
Onafre	see Onofre.
Onastacio	see Anastacio.
Onastasio	see Anastacio.
Onceforo	see Onésimo.

Ondino (Own dee' no) m. EE: Undina, Undine. Lat. "V. of waves." In Roman myth., water sprite given soul when enamored with mortal.

Ondrés	see Andrés.
Onécimo	see Onésimo.
Onecimón	see Onésimo.
Onécino	see Onésimo.
Onefre	see Onofre.
Onefro	see Onofre.
Onéjimo	see Onésimo.
Onel	see Onelia.

Onelia (Owe nay' le ah) f. Comb. of Onofre & Amelia (see both). **Dim:** Onelino. **Var:** Enoelia, Omelia, Onel, Onelimo, Onilia, Urmelia.

Onelimo	see Onelia.
Onelino	see Onelia.
Onemio	see Onésimo.
Onenimo	see Onésimo.

Onenino (Owe nay nee' no) m. Oneno, S. of Benedictine order.

Onénsimo	see Onésimo.
Onerina	see Honoria.
Onésemo	see Onésimo.
Onesiana	see Onésimo.
Onesim	see Onésimo.
Onésime	see Onésimo.

Onésimo (Owe nay' see mo) m. EE: Onesima, Onesimus. Gk. "That which is useful & advantageous."

8 x in DS. 1, bishop of Ephesus in 1st cen. F. 2/16. **Var:** Anécimo, Anésimo, Anésino, Danésimo, Donécimo, Donésimo, Honésimo, Oncéforo, Onécimo, Onecimón, Onécino, Onéjimo, Onemio, Onenimo, Onénsimo, Onésemo, Onesiana, Onesim, Onésime, Onésimus, Onesindo, Onésine, Onesineo, Onesinio, Onésino, Onesirno, Onesmo, Onéssimo, Onéssimus, Oneximo, Onézimo, Onícimo, Onísimo, Onísino, Onnésimo, Onocéfiro, Unésima, Unice.

Onésimus	see Onésimo.
Onesindo	see Onésimo.
Onésine	see Onésimo.
Onesineo	see Onésimo.
Onesinio	see Onésimo.
Onésino	see Onésimo.
Onesirno	see Onésimo.
Onesmo	see Onésimo.
Onéssimo	see Onésimo.
Onéssimus	see Onésimo.
Onesto	see Honesto.
Oneximo	see Onésimo.
Onézimo	see Onésimo.

Onfalia (Own fah' lee ah) f. Gk. "Woman with beautiful navel." **Var:** Omfala.

Ongelita	see Ángel.
Onícimo	see Onésimo.
Onifre	see Onofre.
Onifrio	see Onofre.
Onilia	see Onelia.
Onísimo	see Onésimo.
Onísino	see Onésimo.
Onita	see Ana.
Onnésimo	see Onésimo.

Onnirénico (Oh nee ray' nee co) m. Sp. "Onírico" means "relating to dreams."

Onocéfiro	see Onésimo.
Onofra	see Onofre.

Onofre (Owe no' fray) m. EE: Humphrey, etc. Teut. "Defender of peace." 5 x in DS. 1, 4th cen, hermit. Patron of weavers. F. 6/12. **Var:** Anofre, Anofrio, Anufre, Hinofrio, Honafre, Humfredo, Hunfredo, Nofri, Onafre, Onefre, Onefro, Onifre, Onifrio, Onofra, Onofreo, Onofri, Onofrio, Onofry, Onofvio, Onophro, Onopre, Onufre, Onufri, Unofre.

Onofreo	see Onofre.
Onofri	see Onofre.
Onofrio	see Onofre.
Onofry	see Onofre.
Onofvio	see Onofre.

Onojiro (Owe no hee' roe) m. Oniros, Gk. god of dreams.

Onophro	see Onofre.
Onopre	see Onofre.
Onora	see Honoria.
Onorato	see Honoria.
Onorio	see Honoria.
Onostisio	see Anastacio.
Onselmo	see Anselmo.
Onufre	see Onofre.
Onufri	see Onofre.
Opalimar	see Apolonio.
Opalinaria	see Apolonio.

Opel (Oh pell') f. **EE:** Opal, Opaline. Lat. "Opal." Jewel believed to bring bad luck to bearer.
Ophelio   see **Ofelio.**
Ophilio   see **Ofelio.**
Opidio   see **Elpidio.**
Opimenio   see **Epigmenio.**
Optaciano (Ope tah see ah' no) m. **EE:** Optatianus. Lat. "Optatus, he who is loved." 8 x in DS. 1, among 18 Mm. of Saragossa in 4th cen. F. 4/16.
Optila   see **Optilia.**
Optilia (Ope tee' lee ah) f. Form of Optatus, 7 Ss. of Christian calendar. **Var:** Optila.
Optimo (Ope' tee mo) m. Lat. "Best." **Var:** Optina.
Optina   see **Optimo.**
Oracio   see **Horacio.**
Oracleto   see **Heráclio.**
Orasio   see **Horacio.**
Oratia   see **Horacio.**
Ordando   see **Roldán.**
Orecencia   see **Orencio.**
Orel   see **Aurelio.**
Orencio (Oh rain' see oh) m. **EE:** Orentius. Gk. "He who examines & judges." 4 x in DS. 1, of 3rd cen., from Huescar, Spain. F. 5/1. **Var:** Dorenz, Orecencia, Orentia, Orescencia, Urento.
Orentia   see **Orencio.**
Orescencia   see **Orencio.**
Orestes (Oh raise' tays) m. **EE:** Euristus, Orestes. Gk. "He who lives in mountains." In Gk. legend, conspired with Electra to avenge their father's murder. 7 x in DS.
Orfa (Ore' fah) f. Heb. "Fawn." Chilion's wife & sister-in-law of Ruth.
Orfalinda (Ore' fah leen' dah) f. Comb. of Orfa & Linda (see both). **Var:** Ofalinda, Orfelina, Urlinda.
Orfelina   see **Orfalinda.**
Orfelio   see **Ofelio.**
Orfila   see **Ofelio.**
Orfilia   see **Ofelio.**
Orfina (Ore fee' nah) f. Comb. of Orfa & Josefina (see both).
Oria   see **Aureo.**
Oriol (Oh ree ol') m. Lat. "Color of gold." Joseph Oriol, celebrated priest of 17th cen. from Barcelona. Noted for extreme austerity. F. 3/23. See also Aura.
Orito   see **Jorge.**
Orlando   see **Roldán.**
Orlo   see **Roldán.**
Orlondo   see **Roldán.**
Ornacleto   see **Anacleto.**
Ornaldo   see **Arnoldo.**
Orocio   see **Orosio.**
Oroncio (Oh roan' see oh) m. **EE:** Orontius. Pers. "Runner." 7 x in DS. 1, patron of Lecce, Italy, invoked for rain. F. 8/26. **Var:** Oronzo.
Oronzo   see **Oroncio.**
Orosio (Oh roe' see oh) m. **EE:**

Eurosia, Orosia, Orsius. Gk. "He who lives on mountain." 2 x in DS. 1, V. of Bayonne, France, mart. by Saracens in 8th cen. F. 6/25. **Var:** Orocio.
Orphile   see **Ofelio.**
Orphilia   see **Ofelio.**
Orqidea   see **Orquidea.**
Orquidea (Or key' day ah) f. Lat. "Orchid." **Var:** Orqidea, Orquides, Orquidia, Orquindia.
Orquides   see **Orquidea.**
Orquidia   see **Orquidea.**
Orquindia   see **Orquidea.**
Orsinia   see **Ursula.**
Orsula   see **Ursula.**
Ortemio   see **Artemio.**
Ortencia   see **Hortencia.**
Ortense   see **Hortencia.**
Ortensia   see **Hortencia.**
Ortensión   see **Hortencia.**
Ortenza   see **Hortencia.**
Ortermio   see **Artemio.**
Ortesia   see **Hortencia.**
Ortilio   see **Odilia.**
Ortilla   see **Odilia.**
Ortillia   see **Odilia.**
Ortilo   see **Odilia.**
Ortimio   see **Artemio.**
Ortino   see **Odilia.**
Ortitia   see **Odilia.**
Orturo   see **Arturo.**
Orvidia   see **Ovidio.**
Osbaldo   see **Osvaldo.**
Osbauldo   see **Osvaldo.**
Osboldo   see **Osvaldo.**
Oscar (Oh scar') m. **EE:** Oscar, Oswald, Ozzie, Ang-Sax. "Power of godliness." Fr. S. helped to evangelize Scan. countries in 10th cen. F. 2/3. **Dim:** Noca. **Var:** Ascar, Ascarus. See also Osvaldo.
Oscensio   see **Asunción.**
Oseas   see **Josué.**
Osevia   see **Eusebio.**
Osias (Oh see' ahs) m. **EE:** Ozias, Uzzias. Heb. "God is my strength." 6 x in OT.
Osiel   see **Oziel.**
Osilio   see **Auxilio.**
Osivaldo   see **Osvaldo.**
Osmar   see **Osmaro.**
Osmaro (Ohs mah' roe) m. Teut. "Shining like glory of God." **Var:** Osmar.
Osmin (Ohs mean') m. **EE:** Osman. Ar. "Tender as a pigeon." Founder of Ottoman Empire. Possibly Osmans, 7th cen. Irish V. walled up to preserve chastity.
Osmundo (Ohs moon' doe) m. **EE:** Osmund, etc. Teut. "Divine protector." Bishop of Salisbury in 11th cen. who established basis for sarum rite in Roman liturgy. F. 12/4. **Var:** Esmondo, Ezmundo.
Ospicio   see **Hospicio.**
Ossea   see **Josué.**
Ossie   see **Osvaldo.**
Ossiliae   see **Auxilio.**
Ostine (Ohs tee' nay) f? Form of Ostianus, S. of 6th cen. France. F. 6/30.
Ostogio   see **Eustorgio.**

Ostrid   see **Astrid.**
Osvaldino   see **Osvaldo.**
Osvaldo (Ohs ball' doe) m. EE:
    Oswald, etc. Teut. "He who gov-
    erns with power of God." 2 x in
    DS. 1, 7th cen. king of North-
    umbria, helped evangelize area.
    F. 8/5. **Dim:** Ossie, Osvaldino.
    Var: Aswaldo, Osbaldo, Osbauldo,
    Osboldo, Osivaldo, Oswaldo,
    Uswaldo. See also Oscar.
Oswaldo   see **Osvaldo.**
Otabia   see **Octavio.**
Otabiano   see **Octavio.**
Otanasio   see **Atanasio.**
Otaviano   see **Octavio.**
Otavio   see **Octavio.**
Otaviono   see **Octavio.**
Otavita   see **Octavio.**
Otelio   see **Odilia.**
Otelo   see **Odilia.**
Otemio   see **Artemio.**
Othelia   see **Odilia.**
Othilia   see **Odilia.**
Othniel   see **Otón.**
Othom   see **Otón.**
Othón   see **Otón.**
Othoniel   see **Otón.**
Otilano   see **Odilia.**
Otilario   see **Odilia.**
Otilda   see **Odilia.**
Otilea   see **Odilia.**
Otilio   see **Odilia.**
Otillo   see **Odilia.**
Otilo   see **Odilia.**
Otilono   see **Odilia.**
Otimio   see **Eutimia.**
Otinio   see **Eutimia.**
Otman (Oat' mahn) m. EE: Osman.
    Ar. "Tender as a pigeon."
Oto   see **Otón.**
Otón (Oh tone') m. EE: Ot,
    Othello, Otto. Teut. "Powerful
    lord." 2 x in DS. 1, bishop of
    Bambers, Germany, noted for
    evangelization of Pommeranians.
    F. 7/2. **Dim:** Ottorino, Tilo.
    Var: Odom, Odón, Odonel, Ohtón,
    Othniel, Othom, Othón, Othoniel,

Oto, Otone, Otoniel, Ottón.
Otone   see **Otón.**
Otoniel   see **Otón.**
Ottava   see **Octavio.**
Ottavian   see **Octavio.**
Ottaviana   see **Octavio.**
Ottaviani   see **Octavio.**
Ottilia   see **Odilia.**
Ottiliana   see **Odilia.**
Ottilla   see **Odilia.**
Ottillia   see **Odilia.**
Ottimia   see **Eutimia.**
Ottón   see **Otón.**
Ottorino   see **Otón.**
Otyl   see **Odilia.**
Otylia   see **Odilia.**
Ouidio   see **Ovidio.**
Ovaldina   see **Ubaldo.**
Ovalia   see **Ovelia.**
Oved   see **Ovidio.**
Oveda   see **Ovidio.**
Ovedio   see **Ovidio.**
Ovelia (Oh bay' lee ah) f. Gk.
    "Happy, bright." **Var:** Availia,
    Lovelia, Ovalia, Ovellia,
    Ubelia, Urbila, Uvelia, Velina,
    Velio, Velita.
Ovellia   see **Ovelia.**
Ovencio   see **Juvencio.**
Ovideo   see **Ovidio.**
Ovidid   see **Ovidio.**
Ovidio (Oh bee' dee oh) m. EE:
    Ovid. Lat. "He who takes care of
    sheep." Famous Lat. poet. Anoth-
    er, bishop of Braga, Portugal.
    F. 6/3. **Dim:** Obita. **Var:** Avideo,
    Bidio, Obidio, Obigilio,
    Olivido, Olvido, Orvidia,
    Ouidio, Oved, Oveda, Ovedio,
    Ovideo, Ovidid, Ovido, Ovidro,
    Ovilio, Ubidio.
Ovido   see **Ovidio.**
Ovidro   see **Ovidio.**
Ovilio   see **Ovidio.**
Oziel (Oh zee ell') m. EE: Oziel,
    Uzziel. Heb. "Might of God." 6 x
    in Bible. **Var:** Osiel, Uzelia,
    Uziel.

P

Pabila   see **Paulo.**
Pabillo   see **Paulo.**
Pabis   see **Paulo.**
Pablana   see **Paulo.**
Pablillo   see **Paulo.**
Pablino   see **Paulo.**
Pablita   see **Paulo.**
Pablo   see **Paulo.**
Pacha   see **Eufracio.**
Pacheco   see **Francisco.**
Pacheco   see **Julio.**
Pachi   see **Patricio.**
Pachico   see **Francisco.**
Pachín   see **Francisco.**
Pacho   see **Bonifacio.**
Pacho   see **Francisco.**
Pachu   see **Francisco.**
Paciano (Pah see ah' no) m. EE:

Pacianus. Lat. Peace." 4th cen.
    Sp. bishop & author of theo-
    logical treatises. F. 3/9.
Paciencia (Pah see en' see ah) f.
    EE: Patience. Lat. "Patience &
    tolerance." **Dim:** Pacis. **Var:**
    Pasencia.
Pacificia   see **Pacífico.**
Pacífico (Pah see' fee co) m. EE:
    Pacificus. Lat. "Pax," "peace."
    One who makes peace, **Dim:** Paco.
    Var: Pacificia, Pasífica.
Pacis   see **Paciencia.**
Paco   see **Francisco.**
Paco   see **Pacífico.**
Paco   see **Pascual.**
Pacomio (Pah co' mee oh) m. EE:
    Pachomius. Lat. "Man of eagle."

4th cen. S. & hermit lived in
Egyp. desert & founded several
monasteries. F. 5/14.

Pactrocinia   see **Patrocinio.**
Pacurro   see **Francisco.**
Padra   see **Patrocinio.**
Padrosinia   see **Patrocinio.**
Pafilio   see **Pánfilo.**
Páfilo   see **Pánfilo.**
Págadiz   see **Práxedes.**
Paidomero   see **Baldomero.**
Paito   see **Francisco.**
Pajito   see **Francisco.**
Pala   see **Paulo.**
Palácido   see **Plácido.**
Palbino   see **Balbina.**
Paldomero   see **Baldomero.**
Palemán   see **Palemón.**
Palemón (Pah lay mone') m. **EE:**
Palaemon. Egyp. S. & hermit. F.
1/11. **Var:** Palemán, Palomón.
Palinaria   see **Apolonio.**
Palmira (Pahl mee' rah) f. **EE:**
Palmer. Lat. "Palm." Palm
Sunday. **Var:** Polmira.
Paloma (Pah low' mah) f. **EE:**
Paloma. Lat. "Palumbes," "wild
dove." OT symbol of peace. **Var:**
Aloma, Polomo.
Palomia   see **Apolonio.**
Palomón   see **Palemón.**
Pámfelo   see **Pánfilo.**
Pamfilio   see **Pánfilo.**
Pámfilo   see **Pánfilo.**
Pamfina   see **Pánfilo.**
Pamfirio   see **Pánfilo.**
Pamosena   see **Nepomuceno.**
Pampbilo   see **Pánfilo.**
Pamphiliam   see **Pánfilo.**
Pamphilio   see **Pánfilo.**
Pámphilo   see **Pánfilo.**
Pámphylo   see **Pánfilo.**
Pamposa   see **Pomposo.**
Panatale   see **Pantaleón.**
Panchio   see **Francisco.**
Panchito   see **Francisco.**
Pancho   see **Francisco.**
Pancholo   see **Francisco.**
Panchy   see **Francisco.**
Panciano   see **Ponciano.**
Pancracio (Pahn crah' see oh) m.
EE: Pancratius. Gk. "Who unites
all power." M. in Rome. F. 5/12.
Var: Pancrasio.
Pancrasio   see **Pancracio.**
Pandalia   see **Pantaleón.**
Pandencio (Pahn den' see oh) m.
EE: Pandercio. Pandercio in Gk.
myth. sees all. Another name for
sun, justice & nemesis.
Panezio (Pah nay' see oh) m. **EE:**
Panezio. Gk. "One who does
everything well." Possibly
Renaissance type. **Var:** Panzian.
Panfilio   see **Pánfilo.**
Pánfilo (Pahn' fee low) m. **EE:**
Pamphilius, Panphil. Gk. "Friend
of all." 8th cen. Ital. S. F.
4/28. **Var:** Pafilio, Páfilo,
Pámfelo, Pamfilio, Pámfilo,
Pamfina, Pamfirio, Pampbilo,
Pamphiliam, Pamphilio, Pámphilo,
Pámphylo, Panfilio, Pánfino,
Panflo, Panifilo, Panphilius,
Pánpilla, Paufila, Ponfilio,

Ponfilo.
Pánfino   see **Pánfilo.**
Panflo   see **Pánfilo.**
Panifilo   see **Pánfilo.**
Panina   see **Paulo.**
Panphilius   see **Pánfilo.**
Pánpilla   see **Pánfilo.**
Pánsalo (Pahn' sah low) m. **EE:**
Pansalino. St. Pansalino,
Christian M., died in Spain. F.
1/11.
Panta   see **Pantaleón.**
Pantalcona   see **Pantaleón.**
Pantale   see **Pantaleón.**
Pantaleana   see **Pantaleón.**
Pantalene   see **Pantaleón.**
Pantaleo   see **Pantaleón.**
Pantaleón (Pahn tah lay own') m.
EE: Pantaleon. "One who is a
lion in everything." 3 x in DS.
1, 3rd cen. S. whose name means
"all-compassionate." Milk flowed
from head after decapitation.
Dim: Panta, Pantuca. **Var:**
Panatale, Pandalia, Pantalcona,
Pantale, Pantaleana, Pantalene,
Pantaleo, Pantaleone, Pantalián,
Pantalin, Pantalión, Pantealeón,
Panteleón, Pantiano, Pantileón,
Pantilión, Pantilo, Pantoleón,
Pantoleonis, Pantolión,
Pateleón, Patolenón, Pautaleón,
Pontalone, Pontelone.
Pantaleone   see **Pantaleón.**
Pantalián   see **Pantaleón.**
Pantalin   see **Pantaleón.**
Pantalión   see **Pantaleón.**
Pantealeón   see **Pantaleón.**
Panteleón   see **Pantaleón.**
Pantiano   see **Pantaleón.**
Pantileón   see **Pantaleón.**
Pantilión   see **Pantaleón.**
Pantilo   see **Pantaleón.**
Pantoleón   see **Pantaleón.**
Pantoleonis   see **Pantaleón.**
Pantolión   see **Pantaleón.**
Pantuca   see **Pantaleón.**
Panzian   see **Panezio.**
Panzo   see **Francisco.**
Paoguinto   see **Pioquinto.**
Paola   see **Paulo.**
Paolino   see **Paulo.**
Papías (Pah pee' ahs) m. **EE:**
Papias. Gk. "Venerable father."
7 x in DS. **Var:** Papillas,
Papíos, Phapila.
Papillas   see **Papías.**
Papíos   see **Papías.**
Papolonia   see **Apolonio.**
Paquillo   see **Francisco.**
Paquin   see **Francisco.**
Paquito   see **Francisco.**
Parázedes   see **Práxedes.**
Parcasio (Pahr cah' see oh) m. **EE:**
Parcas. Parcas in Gk. & Roman
myth., god of destiny.
Parfidia   see **Porfirio.**
Parfinia   see **Porfirio.**
Parfirio   see **Porfirio.**
Parfiro   see **Porfirio.**
Parfita   see **Porfirio.**
Paricio   see **Parisio.**
Parisio (Pah ree' see oh) m. **EE:**
Parisius. Form of Paris, causal
figure of Trojan War. 1, 13th

cen. S. F. 6/11. **Var:** Paricio.
Pármeno (Pahr' may no) m. **EE:**
Parmenius, Gk. "Persistent,
enduring." M. of 3rd cen. Persia
F. 4/22.
Parphilia   see **Porfirio.**
Parsibal   see **Parsifal.**
Parsifal (Par see fall') m. **EE:**
Percevale, Percival. Fr. "Pierce
the valley." Hero in poem
"Percevale." Also figure in
Arthurian legend. **Var:** Parsibal.
Pas   see **Paz.**
Pascalo   see **Pascual.**
Pascasio (Pahs cah' see oh) m. **EE:**
Paschasius. Lat. "Paschalis,"
"born during Passover." 4 x in
DS. See also Pascual.
Paschala   see **Pascual.**
Paschalis   see **Pascual.**
Pasco   see **Pascual.**
Pascual (Pahs kwall') m. **EE:**
Paschal. Lat. "Paschalis," "born
during Passover." Easter season.
2 x in DS. **Dim:** Paco, Pasco.
Var: Pascalo, Paschala,
Paschalis, Pascualino, Pascuda,
Pascuelo, Pascula, Pasculia,
Pascuola, Pasehual, Pasenal,
Pasguelina, Pasqual, Pasqualar,
Pasqualia, Pasqualo, Pasquel,
Pasquelina, Pasqula, Pazcual,
Pazqual, Poscuala. See also
Pascasio.
Pascualino   see **Pascual.**
Pascuda   see **Pascual.**
Pascuelo   see **Pascual.**
Pascula   see **Pascual.**
Pasculia   see **Pascual.**
Pascuola   see **Pascual.**
Pasehual   see **Pascual.**
Pasenal   see **Pascual.**
Pasencia   see **Paciencia.**
Pasguelina   see **Pascual.**
Pasífica   see **Pacífico.**
Pasión (Pah see own') mf? **EE:**
Passion, Lat. "Passio," "to
suffer." Christ's passion &
death.
Pasqual   see **Pascual.**
Pasqualar   see **Pascual.**
Pasqualia   see **Pascual.**
Pasqualo   see **Pascual.**
Pasquel   see **Pascual.**
Pasquelina   see **Pascual.**
Pasqula   see **Pascual.**
Pastor (Pahs tore') m. **EE:** Pastor.
Lat. "He who takes care of
sheep." 7 x in DS. 1, abbot in
desert of Scete, refused to see
mother when she visited monas-
tery. **Var:** Pastorela.
Pastorela   see **Pastor.**
Pat   see **Patricio.**
Patarico   see **Patricio.**
Pateleón   see **Pantaleón.**
Patercio   see **Patricio.**
Pati   see **Patricio.**
Paticio   see **Patricio.**
Patiscinia   see **Patrocinio.**
Patolenón   see **Pantaleón.**
Patosinia   see **Patrocinio.**
Patracina   see **Patrocinio.**
Patracinio   see **Patrocinio.**
Patrecio   see **Patricio.**

Patriciana   see **Patricio.**
Patricica   see **Patricio.**
Patricier   see **Patricio.**
Patricinia   see **Patrocinio.**
Patricino   see **Patrocinio.**
Patricio (Pah tree' see oh) m. **EE:**
Pat, Patricia, Patrick, Lat. "Of
noble birth." 2 Irish Ss. Main 1
of 5th cen. converted many to
Christianity. F. 3/17. **Dim:**
Pachi, Pat, Pati, Richi, Ticho,
Tricia. **Var:** Patarico, Patercio,
Paticio, Patrecio, Patriciana,
Patricica, Patricier, Patrico,
Patrisa, Patrisia, Patrisis,
Patritio, Patrito, Patrizio,
Petrice, Petricia, Pitricia.
Patrico   see **Patricio.**
Patrinio   see **Patrocinio.**
Patrisa   see **Patricio.**
Patrisia   see **Patricio.**
Patrisis   see **Patricio.**
Patritio   see **Patricio.**
Patrito   see **Patricio.**
Patrizio   see **Patricio.**
Patro   see **Patrocinio.**
Patrociana   see **Patrocinio.**
Patrocimia   see **Patrocinio.**
Patrocimo   see **Patrocinio.**
Patrocine   see **Patrocinio.**
Patrocinio (Pah tro see' nee oh)
m. **EE:** Patricinius. Lat. "He who
gives his protection." F. 11/14.
Dim: Padra, Patro, Patroni,
Patronia. **Var:** Pactrocinia,
Padrosinia, Patiscinia,
Patosinia, Patracina,
Patracinio, Patricinia,
Patricino, Patrinio, Patrociana,
Patrocimia, Patrocimo,
Patrocine, Patrocinnio,
Patrocino, Patrocnio,
Patroncisia, Patronicinia,
Patronida, Patrosinio,
Patrozina, Patrozinia,
Patrucina, Petrasina, Petrocima,
Petrocimi, Petrocino, Petrozina,
Petrozinia.
Patrocinnio   see **Patrocinio.**
Patrocino   see **Patrocinio.**
Patrocnio   see **Patrocinio.**
Patrolino   see **Petronilo.**
Patroncisia   see **Patrocinio.**
Patroni   see **Patrocinio.**
Patronia   see **Patrocinio.**
Patronicinia   see **Patrocinio.**
Patronida   see **Patrocinio.**
Patrosinio   see **Patrocinio.**
Patrozina   see **Patrocinio.**
Patrozinia   see **Patrocinio.**
Patrucina   see **Patrocinio.**
Patrucio (Pah troo' see oh) m. **EE:**
Patusius. Patusius, Fr. S. of
8th cen. F. 10/3.
Paubio   see **Paulo.**
Paublino   see **Paulo.**
Paublo   see **Paulo.**
Paufila   see **Pánfilo.**
Paulae   see **Paulo.**
Paulam   see **Paulo.**
Paulana   see **Paulo.**
Paulbino (Powl bee' no) m. **EE:**
Paulbino, Comb. of Paulo &
Balbina (see both).
Pauleta   see **Paulo.**

Pauli   see **Paulo.**
Pauliciano   see **Paulo.**
Paulico   see **Paulo.**
Paulinar   see **Paulo.**
Paulino   see **Paulo.**
Paulius   see **Paulo.**
Paulo (Pow' low) m. **EE:** Paul,
  Paula. Lat. "Of small stature."
  35 x in DS. 1, Paul of Tarsus,
  apostle of Rome. F. 6/30. **Dim:**
  Lino, Oalo, Pabila (Pablo),
  Pabillo (Pablo), Pabis (Pablo),
  Pablillo, Pablino (Pablo),
  Pablita (Pablo), Panina,
  Paolino, Paublino, Pauleta,
  Pauli, Paulico, Paulino,
  Pavalita, Pavelita, Pavillo,
  Polín. **Var:** Pablana, Pablo,
  Pala, Paola, Paubio, Paublo,
  Paulae, Paulam, Paulana,
  Pauliciano, Paulinar, Paulius,
  Paulum, Paviana, Pavlo, Payla.
Paulum   see **Paulo.**
Pautaleón   see **Pantaleón.**
Pavalita   see **Paulo.**
Pavelita   see **Paulo.**
Paviana   see **Paulo.**
Pavillo   see **Paulo.**
Pavlo   see **Paulo.**
Paya   see **Leocadia.**
Payito   see **Francisco.**
Payla   see **Paulo.**
Payo   see **Pelagio.**
Paz (Pahs) mf. **EE:** Pax, Peace.
  Lat. "Pax," "peace." Devotion to
  Our Lady of Peace. F. 1/23. **Var:**
  Pas. See also Paciencia.
Pazcual   see **Pascual.**
Pazqual   see **Pascual.**
Pearla   see **Perla.**
Pedrín   see **Pedro.**
Pedro (Pay' droh) m. **EE:** Pete,
  Peter, Petra. Lat. "Rock." 56 x
  in DS. Greatest, Peter the apos-
  tle. F. 6/29. **Dim:** Pedrín,
  Pedromillo, Pedrucho, Pedruco,
  Perico, Periquín, Perucho, Peta
  (Petra), Petrina (Petra),
  Petrita (Petra), Peyo, Peyuço,
  Picho (Petrona), Pico, Pierín,
  Pifa, Piquín, Pit, Piti. **Var:**
  Betra, Pedtra, Petara, Petra,
  Petrae, Petram, Petranelo,
  Petria, Petritam, Petritane,
  Petrolino, Petrona, Petronina,
  Petronio, Petronlo, Petropilo,
  Petros, Petrovido, Petru,
  Petrum, Petruna, Petrus, Pidra,
  Piedro, Piter. See also
  Petronilo.
Pedromillo   see **Pedro.**
Pedrucho   see **Pedro.**
Pedruco   see **Pedro.**
Pedtra   see **Pedro.**
Pefilia (Pay fee' lee ah) f. **EE:**
  Perfilia. Sp. "Perfilar," "to
  adorn" or "to embellish."
Pehonila   see **Petronilo.**
Pela   see **Esperanza.**
Pela   see **Ofelio.**
Pelagio (Pay lah' hee oh) m. **EE:**
  Pelagius. Lat. "He who belongs
  to the sea." 10 x in DS. **Dim:**
  Payo. **Var:** Pelatgie, Pelayo.
Pelagrina   see **Peregrino.**

Pelancha   see **Esperanza.**
Pelanchita   see **Esperanza.**
Pelar   see **Pilar.**
Pelaseo (Pay lah' see oh) m. **EE:**
  Pelasgus. Pelasgico, another
  name for Jupiter in Gk. myth.
Pelatgie   see **Pelagio.**
Pelayo   see **Pelagio.**
Pelegrino   see **Peregrino.**
Peleina (Pay lay' nah) f. **EE:**
  Peleus. Peleo was father of
  Achilles in "Iliad."
Pelo   see **Raul.**
Pelonia   see **Apolonio.**
Pelonoia   see **Apolonio.**
Penélope (Pay nay' low pay) f. **EE:**
  Penelope. Gk. "Type of duck or
  goose noted for red stripes."
Pensita   see **Prudencia.**
Pentea (Pane tay' ah) f. **EE:**
  Pentea. Flower of orchid family.
Pentecostes (Pane tay cohs' tays)
  m. **EE:** Pentecost. From Pente-
  cost, celebrated 40 days after
  Easter. Day on which Holy Spirit
  descended upon apostles.
Peokinda   see **Pioquinto.**
Peoquento   see **Pioquinto.**
Pepa   see **José.**
Pepe   see **José.**
Pepeto   see **Perpetua.**
Pepillo   see **José.**
Pepín   see **José.**
Pepina   see **José.**
Pepito   see **José.**
Pepón   see **José.**
Pera   see **Esperanza.**
Perciliano   see **Prisciliano.**
Perciliano   see **Prisciliano.**
Peregrín   see **Peregrino.**
Peregrine   see **Peregrino.**
Peregrino (Pay ray gree' no) m.
  EE: Peregrinus. Lat. "Rare or
  strange." 9 x in DS. **Dim:** Pina.
  Var: Pelagrina, Pelegrino,
  Peregrín, Peregrine, Perino.
Perfecto (Pare fake' toe) m. **EE:**
  Perfectus, Lat. "Perfect, free
  from sin." 9th cen. Sp. S. mart.
  by Mohammedans in Cordova. F.
  4/18. **Var:** Perfectos, Perfedto,
  Perfetita, Perfeto, Perfetto,
  Perficto, Pirficta.
Perfectos   see **Perfecto.**
Perfedto   see **Perfecto.**
Perfetita   see **Perfecto.**
Perfeto   see **Perfecto.**
Perfetto   see **Perfecto.**
Perficto   see **Perfecto.**
Perfida (Pare fee' dah) f. **EE:**
  Perfida. Lat. "Perfidia" means
  "disloyalty, treachery."
Perfilio   see **Porfirio.**
Perfirio   see **Porfirio.**
Perico   see **Pedro.**
Perino   see **Peregrino.**
Periquín   see **Pedro.**
Perita   see **Esperanza.**
Perla (Pare' lah) f. **EE:** Pearl.
  Lat. "Pernula," "bone." No Ss.
  for popular name of early 20th
  cen. **Var:** Pearla.
Perpetua (Pare pay' too ah) f. **EE:**
  Perpetua, Perpetuus. Lat. "To
  continue without interruption."

2 x in DS. **Dim:** Perta. **Var:**
Pepeto, Perpetuna.

Perpetuna   see **Perpetua.**
Perta   see **Perpetua.**
Perucho   see **Pedro.**
Peseiliano   see **Prisciliano.**
Peta   see **Pedro.**
Petacea   see **Epitacio.**
Petara   see **Pedro.**
Petasho   see **Epitacio.**
Petasio   see **Epitacio.**
Peteo (Pay tay' oh) m. **EE:** Peteus.
Mythological father of Menesteo.
Expelled from Athens & founded
Phocis.
Petolina   see **Petronilo.**
Petonilo   see **Petronilo.**
Petra   see **Pedro.**
Petrae   see **Pedro.**
Petrainla   see **Petronilo.**
Petram   see **Pedro.**
Petranelo   see **Pedro.**
Petranilla   see **Petronilo.**
Petrasina   see **Patrocinio.**
Petrenelo   see **Petronilo.**
Petrenilo   see **Petronilo.**
Petria   see **Pedro.**
Petrice   see **Patricio.**
Petricia   see **Patricio.**
Petrina   see **Pedro.**
Petrinila   see **Petronilo.**
Petrionila   see **Petronilo.**
Petrita   see **Pedro.**
Petritam   see **Pedro.**
Petritane   see **Pedro.**
Petrocima   see **Patrocinio.**
Petrocimi   see **Patrocinio.**
Petrocino   see **Patrocinio.**
Petrolina   see **Petronilo.**
Petrolino   see **Pedro.**
Petromello   see **Petronilo.**
Petromila   see **Petronilo.**
Petromlo   see **Petronilo.**
Petrona   see **Pedro.**
Petronella   see **Petronilo.**
Petronia   see **Petronilo.**
Petronilla   see **Petronilo.**
Petronilo (Pay' troh nee' low) m.
EE: Petronillo, Petronius, Lat.
diminutive of "petronius,
"rocky place." 3 x in DS. **Dim:**
Pituca, Tona. **Var:** Patrolino,
Pehonila, Petolina, Petonilo,
Petrainla, Petranilla,
Petrenelo, Petrenilo, Petrinila,
Petrionila, Petrolina,
Petromello, Petromila, Petromlo,
Petronella, Petronia,
Petronilla. See also Pedro.
Petronina   see **Pedro.**
Petronio   see **Pedro.**
Petronlo   see **Pedro.**
Petropilo   see **Pedro.**
Petros   see **Pedro.**
Petrovido   see **Pedro.**
Petrozina   see **Patrocinio.**
Petrozinia   see **Patrocinio.**
Petru   see **Pedro.**
Petrum   see **Pedro.**
Petruna   see **Pedro.**
Petrus   see **Pedro.**
Peyo   see **Pedro.**
Peyuco   see **Pedro.**
Phaleppa   see **Felipo.**
Phapila   see **Papías.**

Phebe   see **Febe.**
Phelia   see **Félix.**
Phelipa   see **Felipo.**
Phelipe   see **Felipo.**
Phelis   see **Félix.**
Phelisiana   see **Félix.**
Phidencia   see **Fidencio.**
Philberto   see **Filiberto.**
Philemona   see **Filomeno.**
Philemone   see **Filomeno.**
Philiberta   see **Filiberto.**
Philibertus   see **Filiberto.**
Philimena   see **Filomeno.**
Philipa   see **Felipo.**
Philippa   see **Felipo.**
Phillipa   see **Felipo.**
Phillippe   see **Felipo.**
Phillippo   see **Felipo.**
Philomen   see **Filomeno.**
Philomeno   see **Filomeno.**
Philumena   see **Filomeno.**
Philysa   see **Félix.**
Phoebe   see **Febe.**
Piae   see **Pio.**
Piano   see **Cipriano.**
Picardo   see **Picardus.**
Picardus (Pee car' doose) m. **EE:**
Picardus. Lat. "Picardo," region
in northern Gaul. One who lives
in Picardie, France. **Var:**
Picardo.
Picarino (Pee cah ree' no) m. **EE:**
Picarino. Sp. "Picaro," "knav-
ish, roguish." Diminutive "ino"
softens pejorative quality.
Picho   see **Pedro.**
Picho   see **Piedad.**
Pico   see **Pedro.**
Pictoria   see **Víctor.**
Pidra   see **Pedro.**
Pieda   see **Piedad.**
Piedad (Pee aay dahd') f. **EE:**
Pieta, Piety. Lat. "Sense of
duty towards gods." Special
devotion to Nuestra Señora de la
Piedad, Our Lady of Piety. F.
5/11. **Dim:** Picho. **Var:** Pieda,
Piedada, Piedal, Pietá,
Pietatis.
Piedada   see **Piedad.**
Piedal   see **Piedad.**
Piedro   see **Pedro.**
Pierin   see **Pedro.**
Pierio (Pee ay' ree oh) m. **EE:**
Pierius, Pierre. Lat. "Origi-
nating in Pieria, Macedonia."
4th S. of Alexandria, Egypt. F.
11/4. **Var:** Piero.
Piero   see **Pierio.**
Pietá   see **Piedad.**
Pietatis   see **Piedad.**
Pifa   see **Pedro.**
Pifania   see **Epifanio.**
Pifano   see **Epifanio.**
Pil   see **Felipo.**
Pila   see **Pilar.**
Pila   see **Porfirio.**
Pilar (Pee lahr') mf. **EE:** Pilar.
Lat. "Pillar," Sp. V. who
appeared to Santiago over marble
pillar. F. 10/12. **Dim:** Pilarica,
Pili, Pilo, Piluca, Pilucha.
Var: Pelar, Pila, Pilardo,
Pilario, Pilaro, Pileria,
Piliar, Pillar, Pilor.

Pilardela (Pee lahr day' lah) f.
EE: Pilardela. Comb. of Pilar &
Adela (see both).

Pilardo	see **Pilar.**
Pilarica	see **Pilar.**
Pilario	see **Pilar.**
Pilaro	see **Pilar.**
Pileria	see **Pilar.**
Pili	see **Pilar.**
Piliar	see **Pilar.**
Pillar	see **Pilar.**
Pilo	see **Pilar.**
Pilor	see **Pilar.**
Piluca	see **Pilar.**
Pilucha	see **Pilar.**
Pimeneo	see **Epigmenio.**
Pimenio	see **Epigmenio.**
Pimeno	see **Epigmenio.**
Pimimeno	see **Epigmenio.**
Pina	see **Delfino.**
Pina	see **Joaquín.**
Pina	see **José.**
Pina	see **Peregrino.**
Pina	see **Serafín.**

Pindaro (Peen' dah roe) m. EE:
Pindar, Pindarus. Greatest of
Gk. lyric poets c. 500 B.C.

Pine	see **Agripino.**

Pinito (Pee nee' toe) m. EE:
Pinytus. S. & bishop of Crete in
3rd cen. F. 10/10.

Pino	see **Crespín.**

Pío (Pee' oh) m. EE: Pius. Lat.
"One pious & observant of
rules." 12 popes. **Var:** Piae.

Piocinto	see **Pioquinto.**
Piogineto	see **Pioquinto.**
Pioguinto	see **Pioquinto.**
Pioquento	see **Pioquinto.**
Pioquintae	see **Pioquinto.**

Pioquinto (Pee oh keen' toe) m.
EE: Pius V. Comb. of Pio (see) &
Quinto, "fifth." Pope of 16th
cen. **Var:** Biocinto, Paoguinto,
Peokinda, Peoquento, Piocinto,
Piogineto, Pioguinto, Pioquento,
Pioquintae.

Pipe	see **Felipo.**
Pipina	see **José.**
Pipo	see **José.**
Piquín	see **Pedro.**
Pirficta	see **Perfecto.**
Pit	see **Pedro.**
Pita	see **José.**
Pitacio	see **Epitacio.**

Pitana (Pee tah' nah) f. EE:
Pitana, Pitane. In Gk. myth.,
Pitane, daughter of river god.
Bore child to Poseidon.

Pitasio	see **Epitacio.**
Pitazio	see **Epitacio.**
Piter	see **Pedro.**
Piti	see **Pedro.**
Pitín	see **Félix.**
Pito	see **Félix.**

Pitos (Pee' toes) mf. EE: Pitos.
Gk. goddess of persuasion.

Pitricia	see **Patricio.**
Pituca	see **Petronilo.**
Pituro	see **Arturo.**
Piyo	see **Porfirio.**
Plácedo	see **Plácido.**
Placi	see **Plácido.**
Placidad	see **Plácido.**

Plácido (Plah' see doe) m. EE:
Placidus. Lat. "Quiet,
tranquil." 4 x in DS. **Dim:**
Placi, Plasa, Plasio, Plaza.
Var: Blácida, Brácida, Palácido,
Plácedo, Placidad, Placijo,
Placinto, Placiva, Plásido,
Plásidus, Plócida, Plózida.

Placijo	see **Plácido.**
Placinto	see **Plácido.**
Placiva	see **Plácido.**
Plalone	see **Apolonio.**
Planonia	see **Apolonio.**
Plasa	see **Plácido.**
Plásido	see **Plácido.**
Plásidus	see **Plácido.**
Plasio	see **Plácido.**

Platón (Plah tone') m. EE: Plato.
Gk. "Broad." S. mart. in Turkey.
Var: Platone.

Platone	see **Platón.**
Plaza	see **Plácido.**

Plinio (Plee' nee oh) m. EE:
Plinius, Pliny. 1st cen. Roman
author who compiled encyclopedia, "Natural History."

Plócida	see **Plácido.**
Plózida	see **Plácido.**
Plutarcho	see **Plutarco.**

Plutarco (Ploo tahr' co) m. EE:
Plutarch. Gk. "King of riches."
1st cen. Gk. biographer. 3rd
cen. S. mart. in Egypt. **Dim:**
Plutarico. **Var:** Plutarcho,
Plutareo, Plutargeo, Plutargne,
Plutargo, Plutario, Plutarquo,
Plutraca.

Plutareo	see **Plutarco.**
Plutargeo	see **Plutarco.**
Plutargne	see **Plutarco.**
Plutargo	see **Plutarco.**
Plutarico	see **Plutarco.**
Plutario	see **Plutarco.**
Plutarquo	see **Plutarco.**
Plutraca	see **Plutarco.**
Pocho	see **Alfonso.**
Pocho	see **Ambrosio.**
Podencia	see **Potérciano.**
Podenciana	see **Pudenciana.**
Pofilio	see **Porfirio.**
Poincianna	see **Ponciano.**
Pola	see **Amapola.**
Polania	see **Apolonio.**
Polcarpio	see **Policarpo.**
Polda	see **Leopoldo.**
Poldi	see **Leopoldo.**
Pole	see **Apolonio.**
Polecarpos	see **Policarpo.**
Polenario	see **Apolonio.**

Polenciana (Poe lain' see ah' nah)
f. EE: Polenciana. Polencia,
Roman goddess of power.

Poley	see **Apolonio.**
Poli	see **Apolonio.**
Poli	see **Hipólito.**
Poli	see **Policarpo.**
Poliana	see **Apolonio.**
Policaopa	see **Policarpo.**
Policapio	see **Policarpo.**
Policardio	see **Policarpo.**
Policarfio	see **Policarpo.**
Policarfro	see **Policarpo.**
Policaria	see **Policarpo.**
Policarjio	see **Policarpo.**
Policarno	see **Policarpo.**
Policarp	see **Policarpo.**

Policarpio   see **Policarpo.**
Policarpis   see **Policarpo.**
Policarpo (Poe lee car' poe) m.
   EE: Polycarp, Gk. "He who gives
   many fruits (good works)." 3 x
   in DS. **Dim:** Poli, Polo. **Var:**
   Polcarpio, Polecarpos,
   Policaopa, Policapio,
   Policardio, Policarfio,
   Policarfro, Policaria,
   Policarjio, Policarno, Policarp,
   Policarpio, Policarpis,
   Policarpyo, Policipio,
   Policorpia, Policorpo,
   Pollicarpia, Polocarpo,
   Polucarpo, Polycarfo, Polycarp,
   Polycarpe, Polycarpem,
   Polycarpio, Polycarpius,
   Polycart, Polycayso, Polycorpia.
Policarpyo   see **Policarpo.**
Policedes   see **Policeto.**
Policeto (Poe lee say' toe) m. **EE:**
   Polyceute. Gk. "He who has
   caused much affliction." 3rd
   cen. Armenian M. F. 2/13. **Var:**
   Policedes.
Policipio   see **Policarpo.**
Policorpia   see **Policarpo.**
Policorpo   see **Policarpo.**
Polidor   see **Polidoro.**
Polidoro (Poe lee doe' roe) m. **EE:**
   Polydorus. Gk. "He who gives
   many gifts." Priam's son who
   died in Trojan War. 18th cen. S.
   mart. in Cyprus for renouncing
   Mohammedanism. F. 2/3. **Var:**
   Polidor.
Polifo (Poe lee' foe) m. **EE:**
   Polifontes. In myth., Poli-
   fontes, coachman of Layo killed
   by Oedipus.
Polin   see **Apolonio.**
Polin   see **Hipólito.**
Polin   see **Leopoldo.**
Polin   see **Paulo.**
Polina   see **Hipólito.**
Polinar   see **Apolonio.**
Polinario   see **Apolonio.**
Polinarius   see **Apolonio.**
Polinarus   see **Apolonio.**
Poline   see **Apolonio.**
Polinio   see **Apolonio.**
Polito   see **Hipólito.**
Polivario   see **Olivo.**
Pollicarpia   see **Policarpo.**
Pollinaria   see **Apolonio.**
Polmira   see **Palmira.**
Polo   see **Apolonio.**
Polo   see **Hipólito.**
Polo   see **Leopoldo.**
Polo   see **Policarpo.**
Polocarpo   see **Policarpo.**
Polocho   see **Sinforoso.**
Polomia   see **Apolonio.**
Polomo   see **Paloma.**
Polonario   see **Apolonio.**
Polonice (Poe low nee' say) m. **EE:**
   Polynices. In Gk. legend son of
   Oedipus & brother of Antigone.
   Leader of 7 heroes in "Seven
   Against Thebes." **Var:** Polonis.
Polonio   see **Apolonio.**
Polonis   see **Polonice.**
Polonium   see **Apolonio.**
Polucarpo   see **Policarpo.**

Polycarfo   see **Policarpo.**
Polycarp   see **Policarpo.**
Polycarpe   see **Policarpo.**
Polycarpem   see **Policarpo.**
Polycarpio   see **Policarpo.**
Polycarpius   see **Policarpo.**
Polycart   see **Policarpo.**
Polycayso   see **Policarpo.**
Polycorpia   see **Policarpo.**
Polyta   see **Hipólito.**
Pomacena   see **Nepomuceno.**
Pomelio   see **Pompeyo.**
Pomesana   see **Nepomuceno.**
Pomoseno   see **Nepomuceno.**
Pompaso   see **Pomposo.**
Pompeyo (Pome pay' yo) m. **EE:**
   Pompeius, Pompey. Gk. "He who
   leads procession." Famous Roman
   general. 3 x in DS. **Dim:** Pompo.
   Var: Pomelio, Pompilio.
Pompilio   see **Pompeyo.**
Pompo   see **Pompeyo.**
Pomposia   see **Pomposo.**
Pomposo (Pome poe' so) m. **EE:**
   Pomposa, Pomposo. Lat. "Pomp or
   solemnity." 9th cen. Sp. S.
   mart. in Cordova by Moors. F.
   9/19. **Var:** Pamposa, Pompaso,
   Pomposia, Pomposso, Pompossor,
   Pompozo, Pompresa, Pomprosa,
   Ponposo.
Pomposso   see **Pomposo.**
Pompossor   see **Pomposo.**
Pompozo   see **Pomposo.**
Pompresa   see **Pomposo.**
Pomprosa   see **Pomposo.**
Pomuceno   see **Nepomuceno.**
Ponaciano   see **Ponciano.**
Ponceno   see **Ponciano.**
Ponchilla   see **Ponciano.**
Poncho   see **Alfonso.**
Poncho   see **Florencio.**
Poncián   see **Ponciano.**
Ponciano   see **Alfonso.**
Ponciano (Pone see ah' no) m. **EE:**
   Pontian, Pontion. Gk. "Coming
   from the sea." 6 x in DS. **Dim:**
   Chano, Ponchilla. **Var:** Panciano,
   Poincianna, Ponaciano, Ponceno,
   Poncián, Ponciarro, Ponciaus,
   Poncieno, Poncino, Poncio,
   Ponciona, Ponicia, Ponoceno,
   Ponoseno, Ponsiano, Pontiani,
   Pontiano, Pontianus, Ponticena,
   Ponziana, Porciano, Porziano,
   Puniciano.
Ponciarro   see **Ponciano.**
Ponciaus   see **Ponciano.**
Poncieno   see **Ponciano.**
Poncino   see **Ponciano.**
Poncio   see **Ponciano.**
Ponciona   see **Ponciano.**
Ponfilio   see **Pánfilo.**
Ponfilo   see **Pánfilo.**
Ponicia   see **Ponciano.**
Ponoceno   see **Ponciano.**
Ponoseno   see **Ponciano.**
Ponposo   see **Pomposo.**
Ponsiano   see **Ponciano.**
Ponso   see **Alfonso.**
Ponso   see **Ildefonso.**
Pontalone   see **Pantaleón.**
Pontelone   see **Pantaleón.**
Pontiani   see **Ponciano.**
Pontiano   see **Ponciano.**

Pontianus	see	Ponciano.
Ponticena	see	Ponciano.
Ponziana	see	Ponciano.
Popo	see	Rodolfo.
Porciano	see	Ponciano.
Pordirio	see	Porfirio.
Porfeiro	see	Porfirio.
Porfelio	see	Porfirio.
Porferi	see	Porfirio.
Porferio	see	Porfirio.

Porfidio (Pore fee' dee oh) m. EE:
Porfidio. Comb. of Porfirio &
Perfida (see both).

Porfie	see	Porfirio.
Porfijo	see	Porfirio.
Porfilio	see	Porfirio.
Porfinio	see	Porfirio.
Porfino	see	Porfirio.
Porfio	see	Porfirio.

Porfirio (Pore fee' ree oh) m. EE:
Porphyrius, Porphyry. Gk. "He
who is dressed in purple." 7 x
in DS. Dim: Filo, Firo, Pila,
Piyo, Porfie, Porfio. Var:
Parfidia, Parfinia, Parfirio,
Parfiro, Parfita, Parphilia,
Perfilio, Perfirio, Pofilio,
Pordirio, Porfeiro, Porfelio,
Porferi, Porferio, Porfijo,
Porfilio, Porfinio, Porfino,
Porfirius, Porfirro, Porfivio,
Porforio, Porifiria, Porphelia,
Porpheriae, Porphilio, Porphino,
Porphir, Porphirio, Porphrio,
Porphyrio, Porphyrius, Porpirio,
Preferio, Profirio, Profiro,
Purfiria, Purfiris, Purforio.

Porfirius	see	Porfirio.
Porfirro	see	Porfirio.
Porfivio	see	Porfirio.
Porforio	see	Porfirio.
Porifiria	see	Porfirio.
Porphelia	see	Porfirio.
Porpheriae	see	Porfirio.
Porphilio	see	Porfirio.
Porphino	see	Porfirio.
Porphir	see	Porfirio.
Porphirio	see	Porfirio.
Porphrio	see	Porfirio.
Porphyrio	see	Porfirio.
Porphyrius	see	Porfirio.
Porpirio	see	Porfirio.
Porziano	see	Poncio.
Poscuala	see	Pascual.

Poterciano (Poe tare' see ah' no)
m. EE: Potentiantus. Lat.
"Potents," "powerful"? 1st cen.
S. mart. in France where he was
reputedly sent by Christ. F.
12/31. Var: Podencia.

Poya	see	Glorio.
Prácedes	see	Práxedes.
Prácedis	see	Práxedes.
Prácherez	see	Práxedes.
Praédis	see	Práxedes.
Praesiliano	see	Prisciliano.
Prage	see	Práxedes.
Pragedes	see	Práxedes.
Pragedis	see	Práxedes.
Pragediz	see	Práxedes.
Pragelis	see	Práxedes.
Pragenes	see	Práxedes.
Prageres	see	Práxedes.
Pragerez	see	Práxedes.
Prageris	see	Práxedes.

Prágiles	see	Práxedes.
Pragues	see	Práxedes.
Práhedis	see	Práxedes.
Prájede	see	Práxedes.
Prájedes	see	Práxedes.
Prájedis	see	Práxedes.
Prájediz	see	Práxedes.
Prájeres	see	Práxedes.
Prájetes	see	Práxedes.
Prájides	see	Práxedes.
Prájidos	see	Práxedes.
Práscede	see	Práxedes.
Práscedes	see	Práxedes.
Prásedis	see	Práxedes.
Práxcedis	see	Práxedes.
Práxede	see	Práxedes.

Práxedes (Prah' hay days) m. EE:
Prassede, Praxedes. Gk. "Firm of
purpose." 2nd cen. Roman S. who
devoted wealth to poor, F. 5/19.
Dim: Prage, Pragues, Rágedes.
Var: Brácedis, Bráhedez,
Brájedes, Brájeres, Págadiz,
Parázedes, Prácedes, Prácedis,
Prácherez, Praédis, Prágedes,
Prágedis, Prágediz, Prágelis,
Prágenes, Prágeres, Prágerez,
Prágeris, Prágiles, Práhedis,
Prájede, Prájedes, Prájedis,
Prájediz, Prájeres, Prájetes,
Prájides, Prájidos, Práscede,
Práscedes, Prásedis, Práxcedis,
Práxede, Praxedio, Práxedis,
Práxedo, Praxeds, Praxeolis,
Praxepio, Práxida, Práxides,
Práyedes, Prázedez, Préjedes,
Prójades, Prójedes, Próxedes,
Próxidia.

Praxedio	see	Práxedes.
Práxedis	see	Práxedes.
Práxedo	see	Práxedes.
Praxeds	see	Práxedes.
Praxeolis	see	Práxedes.
Praxepio	see	Práxedes.
Práxida	see	Práxedes.
Práxides	see	Práxedes.
Práyedes	see	Práxedes.
Prázedez	see	Práxedes.

Preapiana (Pray ah pee ah' nah) f.
EE: Priapus. Gk. "Relating to
Priapus," another name for
Apollo, promoter of fertility.

Precencio	see	Presencia.
Precentación	see	Presentación.
Preciano	see	Prisciliano.
Precidiano	see	Prisciliano.
Precileana	see	Prisciliano.
Precilianada	see	Prisciliano.
Preciliano	see	Prisciliano.
Precilla	see	Prisco.
Precilliano	see	Prisciliano.

Preciosa (Pray see oh' sah) f. EE:
Precious. Lat. "Pretiosus" means
"precious." Used frequently in
Roman Catholicism: precious
blood of Christ, precious relics
of Ss. Var: Preciosilla,
Precisia.

Preciosilla	see	Preciosa.
Precisia	see	Preciosa.
Predencio	see	Prudencia.

Predicando (Pray dee cahn' doe) m.
EE: Predicando. Lat. "Predicato"
means "action of preaching."

Preferio	see	Porfirio.

Préjedes   see **Práxedes.**
Premetibo   see **Primitivo.**
Premetivo   see **Primitivo.**
Premitivo   see **Primitivo.**
Prenció   see **Presentación.**
Prenda   see **Brandio.**
Prenitivo   see **Primitivo.**
Prensensio   see **Presencia.**
Prescella   see **Prisco.**
Prescila   see **Prisco.**
Prescilia   see **Prisco.**
Presciliano   see **Prisciliano.**
Preseiliana   see **Prisciliano.**
Preseliano   see **Prisciliano.**
Presencia (Pray sane' see ah) f.
  EE: Presencia. Lat. "Presence."
  Major document on Catholic Eu-
  charist that Christ is present
  in Holy Communion. Also presence
  of God in all things. **Var:**
  Precencio, Prensensio,
  Presensio.
Presensio   see **Presencia.**
Presentació   see **Presentación.**
Presentación (Pray sane tah see
  own') mf. **EE:** Presentacion. Lat.
  "Presented." Presentation of
  Christ in temple. **Dim:** Chón,
  Prenció, Presy. **Var:**
  Precentación, Presentació,
  Presentatiana, Presentatión,
  Presentiano, Presintación.
Presentatiana   see **Presentación.**
Presentatión   see **Presentación.**
Presentiano   see **Presentación.**
Presibiano   see **Prisciliano.**
Présides (Pray' see days) m. **EE:**
  Praxedes. Form of Práxedes
  (see)? 4th cen. African M.
Presidiano   see **Prisciliano.**
Presila   see **Prisco.**
Presilián   see **Prisciliano.**
Presilianco   see **Prisciliano.**
Presiliano   see **Prisciliano.**
Presilliano   see **Prisciliano.**
Presintación   see **Presentación.**
Prestiliano   see **Prisciliano.**
Presy   see **Presentación.**
Preto (Pray' toe) m. **EE:** Proteus.
  In Gk. myth. he was god of sea
  who could change into any form.
  If captured, could predict
  future.
Prex   see **Prisciliano.**
Prexiliano   see **Prisciliano.**
Priceilla   see **Prisciliano.**
Pricella   see **Prisco.**
Prici   see **Prisco.**
Pricila   see **Prisco.**
Priciliano   see **Prisciliano.**
Pricilliano   see **Prisciliano.**
Pricus   see **Prisco.**
Pridiliano   see **Prisciliano.**
Prígido   see **Brígido.**
Primativo   see **Primitivo.**
Primetivo   see **Primitivo.**
Primeto   see **Primitivo.**
Primitavo   see **Primitivo.**
Primiterio   see **Primitivo.**
Primitibo   see **Primitivo.**
Primitino   see **Primitivo.**
Primitios   see **Primitivo.**
Primitiro   see **Primitivo.**
Primitiv   see **Primitivo.**
Primitivio   see **Primitivo.**

Primitivo (Pree mee tee' bo) m.
  EE: Primitivus. Lat. "1st one."
  6 x in DS. **Dim:** Primeto,
  Primitiv. **Var:** Premetibo,
  Premetivo, Premitivo, Prenitivo,
  Primativo, Primetivo, Primitavo,
  Primiterio, Primitibo,
  Primitino, Primitios, Primitiro,
  Primitivio, Primitovo, Primivo,
  Primotivo, Prinitino, Prinitivo,
  Prinotivo, Rimitivo. See also
  Primo.
Primitovo   see **Primitivo.**
Primivo   see **Primitivo.**
Primo (Pree' mo) m. **EE:** Primus.
  Lat. "1st born." 4 x in DS. **Var:**
  Prino. See also Primitivo.
Primotivo   see **Primitivo.**
Prinitino   see **Primitivo.**
Prinitivo   see **Primitivo.**
Prino   see **Primo.**
Prinotivo   see **Primitivo.**
Prisalino   see **Prisciliano.**
Priscan   see **Prisco.**
Prisceliano   see **Prisciliano.**
Prisciana   see **Prisciliano.**
Priscidiana   see **Prisciliano.**
Priscifiano   see **Primitivo.**
Prisciliano (Pree see' lee ah' no)
  m. **EE:** Priscilla. Lat. "Pris-
  cus," "old or 1st." 1, 1st cen.
  S. of Rome converted by St.
  Peter. F. 1/16. **Dim:** Chano,
  Chiano, Prex. **Var:** Bircilinia,
  Bresiliano, Brisciliana,
  Brisiliana, Perciliano,
  Percillano, Peseiliano,
  Praesiliano, Preciano,
  Precidiano, Precileana,
  Precilianada, Preciliano,
  Precilliano, Presciliano,
  Preseiliana, Preseliano,
  Presibiano, Presidiano,
  Presilián, Presilianco,
  Presiliano, Presilliano,
  Prestiliano, Prexiliano,
  Priceilla, Priciliano,
  Pricilliano, Pridiliano,
  Prisalino, Prisceliano,
  Prisciana, Priscidiana,
  Priscifiano, Priscilianso,
  Priscille, Priscillianan,
  Priscilliano, Priscilo,
  Priseiliano, Prisiliana,
  Prisilliano, Prizsiliano,
  Procelana, Proesilana,
  Reciliana. See also Prisco.
Priscilianso   see **Prisciliano.**
Priscille   see **Prisciliano.**
Priscillianan   see **Prisciliano.**
Priscilliano   see **Prisciliano.**
Priscilo   see **Primitivo.**
Prisco (Prees' co) m. **EE:** Priscus.
  Lat. "Old or 1st." 7 x in DS.
  Dim: Precilla, Prescella,
  Prescila, Prescilia, Presila,
  Pricella, Prici, Pricila,
  Priseilla, Prisillia, Prisillo,
  Prisscila. **Var:** Pricus, Priscan.
  See also Prisciliano.
Priseiliano   see **Prisciliano.**
Priseilla   see **Prisco.**
Prisiliana   see **Prisciliano.**
Prisillia   see **Prisco.**
Prisilliano   see **Prisciliano.**

Prisillo   see **Prisco.**
Prisscila   see **Prisco.**
Pristen   see **Pristina.**
Pristina (Prees tee' nah) f. **EE:**
  Pristina, Pristine, Sp. "Fresh,"
  original." Hence, "uncorrupted."
  Var: Pristen. See also
  Prisciliano, Prisco.
Prizsiliano   see **Prisciliano.**
Probo (Pro' bo) m. **EE:** Probus.
  Lat. "Recognized for moral
  conduct." 6 x in DS.
Procapio   see **Procopio.**
Prócaro   see **Prócoro.**
Proceliana   see **Prisciliano.**
Proceso (Pro say' so) m. **EE:**
  Processus. Lat. "He who goes
  before." 1st cen. S. converted
  by Ss. Peter & Paul. F. 7/2.
  Var: Processo, Proseso.
Processo   see **Proceso.**
Procobio   see **Procopio.**
Procofino   see **Procopio.**
Procojio   see **Procopio.**
Prócolo   see **Próculo.**
Procopie   see **Procopio.**
Procopio (Pro co' pee oh) m. **EE:**
  Procopius. Gk. "He who pro-
  gresses." 2 x in DS. **Dim:** Copo.
  Var: Procapio, Procobio,
  Procofino, Procojio, Procopie,
  Procopo, Prokopio, Proscopia.
Procopo   see **Procopio.**
Procor   see **Prócoro.**
Prócoro (Pro' co roe) m. **EE:**
  Prochorus. Gk. "He who pros-
  pers." 1st cen. S. mart. at
  Antioch. F. 4/9. **Var:** Prócaro,
  Prócor, Prócur.
Próculo (Pro' coo low) m. **EE:**
  Proclus. Lat. "He who is born
  far from home." 2nd cen. S. of
  Ancyra. **Var:** Prócolo.
Prócur   see **Prócoro.**
Proesilana   see **Prisciliano.**
Profeto (Pro fay' toe) m. **EE:**
  Prophet. Lat. "To preach." One
  with gift of prophecy. **Var:**
  Profio.
Profio   see **Profeto.**
Profirio   see **Porfirio.**
Profiro   see **Porfirio.**
Projades   see **Práxedes.**
Projedes   see **Práxedes.**
Prokopio   see **Procopio.**
Promunciano   see **Pronunciana.**
Pronunciana (Pro noon' see ah
  nah) f. **EE:** Pronunciana. Sp.
  "Pronuncio," clergyman invested
  with powers of official repre-
  sentative of pope. **Var:**
  Promunciano.
Propedis (Pro pay' dees) m. **EE:**
  Propetidas. In Gk. myth.,
  Propetidas, 1 of Amatunte's
  daughters, changed into rock for
  mocking beauty of Venus.
Própero   see **Próspero.**
Prosalio   see **Rosalio.**
Proscopia   see **Procopio.**
Proseso   see **Proceso.**
Prósfero   see **Próspero.**
Prósjero   see **Próspero.**
Prospecto (Pro spake' toe) m. **EE:**
  Prospectus. Lat. "He who fore-

sees or examines."
Próspero (Prose' pay roe) m. **EE:**
  Prosper, Prospero. Lat. "Pros-
  perous, happy." 2 x in DS. **Var:**
  Própero, Prósfero, Prósjero.
Protacio   see **Protasio.**
Protah   see **Proto.**
Protasio (Pro tah' see oh) m. **EE:**
  Protasius. Gk. "He who tries to
  be 1st." 3 x in DS. **Var:**
  Protacio, Protensio.
Protensio   see **Protasio.**
Proto (Pro' toe) m. **EE:** Protus.
  Gk. "1st one." 3 x in DS. **Var:**
  Protah.
Proventio (Pro bane' tee oh) m.
  EE: Proventius. Lat. "Product or
  rent." Divine guidance or care.
Providencio (Pro bee dane' see oh)
  m. **EE:** Providence. Lat. "To see
  ahead." Concept of providence of
  God is 1 of principal points of
  Catholic theology.
Próxedes   see **Práxedes.**
Próxidia   see **Práxedes.**
Prudatio   see **Prudencia.**
Prudences   see **Prudencia.**
Prudencia (Proo dane' see ah) f.
  EE: Prudence, Prudentius. Lat.
  "Wise or prudent." 2 x in DS.
  Dim: Pensita, Pule. **Var:**
  Predencio, Prudatio, Prudences,
  Prudenciana, Prudencis,
  Prudeniso, Prudensiano,
  Prudentiam, Prudentiano,
  Prudentianus, Prudentio,
  Prudento, Prudentrano,
  Prudenzio, Prudincio, Prudino,
  Prudintia, Prundencio,
  Purdencia, Rudencia.
Prudenciana   see **Prudencia.**
Prudencis   see **Prudencia.**
Prudeniso   see **Prudencia.**
Prudensiano   see **Prudencia.**
Prudentiam   see **Prudencia.**
Prudentiano   see **Prudencia.**
Prudentianus   see **Prudencia.**
Prudentio   see **Prudencia.**
Prudento   see **Prudencia.**
Prudentrano   see **Prudencia.**
Prudenzio   see **Prudencia.**
Prudincio   see **Prudencia.**
Prudino   see **Prudencia.**
Prudintia   see **Prudencia.**
Prundencio   see **Prudencia.**
Pubilius   see **Públio.**
Públio (Poob' lee oh) m. **EE:**
  Pubilius. Lat. "Popular, belong-
  ing to the people." 6 x in DS.
  Var: Pubilius.
Pudecitiane   see **Pudenciana.**
Pudenciana (Poo dane' see ah' nah)
  f. **EE:** Pudentiana. Lat.
  "Pudens," "honesty, modesty,"
  2nd cen. Roman S., also called
  Potentiana, buried Mm. & cared
  for poor. F. 5/19. **Var:**
  Podenciana, Pudecitiane.
Pulcheria   see **Pulquerio.**
Pule   see **Prudencia.**
Pulquerio (Pool kay' ree oh) m.
  EE: Pulcheria. Lat. "Pulcheria,"
  "beautiful." 5th cen. S. who
  governed countries subject to
  Constantinople. F. 9/10. **Var:**

Pulcheria.

Pumesano	see **Nepomuceno.**
Puniciano	see **Ponciano.**
Purdencia	see **Prudencia.**
Puresa	see **Purificación.**
Purfiria	see **Porfirio.**
Purfiris	see **Porfirio.**
Purforio	see **Porfirio.**

Purificación (Poo ree fee cah' see own') f. EE: Purification. Sp. "To purify." Purification of Mary 40 days after birth of Christ. F. 2/2. Dim: Chón, Puro. **Var:** Puresa, Purificasión, Purita.

Purificasión	see **Purificación.**
Purita	see **Purificación.**
Puro	see **Purificación.**

Q

Qaerino	see **Quirino.**
Qeferina	see **Quirino.**
Quadal	see **Guadalupe.**
Quadalupe	see **Guadalupe.**
Quadelupe	see **Guadalupe.**
Quadupe	see **Guadalupe.**
Quanda	see **Wanda.**
Quanita	see **Juan.**
Quaquín	see **Joaquín.**

Quasimodo (Kwah see mo' doe) m. EE: Quasimodo. Lat. "Quasi modo geneti infantes" means "like newborn children." Victor Hugo's character in "The Hunchback of Notre Dame."

Quecha	see **Lucrecio.**
Quela	see **Miguel.**
Quela	see **Raquel.**
Quelino	see **Tranquilino.**
Quelita	see **Raquel.**
Quelo	see **Ezequiel.**
Quentín	see **Quinto.**
Queña	see **Eugenio.**
Queotilde	see **Clotilde.**

Querido (Kay ree' doe) m. Sp. "Querer," "to love." Hence, "beloved."

Querimo	see **Quirino.**
Querinae	see **Quirino.**
Querino	see **Quirino.**

Querubín (Kay roo bean') m. EE: Cherub. Heb. "Cherub," type of angel.

Quesino	see **Casiano.**
Queta	see **Enrique.**
Quetano	see **Cayetano.**
Queteriaca	see **Quiterio.**
Quetilda	see **Clotilde.**
Quetita	see **Enrique.**
Quicho	see **Quiterio.**
Quico	see **Engracia.**
Quico	see **Enrique.**
Quico	see **Federico.**
Quico	see **Francisco.**
Quicolín	see **Engracia.**
Quiel	see **Ezequiel.**
Quietano	see **Cayetano.**

Quietus (Key ay' tuce) m. Lat. "Peaceful." 5-year-old S. & M. F. 6/1.

Quilino	see **Tranquilino.**
Quillermo	see **Guillermo.**

Quilmes (Keel' maze) m. Imaginary person with status of S. Patron of those in trouble. **Var:** Cuilmas, Kilmes.

Quilo	see **Aquiles.**
Quilo	see **Virgilio.**

Quimino	see **Quirino.**
Quin	see **Joaquín.**
Quina	see **Aquiles.**
Quincho	see **Joaquín.**
Quinino	see **Quinto.**
Quino	see **Joaquín.**
Quino	see **Virginia.**

Quintera (Keen tay' rah) f. Comb. of Quinto & Quiteria (see both).

Quintil	see **Quinto.**
Quintiliano	see **Quinto.**
Quintilla	see **Quinto.**
Quintin	see **Quinto.**
Quintino	see **Quinto.**
Quinto	see **Enrique.**

Quinto (Keen' toe) m. EE: Quentin, etc. Lat. "Fifth." 5th child. 42 x in DS. **Dim:** Quintil, Quintilla, Quintino. **Var:** Quentín, Quinino, Quintiliano, Quintin, Quintón, Qurcencio. See also Cointa.

Quintón	see **Quinto.**
Quiotilde	see **Clotilde.**
Quique	see **Engracia.**
Quique	see **Enrique.**
Quique	see **Ricardo.**
Quiqui	see **Enrique.**
Quirico	see **Ciríaco.**
Quirieno	see **Quirino.**
Quirin	see **Quirino.**
Quirines	see **Quirino.**
Quirini	see **Quirino.**
Quirinia	see **Quirino.**

Quirino (Key ree' no) m. EE: Quirinus. Lat. "He who carries lance." Diety identified with Romulus, founder of Rome. 8 x in DS. **Var:** Cirriano, Qaerino, Qeferina, Querimo, Querinae, Querino, Quimino, Quirieno, Quirin, Quirines, Quirini, Quirinia, Quirisus, Quirmo, Quirono, Quirrino.

Quirisus	see **Quirino.**
Quirmo	see **Quirino.**
Quiro	see **Eduardo.**
Quirono	see **Quirino.**
Quirrino	see **Quirino.**
Quita	see **Blanca.**

Quiterio (Key tay' ree oh) m. Gk. "Native of Citera." V. M. from border of Spain & France. Popular in northern Spain. F. 2/22. **Dim:** Quicho. **Var:** Guiteria, Guiterria, Queteriaca.

Quito	see **Francisco.**
Qumensindo	see **Gumersindo.**

Qumisindo   see **Gumersindo.**   Qurcencio   see **Quinto.**

R

Rabecca   see **Rebeca.**
Raberto   see **Roberto.**
Rabi (Rah bee') m. Heb. "My
   teacher." In Bible Jesus called
   "Rabbi" at times. **Var:** Rabiba.
Rabiba   see **Rabi.**
Rabu   see **Rabul.**
Rabul (Rah' bool) m. St. Rabulas
   founded monasteries in Phoenicia
   & Constantinople. F. 2/19. **Var:**
   Rabu.
Racael   see **Raquel.**
Racaela   see **Raquel.**
Rach   see **Rafael.**
Racheal   see **Raquel.**
Rachele   see **Raquel.**
Rachelina   see **Raquel.**
Rachell   see **Raquel.**
Racho   see **Horacio.**
Raco   see **Raquel.**
Racquel   see **Raquel.**
Racuel   see **Raquel.**
Radalfo   see **Rodolfo.**
Radelia   see **Rogelio.**
Raechel   see **Raquel.**
Raefaela   see **Rafael.**
Rafa   see **Raul.**
Rafael (Rah fah el') m. EE: Raff,
   Raphael, etc. Heb. "God heals."
   God sent him to guide Tobias. 1
   of 6 archangels & patron of
   travelers. F. 10/24. **Dim:** Fafa,
   Fallo, Falo, Faro, Fay, Fedo,
   Felio, Fule, Lafa, Lito, Lucho,
   Rach, Rafaelina, Rafaelita,
   Raffa, Raffie, Rafi, Rafico,
   Rafito, Rafo, Raphaelita, Rave,
   Tito. **Var:** Raefaela, Rafaelia,
   Rafaelo, Rafail, Rafaila,
   Rafala, Rafalla, Rafeal,
   Rafeala, Rafel, Rafela, Rafelia,
   Rafelinda, Raffael, Rafiela,
   Rafil, Rafsela, Rafuela,
   Ralfeal, Ralfo, Raphaela,
   Raphaele, Raphaelelis,
   Raphaelem, Raphaelia,
   Raphaelilis, Raphaelis,
   Raphaila, Raphel, Raphela,
   Raphelia, Ravella, Raviel,
   Rayphael, Refael.
Rafaelia   see **Rafael.**
Rafaelina   see **Rafael.**
Rafaelita   see **Rafael.**
Rafaelo   see **Rafael.**
Rafagio   see **Refugio.**
Rafail   see **Rafael.**
Rafaila   see **Rafael.**
Rafala   see **Rafael.**
Rafalla   see **Rafael.**
Rafeal   see **Rafael.**
Rafeala   see **Rafael.**
Rafel   see **Rafael.**
Rafela   see **Rafael.**
Rafelia   see **Rafael.**
Rafelinda   see **Rafael.**
Raffa   see **Rafael.**

Raffael   see **Rafael.**
Raffie   see **Rafael.**
Rafi   see **Rafael.**
Rafico   see **Rafael.**
Rafiela   see **Rafael.**
Rafil   see **Rafael.**
Rafina   see **Rufino.**
Rafito   see **Rafael.**
Rafo   see **Rafael.**
Rafsela   see **Rafael.**
Rafuela   see **Rafael.**
Rafufio   see **Refugio.**
Rafugia   see **Refugio.**
Rafujia   see **Refugio.**
Ragaela   see **Raquel.**
Ragedes   see **Práxedes.**
Ragelio   see **Rogelio.**
Ragnel   see **Raquel.**
Ragnela   see **Raquel.**
Raguel   see **Raquel.**
Raguenel   see **Raquel.**
Raimondo   see **Raimundo.**
Raimundo (Rye moon' doe) m, EE:
   Ray, Raymond, etc. Ger. "Wise
   protector. 9 x in DS. 1, of
   12th cen. Catalonia, was doctor
   of church. F. 1/23. **Dim:** Monchi,
   Monchin, Moncho, Mongo, Mundo,
   Ramoncito, Ramuncha. **Var:**
   Raimondo, Rairado, Raminda,
   Ramondo, Ramuido, Ramundo,
   Raymon, Raymondo, Raymunda,
   Raymundus, Reimundo, Remundo,
   Reymondo, Reymundo, Reynunda,
   Romundo. See also Ramón.
Rainaldo   see **Reinaldo.**
Rainelda   see **Reinaldo.**
Rairado   see **Raimundo.**
Rajelis   see **Rogelio.**
Rajelo   see **Rogelio.**
Rajino   see **Regina.**
Raldán   see **Roldán.**
Raldina   see **Roldán.**
Ralfeal   see **Rafael.**
Ralfo   see **Rafael.**
Ramana   see **Ramón.**
Ramas   see **Ramón.**
Ramelia   see **Romilda.**
Rameo   see **Román.**
Ramero (Rah may' roe) m. Could be
   variant of Romero. Also small
   falcon.
Ramesses   see **Ramón.**
Ramico (Rah mee' co) m. Variant of
   Romárico (see). Also diminutive
   of "rama" meaning "branch."
Ramiero   see **Ramiro.**
Ramigio   see **Remigio.**
Ramigis   see **Remigio.**
Ramigo   see **Remigio.**
Ramijio   see **Remigio.**
Ramijo   see **Remigio.**
Ramina   see **Ramón.**
Raminda   see **Raimundo.**
Ramiona   see **Ramón.**
Ramireo   see **Ramiro.**

Ramiro (Rah mee' roe) m. **EE:**
Ramiro. Teut. "Powerful in
army." Ramírez, popular Sp. sur-
name, derives from Ramiro. 1,
Spaniard mart. under Visigothic
Arian Leovigild. **Var:** Ramiero,
Ramireo.

Ramma   see **Ramón.**
Rammón   see **Ramón.**
Ramón (Rah moan') m. **EE:** Ramona,
Raymond. Teut. "Wise protector."
Dim: Mon, Mona (Ramona), Monche,
Monchi, Moncho, Mongo, Monona
(Ramona), Monsete, Moño, Ramas,
Ramonche, Ramuncho. **Var:**
Dramona, Ramana, Ramesses,
Ramina, Ramiona, Ramma, Rammón,
Ramone, Ramonel, Ramonelia,
Ramonia, Ramuna, Raniona,
Rannón, Ranona, Remona, Romona.
See also Raimundo.

Ramonche   see **Ramón.**
Ramoncito   see **Raimundo.**
Ramondo   see **Raimundo.**
Ramone   see **Ramón.**
Ramonel   see **Ramón.**
Ramonelia   see **Ramón.**
Ramonia   see **Ramón.**
Ramuido   see **Raimundo.**
Rámula   see **Rómulo.**
Ramulfo   see **Ranulfo.**
Rámulus   see **Rómylo.**
Ramuna   see **Ramón.**
Ramuncha   see **Raimundo.**
Ramuncho   see **Ramón.**
Ramundo   see **Raimundo.**
Ranaldo   see **Reinaldo.**
Randolfo (Rahn dole' foe) m. **EE:**
Randolph, etc. Teut. "He who
carries shield of power."
Raniona   see **Ramón.**
Rannón   see **Ramón.**
Ranolfo   see **Ranulfo.**
Ranona   see **Ramón.**
Ranulf   see **Ranulfo.**
Ranulfo (Rah newl' foe) m. **EE:**
Ragenulfa. Teut. "Wise warrior."
Ragenulfa, 7th cen. Fr. S. F.
7/14. **Var:** Ramulfo, Ranolfo,
Ranulf, Renolfo, Renulfo. See
also Wulfrano.

Raol   see **Raul.**
Raoul   see **Raul.**
Raphaela   see **Rafael.**
Raphaele   see **Rafael.**
Raphaelelis   see **Rafael.**
Raphaelem   see **Rafael.**
Raphaelia   see **Rafael.**
Raphaelilis   see **Rafael.**
Raphaelis   see **Rafael.**
Raphaelita   see **Rafael.**
Raphaila   see **Rafael.**
Raphel   see **Rafael.**
Raphela   see **Rafael.**
Raphelia   see **Rafael.**
Rapito (Rah pee' toe) m. Diminu-
tive form of Agapito or Rafael
(see both).
Raqkel   see **Raquel.**
Raqual   see **Raquel.**
Raquel (Rah kel') f. **EE:** Rachel,
Rae. Heb. "Ewe." Younger daugh-
ter of Laban. 2nd wife of Jacob.
Dim: Quela, Quelita, Rachelina,
Raco, Requia. **Var:** Racael,

Racaela, Racheal, Rachele,
Rachell, Racquel, Racuel,
Raechel, Ragaela, Ragnel,
Ragnela, Raguel, Raguenel,
Raqkel, Raqual, Raquelio,
Raquelo, Rascel, Rasquel,
Raxsel, Raychal, Requel, Roquel.

Raquelio   see **Raquel.**
Raquelo   see **Raquel.**
Rasaela   see **Raziel.**
Rasalía   see **Rosalío.**
Rascel   see **Raquel.**
Rasindo   see **Rosendo.**
Rasquel   see **Raquel.**
Rasura   see **Rosauro.**
Raudel (Rah dell') m. Sp. "Raudo,"
"abundance, copiousness."
Raul (Rah ool') m. **EE:** Ralph, etc.
Fr., Teut. "Warrior eager for
glory." **Dim:** Fafa, Fallo, Falo,
Faro, Felo, Lulito, Pelo, Rafa,
Raulina, Rulito, Rulo. **Var:**
Raol, Raoul, Raule, Raulio. See
also Rodolfo.

Raule   see **Raul.**
Raulina   see **Raul.**
Raulio   see **Raul.**
Rave   see **Rafael.**
Ravella   see **Rafael.**
Raviel   see **Rafael.**
Raxsel   see **Raquel.**
Raychal   see **Raquel.**
Rayes   see **Reyes.**
Raymaldo   see **Reinaldo.**
Raymón   see **Raimundo.**
Raymondo   see **Raimundo.**
Raymunda   see **Raimundo.**
Raymundus   see **Raimundo.**
Raynaldo   see **Reinaldo.**
Raynoado   see **Reinaldo.**
Rayphael   see **Rafael.**
Raziel (Rah zee el') m. Heb. "My
secret is God." **Var:** Rasaela,
Razuel.
Razuel   see **Raziel.**
Rebbeca   see **Rebeca.**
Rebbecca   see **Rebeca.**
Rebeca (Ray bay' kah) f. **EE:**
Becky, Rebecca. Heb. "To bind."
Wife of Isaac, mother of Jacob &
Esau. 2 x in DS. **Dim:** Bequi,
Bequita. **Var:** Rabecca, Rebbeca,
Rebbecca, Rebecca, Rebekah,
Reebeca, Reveca, Revecca.

Rebecca   see **Rebeca.**
Rebekah   see **Rebeca.**
Recardo   see **Ricardo.**
Recaredo   see **Ricardo.**
Rechard   see **Ricardo.**
Recharda   see **Ricardo.**
Reciliana   see **Prisciliano.**
Redemptión   see **Redención.**
Redención (Ray dane see own') mf.
Sp. "Redemption." Christ's dying
on cross to redeem Christians.
Var: Redemptión.
Redimino (Ray dee mee' no) m. Sp.
"Redimir," "to redeem." **Var:**
Redimiro, Redina.
Redimiro   see **Redimino.**
Redina   see **Redimino.**
Redolfo   see **Rodolfo.**
Redosindo   see **Rudesinda.**
Reducind   see **Rudesinda.**
Reducindo   see **Rudesinda.**

Redusendo	see	**Rudesinda.**
Redusindo	see	**Rudesinda.**
Reebeca	see	**Rebeca.**
Reemberto	see	**Remberto.**
Refael	see	**Rafael.**
Refigio	see	**Refugio.**
Refigua	see	**Refugio.**
Refilla	see	**Refugio.**
Refogio	see	**Refugio.**
Refrigio	see	**Refugio.**
Refufio	see	**Refugio.**
Refuge	see	**Refugio.**

Refugio (Ray foo' hee oh) mf. Lat.
"Refuge." 1 of names of Blessed
V., Nuestra Señora del Refugio
(Our Lady of Refuge). **Dim:** Cuco,
Cuquito, Fucho, Fujo, Guka,
Refugito. **Var:** Rafagio, Rafufio,
Rafugia, Rafujia, Refigio,
Refigua, Refilla, Refogio,
Refrigio, Refufio, Refuge,
Refuguia, Refuigia, Refujio,
Refujo, Refutiano, Refutio,
Refuxio, Refygia, Regugio,
Resugio, Rifuagio, Rufugio,
Rufuia.

Refugito	see	**Refugio.**
Refuguia	see	**Refugio.**
Refuigia	see	**Refugio.**
Refujio	see	**Refugio.**
Refujo	see	**Refugio.**
Refutiano	see	**Refugio.**
Refutio	see	**Refugio.**
Refuxio	see	**Refugio.**
Refygia	see	**Refugio.**

Regalado (Ray gah lah' doe) m.
Lat. "Gift." Sp. "gifted." Peter
Regalado, of 15th cen.
Valladolid, helped reform
Franciscan order. F. 5/13.

Regelso	see	**Rogelio.**
Regenio	see	**Regina.**
Regerio	see	**Rogelio.**
Reges	see	**Reyes.**
Regildo	see	**Reinaldo.**
Regimo	see	**Regina.**

Regina (Ray hee' nah) f. EE:
Regan, Regina, etc. Lat. "Rex"
means "ruler." "Salve Regina" or
"Hail, Holy Queen" 1 of oldest
psalms in western Christianity.
5 x in DS. **Dim:** Gina. **Var:**
Aregina, Eregenia, Rajino,
Regenio, Regimo, Reginal, Regum,
Reguum, Reina, Rejain, Rejinia,
Rejino, Rena, Reyna, Rigino,
Rogino. See also **Régulo, Reyes.**

Reginal	see	**Regina.**
Reginaldo	see	**Reinaldo.**
Reginaldrum	see	**Reinaldo.**
Regino	see	**Reinaldo.**

Regira (Ray hee' rah) f. Lat.
"Regere" means "to rule or to
moderate."

Regirio	see	**Rogelio.**
Regis	see	**Reyes.**
Regita	see	**Reyes.**
Regnol	see	**Reinaldo.**
Regoberto	see	**Rigoberto.**
Reguelo	see	**Régulo.**
Regugio	see	**Refugio.**

Régulo (Ray' goo low) m. EE:
Regula, Regulus. Lat. "Little
king." Roman general in 1st
Punic War. 8 x in DS. 1, 8th

cen. Scottish bishop, brought
relics of St. Andrew to his
country. F. 10/17. **Var:** Reguelo.
See also **Regina, Reyes.**

Regum	see	**Regina.**
Reguum	see	**Regina.**
Rehela	see	**Rogelio.**
Reico	see	**Ricardo.**
Reimeldo	see	**Reinaldo.**
Reimundo	see	**Raimundo.**
Reina	see	**Regina.**

Reinaldo (Ray nahl' doe) m. EE:
Reginald, etc. Teut. "He com-
mands with intelligence." 7 x in
DS. **Dim:** Naldo, Nelda, Nelde,
Neldina, Nélida, Nelta, Nilda,
Ronalita. **Var:** Rainaldo,
Rainelda, Ranaldo, Raymaldo,
Raynaldo, Raynoado, Regildo,
Reginaldo, Reginaldrum, Regino,
Regnol, Reimeldo, Reinando,
Rejinaldo, Renaldo, Renaldus,
Reunaldo, Reymaldo, Reynaldo,
Reynaldo, Reynanda, Reynol,
Rinaldo, Ronaldo, Ronualdo.

Reinando	see	**Reinaldo.**
Reinigia	see	**Remigio.**
Reiss	see	**Reyes.**
Reita	see	**Rito.**
Rejain	see	**Regina.**
Rejas	see	**Reyes.**
Rejelio	see	**Rogelio.**
Rejinaldo	see	**Reinaldo.**
Rejinia	see	**Regina.**
Rejino	see	**Regina.**
Relles	see	**Reyes.**
Rellies	see	**Reyes.**
Remaldo	see	**Rumolda.**

Remberto (Raim bare' toe) m. EE:
Reginbert. Teut. "Outstanding
for advice." 10th cen. bishop of
Seldenburen, Switzerland. F.
12/20. **Var:** Reemberto.

Remedias	see	**Remedio.**

Remedio (Ray may' dee oh) mf. EE:
Remedius. Lat. "That which
cures." Several churches,
Nuestra Señora de los Remedios
(Our Lady of Remedies). 1 in
Mexico has image of V. brought
from Spain during conquest. **Var:**
Remedias, Remedior, Remedius,
Remidios.

Remedior	see	**Remedio.**
Remedius	see	**Remedio.**
Remegio	see	**Remigio.**
Remegra	see	**Remigio.**
Remejio	see	**Remigio.**
Remeo	see	**Roman.**
Remicsela	see	**Remisio.**
Remidios	see	**Remedio.**
Remigin	see	**Remigio.**

Remigio (Ray mee' hee oh) m. EE:
Remigius. Lat. "He who knows how
to row." 5 x in DS. 5th cen. Fr.
bishop who converted King Clovis
I. F. 10/1. **Dim:** Mich. **Var:**
Ramigio, Ramigis, Ramigo,
Ramijio, Ramijo, Reinigia,
Remegio, Remegra, Remejio,
Remigin, Remigius, Remigo,
Remigro, Remiguio, Remijio,
Remijo, Remingia, Remiro,
Remitia, Renegero, Renicia,
Renigio, Renigna, Renigui,

Renijio, Renirgio, Renugio,
Rimigio, Romijio.

Remigius	see **Remigio.**
Remigo	see **Remigio.**
Remigro	see **Remigio.**
Remiguio	see **Remigio.**
Remijio	see **Remigio.**
Remijo	see **Remigio.**
Remingia	see **Remigio.**
Remiro	see **Remigio.**
Remisino	see **Remisio.**

Remisio (Ray mee' see oh) m. Lat. "Remissum," "ability to pardon." **Var:** Remicsela, Remisino.

Remitia	see **Remigio.**
Remona	see **Ramón.**

Remorda (Ray more' dah) f. Lat. "Remodere," "to have remorse."

Rémul (Ray' mool) m. Remulo was leader of Rutulos, tribe that lived in Italy.

Rémulo	see **Rómulo.**
Remundo	see **Raimundo.**
Rena	see **Regina.**
Renaldo	see **Reinaldo.**
Renaldus	see **Reinaldo.**
Renán	see **Renato.**
Renate	see **Renato.**

Renato (Ray nah' toe) m. **EE:** Renatus, etc. Lat. "Born again." 2 x in DS. Both 5th cen. bishops. **Var:** Renán, Renate, Renitta, Reynata, Rinato. See also René.

René (Ray nay') m. **EE:** Rene, Renee. Lat. "Born again." **Dim:** Neco. **Var:** Renissa. See also Renato.

Renegero	see **Remigio.**
Renica	see **Irene.**
Renicia	see **Remigio.**
Renigio	see **Remigio.**
Renigna	see **Remigio.**
Renigui	see **Remigio.**
Renijio	see **Remigio.**
Reniquita	see **Irene.**
Renirgio	see **Remigio.**
Renissa	see **René.**
Renitta	see **Renato.**
Renolfo	see **Ranulfo.**

Renovato (Ray no bah' toe) m. **EE:** Renovatus. Lat. "Restored." Cleansed of all sin as in baptism. Bishop of Merida who converted gluttonous monk. F. 3/31.

Renterio (Rain tay' ree oh) m. Lat. "One who rents (tears)."

Renugio	see **Remigio.**
Renulfo	see **Ranulfo.**
Reparada	see **Reparata.**

Reparata (Ray pah rah' tah) f. **EE:** Reparata. Lat. "He who starts a new life." 2 x in DS. Dove issued from headless trunk of 1, 3rd cen. M. **Var:** Reparada, Reperto.

Repertha	see **Ruperto.**
Reperto	see **Reparata.**
Requel	see **Raquel.**
Requia	see **Raquel.**
Resendo	see **Rosendo.**

Respicio (Race pee' see oh) m. **EE:** Respicius. Lat. "He who observes with care." M. of unknown period. F. 11/10.

Restituto (Race tee too' toe) m. **EE:** Restituta, Restitutus. Lat. "Restored." 17 x in DS. 1, of 3rd cen. Africa, mart. by burning. F. 5/17.

Resugio	see **Refugio.**
Resura	see **Resurección.**

Resurección (Ray soo rake see own') mf. Lat. "To rise again." Christ rising from the dead. **Dim:** Resura.

Reto	see **Margarito.**
Reubén	see **Rubén.**
Reubena	see **Rubén.**
Reunaldo	see **Reinaldo.**
Reveca	see **Rebeca.**
Revecca	see **Rebeca.**
Revera	see **Reveriano.**

Reveriano (Ray bay ree ah' no) m. **EE:** Reverianus. Lat. "He who looks at sacred with respect." S. sent by pope in 3rd cen. to evangelize Gauls. F. 6/1. **Var:** Revera.

Revocata (Ray bo cah' tah) f. **EE:** Revocatus. Lat. "Called again to grace of God." 6 x in DS.

Reyes (Ray' yays) m. Lat. "Kings." Adoration of 3 kings on 1/6. **Dim:** Regita. **Var:** Rayes, Reges, Regis, Reiss, Rejas, Relles, Rellies, Reyez, Reys. See also Régulo, Regina.

Reyez	see **Reyes.**
Reymaldo	see **Reinaldo.**
Reymondo	see **Raimundo.**
Reymundo	see **Raimundo.**
Reyna	see **Regina.**
Reynadlo	see **Reinaldo.**
Reynaldo	see **Reinaldo.**
Reynanda	see **Reinaldo.**
Reynata	see **Renato.**
Reynol	see **Reinaldo.**
Reynunda	see **Raimundo.**
Reys	see **Reyes.**
Ria	see **María.**
Rialino	see **María.**
Rica	see **Ricardo.**

Ricanora (Ree cah no' rah) f. Comb. of Ricardo & Nicanor (see both).

Ricardeta	see **Ricardo.**
Ricardio	see **Ricardo.**

Ricardo (Ree car' doe) m. **EE:** Dick, Richard, Rick, etc. Ger. "Rich & hard." Most famous, Richard the Lion-Hearted of 12th cen. 19 x in DS. **Dim:** Cardo, Cayo, Licaldo, Licalo, Lico, Quique, Reico, Rica (Ricarda), Rich, Richi, Ricia (Ricarda), Ricky, Rico. **Var:** Recardo, Recaredo, Rechard, Recharda, Ricardeta, Ricardio, Ricardum, Ricarla, Ricarrdi, Ricarrdo, Riccardae, Riccardo, Riccareda, Richar, Richardo, Richardus, Ricorda, Ricordio, Riqui, Rirgarda.

Ricardum	see **Ricardo.**
Ricarla	see **Ricardo.**
Ricarrdi	see **Ricardo.**
Ricarrdo	see **Ricardo.**
Riccardae	see **Ricardo.**
Riccardo	see **Ricardo.**

Riccareda   see **Ricardo.**
Rich   see **Ricardo.**
Richar   see **Ricardo.**
Richardo   see **Ricardo.**
Richardus   see **Ricardo.**
Richi   see **Patricio.**
Richi   see **Ricardo.**
Richo   see **Mauricio.**
Ricia   see **Ricardo.**
Ricky   see **Ricardo.**
Rico   see **Alarico.**
Rico   see **Ricardo.**
Ricoberto   see **Rigoberto.**
Ricorda   see **Ricardo.**
Ricordio   see **Ricardo.**
Rida   see **Rito.**
Riducenda   see **Rudesinda.**
Riel   see **Gabriel.**
Rifuagio   see **Refugio.**
Rigaberto   see **Rigoberto.**
Rigelio   see **Rogelio.**
Rígido (Ree' hee doe) m. Lat.
"Severe or inflexible."
Rigino   see **Regina.**
Rigo   see **Rigoberto.**
Rigoberto (Ree go bare' toe) m.
EE: Rigobert. Teut. "Splendid
for his wealth." 7th cen. Arch-
bishop of Rheims, France. F.
1/4. **Dim:** Rigo. **Var:** Regoberto,
Ricoberto, Rigaberto, Rigoverto.
Rigofredo (Ree go fray' doe) m.
Comb. of Rigoberto & Alfredo
(see both).
Rigoverto   see **Rigoberto.**
Rimaldo   see **Rumolda.**
Rimigio   see **Remigio.**
Rimitivo   see **Primitivo.**
Rina   see **Catalina.**
Rinaldo   see **Reinaldo.**
Rinato   see **Renato.**
Riqueta   see **Enrique.**
Riqui   see **Ricardo.**
Rirdolfo   see **Rodolfo.**
Rirgarda   see **Ricardo.**
Risauro   see **Rosauro.**
Risendo   see **Rosendo.**
Rita   see **Margarito.**
Ritae   see **Rito.**
Rito (Ree' toe) m. **EE:** Reta, Rita.
Independent diminutive form of
Margarito. St. Rita of 15th
cen., patroness of desperate
cases. **Var:** Reita, Rida, Ritae,
Ritta. See also Margarito.
Ritta   see **Rito.**
Rober   see **Roberto.**
Roberto (Roe bare' toe) m. **EE:**
Bob, Robert, Roberta, etc. Ger.
"Bright in fame." 18 x in DS. 1,
13th cen. hermit of Knares-
borough, England. F. 9/24. **Dim:**
Berto, Bertunga, Beto, Bobby,
Rober, Tito. **Var:** Raberto,
Roverto, Ruberto. See also
Ruperto.
Robla (Robe' lah) f. Lat.
"Roborare," "to fortify." Strong
person.
Robustiano (Roe boose tee ah' no)
m. **EE:** Robustian, Robustianus.
Lat. "Strong as an oak." M. ven-
erated in Milan, Italy. F. 8/31.
Var: Rogustiano, Rubestiana,
Ruvestiana.

Rocco   see **Roque.**
Roccus   see **Roque.**
Rocel   see **Rosalba.**
Rocelva   see **Rosalba.**
Rocendo   see **Rosendo.**
Rocha   see **Rosauro.**
Rochaz   see **Roque.**
Roche   see **Roque.**
Rochi   see **Rosa.**
Rocho   see **Roque.**
Rochus   see **Roque.**
Rocío (Roe see' oh) m. Lat. "Ros,"
"covered with dew." Title of
Blessed V., Nuestra Señora del
Rocío (Our Lady of the Dew).
Rocke   see **Roque.**
Rodalfo   see **Rodolfo.**
Rodas (Roe' dahs) f. **EE:** Rhoda.
Gk. "Rose." Biblical servant of
Mary & mother of Mark. See also
Rosa, Rosabel, Rosalba, Rosalío,
Rosalindo, Rosara, Rosario,
Rosaura, Rosendo.
Roderiga   see **Rodrigo.**
Rodgia   see **Rodrigo.**
Rodlofo   see **Rodolfo.**
Rodoefo   see **Rodolfo.**
Rodola   see **Rodolfo.**
Rodolfo (Roe dole' foe) m. **EE:**
Rudolf, Rudy. Ger. "Bright in
fame." 2 x in DS. 1 killed by
non-Christians in Bern, Switzer-
land in 13th cen. F. 4/17. **Dim:**
Fito, Fofo, Lulito, Popo, Rolo,
Rudi, Rudina, Rudy, Rulito,
Rulo. **Var:** Radalfo, Redolfo,
Rirdolfo, Rodalfo, Rodlofo,
Rodoefo, Rodola, Rodolpo,
Rodulfo, Rudalfo, Rudelfa,
Rudlofo, Rudulfa, Rudolpho,
Rudolphus, Rudulfo. See also
Raul.
Rodolpo   see **Rodolfo.**
Rodrego   see **Rodrigo.**
Rodrigo (Roe dree' go) m. **EE:**
Roderick, etc. Teut. "Famous for
glory." Root for patronymic
Rodriguez. 9th cen. M. of
Cordoba, Spain denounced by
brother for betraying Islam. F.
3/13. **Dim:** Gigo, Igo. **Var:**
Roderiga, Rodgia, Rodrego,
Rodrigus, Rodrique, Ruderico,
Ruy, Ruyz, Ryrus.
Rodrigus   see **Rodrigo.**
Rodrique   see **Rodrigo.**
Rodulfo   see **Rodolfo.**
Rogaciano (Roe gah see ah' no) m.
EE: Rogatianus, etc. Lat. "En-
treaty." Concept of prayer. 33 x
in DS. Mentioned for witnessing
good confession for Christ. F.
10/26. **Var:** Rogación, Rogarina.
See also Rogato.
Rogación   see **Rogaciano.**
Rogarina   see **Rogaciano.**
Rogato (Roe gah' toe) m. **EE:**
Rogata, Rogatus. Lat. "That
asked of God." 30 x in DS. See
also Rogaciano.
Rogelio (Roe hay' lee oh) m. **EE:**
Roger, etc. Teut. "He of glorious spear." 6 x in DS. 1,
disciple of St. Francis in 13th
cen. F. 3/5. **Dim:** Gela, Geyo,

Rugino. **Var:** Radelia, Ragelio,
Rajelis, Rajelo, Regelso,
Regerio, Regirio, Rehela,
Rejelio, Rigelio, Rogellio,
Rogelto, Rogerio, Rogetio,
Rogilio, Rognelio, Roguedela,
Roguerio, Rohelio, Rojelio,
Rojelo, Rojerio, Rojilio,
Ropelio, Rugelio, Rujelio.

Rogellio   see **Rogelio.**
Rogelto   see **Rogelio.**
Rogerio   see **Rogelio.**
Rogetio   see **Rogelio.**
Rogilio   see **Rogelio.**
Rogino   see **Regina.**
Rognelio   see **Rogelio.**
Rogue   see **Roque.**
Roguedela   see **Rogelio.**
Roguerio   see **Rogelio.**
Rogustiano   see **Robustiano.**
Rohelio   see **Rogelio.**
Rojana (Roe ha' nah) f. Wife of
Alexander the Great.
Rojelio   see **Rogelio.**
Rojelo   see **Rogelio.**
Rojerio   see **Rogelio.**
Rojilio   see **Rogelio.**
Rokil   see **Roque.**
Rolán   see **Roldán.**
Rolando   see **Roldán.**
Roldán (Role don') m. **EE:** Roland,
etc. Ger. "He who comes from
glorious country." Fr. hero of
medieval legend, "Song of Ro-
land." 5 x in DS. 1, probably
same 8th cen. hero, died
fighting Saracens. F. 6/16. **Dim:**
Lando, Olo, Orlo. **Var:** Ordando,
Orlando, Orlondo, Raldán,
Raldina, Rolán, Rolando, Roldón,
Rollón, Rolón, Urlanda.
Roldón   see **Roldán.**
Rollón   see **Roldán.**
Rolo   see **Rodolfo.**
Rolón   see **Roldán.**
Romaldina   see **Romilda.**
Romaldo   see **Romualdo.**
Rómalo   see **Rómulo.**
Romam   see **Román.**
Román (Roe mahn') m. **EE:** Roman,
etc. Lat. "Born in Rome." 45 x
in DS. 1, 4th cen. zealot of
Antioch. F. 11/18. **Dim:** Mancho,
Romanil, Romino. **Var:** Rameo,
Remeo, Romam, Romana, Romanade,
Romanano, Romance, Romanda,
Romandus, Romarico, Romarra,
Romeo, Rumona. See also Rómulo.
Romana   see **Román.**
Romanade   see **Román.**
Romanano   see **Román.**
Romance   see **Román.**
Romanda   see **Román.**
Romandus   see **Román.**
Romanil   see **Román.**
Romarico   see **Román.**
Romarra   see **Román.**
Romedo (Roe may' doe) m. **EE:**
Romedius. 5th cen. hermit of
Trent, Italy.
Romelia   see **Romilda.**
Romelica   see **Romilda.**
Romellia   see **Romilda.**
Romeo   see **Román.**
Romijio   see **Remigio.**

Romilda (Roe meel' dah) f. Teut.
"Glorious heroine." **Dim:**
Romaldina. **Var:** Ramelia,
Romelia, Romelica, Romellia.
Romino   see **Román.**
Romoalda   see **Romualdo.**
Romoldo   see **Rumolda.**
Rómolo   see **Rómulo.**
Romona   see **Ramón.**
Romuald   see **Romualdo.**
Romualdo (Roe moo all' doe) m. **EE:**
Romuald. Teut. "Glorious king."
Founder of Camadolese hermits,
an order with minimal communal
ties. F. 2/7. **Var:** Romaldo,
Romoalda, Romuald, Romulda,
Romundla.
Romul   see **Rómulo.**
Romulda   see **Romualdo.**
Rómulo (Roe' moo low) m. **EE:**
Romulus. Gk. "Full of force." 1
of twin founders of Rome. 16 x
in DS. **Var:** Rámula, Rámulus,
Rémulo, Rómalo, Rómolo, Romul,
Rónulo, Rúmulo. See also Román.
Romundla   see **Romualdo.**
Romundo   see **Raimundo.**
Ronaldo   see **Reinaldo.**
Ronalita   see **Reinaldo.**
Ronanciano (Roe non' see ah' no)
m. 12 Irish Ss. **Dim:** Ronanita.
Ronanita   see **Ronanciano.**
Ronmaldo   see **Rumolda.**
Ronsara   see **Rosauro.**
Ronualdo   see **Reinaldo.**
Rónulo   see **Rómulo.**
Ropelio   see **Rogelio.**
Roperto   see **Ruperto.**
Roque (Roe' kay) m. **EE:** Roch,
Roche, Rochus. Lat. "Rock."
Fig., "he who is like a for-
tress." 4th cen. Ital. patron
against pestilence. F. 8/16.
Var: Rocco, Roccus, Rochaz,
Roche, Rocho, Rochus, Rocke,
Rogue, Rokil.
Roquel   see **Raquel.**
Roralia   see **Aurelio.**
Rory   see **Aurora.**
Ros   see **Rosa.**
Rosa (Roe' sah) f. **EE:** Rose. Lat.
"Rose." Symbolizes martyrdom, V.
Mary, & lost perfection. 17th
cen. Peruvian nun, Rose of Lima,
most famous. F. 8/30. **Dim:**
Chalina, Challo, Charo, Chayo,
Chita, Chocha, Hrosita, Ocha,
Rochi, Rosasina, Roseta,
Rosetta, Rosi, Rosita, Shaba,
Tita, Xaba. **Var:** Chaba,
Chaguita, Ros, Rosado,
Rosaltina, Rosarera, Rosatio,
Rosaudia, Rosaudo, Rosember,
Rosenaldo, Rosizela, Rosmal,
Rosodia, Rosula, Rosunta,
Roszeda, Roza, Rozella, Rozuel.
See also Rodas, Rosalba,
Rosalia, Rosana, Rosario,
Rosaura.
Rosaana   see **Rosana.**
Rosabel (Roe sah bell') f. Comb.
of Rosa (see) & belle, Fr.
"beautiful." **Var:** Rosabello,
Rosbel, Rosibel. See also Rodas.
Rosabello   see **Rosabel.**

Rosaberta (Roe sah bare' tah) f.
  Comb. of Rosa & Berto (see
  both).

Rosado	see **Rosa.**
Rosaelia	see **Rosalío.**
Rosailia	see **Rosalío.**
Rosaisela	see **Rosalío.**
Rosalá	see **Rosalío.**
Rosalanda	see **Rosalindo.**

Rosalba (Roe sahl' bah) f. Lat.
  "Rosa" & "alba" meaning "white
  rose." **Dim:** Chaba, Chalba,
  Rocel. **Var:** Rocelva, Rosalva,
  Rosalval, Roselva. See also
  Rodas, Rosa.

Rosaleo	see **Rosalío.**

Rosaleón (Roe sah lay own') f.
  Comb. of Rosa & León (see both).

Rosalighia	see **Rosalío.**

Rosalindo (Roe' sah leen' doe) m.
  EE: Rosalind, Roselyn. Lat &
  Teut. "Smooth as a rose." **Dim:**
  Chalina, Lina. **Var:** Rosalanda,
  Roselín, Roselino, Roslinda,
  Roslino. See also Rodas,
  Rosamunda.

Rosalío (Roe sah lee' oh) m. **EE:**
  Rosalia, Rosalie. Rosalia, Roman
  feast of roses. Best known
  occasion "Dies Rosationis" when
  entire family placed roses on
  grave. **Dim:** Chala, Chali,
  Chalina, Chalío, Lía. **Var:**
  Prosalío, Rasalía, Rosaelia,
  Rosailia, Rosaisela, Rosalá,
  Rosaleo, Rosalighia, Rosalya,
  Rosela, Roselío, Rosilío,
  Rosolío, Rozalío. See also
  Rodas, Rosalina.

Rosalmira (Roe sahl mee' rah) f.
  Comb. of Rosa (see) & mira, Lat.
  "wonderful."

Rosaltina	see **Rosa.**
Rosalva	see **Rosalba.**
Rosalval	see **Rosalba.**
Rosalya	see **Rosalío.**

Rosamunda (Roe sah moon' dah) f.
  EE: Rosamond, etc. Lat. "Rose of
  the world." Mother of St. Ad-
  jutor of Vernon. F. 4/30. See
  also Rosalindo, Rosendo.

Rosana (Roe sah' nah) f. Comb. of
  Rosa & Ana (see both). **Dim:**
  Rosantino. **Var:** Rosaana,
  Rosania, Rosanna, Rosanro,
  Rosante, Rosauna, Rossana,
  Roszán, Rozanna. See also Rodas,
  Rosa.

Rosando	see **Rosendo.**
Rosania	see **Rosana.**
Rosanna	see **Rosana.**
Rosanro	see **Rosana.**
Rosante	see **Rosana.**
Rosantino	see **Rosana.**
Rosaora	see **Rosario.**
Rosarera	see **Rosa.**

Rosario (Roe sah' ree oh) mf. Lat.
  "Rose garden." Devotional
  prayers honoring V. Also title
  of V. Mary, Nuestra Señora del
  Rosario (Our Lady of the
  Rosary). F. 10/7. **Dim:** Challo,
  Chalo, Charito, Charo, Chayito,
  Chayo. **Var:** Rosaora, Rosiria,
  Rosorio, Rosrio, Rossario. See

also Rodas, Rosa.

Rosarra	see **Rosauro.**
Rosasina	see **Rosa.**
Rosatio	see **Rosa.**
Rosaudia	see **Rosa.**
Rosaudo	see **Rosa.**
Rosauna	see **Rosana.**

Rosauro (Roe sough' roe) m. Lat.
  "Rosa" & "aurea" meaning "rose
  of gold." **Dim:** Chaga, Chaguo,
  Rocha. **Var:** Rasura, Risauro,
  Ronsara, Rosarra. See also
  Rodas, Rosa.

Rosbel	see **Rosabel.**
Roscindo	see **Rosendo.**
Rosela	see **Rosalío.**
Roselin	see **Rosalindo.**
Roselino	see **Rosalindo.**
Roselío	see **Rosalío.**
Roselva	see **Rosalba.**
Rosember	see **Rosa.**
Rosenaldo	see **Rosa.**

Rosendo (Roe sane' doe) m. Teut.
  "Excellent lord." **Dim:** Chendo.
  Var: Chinda, Rasindo, Resendo,
  Risendo, Rocendo, Rosando,
  Roscindo, Rosenedo, Rosentina,
  Rosento, Roseudo, Rosinando,
  Rosindo, Rozenda. See also
  Rodas, Rosamunda, Rudesinda.

Rosenedo	see **Rosendo.**
Rosentina	see **Rosendo.**
Rosento	see **Rosendo.**
Roseta	see **Rosa.**
Rosetta	see **Rosa.**
Roseudo	see **Rosendo.**
Rosi	see **Rosa.**
Rosibel	see **Rosabel.**
Rosilío	see **Rosalío.**
Rosinando	see **Rosendo.**
Rosindo	see **Rosendo.**
Rosiria	see **Rosario.**
Rosita	see **Rosa.**
Rosizela	see **Rosa.**
Roslinda	see **Rosalindo.**
Roslino	see **Rosalindo.**
Rosmal	see **Rosa.**
Rosodja	see **Rosa.**
Rosolío	see **Rosalío.**
Rosorio	see **Rosario.**
Rosrio	see **Rosario.**
Rossana	see **Rosana.**
Rossario	see **Rosario.**
Rosula	see **Rosa.**
Rosunta	see **Rosa.**
Roszán	see **Rosana.**
Roszeda	see **Rosa.**

Roterio (Roe tay' ree oh) m. Teut.
  "Famous in army."

Roumaldo	see **Rumolda.**
Roumalinda	see **Rumolda.**
Roumold	see **Rumolda.**
Roverto	see **Roberto.**

Roxana (Rox ah' nah) f. **EE:**
  Roxanne. Wife of Alexander the
  Great. **Var:** Roxanna.

Roxanna	see **Roxana.**
Roza	see **Rosa.**
Rozalío	see **Rosalío.**
Rozanna	see **Rosana.**
Rozella	see **Rosa.**
Rozenda	see **Rosendo.**
Rozuel	see **Rosa.**
Rubbén	see **Rubén.**
Rubelina	see **Rubén.**

Rubén (Roo bain') m. **EE:** Rube, Rueben, etc. Heb. "Behold a son." Jacob's eldest son & founder of 1 of 12 tribes of Israel. **Dim:** Rubelina, Rubilina. **Var:** Reubén, Reubena, Rubbén, Rubena, Rubene, Rubilma, Rubina, Rubinda, Rubinia, Ruvén.

Rubena	see **Rubén.**
Rubene	see **Rubén.**
Ruberto	see **Roberto.**
Rubestiana	see **Robustiano.**

Rubí (Roo bee') m. **EE:** Ruby, etc. Lat. "Red." Refers to ruby. **Var:** Ruvilina.

Rubilina	see **Rubén.**
Rubilma	see **Rubén.**
Rubina	see **Rubén.**
Rubinda	see **Rubén.**
Rubinia	see **Rubén.**

Rubrico (Roo bree' co) m. **EE:** Rubrik. Lat. "Red sign." Rubrics also directions for order of Catholic Mass.

Ruca	see **Ruth.**
Rudalfo	see **Rodolfo.**
Rudecinda	see **Rudesinda.**
Rudelfa	see **Rodolfo.**
Rudencia	see **Prudencia.**
Rudenia	see **Rudesinda.**
Ruderico	see **Rodrigo.**
Ruderindo	see **Rudesinda.**

Rudesinda (Roo day seen' dah) f. **EE:** Rosendo, Rudesind. Ger. "Glorious military expedition." 10th cen. bishop of Galicia, Spain, who reformed Benedictine order. F. 3/1. **Dim:** Chicho, Chindo. **Var:** Redosindo, Reducind, Reducindo, Redusendo, Redusindo, Riducenda, Rudecinda, Rudenia, Ruderindo, Rudesindum, Rudesindus, Rudicinda, Rudinciada, Rusindo. See also Rosendo.

Rudesindum	see **Rudesinda.**
Rudesindus	see **Rudesinda.**
Rudi	see **Rodolfo.**
Rudicinda	see **Rudesinda.**
Rudilio	see **Rutilio.**
Rudina	see **Rodolfo.**
Rudinciada	see **Rudesinda.**
Rudlofo	see **Rodolfo.**
Rudolfa	see **Rodolfo.**
Rudolpho	see **Rodolfo.**
Rudolphus	see **Rodolfo.**
Rudulfo	see **Rodolfo.**
Rudy	see **Rodolfo.**

Rufecta (Roo fake' tah) f. Comb. of Ruperto & Perfecto (see both).

Rufemio	see **Eufemia.**
Rufena	see **Rufino.**
Rufeo	see **Rufino.**
Ruferio	see **Rufino.**
Ruferto	see **Rufino.**
Ruffo	see **Rufino.**
Rufia	see **Rufino.**
Rufilio	see **Rufino.**
Rufinam	see **Rufino.**
Rufiniano	see **Rufino.**

Rufino (Roo fee' no) m. **EE:** Rufus, etc. Lat. "Rufus," "red." 56 x in DS. 1, Roman mart. in 3rd cen. F. 7/10. **Var:** Rafina, Rufena, Rufeo, Ruferio, Ruferto, Ruffo, Rufia, Rufilio, Rufinam, Rufiniano, Rufinus, Rufo.

Rufinus	see **Rufino.**
Rufo	see **Rufino.**
Rufrosia	see **Eufracio.**
Rufugio	see **Refugio.**
Rufuia	see **Refugio.**
Rugelio	see **Rogelio.**
Rugino	see **Rogelio.**
Ruinalda	see **Rumolda.**
Rujelio	see **Rogelio.**
Rulito	see **Raul.**
Rulito	see **Rodolfo.**
Rulo	see **Raul.**
Rulo	see **Rodolfo.**
Rumaldo	see **Rumolda.**
Rumanda	see **Rumolda.**
Rummela	see **Rumolda.**

Rumolda (Roo mole' dah) f. **EE:** Rombauld, Rumold. Ger. "He who governs with glory." Irish S. of 11th cen. & patron of Malines, Belgium. F. 7/1. **Var:** Remaldo, Rimaldo, Romoldo, Ronmaldo, Roumaldo, Roumalinda, Roumold, Ruinalda, Rumaldo, Rumanda, Rummela, Rumualda.

Rumona	see **Román.**
Rumualda	see **Rumolda.**
Rúmulo	see **Rómulo.**

Ruperto (Roo pear' toe) m. **EE:** Rupert. Teut. "Splendid in advice." 3 x in DS. 1, 8th cen founder & 1st bishop of Salzburg, Austria. F. 3/27. **Dim:** Rupo. **Var:** Repertha, Roperto, Rupertus, Ruporto. See also Roberto.

Rupertus   see **Ruperto.**

Rupino (Roo pee' no) m. Rupinia in Roman myth. was rural goddess.

Rupo	see **Ruperto.**
Ruporto	see **Ruperto.**
Rusindo	see **Rudesinda.**

Rustam (Roo stahm') m. **EE:** Rustam. Major Pers. mythological hero who unitentionally slays son Sohrab. **Var:** Rustem.

Rystem   see **Rustam.**

Rústico (Ruse' tee co) m. Lat. "Belonging to the country." In positive sense, "simple, plain." 19 x in DS. 1, 5th cen. bishop of Narbonne, France, mart. by Goths.

Ruston (Ruse' tone) m. Rustam, celebrated hero of Pers. myth.

Rutelio   see **Rutilio.**

Ruth (Root) f. **EE:** Ruth, etc. Heb. "Compassionate." Biblical heroine who returns to Bethlehem with mother-in-law, Naomi. Married Boaz & became ancestor of David. **Dim:** Ruca, Ruti.

Ruti	see **Ruth.**
Rutibo	see **Rutilio.**
Rutilda	see **Rutilio.**

Rutilio (Roo tee' lee oh) m. **EE:** Rutila, Rutulus. Lat. "He who shines." 5 x in DS. 1 lived in hiding during persecution of Severus. F. 8/2. **Var:** Rudilio, Rutelio, Rutibo, Rutilda, Rutillo, Rutilo.

Rutillo	see Rutilio.	Ruvilina	see Rubí.
Rutilo	see Rutilio.	Ruy	see Rodrigo.
Ruvén	see Rubén.	Ruyz	see Rodrigo.
Ruvestiana	see Robustiano.	Ryrus	see Rodrigo.

S

Saara see Sara.

Sabá (Sah bah') f. EE: Sheba. Lat. form of Ar. "Sheba." Arab region noted for wealth through visit of Queen of Sheba to Solomon, **Dim:** Savita, **Var:** Sabad, Sabán, Sabar, Sabbae. See also Sabás.

Sabad see Sabá.
Sabán see Sabá.
Sabapa see Zapopan.
Sabar see Sabá.

Sabás (Sah bahs') f. EE: Sabba, etc. Heb. "Rest." Sabbath, day of rest. 28 x in DS. 1, 4th cen. Visigoth, tortured & drowned. F. 4/12. **Dim:** Sabitas. **Var:** Sabatis, Sabáz, Sabbás, Sabós, Savás, Zabaz. See also Sabá.

Sabastián see Sebastián.
Sabastiana see Sebastián.
Sabatis see Sabás.
Sabáz see Sabás.
Sabbae see Sabá.
Sabbás see Sabás.
Sabeida see Zobeida.
Sabela see Isabel.
Sabena see Sabino.
Saberio see Sabino.
Sabiano see Sabino.
Sabijina see Sabino.
Sabiniano see Sabino.

Sabino (Sah bee' no) m. EE: Sabina, etc. Lat. "Born in Sabina." Emperor Nero's wife who tried to save beauty by bathing in asses' milk. 49 x in DS. 1, 2nd cen. widow, arrested by Hadrian after conversion. F. 4/29. **Var:** Sabena, Saberio, Sabiano, Sabijina, Sabiniano, Sabinta, Sabinus, Sabra, Sabrino, Saviniano, Savino, Sebrina, Sibino, Suvina, Zabina, Zabriana, Zabrina.

Sabinta see Sabino.
Sabinus see Sabino.
Sabistriana see Sebastián.
Sabitas see Sabás.
Saboba see Zapopan.
Sabós see Sabás.
Sabra see Sabino.
Sabrino see Sabino.
Sabulón see Zabulón.
Saburnino see Saturnino.
Sacarías see Zacarías.
Sacaríes see Zacarías.
Sacario see Sagrario.
Sacarios see Sagrario.
Sacarro see Socorro.
Saccarías see Zacarías.
Sacharío see Zacarías.
Sacorro see Socorro.

Sacramento (Sah crah main' toe) m. Lat. "That which binds or obliges one." In Catholicism, visible sign of inward grace. Lat. root is parent of several surnames: Santos, Sánchez, Sáenz, Saíz, & Sais. **Var:** Sacramentus, Sacremento, Sacrimento, Sacromento. See also Sagrario, Sancho.

Sacramentus see Sacramento.
Sacremento see Sacramento.
Sacrías see Zacarías.
Sacrimento see Sacramento.
Sacromento see Sacramento.
Sacundina see Segundino.

Sadat (Sah daht') m. EE: Sadoth, Shadhost. Heb. "Just, righteous." Biblical ancestor of Christ. 2 x in DS. 1, 10th cen. metropolitan of Syria, killed for refusing to worship sun. F. 2/20.

Sadio see Zaida.
Sadislao see Estanislao.
Sadislas see Estanislao.
Safarena see Ceferino.
Saferina see Ceferino.
Safiá see Sofío.
Safira see Ceferino.
Safirio see Ceferino.
Safopan see Zapopan.
Sagario see Sagrario.

Sagrario (Sah grah' ree oh) m. Lat. "Place of worship." **Var:** Sacario, Sacarios, Sagario, Sagrasio, Sagroria, Sagrua, Secario, Segario, Segreda. See also Sacramento, Sancho.

Sagrasio see Sagrario.
Sagroria see Sagrario.
Sagrua see Sagrario.
Sahra see Sara.
Saida see Zaida.
Saila see Zoilo.
Saladono see Celedonio.
Salamón see Salomón.
Salastina see Celestino.
Salatonia see Celedonio.
Salavador see Salvador.
Salbador see Salvador.
Salbadora see Salvador.
Salbedor see Salvador.
Saledá see Soledad.
Saledad see Soledad.
Saledonio see Celedonio.
Salena see Celina.
Salerino see Celerino.
Salerna see Celerino.

Saleta (Sah lay' tah) f. Salete in Egyp. myth., goddess similar to Minerva.

Salfarino see Ceferino.
Salforino see Ceferino.

162   Salima

|---|---|---|---|

Salima   see Celina.
Salino   see Celina.
Salomán   see Salomón.
Salomé (Sah low may') f. EE:
  Salome, etc. Heb. "Peace."
  Daughter of Herod who requested
  head of St. John the Baptist. 5
  x in DS. 1, wife of Zebedee,
  mother of apostles James & John.
  F. 10/22. **Var:** Salomena,
  Salomene, Salomeo, Salomer,
  Salomera, Salomó, Soloma,
  Soloné. See also Salomón.
Salomena   see Salomé.
Salomene   see Salomé.
Salomeo   see Salomé.
Salomer   see Salomé.
Salomera   see Salomé.
Salomó   see Salomé.
Salomón (Sah low moan') m. EE:
  Sol, Solomon, etc. Heb. "Peace-
  ful." Son of David & Bathsheba &
  king of Israel. 9 x in DS. 1,
  king of Brittany, France, mur-
  dered by rebellious subjects. F.
  6/25. **Dim:** Mon, Moñi. **Var:**
  Salamón, Salomán, Slomón,
  Solomone. See also Salomé.
Salonaho   see Salonia.
Salonia (Sah low' nee ah) f. Roman
  empress abandoned by husband,
  sought consolation of philoso-
  phers & is thought to have pro-
  tected Christians. **Var:**
  Salonaho.
Salos (Sah' lohs) m. Salus in
  Roman myth., goddess of health.
  See also Salud, Salustiano,
  Salvador, Salvino.
Salradón   see Celedonio.
Salso   see Celso.
Salto   see Exaltación.
Salud (Sah lood') mf. Lat. "Un-
  hurt, uninjured." Sanctuary in
  Castellón, Spain, named after la
  Virgen de la Fuente de la Salud
  de Traiguera (Our Lady of the
  Fountain of Good Health). **Dim:**
  Saludino. See also Salos,
  Salustiano, Salvador, Salvino.
Saludino   see Salud.
Salurnino   see Saturnino.
Salustiano (Sah loose' tee ah' no)
  m. EE: Sallustius, Salust. Lat.
  "That offers salvation." 1 S.
  Var: Salustino, Salustio,
  Salustria, Salustriano. See also
  Salos, Salud, Salvador, Salvino.
Salustino   see Salustiano.
Salustio   see Salustiano.
Salustria   see Salustiano.
Salustriano   see Salustiano.
Salvado   see Salvador.
Salvador (Sahl bah dore') m. Lat.
  "One who saves." Christ's sacri-
  fice for mankind's salvation. 3
  x in DS. 1, 16th cen. Sp.
  miracle worker. **Dim:** Chaba,
  Chabalito, Chavo. **Var:**
  Salavador, Salbador, Salbadora,
  Salbedor, Salvado, Salvadora,
  Salvadore, Salvadoren, Salvados,
  Salvadro, Salvaniano, Salvarado,
  Salvardo, Salvardor, Salvator,
  Salvodor, Zlavador. See also

Salos, Salud, Salustiano,
  Salvino.
Salvadora   see Salvador.
Salvadore   see Salvador.
Salvadoren   see Salvador.
Salvados   see Salvador.
Salvadro   see Salvador.
Salvaniano   see Salvador.
Salvarado   see Salvador.
Salvardo   see Salvador.
Salvardor   see Salvador.
Salvator   see Salvador.
Salviano   see Salvino.
Salvino (Sahl bee' no) m. EE:
  Salvinus, Salvius. Lat. "Unhurt,
  uninjured." 14 x in DS. **Var:**
  Salviano, Salvio, Selveno. See
  also Salos, Salud, Salustiano,
  Salvador.
Salvio   see Salvino.
Salvodor   see Salvador.
Sambuena (Sahm bway' nah) f. Comb.
  of Samuel & Buenaventura (see
  both).
Sami   see Samuel.
Samia   see Samuel.
Samjuana   see Sanjuana.
Samuel (Sahm well') m. EE: Sam,
  Samuel, etc. Heb. "Heard of
  God." In OT last of judges of
  Israel. F. 8/20. 10 x in DS.
  Dim: Mel, Sami, Samia. **Var:**
  Samuelo.
Samuelo   see Samuel.
Sanagossa   see Zaragoza.
Sanaida   see Zenaido.
Sancho (Sahn' cho) m. EE: Sanctan,
  Sanctius. Lat. "Sacred, invio-
  lable." Patronymic "Sánchez"
  means "son of Sancho." Squire of
  Don Quixote. 16 x in DS. **Dim:**
  Santino, Santita, Santitas. **Var:**
  Sancta, Sanctae, Sanctio,
  Sanctorum, Sanctos, Sanctum,
  Santa, Santes, Santín,
  Santísimo, Santón, Santona,
  Santos, Santún, Santus. See also
  Sacramento, Sagrario.
Sancta   see Sancho.
Sanctae   see Sancho.
Sanctio   see Sancho.
Sanctorum   see Sancho.
Sanctos   see Sancho.
Sanctum   see Sancho.
Sandalio (Sahn dah' lee oh) m. EE:
  Sandalus, Gk. "He who scatters
  perfume." S. who died in
  Cordoba, Spain. F. 9/3.
Sandara   see Alejandro.
Sandeago   see Santiago.
Sandiago   see Santiago.
Sandiego   see Santiago.
Sandra   see Alejandro.
Sandrah   see Alejandro.
Sanduago   see Santiago.
Sanfuena (Sahn fway' nah) f.
  Transposition of Fuensanta
  (see).
Sangiago   see Santiago.
Sanguana   see Sanjuana.
Saniago   see Santiago.
Sanisildo   see Estanislao.
Sanja   see Sanjuana.
Sanjago   see Santiago.
Sanjana   see Sanjuana.

Sanjargo   see **Santiago**.
Sanjuan   see **Sanjuana**.
Sanjuana (Sahn hua' nah) f. Comb.
  of "san," "saint" & Juan (see).
  Var: Samjuana, Sanguana, Sanja,
  Sanjana, Sanjuan, Sanjuna,
  Sonjuana.
Sanjuna   see **Sanjuana**.
Sanobia   see **Zenobio**.
Sanorina   see **Senorina**.
Sanovio   see **Zenobio**.
Sanpiana (Sahn pee ah' na) f.
  Comb. of "san," "saint" &
  Ulipiano (see). **Var**: Sanpina.
Sanpina   see **Sanpiana**.
Sansón (Sahn sone') m. **EE**: Samson,
  etc. Heb. "Little sun." Judge of
  Israel whose strength related to
  hair. F. 3/26. 3 x in DS.
Santa   see **Sancho**.
Santaana   see **Santana**.
Santago   see **Santiago**.
Santaleón (Sahn tah lay own') m.
  Comb. of Santa & Pantaleón (see
  both).
Santana (Sahn tah' nah) f. Comb.
  of Santa & Ana (see both). **Var**:
  Santaana.
Santava   see **Santiago**.
Santavera (Sahn' tah bay' rah) f.
  Comb. of Santa & Vera (see
  both).
Santeago   see **Santiago**.
Santeno (Sahn tay' no) m. Lat.
  "Native of Saintonge, France."
  Var: Santino.
Santes   see **Sancho**.
Santiaco   see **Santiago**.
Santiada   see **Santiago**.
Santiafa   see **Santiago**.
Santiago (Sahn tee ah' go) m. **EE**:
  Jacob, James, etc. Comb. of
  "san," "saint" & Jacobo (see).
  Dim: Chago, Chango, Chano,
  Didaco (Diego), Diegolino
  (Diego), Dieguín (Diego),
  Dieguito (Diego), Santiaguito,
  Santinguito, Tago, Vego (Diego),
  Yego. **Var**: Antiago, Dieco,
  Diego, Jaimitio, Jaimito,
  Jantiago, Sandeago, Sandiago,
  Sandiego, Sanduago, Sangiago,
  Saniago, Sanjago, Sanjargo,
  Santago, Santava, Santeago,
  Santiaco, Santiada, Santiafa,
  Santiato, Santiego, Santiero,
  Santigio, Santigo, Santiogo,
  Santrago, Senteago, Somtiogo.
  See also Jacobo, Jaime.
Santiaguito   see **Santiago**.
Santiato   see **Santiago**.
Santiego   see **Santiago**.
Santiero   see **Santiago**.
Santigio   see **Santiago**.
Santigo   see **Santiago**.
Santín   see **Sancho**.
Santinguito   see **Santiago**.
Santino   see **Sancho**.
Santino   see **Santeno**.
Santiogo   see **Santiago**.
Santísimo   see **Sancho**.
Santita   see **Sancho**.
Santitas   see **Sancho**.
Santón   see **Sancho**.
Santona   see **Sancho**.

Santos   see **Sancho**.
Santrago   see **Santiago**.
Santún   see **Sancho**.
Santus   see **Sancho**.
Sapapo   see **Zapopan**.
Sapatra   see **Zapopan**.
Sapherino   see **Ceferino**.
Saphias   see **Sofío**.
Sapopa   see **Zapopan**.
Sapopae   see **Zapopan**.
Sapopais   see **Zapopan**.
Sapopan   see **Zapopan**.
Sapope   see **Zapopan**.
Sapopopo   see **Zapopan**.
Sapopra   see **Zapopan**.
Sappana   see **Zapopan**.
Sapriano   see **Cipriano**.
Sara (Sah' rah) f. **EE**: Sadie,
  Sally, Sarah, etc. Heb. "Prin-
  cess." Wife of Abraham who at
  age of 90 gave birth to Isaac.
  F. 8/19. 4 x in DS. **Dim**: Chara,
  Charita, Charrita, Saraita,
  Sarino, Sarita. **Var**: Saara,
  Sahra, Sarea, Sarero, Sares,
  Sarra, Sarrah, Sarres, Sera,
  Serah, Serra, Sora, Sorah,
  Sorita, Zahara, Zara, Zayde,
  Zayra, Zera.
Sarafina   see **Ceferino**.
Saragazza   see **Zaragoza**.
Saragda   see **Zaragoza**.
Saragogo   see **Zaragoza**.
Saragos   see **Zaragoza**.
Saragosam   see **Zaragoza**.
Saragoso   see **Zaragoza**.
Saragossa   see **Zaragoza**.
Saragoza   see **Zaragoza**.
Saraida   see **Zoraida**.
Saraita   see **Sara**.
Sarapita   see **Serapio**.
Sarazoso   see **Zaragoza**.
Sarea   see **Sara**.
Sarefio   see **Serapio**.
Sarepio   see **Serapio**.
Sarero   see **Sara**.
Sares   see **Sara**.
Sarino   see **Sara**.
Sarita   see **Sara**.
Sarito   see **César**.
Sarojoza   see **Zaragoza**.
Saropio   see **Serapio**.
Saroza   see **Zaragoza**.
Sarpia   see **Serapio**.
Sarra   see **Sara**.
Sarrah   see **Sara**.
Sarrazoza   see **Zaragoza**.
Sarres   see **Sara**.
Sasá   see **Saturnino**.
Sasaria   see **César**.
Sásimo   see **Zósimo**.
Sástenes   see **Sóstenes**.
Sástines   see **Sóstenes**.
Sástinez   see **Sóstenes**.
Satanelia (Sah tah nay' lee ah) f.
  From Saturnales, Roman feast in
  honor of Saturn.
Satarino   see **Saturnino**.
Satere   see **Sotero**.
Satero   see **Sotero**.
Satornino   see **Saturnino**.
Sattera   see **Sotero**.
Satuanina   see **Saturnino**.
Satumia   see **Saturnino**.
Satumina   see **Saturnino**.

Saturdino	see **Saturnino**.		Tano, Tato, Xebo. **Var**:	
Saturiana	see **Saturnino**.		Cebastián, Cebastiana,	
Saturimo	see **Saturnino**.		Sabastián, Sabastiana,	
Saturinino	see **Saturnino**.		Sabistriana, Savastián,	
Saturino	see **Saturnino**.		Sebantina, Sebartiana,	
Saturmino	see **Saturnino**.		Sebasbiás, Sebastaín,	
Saturniana	see **Saturnino**.		Sebastaina, Sebastana,	
Saturnín	see **Saturnino**.		Sebastiance, Sebastianna,	

Saturnino (Sah toor nee´ no) m.
EE: Saturn, Saturninus. Lat.
"Protector of crops." In Roman
myth., Saturn god of sowing &
reaping grain. 84 x in DS. **Dim**:
Nino, Sasá, Tunino, Tuno. **Var**:
Cetoninia, Ceturnino, Saburnino,
Salurnino, Satarino, Satornino,
Satuanina, Satumia, Satumina,
Saturdino, Saturiana, Saturimo,
Saturinino, Saturino, Saturmino,
Saturniana, Saturnín,
Saturninun, Saturnio, Saturno,
Saturrino, Saturvina, Saturwino,
Septurnina, Seterino, Seturnino,
Sturnino, Sturrino, Zaturnina.

			Sebastiano, Sebastién, Sebastín,	
			Sebastina, Sebastinus,	
			Sebastión, Sebateán, Sebathana,	
			Sebestiana, Sebistín,	
			Selbastiano, Sevastián,	
			Sevastiana, Sevastrán.	
Saturninun	see **Saturnino**.		Sebastiance	see **Sebastián**.
Saturnio	see **Saturnino**.		Sebastianna	see **Sebastián**.
Saturno	see **Saturnino**.		Sebastiano	see **Sebastián**.
Saturrino	see **Saturnino**.		Sebastién	see **Sebastián**.
Saturvina	see **Saturnino**.		Sebastín	see **Sebastián**.
Saturwino	see **Saturnino**.		Sebastina	see **Sebastián**.

Saúl (Sah ool´) m. EE: Saul,
Solly. Heb. "Longed for." 1st
king of Israel, told of his
death by witch of Endor. 2 x in
DS. **Var**: Saulo.

			Sebastinus	see **Sebastián**.
			Sebastión	see **Sebastián**.
			Sebateán	see **Sebastián**.
			Sebathana	see **Sebastián**.
Saulo	see **Saúl**.		Seberiano	see **Severo**.
Saundra	see **Alejandro**.		Seberino	see **Severo**.
Sauro	see **Isauro**.		Seberiona	see **Severo**.
Sausisla	see **Auxilio**.		Sebero	see **Severo**.
Savara	see **Severo**.		Seberro	see **Severo**.
Savás	see **Sabás**.		Sebestiana	see **Sebastián**.
Savastián	see **Sebastián**.		Sebistín	see **Sebastián**.
Saveida	see **Zobeida**.		Seboba	see **Zapopan**.
Saverio	see **Severo**.		Sebriano	see **Severo**.
Savero	see **Severo**.		Sebrina	see **Sabino**.
Saviniano	see **Sabino**.		Sebuba	see **Zapopan**.
Savino	see **Sabino**.		Secario	see **Sagrario**.
Savita	see **Sabá**.		Secelio	see **Cecilio**.
Sayda	see **Zaida**.		Secilia	see **Cecilio**.
Sazaro	see **César**.		Secindino	see **Segundino**.
Sbella	see **Isabel**.		Secondina	see **Segundino**.
Schalástica	see **Escolástica**.		Seconideo	see **Segundino**.
Scholastice	see **Escolástica**.		Secora	see **Socorro**.
Scipio	see **Escipión**.		Secorro	see **Socorro**.
Scleastiana	see **Escolástica**.		Secrandina	see **Segundino**.
Scolástica	see **Escolástica**.		Secumdina	see **Segundino**.
Scoléstico	see **Escolástica**.		Secunden	see **Segundino**.
Scrafina	see **Ceferino**.		Secundiano	see **Segundino**.
Scraphio	see **Serapio**.		Secundica	see **Segundino**.
Scynthia	see **Cinta**.		Secundila	see **Segundino**.
Seasaro	see **César**.		Secundimo	see **Segundino**.
Sebantina	see **Sebastián**.		Secundino	see **Segundino**.
Sebarano	see **Severo**.		Secundinus	see **Segundino**.
Sebarino	see **Ceferino**.		Secundio	see **Segundino**.
Sebartiana	see **Sebastián**.		Secundirio	see **Segundino**.
Sebasbiás	see **Sebastián**.		Secundius	see **Segundino**.
Sebastaín	see **Sebastián**.		Secundo	see **Segundino**.
Sebastaina	see **Sebastián**.		Secundulo	see **Segundino**.
Sebastana	see **Sebastián**.		Secunduro	see **Segundino**.
			Secunideno	see **Segundino**.
			Secunina	see **Segundino**.

Sebastián (Say bahs tee ahn´) m.
EE: Sebastian, etc. Gk. "Worthy
of veneration." 15 x in DS. 1,
Roman M. killed with arrows. F.
1/20. **Dim**: Bastián, Bastiana,
Chabo, Chano, Chebo, Shebo, Tan,

			Securro	see **Socorro**.
			Sedo	see **Sidonio**.
			Sedonia	see **Sidonio**.
			Sef	see **Ceferino**.
			Sefa	see **José**.
			Sefahrina	see **Ceferino**.
			Sefano	see **Esteban**.
			Sefariano	see **Ceferino**.
			Sefarino	see **Ceferino**.
			Sefelina	see **Ceferino**.
			Seferana	see **Ceferino**.
			Seferenio	see **Ceferino**.
			Sefereno	see **Ceferino**.
			Seferfino	see **Ceferino**.
			Seferiano	see **Ceferino**.

Seferim	see Ceferino.
Seferima	see Ceferino.
Seferin	see Ceferino.
Seferino	see Ceferino.
Sefernio	see Ceferino.
Seferrino	see Ceferino.
Sefevino	see Ceferino.
Seffano	see Ceferino.
Sefia	see Ceferino.
Sefirano	see Ceferino.
Sefireno	see Ceferino.
Seforina	see Ceferino.
Sefredo	see Sigfrido.
Sefrenia	see Ceferino.
Sefriana	see Ceferino.
Sefrinia	see Ceferino.
Sefrino	see Ceferino.
Segandina	see Segundino.
Segario	see Sagrario.
Segerina	see Sergio.
Segiberto	see Sigeberto.
Segismondo	see Segismundo.
Segismund	see Segismundo.

Segismundo (Say hees moon' doe) m.
EE: Sigismund, Sigmund. Teut.
"Victor, guardian." Principal
character in Calderón's "La vida
es sueño" (1635). 6th cen. Bur-
gundian king condemned son to
death. Patron against fever &
hernia. F. 7/17. Dim: Muno. Var:
Segismondo, Segismund,
Sigismundo, Sigmundus.

Segneda	see Zenaido.

Segrada (Say grah' dah) f. Variant
of Sagrada, Lat. "sacratus"
meaning "worthy of veneration &
respect." See also Sacramento,
Sagario.

Segreda	see Sagrario.
Segrefredo	see Sigfrido.
Seguindo	see Segundino.

Segundino (Say' goon dee' no) m.
EE: Secundus. Lat. "Following."
Literally, 2nd child of family.
81 x in DS. 1, of 2nd cen.
Italy, mart. under Hadrian. F.
3/30. Dim: Chundo, Secundila,
Secundulo. Var: Cecundina,
Sacundina, Secindino, Secondina,
Seconideo, Secrandina,
Secumdina, Secunden, Secundiano,
Secundica, Secundimo, Secundino,
Secundinus, Secundio,
Secundirio, Secundius, Secundo,
Secunduro, Secunideno, Secunina,
Segandina, Seguindo, Segundo,
Segunia, Segunta.

Segundo	see Segundino.
Segunia	see Segundino.
Segunta	see Segundino.

Sei (Say) f? Seia, in Roman myth.,
protectress of germinating
seeds.

Seivero	see Severo.
Selaido	see Zenaido.
Selbastiano	see Sebastián.
Selbia	see Silvio.

Selco (Sell' co) m. Selk, in Egyp.
myth., goddess worshipped in
Nubia, Africa.

Seldona	see Celedonio.
Seldonio	see Celedonio.
Seledino	see Celedonio.
Seledomia	see Celedonio.

Seledón	see Celedonio.
Seledonio	see Celedonio.
Seledonis	see Celedonio.
Selema	see Zulema.
Selena	see Celina.
Selenia	see Celina.
Selerino	see Celerino.
Seles	see Celina.

Selésforo (Say lace' foe roe) m.
Comb. of Celestino & Telésforo
(see both).

Selestena	see Celestino.
Selestine	see Celestino.
Selestino	see Celestino.
Selgio	see Sergio.
Selia	see Celio.
Seliam	see Celina.
Selice	see Celina.
Selicita	see Celina.
Selidón	see Celedonio.
Selidonio	see Celedonio.
Selilia	see Celina.
Selina	see Celina.
Selinda	see Celina.
Selistino	see Celestino.
Selita	see Celina.
Seliverto	see Silverio.
Selmo	see Anselmo.
Selodona	see Celedonio.
Selso	see Celso.
Selveno	see Salvino.
Selverdo	see Silverio.
Selverio	see Silverio.
Selvestra	see Silvestre.
Selvestre	see Silvestre.
Selvia	see Silvio.
Selzo	see Celso.
Semetrio	see Simitrio.
Semión	see Zenón.
Semo	see Anselmo.
Semón	see Zenón.
Semona	see Zenón.
Semphoriana	see Ceferino.
Semplicia	see Simplicio.
Sena	see Zenaido.
Sena	see Zenón.
Senaid	see Zenaido.
Senaido	see Zenaido.
Senarda	see Zenaido.
Senarina	see Senorina.
Senaro	see Génaro.
Senavia	see Zenobio.
Senaydo	see Zenaido.

Sencida (Sane see' dah) f. Sp.
adjective "beautiful, adorned."

Sencio	see Inocencio.
Sención	see Asunción.
Seneción	see Asunción.
Seneida	see Zenaido.
Senén	see Zenón.

Senén (Say nen') m. EE: Senan.
Heb. "Pure." 12 x in DS.

Seneronia	see Senorina.
Seniada	see Zenaido.
Senido	see Zenaido.
Senilla	see Zenón.
Seniona	see Zenón.
Senivina	see Genoveva.
Sennón	see Zenón.
Senobio	see Zenobio.
Senofia	see Zenobio.
Senoida	see Zenaido.
Senón	see Zenón.
Senona	see Zenón.
Senone	see Zenón.

Senonio   see **Zenón.**
Senopio   see **Zenobio.**
Senora   see **Senorina.**
Senorana   see **Senorina.**
Senoriana   see **Senorina.**
Senorina (Say no ree' nah) f.
   Ital. "Signorina," "young lady."
   10th cen Portuguese nun & ab-
   bess. F. 4/22. **Var:** Cenerino,
   Cenorina, Cenorio, Sanorina,
   Senarina, Seneronia, Senora,
   Senorana, Senoriana, Sinorina,
   Zenorina.
Senovina   see **Genoveva.**
Senovio   see **Zenobio.**
Sensión   see **Asunción.**
Senteago   see **Santiago.**
Senvio   see **Zenobio.**
Seolasticus   see **Escolástica.**
Seón   see **Zenobio.**
Seonida   see **Zenaido.**
Sepapa   see **Zapopan.**
Separina   see **Ceferino.**
Seperino   see **Ceferino.**
Sephania   see **Ceferino.**
Sepharina   see **Ceferino.**
Sephario   see **Ceferino.**
Sepherino   see **Ceferino.**
Sepherinus   see **Ceferino.**
Sephirino   see **Ceferino.**
Sepora   see **Sippora.**
Sepreano   see **Cipriano.**
Seprián   see **Cipriano.**
Sepriano   see **Cipriano.**
Septimino   see **Séptimo.**
Séptimo (Sape' tee mo) m. **EE:** Sep,
   Septimia, Septimus. Lat. "Sev-
   enth." Literally, 7th child of
   family. 15 x in DS. **Dim:** Septo.
   Var: Septimino.
Septo   see **Séptimo.**
Septurnina   see **Saturnino.**
Sequel   see **Ezequiel.**
Sequiel   see **Ezequiel.**
Sera   see **Ceferino.**
Sera   see **Sara.**
Seraf   see **Serapio.**
Serafana   see **Ceferino.**
Serafén   see **Ceferino.**
Serafena   see **Ceferino.**
Serafica   see **Serapio.**
Serafiel (Say rah fee ell') m.
   Comb. of Sara & Rafael (see
   both).
Serafim   see **Serafín.**
Serafín (Say rah feen') m. **EE:**
   Seraphim, Seraphine. Heb. "Ser-
   pent or flaming angel." 1 of ce-
   lestial beings who stand before
   God in vision of Isaiah. 2 x in
   DS. **Dim:** Pina. **Var:** Cepherina,
   Cerafino, Cerefino, Cererino,
   Ceresfin, Serafim, Serafino,
   Serafirm, Serafrio, Seraphim,
   Seraphin, Seraphina, Serefino,
   Serfemino, Serfina, Serfinos,
   Serfio, Serofín, Serofina,
   Serrarina.
Serafina   see **Ceferino.**
Serafino   see **Serafín.**
Serafio   see **Serapio.**
Serafirm   see **Serafín.**
Serafrio   see **Serafín.**
Seragosa   see **Zaragoza.**
Serah   see **Sara.**

Seraida   see **Zoraida.**
Serap   see **Serapio.**
Serapeo   see **Serapio.**
Serapheina   see **Ceferino.**
Seraphim   see **Serafín.**
Seraphima   see **Ceferino.**
Seraphin   see **Serafín.**
Seraphina   see **Serafín.**
Seraphino   see **Ceferino.**
Seraphio   see **Serapio.**
Serapii   see **Serapio.**
Serapin   see **Serapio.**
Serapina   see **Serapio.**
Serapio (Say rah' pee oh) m. **EE:**
   Serapion, etc. Lat. "Consecrated
   to Serapis," composite Egyp. god
   of healing. 39 x in DS. 1 mart.
   at Alexandria, Egypt. F. 5/19.
   Dim: Lapo, Sarapita, Serap,
   Yapa. **Var:** Cerapio, Cirapio,
   Sarefio, Sarepio, Saropio,
   Sarpia, Scraphio, Seraf,
   Serafica, Serafio, Serapeo,
   Seraphio, Serapii, Serapin,
   Serapina, Serapión, Serapionem,
   Serapo, Serapu, Seripio, Seripo,
   Serofia, Seropio, Seropora,
   Serovio, Serpio, Serppio,
   Serrovio, Sesapio, Sirapio,
   Sorapio, Zarapina, Zarapio,
   Zerapio, Zorapio.
Serapión   see **Serapio.**
Serapionem   see **Serapio.**
Serapo   see **Serapio.**
Serapu   see **Serapio.**
Serbal (Sare bal') mf? Tree of
   rose family. **Var:** Serbol,
   Servol.
Serbando   see **Servando.**
Serbardo   see **Servando.**
Serbaro   see **Servando.**
Serbol   see **Serbal.**
Serdio   see **Sergio.**
Serefino   see **Ceferino.**
Serefino   see **Serafín.**
Serena (Say ray' nah) f. **EE:**
   Serena, Serenity, etc. Lat.
   "Serene, tranquil." 12 x in DS.
   1, reputed wife of notorious
   Christian slayer, Diocletian. F.
   8/16. **Var:** Serenia, Serino,
   Sirenio, Syrina.
Serenia   see **Serena.**
Serenzo (Say rane' so) m. Comb. of
   Serena & Lorenzo (see both).
Serero   see **Severo.**
Serevino   see **Severo.**
Sereyoso   see **Zaragoza.**
Serfemino   see **Serafín.**
Serfina   see **Serafín.**
Serfinos   see **Serafín.**
Serfio   see **Serafín.**
Sergeo   see **Sergio.**
Sergio (Sare' hee oh) m. **EE:**
   Serge, Sergius. Lat. "He who
   protects & shepherds." 33 x in
   DS. 1, of 3rd cen. Rome, be-
   headed. F. 10/7. **Dim:** Checho,
   Checo. **Var:** Cergio, Segerina,
   Selgio, Serdio, Sergeo, Serjio,
   Sirgior, Zergio.
Sericón (Say ree cone') m. Serico,
   inhabitant of Seres, Asia.
Serifín   see **Ceferino.**
Serino   see **Serena.**

Seripio   see **Serapio.**
Seripo   see **Serapio.**
Serjio   see **Sergio.**
Sernando   see **Servando.**
Sernovia   see **Zenobio.**
Serofia   see **Serapio.**
Serofin   see **Serafín.**
Serofina   see **Serafín.**
Seropio   see **Serapio.**
Seropora   see **Serapio.**
Serovio   see **Serapio.**
Serpio   see **Serapio.**
Serppio   see **Serapio.**
Serra   see **Sara.**
Serrando   see **Servando.**
Serrarina   see **Serafín.**
Serrero   see **Severo.**
Serrovio   see **Serapio.**
Serva   see **Servacio.**
Servace   see **Servacio.**
Servacio (Sare bah' see oh) m. EE: Servatius, Lat. "To save, to preserve," 1st bishop of Tongern, Belgium, who predicted invasion of Huns. F. 5/13. **Var:** Cerasio, Cervacio, Serva, Servace.
Serván   see **Servando.**
Servando (Sare bahn' doe) m. EE: Servandus, Lat. "He who should be saved." 3 x in DS. 1, 3rd cen. Spaniard, beheaded for destroying pagan sanctuaries in Leon, Spain. Patron of Cadiz. F. 10/23. **Var:** Cerbando, Cervardo, Serbando, Serbardo, Serbaro, Sernando, Serrando, Serván, Servanedo, Servanto, Servardo, Servendo, Servonda. See also Servilio.
Servanedo   see **Servando.**
Servanto   see **Servando.**
Servardo   see **Servando.**
Servenario   see **Severo.**
Servendo   see **Servando.**
Servera   see **Severo.**
Servey   see **Servilio.**
Servigildo (Sare' bee heel' doe) m. Comb. of Servo & Hermenegildo (see both).
Servileón   see **Severo.**
Servilio (Sare bee' lee oh) m. EE: Servilianus. Lat. "One who serves." Roman family. 4 x in DS. **Dim:** Servitas. **Var:** Cervilia, Cerville, Servey, Servina, Servión, Servulo. See also Servando.
Servina   see **Servilio.**
Servión   see **Servilio.**
Servitas   see **Servilio.**
Servol   see **Serbal.**
Servonda   see **Servando.**
Servulo   see **Servilio.**
Sesadio   see **César.**
Sesánea (Say sah' nee ah) f. Sesan in Bible, son of Jesse & brother of David.
Sesapio   see **Serapio.**
Sésar   see **César.**
Sesareo   see **César.**
Sesario   see **César.**
Seserino   see **César.**
Sesililo   see **Cecilio.**
Sesilium   see **Cecilio.**

Sessaria   see **César.**
Sesto   see **Sixto.**
Seterino   see **Saturnino.**
Setero   see **Sotero.**
Setta (Say' tah) f. Feminine form of Set (Seth), 3rd son of Adam & Eve. Also Seta, sister of Reso & mistress of Mars in Roman myth.
Seturnino   see **Saturnino.**
Sevafín (Say bah feen') m. Comb. of Severo & Josefina (see).
Sevaida   see **Zobeida.**
Sevariana   see **Severo.**
Sevaro   see **Severo.**
Sevastián   see **Sebastián.**
Sevastiana   see **Sebastián.**
Sevastrán   see **Sebastián.**
Seveida   see **Zobeida.**
Sevenano   see **Severo.**
Sevenino   see **Severo.**
Sevennana   see **Severo.**
Seveno   see **Severo.**
Sevenriano   see **Severo.**
Severaina   see **Severo.**
Severano   see **Severo.**
Severeano   see **Severo.**
Severia   see **Severo.**
Severiada   see **Severo.**
Severiano   see **Severo.**
Severino   see **Severo.**
Severious   see **Severo.**
Severito   see **Severo.**
Severo (Say bay' roe) m. EE: Sever, Severin, Severus. Lat. "Austere, severe." 51 x in DS. 1, bishop of Barcelona, Spain, put to death by Arian Visigoths. F. 11/6. **Dim:** Ceberita, Severito. **Var:** Cebera, Ceberiano, Ceboenao, Cervero, Ceverina, Cevero, Savara, Saverio, Savero, Sebarano, Seberiano, Seberino, Seberiona, Sebero, Seberbo, Sebriano, Seivero, Serero, Serevino, Serrero, Servenario, Servera, Servileón, Sevariana, Sevaro, Sevenano, Sevenino, Sevennana, Seveno, Sevenriano, Severaina, Severano, Severeano, Severia, Severiada, Severiano, Severino, Severious, Severum, Severus, Seviriana, Sevoriano, Sevreano, Siberiana, Sivenana, Siverino, Siverio, Sivero, Svero, Zeverino.
Severum   see **Severo.**
Severus   see **Severo.**
Seviriana   see **Severo.**
Sevoriano   see **Severo.**
Sevreano   see **Severo.**
Sexta   see **Sixto.**
Sezario   see **César.**
Sezaro   see **César.**
Sferino   see **Ceferino.**
Shaba   see **Rosa.**
Shebo   see **Eusebio.**
Shebo   see **Sebastián.**
Siama (See ah' mah) f. Feminization of Siam, ancient name of Thailand.
Siberiana   see **Severo.**
Siberto   see **Silverio.**
Sibester   see **Silvestre.**
Sibilo (See bee' low) m. EE:

Sybil, etc. Gk. "One with gift
of prophecy." Wise woman of
ancient Greece whose prophecies
came through divine incantation.
Derivation of Seville, Spain.
Dim: Sila. **Var:** Cibilo, Civilo,
Cybil, Sivila.
Sibino   see **Sabino.**
Sibrado (See brah' doe) m.
Sibrando, beatified abbot of
13th cen.
Sibrián   see **Cipriano.**
Sicadio (See cah' dee oh) m.
Sicatios, in Gk. myth., another
name for Zeus, supreme god.
Sicaria (See cah' ree ah) f. Bene-
dictine V. of Orleans, France of
an unknown period. F. 2/26.
Sicilio   see **Cecilio.**
Sicto   see **Sixto.**
Sidero   see **Desiderio.**
Sididoro   see **Isidoro.**
Sidie   see **Sidonio.**
Sidio   see **Sidonio.**
Sidonio (See doe' nee oh) m. EE:
Sidney, etc. Lat. "Native of
Sidon," ancient Phoen. city.
Dim: Sedo, Sidie, Sidio. **Var:**
Sedonia.
Sidro   see **Isidoro.**
Sidronio (See droe' nee oh) m. EE:
Sidronius, etc. Gk. "Ironsmith."
10 x in DS. 1, Christian poet &
orator of 5th cen. F. 8/23. **Var:**
Cidronea, Cidronis, Sidronius,
Sisdranio.
Sidronius   see **Sidronio.**
Siegfrido   see **Sigfrido.**
Sielia   see **Cecilio.**
Siferino   see **Ceferino.**
Siforiana   see **Sinforiano.**
Sifredo   see **Sigfrido.**
Sifrigedo   see **Sigfrido.**
Sifugeno   see **Sigfrido.**
Sigeberto (See hay bare' toe) m.
EE: Sigebert. Teut. "He who
shines for victories." 1, king
of East Anglia in 7th cen. died
in battle against pagans. F.
9/27. **Var:** Segiberto.
Sigefredo   see **Sigfrido.**
Sigelfrido   see **Sigfrido.**
Sigfredo   see **Sigfrido.**
Sigfrido (Seeg free' doe) m. EE:
Siegfried, Sig. Teut. "He who
assures peace with victories."
Ger. hero of legend "Nibelungen-
lied." 2 x in DS. 1, 11th cen.
Englishman, preached in Sweden &
converted King Olaf. F. 2/15.
Var: Cifredo, Cigifredo,
Sefredo, Segrefredo, Siegfrido,
Sifredo, Sifrigedo, Sifugeno,
Sigefredo, Sigelfrido, Sigfredo,
Sigfridres, Sigifordo, Sigifred,
Sigifredo, Sigifribo, Sigifrido,
Sigisfudo, Sigrado, Sigredo,
Sijefredo, Sijifredo,
Sijisfredo, Silfredo, Sisifredo,
Sugifredo, Zigfredo, Zigifredo.
Sigfridres   see **Sigfrido.**
Sigifordo   see **Sigfrido.**
Sigifred   see **Sigfrido.**
Sigifredo   see **Sigfrido.**
Sigifribo   see **Sigfrido.**

Sigifrido   see **Sigfrido.**
Sigisfudo   see **Sigfrido.**
Sigismundo   see **Segismundo.**
Siglinda (Seeg leen' dah) f. Ger.
"Shield of victory." **Var:**
Zelinda.
Sigmundus   see **Segismundo.**
Sigrado   see **Sigfrido.**
Sigredo   see **Sigfrido.**
Sijefredo   see **Sigfrido.**
Sijifredo   see **Sigfrido.**
Sijisfredo   see **Sigfrido.**
Sila   see **Sibilo.**
Silano (See lah' no) m. S. mart.
in 1st cen. of church. F. 1/2.
Silas (See' lahs) m. EE: Silas.
Lat. "Jungle." Biblical leader
who accompanied Paul on 2
missions. F. 7/13. 4 x in DS.
See also Silvano, Silverio,
Silvestre, Silvino, Silvio.
Silbanio   see **Silvano.**
Silbano   see **Silvano.**
Silbeana   see **Silvano.**
Silberato   see **Silverio.**
Silberio   see **Silverio.**
Silbestre   see **Silvestre.**
Silbestro   see **Silvestre.**
Silbia   see **Silvio.**
Silbiano   see **Silvano.**
Silbino   see **Silvino.**
Silbona   see **Silvino.**
Silferiana   see **Ceferino.**
Silfredo   see **Sigfrido.**
Silia   see **Bacilio.**
Silidonia   see **Celedonio.**
Siliviano   see **Silvino.**
Silván   see **Silvano.**
Silvanilda   see **Silvano.**
Silvanio   see **Silvano.**
Silvano (Seel bah' no) m. EE:
Sylvain, Sylvanus, etc. Lat.
"Forest." Forest deity Sylvanus
protected boundaries of fields.
42 x in DS. 1, of Clairvaux,
France, rewarded by heavenly
visions. F. 2/18. **Var:** Silbanio,
Silbano, Silbeana, Silbiano,
Silván, Silvanilda, Silvanio,
Silvaria, Silviano, Sylbana,
Sylvanos. See also Silas,
Silverio, Silvestre, Silvino,
Silvio.
Silvaria   see **Silvano.**
Silvastre   see **Silvestre.**
Silvenio   see **Silvino.**
Silveno   see **Silvino.**
Silvera   see **Silverio.**
Silverio   see **Silverio.**
Silverio (Seel bay' ree oh) m. EE:
Silverius. Lat. "Jungle." 6th
cen. pope. F. 6/20. **Var:**
Seliverto, Selverdo, Selverio,
Siberto, Silberato, Silberio,
Silvera, Silvirio, Sylverio,
Sylvero. See also Silas,
Silvano, Silvestre, Silvino,
Silvio.
Silversto   see **Silvestre.**
Silverta   see **Silvestre.**
Silverte   see **Silvestre.**
Silverter   see **Silvestre.**
Silvester   see **Silvestre.**
Silvestia   see **Silvestre.**
Silvestre (Seel base' tray) m. EE:

Sylvester, etc. Lat. "He who
lives in forest." 13 x in DS. 1,
4th cen. pope. F. 12/31. **Dim:**
Chivete, Chiveto, Veche, Veto.
Var: Cilvestra, Cilvestre,
Selvestra, Selvestre, Sibester,
Silbestre, Silbestro, Silvastre,
Silverio, Silversto, Silverta,
Silverte, Silverter, Silvester,
Silvestia, Silvestrem,
Silvestria, Silvestro,
Slyvestre, Soester, Sulvester,
Sylbestrio, Sylvesdre,
Sylvestas, Sylvestera,
Sylvestine, Sylvestro. See also
Silas, Silvano, Silverio,
Silvino, Silvio.
Silvestrem   see **Silvestre.**
Silvestria   see **Silvestre.**
Silvestro   see **Silvestre.**
Silviano   see **Silvano.**
Silvino (Seel bee' no) m. **EE:**
Silva, Sylvana, etc. Lat.
"Jungle." 4 x in DS. 1, 7th cen.
Fr. bishop, spent fortune ran-
soming Christian captives from
barbarians. F. 2/17. **Dim:** Vina.
Var: Cilviano, Silbino, Silbona,
Siliviano, Silvenio, Silveno,
Syvinia. See also Silas,
Silvano, Silverio, Silvestre,
Silvio.
Silvio (Seel' bee oh) m. **EE:**
Sylvia, Sylvius, etc. Lat. "For-
est." 12 x in DS. Silvia was
Roman M. & mother of Pope Grego-
ry of 6th cen. F. 11/3. **Dim:**
Chiva, Chivi, Chiviz, Cyvia.
Var: Celvia, Selbia, Selvia,
Silbia, Sylbia, Sylvia. See also
Silas, Silvano, Silverio,
Silvestre, Silvino.
Silvirio   see **Silverio.**
Símaco (See' mah co) m. **EE:**
Symmachus. Gk. "Ally & companion
in battle." 3 x in DS. 1, 6th
cen. pope. F. 7/19.
Simana   see **Simón.**
Simatio   see **Simitrio.**
Simena   see **Simón.**
Simeón   see **Simón.**
Simeona   see **Simón.**
Simeonis   see **Simón.**
Simfonana see **Sinforiano.**
Simforo   see **Sinforiano.**
Simforoso see **Sinforoso.**
Simión   see **Simón.**
Simitrio (See mee' tree oh) m. **EE:**
Symmetrius. Lat. "Measured, mod-
erate." 2nd cen. M. F. 5/26.
Var: Cimitrio, Semetrio,
Simatio.
Simma   see **Simón.**
Simmona   see **Simón.**
Simoenae   see **Simón.**
Simón (See moan') m. **EE:** Simeón,
Simon, etc. Heb. "Hearing." 51 x
in DS. Given name of St. Peter.
F. 10/28. **Dim:** Cima, Moncho,
Simma. **Var:** Chimón, Chimona,
Chimone, Cimona, Simana, Simena,
Simeón, Simeona, Simeonis,
Simión, Simmona, Simoenae,
Simona, Simonan, Simonéo,
Simonis, Somona, Zimón. See also

Jimeno.
Simona   see **Simón.**
Simonan   see **Simón.**
Simonéo   see **Simón.**
Simonis   see **Simón.**
Simpilia   see **Simplicio.**
Simplicio (Seem plee' see oh) m.
EE: Simplicius. Lat. "Simple or
without affectation." 21 x in
DS. 1, 5th cen. pope. F. 3/10.
Var: Cimplicio, Semplicia,
Simpilia, Simplicitas,
Simplisio, Siplicia.
Simplicitas see **Simplicio.**
Simplisio   see **Simplicio.**
Sinaido   see **Zenaido.**
Sinas   see **Sinesio.**
Sinayda   see **Zenaido.**
Sincionite see **Asunción.**
Sindoroso   see **Sinforoso.**
Sindulfo (Seen dool' foe) m. **EE:**
Sindulf, Sindulphus. Teut.
"Trained warrior." 7th cen.
hermit near Rheims, France. F.
10/20.
Sinecio   see **Sinesio.**
Sinesio (See nay' see oh) m. **EE:**
Sinicius. Gk. "Wise, intelli-
gent." Bishop of Soissons,
France. F. 9/1. **Dim:** Sinas. **Var:**
Sinecio.
Sinfariano see **Sinforiano.**
Sinfor   see **Sinforiano.**
Sinforiano (Seen foe' ree ah' no)
m. **EE:** Symphorianus. Gk. "He who
has many gifts." 7 x in DS. 1,
in Gaul, scourged, jailed, &
beheaded for refusing to sacri-
fice to Cybele, goddess of fer-
tility. F. 8/22. **Var:** Cifernio,
Cifirina, Ciforiano, Cifrana,
Cinforiano, Siforiana,
Simfonana, Simforo, Sinfariano,
Sinfor, Sinfornia, Sinoriana,
Zinforiana.
Sinfornia   see **Sinforiano.**
Sinforofa   see **Sinforoso.**
Sinforosae see **Sinforoso.**
Sinforoso (Seen' foe roe' so) m.
EE: Symphorosa. Lat. "To be
useful." 2 x in DS. 1, Roman
matron mart. with 7 sons. F.
7/19. **Dim:** Bocho, Chóforo, Foro,
Polocho. **Var:** Simforoso,
Sindoroso, Sinforofa,
Sinforosae, Sinforsa, Sinfrosia,
Sinphoroso, Symforosa,
Symphorio, Symphorosae,
Symphoroso, Symporoso,
Synforosa, Synphoriano.
Sinforsa   see **Sinforoso.**
Sinfrosia   see **Sinforoso.**
Sinibaldo (See' nee ball' doe) m.
Teut. "Audacious, enterprising."
Dim: Nibaldo.
Sinón   see **Zenón.**
Sinona   see **Zenón.**
Sinonita   see **Zenón.**
Sinoriana   see **Sinforiano.**
Sinorina   see **Senorina.**
Sinovio   see **Zenobio.**
Sinphoroso see **Sinforoso.**
Sintica   see **Sintiques.**
Sintiques (Seen tee' kays) m. Gk.
"Amiable with others." **Var:**

Sintica.
Sipio   see **Cipriano.**
Siplano   see **Cipriano.**
Siplicia   see **Simplicio.**
Sippora (See poe' rah) f. **EE:**
Zippora, Zipporah. Heb. "Small
bird." Daughter of Jethro & wife
of Moses. **Var:** Jsipora, Sepora,
Zipora.
Siprano   see **Cipriano.**
Siprián   see **Cipriano.**
Siprianita   see **Cipriano.**
Sipriano   see **Cipriano.**
Siprino   see **Cipriano.**
Siraco   see **Ciriaco.**
Siralio   see **Cirilo.**
Sirapio   see **Serapio.**
Sirenio   see **Serena.**
Sirgior   see **Sergio.**
Siria   see **Ciriaco.**
Siriaco   see **Ciriaco.**
Siriago   see **Ciriaco.**
Siricio   see **Ciriaco.**
Sirido   see **Cirilo.**
Sirila   see **Cirilo.**
Sirildo   see **Cirilo.**
Sirilio   see **Cirilo.**
Sirio   see **Ciro.**
Siro   see **Ciro.**
Siscto   see **Sixto.**
Sisdranio   see **Sidronio.**
Sisebuto (See say boo' toe) m. **EE:**
Sisebut. Ger. "Victorious lead-
er." Abbot of Cardena, Spain,
who gave shelter to El Cid in
11th cen.
Sisenando (See say nahn' doe) m.
EE: Sisenand. Teut. "Daring for
victory." Mart. when beheaded in
Badajoz, Spain in 9th cen. F.
7/16.
Siseto   see **Sixto.**
Sisifredo   see **Sigfrido.**
Sisilia   see **Cecilio.**
Sisinio (See see' nee oh) m. **EE:**
Sisinnius. Lat. "Native of Sis,
Armenia." 15 x in DS. 1, mart.
by pagans in Nonsberg, Austria
in 4th cen. F. 5/29.
Sistana   see **Sixto.**
Sisteo   see **Sixto.**
Sistine   see **Sixto.**
Sisto   see **Sixto.**
Sistor   see **Sixto.**
Sivenana   see **Severo.**
Siverino   see **Severo.**
Siverio   see **Severo.**
Sivero   see **Severo.**
Sivila   see **Sibilo.**
Sixsto   see **Sixto.**
Sixtino   see **Sixto.**
Sixtio   see **Sixto.**
Sixto (Seeks' toe) m. **EE:** Sextus,
Xystus. Lat. "Sixth." 6th child
of family. 7 x in DS. 3 popes.
Var: Cisterna, Cisto, Cysta,
Cystine, Sesto, Sexta, Sicto,
Siscto, Siseto, Sistana, Sisteo,
Sistine, Sisto, Sistor, Sixsto,
Sixtino, Sixtio, Systo, Xista,
Xistae, Xistao, Xixta, Xysto,
Xystum. See also Sistine.
Sizaris   see **César.**
Slaltonia   see **Celedonio.**
Slena   see **Celina.**

Slomón   see **Salomón.**
Slyvestre   see **Silvestre.**
Snayda   see **Zenaido.**
Soaida   see **Zoraida.**
Sobeda   see **Zobeida.**
Sobeida   see **Zobeida.**
Sobeyda   see **Zobeida.**
Socaria   see **Socorro.**
Socarito   see **Socorro.**
Socaro   see **Socorro.**
Socarro   see **Socorro.**
Soccarro   see **Socorro.**
Soccora   see **Socorro.**
Soccorro   see **Socorro.**
Socerro   see **Socorro.**
Sócimo   see **Zósimo.**
Soco   see **Socorro.**
Sócoma   see **Zósimo.**
Socorio   see **Socorro.**
Socoro   see **Socorro.**
Socorro (So co' roe) f. Lat. "To
run to help." Title of Blessed
V., Nuestra Señora del Perpetuo
Socorro (Our Lady of Perpetual
Help). Image of V. venerated in
Redemptorist church in Rome.
Dim: Choco, Cocó, Coyo, Soco.
Var: Jocorro, Sacarro, Sacorro,
Secora, Secorro, Securro,
Socaria, Socarito, Socaro,
Socarro, Soccarro, Soccora,
Soccorro, Socerro, Socorio,
Socoro, Socorso, Socurro,
Succoro, Succorro, Sucorra,
Sucurro.
Socorso   see **Socorro.**
Sócrates (So' crah tays) m. **EE:**
Socrates. Gk. "Healthy, strong."
Gk. philosopher & 1 of wisest
men of all time. 5 x in DS. 1,
4th cen. British M., suffered
under Diocletian. F. 9/1. **Dim:**
Socro.
Socro   see **Sócrates.**
Socurro   see **Socorro.**
Soester   see **Silvestre.**
Soferino   see **Ceferino.**
Sofero   see **Ceferino.**
Sofí   see **Sofío.**
Sofial   see **Sofío.**
Soficita   see **Sofío.**
Sofina   see **Sofío.**
Sofío (So fee' oh) m. **EE:** Sophia,
Sophie. Gk. "He who has knowl-
edge." 18 x in DS. St. Sophia
mart. with 3 daughters. F. 9/18.
Dim: Chefi, Chofa, Chofi, Fia,
Fifi, Fita, Soficita. **Var:**
Safía, Saphías, Sofí, Sofial,
Sofina, Sonia, Sophiae, Zofía.
See also Sonio.
Sofiria   see **Ceferino.**
Sofirina   see **Ceferino.**
Sofofa   see **Zapopan.**
Sofopa   see **Zapopan.**
Sofronio (So fro' nee oh) m. **EE:**
Sophronia, Sophronius. Gk. "Pru-
dent & sensible." 6 x in DS. 1,
Patriarch of Jerusalem & eminent
theologian of 6th cen. F. 3/11.
Var: Sonfonias.
Sohnya   see **Sonio.**
Soile   see **Zoilo.**
Soilla   see **Zoilo.**
Soilo   see **Zoilo.**

Soilus   see Zoilo.
Soladá   see Soledad.
Soladad   see Soledad.
Solano (So lah' no) m. Lat. "Like
   the eastern wind." St. Francis
   Solano worked among Peruvian
   Indians in 16th cen. F. 7/24.
Solario (So lah' ree oh) m.
   Solaria, flower of lilac family.
Soldad   see Soledad.
Sole   see Soledad.
Solea   see Soledad.
Soledá   see Soledad.
Soledad (So lay dahd') f. Lat.
   "She who likes to be alone."
   Title of V., Nuestra Señora de
   la Soledad (Our Lady of Soli-
   tude). Colonial period Mexican
   church made national church in
   1924. Dim: Chola, Chole,
   Cholita, Saledá, Sole. Var:
   Saledad, Soladá, Soladad,
   Soldad, Solea, Soledá, Soledate,
   Soledod, Soletá, Solidá,
   Solidad, Solidar, Solidera,
   Solidia, Soliludo, Solitá,
   Solitudina, Solitudo, Solodad.
Soledate   see Soledad.
Soledod   see Soledad.
Soledonio   see Celedonio.
Soleida   see Zoraida.
Solema   see Zulema.
Solemna   see Zulema.
Solena   see Zulema.
Soletá   see Soledad.
Solferino   see Ceferino.
Solidá   see Soledad.
Solidad   see Soledad.
Solidar   see Soledad.
Solidera   see Soledad.
Solidia   see Soledad.
Soliludo   see Soledad.
Solima   see Zulema.
Solitá   see Soledad.
Solitudina   see Soledad.
Solitudo   see Soledad.
Solodad   see Soledad.
Solodonio   see Celedonio.
Soloma   see Salomé.
Solomone   see Salomón.
Solone   see Salomé.
Somona   see Simón.
Somtiago   see Santiago.
Sonfonias   see Sofronio.
Sonia   see Sofío.
Sonio (So' nee oh) m. EE: Sonya.
   Russian diminutive of Sofío
   (see). Dim: Chona. Var: Sohnya,
   Sonja, Sonya, Zonia. See also
   Sofío.
Sonja   see Sonio.
Sonjuana   see Sanjuana.
Sonya   see Sonio.
Sopapa   see Zapopan.
Sophiae   see Sofío.
Sopia   see Zapopan.
Sopopa   see Zapopan.
Sopopio   see Zapopan.
Sora   see Sara.
Sorah   see Sara.
Soraida   see Zoraida.
Soraide   see Zoraida.
Soraita   see Zoraida.
Sorapio   see Serapio.
Soriada   see Zoraida.

Sorida   see Zoraida.
Sorita   see Sara.
Sortero   see Sotero.
Sos   see Zósimo.
Sósimo   see Zósimo.
Sóstenas   see Sóstenes.
Sóstenes (Sose' tay nays) m. EE:
   Sosthenes. Gk. "Strong &
   healthy." Ruler of Jewish syna-
   gog of Corinth. F. 9/11. 4 x in
   DS. Var: Sástenes, Sástines,
   Sástinez, Sóstenas, Sóstenez,
   Sóstenis, Sósteno, Sóstines,
   Sóstinez, Sóstmes, Sóstonos,
   Sústenes, Sústenos.
Sóstenez   see Sóstenes.
Sóstenis   see Sóstenes.
Sósteno   see Sóstenes.
Sóstines   see Sóstenes.
Sóstinez   see Sóstenes.
Sóstmes   see Sóstenes.
Sóstonos   see Sóstenes.
Sotelo   see Sotero.
Soter   see Sotero.
Soterade   see Sotero.
Soterio   see Sotero.
Sotero (So tay' roe) m. EE: Soter.
   Gk. "Savior." 3 x in DS. 1, 2nd
   cen. pope. Dim: Sotes. Var:
   Satere, Satero, Sattera, Setero,
   Sortero, Sotelo, Soter,
   Soterade, Soterio, Soterus,
   Sotorel, Sotoro, Sotro, Soturo,
   Suterio, Sutero, Zotero.
Soterus   see Sotero.
Sotes   see Sotero.
Sotorel   see Sotero.
Sotoro   see Sotero.
Sotro   see Sotero.
Soturo   see Sotero.
Sovaida   see Zobeida.
Soveda   see Zobeida.
Sovedia   see Zobeida.
Soveido   see Zobeida.
Sovia   see Zobeida.
Sovida   see Zobeida.
Sovita   see Zobeida.
Soylo   see Zoilo.
Sozano   see Susano.
Sperancia   see Esperanza.
Speranza   see Esperanza.
Sperión   see Espiridión.
Spes (Space) f. Lat. "Hope." 1 of
   3 mart. daughters of St. Sophia.
   10-year-old Spes cast into fur-
   nace & then decapitated. F. 8/1.
Spifamia   see Epifanio.
Spigmenio   see Epigmenio.
Spiridine   see Espiridión.
Spiridio   see Espiridión.
Spiridión   see Espiridión.
Spiridione   see Espiridión.
Spiridionis   see Espiridión.
Spiridionus   see Espiridión.
Spiridón   see Espiridión.
Spiridonio   see Espiridión.
Spiridrán   see Espiridión.
Spiriona   see Espiridión.
Spirita (Spee ree' tah) f. Lat.
   "Spirit." Holy Spirit, 3rd
   person of Christian Trinity.
   Frequent in Bible.
Spolonia   see Apolonio.
Spriana   see Espiridión.
Sprindión   see Espiridión.

Sragosa	see Zaragoza.	Sumerando	see Gumersindo.
Srylo	see Cirilo.	Sumersindo	see Gumersindo.

Stacteo (Stahk' tay oh) m.
Stacteus, Roman M. F. 9/28.

Stalfo	see Astolfo.
Stanacia	see Atanasio.
Stanasia	see Atanasio.
Stancio	see Constancio.
Staneslaus	see Estanislao.
Stanidlado	see Estanislao.
Stanilada	see Estanislao.
Stanisla	see Estanislao.
Stanislace	see Estanislao.
Stanislado	see Estanislao.
Stanislao	see Estanislao.
Stanislaus	see Estanislao.
Stanislav	see Estanislao.
Stanislava	see Estanislao.
Stanislio	see Estanislao.
Stanisloa	see Estanislao.
Stanislor	see Estanislao.
Stanzo	see Constancio.
Steban	see Esteban.
Stefa	see Esteban.
Stefana	see Esteban.
Steperina	see Esteban.
Stephano	see Esteban.
Stephona	see Esteban.
Stifana	see Esteban.
Stnaisloo	see Estanislao.
Sturnino	see Saturnino.
Sturrino	see Saturnino.

Subigen (Soo bee' hen) m. Subigo,
in Gk. & Roman myth., deity of
wedding night.

Succoro	see Socorro.
Succorro	see Socorro.
Suciano	see Susano.
Sucorra	see Socorro.
Sucurro	see Socorro.
Sudi	see Susano.
Suelito	see Consuelo.
Suelo	see Consuelo.

Sueño (Swain' yo) m. Lat. "Act of
sleeping." Refers to dream.

Sugifredo	see Sigfrido.
Suilielma	see Zulema.
Sulemia	see Zulema.
Sulemo	see Zulema.
Sulenia	see Zulema.
Sulerma	see Zulema.
Sulerna	see Zulema.
Sulia	see Zulema.
Sulima	see Zulema.
Sulpecio	see Sulpicio.

Sulpicio (Sool pee' see oh) m. EE:
Sulpice, Sulpitius. Lat. "Be-
longing to Sulpicia family." 7 x
in DS. 1, Archbishop of Bourges,
France, in 7th cen. F. 1/17.
Var: Sulpecio.

Suluma	see Zulema.
Sulvester	see Silvestre.
Suly	see Zulema.

Sunción	see Asunción.

Superiordina (Soo pay ree or dee'
nah) f. Lat. "Superior" means
"to surpass." St. Superio mart.
in France in 9th cen. F. 6/26.

Susa   see Susano.

Susano (Soo sah' no) f. EE: Susan,
Susanna, etc. Heb. "Lily." Woman
who took care of Christ. 16 x in
DS. 3rd cen. M. who refused to
marry pagan. F. 8/11. Dim:
Chano, Sozano, Suciano, Sudi,
Susa, Suse, Susi, Susy. Var:
Susonio, Sussana, Susuie,
Suzanea, Suzanna, Suzano,
Zuzama, Zuzana, Zuzanna.

Suse	see Susano.
Susi	see Susano.
Susimo	see Zósimo.
Susonio	see Susano.
Syssana	see Susano.
Sustenes	see Sóstenes.
Sustenos	see Sóstenes.
Susu	see Ursula.
Susuie	see Susano.
Susy	see Susano.
Suterio	see Sotero.
Sutero	see Sotero.
Suvina	see Sabino.
Suzanea	see Susano.
Suzanna	see Susano.
Suzano	see Susano.
Svero	see Severo.
Sylbana	see Silvano.
Sylbestrio	see Silvestre.
Sylbia	see Silvio.
Sylina	see Celina.
Sylvanos	see Silvano.
Sylverio	see Silverio.
Sylvero	see Silverio.
Sylvesdre	see Silvestre.
Sylvestas	see Silvestre.
Sylvestera	see Silvestre.
Sylvestine	see Silvestre.
Sylvestro	see Silvestre.
Sylvia	see Silvio.
Symforosa	see Sinforoso.
Symphorio	see Sinforoso.
Symphorosae	see Sinforoso.
Symphoroso	see Sinforoso.
Symporoso	see Sinforoso.
Synforosa	see Sinforoso.
Synida	see Zenaido.
Synphoriano	see Sinforoso.
Synthia	see Cinta.
Sypherina	see Ceferino.
Syprian	see Cipriano.
Syria	see Ciriaco.
Syriaco	see Ciriaco.
Syrina	see Serena.
Systo	see Sixto.
Syvinia	see Silvino.

T

Tabatha   see **Tabita**.
Tabita (Tah bee' tah) f. **EE**: Tab, Tabby, Tabitha. Aramiac, "Gazelle." Christian woman of Joppa who helped poor. Resurrected by St. Peter. Also known as Dorcas. F. 10/25. **Var**: Tabatha, Tabitha.
Tabitha   see **Tabita**.
Tabo   see **Gustavo**.
Tacha   see **Anastacio**.
Tachito   see **Anastacio**.
Tacho   see **Natalio**.
Tacho   see **Tránsito**.
Taciana   see **Tacio**.
Tacio (Tah' see oh) m. **EE**: Tatius. Gk. "Active, diligent." Sabine king who wanted to avenge rape of Sabines. 1 x in DS. Pers. M. F. 9/19. **Var**: Taciana, Tactto.
Taco   see **Eustaquio**.
Tactto   see **Tacio**.
Tadeo (Tah day' oh) m. **EE**: Tad, Thaddeus, etc. Heb. "Praising God." 7 x in DS. 1, apostle of Christ, preached in Mesopotamia & mart. F. 10/28. **Dim**: Tadi, Tato. **Var**: Thadeo.
Tadi   see **Tadeo**.
Tadislao   see **Estanislao**.
Tago   see **Santiago**.
Tail   see **Tales**.
Taila   see **Tales**.
Tais (Tah' ees) m. **EE**: Thais, Thaisa. Gk. "Very beautiful." 2 famous courtesans: mistress of Alexander the Great; 1st cen. nun converted by seducer. F. 10/8.
Talefero   see **Telésforo**.
Talentina (Tah lane tee' nah) f. Lat. "Talentum" means "gifted naturally."
Tales (Tah' lace) f. **EE**: Thales, Thalia. Gk. "She who comes forth with splendor." In Gk. myth., Thalia, Muse of comedy & 1 of Graces. **Var**: Tail, Taila, Telia.
Talia   see **Natalio**.
Talino   see **Natalio**.
Talisfora   see **Telésforo**.
Talitha (Tah lee' tha) f. Heb. "Talitha cumi" means "child arise." Christ's words spoken to resurrect daughter of Jairo.
Tamara (Tah mah' rah) f. **EE**: Tamara, etc. Heb. "That which gives pleasant shelter." 5 x in Bible. 1, sister of Absalom. In DS, bishop of Africa. **Var**: Tomara.
Tamás   see **Tomás**.
Tamasa   see **Tomás**.
Tamascio   see **Tomás**.
Tamerlán (Tah mare lahn') m. **EE**: Tamerlane, Timur. Mongolian, "Cripple Timur." 14th cen. Mongolian conqueror with kingdom

from Volga to Great Wall of China.
Tan   see **Sebastián**.
Tanacio   see **Atanasio**.
Tanas   see **Estanislao**.
Tancha   see **Constancio**.
Tancho   see **Tránsito**.
Tancredo (Tahn cray' doe) m. **EE**: Tancred. Teut. "Wise counselor." 10th cen. crusader in capture of Antioch & Jerusalem. Also 9th cen. hermit of Cambridgeshire, England, killed by pagan Danes. F. 4/9.
Taneslado   see **Estanislao**.
Tani   see **Estanislao**.
Tani   see **María**.
Tanis   see **Estanislao**.
Tanisla   see **Estanislao**.
Tanislado   see **Estanislao**.
Tanislodo   see **Estanislao**.
Tanix   see **Estanislao**.
Tano   see **Cayetano**.
Tano   see **Estanislao**.
Tano   see **Sebastián**.
Tanquiliano   see **Tranquilino**.
Tansilado   see **Estanislao**.
Taraco (Tah rah' co) m. **EE**: Tarachus. Form of Tarachus, Roman M. F. 10/11.
Tarasio (Tah rah' see oh) m. **EE**: Tarasius. Gk. "Restless." 4 x in DS. 1, 4th cen. Patriarch of Constantinople, tried to reunite Byzantine & Roman churches. F. 2/25.
Tarbio   see **Toribio**.
Tarcisio   see **Tarsicio**.
Taribio   see **Toribio**.
Tarquino (Tar key' no) m. **EE**: Tarquin, Tarquinus. Lat. "Native of Tarquinium." 1 of most important cities of Etruscan League. Also Etruscan family that ruled Rome c. 500 B.C. **Var**: Tarquivo.
Tarquivo   see **Tarquino**.
Tarsicio (Tar see' see oh) m. **EE**: Tarsicia, Tarsiscius. Lat. "Native of Tarsus." 4 x in DS. 1, Roman M., clubbed to death for wanting to carry Eucharist to Christian prisoners. F. 8/15. **Var**: Tarcisio.
Tarsila (Tar see' lah) f? **EE**: Tarsilia, Tarsilla. Gk. "He who weaves willows," or "native of Tarsus." 6th cen. Roman S. led life of mortification & rewarded with heavenly visions. F. 12/24.
Tasio   see **Anastacio**.
Tasito   see **Tránsito**.
Tatá   see **Altagracia**.
Tatiano (Tah tee ah' no) m. **EE**: Tantianus. Lat. "Taciano," "of Tatius family." 8 x in DS. 1, 3rd cen. Roman M. F. 1/12.
Tato   see **Anastacio**.

Tato   see **Bernal.**
Tato   see **Eduardo.**
Tato   see **Sebastián.**
Tato   see **Tadeo.**
Tato   see **Tránsito.**
Taurino (Tah ooh ree' no) m. EE:
   Taurian, Taurinus. Lat. "Afi-
   cionado of bulls." 3 x in DS. 1,
   4th cen. bishop of Evereux,
   France. F. 8/11.
Taviano   see **Octavio.**
Tavín   see **Gustavo.**
Tavio   see **Octavio.**
Tavito   see **Gustavo.**
Tavito   see **Octavio.**
Tavo   see **Gustavo.**
Tavo   see **Octavio.**
Tayetano   see **Cayetano.**
Te   see **Clemente.**
Tea   see **Tereso.**
Teadoro   see **Teodoro.**
Teafilo   see **Teófilo.**
Teatimo (Tay ah tee' mo) m.
   Teatino, religious order dedi-
   cated to reconcile condemned to
   God.
Teb   see **Esteban.**
Tebacio   see **Tiburcio.**
Teburcio   see **Tiburcio.**
Techa   see **Tereso.**
Teche   see **Ester.**
Teche   see **Tereso.**
Teclo (Tay' clo) m. EE: Thecla,
   etc. Gk. "God's glory." 31 x in
   DS. 1st female M., convert of
   St. Paul, noted for 3 torments:
   eviction, thrown to wild
   animals, & burned at stake. F.
   9/23. **Var:** Thecla.
Tedalia   see **Teódulo.**
Tedfilo   see **Teófilo.**
Tedi   see **Teodoro.**
Tedlo   see **Teódulo.**
Teferiano   see **Ceferino.**
Teferino   see **Ceferino.**
Tela   see **Estela.**
Telásforo   see **Telésforo.**
Telefonso   see **Telesfonso.**
Teléfor   see **Telésforo.**
Teléforo   see **Telésforo.**
Teleóforo   see **Telésforo.**
Telephoro   see **Telésforo.**
Teles   see **Telésforo.**
Telésara   see **Telésforo.**
Telésfaro   see **Telésforo.**
Telesfeo   see **Telésforo.**
Telésfero   see **Telésforo.**
Telésfono   see **Telésforo.**
Telesfonso (Tay lace fone' so) m.
   Comb. of Telésforo & Alfonso or
   Ildefonso (see all). **Var:**
   Telefonso.
Telesfor   see **Telésforo.**
Telesford   see **Telésforo.**
Telésforo (Tay lace' foe roe) m.
   EE: Telesphorus. Gk. "He who is
   successful." 2 x in DS. 1, 2nd
   cen. pope, introduced custom of
   midnight Mass on Christmas day.
   F. 1/5. **Dim:** Teles. **Var:**
   Elésforo, Taléfor, Talísfora,
   Telásforo, Teléfor, Teléforo,
   Teleóforo, Telephoro, Telésara,
   Telésfaro, Telesfeo, Telésfero,
   Telésfono, Telesfor, Telesford,

Telésora, Teléspherum,
Telésphontes, Telésphor,
Telésphoro, Teléssoro, Telífora,
Telísforo, Télsforo, Thelephoro,
Thelésforo, Thelésphoro,
Tlésfore.
Telésora   see **Telésforo.**
Teléspherum see **Telésforo.**
Telésphontes see **Telésforo.**
Telésphor   see **Telésforo.**
Telésphoro   see **Telésforo.**
Teléssoro   see **Telésforo.**
Telia   see **Tales.**
Telífora   see **Telésforo.**
Telio   see **Eleuterio.**
Telísforo   see **Telésforo.**
Telita   see **Estela.**
Tella   see **Eleuterio.**
Tellus (Tay' lus) m. Lat. "Earth."
   Personification of earth, nour-
   ishing goddess.
Telma (Tell' mah) f. EE: Thel,
   Thelma. Gk. "Will." Also femi-
   nine form of Telmo, variant of
   Antelmo (see). **Dim:** Chemo, Mita,
   Temo. **Var:** Thelmo.
Télsforo   see **Telésforo.**
Teluca   see **Tereso.**
Telvina   see **Etelvina.**
Temístocles (Tay mee' stoke lays')
   m. EE: Themistocles. Gk. "Glori-
   ous for justice." Statesman,
   naval commander of Athens c. 500
   B.C. In DS, 3rd cen. Lycian
   shepherd mart. for refusing to
   reveal Christian's hiding place.
   F. 12/21. **Dim:** Chamico, Temoc.
Temo   see **Telma.**
Temoc   see **Temístocles.**
Temotio   see **Timoteo.**
Tempora (Tame poe' rah) f. Lat.
   "Time." Fasting period at
   beginning of each season. In
   English, Ember days.
Tenalado   see **Estanislao.**
Tenaro (Tay nah' roe) m. In Roman
   myth., hill in Lacinia with
   temple to Neptune.
Tenasio   see **Atanasio.**
Tencha   see **Hortencia.**
Tenche   see **Hortencia.**
Tenchi   see **Hortencia.**
Tencho   see **Terencio.**
Tendolinda   see **Teodolinda.**
Teneslardo   see **Estanislao.**
Teneston (Tay nace' tone) m. Form
   of Tenes or Teneo, sometimes
   considered father of Apollo in
   Gk. myth.
Teno   see **Tenorio.**
Tenorio (Tay no' ree oh) m. Prota-
   gonist of play "El Burlador de
   Sevilla." Also, male lover. **Dim:**
   Teno.
Tente   see **Clemente.**
Tente   see **Vicente.**
Teo   see **Doroteo.**
Teo   see **Mateo.**
Teo (Tay' oh) m. Gk. "God." Rather
   than separate, name often com-
   bined with others as in Teodoro
   & Teofilo (see).
Teobaldo (Tay oh bahl' doe) m. EE:
   Theobalt, Tybalt. Teut. "Valiant
   prince among his people." 9 x in

DS. 1, hermit of Champagne, France, made pilgrimages to Rome & Compostella, Spain. Patron of charcoal burners. F. 7/1. **Var:** Teoblo.

Teoblo	see **Teobaldo.**
Teoboro	see **Teodoro.**
Teodala	see **Teodulo.**
Teodara	see **Teodoro.**

Teodardo (Tay oh dar' doe) m. **EE:** Theodard. Teut. "He who is force & valor of his people." 2 x in DS. 1, bishop of Maestricht, Germany, killed while trying to redress wrongs. F. 9/10.

Teodario	see **Teodoro.**
Teodero	see **Teodoro.**
Teodilda	see **Teotilde.**
Teodita	see **Teodoro.**
Teodocio	see **Teodoro.**
Teodola	see **Teodulo.**

Teodolinda (Tay oh doe leen' dah) f. **EE:** Theodelinde. Teut. "She who is amiable with her people." **Dim:** Delina, Deolinda, Linda. **Var:** Tendolinda, Teollinda, Theodina, Tiodolinda.

Teodomiro (Tay oh doe mee' roe) m. **EE:** Theodimir, Thetmar. Teut. "Famous among his people." 3 x in DS. 1, from Carmona, Spain, beheaded by Moors in 9th cen. F. 7/25. **Dim:** Diomira, Dionires.

Teodorico	see **Teodoro.**
Teodorilde	see **Teodoro.**
Teodorio	see **Teodoro.**

Teodoro (Tay oh doe' roe) m. **EE:** Ned, Teddy, Theodore. Gk. "Gift of gods." 146 x in DS. 1, great military S. of Eastern church of 4th cen. F. 11/9. **Dim:** Dores, Doro, Doya, Tedi, Teodita, Tiedra. **Var:** Deodoro, Deudoria, Teadoro, Teoboro, Teodara, Teodario, Teodero, Teodocio, Teodorico, Teodorilde, Teodorio, Teodro, Teodrora, Teogora, Teovoro, Theador, Theadora, Theadori, Theadorita, Theidor, Thiodosa, Tieodoro, Tiodoria, Tiodoro, Todoro, Tridoro, Trodoro.

Teodos	see **Teodosio.**
Teodosiana	see **Teodosio.**

Teodosio (Tay oh doe' see oh) m. **EE:** Theodosia, Theodosius. Gk. "Like gift from God." 4th cen. Roman emperor. Influential in condemning Arianism & in forming Nicene Creed. 34 x in DS. **Dim:** Odosia, Teodos, Tocho. **Var:** Teodosiana, Teodozo, Terdosio, Tiodoso, Tiodoza, Todosia.

Teodozo	see **Teodosio.**
Teodro	see **Teodoro.**
Teodrora	see **Teodoro.**

Teodulo (Tay oh' due low) m. **EE:** Theodula, Theodulus. Gk. "Servant of God." 25 x in DS. 1, prefect of Constantinople in 4th cen. Spent 40 years on pillar near Edessa, Greece. F. 5/28. **Var:** Tedalia, Tedlo, Teodala, Teodola, Theadolfa, Theodula, Tiodola, Tiodula.

Teofanes (Tay oh' fah nays) m. **EE:** Theophanes. Gk. "To whom God has revealed himself." 18 x in DS. 1, Archbishop of Nice in 9th cen. Mart. by having verses punctured into face. F. 10/11.

Teofel	see **Teofilo.**
Teofelo	see **Teofilo.**
Teofeto	see **Teofilo.**
Teofil	see **Teofilo.**
Teofilio	see **Teofilo.**
Teofiln	see **Teofilo.**

Teofilo (Tay oh' fee low) m. **EE:** Phil, Theophilus. Gk. "Beloved of God." Luke addressed Gospel and Acts of Apostles to Teofilo. 47 x in DS. 1 contracts with Satan but V. frees him. F. 2/4. **Dim:** Fico, Filo, Teofito, Tofi, Tofia. **Var:** Teafilo, Tedfilo, Teofel, Teofelo, Teofeto, Teofil, Teofilio, Teofiln, Teofilus, Teofina, Teofolo, Teophelo, Teophil, Teophila, Teophiloso, Theofil, Theofilo, Theofilus, Theophilda, Theophilia, Theophilo, Theophilus, Thiofila, Tiofelo, Tiofilio, Tiofilo, Tiofilo.

Teofilus	see **Teofilo.**
Teofina	see **Teofilo.**
Teofito	see **Teofilo.**
Teofolo	see **Teofilo.**

Teofrasto (Tay oh frahs' toe) m. **EE:** Theophrastus. Gk. "He who speaks in name of God." Successor of Aristotle c. 372 B.C. In DS, died with St. Athenogenes of Armenia in 4th cen. F. 7/17.

Teofrido (Tay oh free' doe) m. **EE:** Theofried. Teut. "Counselor of his people." Form of Teodofredo, Fr. nun of 7th cen. F. 10/8. **Var:** Theaphid.

Teogenes (Tay oh' hay nays) m. **EE:** Theogenes, etc. Gk. "Born of God." 5 x in DS. 1 mart. when beheaded by Diocletian in Cyzicus, Asia Minor. F. 4/28.

Teogora	see **Teodoro.**
Teollinda	see **Teodolinda.**

Teonilia (Tay oh nee' lee ah) f. St. Theonilla, mart. in Aegae, Greece.

Teophelo	see **Teofilo.**
Teophil	see **Teofilo.**
Teophila	see **Teofilo.**
Teophiloso	see **Teofilo.**
Teotilda	see **Teotilde.**

Teotilde (Tay oh teel' day) m. Comb. of Teofilo or Teodoro & Clotilde (see all). **Var:** Teodilda, Teotilda.

Teotimo (Tay oh' tee mo) m. **EE:** Theotima, Theotimus. Gk. "He who knows how to honor God." 7 x in DS. 1, 5th cen. convert from paganism. Rejected some of writings of Origen. F. 4/20.

Teovigildo (Tay oh bee heel' doe) m. Comb. of Teofilo or Teodoro & Leovigildo (see all).

Teovoro	see **Teodoro.**
Tera	see **Tereso.**
Terasa	see **Tereso.**

Terdosio	see	**Teodosio.**
Tere	see	**Tereso.**
Terecina	see	**Tereso.**
Terela	see	**Tereso.**
Terenciano	see	**Terencio.**

Terencio (Tay rane' see oh) m. **EE:**
Terentius, etc. Lat. "Native of
Taranto, Italy." Writer of come-
dies in Rome c. 185 B.C. 19 x in
DS. 1 beheaded in 3rd cen.
Africa. F. 4/10. **Dim:** Tencho,
Terentilo, Teres. **Var:**
Terenciano, Terenta, Tererso,
Terocencia.

Terenta	see	**Terencio.**
Terentilo	see	**Terencio.**
Tererso	see	**Terencio.**
Teres	see	**Terencio.**
Teresia	see	**Tereso.**
Teresito	see	**Tereso.**

Tereso (Tay ray' so) m. **EE:**
Teresa, Therse, etc. Gk. "Hunt-
ress." 8 x in DS. Teresa, 16th
cen. Sp. mystic, reformed
Carmelite order. F. 10/15. **Dim:**
Tea, Techa, Teche, Teluca, Tera,
Tere, Terela, Teresito, Terry,
Tessa, Teté, Teteya, Tire, Zita.
Var: Terasa, Terecina, Teresia,
Tereza, Terezia, Terrsa,
Tersifa, Terusa, Therese,
Theresia, Thereso, Therezo,
Tresa.

Tereza	see	**Tereso.**
Terezia	see	**Tereso.**

Termín (Tare meen') m. **EE:**
Terminus. In myth., Termino, god
that protects boundaries of
fields.

Termutiz (Tare moo' tease) m.
Termutis, figure in Gk. myth.

Terocencia	see	**Terencio.**
Terrsa	see	**Tereso.**
Terry	see	**Tereso.**

Tersa (Taire' sah) ? **EE:** Tirsah.
Could be form of Tirsah, blind
person at time of Moses. Also
royal city of Canaan. Another
diminutive of Tereso (see).

Tersifa	see	**Tereso.**

Tertuliano (Tare too lee ah' no)
m. **EE:** Tertullian. Lat. "Son of
Tertulio." Roman theologian of
2nd cen. 8 x in DS. 1, Roman M.,
tortured & beheaded. F. 8/4.

Terusa	see	**Tereso.**

Tesaura (Tay sough' rah) f. Lat.
"Treasury." Comb. of Tessa,
diminutive form of Teresa (see),
& "aurea," Lat. "gold."

Tessa	see	**Tereso.**
Teté	see	**Estela.**
Teté	see	**Ester.**
Teté	see	**Tereso.**
Teteya	see	**Tereso.**
Tey	see	**Ester.**
Teya	see	**Doroteo.**
Teyo	see	**Eleuterio.**
Teyo	see	**Emeterio.**
Teyo	see	**Timoteo.**
Thadeo	see	**Tadeo.**
Theadolfa	see	**Teodulo.**
Theador	see	**Teodoro.**
Theadora	see	**Teodoro.**
Theadori	see	**Teodoro.**
Theadorita	see	**Teodoro.**
Theaphid	see	**Teofrido.**
Thecla	see	**Teclo.**
Theidor	see	**Teodoro.**
Theléphoro	see	**Telésforo.**
Thelésforo	see	**Telésforo.**
Thelésphoro	see	**Telésforo.**
Thelmo	see	**Telma.**
Thematheo	see	**Timoteo.**
Theodina	see	**Teodolinda.**
Theodula	see	**Teodulo.**
Theofil	see	**Teofilo.**
Theofilo	see	**Teofilo.**
Theofilus	see	**Teofilo.**
Theophilda	see	**Teofilo.**
Theophilia	see	**Teofilo.**
Theophilo	see	**Teofilo.**
Theophilus	see	**Teofilo.**
Therburcio	see	**Tiburcio.**
Therese	see	**Tereso.**
Theresia	see	**Tereso.**
Thereso	see	**Tereso.**
Therezo	see	**Tereso.**

Thila (Tee' lah) f. Form of Tillo,
S. of 7th cen. France, invoked
against fever & sickness of
children. F. 1/7. May be diminutive of Domitilo (see).

Thimoteo	see	**Timoteo.**
Thimotheos	see	**Timoteo.**
Thiodosa	see	**Teodoro.**
Thiofila	see	**Teofilo.**
Thomacita	see	**Tomás.**
Thomasa	see	**Tomás.**
Thomasita	see	**Tomás.**
Thorburcio	see	**Tiburcio.**
Thoribio	see	**Toribio.**
Thorivis	see	**Toribio.**
Thuribio	see	**Toribio.**
Tibercia	see	**Tiburcio.**
Tiberesa	see	**Tiburcio.**

Tiberio (Tee bay' ree oh) m. **EE:**
Tibe, Tiber, Tiberius. Lat.
"Born near Tiber." 2nd Roman
emperor called Tiberius Caesar
in Bible. 4 x in DS. 1, general
of order of Humiliates, lay
penitential association. F.
1/21. **Dim:** Bucho.

Tibersio	see	**Tiburcio.**
Tibertia	see	**Tiburcio.**
Tibircio	see	**Tiburcio.**
Tibo	see	**Tiburcio.**
Tiborcio	see	**Tiburcio.**
Tiborio	see	**Tiburcio.**
Tibruscia	see	**Tiburcio.**
Tibrusia	see	**Tiburcio.**
Tibucio	see	**Tiburcio.**
Tibullo	see	**Tibulo.**

Tibulo (Tee' boo low) m. **EE:**
Tibullus. Lat. "He who is outstanding." Roman poet of 1st
cen. **Var:** Tibullo.

Tiburcio (Tee boor' see oh) m. **EE:**
Tiburtinus, Tiburtius. Lat.
"Born in Tivoli, Rome." 5 x in
DS. 1, Roman betrayed by apos-
tate & executed. F. 8/11. **Dim:**
Burcilla, Tibo, Tiburtino, Tivo.
Var: Devorcio, Devorsia,
Diburtio, Divertio, Divorsia,
Divortio, Divortis, Divurecia,
Divursio, Tebacio, Teburcio,
Therburcio, Thorburcio,
Tibercia, Tiberesa, Tibersio,

Tibertia, Tibircio, Tiborcio,
Tiborio, Tibruscia, Tibrusia,
Tibucio, Tiburecia, Tiburia,
Tiburrcia, Tiburrio, Tiburro,
Tibursio, Tiburtio, Tiburtisa,
Tiburtium, Tiburto, Tiburzia,
Tibusio, Tibuzio, Tibyrcio,
Tilurcio, Tivorcio, Tivurcio,
Tivursio, Tubircio, Tuburcio,
Tuburtia, Turvicio.

Tiburecia	see **Tiburcio**.
Tiburia	see **Tiburcio**.
Tiburrcia	see **Tiburcio**.
Tiburrio	see **Tiburcio**.
Tiburro	see **Tiburcio**.
Tibursio	see **Tiburcio**.
Tiburtino	see **Tiburcio**.
Tiburtio	see **Tiburcio**.
Tiburtisa	see **Tiburcio**.
Tiburtium	see **Tiburcio**.
Tiburto	see **Tiburcio**.
Tiburzia	see **Tiburcio**.
Tibusio	see **Tiburcio**.
Tibuzio	see **Tiburcio**.
Tibyrcio	see **Tiburcio**.
Ticha	see **Beatriz**.
Ticha	see **Leticia**.
Tichi	see **Beatriz**.
Ticho	see **Patricio**.

Ticiano (Tee see ah' no) m. EE:
Titian. Lat. "Son of Titus."
Biblical disciple of St. Paul.
F. 1/4. 8 x in DS. See also
Tito.

Tico	see **Alberto**.
Tico	see **Eutiquio**.
Tiedra	see **Teodoro**.
Tieodoro	see **Teodoro**.
Tiffy	see **Antonio**.

Tigrio (Tee' gree oh) m. EE:
Tigris, Tigrius. Lat. "Tigrino,"
"born near Tigris River." 2 x in
DS. 1, falsely accused of cathedral arson, scourged, imprisoned, & finally exiled. F. 1/12.

Tila	see **Clotilde**.
Tila	see **Matilde**.
Tila	see **Odilia**.
Tilán	see **Atilano**.
Tilano	see **Atilano**.
Tilda	see **Clotilde**.
Tilda	see **Matilde**.
Tilde	see **Clotilde**.
Tilde	see **Matilde**.
Tilde	see **Odilia**.
Tildita	see **Matilde**.
Tiliana	see **Atilano**.
Tilín	see **Matilde**.
Tilita	see **Atilano**.
Tilla	see **Odilia**.
Tilo	see **Domitilo**.
Tilo	see **Estanislao**.
Tilo	see **Otón**.
Tilurcio	see **Tiburcio**.
Timateo	see **Timoteo**.
Times	see **Timoteo**.
Timeteo	see **Timoteo**.
Timías	see **Timoteo**.
Timimeo	see **Timoteo**.
Timiro	see **Timoteo**.
Timiteo	see **Timoteo**.
Timo	see **Timoteo**.
Timodeo	see **Timoteo**.
Timoleo	see **Tolomeo**.
Timolteo	see **Timoteo**.

Timón (Tee moan') m. EE: Timon.
Gk. "He who is venerated &
honored." In Bible one of 7
chosen to relieve apostles of
secular work. F. 4/19.

Timona	see **Timoteo**.
Timot	see **Timoteo**.
Timotello	see **Timoteo**.

Timoteo (Tee mo tay' oh) m. EE:
Tim, Timothy. Gk. "Honoring
God." 51 x in DS. Early Chris-
tian & friend of St. Paul. F.
1/24. **Dim:** Teyo, Timo, Timona,
Timot. **Var:** Temotio, Themathea,
Thimoteo, Thimotheos, Timateo,
Times, Timeteo, Timías, Timimeo,
Timiro, Timiteo, Timodeo,
Timolteo, Timotello, Timotheus,
Timotio, Tomoteo, Trimoteo.

Timotheus	see **Timoteo**.
Timotio	see **Timoteo**.

Timur (Tee moor') m. EE:
Tamerlane, Timur. Tamerlane,
Mongol conqueror of 14th cen.

Tin	see **Agusto**.
Tin	see **Martín**.
Tin	see **Valente**.
Tina	see **Clemente**.
Tina	see **Cristián**.
Tina	see **Ernesto**.
Tina	see **Leontina**.
Tina	see **Martín**.
Tincho	see **Agusto**.

Tindaro (Teen' dah roe) m. In
myth., legendary king of Sparta
& husband of Leda.

Tini	see **Trinidad**.
Tinica	see **Agusto**.
Tinidad	see **Trinidad**.
Tino	see **Agusto**.
Tino	see **Argentina**.
Tino	see **Constancio**.
Tino	see **Faustino**.
Tino	see **Florencio**.
Tino	see **Fortuno**.
Tino	see **Justino**.
Tino	see **Valente**.
Tinuch	see **Agusto**.
Tiodola	see **Teodulo**.
Tiodolinda	see **Teodolinda**.
Tiodoria	see **Teodoro**.
Tiodoro	see **Teodoro**.
Tiodoso	see **Teodosio**.
Tiodoza	see **Teodosio**.
Tiodula	see **Teodulo**.
Tiofelo	see **Teófilo**.
Tiofilio	see **Teófilo**.
Tiofilo	see **Teófilo**.
Tiquio	see **Eutiquio**.
Tircio	see **Tirso**.
Tire	see **Tereso**.

Tireo (Tee' ray oh) m. Another
name for Apollo, guardian of
doors.

Tirso (Teer' so) m. EE: Thyrsus.
Gk. "Crowned with vines." Grape-
topped wand used in Dionysian
rites. 9 x in DS. 1 belonged to
Theban legion & was massacred at
Treves in 3rd cen. F. 10/4. **Var:**
Tircio, Tirsozo, Tirzah, Tirzo,
Tyrso, Tyrsus.

Tirsozo	see **Tirso**.
Tirubio	see **Toribio**.
Tirzah	see **Tirso**.

Tirzo   see **Tirso.**
Tis   see **Beatriz.**
Tiso (Tee' so) m. Tisoa, nymph in
  Gk. myth. **Var:** Tisso.
Tisso   see **Tiso.**
Tita   see **Ángel.**
Tita   see **Cristián.**
Tita   see **Margarito.**
Tita   see **Matilde.**
Tita   see **Rosa.**
Titay   see **Margarito.**
Tite   see **Tito.**
Titico   see **Víctor.**
Titina   see **Alberto.**
Titina   see **Cristián.**
Titina   see **Ernesto.**
Titina   see **Leontina.**
Titio (Tee' tee oh) m. In Gk.
  myth. Zeus' son who tried to
  rape Artemis.
Tito   see **Agusto.**
Tito   see **Alberto.**
Tito   see **Andrés.**
Tito   see **Carlos.**
Tito   see **Héctor.**
Tito   see **Humberto.**
Tito   see **Rafael.**
Tito   see **Roberto.**
Tito (Tee' toe) m. **EE:** Titus. Lat.
  "Safe." Roman emperor who
  destroyed Jerusalem. 6 x in DS.
  Early Christian missionary &
  friend of St. Paul. F. 1/4. **Var:**
  Tite. See also Ticiano.
Tivo   see **Tiburcio.**
Tivorcio   see **Tiburcio.**
Tivurcio   see **Tiburcio.**
Tivursio   see **Tiburcio.**
Tix   see **Beatriz.**
Tlésfore   see **Telésforo.**
Tlófilo   see **Teófilo.**
Tobal   see **Cristóbal.**
Tobalito   see **Cristóbal.**
Tobe   see **Tobías.**
Tobiana   see **Tobías.**
Tobías (Toe bee' ahs) m. **EE:**
  Tobias, Toby. Heb. "Yahweh is
  good." 4 x in Bible. 4 x in DS.
  1, afflicted & cured of blind-
  ness by God through archangel
  Raphael. F. 9/13. **Dim:** Tovita.
  Var: Tobe, Tobiana, Tobibías.
Tobibías   see **Tobías.**
Tocho   see **Héctor.**
Tocho   see **Teodosio.**
Todoro   see **Teodoro.**
Todosia   see **Teodosio.**
Tofi   see **Teófilo.**
Tofia   see **Teófilo.**
Toila (Toy' lah) f. Could be form
  of Tola, 8th cen. Irish S. F.
  3/30.
Tola   see **Bartolomé.**
Tola   see **Víctor.**
Tolasa (Toe lah' sah) f. Form of
  Tolosha, mart. in Egypt with
  brother Pachomius. F. 12/18.
Toli   see **Bartolomé.**
Tolita   see **Víctor.**
Tolivia   see **Olivo.**
Tolomeo (Toe low may' oh) m. **EE:**
  Ptolemaeus, Ptolemy. Gk. "Power-
  ful in battle." Macedonian
  dynasty of Egypt. Last was Cleo-
  patra. 9 x in DS. 1, Roman

priest, beheaded for instructing
pagan woman in his religion. F.
10/19. **Var:** Timoleo.
Tolvino   see **Etelvina.**
Tomana   see **Tomás.**
Tomara   see **Tamara.**
Tomás (Toe mahs') m. **EE:** Thomas,
  Thomasa, Tom. Heb. "Twin."
  Apostle known as "Doubting Thom-
  as." 81 x in DS. 1, St. Thomas
  Aquinas, doctor of church.
  Another, Thomas à Becket,
  Archbishop of Canterbury, mart.
  by Henry VIII. **Dim:** Chumo, Max,
  Maxico, Thomacita, Thomasita,
  Tomesito, Tomi, Tomito. **Var:**
  Tamás, Tamasa, Tamascio,
  Thomasa, Tomana, Tomasena,
  Tomasila, Tomasina, Tomaso,
  Tomasso, Tomaz, Tomaza,
  Tomazcio, Tomesa, Tomesano,
  Tomeseta, Tommasa, Tomosa.
Tomasena   see **Tomás.**
Tomasila   see **Tomás.**
Tomasina   see **Tomás.**
Tomaso   see **Tomás.**
Tomasso   see **Tomás.**
Tomaz   see **Tomás.**
Tomaza   see **Tomás.**
Tomazcio   see **Tomás.**
Tomesa   see **Tomás.**
Tomesano   see **Tomás.**
Tomeseta   see **Tomás.**
Tomesito   see **Tomás.**
Tomi   see **Tomás.**
Tomito   see **Tomás.**
Tommasa   see **Tomás.**
Tomosa   see **Tomás.**
Tomoteo   see **Timoteo.**
Tona   see **Petronilo.**
Tonche   see **Antonio.**
Toncho   see **Antonio.**
Toni   see **Antonio.**
Tonico   see **Antonio.**
Tonin   see **Antonio.**
Tonio   see **Antonio.**
Tono   see **Antonio.**
Tonsa   see **Encarnación.**
Tony   see **Antonio.**
Toñico   see **Antonio.**
Toñin   see **Antonio.**
Toño   see **Antonio.**
Toolis   see **Gertrudis.**
Torbilia   see **Toribio.**
Torbio   see **Toribio.**
Torcuato (Tore qua' toe) m. **EE:**
  Torquatus. Lat. "He who has
  received garland." 3 x in DS. 1,
  disciple, sent by Sts. Peter &
  Paul to Spain. F. 5/15.
Torebea   see **Toribio.**
Torebio   see **Toribio.**
Torib   see **Toribio.**
Toribes   see **Toribio.**
Toribie   see **Toribio.**
Toribin   see **Toribio.**
Toribio (Toe ree' bee oh) m. **EE:**
  Turibius. Gk. "He who carves
  arches." 3 x in DS. 1, 5th cen.
  bishop of Astorga, condemned
  teachings of Priscillianists. F.
  4/16. **Var:** Doribeo, Dorivia,
  Tarbio, Taribio, Thoribio,
  Thorivis, Thuribio, Tirubio,
  Torbilia, Torbio, Torebea,

Torebio, Torib, Toribes,
Toribie, Toribin, Toribis,
Toribo, Torilio, Toriria,
Toriva, Toriveo, Torivio,
Torivis, Torivivo, Torlivia,
Torovio, Torribea, Torribio,
Torribo, Torrio, Torrivia,
Turbio, Turibio, Turibius,
Turribio.

Toribis   see **Toribio.**
Toribo   see **Toribio.**
Torico   see **Víctor.**
Torilio   see **Toribio.**
Toriria   see **Toribio.**
Toriva   see **Toribio.**
Toriveo   see **Toribio.**
Torivio   see **Toribio.**
Torivis   see **Toribio.**
Torivivo   see **Toribio.**
Torlivia   see **Toribio.**
Torman (Tore' mahn) m. In DS, sons
of Torman identified as entry in
martyrology of Donegal, Ireland.
F. 3/10.

Torovio   see **Toribio.**
Torribea   see **Toribio.**
Torribio   see **Toribio.**
Torribo   see **Toribio.**
Torrio   see **Toribio.**
Torrivia   see **Toribio.**
Tota   see **Carlos.**
Totó   see **Antonio.**
Totó   see **Moisés.**
Totoya   see **Víctor.**
Tovita   see **Tobías.**
Toya   see **Custodia.**
Toya   see **Víctor.**
Toyano   see **Víctor.**
Trachilino   see **Tranquilino.**
Traguilaro   see **Tranquilino.**
Trancilmo   see **Tranquilino.**
Tráncito   see **Tránsito.**
Trancolino   see **Tranquilino.**
Tranguilimo see **Tranquilino.**
Tranguilino see **Tranquilino.**
Tranislao   see **Estanislao.**
Trankelino   see **Tranquilino.**
Trankilino   see **Tranquilino.**
Tranquelino see **Tranquilino.**
Tranquileno see **Tranquilino.**
Tranquiliano see **Tranquilino.**
Tranquilimo see **Tranquilino.**
Tranquilinia see **Tranquilino.**
Tranquilino (Trahn key lee' no) m.
EE: Tranquillinus, etc. Lat.
"Quiet, calm." 3 x in DS. 1, 3rd
cen. M. stoned to death while
praying at tomb of St. Paul. F.
7/6. **Dim:** Kilina, Kilo, Quelino,
Quilino. **Var:** Hanquilino,
Tanquiliano, Trachilino,
Traguilaro, Trancilmo,
Trancolino, Tranguilimo,
Tranguilino, Trankelino,
Trankilino, Tranquelino,
Tranquileno, Tranquiliano,
Tranquilimo, Tranquilinia,
Tranquillcia, Tranquillina,
Tranquillo, Tranquitina,
Tranqulano, Tranzuillino,
Traquilaro, Traquilino,
Traquilivo, Trenquiliano,
Trincalina, Trinquilino.
Tranquillcia   see **Tranquilino.**
Tranquillina   see **Tranquilino.**

Tranquillo   see **Tranquilino.**
Tranquitina   see **Tranquilino.**
Tranqulano   see **Tranquilino.**
Tránsit   see **Tránsito.**
Tránsito (Trahn' see toe) f. Lat.
"Passage, transfer." Death of
Blessed V. & passage into heav-
en. F. 8/15. **Dim:** Tacho, Tancho,
Tásito. **Var:** Tato, Tráncito,
Tránsit, Tranzitas.
Tranzitas   see **Tránsito.**
Tranzuillino see **Tranquilino.**
Traquilaro   see **Tranquilino.**
Traquilino   see **Tranquilino.**
Traquilivo   see **Tranquilino.**
Trasíbulo (Trah see' boo low) m.
EE: Thrasybulus, Gk. "He with
bold decisions." Gk. soldier &
statesman.
Treinidad   see **Trinidad.**
Tremandez   see **Tremendo.**
Tremando   see **Tremendo.**
Tremendo (Tray mane' doe) m. Lat.
"Worthy of respect & reverence."
Var: Tremandez, Tremando.
Trena (Tray' nah) f. Lat. "Trina,"
"triple." 1 of set of triplets
or 3rd child of family. **Var:**
Trenia.
Trenedad   see **Trinidad.**
Trenia   see **Trena.**
Trenidad   see **Trinidad.**
Trenquiliano see **Tranquilino.**
Tresa   see **Tereso.**
Tresiliana (Tray see lee ah' nah)
f. Sp. "Tresillo" is diminutive
of "three." Hence, 3rd child of
family.
Trestán   see **Tristán.**
Trevia (Tray' bee ah) f. Plant
with flowers.
Trevo (Tray' bo) m. Form of
Treves. Many Christians mart.
here in 3rd cen.
Triboniano (Tre bo nee ah' no) m.
EE: Tribonian. Famous Roman
lawyer of 5th cen.
Tricia   see **Patricio.**
Trida (Tree' dah) f. Form of
Tridian, patron of church of
Wales. **Var:** Tridina.
Trididad   see **Trinidad.**
Tridina   see **Trida.**
Tridoro   see **Teodoro.**
Trifán   see **Trifonio.**
Trifón   see **Trifonio.**
Trifonio (Tree foe' nee oh) m. EE:
Tryphon. Gk. "Delicate, ele-
gant." 10 x in DS. 1, Patriarch
of Constantinople in 10th cen.
F. 4/19. **Var:** Trifán, Trifón.
Trimoteo   see **Timoteo.**
Trina   see **Catalina.**
Trinadad   see **Trinidad.**
Trincalina   see **Tranquilino.**
Trindidad   see **Trinidad.**
Trine   see **Trinidad.**
Trinedad   see **Trinidad.**
Trinedada   see **Trinidad.**
Trineo   see **Trinidad.**
Trini   see **Catalina.**
Trini   see **Trinidad.**
Triniadad   see **Trinidad.**
Trinidá   see **Trinidad.**
Trinidad (Tree nee dahd') m. Lat.

"3 in 1." Central doctrine of Christian religion. God is 1 but has 3 distinct persons: Father, Son, & Holy Spirit. F. 1st Sunday after Pentecost. **Dim:** Tini, Trine, Trineo, Trini, Trinie, Trinitá, Trinitas, Trino, Triny. **Var:** Tinidad, Treinidad, Trenedad, Trenidad, Trididad, Trinadad, Trindidad, Trinedad, Trinedada, Triniadad, Trinidá, Trinidada, Trinidadnie, Trinidás, Trinidat, Trinidé, Trinis, Trinistina, Trinitad, Trinitate, Trinitatis. See also Trinotera.

Trinidada	see **Trinidad.**
Trinidadnie	see **Trinidad.**
Trinidás	see **Trinidad.**
Trinidat	see **Trinidad.**
Trinidé	see **Trinidad.**
Trinie	see **Trinidad.**
Trinis	see **Trinidad.**
Trinistina	see **Trinidad.**
Trinitá	see **Trinidad.**
Trinitad	see **Trinidad.**
Trinitas	see **Trinidad.**
Trinitate	see **Trinidad.**
Trinitatis	see **Trinidad.**
Trino	see **Trinidad.**

Trinotera (Tree no tay' rah) f. Religious order dedicated to promoting devotion to Holy Trinity. In early days, rescued Christians held captive by Moslems. See also Trinidad.

Trinquilino	see **Tranquilino.**
Triny	see **Trinidad.**

Trisema (Tree say' mah) f. Flowering plant.
Tristán (Trees tahn') f. **EE:** Tristam, Tristan. Lat. "He who is God." In Arthurian legend, fell in love with Iseult. **Var:** Trestán, Tristano.

Tristano	see **Tristán.**
Trodoro	see **Teodoro.**
Trudel	see **Gertrudis.**

Trunfo (Troon' foe) m. Lat. "Triumphus" means "triumph."

Tubircio	see **Tiburcio.**
Tuburcio	see **Tiburcio.**
Tuburtia	see **Tiburcio.**
Tuca	see **Berta.**

Tucilla (Too see' lah) f. Tucia, in Roman myth., Vestal V. of great beauty.

Tuco	see **Antonio.**
Tuelis	see **Ángel.**
Tule	see **Gertrudis.**
Tulenia	see **Tulio.**
Tules	see **Gertrudis.**
Tulez	see **Gertrudis.**
Tulia	see **Gertrudis.**
Tuliana	see **Tulio.**

Tulio (Too' lee oh) m. **EE:** Tullia, Tullius, etc. Lat. "Risen from the ground." 3 x in DS. 1 of 5th cen. Lyons, France. F. 10/5. **Var:** Tulenia, Tuliana. See also Gertrudes.

Tulis	see **Gertrudis.**
Tulitas	see **Gertrudis.**
Tuliz	see **Gertrudis.**
Tulles	see **Gertrudis.**
Tulo	see **Gertrudis.**
Tuly	see **Gertrudis.**
Tunacia	see **Atanasio.**
Tuncho	see **Antonio.**
Tuni	see **Fortuno.**
Tunino	see **Saturnino.**
Tuno	see **Saturnino.**
Turbio	see **Toribio.**
Turi	see **Arturo.**
Turibio	see **Toribio.**
Turibius	see **Toribio.**
Turin	see **Arturo.**
Turis	see **Arturo.**
Turix	see **Arturo.**

Turnina (Toor nee' nah) f. Turnin, Irish priest & S. of 8th cen., did missionary work in Low Countries.

Turribio	see **Toribio.**
Turvicio	see **Tiburcio.**
Tuto	see **Agusto.**
Tuto	see **Arturo.**
Tuto	see **Gertrudis.**
Tuto	see **Justino.**
Tutu	see **Gertrudis.**
Tuyo	see **Arturo.**
Tyrso	see **Tirso.**
Tyrsus	see **Tirso.**

U

Ubaldino see **Ubaldo.**
Ubaldo (Ooh ball' doe) m. **EE:** Walde, Waldo. Ger. "To wield" or "one who rules." 3 x in DS. 1, bishop of Gubbio in 12th cen. F. 5/16. **Dim:** Uva. **Var:** Eubaldo, Eusbaldo, Galdeno, Galdino, Galdro, Gualdina, Hubaldo, Ovaldina, Ubaldino, Urbaldo, Usbaldo, Usballo, Uvald, Uvaldina, Uvaldo, Uvasldo, Uvildina, Waldino, Waldo. See also Vivaldo.

Ubelia	see **Ovelia.**
Ubence	see **Juvencio.**
Ubencio	see **Juvencio.**
Ubense	see **Juvencio.**
Ubensi	see **Juvencio.**
Uberto	see **Humberto.**

Ubiado (Ooh bee ah' doe) m. Participle of Sp. verb "ubiar" meaning "to aid, to succor."

Ubidio	see **Ovidio.**
Ubigilio	see **Virgilio.**

Ubil (Ooh beel') m. Caretaker of King David's camels. Also known as Abias & Oubias. **Var:** Uvil.

Uca	see **María.**
Ucuberto	see **Cutberto.**
Udelbina	see **Etelvina.**

Udelfonsa	see Ildefonso.
Udelia	see Odilia.
Udelvina	see Etelvina.
Udilia	see Odilia.
Udilón	see Odilia.
Uegenio	see Eugenio.
Uelalia	see Eulalio.
Ufascia	see Eufracio.
Ufelia	see Ofelio.
Ufemia	see Eufemia.
Ufenia	see Eufemia.
Ufilia	see Ofelio.
Ufracia	see Eufracio.
Ufrasia	see Eufracio.
Ufricina	see Eufrosina.
Ufrosia	see Eufracio.
Ugenio	see Eugenio.
Ugnacio	see Ignacio.
Ugón	see Hugo.
Uhenio	see Eugenio.
Uidalia	see Odilia.
Ula	see Ladislao.
Ula	see Ladislao.
Ulalio	see Eulalio.
Ularia	see Eulalio.
Ularia	see Hilario.
Ulda	see Holda.
Uldarico	see Ulrico.
Uldirico	see Ulrico.
Ulelea	see Eulalio.
Ulemia	see Eumelia.

Ulfrido (Ool free' doe) m. EE: Wilfred, etc. Teut. "Warrior who brings peace with sword." In DS, 11th cen. Englishman who evangelized in Sweden. Killed by pagans for destroying idol of Thor. F. 6/18.

Ulgario	see Olegario.
Ulia	see Eulalio.
Ulián	see Julio.
Ulibia	see Olivo.
Ulices	see Ulises.

Ulielmi (Ooh lee ell' mee) f. EE: Ulalume. Sp. "Ulalume," name coined by Poe for poem of same name written in 1847.

Ulio   see Julio.

Ulipiano (Ooh lee pee ah' no) m. EE: Ulpianus, Vulpianus. Lat. "Relating to fox." 1, M. of Tyre, placed in sack with dog & snake & cast into river. F. 4/3.

Ulises (Ooh lee' says) m. EE: Ulix, Ulysses. Lat. "One who hates." Latin for Odysseus, Gk. hero of "Odyssey," story of his return voyage after Trojan War. **Dim:** Licho. **Var:** Ulices. See also Odessa.

Ullallio	see Eulalio.
Ulogia	see Eulogio.
Ulojio	see Eulogio.

Ulrico (Ool ree' co) m. EE: Ulrich, etc. Teut. "Rich & noble as prince." 9 x in DS. 1, bishop of Augsburg, Germany in 9th cen. F. 7/4. **Var:** Uldarico, Uldirico.

Ululio	see Eulalio.
Umasenda	see Gumersindo.
Umbelina	see Umberlina.

Umberlina (Oom bare lee' nah) f. Lat. "She who gives sheltering shadow." In DS, St. Bernard's sister who rejected world &

became Benedictine nun in 12th cen. F. 2/12. **Var:** Humbelina, Umbelina.

Umberto	see Humberto.
Umecindae	see Gumersindo.
Umecindi	see Gumersindo.
Umelda	see Hermenegildo.
Umesindo	see Gumersindo.
Umesinta	see Gumersindo.
Umicindae	see Gumersindo.
Umicindi	see Gumersindo.
Umocinda	see Gumersindo.
Unberto	see Humberto.
Uneberto	see Humberto.
Unesima	see Onésimo.
Uness	see Inés.
Unice	see Onésimo.
Univerto	see Humberto.
Unofre	see Onofre.
Uofilo	see Ofelio.
Upa	see Guadalupe.
Upe	see Guadalupe.
Upidio	see Elpidio.
Upolonia	see Apolonio.

Urania (Ooh rah' nee ah) f. EE: Uranus. Gk. "Sky." In Gk. myth., 1st ruler of universe. 7th planet in distance from sun. 1 S. F. 5/19. **Var:** Urano.

Urano	see Urania.
Urba	see Urbano.
Urbaldo	see Ubaldo.
Urbania	see Urbano.
Urbanns	see Urbano.

Urbano (Oor bah' no) m. EE: Orban, Urban, Urbane. Lat. "He who is courteous." 8 popes. 30 x in DS. 1, 3rd cen. pope. F. 5/25. **Var:** Eurbana, Eurvana, Urba, Urbania, Urbanns, Urbanum, Urbanus, Urvano.

Urbanum	see Urbano.
Urbanus	see Urbano.
Urberto	see Herberto.
Urbila	see Ovelia.
Urcina	see Ursula.
Urcula	see Herculano.
Urento	see Orencio.
Ureula	see Aurelio.
Urial	see Uriel.

Urias (Ooh ree' ahs) m. EE: Uriah, Urian, Urias. Heb. "My light is Yahweh." In Bible, King David plotted his death for lust of Uriah's wife, Bathsheba.

Uriel (Ooh ree ell') m. EE: Uriel. Heb. "Powerful light of God." In Bible, husband of Tamar. In Milton's "Paradise Lost," angel of sun. In DS, archangel who showed Enoc revolutions of heavenly bodies. **Var:** Jurelia, Urial.

Urlanda	see Roldán.
Urlinda	see Orfalinda.
Urlisa	see Ursula.
Urmelia	see Onelia.
Ursala	see Ursula.
Ursela	see Ursula.
Urselia	see Ursula.
Ursinia	see Ursula.
Ursino	see Ursula.
Ursline	see Ursula.
Urso	see Ursula.
Ursola	see Ursula.
Ursual	see Ursula.

Ursuela   see Órsula.
Ursul   see Úrsula.
Úrsula (Oore' soo lah) f. EE:
   Ursula, etc. Lat. "Little she-
   bear." 15 x in DS. 1, of 10th
   cen., refused to marry leader of
   Huns & was mart. with 11,000
   companions. F. 10/21. Dim: Susu.
   Var: Eursa, Orsinia, Orsula,
   Orcina, Urlisa, Ursala, Ursela,
   Urselia, Ursinia, Ursino,
   Ursline, Urso, Ursola, Ursual,
   Ursuela, Ursul, Ursulina,
   Ursuls, Urula, Urzula, Ussulo,
   Usula.
Ursulina   see Úrsula.
Ursuls   see Úrsula.
Urula   see Úrsula.
Urvano   see Urbano.
Urzula   see Úrsula.
Usavia   see Eusebio.
Usbaldo   see Ubaldo.
Usballo   see Ubaldo.
Usebio   see Eusebio.
Usevio   see Eusebio.
Usibio   see Eusebio.
Usidoro   see Isidoro.
Usidro   see Isidoro.
Ussulo   see Úrsula.
Ustacia   see Eustacio.
Ustalia   see Eustalio.
Ustaque   see Eustaquio.
Ustaquio   see Eustaquio.

Ustasio   see Eustacio.
Ustin   see Agusto.
Ustiquio   see Eustaquio.
Ustochia   see Eustaquio.
Ustolia   see Eustalio.
Ustorgio   see Eustorgio.
Ustoria   see Eustorgio.
Usuardo (Ooh soo are' doe) m. 9th
   cen. Fr. monk.
Usula   see Úrsula.
Uswaldo   see Osvaldo.
Ute (Ooh' tay) m. Planet.
Utenio   see Eutimia.
Uticio   see Eutiquio.
Utikio   see Eutiquio.
Utilio   see Odilia.
Utimio   see Eutimia.
Utumio   see Eutimia.
Uva   see Ubaldo.
Uvald   see Ubaldo.
Uvaldina   see Ubaldo.
Uvaldo   see Ubaldo.
Uvasldo   see Ubaldo.
Uvelia   see Ovelia.
Uvence   see Juvencio.
Uvencio   see Juvencio.
Uvil   see Ubil.
Uvildina   see Ubaldo.
Uxa   see Eufemia.
Uxo   see Eugenio.
Uzelia   see Oziel.
Uziel   see Oziel.

V

Vacilio   see Bacilio.
Vacilla   see Bacilio.
Vacunda   see Facundo.
Vala (Bah' lah) m. EE: Vala. Small
   planetoid. Also god in Indian
   myth.
Valante   see Valente.
Valantin   see Valente.
Valbina   see Balbina.
Valdamar   see Baldomero.
Valdamero   see Baldomero.
Valde   see Baldomero.
Valdemar   see Baldomero.
Valdemares   see Baldomero.
Valdemaro   see Baldomero.
Valdemena   see Baldomero.
Valdemero   see Baldomero.
Valdemor   see Baldomero.
Valdenar   see Baldomero.
Valdera   see Baldomero.
Valderis   see Baldomero.
Valderma   see Baldomero.
Valdermar   see Baldomero.
Valdimar   see Baldomero.
Valdino   see Baldomero.
Valdmar   see Baldomero.
Valdo   see Baldomero.
Valdomao   see Baldomero.
Valdomar   see Baldomero.
Valdomiro   see Baldomero.
Valeano   see Valerio.
Valediano   see Valerio.
Valemtin   see Valente.
Valén   see Belén.

Valenda   see Belinda.
Valendina   see Valente.
Valenia   see Valerio.
Valenina   see Valerio.
Valenlin   see Valerio.
Valenta   see Valente.
Valente (Bah lain' tay) m. EE:
   Val, Valentine. Lat. "Strong." 3
   Roman emperors. 51 x in DS. 1,
   3rd cen. Roman M., patron of
   lovers. Feast thought to be day
   birds paired. F. 2/14. Dim: Tin,
   Tino. Var: Balante, Balente,
   Balentin, Balentine, Balentino,
   Balento, Balintin, Valante,
   Valantin, Valemtin, Valendina,
   Valenta, Valentén, Valentiano,
   Valentin, Valentiniano,
   Valentino, Valentio, Valentón,
   Valentura, Valinina, Valintin,
   Valintina, Valintine, Valnetin,
   Velente, Velentina.
Valentén   see Valente.
Valentiano   see Valente.
Valentin   see Valente.
Valentiniano   see Valente.
Valentino   see Valente.
Valentio   see Valente.
Valentón   see Valente.
Valentura   see Valente.
Valerianna   see Valerio.
Valeriano   see Valerio.
Valerimio   see Valerio.
Valerin   see Valerio.

Valerio (Bah lay' ree oh) m. **EE:**
Val, Valerian, Valery. Lat. "To
be valiant." 3rd cen. Roman
emperor. 39 x in DS. 1, bishop
of Saragossa, Spain in 3rd cen.
F. 1/28. **Var:** Baleriano,
Balerio, Valeano, Valediano,
Valenia, Valenina, Valenlin,
Valerianna, Valeriano,
Valerimio, Valerín, Valeriona,
Valeritas, Valero, Valiria,
Valiriano, Vallerio.

Valeriona	see **Valerio.**
Valeritas	see **Valerio.**
Valero	see **Valerio.**
Valgamero	see **Baldomero.**
Valgumero	see **Baldomero.**

Validiano (Bah lee dee ah' no) m.
EE: Validiano, Possibly variant
of Biridiano (see).

Valinda	see **Belinda.**
Valinina	see **Valente.**
Valintín	see **Valente.**
Valintina	see **Valente.**
Valintine	see **Valente.**
Valiria	see **Valerio.**
Valiriano	see **Valerio.**
Vallerio	see **Valerio.**
Valnetín	see **Valente.**

Valoniano (Bah low nee ah' no) m.
EE: Valonian. Valonia, nymph &
goddess of valleys in Roman
myth.

Valtazar	see **Baltasar.**
Valtesar	see **Baltasar.**
Valvino	see **Balbina.**

Valydia (Bah lee' dee ah) f. **EE:**
Valada, Valida. Valida, or
Valada, 11th cen Arab princess
who excelled in elocution &
poetry. Comb. of Lidia & Valerio
(see both).

Vancente	see **Vicente.**
Vanceslao	see **Venceslao.**
Vanda	see **Wanda.**

Vandelia (Bahn day' lee ah) f. **EE:**
Vandelia. Plant with flowers.
Var: Bandelia.

Vanencio	see **Venancio.**
Vanera	see **Vanora.**
Vangelina	see **Evangelina.**
Vanifacia	see **Bonifacio.**
Vanita	see **Wanda.**

Vanora (Bah no' rah) f. **EE:**
Vanora. Celt. "White wave." **Var:**
Vanera.

Vantura	see **Venturo.**
Varito	see **Eduardo.**
Varónica	see **Verónico.**
Vartolo	see **Bartolomé.**
Várvara	see **Bárbara.**
Várvera	see **Bárbara.**
Vasilio	see **Bacilio.**
Vasilisa	see **Bacilio.**
Vaudelio	see **Baudilio.**
Vautista	see **Bautista.**
Ve	see **Javier.**
Veatrés	see **Beatriz.**
Veatrís	see **Beatriz.**
Veatriz	see **Beatriz.**
Vecelada	see **Venceslao.**
Vecenta	see **Vicente.**
Veceslado	see **Venceslao.**
Veche	see **Silvestre.**
Veda	see **Beda.**

Vedal	see **Vidal.**
Vego	see **Santiago.**
Veicente	see **Vicente.**
Velente	see **Valente.**
Velentina	see **Valente.**
Velia	see **Eva.**
Velina	see **Ovelia.**
Velinda	see **Belinda.**
Velino	see **Belino.**
Velio	see **Ovelia.**
Velita	see **Ovelia.**
Vellino	see **Belino.**
Venanaucio	see **Venancio.**

Venancio (Bay nahn' see oh) m. **EE:**
Venantius. Lat. "He who likes to
hunt." 11 x in DS. 1, 3rd cen.
M. of Camerino, Italy. Thrown to
wild beasts & eventually behead-
ed. F. 5/18. **Dim:** Nancho. **Var:**
Benancio, Benansio, Benantia,
Benanza, Benanzio, Benarencia,
Vanencio, Venanaucio, Venanio,
Venanjia, Venantio, Venantus,
Venanzco, Venarcio, Venazia,
Venuncio, Vernancia, Verninzo.

Venanio	see **Venancio.**
Venanjia	see **Venancio.**
Venantio	see **Venancio.**
Venantus	see **Venancio.**
Venanzco	see **Venancio.**
Venarcio	see **Venancio.**
Venardo	see **Bernal.**
Venastiano	see **Venustiano.**
Venazia	see **Venancio.**
Vencealao	see **Venceslao.**
Vencelado	see **Venceslao.**
Vencelano	see **Venceslao.**
Vencelao	see **Venceslao.**
Vencelas	see **Venceslao.**
Vencelaus	see **Venceslao.**
Vencella	see **Venceslao.**
Vencelso	see **Venceslao.**
Vencente	see **Vicente.**
Vences	see **Venceslao.**
Venceskao	see **Venceslao.**
Venceslado	see **Venceslao.**
Venceslaha	see **Venceslao.**
Venceslan	see **Venceslao.**

Venceslao (Bane sace' lah oh) m.
EE: Wenceslaus, Wenzel. Slav.
"He who is crowned with glory."
Patron S. of Bohemia. F. 9/28.
Dim: Bences, Benche, Benses,
Bensis, Chelago, Chelao, Chelo,
Guences, Huenche, Vences,
Wences, Wense. **Var:** Benalado,
Benaslado, Bencelado,
Benceslao, Bensala, Bensclado,
Benselado, Benselaso, Bensilao,
Benzalao, Benzelada, Enselao,
Guenseslado, Juvensceslas,
Mencelado, Nenselada, Vanceslao,
Vecelada, Veceslado, Vencealao,
Vencelado, Vencelano, Vencelao,
Vencelas, Vencelaus, Vencella,
Vencelso, Venceskao, Venceslado,
Venceslaha, Venceslan,
Venceslaos, Vencesslas,
Venceslaus, Vencesslo, Vencesloa,
Vencesslon, Vencestiriano,
Vencilado, Vencilao, Vencistas,
Venelado, Venerlao, Veneslau,
Veneslaur, Venezeslada,
Venizelos, Venselado, Venselans,
Venserlado, Vensesslado,

Vensulado, Venzelano, Venzeslao,
Vincelaus, Vincelado,
Vinceslas, Vinceslav, Vinceslow,
Vinzalas, Vonceslaa, Wanceslada,
Welesse, Wenaslao, Wencelado,
Wencelao, Wencelaus, Wenceloa,
Wencelso, Wencerlada,
Wencesdada, Wencesladam,
Wenceslado, Wenceslaeo,
Wenceslai, Wenceslana,
Wenceslar, Wenceslar, Wenceslas,
Wenceslau, Wenceslaus,
Wenceslendo, Wenceslo,
Wencesloa, Wencezlaus,
Wencislado, Wencislov,
Wendislada, Weneeslao,
Weneslada, Weneslao, Wenesyada,
Wenselado, Wenselao, Wenselau,
Wensellao, Wenserlado,
Wenseslado, Wenseslao,
Wenseslar, Wenseslas,
Wenseslaus, Wenseslo,
Wensislado, Wenslada, Wenuelada,
Wenzelado, Wenzelau, Wenzeslado,
Wenzeslao, Wenzeslar, Wenzeslau,
Wenzeslos, Wenzislaus,
Wenzislous, Wescenlao,
Wesceslau, Wincenlada,
Winceslado, Winceslao,
Wineslade, Winieslado.

Venceslaos	see	**Venceslao.**
Venceslas	see	**Venceslao.**
Venceslaus	see	**Venceslao.**
Venceslo	see	**Venceslao.**
Vencesloa	see	**Venceslao.**
Venceslon	see	**Venceslao.**
Vencestiriano	see	**Venceslao.**
Vencilado	see	**Venceslao.**
Vencilao	see	**Venceslao.**
Vencinte	see	**Vicente.**
Vencistas	see	**Venceslao.**
Venecio	see	**Benicio.**
Venelado	see	**Venceslao.**
Venera	see	**Venerio.**

Veneranda (Bay nay rahn' dah) f.
EE: Veneranda. Lat. "He who is
worthy of respect." 7 x in DS.
1, V. M. of Gaul. F. 11/14. **Var:**
Benaranda, Beneranda, Beranda.
Venerio (Bay nay' ree oh) m. EE:
Venerius. Lat. "He who inspires
love." 4 x in DS. 1, Archbishop
of Milan in 3rd cen. F. 5/4.
Var: Venera.

Venerlao	see	**Venceslao.**
Veneslau	see	**Venceslao.**
Veneslaur	see	**Venceslao.**
Venezeslada	see	**Venceslao.**
Venicio	see	**Benicio.**
Venigno	see	**Benigno.**
Venilde	see	**Benilde.**
Veningna	see	**Benigno.**
Venino	see	**Benigno.**
Venisio	see	**Benicio.**
Venito	see	**Benito.**
Venizelos	see	**Venceslao.**
Venjamin	see	**Benjamin.**
Venselado	see	**Venceslao.**
Venselans	see	**Venceslao.**
Vensento	see	**Vicente.**
Venserlado	see	**Venceslao.**
Venseslado	see	**Venceslao.**
Vensulado	see	**Venceslao.**
Ventrua	see	**Venturo.**

Ventura	see	**Bonavento.**
Ventureno	see	**Venturo.**
Venturino	see	**Bonavento.**
Venturino	see	**Venturo.**
Venturio	see	**Venturo.**
Venturita	see	**Bonavento.**

Venturo (Bane too' roe) m. EE:
Ventura, Venture. Lat. "He who
has luck." 3 x in DS. 1, from
13th cen. Umbria, killed by
woodcutter whom he corrected for
cursing. F. 1st Sunday in Sept.
Var: Benturo, Vantura, Ventrua,
Ventureno, Venturino, Venturio.

Venuncio	see	**Venancio.**

Venus (Bay' noose) f. EE: Venus.
Lat. "That which is pleasing."
Roman goddess of love, Vulcan's
wife, mother of Cupid. **Var:**
Benus. See also Venustiano.
Venustiano (Bay noose' tee ah' no)
m. EE: Venustian. Lat. "Venusto"
means "love object." 11 x in DS.
1, governor of Tuscany, Italy,
converted to Christianity by St.
Sabinus who cured his eyes. F.
12/30. **Var:** Bennotiano,
Bennstriano, Benostiano,
Benusteana, Benustiano,
Benustriano, Venastiano,
Venustienio, Venustriano,
Venutiano. See also Venus.

Venustienio	see	**Venustiano.**
Venustriano	see	**Venustiano.**
Venutiano	see	**Venustiano.**
Venzelano	see	**Venceslao.**
Venzeslao	see	**Venceslao.**
Veralda	see	**Bernal.**
Veralina	see	**Vero.**
Verardo	see	**Bernal.**

Veremundo (Bay ray moon' doe) m.
EE: Veremund. Lat. "He who is
pure & clean." 2 x in DS. 1,
bishop of Hirach, Spain, noted
for chastity & gift of miracles.
F. 3/8.

Verenguela	see	**Berenguela.**
Vergil	see	**Virgilio.**
Virginia	see	**Virginia.**
Vericio	see	**Bernicia.**
Verina	see	**Vero.**
Verisimo	see	**Vero.**
Verjinia	see	**Virginia.**

Verlita (Bare lee' tah) f. EE:
Verlita. Form of Berilo (beryl),
type of precious stone.

Vernadine	see	**Bernal.**
Vernado	see	**Bernal.**
Vernaldo	see	**Bernal.**
Vernancia	see	**Venancio.**
Vernardino	see	**Bernal.**
Vernavela	see	**Bernabé.**
Verninzo	see	**Venancio.**

Vero (Bay' roe) m. EE: Vera,
Veradas, Verity. Lat. "True." S.
venerated in Clermont, France.
F. 1/24. **Var:** Veralina, Verina,
Verisimo, Verulo, Vira.
Verona (Bay roe' nah) f. EE:
Verona, Veronus. City in Italy.
Also religious society devoted
to missionary work. 4 x in DS.
Var: Veroniam.

Veroniam	see	**Verona.**

Veronico (Bay roe' nee co) m. EE:

Bernice, Veronica. Gk. "She who brings victory." 7 x in DS. 1 succored Christ on way to Calvary. Received imprint of His face on her veil. F. 2/4. **Var:** Berónico, Varónica.

Verta   see **Berta.**
Vertudes   see **Virtudes.**
Verulo   see **Vero.**
Vesent   see **Vicente.**
Vespasiano (Base pah see ah' no) m. **EE:** Vespasian. Lat. "Wasp." Roman emperor, founder of Flavius family.
Vesta (Bays' tah) f. **EE:** Vesta. Lat. "Clothed with authority." Roman goddess of hearth whose temple was attended by Vestal Vv. **Var:** Besta.
Vetaria (Bay tah' ree ah) f. **EE:** Vetaria. Possibly form of Vetturius, S. mart. in Scilla, Italy, in 2nd cen.
Veto   see **Alberto.**
Veto   see **Silvestre.**
Veva   see **Genoveva.**
Veviana   see **Bibiano.**
Viana   see **Bibiano.**
Vianca   see **Blanca.**
Vianes (Bee ah' nays) m? **EE:** Vianes. Native of Viana, city in Navarre & Orense provinces, Spain.
Viatrice   see **Beatriz.**
Viatricia   see **Beatriz.**
Viatrix   see **Beatriz.**
Vibiano   see **Bibiano.**
Vibiena   see **Bibiano.**
Vibrano   see **Bibiano.**
Vica   see **Virginia.**
Vicencio   see **Vicente.**
Vicente (Bee sane' tay) m. **EE:** Vince, Vincent, etc. Lat. "He who has gained victory." 61 x in DS. Vincent of Saragossa, 1 of most illustrious Mm. of Spain. F. 1/22. **Dim:** Chenche, Chenta, Chente, Chentillo, Chicho, Tente, Viche. **Var:** Becentia, Besente, Besento, Bicenta, Bicente, Bicinthia, Biocento, Biscente, Bisenta, Bisente, Bisentes, Bisenti, Bizenta, Vancente, Vecenta, Veicente, Vencente, Vencinte, Vensento, Vesent, Vicencio, Vicentia, Vicenticus, Vicentino, Vicentius, Vicento, Vicienta, Vicientio, Vicinta, Vincencia, Vincensio, Vincenta, Vincente, Vincentio, Vincenzio, Vincetzius, Vincienta, Vincinta, Vinsenta, Vinzeato, Visante, Visent, Visenta, Visente, Visinta, Visinte, Vizente.
Vicentia   see **Vicente.**
Vicenticus   see **Vicente.**
Vicentino   see **Vicente.**
Vicentius   see **Vicente.**
Vicento   see **Vicente.**
Vicerbo   see **Viterbo.**
Viche   see **Euridice.**
Viche   see **Vicente.**
Vicho   see **Víctor.**
Vicienta   see **Vicente.**

Vicientio   see **Vicente.**
Vicinta   see **Vicente.**
Vicitación   see **Visitación.**
Vico   see **Víctor.**
Victariana   see **Víctor.**
Victena   see **Víctor.**
Victo   see **Víctor.**
Victolina   see **Víctor.**
Víctor (Beak' tor) m. **EE:** Vic, Victor, Victoria. Lat. "Conqueror, victor." 230 x in DS. **Dim:** Bique (Victoria), Bito, Bitulo, Lina (Victorina), Titico, Tola, Tolita, Torico, Totoya (Victoria), Toya (Victoria), Toyano (Victoriano), Vicho, Vico, Viqui (Victoria), Vitico, Vitín, Vito, Vituca (Victoria). **Var:** Bictar, Bictor, Bictoria, Bitaria, Bitoria, Bitoriano, Bitriana, Pictoria, Victariana, Victena, Victo, Victolina, Victorana, Victorem, Victoria, Victoriano, Victorianum, Victorihno, Victorinas, Victorino, Victro, Vifforiano, Viktoriana, Viktorio, Viltoriano, Vithorina, Vithorio, Vítor, Vitorianno, Vitoriano, Víttor, Vittoriano, Vittorio.
Victorana   see **Víctor.**
Victorem   see **Víctor.**
Victoria   see **Víctor.**
Victoriano   see **Víctor.**
Victorianum   see **Víctor.**
Victorihno   see **Víctor.**
Victorinas   see **Víctor.**
Victorino   see **Víctor.**
Victro   see **Víctor.**
Vidad   see **Vidal.**
Vidah   see **Vidal.**
Vidal (Bee doll') m? Lat. "He who is agile & strong." Form of "vital" meaning "he who has life." 52 x in DS. 1 mart. in 3rd cen. F. 11/4. **Dim:** Vita. **Var:** Bedal, Bidad, Bidal, Bidala, Bidalda, Bidar, Bitalia, Bito, Bitor, Vedal, Vidad, Vidah, Vidalia, Vidalina, Vidalo, Videl, Videlio, Vidola, Vital, Vitala, Vitaliano, Vitalico, Vitalina, Vitalio, Vitalis, Vitallo, Vitol, Vitolia, Vitona, Vítor, Vitus.
Vidalia   see **Vidal.**
Vidalina   see **Vidal.**
Vidalo   see **Vidal.**
Vidar (Bee dahr') m. In Scan. myth., god who walked through air & over water. Also god of silence & discretion. **Var:** Vitar.
Videl   see **Vidal.**
Videlio   see **Vidal.**
Vidola   see **Vidal.**
Vierginia   see **Virginia.**
Vifforiano   see **Víctor.**
Vigberto   see **Wigberto.**
Vigido   see **Brígido.**
Vigilio   see **Virgilio.**
Vijelio   see **Virgilio.**
Vijes   see **Eduvigis.**
Viktoriana   see **Víctor.**

Viktorio	see	**Víctor.**
Vila	see	**Elviro.**
Vilfredo	see	**Wilfrido.**
Vilfrido	see	**Wilfrido.**
Vilialdo	see	**Wilebaldo.**
Villebaldo	see	**Wilebaldo.**
Villehaldo	see	**Wilebaldo.**
Villo	see	**Virgilio.**
Vilma	see	**Guillermo.**
Vilmar	see	**Wilma.**
Viltoriano	see	**Víctor.**
Vina	see	**Etelvina.**
Vina	see	**Silvino.**
Vinardo	see	**Bernal.**
Vincelaus	see	**Venceslao.**
Vincencia	see	**Vicente.**
Vincensio	see	**Vicente.**
Vincenta	see	**Vicente.**
Vincente	see	**Vicente.**
Vincentio	see	**Vicente.**
Vincenzio	see	**Vicente.**
Vinceslado	see	**Venceslao.**
Vinceslas	see	**Venceslao.**
Vinceslav	see	**Venceslao.**
Vinceslow	see	**Venceslao.**
Vincetzius	see	**Vicente.**
Vincienta	see	**Vicente.**
Vincinta	see	**Vicente.**

Vinefrida (Bee' nay free' dah) f. EE: Winifred, etc. Ger. "Friend of peace." 2 x in DS. 1, of 7th cen. Wales, mart. for defending chastity. F. 11/3. **Dim:** Vynfa.

Vinicio (Bee nee' see oh) m. EE: Vinicius. Of Etruscan origin. **Var:** Vinusla.

Vinsenta	see	**Vicente.**
Vinusla	see	**Vinicio.**
Vinzalas	see	**Venceslao.**
Vinzeato	see	**Vicente.**

Viola (Bee oh' lah) f. EE: Viol, Violet, etc. Lat. "Violet." 1 M. in DS. F. 5/3. **Dim:** Violetita, Yloy, Yola. **Var:** Biola, Biolanda, Violanda, Violandia, Violanta, Violante, Violeta, Violina. See also Yolanda.

Violanda	see	**Viola.**
Violandia	see	**Viola.**
Violanta	see	**Viola.**
Violante	see	**Viola.**
Violeta	see	**Viola.**

Violeta (Bee oh lay' tah) f. EE: Violet. Lat. "She who causes rejoicing." Also flower with purplish-blue petals. **Var:** Violetta, Violeva.

Violetita	see	**Viola.**
Violetta	see	**Violeta.**
Violeva	see	**Violeta.**
Violina	see	**Viola.**
Vique	see	**Virgilio.**
Viqui	see	**Víctor.**
Vira	see	**Vero.**
Virdana	see	**Viridiana.**
Virgelio	see	**Virgilio.**
Virgena	see	**Virginia.**
Virgenia	see	**Virginia.**
Virgia	see	**Virgilio.**

Virgilio (Beer hee' lee oh) m. EE: Vergil, Virg, etc. Lat. "Virginal or unbloomed." Roman poet who authored "Aeneid." 2 x in DS. 1, bishop of Salzburg, Austria in 8th cen. F. 11/27. **Dim:** Gilo, Guilo, Lilo, Quilo, Villo, Vique. **Var:** Bergelio, Birgilio, Ubigilio, Vergil, Vigilio, Vijelio, Virgelio, Virgia.

Virginia (Beer hee' nee ah) f. EE: Ginger, Virginia, etc. Lat. "Pure." Virginius, powerful Roman family. Virgo, 6th sign of zodiac, from same root. M. whose body was found in 19th cen. F. 5/5. **Dim:** Gina, Ginia, Ginita, Quino, Vica. **Var:** Berginia, Birginio, Verginia, Verjinia, Viergenia, Virgena, Virgenia, Virginnia, Virinia. See also Virgo.

Virginnia   see **Virginia.**

Virgo (Beer' go) f. Lat. "Virgin." Also zodiacal constellation. See also Virginia.

Viriana   see **Viridiana.**

Viridiana (Bee ree' dee ah' nah) f. Ital. S. belonging to 3rd order of St. Francis. Known for penitence & miracles. **Var:** Virdana, Viriana, Virriana.

Virinia	see	**Virginia.**
Virriana	see	**Viridiana.**
Virtrudes	see	**Virtudes.**

Virtudes (Beer too' days) m. Lat. "Virtues" or "manliness," specific quality that gives man strength. Christian virtues are faith, hope, & charity. Angels of 2nd order that God employs for stupendous works. **Var:** Birtudes, Vertudes, Virtrudes.

Virucha	see	**Elviro.**
Visante	see	**Vicente.**
Visent	see	**Vicente.**
Visenta	see	**Vicente.**
Visente	see	**Vicente.**
Visinta	see	**Vicente.**
Visinte	see	**Vicente.**

Visitación (Bee see tah see own') f. Commemorates Mary's visit to Elizabeth. Inspired by Holy Ghost, Elizabeth greeted Mary as mother of Lord. F. 5/31. **Var:** Bisitación, Vicitación.

Vita	see	**Vidal.**
Vital	see	**Vidal.**
Vitala	see	**Vidal.**
Vitaliano	see	**Vidal.**
Vitalico	see	**Vidal.**
Vitalina	see	**Vidal.**
Vitalio	see	**Vidal.**
Vitalis	see	**Vidal.**
Vitallo	see	**Vidal.**
Vitar	see	**Vidar.**

Viterbo (Bee tare' bo) m. Place where V. venerated for delivering city from 4 days of unexplained darkness. **Var:** Berterbo, Biterbo, Bitervo, Vicerbo, Vitervo.

Vitervo	see	**Viterbo.**
Vithorina	see	**Víctor.**
Vithorio	see	**Víctor.**
Vitico	see	**Víctor.**
Vitin	see	**Víctor.**
Vito	see	**Víctor.**
Vitol	see	**Vidal.**
Vitolia	see	**Vidal.**
Vitona	see	**Vidal.**

Vítor   see **Víctor.**
Vítor   see **Vidal.**
Vitorianno   see **Víctor.**
Vitoriano   see **Víctor.**
Víttor   see **Víctor.**
Vittoriano   see **Víctor.**
Vittorio   see **Víctor.**
Vituca   see **Víctor.**
Vitus   see **Vidal.**
Vivaldo (Bee ball' doe) m. Ger. "Bold in battle." Hermit of Tuscany who lived in hollow tree after master's death. F. 5/11. See also Ubaldo.
Vivano   see **Viviano.**
Vivia   see **Viviano.**
Vivián   see **Viviano.**
Vivianna   see **Viviano.**
Viviano (Bee' bee ah' no) m. EE: Viv, Vivian, etc. Lat. "Alive." Vivia Perpetua, Roman matron & M, who became St. Perpetua. F. 3/7. **Dim:** Bibi, Nano. **Var:** Aviviano, Bebián, Bebiano, Bibano, Bibián, Bibiana,

Bibiani, Bibianna, Bibino, Bibrano, Bivián, Biviana, Vivano, Vivia, Vivián, Vivianna, Viviario, Vivieno, Vivina, Viviona.
Viviario   see **Viviano.**
Vivieno   see **Viviano.**
Vivina   see **Viviano.**
Viviona   see **Viviano.**
Vivita   see **Elviro.**
Vivita   see **Natalio.**
Vizente   see **Vicente.**
Vladislav   see **Ladislao.**
Vlas   see **Blas.**
Voldemer   see **Baldomero.**
Vonceslaa   see **Venceslao.**
Vonifacio   see **Bonifacio.**
Vonifaisa   see **Bonifacio.**
Vrígido   see **Brígido.**
Vríjeda   see **Brígido.**
Vuena   see **Bonavento.**
Vulfra   see **Wulfrano.**
Vulfrano   see **Wulfrano.**
Vulstano   see **Wolstano.**
Vynfa   see **Vinefrida.**

W

Wakín   see **Joaquín.**
Waldemar   see **Baldomero.**
Waldemero   see **Baldomero.**
Waldenor   see **Baldomero.**
Waldino   see **Ubaldo.**
Waldo   see **Ubaldo.**
Waldomero   see **Baldomero.**
Walfredo   see **Wilfrido.**
Walfrido   see **Wilfrido.**
Wanceslada   see **Venceslao.**
Wanda (Wahn' dah) f. EE: Wanda, Wandis, Wendy. Teut. "Wanderer." Wando, 8th cen. abbot of Fontanelle, Belgium. F. 4/17. **Dim:** Vanita. **Var:** Quanda, Vanda.
Wanita   see **Juan.**
Washington (Wah shing tone') m. EE: Washington. Teut. "Wassing," "wise, knowing." English place & family name. **Dim:** Guacho, Guasho.
Waterio   see **Gualterio.**
Welesse   see **Venceslao.**
Wenaslao   see **Venceslao.**
Wencelado   see **Venceslao.**
Wencelao   see **Venceslao.**
Wencelaus   see **Venceslao.**
Wenceloa   see **Venceslao.**
Wencelso   see **Venceslao.**
Wencerlada   see **Venceslao.**
Wences   see **Venceslao.**
Wencesdada   see **Venceslao.**
Wencesladam   see **Venceslao.**
Wenceslado   see **Venceslao.**
Wenceslaeo   see **Venceslao.**
Wenceslai   see **Venceslao.**
Wenceslana   see **Venceslao.**
Wenceslao   see **Venceslao.**
Wenceslar   see **Venceslao.**
Wenceslas   see **Venceslao.**
Wenceslau   see **Venceslao.**
Wenceslaus   see **Venceslao.**

Wenceslendo   see **Venceslao.**
Wenceslo   see **Venceslao.**
Wencesloa   see **Venceslao.**
Wencezlaus   see **Venceslao.**
Wencislado   see **Venceslao.**
Wencislov   see **Venceslao.**
Wendislada   see **Venceslao.**
Weneeslao   see **Venceslao.**
Weneslada   see **Venceslao.**
Weneslao   see **Venceslao.**
Wenesyada   see **Venceslao.**
Wense   see **Venceslao.**
Wenselado   see **Venceslao.**
Wenselao   see **Venceslao.**
Wenselau   see **Venceslao.**
Wensellao   see **Venceslao.**
Wenserlado   see **Venceslao.**
Wenserlao   see **Venceslao.**
Wenseslad   see **Venceslao.**
Wenseslado   see **Venceslao.**
Wenseslao   see **Venceslao.**
Wenseslar   see **Venceslao.**
Wenseslas   see **Venceslao.**
Wenseslaus   see **Venceslao.**
Wenseslo   see **Venceslao.**
Wensislado   see **Venceslao.**
Wenslada   see **Venceslao.**
Wenuelada   see **Venceslao.**
Wenzelado   see **Venceslao.**
Wenzelau   see **Venceslao.**
Wenzeslado   see **Venceslao.**
Wenzeslao   see **Venceslao.**
Wenzeslar   see **Venceslao.**
Wenzeslau   see **Venceslao.**
Wenzeslos   see **Venceslao.**
Wenzislaus   see **Venceslao.**
Wenzislous   see **Venceslao.**
Wescenlao   see **Venceslao.**
Wesceslau   see **Venceslao.**
Wichi   see **Luis.**
Wicho   see **Luis.**
Wigberto (Weeg bare' toe) m. EE:

Wigbert. Ger. "Glory of war." 2 x in DS. 1, 8th cen. British monk, went to Germany following call of St. Boniface. F. 8/13. **Var:** Vigberto.

Wilebaldo (Wee' lay ball' doe) m. **EE:** Willebald, Willibald. Teut. "Daring & strong of will." 8th cen. British S. appointed apostolic missionary to Germany. F. 7/7. **Dim:** Balo, Guilde. **Var:** Bibaldo, Bilebalbo, Gilevaldo, Gilibaldo, Gilivaldo, Guibebaldo, Guilebaldo, Guilevaldo, Guilibaldo, Guilibardo, Guillibaldo, Vilialdo, Villebaldo, Villehaldo, Wilehaldo, Willebaldo, Willehado.

Wilehaldo   see **Wilebaldo**.
Wilfido   see **Wilfrido**.
Wilfredo   see **Wilfrido**.
Wilfrido (Weel free' doe) m. **EE:** Wilfred, Wilfrid. Ger. "Resolute peacemaker." 7th cen. Archbishop of York, England & 1 of greatest men of age. F. 10/12. **Var:** Guiffredo, Guilfredo, Vilfredo, Vilfrido, Walfredo, Walfrido, Wilfido, Wilfredo, Wilfrieda, Wolfido.

Wilfrieda   see **Wilfrido**.
Wilhelmio   see **Guillermo**.
Wilhelmo   see **Guillermo**.
Willebaldo   see **Wilebaldo**.
Willehado   see **Wilebaldo**.
Williberto (Wee' lee bare' toe) m.

EE: Wilbert. Comb. of Willebaldo & Berto (see both).
Wilma (Weel' mah) f. **EE:** Wilhelmina, Wilma, etc. Ger. "Chosen protector." **Var:** Vilmar. See also Guillermo.
Wincenlada   see **Venceslao**.
Winceslado   see **Venceslao**.
Winceslao   see **Venceslao**.
Winebertus (Wee nay bare' toose) m. Comb. of Vinefreda & Berto (see both). **Var:** Winiverto.
Wineslade   see **Venceslao**.
Winieslado   see **Venceslao**.
Winiverto   see **Winebertus**.
Wolfango   see **Wulfrano**.
Wolfgang   see **Wolfgango**.
Wolfgango (Woolf gahn' go) m. **EE:** Wolfgang. Teut. "Departing wolf." 10th cen. bishop of Ratsibon, Germany. F. 10/13. **Var:** Wolfgang.
Wolfido   see **Wilfrido**.
Wolfo   see **Wulfrano**.
Wolfran   see **Wulfrano**.
Wolstano (Wool stah' no) m. **EE:** Wulstan, etc. Ang-Sax. "Firm as rock." 11th cen. bishop of Worcester, England & now patron of that city. F. 1/19. **Var:** Vulstano.
Wulalia   see **Eulalio**.
Wulfrano (Wool frah' no) m. **EE:** Wolfram. Teut. "Wolf raven." **Dim:** Vulfra, Wolfo. **Var:** Bulfrano, Vulfrano, Wolfango, Wolfran. See also Ranulfo.

X

Xaba   see **Rosa**.
Xabiel   see **Javier**.
Xabier   see **Javier**.
Xabiera   see **Javier**.
Xacino   see **Jacinto**.
Xacoba   see **Jacobo**.
Xaime   see **Jaime**.
Xandra   see **Alejandro**.
Xano   see **Jano**.
Xanthippi   see **Xantipa**.
Xantipa (Hahn tee' pah) f. **EE:** Xanthippe, Xantippe. Gk. "Yellow horse." Socrates' wife, noted for quarrelsome disposition. Yellow-blooming Xanthium named in her honor. **Var:** Xanthippi.
Xasinto   see **Jacinto**.
Xaverio   see **Javier**.
Xavier   see **Javier**.
Xavior   see **Javier**.
Xcristóbal   see **Cristóbal**.
Xebo   see **Sebastián**.
Xenaida   see **Zenaido**.
Xenar   see **Génaro**.
Xenobio   see **Genoveva**.
Xenov   see **Genoveva**.
Xenovio   see **Genoveva**.
Xerardo   see **Gerardo**.
Xerón   see **Jerónimo**.
Xerónima   see **Jerónimo**.

Xertrudez   see **Gertrudis**.
Xesaria   see **César**.
Xicotencatl   see **Xicotenga**.
Xicotenga (See coo ten' gah) m? Bernal Díaz del Castillo in "True History" named leader of Tlaxcaltecas, a pre-Columbian Mexican tribe. **Var:** Xicotencatl.
Xil   see **Gilberto**.
Ximena   see **Jimeno**.
Xintu   see **Jacinto**.
Xiomara   see **Guiomar**.
Xipto (Seep' toe) m. Shortened form of Xipe-Totec, Mexican god of silversmiths.
Xista   see **Sixto**.
Xistae   see **Sixto**.
Xistao   see **Sixto**.
Xixta   see **Sixto**.
Xlut   see **Eleuterio**.
Xóchil (So' cheel) f? Aztec. "Xochila" means "where flowers abound." **Var:** Xochipil, Xochithil.
Xochipil   see **Xochil**.
Xochithil   see **Xochil**.
Xorge   see **Jorge**.
Xotabel   see **Cristóbal**.
Xpil   see **Felipo**.
Xptóbal   see **Cristóbal**.

Xptobalina	see Cristóbal.	Xysto	see Sixto.
Xrenio	see Irene.	Xystum	see Sixto.

Y

Yaco	see Ciríaco.	Yldalecio	see Indalecio.
Yacobia	see Jacobo.	Yldaphonzo	see Ildefonso.
Yacundo	see Jucundo.	Yldefonso	see Ildefonso.
Yadelicio	see Indalecio.	Yldefonzo	see Ildefonso.
Yana	see María.	Yldephonsa	see Ildefonso.
Yano	see Cipriano.	Yldephoso	see Ildefonso.
Yano	see Jano.	Yldifonza	see Ildefonso.
Yanuario	see Jano.	Yledefonso	see Ildefonso.
Yapa	see Serapio.	Ylefonsa	see Ildefonso.
Yaya	see Adelaido.	Yloanda	see Yolanda.
Yayo	see Arturo.	Ylonda	see Yolanda.
Yayo	see Eduardo.	Yloy	see Viola.
Yayo	see Eulalio.	Ylupe	see Guadalupe.
Yazmín	see Jazmin.	Ymelda	see Imelda.
Ybencio	see Juvencio.	Ynacencio	see Inocencio.
Ybette	see Ivés.	Ynación	see Ignacio.
Ybona	see Ivés.	Ynaiso	see Ignacio.
Ycario	see Icario.	Yncarnación	see Encarnación.
Ycarrio	see Icario.	Yndalecio	see Indalecio.
Ycidro	see Isidoro.	Yndalesio	see Indalecio.
Yda	see Ida.	Yndalicio	see Indalecio.
Ydalia	see Idalia.	Yndalisio	see Indalecio.
Ydelia	see Idalia.	Yndelacio	see Indalecio.
Ydia (Ee' dee ah) f. Idia in		Yndelecio	see Indalecio.
myth., mother of Medea &		Ynéss	see Inés.
Absirto. Also known as Oceanide.		Ynez	see Inés.
Ydolfo	see Adolfo.	Ynnocente	see Inocencio.
Ydolina	see Idolina.	Ynocencio	see Inocencio.
Ydubiges	see Eduvigis.	Ynocensio	see Inocencio.
Ydubijes	see Eduvigis.	Ynocente	see Inocencio.
Yeda (Yay' dah) f. Could be form		Ynoscencio	see Inocencio.
of Yedayah, 2 x in OT.		Ynoscente	see Inocencio.
Yego	see Santiago.	Ynosencio	see Inocencio.
Yelubiges	see Eduvigis.	Ynslalesio	see Indalecio.
Yemo	see Anselmo.	Yñacio	see Ignacio.
Yenerita	see Génaro.	Yoaquin	see Joaquín.
Yenobio	see Genoveva.	Yocundo	see Jucundo.
Yenobis	see Genoveva.	Yohanmes	see Juan.
Yertrudis	see Gertrudis.	Yola	see Viola.
Yevette	see Ivés.	Yola	see Yolanda.
Yeyo	see Aurelio.	Yolanda (Yoh lawn' dah) f. EE:	
Yeyo	see Desiderio.	Yolanda. Gk. "Yole," "beautiful	
Ygancio	see Ignacio.	as violet." Dim: Yola, Yoli,	
Ygenio	see Higinio.	Yolie, Yoliz. Var: Eulanda,	
Ygidroro	see Isidoro.	Iolanda, Jolanda, Jolina,	
Yginio	see Higinio.	Jolinda, Jorlanda, Llolanda,	
Ygnacencio	see Inocencio.	Ylanda, Yloanda, Ylonda,	
Ygnacio	see Ignacio.	Yoldina, Yollando, Yolonda,	
Ygnacito	see Ignacio.	Yoly. See also Viola.	
Ygnacus	see Ignacio.	Yoldina	see Yolanda.
Ygnaico	see Ignacio.	Yoli	see Yolanda.
Ygnasio	see Ignacio.	Yolie	see Yolanda.
Ygnés	see Ignacio.	Yoliz	see Yolanda.
Ygnocencio	see Inocencio.	Yollando	see Yolanda.
Ygnocio	see Ignacio.	Yolonda	see Yolanda.
Yigenia	see Higinio.	Yoly	see Yolanda.
Yilda	see Hildo.	Yoni	see Juan.
Yimi	see Jaime.	Yonocencia	see Inocencio.
Yisadore	see Isidoro.	Yovanna	see Juan.
Yisdero	see Isidoro.	Yoya	see Aurora.
Yismael	see Ismael.	Yoya	see Glorio.
Ylalio	see Eulalio.	Yoya	see Jorge.
Ylanda	see Yolanda.	Yoyi	see Jorge.
Ylario	see Hilario.	Yoyo	see Jorge.
Yldafonso	see Ildefonso.	Ypolario	see Apolonio.

Ypólito	see	Hipólito.
Ypóloto	see	Hipólito.
Yrena	see	Irene.
Yrene	see	Irene.
Yreneo	see	Irene.
Yrenia	see	Irene.
Yrinea	see	Irene.
Ysa	see	Isidoro.
Ysaac	see	Isaac.
Ysaax	see	Isaac.
Ysabel	see	Isabel.
Ysac	see	Isaac.
Ysadora	see	Isidoro.
Ysaís	see	Isaías.
Ysamrel	see	Ismael.
Ysaure	see	Isauro.
Ysauro	see	Isauro.
Ysavel	see	Isabel.
Ysay	see	Isaí.
Ysedora	see	Isidoro.
Ysedro	see	Isidoro.
Ysevio	see	Eusebio.
Ysidalesio	see	Indalecio.
Ysidero	see	Isidoro.
Ysidor	see	Isidoro.
Ysidoro	see	Isidoro.
Ysidro	see	Isidoro.
Ysmael	see	Ismael.
Ysmaela	see	Ismael.

Ysos (Ee' soes) m. In myth.,
Isoso, son of Priam, king of
Troy.

Ysrael	see	Israel.
Ysrrael	see	Israel.
Yssa	see	Isabel.
Yssaach	see	Isaac.
Yssac	see	Isaac.
Yuana	see	Juan.
Yuanita	see	Juan.
Yubencio	see	Juvencio.
Yudalecio	see	Indalecio.
Yudel	see	Odilia.
Yudelia	see	Odilia.
Yudi	see	Judit.
Yulius	see	Julio.
Yulos	see	Julio.
Yuvencio	see	Juvencio.
Yuyo	see	Arturo.
Yuyo	see	Julio.
Yuyu	see	Julio.
Yvés	see	Ivés.
Yvesette	see	Ivés.
Yvette	see	Ivés.
Yvone	see	Ivés.
Yvonne	see	Ivés.
Yvonny	see	Ivés.
Yza	see	Isabel.
Yzabel	see	Isabel.
Yzabela	see	Isabel.

Z

Zabaz	see	Sabás.
Zabina	see	Sabino.
Zabriana	see	Sabino.
Zabrina	see	Sabino.

Zabulón (Zah boo loan') m. EE:
Zebulon, etc. Heb. "Dwelling."
Son of Jacob & Leah & founder of
1 of 12 tribes of Israel. **Var:**
Sabulón, Zebuló.

Zacagosa	see	Zaragoza.
Zacaréas	see	Zacarías.
Zacarian	see	Zacarías.

Zacarías (Zah cah ree' ahs) m. EE:
Zach, Zachary. Heb. "Yahweh hath
remembered." In Bible, last king
of Israel. 42 x in DS. 1, hus-
band of Elizabeth & father of
John the Baptist. F. 11/5. **Var:**
Sacarías, Sacaries, Saccarías,
Sacharío, Sacrías, Zacaréas,
Zacarian, Zacaríaz, Zacarica,
Zacarío, Zacaríos, Zacarís,
Zacaríus, Zacarría, Zacarrías,
Zaccharia, Zacharial, Zacharías,
Zacheo, Zachurías, Zackry,
Zaquarías, Zucarino.

Zacaríaz	see	Zacarías.
Zacarica	see	Zacarías.
Zacarío	see	Zacarías.
Zacaríos	see	Zacarías.
Zacarís	see	Zacarías.
Zacaríus	see	Zacarías.
Zacarría	see	Zacarías.
Zacarrías	see	Zacarías.
Zaccharia	see	Zacarías.
Zacharial	see	Zacarías.
Zacharías	see	Zacarías.
Zacheo	see	Zacarías.
Zachurías	see	Zacarías.
Zackry	see	Zacarías.
Zacobia	see	Jacobo.
Zaelia	see	Azalia.
Zaferina	see	Ceferino.
Zahara	see	Sara.

Zaida (Sigh' dah) f. Ar. "Hunt-
ress." Moorish king's daughter
who took name Isabel when
converted to Christianity. **Var:**
Sadio, Saida, Sayda, Zeida.

Zaila	see	Zoilo.
Zalema	see	Zulema.
Zalia	see	Zoilo.
Zaloma	see	Zulema.
Zandra	see	Alejandro.

Zaneta (Zah nay' tah) f. Form of
Zanitas, S. mart. in Persia
(Iran). F. 3/27. **Var:** Zenita.

Zanona	see	Zenón.
Zap	see	Zapopan.
Zapapa	see	Zapopan.
Zapapan	see	Zapopan.
Zapapana	see	Zapopan.
Zapepan	see	Zapopan.
Zapipo	see	Zapopan.
Zapoba	see	Zapopan.
Zapohan	see	Zapopan.
Zapopa	see	Zapopan.
Zapopam	see	Zapopan.

Zapopan (Zah poe' pahn) f. Nuestra
Señora de Zapopan (Our Lady of
Zapopan) is sanctuary located in
Jalisco, Mexico & dedicated in
1730. During rebellion, friar
calmed Indians by showing them

image of Christ & V. **Dim:** Sopia,
Zap. **Var:** Sabapa, Saboba,
Safopan, Sapapo, Sapatra,
Sapopa, Sapopae, Sapopais,
Sapopan, Sapope, Sapopopo,
Sapopra, Sappana, Seboba,
Sebuba, Sepapa, Sofofa, Sofopa,
Sopapa, Sopopa, Sopopio, Zapapa,
Zapapan, Zapapana, Zapepan,
Zapipo, Zapoba, Zapohan, Zapopa,
Zapopam, Zapopana, Zapopani,
Zapope, Zapopian, Zapropan.

Zapopana	see	**Zapopan.**
Zapopani	see	**Zapopan.**
Zapope	see	**Zapopan.**
Zapopian	see	**Zapopan.**
Zapropan	see	**Zapopan.**
Zaquarías	see	**Zacarías.**
Zara	see	**Sara.**
Zaracoza	see	**Zaragoza.**
Zaragos	see	**Zaragoza.**
Zaragosa	see	**Zaragoza.**
Zaragosae	see	**Zaragoza.**
Zaragossa	see	**Zaragoza.**

Zaragoza (Zah' rah go' sah) f.
Lat. "Caesar Augustus." City in
Spain named for Caesar Augustus.
Mainly surname, popularized as
christening form because of
Mexican general Zaragoza, hero
of Battle of Puebla in 1862.
Var: Ceragoza, Garagoza,
Laragosa, Sanagossa, Saragazza,
Saragda, Saragogo, Saragos,
Saragosam, Saragoso, Saragossa,
Saragoza, Sarazoso, Sarojoza,
Saroza, Sarrazoza, Seragosa,
Sereyoso, Sragosa, Zacagosa,
Zaracoza, Zaragos, Zaragosa,
Zaragosae, Zaragossa, Zarajoza,
Zarangosa, Zarasossa, Zarazoza,
Zargoza, Zaroza.

Zaraida	see	**Zoraida.**
Zarajoza	see	**Zaragoza.**
Zarangosa	see	**Zaragoza.**
Zarapina	see	**Serapio.**
Zarapio	see	**Serapio.**
Zarasossa	see	**Zaragoza.**
Zarazoza	see	**Zaragoza.**

Zarazza (Zah rah' zah) f. Zaraza,
a flower.

Zargoza	see	**Zaragoza.**
Zarida	see	**Zoraida.**
Zaroza	see	**Zaragoza.**
Zastolo	see	**Casto.**
Zaturnina	see	**Saturnino.**
Zaudalupe	see	**Guadalupe.**
Zavier	see	**Javier.**
Zayde	see	**Sara.**
Zayra	see	**Sara.**
Zebuló	see	**Zabulón.**
Zefarana	see	**Ceferino.**
Zefarino	see	**Ceferino.**
Zefenira	see	**Ceferino.**
Zeferimo	see	**Ceferino.**
Zeferín	see	**Ceferino.**
Zeferino	see	**Ceferino.**
Zeferinus	see	**Ceferino.**
Zeferna	see	**Ceferino.**
Zefernio	see	**Ceferino.**
Zefirima	see	**Ceferino.**
Zefirino	see	**Ceferino.**
Zefreno	see	**Ceferino.**
Zefrino	see	**Ceferino.**
Zeida	see	**Zaida.**

Zeladomio	see	**Celedonio.**
Zelafina	see	**Ceferino.**
Zeledonia	see	**Celedonio.**
Zelia	see	**Celio.**
Zelinda	see	**Siglinda.**
Zelmo	see	**Anselmo.**
Zelsa	see	**Celso.**
Zena	see	**Zenobio.**
Zenabia	see	**Zenobio.**

Zenaido (Zay nye' doe) m. **EE:**
Zenaida, etc. Gk. "Pertaining to
Zeus." Daughter of Zeus in Gk.
myth. **Dim:** Naida (Zenaida), Sena
(Zenaida). **Var:** Cenaida,
Cenaide, Cenanida, Cenaydo,
Cenida, Sanaida, Segneda,
Selaido, Senaid, Senaido,
Senarda, Senaydo, Seneida,
Seniada, Senido, Senoida,
Seonida, Sinaido, Sinayda,
Snayda, Synida, Xenaida,
Zenaldo, Zenalfo, Zenarda,
Zenario, Zeneida, Zenido,
Zenoida. See also Zenón,
Zenobio.

Zenaldo	see	**Zenaido.**
Zenalfo	see	**Zenaido.**
Zenarda	see	**Zenaido.**
Zenario	see	**Zenaido.**

Zenda (Zain' dah) f? Ancient Indo-
European language of Persia. Al-
so mythical castle in Alexander
Dumas' "Prisoner of Zenda."

Zeneida	see	**Zenaido.**
Zenen	see	**Zenón.**
Zenido	see	**Zenaido.**
Zenita	see	**Zaneta.**
Zennia	see	**Zenobio.**
Zennovia	see	**Zenobio.**
Zenobi	see	**Zenobio.**
Zenobie	see	**Zenobio.**
Zenobino	see	**Zenobio.**

Zenobio (Zay no' bee oh) m. **EE:**
Zenobia, etc. Lat. "Belonging to
Jupiter." 7 x in DS. 1, 5th cen.
bishop of Florence, Italy. F.
5/25. **Dim:** Seón, Zena (Zenobia),
Zennia (Zenobia). **Var:** Cenabio,
Cenavia, Cenbio, Cenenobia,
Cenobiae, Cenobii, Cenobil,
Cenobio, Cenovina, Cenovio,
Cenvio, Cerobio, Cerrovio,
Cevobia, Cinivio, Cinnonia,
Cinobia, Sanobia, Sanovio,
Senavia, Senobio, Senofia,
Senopio, Senovio, Senvio,
Sernovia, Sinovio, Zenabia,
Zennovia, Zenobi, Zenobie,
Zenobino, Zenobius, Zenovina,
Zenovio, Zevobio. See also
Zenaido, Zenón.

Zenobius	see	**Zenobio.**
Zenoida	see	**Zenaido.**

Zenón (Zay nown') m. **EE:** Zeno. Gk.
"Lively one." Gk. philosopher
who founded Stoicism. **Dim:**
Cenita (Zenona), Sena (Zenona),
Senilla (Zenona), Zona (Zenona).
Var: Cemona, Cenón, Cenona,
Semión, Semón, Semona, Senén,
Seniona, Sennón, Sinón, Senona,
Senone, Senonio, Sinón, Sinona,
Singnita, Zanona, Zenén, Zenona,
Zinón. See also Zenaido,
Zenobio.

Zenona   see **Zenón.**
Zénora   see **Génaro.**
Zénore   see **Génaro.**
Zenorina   see **Senorina.**
Zenovina   see **Zenobio.**
Zenovio   see **Zenobio.**
Zeón (Zay own') m. In Byzantine rite, small metal vessel used before Holy Communion. **Dim:** Zeonilla.
Zeonilla   see **Zeón.**
Zeperino   see **Ceferino.**
Zepheayea   see **Ceferino.**
Zepherena   see **Ceferino.**
Zepherino   see **Ceferino.**
Zepheryna   see **Ceferino.**
Zephimno   see **Ceferino.**
Zephoino   see **Ceferino.**
Zephyrinae   see **Ceferino.**
Zephyrino   see **Ceferino.**
Zephyrinum   see **Ceferino.**
Zephyrinus   see **Ceferino.**
Zeprina   see **Ceferino.**
Zera   see **Sara.**
Zerada   see **Zoraida.**
Zerafín   see **Ceferino.**
Zeraida   see **Zoraida.**
Zerapina   see **Ceferino.**
Zerapio   see **Serapio.**
Sergio   see **Sergio.**
Zeríbio (Zay ree' bee oh) m. Comb. of Sergio & Toribio (see both).
Zerlinda (Zare leen' dah) f. "Zerline," 3 act opera by Daniel Auber, 19th cen. Fr. composer.
Zerofria   see **Ceferino.**
Zesaria   see **César.**
Zeverino   see **Severo.**
Zevobio   see **Zenobio.**
Zezaria   see **César.**
Ziek   see **Ezequiel.**
Ziferina   see **Ceferino.**
Zigfredo   see **Sigfrido.**
Zigifredo   see **Sigfrido.**
Zimón   see **Simón.**
Zina   see **Zinnia.**
Zinforiana   see **Sinforiano.**
Zinnia (Zee' nee ah) f. Purple or lilac flower, native to U.S. & Mexico. **Var:** Cinnia, Ezenia, Zina.
Zinón   see **Zenón.**
Ziola   see **Zoilo.**
Zipora   see **Sippora.**
Zipriana   see **Cipriano.**
Ziprianes   see **Cipriano.**
Zita   see **Félix.**
Zita   see **Tereso.**
Zita (Zee' tah) f. **EE:** Sitha, Zita, Zite. Heb. "Mistress." 13th cen. Ital. patroness of domestic servants. F. 4/27.
Zlavador   see **Salvador.**
Zobeida (Zoe bay' dah) f. **EE:** Zobeide. Ar. "Rich as cream." Wife of Haroun-Al-Raschid in Arabian Nights. **Dim:** Sovia, Sovita. **Var:** Cevaida, Sabeida, Saveida, Sevaida, Seveida, Sobeda, Sobeida, Sobeyda, Sovaida, Soveda, Sovedia, Soveido, Sovida, Zoveida.
Zoé (Zoe aay') f. **EE:** Zoe, etc. Gk. "Life." Byzantine empress. Gk. equivalent to Biblical Eve.

2 x in DS. 1, starved & suffocated with smoke. F. 7/5. See also Zoilo, Zósimo, Zótico.
Zofía   see **Sofío.**
Zoili   see **Zoilo.**
Zoilo (Zoy' low) m. **EE:** Zoilus. Gk. "Life." Gk. rhetoritician & critic of Homer of 4th cen. B.C. 12 x in DS. 1, of 4th cen. Cordova, Spain, beheaded by Diocletian. F. 6/27. **Dim:** Chola (Zoila), Zoili. **Var:** Saila, Soile, Soilla, Soilo, Soilus, Soylo, Zaila, Zalia, Ziola, Zolla, Zoyla. See also Zoé, Zótico.
Zolla   see **Zoilo.**
Zona   see **Zenón.**
Zonia   see **Sonio.**
Zoraida (Zoe rye' dah) f. Ar. "Captivating woman." In 1822, Donizetti presented 1st great successful opera, "Zoraida Di Granata." Another, in Cervantes' "Don Quixote." **Var:** Noraida, Saraida, Seraida, Soaida, Soleida, Soraida, Soraide, Soraita, Soriada, Sorida, Zaraida, Zarida, Zerada, Zeraida, Zorida, Zorila.
Zorapio   see **Serapio.**
Zorida   see **Zoraida.**
Zorila   see **Zoraida.**
Zornia (Zore' nee ah) f. Plant genre.
Zoroastro (Zoe' roe ahs' troe) m. **EE:** Zarathustra, Zoroaster. Pers. "Living star." Prophet of ancient Iran & founder of religion Zoroastrianism.
Zósimo (Zoe' see mo) m. **EE:** Zosimus. Gk. "Full of life & vigor." 5th cen. Gk. historian. 24 x in DS. 1, 7th cen. bishop of Syracuse, noted for love of poor. F. 11/30. **Dim:** Sos. **Var:** Sásimo, Sócimo, Sócoma, Sósimo, Súsimo, Zózimo. See also Zoé, Zoilo, Zótico.
Zotero   see **Sotero.**
Zótico (Zoe' tee co) m. **EE:** Zoticus. Gk. "That which is vital." 22 x in DS. 1 lived in Rome & built hospital for poor & orphaned. Tied to wild horse & dragged to death for resisting Arians. F. 12/31. See also Zoé, Zoilo, Zósimo.
Zoveida   see **Zobeida.**
Zoyla   see **Zoilo.**
Zózimo   see **Zósimo.**
Zucarino   see **Zacarías.**
Zuelema   see **Zulema.**
Zuelma   see **Zulema.**
Zuiliana   see **Zulema.**
Zula   see **Zulema.**
Zulahika   see **Zuleica.**
Zulaica   see **Zuleica.**
Zuleica (Zoo lay' cah) f. **EE:** Zuleika. Ar. "Fair." **Var:** Zulahika, Zulaica.
Zulema (Zoo lay' mah) f. Heb. "Peace." **Dim:** Sulia, Suly, Zula, Zuly. **Var:** Asulema, Selema, Solema, Solemna, Solena, Solima,

Suilielma, Sulemia, Sulemo,
Sulenia, Sulerma, Sulerna,
Sulima, Suluma, Zalema, Zaloma,
Zuelema, Zuelma, Zuiliana,
Zulemna, Zulena, Zulenra,
Zulerma, Zulia, Zulima.

Zulemna	see **Zulema.**
Zulena	see **Zulema.**
Zulenra	see **Zulema.**
Zulerma	see **Zulema.**
Zulia	see **Zulema.**
Zulima	see **Zulema.**
Zuly	see **Zulema.**
Zumersindo	see **Gumersindo.**
Zuzama	see **Susano.**
Zuzana	see **Susano.**
Zuzanna	see **Susano.**

Appendix: Frequency Count of Mexican American Baptismal Names

The following names were taken from the San Antonio Catholic Chancery, which archives all of the baptismal records of thirty south Texas counties. Since the Martínez name appears more frequently than any other Spanish surname, it may be considered representative of the entire Mexican American population. These 2,175 baptismal names (1,123 female and 1,052 male) span the years 1847 to 1980 and represent over 18,000 individuals.

The names are ranked and listed alphabetically by categories of decreasing frequency. Each of the five categories has the names and also a summary of the total number of individuals represented and their percentage of the 18,000. Following the tabular account is an analysis.

FEMALE NAMES

Frequency of 200 or more

Guadalupe
Margarita
María
Mary

Includes 1,967 females or 19% of the total.

Frequency of 150–199

Gloria
Juanita
Marta, Martha

Includes 475 females or 5% of the total.

Frequency of 100–149

Francisca
Juana
Linda
Manuela
Rosa

Includes 591 females or 6% of the total.

Frequency of 50–99

Aurora	Elizabeth	Josefina
Carmen	Ester, Esther	Laura
Cynthia	Eva	Leonor
Diana	Irene	Leticia
Dolores	Irma	Lidia, Lydia
Dora	Isabel	Lisa, Liza

Lucia	Olga	Sandra
Lusia	Olivia	Sylvia
Margareta	Patricia	Teresa
Michelle	Paula	Victoria
Mónica	Petra	Virginia
Norma	Rebecca	Yolanda

Includes 2,298 names or 22% of the total.

Frequency of 15-49

Alma	Estela	Melissa
Ascención	Evangelina	Mercedes
Bárbara	Felicitas	Minerva
Beatrice	Felipa	Nancy
Berta, Bertha	Genoveva	Natividad
Blanca	Graciela	Nora
Candelaria	Gregoria	Ofelia
Carolina	Herlinda, Erlinda	Oralia
Cecilia	Herminia	Rachel
Celia	Hortencia	Rafaela
Christine	Jesusa	Ramona
Concepción	Jesusita	Raquel
Consuelo	Josefa	Rita
Cristina	JoAnn	Romana
Debra	Julia	Rosalinda
Delfina	Lilia	Rosario
Delia	Liza	Rose
Dominga	Lucinda	San Juanita
Elena	Lucy	Sara
Elia	Lupe	Silvia
Elida	Luz	Sofía
Elisa	Marcelina	Sonia
Eloisa	Mariana	Theresa
Elvira	Maricela	Tomasa
Emma	Martina	Trinidad
Ernestina	Matilde	Verónica
Esmeralda	Melinda	Yvonne
Esperanza		

Includes 2,182 names or 21% of the total.

The five sets of frequency lists cover 73% of the females. The 1,004 names not listed because of low incidence cover 27% of Mexican American females. Unsurprisingly, approximately 11% (119) of the names serve 73% of the female population; a high 89% of the total names identifies only 27% of the female population of this ethnic group.

MALE NAMES

Frequency of 200 or more

Guadalupe	José	Luis
Jesús	Juan	Manuel

Includes 2,412 males or 22% of the total.

Frequency 150-199

David	Michael	Pedro
Francisco	Miguel	Roberto
Martín		

Includes 1,236 males or 11% of the total.

Frequency 100–149

Carlos	Ramón	Robert
Daniel	Raúl	Rodolfo
Mario	Ricardo	

Includes 1,040 names or 9% of the total.

Frequency of 50–99

Armando	George	Mark
Arturo	Gilberto	Oscar
Domingo	Héctor	Pablo
Eduardo	John	Richard
Enrique	Joseph	Santiago
Ernesto	Julián	Santos
Felipe	Louis	Tomás
Fernando	Marcos	Víctor

Includes 2,189 males or 20% of the total.

Frequency 15–49

Arnulfo	Jaime	Máximo
Arthur	James	Mike
Benito	Javier	Nicolás
Benjamín	Jesse	Pascual
Bernardo	Jimmy	Paul
Celestino	Joe	Paulo
Christopher	Johnny	Rafael
Conrado	Jorge	Ralph
Cruz	Julio	Ramiro
Eduardo	Lázaro	Raymond
Elías	Larry	Raymundo
Emilio	Leandro	Refugio
Ernesto	Leo	René
Esteban	León	Reyes
Eugenio	Leonard	Reynaldo
Federico	Leonardo	Rogelio
Felix	Leopoldo	Roger
Fidel	Leroy	Roland
Frank	Lionel	Rosendo
Gabriel	Lorenzo	Roy
Genaro	Lucio	Rudy
Gerardo	Lupe	Salvador
Gilbert	Magadaleno	Samuel
Gregorio	Marcelino	Simón
Guillermo	Marco	Thomas
Henry	Margarito	Trinidad
Ignacio	Matías	Valentin
Isidro	Mauro	Vicente
Ismael		

Includes 2,670 males or 21% of the total.

The five frequency lists, totaling 131 names, cover 83% of the total number of males. The names not listed because of low frequency (921) represent 17% of the male population. The same disproportion evident among females is at work here. A small pool of names covers by far the majority of the male population.

Glossary

Aagar	see	Agar
Aaron	see	Aarón
Abachum	see	Abacum
Aban	see	Abán
Abby	see	Abegail
Abdenago	see	Abdénago
Abdias	see	Abdías
Abdiel	see	Abdiel
Abdon	see	Abdón
Abdul	see	Abdulia
Abdullah	see	Obdulio
Abe	see	Abraham
Abel	see	Abel
Abelard	see	Abelardo
Abelbald	see	Abelibaldo
Abelicio	see	Abelicio
Abell	see	Abel
Abella	see	Abil
Abenamar	see	Abenamar
Aberardo	see	Aberardo
Abercius	see	Abursia
Abigail	see	Abegail
Abimelech	see	Abimelech
Abiram	see	Abirio
Abiron	see	Abirio
Abishalom	see	Absalón
Able	see	Abel
Abraham	see	Abraham
Abram	see	Abraham
Abrasia	see	Abrasia
Absalom	see	Absalón
Abundius	see	Abundio
Acacius	see	Acacio
Acario	see	Acacio
Acathius	see	Acacio
Achilles	see	Aquiles
Achilleus	see	Aquiles
Aciano	see	Aciano
Acindynus	see	Acinta
Aciono	see	Aciono
Acisclus	see	Acisclo
Acorinio	see	Acorinio
Ada	see	Adina
Adabelia	see	Adabelia
Adactus	see	Adaucto
Adadea	see	Adadea
Adalbert	see	Adalberto
Adalcira	see	Alcir
Adalgisus	see	Adolgiza
Adam	see	Adán
		Adame
Adambert	see	Adamberto

Adamnon	see	Adame
Adanelia	see	Adanelia
Adauctus	see	Adaucto
Adela	see	Adela
		Adelaido
Adelaide	see	Adelaido
Adele	see	Adela
		Adelaido
Adelemus	see	Adilmira
Adeline	see	Adela
Adelmar	see	Edelmira
Adelphe	see	Adelfo
Adelphius	see	Adelfo
Ademar	see	Ademar
Adeodatus	see	Adeodato
Adfilius	see	Afilio
Adhelm	see	Adelmo
Adolf	see	Adolfo
Adolph	see	Adolfo
Adolphus	see	Adolfo
Adon	see	Adón
		Adonís
Adonais	see	Adón
		Adonís
Adonald	see	Adonaldo
Adonario	see	Adonario
Adonijah	see	Adonías
Adonis	see	Adón
		Adonís
Adrian	see	Adrián
Adronicus	see	Adrónico
Adulia	see	Adulio
Adulio	see	Adulio
Aedesius	see	Edesio
Aeneas	see	Eneas
Aeschill	see	Esquilo
Aeschylus	see	Esquilo
Aferino	see	Aferino
Agape	see	Agapito
Agapius	see	Agapito
Agate	see	Ágata
Agatha	see	Ágata
Agathon	see	Agatón
Ageo	see	Haggeo
Aggaeus	see	Ageo
Aggeus	see	Ageo
Aggie	see	Ágata
Agilaeus	see	Agileo
Agilbert	see	Agilberto
Agilbertus	see	Agilberto
Agleus	see	Agileo
Agnes	see	Inés

Agobard	see Agobardo	Americus	see Américo
Agraciana	see Agraciana	Amias	see Amadeo
Agretina	see Agretina	Aminta	see Aminta ·
Agricola	see Agrícola	Amora	see Amora
Agricolus	see Agrícola	Amorosella	see Amorosella
Agrippa	see Agripino	Amos	see Amós
Agrippinus	see Agripino	Amparo	see Amparo
Agueleo	see Agueleo	Ampelius	see Ampelio
Aguinald	see Aguinaldo	Amy	see Amada
Ahasuerus	see Asuero	Anacarius	see Anacario
Aida	see Aída	Anacletus	see Anacleto
Aimee	see Amada	Analilia	see Analilia
Aisha	see Aixa	Ananias	see Ananías
Aishah	see Aixa	Anastasia	see Anastacio
Aislara	see Aislara	Anatole	see Anatolio
Al	see Alberto	Anatoly	see Anatolio
	Alfredo	Ancient	see Anciano
Aladdin	see Aladino	Ancira	see Ancirea
Alalita	see Alalita	Andelius	see Andelio
Alamar	see Alamar	Andorra	see Andora
Alan	see Alano	Andrew	see Andrés
Alaric	see Alarico	Andronicus	see Andrónico
Alba	see Albino	Andy	see Andrés
Alban	see Albano		Leandro
Albanus	see Albano	Anelda	see Anelda
Alberic	see Alberico	Anfiano	see Anfanio
Albert	see Alberto	Anfilo	see Anfilo
Albetto	see Albetto	Angel	see Ángel
Albinia	see Elviro	Angela	see Ángel
Albion	see Albino	Angelo	see Ángel
Alcibiades	see Alcibíades	Aniano	see Aniano
Aldegund	see Aldegundo	Anicetus	see Aniceto
Aldhelm	see Adelmo	Anisius	see Anisio
Aldo	see Aldo	Anita	see Ana
Aldoud	see Aldo	Annabelle	see Anabel
Aleatero	see Aleatero	Annabert	see Aniberto
Alelina	see Alelina	Anne	see Ana
Alentin	see Alentín	Annelise	see Analissa
Alex	see Alejandro	Annunciation	see Anunciación
Alexander	see Alejandro	Anoreus	see Anores
Alf	see Alfredo	Ansbert	see Ansberto
Alfenia	see Alfenia		Austreberto
Alfred	see Alfredo	Anselm	see Anselmo
Algisus	see Adolgiza	Antenorus	see Antenor
Alice	see Alicio	Anthelmus	see Antelmo
Alindardo	see Alindardo	Antherus	see Antero
Alipius	see Alipio	Anthony	see Antonio
Alirio	see Alirio	Antimius	see Antimio
Allen	see Alano	Antimus	see Antimio
Alma	see Alma	Antioch	see Antíoco
Almachius	see Almaquio	Antiochus	see Antíoco
Almaiza	see Almaiza	Antipater	see Antipatio
Alonzo	see Alfonso	Antony	see Antonio
Aloysius	see Aloisio	Aphrodite	see Afrodisio
Alpha	see Alfa	Aplica	see Aplica
Alphege	see Elfego	Apolinar	see Apolonio
Alphonse	see Alfonso	Apollo	see Apolo
Altagracia	see Altagracia	Apparition	see Aparicio
Alva	see Elviro	Apphianus	see Apiano
Alvanus	see Alvanus	Appianus	see Apiano
Alvarus	see Álbaro	Apuleius	see Apuleyo
Alviso	see Alviso	Aquila	see Acilino
Alypius	see Alipio	Aquilinus	see Aquilino
Amabilis	see Amable	Arabella	see Arabela
Amable	see Amable	Araminda	see Armida
Amadeus	see Amadeo	Arcadius	see Arcadio
Amanda	see Amanda	Arcanus	see Arcano
Amantius	see Amancio	Archelaus	see Archeláo
Amapola	see Amapola	Archibald	see Archibaldo
Amarantius	see Amaranto	Archie	see Archibaldo
Amariah	see Mireya	Archimedes	see Arquímedis
Amaryllis	see Amarilis	Argentina	see Argentina
Amasius	see Amasio	Arian	see Ariano
Ambrose	see Ambrosio	Ariel	see Ariela
Amelia	see Amalio	Ariolo	see Aryiola

Ariosto	see	Ariosto
Aristide	see	Aristeo
Aristotle	see	Aristóteles
Arius	see	Ariano
Armand	see	Armando
Armin	see	Arminio
Armina	see	Herminio
		Irma
Arminta	see	Armida
Armon	see	Germán
Arno	see	Arno
Arnold	see	Arnoldo
Arnot	see	Arno
Arnott	see	Arno
Arnulph	see	Arnulfo
Arnulphus	see	Arnulfo
Aron	see	Aarón
Arsenius	see	Arsenio
Art	see	Arturo
Artemas	see	Artemio
Artemis	see	Artemio
Arthur	see	Arturo
Ascanius	see	Ascanio
Asclepiades	see	Asclepiades
Ascylus	see	Acisclo
Asella	see	Acela
		Aselo
Asenath	see	Asenet
Asmus	see	Erasmo
Aspasia	see	Aspasia
Aspatia	see	Aspasia
Assumption	see	Asunción
Asta	see	Astrid
Asteria	see	Asterio
Asterius	see	Asterio
Astolf	see	Astolfo
Astrid	see	Astrid
Astrogild	see	Astrogildo
Atahualpa	see	Atahualpa
Atalus	see	Átalo
Athanasia	see	Atanasio
Athanasius	see	Atanasio
Athenogenes	see	Atenógenes
Atreus	see	Atreo
Attila	see	Atilano
Attilus	see	Átalo
Aubin	see	Albino
Audentius	see	Audencio
		Audenia
Audifax	see	Audifaz
Audoenus	see	Audona
Audomar	see	Audomero
Augurius	see	Augurio
August	see	Agusto
Augustine	see	Agusto
Aura	see	Aura
Aural	see	Aura
Aurelius	see	Aurelio
Aureus	see	Aureo
Aurora	see	Aurora
Ausalia	see	Ausalia
Austrabert	see	Ansberto
Austrebert	see	Austreberto
Autharius	see	Autario
Autonoe	see	Autonia
Auxentius	see	Ausencio
Auxilia	see	Auxilio
Auxilius	see	Auxilio
Avaceli	see	Avaceli
Avelin	see	Abelino
Aventinius	see	Abenicio
Aventinus	see	Avento
Avertanus	see	Abertano
Avitus	see	Avito
Ayesha	see	Aixa
Azael	see	Azael
Azalea	see	Azalia
Azrael	see	Azarel
Azusena	see	Azusena
Babette	see	Bárbara
Babtist	see	Bautista
Babylas	see	Babil
Balbina	see	Balbina
Balbinus	see	Balbina
Balthasar	see	Baltasar
Balthazar	see	Baltasar
Baptist	see	Bautista
Barbara	see	Bárbara
Barbosa	see	Barbosa
Bardomianus	see	Bardomiano
Barnabas	see	Bernabé
Barnaby	see	Bernabé
Bart	see	Bartolomé
Bartholomew	see	Bartolomé
Basil	see	Bacilio
Bathsheba	see	Betsabé
Baudelius	see	Baudilio
Baudencio	see	Baudencio
Baylon	see	Bailón
Beata	see	Beato
Beatrice	see	Beatriz
Beatrix	see	Beatriz
Beatus	see	Beato
Becky	see	Rebeca
Bede	see	Beda
Bee	see	Abejundio
Befania	see	Befania
Begonia	see	Begonia
Belda	see	Belda
Beliarosa	see	Beliarosa
Belinda	see	Belinda
Belisarius	see	Belisario
Bella	see	Arabela
		Belia
		Isabel
Bellarmine	see	Belarmino
Belle	see	Arabela
		Belia
		Isabel
Bellina	see	Belino
Bellinus	see	Belino
Belota	see	Belotta
Belva	see	Belia
Ben	see	Benito
		Benjamín
Bendix	see	Benedicto
Benecio	see	Benecio
Benedict	see	Benedicto
Benedicta	see	Benito
Benerita	see	Benerita
Beni	see	Benigno
Benigna	see	Benigno
Benignus	see	Benigno
Benildis	see	Benilde
Benjamin	see	Benjamín
Benny	see	Benjamín
Bercharius	see	Bercario
Berengario	see	Berenguela
Berenice	see	Bernicia
Bernald	see	Bernal
Bernard	see	Bernal
Bernice	see	Bernicia
		Verónico
Bert	see	Alberto
		Beltrán
		Bertrán
		Cutberto
		Gilberto
		Herberto
		Norberto

Bertha	see	Berta
Berthold	see	Bertoldo
Bertie	see	Berta
Bertold	see	Bertoldo
Bertram	see	Beltrán
		Bertrán
Bertrand	see	Beltrán
		Bertrán
Beryl	see	Berilo
Beryle	see	Berilo
Berylee	see	Berilo
Besnardis	see	Besnardo
Betario	see	Betario
Bethany	see	Bethania
Bethelem	see	Belén
Bethulia	see	Betulia
Bettina	see	Berta
Betty	see	Elisabeth
Beula	see	Bula
Beulah	see	Bula
Beverly	see	Bevelina
Bibeanela	see	Bibeanela
Bildad	see	Bildá
		Biliad
Bill	see	Guillermo
Blanch	see	Blanca
Blanche	see	Blanca
Blandina	see	Blandina
Blase	see	Blas
Blaze	see	Blas
Bob	see	Roberto
Bolivar	see	Bolívar
Bonajunta	see	Bonajunta
Bonaventure	see	Benvenido
		Bonavento
Bonfilius	see	Bonfilio
Boniface	see	Bonifacio
Bonnie	see	Bona
Borgita	see	Borgita
Boris	see	Boris
Borromeo	see	Borromeo
Brand	see	Brandio
Branla	see	Branla
Braulio	see	Braulia
Brendan	see	Brandio
Brice	see	Bricio
Brictius	see	Bricio
Bridget	see	Brígido
Brigid	see	Brígido
Briseis	see	Briseida
Bronislava	see	Bronislava
Brunhilda	see	Brunilda
Brunhilde	see	Brunilda
Bruno	see	Bruno
Brush	see	Ambrosio
Bruto	see	Bruto
Brutus	see	Bruto
Bryce	see	Bricio
Bulmar	see	Bulmaro
Caballinus	see	Cabalina
Caesar	see	César
Cafirio	see	Cafirio
Caius	see	Cayo
Cajetan	see	Cayetano
Cajus	see	Cayo
Calixtus	see	Calixto
Calliope	see	Caliopa
Callista	see	Calixto
Calma	see	Calma
Calvin	see	Calvino
Cameron	see	Camerino
Camilla	see	Camelia
		Camilo
Camille	see	Camelia
		Camilo
Camiria	see	Camiria
Candelario	see	Candelario
Candide	see	Candido
Candor	see	Candor
Caniacian	see	Caniacián
Cantius	see	Cancio
Canute	see	Canuto
Caparina	see	Caparina
Caporino	see	Caporino
Caracalla	see	Carácala
Cardina	see	Cardina
Carina	see	Carino
Carissa	see	Caridad
		Carisa
Carl	see	Carlos
Carmel	see	Carmen
Carmen	see	Carmen
Carol	see	Carolina
Caroline	see	Carolina
Carparem	see	Carparem
Carphorus	see	Carpóforo
Carpus	see	Carpio
Carrie	see	Carolina
Casilda	see	Casildo
Casimir	see	Casimiro
Casinao	see	Casinao
Casinciro	see	Casinciro
Casisno	see	Casisno
Cass	see	Casimiro
Cassandra	see	Casandra
Cassianus	see	Casiano
Cassie	see	Casandra
Cassius	see	Casio
Castalia	see	Castalia
Castimer	see	Casimiro
Castor	see	Cástoro
Castus	see	Casto
Catalus	see	Cátulo
Catedra	see	Cátedra
Catelia	see	Catelia
Catherine	see	Catalina
Cathy	see	Catalina
Cato	see	Catón
Cecil	see	Cecilio
Cecyl	see	Cecilio
Celedonus	see	Celedonio
Celerina	see	Celerino
Celerinus	see	Celerino
Celestine	see	Celestino
		Celia
Celia	see	Celina
Celsus	see	Celso
Censurius	see	Censurio
Cerbonius	see	Cerbonio
Ceres	see	Ceres
Charalampus	see	Caralampio
Charitina	see	Caritina
Charity	see	Caridad
Charles	see	Carlos
Chastina	see	Casto
Cherub	see	Querubín
Chris	see	Cristóbal
Christ	see	Cristo
Christian	see	Cristián
Christopher	see	Cristóbal
Christophorus	see	Crisóforo
Chronita	see	Chronita
Chrysantus	see	Crisanto
Chrysogonus	see	Crisógono
Chrysologus	see	Crisólogo
Chuck	see	Carlos
Chysostom	see	Crisóstomo
Cicero	see	Cicerón
Ciprian	see	Cipriano
Circe	see	Cirz

Cissie	see	Cecilio
Clair	see	Clara
Clara	see	Clara
Clare	see	Clara
Claude	see	Claudio
Claudelario	see	Claudelario
Claudius	see	Claudio
Claus	see	Nicolás
Cleander	see	Cleandro
Cleatus	see	Cleandro
Clelia	see	Clelia
Clem	see	Clemente
Clemens	see	Clemente
Clement	see	Clemente
Cleo	see	Cleopatra
Cleopatra	see	Cleopatra
Cleophas	see	Cleofás
Cletus	see	Cleto
Cloelia	see	Clelia
Clotaire	see	Clotario
Clotarius	see	Clotario
Clothildis	see	Clotilde
Clotildis	see	Clotilde
Clovis	see	Clovio
Coelestius	see	Celestino
Colette	see	Coleta
Collette	see	Coleta
Columba	see	Columba
Columbus	see	Colón
		Columba
Commodus	see	Cómodo
Con	see	Conrado
Conception	see	Concepción
Concordio	see	Concordio
Concordius	see	Concordio
Connie	see	Constancio
		Consuelo
Conrad	see	Conrado
Constantine	see	Constancio
Consuela	see	Consolación
Consuelo	see	Consolación
		Consuelo
Cora	see	Corina
Coral	see	Coral
Coraline	see	Coral
Cordelia	see	Cordilio
Corine	see	Corina
Cornel	see	Cornelio
Cornelius	see	Cornelio
Cosimo	see	Cosme
Cosmas	see	Cosme
Cosmo	see	Cosme
Credence	see	Credenciana
Crescentianus	see	Crescencio
Creusa	see	Cresusa
Crispian	see	Crepino
		Crespín
Crispin	see	Crepino
		Crespín
Crispridion	see	Crispridión
Crux	see	Cruz
Cruz	see	Cruz
Cuauhtemoc	see	Cuauhtémoc
Cunigundis	see	Cunegunda
Cuprian	see	Cupriano
Curt	see	Curcio
Curtis	see	Curcio
Cuthbert	see	Cutberto
Cy	see	Ciro
Cynllo	see	Cynilo
Cynth	see	Cinta
Cynthia	see	Cinta
Cynthie	see	Cinta
Cyprian	see	Cipriano
Cyrenia	see	Cirenia

Cyriaca	see	Ciríaco
Cyriacus	see	Ciríaco
Cyrian	see	Cyriano
Cyril	see	Cirilo
Cyrilla	see	Cirilo
Cyrus	see	Ciro
Dacius	see	Dacio
Dagobert	see	Dagoberto
Dahlia	see	Dalia
Dalmatius	see	Dalmacio
Dalmatus	see	Dalmacio
Damaris	see	Damario
Damasus	see	Dámaso
Damien	see	Damián
Damon	see	Damián
Daniel	see	Daniel
Danielle	see	Daniel
Dante	see	Dante
Dantus	see	Dante
Darian	see	Darío
Darigildo	see	Darigildo
Darius	see	Darío
Dativa	see	Dativa
Dativus	see	Dativa
Datum	see	Dadillo
Dave	see	David
David	see	David
Davigildo	see	Davigildo
Davy	see	David
Debbie	see	Débora
Deborah	see	Débora
Decius	see	Decio
Deianira	see	Deyanira
Dejanira	see	Deyanira
Delfidio	see	Delfidio
Delfina	see	Delfino
Delgadino	see	Delgadino
Delia	see	Cordilio
Deliada	see	Delida
Delicia	see	Delicia
Delizea	see	Delicia
Deloris	see	Dolores
Delphinus	see	Delfino
Demeter	see	Demetino
		Demetrio
Demetrius	see	Demetrio
Democles	see	Democles
Demophilus	see	Demófilo
Demosthenes	see	Demóstenes
Dennis	see	Dionisio
Deodatus	see	Deodato
Deogratias	see	Deogracias
Desiderius	see	Desiderio
Destiny	see	Destina
Devine	see	Divino
Di	see	Diana
		Dina
Diamanta	see	Diamantina
Diana	see	Diana
Diane	see	Diana
Dianora	see	Dionora
Dicasio	see	Dicasio
Dick	see	Ricardo
Didius	see	Didio
Digna	see	Digna
Dignus	see	Digna
Dimas	see	Dimaso
Dimecio	see	Dimecia
Dina	see	Dina
		Dionora
Dinah	see	Dina
Dinorah	see	Dionora
Diodemaro	see	Dicmar
Diodorus	see	Diodoro
Diogenes	see	Diógenes

Diomede	see	Diomedes
Diomedes	see	Diomedes
Dion	see	Dione
Dionysius	see	Dionisio
Dioscuri	see	Dioscoro
Dioscurus	see	Dioscoro
Dismas	see	Dimás
Dita	see	Edita
Divine	see	Adibina
		Divino
Divitianus	see	Divisio
Dolores	see	Dolores
Dometian	see	Domecia
Dometius	see	Domecia
		Domitilo
Dominic	see	Domingo
Dominick	see	Domingo
Dominius	see	Domis
Domino	see	Domnino
Don	see	Donaldo
Dona	see	Domnino
Donald	see	Donaldo
Donatus	see	Donaciano
		Donato
Donna	see	Domnino
Doralice	see	Doraliza
Doralva	see	Doralva
Dorceo	see	Dorasio
Dorofelia	see	Dorofelia
Dorolinda	see	Dorolinda
Dorothea	see	Doroteo
Dorothy	see	Doroteo
Dositheus	see	Dositeo
Dot	see	Doroteo
Drucilla	see	Drusila
Drusilla	see	Drusila
Duella	see	Duella
Dula	see	Dulas
Dulalio	see	Dulalio
Dulas	see	Dulas
Dulcia	see	Dulce
Dulcina	see	Dulce
Dulcy	see	Dulce
Dunstan	see	Dunstano
Duran	see	Dante
Dymphna	see	Dimpna
Dympna	see	Dimpna
Ebbie	see	Ebenezer
Eben	see	Ebenezer
Ebenezer	see	Ebenezer
Ecelso	see	Ecelso
Econina	see	Econina
Ed	see	Edgardo
Edam	see	Adán
Edbert	see	Edberto
Edda	see	Eda
Eddie	see	Edgardo
		Eduardo
Edelfrida	see	Edelfrida
Edenia	see	Edenia
Edesius	see	Edesio
Edgar	see	Edgardo
Edicacion	see	Edicación
Edilio	see	Edilio
Edissa	see	Edissa
Edisteo	see	Edisteo
Edith	see	Edita
Edmund	see	Edmundo
Edna	see	Edna
Edolina	see	Edolina
Edonila	see	Edonila
Eduplidio	see	Eduplidio
Edward	see	Eduardo
Edythe	see	Edita
Eferino	see	Eferino

Effe	see	Eufemia
Egidius	see	Egidio
Egipciacas	see	Egipciacas
Eglantina	see	Eglantina
Eglantine	see	Eglantina
Ela	see	Ela
Elactio	see	Elactio
Eladius	see	Heladio
Elario	see	Elario
Elba	see	Elba
Eleazar	see	Eleazar
		Lázaro
Elebonia	see	Elebonia
Electa	see	Electa
Electra	see	Electra
Electus	see	Electa
Elementro	see	Elementro
Eleonor	see	Eleonor
Eleutherius	see	Eleuterio
Eleveo	see	Eleveo
Eleverio	see	Eleverio
Elfido	see	Elfido
Elfina	see	Elfina
Elfrida	see	Elfrida
Eliakim	see	Eliácim
Eliberto	see	Eliberto
Elidam	see	Elidam
Elido	see	Elido
Eligius	see	Eligio
Elijah	see	Elías
Eliphaz	see	Elífaz
Elipio	see	Elipio
Elisha	see	Eliseo
Elisodoro	see	Elisodoro
Elita	see	Electa
Eliud	see	Eliud
Elizabeth	see	Elisabeth
Ellen	see	Elena
Ellis	see	Eliseo
Elodie	see	Elodio
Eloi	see	Eligio
Eloine	see	Eloina
Eloise	see	Eloiso
Elphege	see	Elfego
Elpidius	see	Elpidio
Eludio	see	Eludio
Elura	see	Elura
Elvas	see	Elvia
Elvenia	see	Elvenia
Elvia	see	Elvia
Elvira	see	Elviro
Elvisa	see	Elvisa
Emana	see	Emana
Emancipation	see	Emancipación
Emanuel	see	Manuel
Emasa	see	Emasa
Emerald	see	Esmeralda
Emeranbiana	see	Emeranbiana
Emerio	see	Emerico
Emerito	see	Eméreo
Emestina	see	Emestina
Emeterius	see	Emeterio
Emetherius	see	Emeterio
Emil	see	Emilio
Emile	see	Amalio
		Emilio
Emma	see	Emma
Emmanuel	see	Manuel
Emosita	see	Emosita
Emygdius	see	Emigdio
Endor	see	Endoro
Endora	see	Endoro
Endovico	see	Endovico
Eneida	see	Eneida
Enerina	see	Enerina

Enfiania	see	Enfiania
Englebert	see	Angilberto
Enidena	see	Enidena
Enoch	see	Enoc
Enula	see	Enula
Enviso	see	Enviso
Epelmiro	see	Epelmiro
Ephraem	see	Efraín
Ephraim	see	Efraín
Epidano	see	Epidano
Epidus	see	Epidus
Epigmenius	see	Epigmenio
Epimachus	see	Epímaco
Epimanuel	see	Epimanuel
Epimencio	see	Epimencio
Epimenus	see	Epimeno
Epinicina	see	Epinicina
Epiphanius	see	Epifanio
Episteme	see	Epistema
Epitatius	see	Epitacio
Equitoria	see	Equitoria
Erasmus	see	Erasmo
Erastus	see	Erasto
Eredius	see	Eredina
Eremia	see	Eremia
Eremita	see	Eremita
Erendira	see	Eréndira
Ergastulo	see	Ergástulo
Erhard	see	Eradio
Eric	see	Eurico
Erland	see	Herlindo
Ermelindis	see	Hermelinda
Ermunia	see	Ermunia
Ernest	see	Ernesto
Ernie	see	Ernesto
Ersilisa	see	Ersilisa
Erudo	see	Erudo
Erulia	see	Erulia
Erwin	see	Herwin
Esau	see	Esaú
Escalentaria	see	Escalentaria
Escilia	see	Escilia
Esdra	see	Esdras
Esenia	see	Esenia
Esmeralda	see	Esmeralda
Esmeregildo	see	Esmeregildo
Esmero	see	Esmero
Esmirna	see	Esmyrna
Espirmenia	see	Espirmenia
Esquipulas	see	Esquipulas
Essie	see	Ester
Estacita	see	Estacita
Estanislaus	see	Estanislao
Estema	see	Estema
Esther	see	Ester
Estimio	see	Estimio
Eston	see	Estón
Estraberto	see	Estraberto
Ethelburge	see	Edelburga
Etheluin	see	Etelvina
Euald	see	Eudaldo
Eubio	see	Eubio
Eucardio	see	Eucardio
Eucharius	see	Eucario
Euclid	see	Euclides
Euclorio	see	Euclorio
Eudo	see	Eudina
Eudocio	see	Eudocio
Eudonia	see	Eudonia
Eudoro	see	Eudoro
Eudoxa	see	Eudocio
Eugene	see	Eugenio
Eugenia	see	Eugenio
Eulalia	see	Eulalio
Eulalius	see	Eulalio
Eulgencio	see	Eulgencio
Eulogius	see	Eulogio
Eumelia	see	Eumelia
Eumenius	see	Eumenia
Eumenzio	see	Eumenzio
Eumicia	see	Eumicia
Eunice	see	Eunice
Euphemia	see	Eufemia
Euphorio	see	Euphorio
Euphrasic	see	Eufracio
Euphrosyne	see	Eufrosina
Eupraxic	see	Eufracio
Euristus	see	Orestes
Eurosia	see	Orosio
Euryalus	see	Eurialo
Eurydice	see	Eurídice
Eusebic	see	Eusebio
Eusebius	see	Eusebio
Eustace	see	Eustacio
Eustachius	see	Eustaquio
Eustacia	see	Eustaquio
Eustadio	see	Eustadio
Eustavio	see	Eustavio
Eustefa	see	Eustefa
Eustella	see	Estela
Eustis	see	Eustacio
Eustochium	see	Eustoquio
Eustochius	see	Eustoquio
Eustoilus	see	Eustalio
Eustolia	see	Eustalio
Eustrogius	see	Eustorgio
Euthalia	see	Eutalia
Euthymia	see	Eutimia
Euthymius	see	Eutimia
Euticius	see	Eutiquio
Eutropia	see	Eutropia
Eutropius	see	Eutropia
Eutychius	see	Eutiquio
Eva	see	Eva
Evald	see	Eudaldo
Evangeline	see	Evangelina
Evaristo	see	Evaristo
Evaristus	see	Abaristo
Eve	see	Eva
Eveline	see	Eva
Evellius	see	Evelio
Eveno	see	Eveno
Eventius	see	Evencio
Everard	see	Eberardo
Everett	see	Eberardo
		Everardo
Everhard	see	Everardo
Evidio	see	Evidio
Evodius	see	Evodio
Evodus	see	Evodio
Evotius	see	Evodio
Eximenio	see	Eximenio
Expectation	see	Expectación
Expeditus	see	Expedito
Exultation	see	Exaltación
Ezechias	see	Ezequías
Ezechiel	see	Hesiquio
Ezekiah	see	Ezequiel
Ezekial	see	Ezequiel
Ezra	see	Esdras
Ezrah	see	Esdras
Fabian	see	Fabián
Fabiola	see	Fabiola
Fabricianus	see	Fabriciano
Facundus	see	Facundo
Faith	see	Fe
Falconia	see	Falconia
Famoso	see	Famoso
Fanasa	see	Fanasa
Fanita	see	Fanita

Faragon	see	Faragón	Generosa	see	Generosa
Fariamo	see	Fariamo	Genessee	see	Genessio
Farid	see	Farid	Genevieve	see	Genoveva
Farrah	see	Fara	Genio	see	Genio
Faust	see	Faustino	George	see	Jorge
Faustina	see	Faustino	Georgia	see	Jorge
Febronius	see	Febronio	Gerald	see	Geraldo
Felicia	see	Félix	Gerard	see	Gerardo
Felix	see	Félix	Gereon	see	Gereón
Ferdinand	see	Fernando	Gerino	see	Gerino
		Hernanda	Germinal	see	Germinal
Ferrer	see	Ferrer	Gerofina	see	Gerofina
Festivity	see	Festividad	Gerontius	see	Geronicio
Festus	see	Festo	Gerry	see	Gerardo
Fiacre	see	Fiacro	Gert	see	Gertrudis
Fidel	see	Fidel	Gertrude	see	Gertrudis
Fidentius	see	Fidencio	Geruntius	see	Geronicio
Firmian	see	Fermín	Gervaldina	see	Gervaldina
Flaminia	see	Flaminio	Gevaro	see	Gevaro
Flavia	see	Flavio	Gideon	see	Gedeón
Flavius	see	Flavio	Gilbert	see	Gilberto
Flo	see	Florencio	Gildard	see	Gildardo
Flora	see	Florencio	Ginger	see	Virginia
Florence	see	Florencio	Giolia	see	Giolia
Floribert	see	Floriberto	Giselle	see	Gisela
Flormenegilda	see	Flormenegilda			Iselda
Fornasa	see	Fornasa	Glaphyra	see	Gláfiro
Fortunatus	see	Fortunato	Gloria	see	Glorio
Fortune	see	Fortino	Glycera	see	Glicerio
		Fortuno	Godfrey	see	Godofredo
Fran	see	Francisco	Godislav	see	Godislao
Francis	see	Francisco	Godiva	see	Godeliva
Frank	see	Francisco	Goliath	see	Goliat
Fred	see	Manfredo	Gontran	see	Gontrán
Frederick	see	Federico	Gonzago	see	Gonzago
Frigidius	see	Frigio	Goodman	see	Hombono
Fringustina	see	Fringustina	Gordius	see	Gordiano
Fronintino	see	Fronintino	Gorgonius	see	Gorgonio
Froylan	see	Froilán	Grace	see	Engracia
Fructuosus	see	Fructuoso			Graciela
Frumentius	see	Frumencio	Gracienne	see	Engracia
Fulgentius	see	Fulgencio	Gramecia	see	Gramecia
Fulvia	see	Fulvio	Grania	see	Grania
Fulvius	see	Fulvio	Gratia	see	Graciela
Furius	see	Furius	Gratiana	see	Grata
Fuscianus	see	Fusciano	Greg	see	Gregorio
Gabe	see	Gabriel	Gregino	see	Gregino
Gabinius	see	Gabino	Gregory	see	Gregorio
Gabinus	see	Gabino	Grevea	see	Grevea
Gabriel	see	Gabriel	Grifonio	see	Grifonio
Gabriella	see	Gabriel	Grimald	see	Grimalda
Gaetan	see	Cayetano	Griselda	see	Griselda
Gail	see	Abegail	Guadalupe	see	Guadalupe
Gaiseric	see	Gensérico	Guarian	see	Guarino
Galaction	see	Galación	Gudelio	see	Gudelio
Galbert	see	Gualberto	Gudemilia	see	Gudemilia
Galen	see	Galeno	Gudrun	see	Gudran
Galenus	see	Galieno	Guinevere	see	Ginebra
Gall	see	Galo	Guiomar	see	Guiomar
Gallienus	see	Galieno	Gumbert	see	Gumbertus
Gallus	see	Galo	Gumersind	see	Gumersindo
Gamaliel	see	Gamaliel	Gummar	see	Gumaro
Garcia	see	García	Gundisalvus	see	Gonzalo
Garibald	see	Garibaldo	Gus	see	Agusto
Gascon	see	Gastón			Gustavo
Gaspar	see	Gaspar	Gustav	see	Gustavo
Gaston	see	Gastón	Guy	see	Guido
Gaudentia	see	Gaudencio	Guyon	see	Guido
Gaudentius	see	Gaudencio	Guzman	see	Guzmán
Gebhardt	see	Gebhardo	Hadrian	see	Adrián
Gellaseo	see	Gelasio	Hagar	see	Agar
Gellasio	see	Gelasio	Haggai	see	Ageo
Geminianus	see	Gemino	Haidee	see	Haidee
Genaida	see	Genaida	Hal	see	Haroldo
Gene	see	Eugenio	Hamilcar	see	Amílcar

Hamon	see Hamión	Hortense	see Hortencia
Hank	see Enrique	Hospitius	see Hospicio
Hannah	see Ana	Huey	see Hugo
Hannibal	see Aníbal	Hugh	see Hugo
Hanoch	see Enoc	Huldah	see Holda
Happy	see Alegra	Humbert	see Humberto
Hario	see Hario	Humphrey	see Onofre
Harold	see Haroldo	Hy	see Hirán
Harry	see Enrique		Iram
	Haroldo	Hyacinth	see Jacinto
Hasdrubal	see Asdrúbal	Hygieia	see Higinio
Hazael	see Hazael	Hyginius	see Higinio
Hazel	see Abelino	Hyxta	see Histo
Hebacuc	see Hebacuc	Iberia	see Iberia
Heck	see Héctor	Icarus	see Icario
Hector	see Héctor	Ida	see Ida
Heda	see Eduvigis	Idalia	see Idalia
Hedda	see Eda	Idella	see Ida
Hedora	see Joram	Idemia	see Idemia
Hedwig	see Eda	Idolina	see Idolina
	Eduvigis	Idonia	see Idonia
Hegesippus	see Hegesipo	Idyll	see Idilio
Helen	see Elena	Ienero	see Ienero
Helga	see Helga	Ignace	see Ignacio
Heliodorus	see Heliodoro	Ignatius	see Ignacio
Helma	see Hilma	Ignestacio	see Ignestacio
Heloise	see Eloiso	Ike	see Isaac
Hemico	see Hemico	Ildephonsus	see Ildefonso
Henedina	see Henedina	Illustrious	see Ilustre
Heneldina	see Enedina	Ilona	see Ilona
Henry	see Enrique	Iluminado	see Iluminado
Heraclitus	see Heráclito	Imelda	see Imelda
Herbert	see Herberto	Imelde	see Imelda
Herculanus	see Herculano	Imperio	see Imperio
Hercules	see Heráclio	Incarnate	see Encarnación
Herman	see Armando	Indaletius	see Indalecio
	Germán	Indiana	see Indiana
	Hermán	Inebel	see Inebel
	Herminio	Ines	see Inés
Hermelo	see Hermelo	Infinity	see Infinio
Hermengild	see Hermenegildo	Ingenious	see Engenio
Hermes	see Hermes	Ingres	see Ingres
Hermine	see Irma	Iniciano	see Iniciano
Hermogenes	see Hermógenes	Innocent	see Inocencio
Herod	see Herodes	Innumerable	see Innumerbilio
Herodotus	see Herodoto	Iphigene	see Ifigenia
Heron	see Herón	Iphigenia	see Ifigenia
Hersilia	see Hersilia	Ira	see Ira
Herwin	see Herwin	Iracema	see Iracema
Hesiod	see Hesíodo	Irah	see Ira
Hester	see Ester	Irene	see Irene
Hezekiah	see Ezequías	Iris	see Iris
	Hesiquio	Irma	see Herminio
Hilary	see Hilario		Irma
Hild	see Hildo	Irvin	see Ervino
Hilda	see Hildo	Isa	see Isaías
Hildebert	see Hildeberto	Isaac	see Isaac
Hildebrand	see Hildebrando	Isabel	see Isabel
Hildegard	see Hildigardo	Isaiah	see Isaías
Hilma	see Hilma	Isander	see Isandro
Hippocrates	see Hipócrates	Isaurus	see Isauro
Hippolytus	see Hipólito	Iseratiam	see Iseratiam
Hiram	see Hirán	Ishmael	see Ismael
	Iram	Isidore	see Isidoro
Histo	see Histo	Isis	see Isis
Hixta	see Histo	Ismael	see Ismael
Homer	see Homero	Ismene	see Ismeme
Homobonus	see Hombono	Isolde	see Isolina
Honestus	see Honesto	Israel	see Israel
Honor	see Honoria	Issachar	see Isachar
Honora	see Honoria	Itaciona	see Itaciona
Hope	see Esperanza	Itha	see Ita
Horace	see Horacio	Itinarino	see Itinarino
Horatio	see Horacio	Itza	see Itzá
Hormisdas	see Hormisdas	Ivara	see Ivara

Izzy	see	Isidoro	Justina	see	Justino
		Israel	Justus	see	Justino
Jacaranda	see	Jacaranda	Juvenal	see	Juvenal
Jacinth	see	Jacinto	Juvenalis	see	Juvenal
Jack	see	Jacinto	Juventius	see	Juvencio
		Juan	Kay	see	Catalina
Jacob	see	Jacobo	Kelliopi	see	Caliopa
		Santiago	Kenneth	see	Inocencio
Jacobina	see	Jacobo	Kit	see	Cristóbal
Jaime	see	Jaime	Knute	see	Canuto
Jair	see	Jairo	Laban	see	Labán
Jairus	see	Jairo	Laertes	see	Laercio
James	see	Jacobo	Lambert	see	Lamberto
		Jaime	Landelin	see	Laudelina
		Santiago	Landrada	see	Landrada
Janarius	see	Génaro	Laura	see	Lauro
Jansen	see	Jansenio	Laurel	see	Lauro
Jansenius	see	Jansenio	Lavinia	see	Lavinia
Januarius	see	Jano	Lawrence	see	Lorenzo
Janus	see	Jano	Lazar	see	Lázaro
Japhet	see	Jafet	Lazarus	see	Eleázar
Japheth	see	Jafet			Lázaro
Jarvis	see	Gervasio			
Jasmine	see	Jazmín	Lea	see	Lea
Jason	see	Jacián	Leah	see	Lea
Jasper	see	Gaspar	Leander	see	Leandro
Javier	see	Javier	Leda	see	Leda
Jeff	see	Godofredo	Lee	see	Lea
Jeffrey	see	Godofredo			Leandro
Jehoram	see	Joram	Lehi	see	Lehi
Jehoshaphat	see	Josefat	Leila	see	Leila
Jemuel	see	Jemuel	Len	see	Leonardo
Jennifer	see	Genoveva	Leocadius	see	Leocadia
Jeremiah	see	Jeremías	Leodagar	see	Ludgarda
Jeremy	see	Jeremías	Leodegar	see	Leodegario
Jericho	see	Jericó	Leon	see	León
Jeroboam	see	Jeroboam	Leonard	see	Leonardo
Jerome	see	Jerónimo	Leonides	see	Leonides
Jeronimo	see	Jerónimo	Leonor	see	Eleonor
Jerry	see	Geraldo			Leonor
		Gerardo	Leontine	see	Leontina
		Jeremías	Leopardus	see	Leopardo
		Jerónimo	Leopold	see	Leopoldo
Jerusha	see	Jerusa	Leovigild	see	Leovigildo
Jerushah	see	Jerusa	Lesbia	see	Lesbia
Jess	see	Isaí	Leslie	see	Ladislao
Jessamyn	see	Jazmín	Leticia	see	Leticia
Jesse	see	Isaí	Letty	see	Leticia
Jesus	see	Jesús	Lewis	see	Luis
Jill	see	Julio	Liberatus	see	Liberato
Jo	see	José	Liberius	see	Liberio
Joachim	see	Joaquín	Licinius	see	Licinio
Job	see	Job	Liddy	see	Lidio
Joe	see	José	Ligorius	see	Ligorio
Joel	see	Joel	Lillian	see	Lilia
John	see	Juan	Linus	see	Lino
Jonah	see	Jonás	Lioba	see	Lioba
Jonas	see	Jonás	Lionel	see	León
Jonathan	see	Jonatán	Lon	see	Alfonso
Joram	see	Joram	Longinus	see	Longinos
Jordan	see	Jordán	Loreta	see	Loreto
Joseph	see	José	Lorraine	see	Lorena
Josh	see	Josué	Lothair	see	Lotario
Joshua	see	Josué	Lothar	see	Lotario
Josiah	see	Josías	Louis	see	Luis
Jovian	see	Joviano	Love	see	Liduvino
Jucunda	see	Jucundo	Lucas	see	Luz
Jucundus	see	Jucundo	Lucia	see	Lucía
Judas	see	Judas	Lucian	see	Lucano
Jude	see	Judas	Lucifer	see	Lucifer
Judith	see	Judit	Lucille	see	Lucía
Julie	see	Julio	Lucinda	see	Lucinda
Julius	see	Julio	Lucius	see	Lucas
Junal	see	Jubal	Lucrece	see	Lucrecio
Justin	see	Justino	Lucretia	see	Lucrecio
			Ludmilla	see	Ludmila

Ludwig	see Ludovico		Maturin	see Maturiano
Lugidianus	see Eluanita		Maude	see Matilde
Luke	see Lucas		Maura	see Mauro
	Luz		Maurelius	see Maurilio
Lulu	see Lucía		Maurice	see Mauricio
Luperculus	see Lupercio		Maurus	see Mauro
Lupercus	see Lupercio		Maxim	see Maximiano
Lutgard	see Ludgarda		Maximianus	see Maximiano
Luthario	see Lutero		Maximilian	see Maximiliano
Luther	see Lutero		Maximus	see Máximo
Luvenia	see Liduvino		May	see Maya
Lycas	see Lica		Mechthild	see Mechilda
Lycurgus	see Licurgo		Medard	see Medardo
Lydell	see Lidio		Medran	see Medrano
Lydia	see Lidio		Melanchthon	see Melantón
Lysander	see Isandro		Melanie	see Melanio
	Lisandro		Melba	see Melba
Macaria	see Macario		Melchiades	see Melquíades
Macarius	see Macario		Melchior	see Melchor
Maccabee	see Macabeo		Meletius	see Melesio
Macedonia	see Macedonio		Melicent	see Melisendo
Macedonius	see Macedonio		Melinda	see Melinda
Maclovius	see Maclovio		Melissa	see Melisa
Macrinus	see Macrino		Mellitus	see Melito
Madron	see Medrano		Melody	see Melodio
Maecenas	see Mecenas		Memorianus	see Memorio
Magadalene	see Magdaleno		Mennas	see Menas
Magdeline	see Magdaleno		Mercedes	see Mercedes
Magloire	see Maglorio		Mercury	see Mercurio
Maglorius	see Maglorio		Mercy	see Mercedes
Magnus	see Magno		Mered	see Merede
Maia	see Maya		Merle	see Merle
Maieul	see Mayolo		Merrit	see Emerenciana
Malachi	see Malaquías		Merritt	see Eméreo
Malachy	see Malaquías			Emerenciana
Malchus	see Malco		Mervin	see Ervino
Malvina	see Malvina		Messalina	see Mesalina
Malvinia	see Malvina		Methodius	see Metodio
Mamertinus	see Mamerto		Metrobius	see Metrobio
Mamertus	see Mamerto		Michael	see Miguel
Mandy	see Amanda		Michah	see Miqueas
Manfred	see Manfredo		Michelle	see Miguel
Marcella	see Marcelino		Mike	see Miguel
March	see Marcos		Milburga	see Milburga
Marcia	see Marcia		Milkiades	see Melquíades
Marciana	see Marciana		Millicent	see Melisendo
Marcianus	see Marciana		Minerva	see Minerva
Marculf	see Marcolfo		Minnie	see Minerva
Mardon	see Mardonio		Miriam	see Miriam
Mardonius	see Mardonio		Mishael	see Misael
Margaret	see Margarito		Modestus	see Modesto
Margie	see Margarito		Moe	see Moisés
Marianus	see Mariana		Moira	see Moirio
Marino	see Marino		Mona	see Mónico
Marinus	see Marino		Monica	see Mónico
Marisa	see Marisa		Mordecai	see Mardoqueo
Marius	see Mario		Morris	see Mauricio
Mark	see Marcos		Moses	see Moisés
Marne	see Matrona		Mucius	see Mucio
Martha	see Marta		Myra	see Mira
Martial	see Marcial		Myrna	see Mirna
Martialis	see Marcial		Nabor	see Nabor
Martin	see Marcos		Nahum	see Nahum
	Martín		Naomi	see Noemí
Marty	see Marta		Nap	see Napoleón
Martyrius	see Martirio		Naphtali	see Neftalí
Marvel	see Maravilla		Napoleon	see Napoleón
Marvin	see Ervino		Narcisse	see Narciso
Mary	see María		Narcissus	see Narciso
Materna	see Materno		Narnius	see Narno
Mathilde	see Matilde		Narnus	see Narno
Matt	see Mateo		Natalia	see Natalio
Matthew	see Mateo		Natalie	see Natalio
Matthias	see Matías		Nathan	see Nataniel
Matty	see Marta		Nathaniel	see Nataniel

Nazarius	see	Nazario
Nectarius	see	Nectario
Ned	see	Eduardo
		Teodoro
Nehemiah	see	Nehemías
Nemesius	see	Nemesio
Nemorius	see	Nemorio
Nemuel	see	Jemuel
Neon	see	Neón
Nepomucene	see	Nepomuceno
Nepos	see	Nepote
Nereus	see	Néreo
Nero	see	Nerón
Nestor	see	Néstor
Nettie	see	Natalio
Nevius	see	Nevio
Newell	see	Noel
Nicander	see	Nicandro
Nicanor	see	Nicanor
Nicasius	see	Nicasio
Nicephorus	see	Nicéforo
Niceras	see	Nicerata
Nicetas	see	Niseto
Nicholas	see	Nicolás
Nick	see	Nicodemus
		Nicolás
Nicodemus	see	Nicodemus
Nicomedia	see	Nicomedes
Nino	see	Nino
Nithard	see	Nitardo
Noah	see	Noé
Noami	see	Noemí
Noel	see	Noel
Noey	see	Noé
Nonnosus	see	Nono
Nonnus	see	Nono
Nora	see	Honoria
Norbert	see	Norberto
Novatus	see	Novatus
Nowell	see	Noel
Nydia	see	Nidia
Nympha	see	Ninfa
Nymphas	see	Ninfa
Obed	see	Obed
Obert	see	Oberto
Octavian	see	Octavio
Octavius	see	Octavio
Odessa	see	Odessa
Odile	see	Odilia
Odo	see	Eudina
Olaf	see	Olav
Olav	see	Olav
Olga	see	Olga
		Olivo
Olive	see	Olivo
Olivia	see	Olivo
Ollegarius	see	Olegario
Olympia	see	Olimpia
Omar	see	Omar
Omega	see	Omega
Onesima	see	Onésimo
Onesimus	see	Onésimo
Opal	see	Opel
Opaline	see	Opel
Ophelia	see	Ofelio
Optatianus	see	Optaciano
Ora	see	Aurelio
Orban	see	Urbano
Orel	see	Aurelio
Orentius	see	Orencio
Orestes	see	Orestes
Orontius	see	Oroncio
Orosia	see	Orosio
Orsius	see	Orosio
Oscar	see	Oscar

Osman	see	Osmín
		Otman
Osmund	see	Osmundo
Oswald	see	Oscar
		Osvaldo
Ot	see	Otón
Othello	see	Otón
Ottilie	see	Odilia
Otto	see	Otón
Ovid	see	Ovidio
Ozias	see	Osías
Oziel	see	Oziel
Ozzie	see	Oscar
Pachomius	see	Pacomio
Pacianus	see	Paciano
Pacificus	see	Pacífico
Palaemon	see	Palemón
Palmer	see	Palmira
Paloma	see	Paloma
Pamphilius	see	Pánfilo
Pancratius	see	Pancracio
Pandercio	see	Pandencio
Panezio	see	Panezio
Panphil	see	Pánfilo
Pansalino	see	Pánsalo
Pantaleon	see	Pantaleón
Papias	see	Papías
Parcas	see	Parcasio
Parisius	see	Parisio
Parmenius	see	Pármeno
Paschal	see	Pascual
Paschasius	see	Pascasio
Passion	see	Pasión
Pastor	see	Pastor
Pat	see	Patricio
Patience	see	Paciencia
Patricia	see	Patricio
Patricinius	see	Patrocinio
Patrick	see	Patricio
Patusius	see	Patrucio
Paul	see	Paulo
Paula	see	Paulo
Paulbino	see	Paulbino
Pax	see	Paz
Peace	see	Paz
Pearl	see	Perla
Peggy	see	Margarito
Pelagius	see	Pelagio
Pelasgus	see	Pelaseo
Peleus	see	Peleina
Penelope	see	Penélope
Pentea	see	Pentea
Pentecost	see	Pentecostes
Percevale	see	Parsifal
Percival	see	Parsifal
Peregrinus	see	Peregrino
Perfectus	see	Perfecto
Perfida	see	Perfida
Perfilia	see	Pefilia
Perpetua	see	Perpetua
Perpetuus	see	Perpetua
Pete	see	Pedro
Peter	see	Pedro
Peteus	see	Peteo
Petra	see	Pedro
Petronillo	see	Petronilo
Petronius	see	Petronilo
Pharoah	see	Faraón
Pheres	see	Fereso
Phil	see	Felipo
		Teófilo
Philadelphus	see	Filadelfo
Philagonia	see	Filogonio
Philbert	see	Filiberto
Philemon	see	Filemón

Philip	see	Felipo	Protus	see	Proto
Philippa	see	Felipo	Proventius	see	Proventio
Philomela	see	Filomeno	Providence	see	Providencio
Philomeno	see	Filomeno	Prudence	see	Prudencia
Phineas	see	Fineas	Prudentius	see	Prudencia
Phocas	see	Focas	Ptolemaeus	see	Tolomeo
Phoebe	see	Febe	Ptolemy	see	Tolomeo
Phoedra	see	Fedro	Pubilius	see	Público
Phoenix	see	Fénix	Pudentiana	see	Pudenciana
Picardus	see	Picardus	Pulcheria	see	Pulquerio
Picarino	see	Picarino	Purification	see	Purificación
Pierius	see	Pierio	Quasimodo	see	Quasimodo
Pierre	see	Pierio	Quentin	see	Quinto
Pieta	see	Piedad	Quirinus	see	Quirino
Piety	see	Piedad	Rachel	see	Raquel
Pigmenius	see	Epigmenio	Rae	see	Raquel
Pilar	see	Bilar	Raff	see	Rafael
		Pilar	Ragenulfa	see	Ranulfo
Pilardela	see	Pilardela	Ralph	see	Raul
Pindar	see	Píndaro	Ramiro	see	Ramiro
Pindarus	see	Píndaro	Ramona	see	Ramón
Pinytus	see	Pinito	Randolph	see	Randolfo
Pitana	see	Pitana	Raphael	see	Rafael
Pitane	see	Pitana	Rasmus	see	Erasmo
Pitos	see	Pitos	Ray	see	Raimundo
Pius	see	Pío	Raymond	see	Raimundo
Pius V	see	Pioquinto			Ramón
Placidus	see	Plácido	Rebecca	see	Rebeca
Plato	see	Platón	Regan	see	Regina
Plinius	see	Plinio	Regina	see	Regina
Pliny	see	Plinio	Reginald	see	Reinaldo
Plutarch	see	Plutarco	Reginbert	see	Remberto
Polenciana	see	Polenciana	Regula	see	Régulo
Polifontes	see	Polifo	Regulus	see	Régulo
Polycarp	see	Policarpo	Remedius	see	Remedio
Polyceute	see	Policeto	Remigius	see	Remigio
Polydorus	see	Polidoro	Renatus	see	Renato
Polynices	see	Polonice	Rene	see	René
Pompeius	see	Pompeyo	Renee	see	René
Pompey	see	Pompeyo	Renovatus	see	Renovato
Pomposa	see	Pomposo	Reparata	see	Reparata
Pomposo	see	Pomposo	Respicius	see	Respicio
Pontian	see	Ponciano	Restituta	see	Restituto
Pontion	see	Ponciano	Restitutus	see	Restituto
Porfidio	see	Porfidio	Reta	see	Rito
Porphyrius	see	Porfirio	Reverianus	see	Reveriano
Porphyry	see	Porfirio	Revocatus	see	Revocata
Potentiantus	see	Poterciano	Rhoda	see	Rodas
Prassede	see	Práxedes	Richard	see	Ricardo
Praxedes	see	Práxedes	Rick	see	Ricardo
		Présides	Rigobert	see	Rigoberto
Precious	see	Preciosa	Rita	see	Rito
Predicando	see	Predicando	Robert	see	Roberto
Presencia	see	Presencia	Roberta	see	Roberto
Presentacion	see	Presentación	Robustian	see	Robustiano
Priapus	see	Preapiana	Robustianus	see	Robustiano
Primitivus	see	Primitivo	Roch	see	Roque
Primus	see	Primo	Roche	see	Roque
Priscilla	see	Prisciliano	Rochus	see	Roque
Priscus	see	Prisco	Roderick	see	Rodrigo
Pristina	see	Pristina	Rogata	see	Rogato
Pristine	see	Pristina	Rogatianus	see	Rogaciano
Probus	see	Probo	Rogatus	see	Rogato
Processus	see	Proceso	Roger	see	Rogelio
Prochorus	see	Prócoro	Roland	see	Roldán
Proclus	see	Próculo	Roman	see	Román
Procopius	see	Procopio	Rombauld	see	Rumolda
Pronunciana	see	Pronunciana	Romedius	see	Romedo
Propetidas	see	Propedis	Romuald	see	Romualdo
Prophet	see	Profeto	Romulus	see	Rómulo
Prospectus	see	Prospecto	Rosalia	see	Rosalío
Prosper	see	Próspero	Rosalie	see	Rosalío
Prospero	see	Próspero	Rosalind	see	Rosalindo
Protasius	see	Protasio	Rosamond	see	Rosamunda
Proteus	see	Preto	Rose	see	Rosa

Roselyn	see Rosalindo	Simeon	see Simón
Rosendo	see Rudesinda	Simon	see Jimeno
Roxanne	see Roxana		Simón
Rube	see Rubén	Simplicius	see Simplicio
Rubrik	see Rubrico	Sindulf	see Sindulfo
Ruby	see Rubí	Sindulphus	see Sindulfo
Rudesind	see Rudesinda	Sinicius	see Sinesio
Rudolf	see Rodolfo	Sisebut	see Sisebuto
Rudy	see Rodolfo	Sisenand	see Sisenando
Rueben	see Rubén	Sisinnius	see Sisinio
Rufus	see Rufino	Sitha	see Zita
Rumold	see Rumolda	Socrates	see Sócrates
Rupert	see Ruperto	Sol	see Salomón
Rustam	see Rustam	Solly	see Saúl
Ruth	see Ruth	Solomon	see Salomón
Rutila	see Rutilio	Sonya	see Sonio
Rutulus	see Rutilio	Sophia	see Sofío
Sabba	see Sabás	Sophie	see Sofío
Sabina	see Sabino	Sophronia	see Sofronio
Sadie	see Sara	Sophronius	see Sofronio
Sadoth	see Sadat	Sosthenes	see Sóstenes
Sallustius	see Salustiano	Soter	see Sotero
Sally	see Sara	Spash	see Aspasia
Salome	see Salomé	Spiridion	see Espiridión
Salust	see Salustiano	Stacy	see Anastacio
Salvinus	see Salvino		Eustacio
Salvius	see Salvino	Stan	see Estanislao
Sam	see Samuel	Stella	see Estela
Samson	see Sansón	Stephen	see Esteban
Samuel	see Samuel	Steven	see Esteban
Sanctan	see Sancho	Strabo	see Estrabón
Sanctius	see Sancho	Stradivarius	see Estradivario
Sandalus	see Sandalio	Stuart	see Estuardo
Sarah	see Sara	Sulpice	see Sulpicio
Saturn	see Saturnino	Sulpitius	see Sulpicio
Saturninus	see Saturnino	Susan	see Susano
Saul	see Saúl	Susanna	see Susano
Scholastica	see Escolástica	Sybil	see Sibilo
Scipio	see Escipión	Sylvain	see Silvano
Sebastian	see Sebastián	Sylvana	see Silvino
Secundus	see Segundino	Sylvanus	see Silvano
Selena	see Celina	Sylvester	see Silvestre
Selma	see Anselmo	Sylvia	see Silvio
Senan	see Senén	Sylvius	see Silvio
Sep	see Séptimo	Symmachus	see Símaco
Septimia	see Séptimo	Symmetrius	see Simitrio
Septimus	see Séptimo	Symphorianus	see Sinforiano
Seraphim	see Serafín	Symphorosa	see Sinforoso
Seraphine	see Serafín	Tab	see Tabita
Serapion	see Serapio	Tabby	see Tabita
Serena	see Serena	Tabitha	see Tabita
Serenity	see Serena	Tad	see Tadeo
Serge	see Sergio	Tamara	see Tamara
Sergius	see Sergio	Tamerlane	see Tamerlán
Servandus	see Servando		Timur
Servatius	see Servacio	Tancred	see Tancredo
Servilianus	see Servilio	Tantianus	see Tatiano
Sever	see Severo	Tarachus	see Taraco
Severin	see Severo	Tarasius	see Tarasio
Severus	see Severo	Tarciscius	see Tarsicio
Sextus	see Sixto	Tarquin	see Tarquino
Shadhost	see Sadat	Tarquinus	see Tarquino
Sheba	see Sabá	Tarsicia	see Tarsicio
Si	see Jimeno	Tarsilia	see Tarsila
Sidney	see Sidonio	Tarsilla	see Tarsila
Sidronius	see Sidronio	Tatius	see Tacio
Siegfried	see Sigfrido	Taurian	see Taurino
Sig	see Sigfrido	Taurinus	see Taurino
Sigebert	see Sigeberto	Teddy	see Teodoro
Sigismund	see Segismundo	Telesphorus	see Telesforo
Sigmund	see Segismundo	Terentius	see Terencio
Silas	see Silas	Teresa	see Tereso
Silva	see Silvino	Terminus	see Termín
Silverius	see Silverio	Tertullian	see Tertuliano
Simeon	see Jimeno	Thaddeus	see Tadeo

Thais	see Tais	Urias	see Urías
Thaisa	see Tais	Uriel	see Uriel
Thales	see Tales	Ursula	see Úrsula
Thalia	see Tales	Ute	see Jutta
Thecla	see Teclo	Uzzias	see Osías
Thel	see Telma	Uzziel	see Oziel
Thelma	see Telma	Val	see Valente
Themistocles	see Temístocles		Valerio
Theobalt	see Teobaldo	Vala	see Vala
Theodard	see Teodardo	Valada	see Valydia
Theodelinde	see Teodolinda	Valentine	see Valente
Theodimir	see Teodomiro	Valerian	see Valerio
Theodore	see Teodoro	Valery	see Valerio
Theodosia	see Teodosio	Valida	see Valydia
Theodosius	see Teodosio	Validiano	see Validiano
Theodula	see Teódulo	Valonian	see Valoniano
Theodulus	see Teódulo	Vandelia	see Vandelia
Theofried	see Teofrido	Vanora	see Vanora
Theogenes	see Teógenes	Vasily	see Bacilio
Theophanes	see Teófanes	Venantius	see Venancio
Theophilus	see Teófilo	Veneranda	see Veneranda
Theophrastus	see Teofrasto	Venerius	see Venerio
Theotima	see Teótimo	Ventura	see Venturo
Theotimus	see Teótimo	Venture	see Venturo
Therse	see Tereso	Venus	see Venus
Thetmar	see Teodomiro	Venustian	see Venustiano
Thomas	see Tomás	Vera	see Vero
Thomasa	see Tomás	Veradas	see Vero
Thrasybulus	see Trasíbulo	Veremond	see Bermudo
Thyrsus	see Tirso	Veremund	see Veremundo
Tibe	see Tiberio	Vergil	see Virgilio
Tiber	see Tiberio	Verity	see Vero
Tiberius	see Tiberio	Verlita	see Verlita
Tibullus	see Tíbulo	Verona	see Verona
Tiburtinus	see Tiburcio	Veronica	see Verónico
Tiburtius	see Tiburcio	Veronus	see Verona
Tiffany	see Epifanio	Vespasian	see Vespasiano
Tigris	see Tigrio	Vesta	see Vesta
Tigrius	see Tigrio	Vetaria	see Vetaria
Tilly	see Matilde	Vianes	see Vianes
Tim	see Timoteo	Vic	see Víctor
Timon	see Timón	Victor	see Víctor
Timothy	see Timoteo	Victoria	see Víctor
Timur	see Tamerlán	Vince	see Vicente
	Timur	Vincent	see Vicente
Tirsah	see Tersa	Vinicius	see Vinicio
Tish	see Leticia	Viol	see Viola
Titian	see Ticiano	Violet	see Viola
Titus	see Tito		Violeta
Tobias	see Tobías	Virg	see Virgilio
Toby	see Tobías	Virginia	see Virginia
Tom	see Tomás	Viv	see Viviano
Torquatus	see Torcuato	Vivian	see Viviano
Tranquillinus	see Tranquilino	Vivianus	see Bibiano
Tribonian	see Triboniano	Vladimir	see Baldomero
Tristam	see Tristán	Vulpianus	see Ulipiano
Tristan	see Tristán	Walde	see Ubaldo
Trudy	see Gertrudis	Waldemar	see Baldomero
Tryphon	see Trifonio	Waldo	see Ubaldo
Tullia	see Tulio	Walter	see Gualterio
Tullius	see Tulio	Wanda	see Wanda
Turibius	see Toribio	Wandis	see Wanda
Tybalt	see Teobaldo	Washington	see Washingtón
Ulalume	see Ulielmi	Wenceslaus	see Venceslao
Ulix	see Ulises	Wendy	see Wanda
Ulpianus	see Ulipiano	Wenzel	see Venceslao
Ulrich	see Ulrico	Wigbert	see Wigberto
Ulysses	see Ulises	Wilbert	see Williberto
Undina	see Ondino	Wilfred	see Ulfrido
Undine	see Ondino		Wilfrido
Uranus	see Urania	Wilfrid	see Wilfrido
Urban	see Urbano	Wilhelmina	see Wilma
Urbane	see Urbano	Will	see Guillermo
Uriah	see Urías	Willebald	see Wilebaldo
Urian	see Urías	William	see Guillermo

Willibald	see	Wilebaldo	Zeke	see	Ezequiel
Wilma	see	Wilma			Hesiquio
Winifred	see	Vinefrida	Zenaida	see	Zenaido
Wolfgang	see	Wolfgango	Zeno	see	Zenón
Wolfram	see	Wulfrano	Zenobia	see	Zenobio
Wulstan	see	Wolstano	Zephyr	see	Ceferino
Wyatt	see	Guido	Zephyrin	see	Ceferino
Xanthippe	see	Xantipa	Zippora	see	Sippora
Xantippe	see	Xantipa	Zipporah	see	Sippora
Xavier	see	Javier	Zita	see	Zita
Xenophon	see	Jenofonte	Zite	see	Zita
Xystus	see	Sixto	Zobeide	see	Zobeida
Yolanda	see	Yolanda	Zoe	see	Zoé
Ytha	see	Ita	Zoilus	see	Zoilo
Yvette	see	Ivés	Zoroaster	see	Zoroastro
Zach	see	Zacarías	Zosimus	see	Zósimo
Zachary	see	Zacarías	Zoticus	see	Zótico
Zarathustra	see	Zoroastro	Zuleika	see	Zuleica
Zebulon	see	Zabulón			

Bibliography

Like all bibliographies, the following has two purposes. It credentials the author's efforts by verifying his scholarship; it provides additional sources of information for the user interested in pursuing the various aspects of the subject.

The organization of the bibliography reflects the steps in the compiling of a name dictionary: the collecting of the names and subsequently, their identification. Under the former are listed first the primary sources or those documents which have not yet reached the stage of print. The main example is the Catholic Chancery of San Antonio, Texas. Less fruitful sources were birth and death registers of both religious and secular institutions.

In this collection of names, two other sources, both secondary, deserve comment. The most numerous, the phone directory, is ubiquitous but also sex and age biased. Yet its presence means the inclusion of many geographical areas that the author was unable to visit. Approximately 182 of these indispensable references are listed with date of publication and they represent 756 locales from the following states: Arizona, 6; California, 127; Colorado, 24; Nevada, 2; New Mexico, 103; and Texas, 494.

More difficult to find for the abstraction of names are the non-directory sources such as dictionaries, genealogies and histories of names. Approximately 15 of these studies supplement the phone books.

Part II, the identification of names, incorporates two types of items of a cognate nature. Books that provided the information for the annotation of each name are included. Etymology, saint lore and historical data comprise the contributions of these works. A subsidiary of this is the final list of those items that do not describe names but provide a context for their understanding. Such a work is Carmen García Rodríguez' El culto de los santos en la España romana y visigoda.

It is hoped that this two-part classification and subdivisions for the many items used in this study will aid those interested in name lore. A simple alphabetical listing, although easier for the author, lacks the focus for immediate retrieval either of locational or definitional sources.

I.   Collecting of Names
     A.   Primary sources
     B.   Secondary sources (phone directories)
     C.   Secondary sources (non-phone directories)
II. Identification of Names
     A.   Sources for definitions or supplemental information
     B.   Sources for understanding of first names

I. COLLECTING OF NAMES
A. PRIMARY SOURCES

San Antonio, Texas. Archdiocese of San Antonio. Catholic Archives.
    San Fernando Cathedral: "Index of Baptisms, 1800–1877."
San Antonio, Texas. Archdiocese of San Antonio. "Milam Park
    Cemeteries, 1808–1860."
San Antonio, Texas. Archdiocese of San Antonio. San Fernando Cathedral
    ("Baptisms, Confirmations, Marriages, 1731–1798.")
San Antonio, Texas. Archdiocese of San Antonio. "San Fernando
    Cathedral Census Book thru Ca. 1901."
San Antonio, Texas. Archdiocese of San Antonio. San Fernando
    Cathedral. "Index to Baptisms Performed in the Missions of San
    Jose, San Juan, San Francisco de la Espada, and the Purísima
    Concepción from 1873–June 1907, 1909–1933."
San Antonio, Texas. Archdiocese of San Antonio. "San Fernando
    Cathedral: Marriage Index 1798–1911."
San Antonio, Texas. Archdiocese of San Antonio. Catholic Archives.
    "San Fernando Cathedral Records Cemeteries 1761–1808."
San Antonio, Texas. Archdiocese of San Antonio. Catholic Archives.
    San Fernando Cathedral Records. "Confirmations June 13, 1886–June
    9, 1903."
San Antonio, Texas. Catholic Chancery. "Baptismal Records, 1847–
    1980."
San Antonio, Texas. San Antonio Texas East Stake. 4th Ward. Church of
    Jesus Christ of Latter Day Saints. Membership Record.
San Antonio, Texas. La Trinidad United Methodist Church. "Libro de
    Registro de las Estación de San Antonio. Iglesia Metodista
    Episcopal del Sur."
San Antonio, Texas. La Trinidad United Methodist Church. "The No. 3
    Church Register of the Misión de San Antonio, Texas. Methodist
    Episcopal Church, South. June 9, 1884–January 1909."
San Antonio, Texas. La Trinidad United Methodist Church. "Official
    Church Records. Membership Record. March 15, 1938–March 31,
    1948."
San Antonio, Texas. La Trinidad United Methodist Church. "The Official
    Membership and Church Record of the Methodist Church, August 11,
    1949–September 12, 1971."
San Antonio, Texas. La Trinidad United Methodist Church. "Registro de
    Iglesia Metodista Mexicana San Antonio, Texas. Metodista Episcopal
    del Sur, 1921–1927."
San Antonio, Texas. La Trinidad United Methodist Church. Metodista
    Episcopal del Sur. El Mesías. "Registro de iglesia, October,
    1922.
San Antonio, Texas. Stake Library of the Church of Jesus Christ of
    Latter Day Saints. 1980.
Santa Fe, New Mexico. New Mexico State Library. "Death Register.
    Santa Fe County, 1907–1927."
Santa Fe, New Mexico. New Mexico State Library. "Birth Register. Taos
    County, 1907–1941?"

B. SECONDARY SOURCES (PHONE DIRECTORIES)

Arizona Phone Directories

Mountain States Telephone and Telegraph Company

Cochise County, Arizona and Vicinity. 1977.
Gallup, Grants, Sanders. 1978.
Nogales, Patagonia, Tubac, (and) Nogales, Sonora. 1977.
Phoenix Metropolitan. 1978.
Tucson. 1975.

Arkansas Phone Directories

General Telephone Company of the Southwest

Texarkana, Redwater, DeKalb, New Boston, Fouke, Garland, (and)
    Texarkana. 1977.

California Phone Directories

General Telephone of California

Alhambra, Altadena, Arcadia, Azusa, Baldwin Park, Bassett, Bradbury,
    Brea, Commerce, Covina, Duarte, El Monte, Flintridge, Glendora,
    Hacienda Heights, Industry, Irwindale, La Canada, La Habra, La
    Habra Heights, La Mirada, La Puente, Los Nietos, Monrovia,
    Montebello, Monterey Park, etc. 1977.
Azusa, Baldwin Park, Covina, Glendora, Hacienda Heights, Industry,
    Irwindale, La Puente, Lowland Heights, West Covina and portions of
    San Dimas and Walnut. 1977.
Bel Air, Beverlywood, Brentwood, Century City, Cheviot Hills, Culver
    City, Los Angeles, Malibu, Marina del Mar, Mar Vista, Pacific
    Palisades, Palms, Playa del Rey, Rancho Park, Santa Monica,
    Topanga, Venice, West Hollywood, West Los Angeles, Westwood. 1979.
Downey, Anaheim, Artesia, Bell, Bell Gardens, Bellflower, Buena Park,
    Carson, Carritos, Commerce, Compton, Cudahy, Cypress, Dominguez,
    Fullerton, Garden Grove, Gardenia, Hawaiian Gardens, Hollydale,
    Lakewood, La Mirada, La Plama, Long Beach, Los Alamitos, Los
    Angeles, Lynwood, Maywood, Norwalk, Paramount, Pico Rivera, Santa
    Fe Springs, South Gate, Stanton, Whittier, (and) Willowbrook. 1977.
Long Beach Area. 1977.
Los Angeles (Bellflower Area). 1977.
Los Angeles Northeast, Sierra Madre and portions of Arcadia and
    Pasadena. 1977.
Los Angeles (Northwestern Area. Arleta, Granada Hills, Lake View,
    Terrace, Mission Hills, Pacoima, San Fernando, Sylmar and portions
    of Chatsworth, Northridge, Panorama City, (and) Sepulveda). 1978.
Los Angeles (South Bay Area, Redondo). 1977.
Los Angeles (Western Area). 1978.
Los Angeles (Western Area, Malibu). 1978.
Sunland-Tujunga. 1978.

Pacific Telephone and Telegraph Company

Alhambra, Arcadia, (and) El Monte. 1977.
Bakersfield, Arvin, Delano, Edwards, Lebec, Mojave, Rosamond, Shafter,
    Tehachapi, Walker Basin and Wasco. 1978.
Beverly Hills. 1978.
Fresno, Madera, Mariposa, and Merced Counties. 1978.
Los Angeles (Airport Area). 1977.
Los Angeles, Burbank, Glendale, (and) La Crescenta. 1978.
Los Angeles Central. 1975.
Los Angeles (Mid Cities). 1977.
Los Angeles (Pasadena, Altadena, San Marino, (and) Portion of South
    Pasadena. 1977.
Los Angeles South Bay. 1977.
Riverside, Corona, (and) Norco. 1974.
Sacramento, Broderick, Bryte, Carmichael, Elverta, Florin, Mather Air
    Force Base, McClellan Air Force Base, North Highlands, North
    Sacramento, Rancho Cordova, Rio Linda and West Sacramento. 1977.
San Diego North County. 1977.
San Diego (Suburban). 1977.
San Francisco Including Daly City, Brisbane and Colma. 1977.

Colorado Phone Directories

The Mountain States Telephone and Telegraph Company

Allison, Bayfield, Cortez, Dolores, Durango, Fort Lewis, Ignacio,
    Mancos, Marvel, Mesa Verde, Pagosa Springs, Pleasant View, Rico,
    (and) Silverton. 1977.
Denver and the Greater Metropolitan Area. 1975.
Pueblo, Pueblo West, Avondale, Beulah, Blende, Boone, (and) Vineland.
    1978.
Trinidad, Aguilar, Branson, (and) Weston. 1978.

Nevada Phone Directories

Central Telephone Company, Nevada Division

Las Vegas, North Las Vegas, Boulder City and Neighboring Nevada

Communities. 1978.

New Mexico Phone Directories

Continental Telephone Company of the West

Abiquiu, Canjilon, Chama, Chimayo, Cuba, Dixon, Dulce, El Rio, Española,
    Gallina, Jemez Springs, Lindrith, Lybrook, Ojo Caliente San Ysidro,
    Tierra Amarilla, Trucyas, Vallecito, (and) Velarde. 1978.
Alto, Capitan, Mescalero, (and) Ruidoso Downs. 1977.

General Telephone Company of the Southwest

Eunice, Hobbs, (and) Jal. 1978.
Lovington. 1978.
Paint Rock, Wingate, Ballinger, Rowena, Crews, Talpa, Winters, (and)
    Bradshaw. 1979.

Leaco Rural Telephone Co-op, Inc.

Tatum and Maljamar. 1977.

The Mountain States Telephone and Telegraph Company

Alamogordo, Carrizozo, Cloudcroft, Mayhill, Tularosa. 1978.
Albuquerque. 1975.
Anthony, Canutillo and La Mesa. 1978.
Artesia, Cottonwood, Hope, Lakewood, (and) Loco Hills. 1978.
Belen, Bosque Farms, Isleta, (and) Los Lunas. 1977.
Clovis, Portales, Arch, Bellview, Causey, Dora, Elida, Farwell, Floyd,
    Ft Sumner, Grady, Melrose, Milnesand, Oklahoma Lane, Pleasant Hill,
    Ragland, Ranchvale, South Clovis, Texico, (and) Weber City. 1977.
Deming, Lordsburg, Silver City Area, Animas, Cliff, Columbus, Gila,
    Glenwood, Luna, Playas, (and) Reserve. 1978.
El Paso, Anthony, Canutillo, Clint, Dell City, Desert Haven, Fabens,
    Fort Bliss, Fort Hancock, Guadalupe Peak, Juarez, Mile High, (and)
    Tornillo. 1978.
Estancia, Moriarty, Mountainair, Santa Rosa, (and) Vaughn. 1978.
Farmington, Aztec, (and) Bloomfield. 1978.
Gallup, Grants, (and) Sanders. 1978.
Las Cruces, Hatch, La Mesa, Mesilla, (and) Organ. 1978.
Socorro, Datil, Magdalena, (and) Quemado. 1978.
Taos, Peñasco, Questa, (and) Red River. 1978.
Tucumcari, Conchas Dam, Logan, Nara Visa, (and) San Jon. 1978.

Texas Phone Directories

Continental Telephone Company of Texas

Andrews (and) Frankel City. 1978.
Crockett, Austonio, Grapeland, Kennard, Lovelady, (and) Pennington.
    1978.
Fairfield, Buffalo, Centerville, Leona, Marquez, Oakwood, Richland,
    Streetman, Bedias, Franklin, Hilltop Lakes, Iola, Normangee, North
    Zulch, (and) Donie. 1977.

General Telephone Company of the Southwest

Agua Dulce, Bishop, Orange Grove, (and) Robstown. 1977.
Alta Loma, Algoa, Arcadia, Alvin, Apollo Zone, Bacliff, San Leon,
    Dickinson, Friendswood, Hitchcock, Kemah, Clark Lake Forest, Clear
    Lake Shores, El Lago, Taylor Lake Village, League City, Webster,
    Nassau Bay, (and) Seabrook. 1978.
Amherst, Anton, Littlefield, Olton, Spade, Springlake, Sudan,
    Whitharral, Fieldton, (and) Bula. 1977.
Aransas Pass (and) Ingleside. 1978.
Archer City, Bryson, Holliday, Jermyn, Megargel, Newcastle, Olney,
    Throckmorton, Elbert, Eliasville, Orth, and Woodson. 1978.
Argyle, Bartonville, Denton, Justin, Pilot Point (and) Toiga. 1978.
Austwell-Tivoli, Bloomington-Placedo, Point Comfort, Port O'Connor, Port
    Lavaca, Seadrift, Vanderbilt. 1978.
Ballinger, Paint Rock, Rowena, Talpa, Norton, Bradshaw, Winters, Crews,
    (and) Wingate. 1979.

Ballinger, Talpa, Paint Rock, Rowena, (and) Norton. 1978.
Barnhart, El Dorado, Ozona, Big Lake, (and) Soma. 1978.
Baytown, Beach City, Crosby, Highlands, Huffman, (and) Mont Belview.
    1977.
Blackwell, Bronte, Carlsbad, Christoval, Eden, Forsan, Mertzon, Miles,
    Eola, Robert Lee, San Angelo, Sterling City, (and) Water Valley.
    1978.
Blanco, Buda, Dripping Springs, Johnson City, Kyle, Round Mountain,
    (and) Wimberley. 1978.
Boerne, Balcones, Kenberg, (and) Sabina. 1978.
Booker, Darrouzett, Follett, Higgins, Lubscomb, Perrytown, (and)
    Spearman. 1978.
Bovina, Earth, Friona, Muleshoe, Olton, (and) Springlake. 1977.
Brownfield, Meadown, Ropesville, Ausborne, Union, (and) Wheatley. 1977.
Bryan, College Station, Kurten, (and) Snook-Tunis. 1977.
Charlotte, Dilley, Fowlerton, George West, Millett, Jourdanton,
    Somerset, Three Rivers, (and) Tilden. 1977.
Claude, Groom, Goodnight, Panhandle, (and) White Deer. 1978.
Dallas, Fort Worth Airport, (and) Irving. 1978.
Del Rio. 1977.
Dodson (and) Wellington. 1978.
Falfurrias, Mirando City, Premont, (and) Encino. 1977.
Fayetteville, La Grange, Schulenburg, Weimar, Borden, High Hill, Hostyn,
    Moravia, Plum, (and) Warrenton. 1978.
Fredericksburg, Stonewall, Willow City, (and) Doss. 1978.
Georgetown, Granger, Jarrell, San Gabriel, (and) Thronedale-Thrall.
    1978.
Gilmer, Bettie, Pine Acres, Pritchett, (and) Rosewood. 1978.
Gonzales, La Vernia, (and) Nixon, Smiley, Waelder, Saturn, Cost-
    Leesville, Saturn. 1978.
Gregory, Odem, Portland, (and) Taft. 1978.
Groveton, New Waverly, Panorama Village, Shepherd, Trinity, Willis,
    Coldspring, (and) Evergreen. 1978.
Hallsville (and) Kilgore. 1978.
Jacksonville, New Summerfield, Rusk, (and) Hudson. 1978.
Mason, Fredonia, Katemcy, Pontotoc, (and) Streeter. 1978.
Paint Rock, Wingate, Ballinger, Rowena, Crews, Talpa, Winters, (and)
    Bradshaw. 1979.
Texarkana, Redwater, DeKalb, New Boston, Fouke, Garland, (and)
    Texarkana. 1977.

              Guadalupe Valley Telephone Cooperative, Inc.

Balcones, Bulverde, Cost, Cranes Mill, Hancock, Kenberg, Kingsbury,
    Leesville, Rocky Creek, Sabina, Sattler, Saturn, Smithsons Valley
    (and) Westhoff. 1978.

                 Gulf States United Telephone Company

Anderson, Navasota, Plantersville, Richards, Shiro, (and) Washington.
    1978.
Commerce, Cooper, (and) East Texas State University. 1977.
Hamilton, Lamkin, (and) Pottsville. 1978.
Overton, Arp, New London, Price, (and) Troup. 1978.

                     Home Telephone Company

Humble, South Humble, Kingwood, Porter, Porter Heights, Crosty-Huffman,
    (and) Splendora. 1978.

                  Kerrville Telephone Company

Kerrville (and) Harper. 1978.

                 Lake Dallas Telephone Co., Inc.

Lake Dallas, Corinth, Hickory Creek, (and) Shady Shores. 1978.

                 Lufkin Telephone Exchange, Inc.
Lufkin, Apple Springs, Central, Diboll, Etoile, Fuller Springs, Hudson,
    (and) Wells. 1977.

          Mountain States Telephone and Telegraph Company

El Paso, Anthony, Canutillo, Clint, Dell City, Fabens, Fort Bliss, Fort

Hancock, Guadalupe Peak, Juarez, Tornillo. 1978.

Pacific Northwest Bell Telephone Company

Olympia, Lacey, {and} Tumwater. 1977.

San Marcos Telephone Company, Inc.

San Marcos {and} Martindale. 1970.

Southwestern Bell Telephone Company

Abilene, Hamby, Hawley and Potosi. 1978.
Alice, Benavides, Freer and San Diego. 1977.
Alpine, Fort Davis, Marfa, Marathon, Sanderson, Alamita, Big Canyon, and
    Calamity Creek. 1977.
Amarillo, Canyon, Cleta and Umbarger. 1978.
Angleton, Bailey's Prairie {and} Danbury. 1978.
Anson, Hamlin, {and} Stamford. 1978.
Bandera, Castroville, Devine, Hondo, LaCoste, Lytle, Medina Lake,
    Natalia, Pipe Creek, Yancey, Medina, {and} Tarpley. 1977.
Bay City {and} Matagorda. 1978.
Beaumont. 1977.
Beeville {and} Skidmore. 1978.
Big Spring, Ackerly, Lomax, Luther, Coahoma, and Sand Springs. 1978.
Borger, Skellytown, Stinnett, Fritch, {and} Sanford. 1978.
Columbus. 1978.
Corpus Christi. 1978.
Denison, Pottsboro, {and} Sherman. 1976.
Eagle Pass {and} Piedras Negras, Mexico. 1977.
Edna. 1977.
Fort Worth. 1978.
Goliad. 1978.
Graham. 1977.
Grand Prairie. 1978.
Greenville, Campbell, {and} Cash. 1977.
Helotes. 1977.
Hereford, Dawn, Frio, Milo Center, Summerfield, {and} Westway. 1978.
Hillsboro, Itasca, {and} Brandon. 1978.
Houston (North Suburban) {and} Katy. 1977.
Houston Southwest, Suburban Richmond, Rosenberg, Alief, Barker, Blue
    Ridge, Buffalo, Smithers Lake, {and} Valley Lodge. 1978.
Italy. 1978.
Kenedy, Karnes City, Runge, {and} Falls City. 1977.
Kermit {and} Wink. 1978.
Kingsville. 1977.
Laredo {and} Encinal. 1977.
Lockhart. 1977.
McKinney, Allen, Anna, Cleina, Frisco, Little Elm, Princeton, Prosper,
    the Colony. 1977.
Marion. 1974.
Marshall {and} Karnack. 1977.
Meridian. 1978.
Mexia, Teague, {and} Wortham. 1978.
Midland {and} Midkiff. 1978.
Mineral Wells {and} Millsap. 1977.
Monahans, Grandfalls, {and} Pyote. 1978.
Nacogdoches. 1977.
New Braunfels. 1978.
Odessa {and} Goldsmith. 1978.
Orange. 1977.
Pampa, Skellytown, {and} Lefors. 1978.
Paris, Blossom, and Deport. 1977.
Pasadena, Deer Park, {and} South Houston. 1977.
Plainview, Hale Center, Cotton Center, Edmonson, Halfway, {and} Happy
    Union. 1977.
Port Arthur, Griffing Park, Groves, Lakeview, Pear Ridge, {and} Sabine
    Pass. 1977.
Refugio, Woodsboro, {and} Bayside. 1977.
Richardson. 1978.
San Antonio. 1975.
Seguin, Marion, {and} Kingsbury. 1978.
Shamrock. 1977.
Silsbee, Kountze, Lumberton and Evadale. 1978.
Sinton. 1977.

Snyder {and} Hermleigh. 1977.
Sweetwater, Roscoe, {and} Nolan. 1977.
Taylor. 1978.
Temple, Belton, Bartlett, {and} Troy. 1978.
Terrell {and} Forney. 1977.
Texas City, LaMarque, Galveston, Port Bolivar, and Hitchcock. 1977.
Tyler. 1977.
Universal City, Converse, Schertz, Bracken, Cibolo, Garden Ridge, St.
    Hedwig, {and} Selma. 1978.
Uvalde, Batesville, Brackettville, LaPryor, {and} Sabinal. 1977.
Victoria. 1978.
Waco, Eddy, Mart, McGregor, Moody, {and} West. 1978.
Waxahachie. 1977.
Wichita Falls, Archer City, Burkburnett, Byers, Charlie, Henrietta,
    Holliday, Iowa Park, Lake Arrowhead, Lake Kickapoo, Petrolia, {and}
    Scotland. 1978.
Wortham. 1975.
Yoakum, Hallettsville, Flatonia, Moulton, Shiner, {and} Moravia. 1978.

Mexico Phone Directories

Mountain States Telephone and Telegraph Company

Nogales, Patagonia, Tubac, {and} Nogalas, Sonora. 1977.

Southwestern Bell Telephone Company

Eagle Pass {and} Piedras Negras, Mexico. 1977.

C. SECONDARY SOURCES (NON-PHONE DIRECTORIES)

Appleton's Revised English-Spanish and Spanish-English Dictionary. 4th
    edition. N.Y.: Appleton-Century-Crofts, 1965.
California Pioneer Register and Index 1542-1848. Including Inhabitants
    of California 1796-1800 and List of Pioneers Extracted from the
    History of California by Hubert Howe Bancroft. Baltimore: Reginal
    Pub. Co. 1964.
Chabot, Frederick C. With the Makers of San Antonio; Genealogies of the
    Early Latin, Anglo-American, and German Families with Occasional
    Biographies, each Group being Prefaced with a Brief Historical
    Sketch and Illustration. San Antonio, Tx: Artes Gráficas, 1937.
Chavez, Fray Angélico. Origins of New Mexico Families in the Spanish
    Colonial Period in Two Parts: The Seventeenth (1598-1693) and the
    Eighteenth (1693- 1821) Centuries. Santa Fe: Historical Society
    of New Mexico. 1954.
Conferencia anual Río Grande La Iglesias Metodista Unida. Cuadragésima
    Séptima Sesión, Junio 11-14, 1976. Southwestern University,
    Georgetown, Texas.
De Leon, Arnoldo. Apuntes Tejanos. Published for the Texas State
    Historical Association by University Microfilms International,
    1978.
Mexican American Task Force of the Synod of Texas. The Mexican American
    Churches in the Synod of Texas. Kingsville, Texas: Presbyterian
    Pan American School, 1971.
New Mexico Cemeteries. Vol. I. Bernalillo County, Mount Calvary.
    Compiled by Mary Brewer. Albuquerque, N.M.: New Mexico
    Genealogical Society, Inc., 1979.
New Mexico 1850 Territorial Census. 4 vols. Albuquerque, N.M.: New
    Mexico Genealogical Society, 1976.
New Revised Velázquez Spanish and English Dictionary. By Mariano
    Velázquez de la Cadena, Eduard Gray and Juan L. Iribar. Chicago:
    Follett Publishing Co. 1964.
Standard English-Spanish and Spanish-English Dictionary by Emilo M.
    Martínez Amador. Boston: D.C. Heath and Company, 1958.
Taylor, Virginia H. Index to Spanish and Mexican Land Grants. Texas:
    General Land Office, 1976.
United Presbyterian Church in the United States of America. The Program
    Agency. Directory of Latino Pastors of the United Presbyterian
    Church in the U.S.A. and Puerto Rico (photocopy) New York: Mission

Service Unit on Church and Race, 1974.

II. IDENTIFICATION OF NAMES
A. SOURCE FOR DEFINITION OF SUPPLEMENTAL INFORMATION

Alonso, Martín. Enciclopedia del idioma, 4 vols. Madrid: Aguilar,
    1958.
American Name Society. Names, Vols. 1-26.
Arthur, William A. Etymological Dictionary of Family and Christian
    Names. New York: Sheldon, Blakeman and Co., 1857.
Attwater, Donald. (comp.) Names and Name Dates. London: Burns Oates
    and Washbourne Ltd., 1939.
Attwater, Donald. The Penguin Dictionary of Saints. Middlesex,
    England: Penguin Books, Inc., 1975.
The Book of Saints: A Dictionary of Servants of God Canonised by the
    Catholic Church. Compiled by the Benedictine Monks of St.
    Augustine's Abbey, Ramsgate. 3rd edition. New York: Macmillan
    Company, 1944.
Boyd-Bowman, Peter. "Cómo obra la fonética infantil en la formación de
    los hipocorísticos." Nueva Revista de Filología Hispánica Año IX,
    Num. 4, 1955. pp. 337-366.
Boyd-Bowman, Peter. "Los nombres de pila en México desde 1540 hasta
    1950." Nueva Revista de Filología Hispánica. El celos de Mexico
    and The Univ. of Texas. 19:1, 1970 p 12-48.
Butler, Alban. Lives of the Saints. New ed. rev. and copiously
    supplemented by Herbert Thurston. 12 V. N.Y.: Kenedy, 1925-38.
Collins Gem Dictionary of First Names. London: Collins, 1976.
Corominas, J. Diccionario crítico etimológico de la lengua Castellana.
    4 vols. Berna: Editorial Francke, 1954.
Coulson, John ed., The Saints: A Concise Biographical Dictionary.
    N.Y.: Hawthorn Books, (1958).
Diccionario de los santos ordenado y presentado por Dom Philippe
    Rovillard. Translated by Oriol Valls Subirà. Haute Provence,
    France, Editions Robert Morel, 1963?
Diccionario Enciclopedico U.T.E.H.A. 10 vols. México: Unión
    tipográfica Editorial Hispano Americano, 1968.
Dictionary of Saints. Compiled by Donald Attwater. Based on Butler's
    Lives of the Saints. New York: P.J. Kenedy and Sons, 1958.
Directorio para las oficinas del Servicio Público de correos de la
    República Mexicana. Mexico. Imprenta de José María Sandoval,
    1876.
Drake, Maurice and Wilfred. Saints and Their Emblems. London: J.B.
    Lippencott Company, 1916.
Egger, Carol: Lexicon Nominum Virorum et Mulierum. Romae: Societas
    Libraria "Studium", 1957.
Enciclopedia de la Biblia. 7 vols. Barcelona: Ediciones Garriga,
    S.A., 1964.
Enciclopedia de referencia católica. 6 vols. Charlotte, N.C.: C.D.
    Stampley Enterprises, Inc., 1970.
Enciclopedia universal europeo americano. 70 vols. Madrid: Espasa-
    Calpe, S.A., (1907?-33).
Espinosa, Aurelio M. "Nombres de bautismo nuevo mejicanos. Algunas
    observaciones sobre su desarrollo fonético." Revue de
    Dialectologie Romane (Belgium/Germany) S, 1913, p. 356-373.
Grassi, M.D. Etimología de los nombres propios. La Habana, Cuba, 1937.
Grassi, M.D. Latin y griego vulgarizados en un breve estudio de la
    formación de las palabras en español, Etimología de los nombres
    propios. (La Habana, Escuela tipográfica de la Institución
    benéfica "Manuel Inclán", 1937).
Hardon, John A. Modern Catholic Dictionary. Garden City, N.Y.:
    Doubleday and Co., Inc., 1980.
Holweck, Frederick George. A Biographical Dictionary of the Saints.
    St. Louis, Mo.: B. Herder Book Co., 1924.
Kolatch, Alfred J. The Name Dictionary: Modern English and Hebrew
    Names. New York: Jonathan David, 1967.
Lopez de Mesa, Luis. Rudimentos de Onomatología. Bogotá: Imprenta del
    Banco de la República, 1961.
Martirología que contiene los nombres de todos los santos y beatos de la
    Iglesia romana y de las órdenes religiosas. Panamá: Imprenta del
    Star and Herald, 1896.
Menéndez Pidal, Ramón. "Onomástica inspirada en el culto mariánico."
    Cuadernos del idioma, Vol. 1, No 1-4, 1965-66. pp. 9-16.
Musser, Benjamin Francis. What Is Your Name? The Catholic Church and

Nomenclature. Manchester, N.H., 1937.
New Catholic Encyclopedia. 15 vols. N.Y.: McGraw-Hill Book Company,
    1967.
The New Century Cyclopedia of Names. Edited by Clarence L. Barnhart
    with the assistance of William D. Halsey. 3 V. New York:
    Appleton-Century-Crofts, Inc., 1954.
Plowden, C. Chicheley. A Manual of Plant Names. N.Y.: Philosophical
    Library, 1970.
Pollock, Saul. Spanish and Mexican Given Names: A Compendium of
    Baptismal Names; Colloquial, Diminutive, and Familiar Forms; Pet
    Names, Nicknames; Coined and Corrupted Forms. Los Angeles:
    Committee for Social Research, 1940.
Quadflieg, Joseph. The Saints and Your Name. N.Y.: Pantheon, 1958.
Robelo, Cecilio A. Diccionario de Aztequismos. México: Ediciones
    Fuente Cultural, 1952.
Roeder, Helen. Saints and Their Attributes; with a Guide to Localities
    and Patronage. London: Longman, Green. (1955).
Sainz de Robles, Federico Carlos. Ensayo de un diccionario universal,
    precidido de un estudio acerca de los mitos y de las religiones
    paganas. Madrid: M. Aguilar, 1944.
Salazar G., Salvador. Nombres para el bebé. México: Editorial Diana,
    1979.
Serdoch, Pedro L. y Igonda, Colman Marcelo. Diccionario onomatológico
    con etimología de 2500 nombres propios. Mendoza, Argentina:
    Talleres Gráficas Jorge Best, 1952.
Sleigh, Linwood. The Book of Girls' Names. London: G.G. Harrap
    (1962).
Smith, Edward Francis. Baptismal and Confirmation Names. New York:
    Benziger Brothers, Inc., 1935.
Smith, Elsdon C. Personal Names; A Bibliography. New York, New York
    Public Library, 1952.
Steiner, Mary Florence. "An Etymological Study of Old Spanish Personal
    Names." (Ph.D. diss. Northwestern University, 1953).
Stewart, George R. American Given Names. New York: Oxford University
    Press, 1979.
Swan, Helena. Girls' Christian Names; Their History, Meaning, and
    Association. Rutland, Vermont: Charles E. Tuttle Co., 1973.
Tibón, Gutierre. Diccionario etimológico comparado de nombres propios
    de personas. México: Unión tipográfica Editorial Hispano
    Americano, 1956.
Toro y Gisbert, Miguel de Ortología Castellana de nombres propios.
    Paris: Librería Paul Ollendorff. [19].
United States Board on Geographic Names. Spain and Andorra.
    Washington, D.C.: Office of Geography, Department of the Interior.
    1961.
United States Department of Justice. Immigration and Naturalization
    Service. Foreign Versions, Variations and Diminutives of English
    Names.- Foreign Equivalents of United States Military and Civilian
    Titles. Washington, D.C.: GPO, 1969.
Van Wijk, H.L.A. "Los hipocorísticos hondureños." Romantische Jahrbuch
    Vol. XV, 1964, pp. 303-313.
Vidal de Battini, Elena. El habla rural de San Luis Argentina." Buenos
    Aires, 1949.
Webster's Dictionary of Proper Names. Geoffrey Payton, (comp.)
    Springfield, Mass.: G. & G. Merriam Co., 1970.
Weidenhan, Joseph L. Baptismal Names. 4th edition. Book Tower,
    Detroit. Gale Research Co., 1968.
Wells, Evelyn. What to Name the Baby (A Treasury of Names) 1500 Names
    to Choose From. Garden City, N.Y.: Doubleday and Co., Inc., 1946.
Williams, Thomas David. A Concordance of Proper Names in the Holy
    Scripture. St Louis, Mo., London. B. Herder Book Co., 1923.
Withycombe, E.G. The Oxford Dictionary of English Christian Names. 3rd
    edition. Oxford: Clarendon Press, 1977.
Yonge, Charlotte May. History of Christian Names. New ed. rev. London:
    Macmillan and Co., 1884.

B. SOURCES FOR UNDERSTANDING FIRST NAMES

Alonso, Amado. "La lingüística de nuestro diminutivo." Revista
    Humanidades, vol XXI, p. 35-41, Facultad de Humanidades, La Plata,
    1930.
Anderson, C.P. The Name Game N.Y.: Simon and Schuster, 1977,
Beaujón, Oscar. Santoral de la medicina. Caracas: Tipografía Vargas,

        S.A. 1969.
Berry, Ana M. Leyendas de las vidas de los santos. Buenos Aires:
        Poseidón, 1952.
Botero Restrepo, Samuel María. Los sesenta y tres santos americanos.
        Medellín: Editorial Bedout, 1956.
Brown, Peter. The Cult of the Saints; Its Rise and Function in Latin
        Christianity. Chicago: University of Chicago Press, 1981.
Century Cyclopedia of Names. Edited by Benjamin E. Smith. New York:
        The Century Co., 1894-97.
Davis, John D. Dictionary of the Bible. 4th edition revised. Grand
        Rapids, Michigan: Baker Book House, 1972.
Delehaye, Hippolyte. The Legends of the Saints. Univ. of Notre Dame,
        1961.
De Miguel Raimundo y Marqués de Moresch. Nuevo diccionario latino-
        español etimológico. Madrid: V. Suárez 1940.
Diccionario de la lengua española. 17th edition. 2 vols. Madrid:
        Real Academia Española, 1947.
Dunkling, Leslie Alan. First Names First. New York: Universe Books,
        1977.
García Rodríguez, Carmen. El culto de los santos en la España romana y
        visigoda. Madrid: Consejo Superior de Investigaciones
        Científicas, 1966.
Guilday, Peter. A History of the Councils of Baltimore (1791-1884).
        New York: Macmillan Company, 1932.
Kolatch, Alfred J. Dictionary of First Names. Middle Village, N.Y.:
        Jonathan David Publishers, Inc., 1980.
Long, Harry Alfred. Personal and Family Names. London: Hamilton,
        Adams and Co., 1883.
Partridge, Eric. Name This Child; a Dictionary of English (and
        American) Christian Names. London: Methuen and Co., ltd., {1936}.
Pei, Mario and Gaynor, Frank. Dictionary of Linguistics. Totowa, N.J.:
        Littlefield, Adams and Co., 1975.
Rajea, Elizabeth M. The Study of Names in Literature: A Bibliography.
        New York: K.G. Saur Publishing, Inc., 1978.
Stewart, George R. Names on the Globe. New York: Oxford University
        Press, 1975.

About the Compiler

RICHARD D. WOODS is a Professor of Foreign Languages at Trinity University, San Antonio, Texas. He is the author of *Latin America in English—Language Reference Books, Reference Materials on Latin America in English*, and *Spanish Surnames in the Southwestern United States* as well as articles on Spanish-American literature and Mexican-American bibliography.